Microsoft® Exchange Server 5

Greg Todd, et al.

W9-CQG-081

SAMS
PUBLISHING

201 West 103rd Street
Indianapolis, IN 46290

UNLEASHED

To "my girls," Shelly and Katie.

Copyright © 1997 by Sams Publishing

FIRST EDITION

International Standard Book Number: 0-672-31034-1

Library of Congress Catalog Card Number: 96-72004

2000   99   98   97   4   3   2

Interpretation of the printing code: the rightmost double-digit number is the year of the book's printing; the rightmost single-digit, the number of the book's printing. For example, a printing code of 97-1 shows that the first printing of the book occurred in 1997.

Composed in New Century Schoolbook and MCPdigital by Macmillan Computer Publishing

Printed in the United States of America

President, Sams Publishing	*Richard K. Swadley*
Publishing Manager	*Dean Miller*
Director of Editorial Services	*Cindy Morrow*
Director of Marketing	*Kelli Spencer*
Product Marketing Managers	*Wendy Gilbride*
	Kim Margolius
Assistant Marketing Managers	*Jennifer Pock*
Marketing Coordinator	*Linda Beckwith*

Acquisitions Editor
Kim Spilker

Development Editor
Sunthar Visuvalingam

Software Development Specialist
Patty Brooks

Production Editor
Nancy Albright

Indexer
Cheryl Jackson

Technical Reviewer
Robert Reinsch

Editorial Coordinators
Mandie Rowell
Katie Wise

Technical Edit Coordinator
Lynette Quinn

Resource Coordinator
Deborah Frisby

Editorial Assistants
Carol Ackerman
Andi Richter
Rhonda Tinch-Mize

Cover Designer
Jason Grisham

Book Designer
Gary Adair

Copy Writer
David Reichwein

Production Team Supervisors
Brad Chinn
Charlotte Clapp

Production
Gene Redding
Deirdre Smith
Andrew Stone

Contents

10 Migrating from Lotus cc:Mail 233

11 Migrating from Microsoft Mail 257

Microsoft Exchange 5.0 Unleashed—Quick Reference

Microsoft Exchange Server 5.0 Unleashed makes it easy to find everything you need to make Microsoft Exchange work for you, including Architecture, Compatibility, Cross-Platform, Future Directions, New to Version 5.0, Performance, Security, Standards, Troubleshooting, Warnings, Tips, and Notes. Entries are grouped under alphabetical categories under the different main topics. When you turn to the corresponding chapters, you'll immediately find the information marked by an icon. You can use these lists either for hasty lookups or to explore a particular aspect of Microsoft Exchange from every possible angle.

Architecture

Compatibility

Cross-Platform

Future Directions

New to Version 5.0

Performance

Security

Standards

Troubleshooting

Foreword

When I ship a major release of a product, I like to take a few moments to reflect on where we have come.

The day we signed off the release of Exchange 5.0 was no different than most signoff days in the Exchange group. We signed off the release at 9:00 a.m. in the morning in the atrium of our building. 9:00 a.m. signoffs have become a tradition in the Exchange group. We choose 9:00 a.m. because this allows the art committee to remove all the artwork in the building the night before. Allows for the champagne and beer to start flowing early; therefore, it doesn't get too warm. Allows for everyone on the project team to put in their best-looking navel-rings. Then when they get thrown in the fountains outside the building, they are in their best attire. And finally, allows Microsoft security plenty of time to call me by 4:00 p.m. (shift change for them), to tell me that there is a riot going on in the building, people are throwing themselves through walls, furniture is being thrown off the third-floor balconies, and so forth. Of course, after calming security down, I explain to them that this is not a riot or mutiny, we just released the next major version of the Exchange product—send me the repair and cleaning bills, please.

Given this, I wasn't really able to reflect until about 5 p.m. that day on where we have come since the early days of Exchange. Here is what I thought about that day.

About 10 years ago, I read a book entitled *Steve Jobs: The Journey is the Reward* about Steve Jobs and his adventures at Apple Computer. For some reason, that title has stayed with me over the years. It's really true; it's not the ship-day that makes the project, it's the journey we were on throughout the project that makes the legends and the special memories.

In late 1991, we officially started the Exchange Server project. I dug through some old e-mails and found what I believe is the e-mail that kicked it off. The following e-mail is a request from Paul Maritz to get together and discuss how we were going to build a winning product in the e-mail space. You will see a couple of things in the e-mail:

- Microsoft is a great place, given how we can candidly speak to our VPs. Seriously, I was happy someone at the exec level finally bought into the ideas we were passing around.
- Most projects don't have grand unification ideas behind them when they start up; things just start out as simple ideas. I guarantee you, on that day in 1991, I wasn't dreaming of what it would be like to ship Exchange Server 5.0.

Here is the e-mail:

> From:Brian Valentine
> Sent:Friday, December 20, 1991 6:50 AM
> To:Paul Maritz
> Subject:RE: project spitfire
>
> Glad to see it is possible for a VP at this company t*o pull* their head out every once and a while and wake up and *smell the* MTA :-)
>
> I'll set the meeting up.
>
> brian
>
> | From:Paul Maritz Thu Dec 19 20:43:51 1991
> | To:Brian Valentine
> | Subject:project spitfire
>
> | Date:Thu Dec 19 20:43:26 1991
>
> | I have just spent a week on the road talking to net specialists.
> | I have learnt a lot, which I will write up separately, but one thing
> | did become clear. Unless we get some form of scalable mail server
> | we are dead ducks. I think you and I need to figure out how we get
> | things done. Time for some career threatening moves - gets too boring
> | otherwise. WE just need to be smart about how we set about things.
>
> | Let's get some time together - are you in Mon/Tues?

It wasn't long after that day in late 1991 when we agreed upon the vision for Exchange: *Build the world's fastest, most scalable, most reliable, easiest-to-administer messaging and collaboration platform that can connect the world.* That vision still lives on today, but the journey is far from over and has taken us along a path that is quite different from where we started out in 1991. Initially, we were building a scalable client-server messaging product that could replace all the legacy e-mail systems that customers had deployed around their companies. When you look closely at Exchange Server 5.0, you will see it's still rooted in being the world's best messaging and group scheduling product. Along the journey, although customer requirements have changed, competitive products have come and gone, and collaboration (groupware) among PC users has become a requirement. In addition to all that, perhaps the most exciting thing to come along has been the Internet. The Internet has morphed e-mail from being a communication tool within an organization into becoming the ubiquitous tool for non–real-time communication between people around the world. Therefore, to have a successful product today, you must have rich scalable e-mail with integrated group scheduling, but you also have to integrate collaboration services over standard internet protocols—all the while providing a rich applications development platform. You will see all of this in Exchange Server 5.0.

We have had great success with the product since shipping Exchange Server 4.0 on April 2, 1996. Customers have been deploying Exchange in large numbers, and the product has been able to live up to the requirements of those customers. Exchange is really the first product delivered in the industry that has allowed these customers to move from their legacy products and problems to a PC-based client-server messaging platform across their entire organization. Exchange delivers solutions from organizations of 10 PCs to 250,000 PCs and beyond. Exchange Server 5.0 is the next logical stepping stone along the journey for our customers and us. We have high expectations for the product, and I am very confident that the architecture we have in place will continue to deliver on our vision for the product many years into the next millenium.

There is no way I could ever write a Foreword for a book talking about the Exchange journey without also mentioning my group. They are a fantastic group of engineers that I wouldn't trade for any other group in the industry. I have been called Mom in the group for some time now. I like to think it's because when the crunch times come, I keep everyone in the group sheltered (who needs to go home?), well-fed (dinners each night and three squares on the weekends), and clothed (there's a new Exchange teeshirt just about every month). Some others may tell you the reason I'm called Mom is that I'm a real Mother. . . well. . .you-know-what, but that's not true, trust me. What all this boils down to is that the Exchange group is made up of great engineers that work hard because the dynamics of the business we are in requires it. But we also like to have fun doing it. If you have heard rumors of the weekly Exchange group's Friday 3 p.m. status meetings, they are most likely true. I have dressed up as Elvis, Jake of the Blues Brothers, Santa Claus, and the Easter Bunny—even in a hula skirt with the full complement of a coconut bikini top. I have brought in a heavy-metal band to sing the Exchange song right after the Microtunes (Microsoft's choir) sang it. I have participated in a Jell-O tug-of-war though 500 gallons of cherry Jell-O. Our motto is: You name it—we, the Exchange group, have done it. I have a ton of great memories of times like these with my group that really brings home "the journey is the reward."

From Day One in the Exchange group, we sat out to change the way people work. Exchange Server 5.0 is a great product that delivers unique functionality allowing people to change the way they work together and become more efficient in their communications with others. The journey is not over, though. The customers keep asking for more, the competition never sits still, and the industry is always changing; therefore, we can't sit back and just watch. We must and will continue to innovate and build the greatest products available.

I grew up in a small town where PCs barely exist even today, where in my wildest dreams I could not have imagined that I would have an opportunity to be where I am today. I'm leading a great team of people that are building a product line that is going to change the way people work—all the while having the time of my life. That is more of a reward than I could have ever hoped for on any journey. Finally, I couldn't reflect back without thanking my wife Geri and my two sons Jake and Chris for having the patience with me during all those late nights that kept me at work. Last but not least, a final thanks to God for giving me the wisdom to make it this far and the blessings to live and tell about it.

One last thing before I end. You most likely have this book in your hands right now because you have or will soon have purchased Exchange Server, and this book is a great reference to help you in using the product. I want to personally thank you for your purchase of Microsoft's Exchange Server. We built the product for our customers with the help of many of our early adopter customers. Without our customers, we don't exist. Thank you!

Acknowledgments

> Either write something worth reading or do something worth writing about.
> — Benjamin Franklin

As I write these words, the creation of *Microsoft Exchange Server 5 Unleashed* is almost complete. And when I reflect upon all the effort that has gone into the making of this book, it generates a real appreciation for everyone involved. Truly, it is a talented and extraordinary group of people that I had the privilege of working with. They helped make this project a success, and without them, this book would surely have never seen the light of day.

First and foremost, I want to express heartfelt gratitude to my family: my wife Shelly and my daughter Katie. You are the two most special people in the world. Shelly, thank you for your love, inspiration, and strength, especially over the past months. I could not have completed this project without your support. You are the best. Katie, thank you for bringing an inexplicable joy into my life that only a child can. Just a year ago you were visiting us for the first time. Since then, it has been a complete delight to watch you grow.

What book about Exchange Server would be complete without some involvement from the people who actually built the thing? Indeed, they have really done something worth writing about. I want to extend a special word of thanks to my friends in the Exchange Product Unit at Microsoft who poured so much excellent work into this book. It's been a real treat working with each of you:

> To my good friend, Eric Lockard—who is a darned good writer in his own right, and Exchange Server expert extraordinaire—thank you for your invaluable support with this project and for letting me recruit you to write a couple of chapters. You made a difference.

> To the incredibly knowledgeable contributing authors—Ken Ewert, Paul Garner, Kevin Kaufmann, Eric Lockard, Brian Murphy, Jim Reitz, and Doug Strauss—many thanks to each of you for stepping up to the challenge and for your felicitous contributions. I appreciate you guys lending your expertise to this project and getting the job done in the midst of incredibly busy schedules.

To Linda Hirsh and Elisa Shotwell for helping me with things "behind the scenes." Thanks for being so accommodating when I needed your assistance—you're great.

To Brian Valentine, thanks for writing the Foreword, which gives us non-Microsofties an engaging glimpse inside the world of Exchange development. And further thanks for supporting the participation of your group members in this project—they really helped take this book to the next level.

Of course, there are other people in the world that know Exchange Server besides people in Building 16. Thanks to veteran Exchange guy Robert Henriksen, who contributed to my first Exchange book, and who agreed to make a return appearance in this book. Thanks also to those original contributors of chapters for *Microsoft Exchange Server Survival Guide* whose work was selected to be revised and incorporated into this book: Diane Andrews, Rick Andrews, Kimmo Bergius, David Mosier, Wesley Peace, Ron Sonntag, and Ray Sundstrom.

No book can make it to the shelves without the support of a great publisher, so I would like to pay a huge debt of gratitude to the venerable crew at Sams Publishing. I would especially like to thank some folks there who have endured for the last several months, seeing this book through: Kim Spilker, Sunthar Visuvalingam, Lynette Quinn, Deborah Frisby, Patty Brooks, Cheryl Dietsch, Carol Ackerman, and Dean Miller. Also thanks to the proofers, layout folks, and others who work so diligently to make these pages palatable. You at Sams put forth a monumental effort that helped make this book a reality.

Next I want to express sincere thanks to Nancy Albright for her tireless work coordinating production edit and author review. It was a bit demanding this time out, but you did a super job and you were great to work with. Also thanks to Bob Reinsch for tech edit.

Thank you to my friends at Keyfile Corporation—Cindy Maxwell, Dave Lakness, and Dave Chestnutt—for your indispensable assistance, support, and expert advice on Keyflow during this project.

I'd like to give a special acknowledgment to my management at BMC Software—Julian Waits, Director of Corporate Development, and Bob Beauchamp, Vice President of Business Strategy—for your gracious support of my efforts, and for your exceptional insight and leadership. We're 10 feet tall and bulletproof!

Also, I'd like to express a warm thank you to various friends, family members, and coworkers who have encouraged me throughout the process of completing this book—you know who you are. It definitely helps.

And finally, I want to offer thanks to God, both for the opportunity to undertake this project and for the talents He gave me to complete it.

Greg Todd
June 5, 1997

About the Authors

Greg Todd (gregt@bmc.com) holds a B.S. in Computer Engineering from the University of South Florida. He currently works in the Corporate Development Group at BMC Software in Houston, Texas, handling emerging Microsoft and NT technologies. Previously, Greg was a Systems Engineer at Compaq Computer Corporation for six years.

Greg got his start with computers as a high school freshman when he purchased his first computer, a brand new TRS-80 Level II 16K system, and taught himself to program BASIC. Since then he has spent over 12 years working in the industry. During this time he has written software, worked extensively with networks and operating systems, authored white papers, presented technical sessions at industry events, and participated as a contributing author on other technical books. Additionally, Greg is the author of *Microsoft Exchange Server Survival Guide*, Sams Publishing, 1996. In his spare time, you will find Greg spending time with his family or his Rottweiler, Zak. Or you might find him hiding out in his home studio, experimenting with technology, music, and other fun stuff.

Paul Garner is currently working on the next versions of Outlook, after three eventful years as a Program Manager on the Exchange Server team. It has been said—though he hasn't yet identified by whom—that he has left the plumbers' union to do interior design. He pioneered the use of Exchange in building powerful Web applications and supervised the development of the first Web site to use Exchange-based discussions on the Internet. He doesn't deny leading the development of the Exchange portion of the BackOffice SDK. A citizen of the UK, Paul spent the previous three years at Microsoft Consulting Services (MCS) in that country, helping people plan and implement large-scale networks and messaging systems based on the predecessor to Exchange, MS Mail. Paul slipped the schedule on his house remodel several weeks while contributing to this book, but after building the next generation of messaging and groupware products, writing, and refinishing floors, he would love to get some time to spend racing his Olson 30 sailboat. His e-mail address is paulgar@microsoft.com.

Ken Ewert is a test manager who has worked for Microsoft for the last five years, focused on various messaging projects, including Microsoft Mail and Exchange. Ken can be considered one of the first Exchange Administrators in the world and is an authority on planning, topology configuration, and operational issues. Ken has been a key player in Microsoft's internal migration to Exchange, offering his insight and guidance on configuration, troubleshooting, and operational issues. His role within the Exchange group includes working with corporate early adopters of Exchange technology, as well as managing the 1000+ user/multi-site topology (the Dogfood lab) that runs prerelease versions of Exchange software in a Microsoft production environment. He can be reached at kene@microsoft.com.

Robert Henriksen is a network consultant and MIS Director for the University of Houston Law Center (http://www.law.uh.edu). He is a Microsoft Certified Product Specialist in

Windows NT, specializing in NT-based networks, remote access, Exchange, and ISDN. He can be reached at Rhenriksen@uh.edu.

Kevin K. Kaufmann is Program Manager for Microsoft Corporation in the Exchange product group. He graduated in 1990 from California State University, Northridge, with a Bachelor of Science in Computer Science and minor in Mathematics. In total, he has been working with the Exchange server product for the past three and a half years—first as the technical liaison between the Product Support group and the Exchange Product group to insure supportability, and then, after shipping Exchange 4.0, as an Escalation Engineer for the Exchange product. As a Program Manager, he has worked on the Exchange 5.0 Administration program, and his current focus is on the integration/unification of Exchange Directory service into the Windows NT 5.0 Directory service. His other interests include operating systems, Internet applications, racquetball, reading, and learning about new technologies. Kevin is married to Laurie Ruth Kaufmann, whom he refers to as "the most important person in my life and my best friend." As of August 16, 1996, he is the very proud father of Megan Sarah Kaufmann, "who has brought unbounded happiness and true meaning to our lives. I would be remiss not to mention the fourth member of the family, Hayley," he adds, "our slightly overweight but very lovable Chinese Pug."

Much to his surprise, **Eric Lockard** continues to work on messaging, groupware, and networking technologies at Microsoft as he has for almost all his career since joining the company in 1989. Arguably the first person working on Exchange Server at Microsoft, he is responsible (and can thus be conveniently blamed) for many aspects of the Exchange Server design and architecture, including, indirectly, the ridiculous and somewhat embarrassing thickness of this book. Currently the manager and head taskmaster of the Exchange Server Core Services and Storage Product Unit, Eric has been involved with most aspects of Exchange Server in his previous and slightly less title-inflated roles as Group Program Manager and Performance Manager for the Exchange Business Unit.

When not chained to his desk or his ISDN line, Eric enjoys brewing his own beer, playing chess, racing sailboats, and spending time with his family—although if his wife asks, not necessarily in that order. Eric holds degrees in Electrical Engineering, Mathematics, and Computer Science from universities that were foolish enough to admit him.

Brian Murphy has been working with messaging technology for almost ten years. Currently a program manager in the Exchange Server group, Brian spent time as a test manager supporting and advising Early Adopters during the Exchange 4.0 release, and he was the first certified Escalation Engineer focused on Microsoft Mail and Exchange.

Prior to his five years at Microsoft, Brian worked for Memorex Telex as network manager for a Novell NetWare implementation integrating Microsoft Mail 2.1 with an existing VM/Notes system, which is still in operation today. Although he feels he spent far too much time running operations for the two IBM VM systems there, Brian feels some small satisfaction knowing that the messaging system that was put in place seven years ago is still going strong.

A native of Sydney, Australia, Brian moved to Redmond, Washington, in the Spring of 1995. Although people don't always understand his accent, his typing is comprehensible, and he can be reached at `Brianmur@microsoft.com`.

Jim Reitz is a Program Manager in the Exchange product unit at Microsoft, responsible for security features of the product. He was previously an Architectural Engineer for Microsoft US's Central Region. Prior to joining Microsoft, Jim held Product Management positions in the LAN and document imaging industries.

Doug Strauss is currently the test lead for the Microsoft Exchange Internet Mail Service. He lived in Concord, California, from the age of 10 until graduating from high school. He then attended Oregon State University in Corvallis and majored in Computer Science, with a minor in Speech Communication, as well as working in many labs helping students and doing some sys admin work for the UNIX hosts. After school, he started Microsoft Product Support Services, supporting all Macintosh products, and eventually focused on Microsoft Mail for AppleTalk networks. When Microsoft acquired Consumer Software, he started working with Microsoft Mail for PC Networks and eventually focused on gateway support for X.400, SMTP, and FFAPI. In 1995, he moved to testing for Exchange Internet Mail Connector 4.0 and future versions, after that as the lead. Currently, Doug lives with his lovely wife Alicia Falsetto in Redmond, Washington. "It is to Alicia that I dedicate my chapter and love," he reports, "for putting up with all the weekends and evenings she was left alone while I worked on shipping the IMC and IMS."

Tell Us What You Think!

As a reader, you are the most important critic and commentator of our books. We value your opinion and want to know what we're doing right, what we could do better, what areas you'd like to see us publish in, and any other words of wisdom you're willing to pass our way. You can help us make strong books that meet your needs and give you the computer guidance you require.

Do you have access to CompuServe or the World Wide Web? Then check out our CompuServe forum by typing GO SAMS at any prompt. If you prefer the World Wide Web, check out our site at http://www.mcp.com.

> **NOTE**
>
> If you have a technical question about this book, call the technical support line at 317-581-4669.

As the team leader of the group that created this book, I welcome your comments. You can fax, e-mail, or write me directly to let me know what you did or didn't like about this book—as well as what we can do to make our books stronger. Here's the information:

FAX: 317-581-4669

E-mail: opsys_mgr@sams.mcp.com

Mail: Dean Miller
         Comments Department
         Sams Publishing
         201 W. 103rd Street
         Indianapolis, IN 46290

Introduction

Microsoft Exchange Server has had a busy first year. Since its introduction in April 1996, Exchange has become quite popular. In fact, it is the most popular product in the Microsoft BackOffice suite. Over half the Fortune 50 companies are actively involved in deploying Exchange. Microsoft is investing a large amount of money in marketing and development for the product. Millions of client seats and tens of thousands of server seats have been sold. There are currently about 140 ISV solutions for the product, some of which are covered in Appendix A, "Third-Party Add-On Products," of this book.

Microsoft has a dedicated Web site for Exchange, called the Microsoft Exchange Community, at www.exchangeserver.com. This is in addition to the pages they maintain on www.microsoft.com/exchange. Exchange Server has become a major component of Microsoft's collaborative computing strategy, and it has been endowed with robust Internet protocol support in its latest revision. Finally, as you might expect, Microsoft is busily at work on revisions to the code for upcoming releases, which will make Exchange even better.

Clearly, things are not standing still in the world of Exchange Server.

Why Exchange Unleashed?

Why, indeed? That question crossed my mind several times during the course of producing this book—usually late at night when everyone else was quietly sleeping, or on beautiful spring days here in The Woodlands.

I could tell you that Exchange Server 5.0 represents a major milestone in the progress of Microsoft's messaging products. And that in this major release, Microsoft has built on the solid foundation of Exchange 4.0 to produce a better and more enriched product—a product that embraces Internet standards and adds features that let you communicate and collaborate.

That would be true enough. But why would someone sit down and write such a tome as this? There are a few reasons.

It's a known fact that people generally like books—you know, something they actually can hold in their hands and refer to without having to boot a computer. A book's the most approachable piece of hardware available. That's fortunate for us authors, because there's always something cool to write about.

Flip a few pages and browse the Table of Contents if you haven't already. Microsoft has put a lot of neat stuff in Exchange Server. If you know anything about Exchange, I'll wager that you will find something that grabs your attention. Whether it's public folders or advanced security, e-mail migration or active server integration, performance or troubleshooting—there's bound to be something of interest in these pages. Even if you're an Exchange veteran, there's probably something you can learn from the wealth of talent represented in this book.

You may be familiar with my prior work, *Microsoft Exchange Server Survival Guide*, Sams Publishing, 1996. ESG, as I refer to it, concentrated on the server aspects of Exchange Server 4.0, and it was oriented largely toward the Exchange administrator. That was great for a *Survival Guide*, but an *Unleashed* book needs to go further. This book takes the knowledge in ESG and expands it, broadens the audience, increases the coverage, and updates you on what is new for Exchange 5.0. *Microsoft Exchange Server 5.0 Unleashed* is a work dedicated to helping you get the most out of Exchange Server, no matter who you are.

We both know there is only so much any mortal can glean from the regular product documentation and from trial and error. Sometimes it's good to turn to an outside source for another view on things. Sometimes it's good to get a sanity check on that project you're about to undertake, to get a jump on what to expect before it happens to you. And if you sit back and say, "Ah, *now* I get it," just once while reading this, that will make the effort worthwhile.

I have several goals for this book. Among them are the following:

- Introduce the new features found in Exchange 5.0, especially those that are Internet-related
- Cover public folders and Internet Mail Service
- Cover advanced messaging security comprehensively
- Provide insight for successful Exchange rollout
- Cover migrating from cc:Mail and MS Mail to Exchange
- Cover Exchange 4.0-to-5.0 migration and coexistence
- Provide detailed guidance about backup and recovery
- Illustrate a real-world Exchange application, such as workflow
- Discuss how Exchange fits into the Active Server platform
- Update the ISV product information and demos

Who Should Read This Book?

Although there are many books available on Exchange, few of them really get into the heart of the *server* side of the product the way *Microsoft Exchange Server 5 Unleashed* does.

Exchange administrators, technical decision makers, integrators, consultants, strategists—this book is for professionals involved in deploying, configuring, managing, troubleshooting, integrating, or developing for Exchange Server. And like the Exchange product itself, this book works great in large and small installations alike. That's right, a scalable book.

The majority of the readers are likely to be mid- to advanced-level professionals currently responsible for messaging or collaboration functions in a primary, hands-on capacity. A typical reader will be responsible for replacing or integrating Microsoft Mail or some other existing system with Exchange Server—or, perhaps, might be rolling out Exchange Server for the first time. That reader will have an interest both in connecting to the Internet and in leveraging standard Internet protocols, and will need some direction about what hardware to purchase in the future and how to maximize performance with what he or she already owns.

Today, the typical Exchange Server installation—the "sweet spot" I call it—will support an average of 200–500 users on a single server. Of course, the book doesn't ignore the larger-scale users, but the really huge installations typically have other resources, such as VARs, consultants, and so on, at their disposal. The rest of the users—especially the really small ones—may have to fend more for themselves, and that's where this book will become valuable.

What to Expect

An exhaustive approach would be overwhelming. Such an approach is the one Microsoft had to use when creating the Exchange product documentation. Such an approach is not one I employed for this project, so I made some assumptions about the target users and the typical installation. Exchange Server scales from small, single-server sites of a few dozen users all the way up to enormous multiple-server, multiple-site organizations with hundreds of thousands of users. Microsoft's documentation for Exchange must cover this full range of possibilities. As a result, a major part of the product documentation necessarily deals with issues concerning large-scale systems. These issues are usually quite involved, and (fortunately) they do not represent the issues that the majority of users will encounter.

Rather, I've positioned this book both to complement the product documentation—*not* to supplant it—and to address needs of the majority of users. Instead of simply focusing on the *how*, as documentation tends to do, I want to give the reader a feel for *why*, *when*, and *where* a particular topic applies.

For example, if there's a useful tool or feature in the product, I will certainly explain how to use it. In addition, though, you also learn *why* it is beneficial or useful, *when* it should be used, and *where* it should be applied. This approach makes *Microsoft Exchange Server 5 Unleashed* more broadly relevant and useful than basic documentation.

A Word About "et al."

With all the aforementioned goals for this book, obviously *Microsoft Exchange Server 5 Unleashed* was not written in a vacuum. Nor was it penned single-handedly—a product so vast as Exchange would be very difficult for one person to cover adequately.

In an attempt to make this book of highest quality, I asked for some help from some of my friends in the business. The result was a comprehensive work by a collection of exceptional talent that really knows their stuff. There are several contributing authors in this project, many of whom are key players who work at Microsoft in the Exchange Product Unit itself. Others are veteran Exchange users, consultants, administrators, and the like who have written about the subject before, and who understand quite well the real-world issues of Exchange. I am privileged to know each one and to have gotten the opportunity to work with such a great group on this project.

The bottom line? You get a great lineup of writers who worked very hard to help me make this book the best one available anywhere. Each contributor brings a unique set of expertise and style to the book—along with a professional perspective—while the magicians at Sams have helped me retain coherency and consistency throughout.

The Future of Exchange

How useful will *Microsoft Exchange 5 Unleashed* be, even after the next versions of Exchange Server and Windows NT Server ship? If we've done our jobs right, it will be very useful—even essential—as a foundation to build upon. Just as Exchange 5.0 is built upon the foundation laid by Exchange 4.0, this book builds upon the foundation laid by Exchange 4.0. To be sure, it is centered around concepts and features you must understand to be effective with Exchange 5.0. But those concepts and ideas aren't going to just go away when a new version ships—they will merely be extended and built upon.

The result? Instead of becoming outdated knowledge, what you learn in *Microsoft Exchange Server 5 Unleashed* will form a valuable foundation for understanding future enhancements, both to Exchange Server and to Windows NT. Things will change with the next version of Exchange—you can be assured of that—but many of those changes will be built upon ideas already presented in this book. Along the way, you will gradually increase your knowledge and expertise as the new versions arrive. And who knows—maybe there will even be another edition of this book to help you then, too.

The Layout of This Book

Before you get into reading the book, you should have an overview of how the book is laid out. The book is divided into seven sections:

■ *Part I: Overview*

This section provides an overview of Exchange Server—including what's new in Exchange 5.0—and it gives the reader insight into how to apply the book. Chapter 1 provides the highest-level overview, and it effectively sets the stage for the book. The remaining chapters in the section fill in more detail, focusing on Exchange architecture and Exchange concepts as they relate to server, clients, and messaging. This section is important for completeness, although you might know some of this material already, and it provides a good foundation for later chapters where the ideas are covered in more detail.

■ *Part II: Planning*

Planning is essential to a successful installation of Exchange Server, especially as the
deployments get larger. Being successful with Exchange requires that you make several
decisions before you begin installation. Some of these are critical, and changing your
mind could mean a lot of lost time, or even starting over again. The Planning section
focuses on giving you the information to install Exchange the right way, whether it is
for a new installation, for migration from an existing e-mail system, or for integration
with the Internet. This section also considers all the major factors that affect server
performance, and it gives you ways to configure Exchange for the best performance.
New features in Exchange 5.0 will be presented so the reader can plan appropriately
for those as well. There's not a lot of "drilling down" into the nuts and bolts of how
things are actually installed—this is a planning section.

■ *Part III: Implementation*

The Implementation section covers real nuts-and-bolts issues in Exchange. Although
the section is lengthy, it covers installation and one-time (or seldom-performed)
system-level tasks that you do primarily during installation. There are many concepts
presented in this part of the book that are fundamental to the operation of Exchange
Server. For example, the topic of installing and configuring Exchange clients and
servers is covered. There are chapters on connecting Exchange to other Exchange sites
and to external mail systems. There is even a chapter dedicated to the Internet Mail
Service. Probably, there are some parts that don't pertain directly to you, but you can
simply skip them.

■ *Part IV: Administration*

Administration comprises those tasks the reader must perform on an ongoing basis, so
the Administration section contains more of the real nuts and bolts you might need in
order to administrate Exchange. The section is fairly lengthy, and it provides information about various aspects of administration so the reader can be more effective at day-
to-day activities with Exchange. Here, you will find detailed information about
advanced security, public folders, backup and recovery, user management, and
Exchange Directory topics. In addition, there are numerous tips, tricks, and background information. Like the rest of the book, this section is not intended to replace
the Exchange documentation, but to complement it.

■ *Part V: Maintenance and Troubleshooting*

The Maintenance and Troubleshooting section is mainly concerned with helping the
reader resolve problems with an Exchange implementation. It certainly does not
pretend to provide all the answers, but it will arm the reader with the principles and
the tools needed to have a fighting chance against those nasty problems that can come
up from time to time.

- *Part VI: More Than Just E-Mail*

  Exchange Server really is more than just e-mail. It is also positioned as the best Internet protocol server, in addition to providing an entire infrastructure for messaging, collaboration, and developing applications. There is an assortment of topics covered in this section, including chapters for workflow, Active Server integration, electronic forms design, and LoadSim—Microsoft's Exchange load simulator. Although a complete book could really be dedicated to this collection of topics alone, this section will help shed some light on these subjects for the reader. They are pretty interesting, so I encourage you to check this section out.

- *Part VII: Appendixes*

  Finally, the appendixes serve their usual purpose of supporting the rest of the book. Appendix A, "Third-Party Add-On Products," is a reference to some of the many solutions that are available from the many Exchange ISVs. Appendix B, "Command Reference," is a reference of commonly used Exchange commands and utilities. Appendix C is a glossary of terms you should know that are contained in this book.

Where Do You Go from Here?

You probably won't just sit down and read this book cover to cover, especially if you are standing in the bookstore right now reading this Introduction. More likely, you will find topics of interest, start reading about them, and then get pulled into other sections of the book. You will eventually end up reading the whole thing—maybe even more than once. It's been known to happen. Ultimately, I hope you find it a valuable reference for answering your Exchange questions—it might not hold all the answers, but I'm confident it will provide more than you have now:

- Regardless of your expertise level, read Chapter 1, "Overview of Microsoft Exchange Server 5.0." This chapter serves as a great introduction for Exchange and for the rest of the book.

- Skim Chapter 2, "Electronic Messaging Concepts," to ensure you are familiar with some of the general terms and ideas surrounding electronic messaging.

- Read Chapter 3, "Exchange Server Components," and Chapter 4, "Exchange Client Components." You should read these closely if you are new to the world of Exchange Server.

- If you are planning a new Exchange system, learning about the Internet, upgrading, migrating, or learning about Exchange in general, I suggest reading all of Part II, "Planning," and exploring the chapters in Part III, "Implementation."

- If you are interested in Exchange administration topics, be sure to read Chapter 5, "Administrative Concepts." Additionally, read Part IV, "Administration," and explore the chapters in Part III, "Implementation," and Part V, "Maintenance and Trouble-shooting."

- If you are replacing Lotus cc:Mail or MS Mail with Exchange, be sure to read Chapter 10, "Migrating from Lotus cc:Mail," and Chapter 11, "Migrating from Microsoft Mail," as applicable.
- If you have performance or scaling issues, or if you are having general problems with Exchange, read Chapter 6, "Planning for Optimal Server Performance," and Part V, "Maintenance and Troubleshooting." You might also refer to Chapter 29, "Understanding and Using LoadSim," especially if you plan to embark upon your own Exchange performance tests and analyses.
- Finally, if you are an advanced Exchange user, or if you're just curious about some of the other neat things Exchange can do, check out Part VI, "More Than Just E-Mail."

Good luck. It is my sincere wish that you benefit from reading *Microsoft Exchange Server 5 Unleashed.*

Conventions Used in This Book

The following conventions are used in this book:

Computer font indicates commands, parameters, statements, and text you see onscreen.

Italic font is used to introduce new terms.

There are several icons in the book to help you quickly identify text you might want to read:

Architecture *Architecture* icons provide information on the underlying structure, or architecture, of Exchange Server and its components.

Compatibility *Compatibility* icons highlight features or components of Exchange that provide compatibility with Exchange Server 4.0 or other legacy components.

Cross-Platform *Cross-Platform* icons indicate those features or functions of Exchange that work across Windows and non-Windows platforms.

Future Directions *Future Directions* icons provide some insight into the future of the Exchange Server product. This information might be useful if you are trying to work around a current limitation or plan for the future.

New to Version 5.0 *New to Version 5.0* icons show those features, functions, or components that were not available prior to Exchange 5.0.

Performance *Performance* icons highlight text that discusses a topic where you might be able to affect the performance of Exchange.

Security *Security* icons indicate features, functions, and information that pertain to maintaining a secure Exchange Server environment.

Standards *Standards* icons highlight areas of Exchange 5.0 where existing industry standards have been followed or adhered to in the product.

Troubleshooting icons provide you with insight to address issues surrounding problems you might encounter with Exchange Server.

Troubleshooting

In addition, the following boxes appear now and then:

NOTE

Notes provide information that is relevant to the subject matter but needs to be specifically called out.

TIP

Tips offer useful hints and information that might make life with Exchange a bit easier.

CAUTION

Caution boxes provide cautions and consequences to particular actions.

WARNING

Warning boxes advise you of potential problems and help you solve them.

IN THIS PART

PART

I

Overview

Overview of Microsoft Exchange Server 5.0

by Eric Lockard

IN THIS CHAPTER

CHAPTER 1

Exchange Server is, at its core, an engine that enables people to communicate and share information. It's a very powerful and reliable engine, to be sure, with many features and powerful functionality for both end users and administrators alike. But its main goals are simply stated: to provide easy, yet powerful, ways for people to communicate and collaborate with one another and to provide a rich platform for authoring collaborative applications.

Electronic mail is certainly one of the primary means of electronic communication today, and Exchange Server is perhaps best known as a solid, high-performance client-server e-mail system. Version 5.0 expands Exchange's strengths in this area, adding support for standard Internet protocols and message formats and thereby supporting almost all e-mail client applications in existence on just about any platform or operating system. Version 5.0 also adds additional connectivity and migration options from proprietary e-mail systems beyond those provided in version 4.0, as well as a host of new administrative and end user e-mail–related features.

Version 5.0 also expands upon the Public Folder functionality included in version 4.0 and unifies this with Internet News. This unification facilitates powerful scenarios, where users can interact with Internet newsgroups and discussions, using the same powerful mechanisms they use for other public folder applications or their personal mailbox. At the same time, Public Folder information is now available to Internet News clients and hosts that speak only the standard news protocol. Companies can now share and replicate not only Internet news, but any Public Folder information between their organizations, using the standard Internet News protocols. Exchange Server Public Folders have become, with version 5.0, universally accessible discussion and collaboration repositories, and Exchange provides a host of powerful features—from security and server-based rules to moderated groups to facilitate rich collaboration.

But perhaps where Exchange Server 5.0 truly delivers the most exciting new functionality is in its integration with the World Wide Web. In addition to providing a turnkey e-mail and collaboration client for Internet World Wide Web browsers on any platform, Exchange actually provides a rich set of application interfaces for exposing any Exchange data to the Web. Known as *Active Messaging,* these interfaces allow collaborative application authors to use Windows NT Server "Active Server Pages" technology to blur the line between traditional Web sites and traditional groupware applications. It's now easy to add discussions or rich workgroup functionality to your intranet Web sites or expose your corporate directory on your corporate Internet Web site. In short, Microsoft has brought the functionality of Exchange Server to the world of the Web.

What's in a Name?

Microsoft uses the name *Exchange* for two separate products. The first, the topic of this book, is the Microsoft Exchange Server that is part of Microsoft BackOffice. Exchange Server includes both a server and a suite of clients that connect to it. There are actually two different clients for Windows 95 and Windows NT included with Exchange Server: an updated version of the Exchange Client that shipped with version 4.0 of Exchange Server and a brand new client, Microsoft Outlook, which also ships as part of Microsoft Office 97.

Microsoft also uses the term *Exchange* to refer to the feature-limited Exchange client included free with Windows 95 and Windows NT, sometimes referred to as the Windows *Inbox*.

Although either client can be used with the Exchange Server, the newer version of the Exchange client that comes with Exchange Server includes advanced features, such as Inbox rules, that take advantage of Exchange Server functionality.

To round out the confusion, due to the flexibility of the underlying Windows Messaging System (also known as the Windows Messaging API or MAPI), either client can be used with other compatible mail servers, and other third-party clients can be used with the Exchange Server. The server and client features are covered in detail in Chapters 3, "Exchange Server Components," and 4, "Exchange Client Components."

What's New in Version 5.0?

New to
Version 5.0

In the first beta release, what is now known as Exchange Server version 5.0 was originally referred to as version 4.1 and was intended to be a reasonably limited and timely update to the 4.0 version. However, as Microsoft added features and functionality, in part as a result of the growing popularity of the Internet, the release grew in size and richness. Microsoft called it version 4.5 by the second beta release. By the final release to manufacturing, less than a year after version 4.0 was released, it was known as version 5.0—and rightfully so.

Version 5.0 represents a significant update release of Microsoft's Exchange Server. Microsoft has added new functionality in many areas, including the following:

■ *Internet mail client connectivity.* Exchange includes built-in support for the Internet Post Office Protocol version 3 (POP3). This means that Exchange Server can now be used to host a multitude of Internet Mail clients, including Microsoft's Internet Explorer Internet Mail client, Netscape Navigator, Eudora Pro Mail, and a host of others. Many of these clients are available free as shareware (such as Eudora Light Mail) or come prepackaged with various operating systems.

■ *Internet directory service connectivity.* Exchange includes built-in support for the Lightweight Directory Access Protocol version 2 (LDAP). This means that Exchange Server can host Internet client applications that use this protocol (such as Microsoft's Internet Explorer Internet Mail client or Netscape Navigator) to look up e-mail addresses or other information about users, based on their name, company, title, or other specification.

■ *Internet Network News connectivity.* Exchange includes built-in support for the Network News Transport Protocol (NNTP). This means that not only can Exchange Server host Internet News client applications (such as Eudora, Microsoft's Internet Explorer Internet News client, Netscape Navigator, MicroPlanet Gravity, and so forth) but also act as an NNTP host server. Exchange Server can become your Internet News server serving your intranet NNTP clients as well as communicating with Internet NNTP hosts to replicate newsgroups.

- *Internet World Wide Web integration.* Exchange includes built-in support for the World Wide Web. Not only can Exchange Server provide secure e-mail, directory, and public folder access for just about any computer with a Web browser, but Exchange also provides a rich set of interfaces for authoring Web-centric Internet groupware applications. It's difficult to overstate the importance of this capability. By bringing the richness of Exchange to Web browser clients, a whole world opens up for users both inside and outside the organization. Roaming users can securely access their mail and schedules via any Web browser inside or outside the company, without installing special software or configuring server and account names, by simply connecting to a URL. Your corporate Web site can provide corporate directory information for prospective customers to look up the right contacts. Intranet applications can take advantage of Exchange functionality to add discussion groups or e-mail or directory integration to your intranet Web sites or provide a corporate organization chart. The possibilities are almost endless, and you can expect Microsoft to continue to invest in this area.

- *The Microsoft Outlook client.* Included with Exchange Server is a new Windows client called Outlook. Outlook, which is also available as part of Microsoft Office 97, is a powerful new e-mail, scheduling, and groupware application that takes full advantage of Exchange Server functionality. It provides a rich, integrated authoring environment for developing sophisticated groupware applications, as well as great integration with Microsoft Office.

- *Macintosh Exchange client.* As part of version 5.0, Microsoft has completed its Macintosh Exchange client offering by providing a Macintosh version of Schedule+ 7.0, which works with Exchange Server.

- *Lotus cc:Mail connectivity.* Included with Exchange Server is a new gateway—what Microsoft calls a "connector," which provides mail and directory interoperation between Lotus cc:Mail e-mail systems and Exchange Server as well as migration tools for migrating your users to Exchange Server.

- *Person-to-person public key exchange.* Exchange Server utilizes public key technology to provide digital signatures and message encryption. However, in version 4.0, Exchange users were limited to only exchanging signed or encrypted messages with other Exchange users in their organization. As part of version 5.0, Microsoft has provided an easy way for users in different Exchange Server organizations to exchange their public certificates, allowing users in different organizations to exchange digitally signed or encrypted messages.

NOTE

Software designed for collaboration and information sharing is called *groupware*. Exchange is an ambitious entry in this field. The first in this field—indeed, the product that in many ways defined the field itself—is IBM's Lotus Notes. Exchange and Notes are quite different products, however, each with a distinct approach to the problem of collaboration and sharing information.

Exchange has historically approached groupware from a messaging foundation; it is an e-mail system first. It has a complete, well-designed interface for sending, receiving, and managing e-mail and for distributed scheduling. There is a strong focus on integrating smoothly with legacy e-mail systems. In the Microsoft view, e-mail is the mechanism and underlying metaphor for sharing information.

In contrast, Notes began as a more database-centric (although neither Notes nor Exchange are really databases in the relational sense) general-purpose application for sharing information. E-mail—in the sense of sending messages back and forth between users—is just one kind of information to share. In the Lotus view, e-mail is an application that can be built with Notes. Indeed, the e-mail interface provided by Lotus (built on top of Notes) is often criticized and has historically been viewed as weak when compared to applications directly targeted at e-mail.

Although perspectives differ, there are strong parallels between Exchange and Notes. Both provide a distributed, messaging and groupware, infrastructure. Both provide development tools for building groupware applications. As the market for messaging and groupware expands, the two products will become strongly competitive. The result will be better products for both Exchange and Notes users.

Current Features and Benefits

Architecture

The following is a brief summary of the major features and benefits of Exchange Server version 5.0:

- *Scalable architecture.* A distributed, replicated, client-server architecture enables Exchange Server to scale from the smallest of single-server offices to very large systems with hundreds of servers and hundreds of thousands of users. Additionally, Exchange utilizes an advanced, transaction-log–based data store that provides tremendous fault tolerance and reliability, not to mention blazing performance. As a result, Exchange can handle your most mission-critical applications and grow with your business, no matter how large it becomes.

NOTE

A system such as Exchange Server is said to be distributed when information on multiple servers can be viewed and navigated in a seamless way by users without those users having to explicitly connect to each of the various underlying physical servers. The distributed system provides a unified namespace and takes care of connecting to the right

continues

continued

physical server to retrieve the right data in the user's logical namespace. In other words, the way data is logically organized for users of that data is completely independent of the underlying physical location of that data. Indeed, one of the primary advantages of most distributed systems is the ability for an administrator to change the underlying physical storage—for example, rename a server or move data from one physical server to another—without changing the users' notions of where that data resides in their logical world. Another advantage is the ability to present users with a consistent, logical view across much more data than could possibly reside on any single machine. To users, the system looks like a single giant computer. The World Wide Web is another good example of a distributed system.

A distributed system is said to be replicated when there may exist multiple server-based copies of data in the system and the system automatically maintains and synchronizes the multiple copies. Users generally don't know or care which replica of the data they connect to (the system generally determines which replica is most appropriate for the user, based on network topology, system load, or other information). Administrators can create new replicas and delete others as needed without the users generally even being aware of their existence. To users, it looks as if there is only a single instance of any piece of data in the system at any point in time. To administrators, it offers the flexibility to optimally configure the system for various loading, geographical, or topological configurations.

Some replicated systems, such as Exchange Server, also allow for users to maintain local or offline replicas where users maintain local copies of various server-based folders on their personal machine. This allows for offline usage where users can access their e-mail, schedule, groupware applications, and so forth, while disconnected from the network, by accessing their locally replicated data. The system provides for synchronizing changes made by the user while offline with the server-resident copies when the user goes online again.

■ *Operating system integration.* Exchange leverages the power of the Windows NT Server operating system. NT provides superior networking, administration, and security support as well as tools for monitoring and optimizing Exchange operation. By providing both pieces, Microsoft achieves a level of integration that would be difficult or impossible for another mail system to match.

■ *Distributed connectivity.* Exchange is a distributed system, which means that you can add servers as needed to suit your geographical or network topology requirements and still provide a single-system image to users and administrators. You can connect Exchange servers between sites to build a single mail system for your organization. This is made possible by built-in directory synchronization and database replication. Microsoft also provides optional "connector" software that lets Exchange connect to and exchange mail with Microsoft Mail systems, cc:Mail systems, X.400 protocol systems (large-scale mini- and mainframe systems), and SMTP protocol systems (the Internet).

- *Centralized administration.* Exchange provides powerful administration features. Administration is centralized—all servers in an organization can be administered from a single location. The practical benefits of this are enormous, allowing for easy administration of the potentially hundreds of servers and hundreds of thousands of users in an Exchange Server organization.

- *Message and transport security.* Exchange includes built-in public key encryption technology for protecting the contents of messages. Messages also can include digital signatures that ensure they are authentic and have not been modified by tampering. A Key Management Server provides and manages encryption keys and signatures. Exchange further leverages built-in NT security to prevent unauthorized user access to the mail system or its directories and files.

- *Migration tools.* Exchange provides a rich set of tools for converting from a wide range of third-party mail systems. Current tools enable you to move from IBM PROFS and OfficeVision, DEC All-In-1, Lotus cc:Mail, and Microsoft Mail (DOS and Macintosh OS versions).

- *Forms.* Exchange supports forms—essentially, messages with built-in fields and controls. Exchange provides a separate application, called Forms Designer, that lets you create and maintain forms for tracking, reporting, and organizing routine information. The new Microsoft Outlook client also includes a built-in, advanced forms development environment, which integrates with Microsoft Office 97.

- *Client support for Windows 95, Windows NT, Windows 3.x, Apple Macintosh, and even computers running plain old DOS.* The Exchange Server product includes client software versions for all these operating systems. Tight integration with the desktop operating system means that Exchange users can send and receive any information—not just text messages. This also means that Exchange can be used to organize and store information on a level not possible with the operating system alone. For example, you can store all information about a project—messages, data files, documents, diagrams, and so on—within an Exchange *folder* and automatically replicate that folder between the server and client machines and to other locations within your organization.

- *Built-in groupware.* Exchange supports *public folders.* These are distributed and potentially replicated server-based folders that all users anywhere in the organization can access. Users can choose to replicate specific public folders locally to their client machines for offline usage, and administrators can choose to have Exchange automatically maintain multiple server-based replicas for wider availabilty or access. When combined with forms, views, rules, and access permissions, public folders provide a rich infrastructure for authoring collaborative, groupware applications. An application author can create folders and design forms for use with those folders, as well as control access permissions, create named views, or add server-based processing via rules. Users of the folder application can then post new items, such as customer records or whatever the application allows, or update existing items using custom forms. Various built-in forms and sample applications are provided to help you get started designing your own groupware applications.

■ *Third-party integration.* Exchange Server supports a rich standard C and C++ language programming interface (MAPI) as well as a Common Object Model (COM) interface (Active Messaging) for programmers who use Visual Basic, Active Server Pages, or other COM-development environments. Exchange Server also provides mechanisms for adding extensions to the Exchange clients (including Microsoft Outlook) and the Administrator program. An Exchange Server features prominently in the Microsoft BackOffice SDK, which includes sample code and applications for developing extensions to Exchange. This means a huge number of third-party products, from messaging gateways to voice mail and fax systems, are available from third parties, with more showing up every day. If you are looking for sophisticated production workflow, content indexing, document management, a gateway to your funky legacy messaging system, or any other additional capabilities beyond those provided in the core Exchange Server product, chances are it is available from a third-party software vendor. The Exchange Web site (`http://www.microsoft.com/exchange`) has plenty of information on third-party products. Check it out!

■ *Integrated scheduling.* The Exchange client is tightly integrated with Microsoft Schedule+. Microsoft Outlook also includes rich integrated scheduling capabilities, which interoperate with Schedule+. Users' appointment schedules and to-do lists can be shared across your organization. Users can view each other's free and busy times, even in different sites and geographical locations, as well as access calendar details (given appropriate permissions). Users can determine when attendees have free time and automatically schedule meetings at the right time. Conference rooms and other shared resources can be selected and scheduled at the same time.

Exchange Futures

Although this version of Exchange delivers a lot, there are more features Microsoft has promised will be delivered in a release before the end of 1997:

■ *Database improvements.* Exchange Server versions 4.0 and 5.0 both have a limitation of 16GB of private mailbox storage and another 16GB of public storage per server. Exchange Server does provide per-user storage quotas and also maintains only a single instance of physical messages and attachments in the database, independent of how many logical instances may exist, so the actual logical storage available to users may actually be several times the 16GB physical limit. However, given the type of high-end server hardware you can buy today, this limit turns out to be the eventual scalability limit, preventing hosting more than a few thousand users per server. Microsoft has promised that it will deliver a version of Exchange Server that essentially removes all database size limitations by the end of 1997. Indeed, this release of Exchange Server should already be in beta test by the time this book is published. Microsoft has also stated that the same release will include enhanced multiprocessor scalability and memory management improvements, allowing for extremely large servers with upwards of 10,000 users, as well as reduced working set requirements on smaller, branch office or departmental servers.

■ *Support for the IMAP4 rev1 protocol.* IMAP4 rev1, the Internet Messaging Application Protocol version 4 revision 1, is the latest draft of the up-and-coming Internet protocol for accessing e-mail and shared folders. Unlike the POP3 protocol, which provides only very limited download capabilities, IMAP4 allows for more sophisticated concepts such as server-resident folders. It's the first Internet e-mail protocol that presumes that users can keep and manage their e-mail on the server indefinitely. Microsoft has indicated that support for IMAP4 will be in the same 1997 release.

■ *Online message and folder restore.* Today's Exchange provides full, differential, and partial backup and restore of the entire server. This is fine for disaster scenarios, but doesn't address the more common case of users accidentally deleting an item or folder in their mailbox or even a public folder. Microsoft has indicated they will provide a solution to this problem in the next release, utilizing an online repository of deleted "zombie" items and folders from which users or the administrator can retrieve accidentally deleted items for some administrator-defined period of time after items have been deleted.

■ *Server-based scripting.* The version 8.01 Outlook client (the Outlook version that comes with Exchange Server 5.0) allows users to author forms that include client-side functionality, or script. This is very handy for doing things such as field validation in groupware applications (for example, the price of an item must be > $100 or it cannot be created) but it falls short of providing a complete solution for certain types of applications. What's needed is a way for application authors to tell the server to execute script on their behalf when certain events happen. For example, purchase orders above a certain amount may need to be sent to a special approver, based on who is submitting the purchase order. The server should be able to execute this logic as part of the overall application, and the application author should be able to specify this. The term "workflow" is often used to describe this class of applications, which embody server-side business process automation logic. Microsoft has indicated that support for server-side scripting will be available in 1997.

Summary

This chapter has given you a brief overview of Microsoft's Exchange Server version 5.0. From the size of the book you're holding, you can probably tell it's quite an involved product, with tons of functionality—and we've barely begun to scratch the surface! But don't feel daunted. For all its power and richness, Exchange Server is actually quite easy to set up and use. A little education before you start, however, will go a long way toward mitigating headaches down the road. So without further ado, let's move on to an overview of Exchange Server concepts.

Electronic Messaging Concepts

by Greg Todd

Messaging Concepts and Terminology

As we discussed in the last chapter, "Overview of Microsoft Exchange Server 5.0," Exchange 5.0 is more than just your basic electronic mail software. It is a powerful foundation that is designed to serve as an Internet protocol server, an Active Server development platform, and yes, even a messaging server.

You may be wondering what the big deal is. After all, we're really talking about electronic mail (e-mail), right? Well, not anymore. Exchange 4.0 set a high standard for messaging because it was capable of much more than just handling simple e-mail. For example, it could handle messages of all types—voice mail, fax, or e-mail. Certainly, the more correct term for Exchange is a *messaging system*, although it can be used as an e-mail system. And Exchange 5.0 fits the bill quite well as either one because its roots lie in messaging technology.

With these thoughts in mind, this chapter is intended to provide a foundation for understanding messaging by reviewing basic e-mail concepts and terminology. Much of this general material applies to all e-mail systems, including Exchange. The remaining chapters of this book assume that you understand the basic material presented here. So when I describe how to implement these concepts in the context of Exchange, you will be able to follow along better.

Take a few moments and flip through this chapter, especially if you are sort of new to this e-mail thing. It covers a broad range of topics, beginning with definitions of fundamental electronic mail terms and Exchange Server terms. The chapter ends with a brief overview of network communication, data replication, and other issues involved in interconnecting e-mail systems. Don't worry though—these topics are covered in more detail throughout the book.

I also encourage you to check out the Glossary in Appendix C—there are many useful definitions found there.

Basic Terminology

An electronic mail system has much in common with the real U.S. Postal Service, and several of the terms are similar. You could think of *Exchange* as the entire system and the *Exchange client* and *Exchange server* as the client and server components of Exchange, respectively. The following are some other terms used in this book:

- *E-mail system.* Although it is intended to handle much more than simple e-mail, Exchange comprises the software portion of an entire e-mail system. And there are others as well, such as Banyan VINES and Lotus cc:Mail. In a broader sense, the term e-mail system embodies the entire collection of software, hardware, and communications infrastructure that makes it possible to send and receive messages.

- *Message.* Message is a general term. Information sent by the e-mail system is always in the form of a message, regardless of how little the message looks like traditional e-mail. Sometimes the terms message and e-mail are used interchangeably, although an e-mail is really a type of message. A message could be most anything: a simple text message, an electronic fax, or voice data.

- *Mailbox.* The delivery destination of a message is typically called a mailbox. Mailboxes are created and managed by the administrator, and they are maintained and controlled by the server. Each user accesses his or her mailbox by using client software. You cannot send and receive e-mail unless you have a mailbox located somewhere, just like the real postal service.

- *Mailbox owner.* A person who uses a designated mailbox in the e-mail system is a mailbox owner, usually referred to as a *client* or a *user.* Users play two roles, recipient and sender.

- *Address.* Every user in an e-mail system must have an address. This is quite analogous to your home address, used by the U.S. Postal Service. There are several different types of e-mail addresses, depending on what type of e-mail system you are using. However, they all serve the same function.

- *Sender.* The originator of a message is the sender. Messages are addressed by the sender to one or more recipients.

- *Recipient.* The one who receives a message is a recipient. It is the recipient's address that the sender uses to send the message.

- *E-mail–aware application.* These are applications that are aware of an available e-mail system and integrate with it where useful and appropriate. For example, Microsoft Office 97 lets you send the current document directly from within an Office application to an e-mail recipient.

- *Distribution lists.* Sometimes it is useful to have a list of recipient addresses grouped together for a mass mailing. So, a list of one or more recipients comprises a distribution list, also called a mailing list. Exchange and other e-mail systems enable distribution lists to include other distribution lists. For example, "All Employees" might include "Home Office" and "Branch Office."

E-Mail Functional Structure

As shown in Figure 2.1, an e-mail system fundamentally consists of a server with a central directory and message storage space. In addition, there is client software that handles access to your mailbox, which contains the messages in the server.

The high-level functional structure of an e-mail system is fairly simple, with only a handful of major components. The server side has a centrally shared directory of possible recipients and storage space for the messages themselves. The client side has software that lets users compose and send messages as well as receive and read them. Certainly this is expanded upon with more complex systems, but these components provide the foundation for a messaging system.

FIGURE 2.1.

Fundamentally, an e-mail system consists of a server with a central directory and message storage space plus client software for handling access to the server.

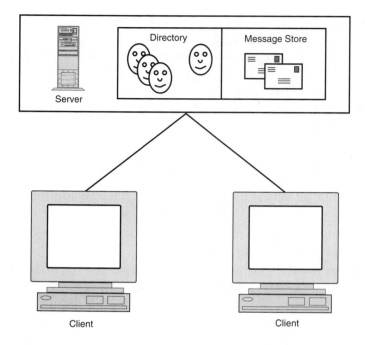

Exchange Administrative Structure

Now let's move from the general to the specific, as it applies to Exchange Server. There are several important terms that describe the high-level administrative structure of Exchange itself:

- *Organization.* Your business, taken as a complete, functioning structure, is an enterprise, or organization. The term organization is clearer, and it is the term used in Exchange—and throughout this guide—to describe the largest administrative unit in Exchange.

- *Site.* The next largest administrative unit in Exchange after the organization is a site. A site in the traditional sense is usually one geographical location, such as Houston, Seattle, or Tampa. An Exchange site is no different. Just as a real organization can have one physical site or many, so it is with Exchange organizations and sites. Sites are typically connected through a high-bandwidth wide area network. However, administrative granularity is not a good reason by itself to draw Exchange site boundaries. The underlying network topology is the single largest contributing factor to how site boundaries are defined. For example, Microsoft has a single Exchange site for all of its physical sites in North America because of its fast WAN implementation.

- *Server.* The next largest administrative unit in Exchange after the site is a server. Put simply, a server is the Windows NT Server computer providing messaging service for a group of users. A site can have one or more servers. Within a site, multiple servers are typically connected through a local area network because the communication between servers in a site necessitates LAN speeds.

■ *Recipient.* The lowest-level administrative unit in Exchange is the recipient. Each Exchange server contains one or more recipients, and each recipient usually represents a user's mailbox. One exception to this intuitive rule is a distribution list. In Exchange, a distribution list is also considered a recipient, and it is treated as such by the directory.

■ *Directory.* What good would an e-mail system be without a way to look up who is in the system? Modern e-mail systems must provide a way to keep track of all the users in the system so everyone can find the correct address for their e-mail. In Exchange, this is called the directory or the address book. There are a variety of ways the directory concept is implemented across various e-mail systems, depending upon the level of sophistication required.

■ *Foreign e-mail system.* An e-mail system or service external to the Exchange organization is referred to as foreign. The Internet, MS Mail, and cc:Mail are all great examples of foreign e-mail systems. Exchange is connected to a foreign e-mail system by a *connector.*

■ *Connector.* In Exchange, a gateway is called a connector. In a general sense, gateways connect different e-mail systems and e-mail services to each other, and they can be used both within and outside the company. For example, a Simple Mail Transfer Protocol (SMTP) gateway lets users within the company communicate with people outside the company using the Internet. In Exchange, this gateway is called the Internet Mail Connector, or IMC. Similarly, if a company uses of a mix of different e-mail systems—for example, Exchange at one physical site and Microsoft Mail at another—a gateway interconnects the two e-mail systems within the organization. In Exchange, this gateway is called the PC Mail Connector. The connector handles the mail format translation between Exchange and the foreign e-mail system. With Exchange Server 5.0, Microsoft provides connectors for SMTP, Microsoft Mail, X.400, and cc:Mail.

Figure 2.2 shows a diagram of a general e-mail system to help you put these terms in context. Conveniently, the high-level administrative structure of Exchange generally reflects the geographic structure of a company. When you plan your own system, you should develop a similar diagram, starting at the highest level with the organization, working your way down to the sites and the server(s) that make up each site.

Of course, many companies are located at a single physical site and served by a single server. But it doesn't hurt to think ahead, because your company is probably going to grow, right? Fortunately, the engineers at Microsoft elegantly designed Exchange Server to scale from small companies with a few dozen users to large ones with many thousands of users.

FIGURE 2.2.

A messaging system such as Exchange Server serves your entire enterprise.

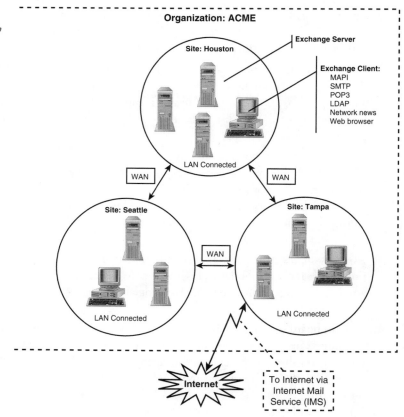

More Terminology

You didn't think we were done yet, did you? I hope not, because there is plenty more to go over. Now I'd like to move into more coverage of the concepts introduced so far.

The following sections discuss the basic components of an Exchange messaging system in a bit more detail. The terminology presented will be relevant to Exchange, so it should help you get a better handle on "Exchange-speak." However, many of these concepts will apply to other e-mail systems, though they may be given different names or implemented slightly differently.

Directories and Address Books

Exchange creates and maintains an internal directory of every recipient in the organization. This information is made available to users in a more user friendly form called an *address book.*

There are two main types of address books in Exchange:

- *Global address book.* This is the master list of every recipient in the organization—all mailbox owners, distribution lists, custom recipients, and public folders. The global address book is generally available to every mailbox owner in the organization.

- *Personal address book.* Exchange and most other e-mail systems support the use of a personal address book so users can have recipients that do not exist in the Global address book. Users can add their own private distribution lists and custom recipients to a personal address book that is stored on their own computer.

I defined two common types of recipients at the beginning of this chapter: individual mailboxes identified by owner name and distribution lists. Exchange and most other e-mail systems support two additional types of recipients:

- *Custom recipient.* A custom recipient is the address of a recipient on a foreign e-mail system. These addresses are also stored in an address book for convenience. Of course, a connector (gateway) must exist to deliver messages to the foreign e-mail system. exchsupp@microsoft.com is an example of a useful, real-life custom recipient where you can send ideas, suggestions, and questions directly to the Exchange development team.

- *Public folder.* A public folder functions as a type of public posting area, or electronic bulletin board. Messages addressed to a public folder are accessible by multiple users at the same time. As you might imagine, public folder technology forms the basis for information sharing and group collaboration. Check out Chapter 24, "Public Folders," for more details.

Aliases

An individual's mailbox is identified by the Display Name of the owner. The Display Name can be anything the owner wants the Exchange world to see, such as the owner's first and last name. It could also be something like The Lead Administrator or Duke's Honey. For convenience, names are often given a short form—an *alias*—for internal use in the e-mail system. The alias is the primary entry in the address book, and it is quicker to type and easier to remember.

There are several conventional ways to generate an alias from a full name. For example, Rodney Todd can be shortened to rodneyt, rtodd, or rt. When you add a new user to a system, Exchange can create an alias automatically, using the first name plus the last initial, the first initial plus the last name, or initials only. No alias—using the full name, in other words—is also an option.

Ideally, an alias uniquely identifies the mailbox owner, but this isn't always possible with such simple renderings of names. For example, the first name/last initial method yields ambiguous results for Rodney Todd and Rodney Thompson. If you try to use rodneyt for both names, Exchange will force the second one to be unique, such as rodneyt2.

Note that an alias is not limited to shortened variations of a full name. Unlike phone numbers or postal addresses, there is no universal scheme or central authority to assign e-mail addresses or enforce consistency. Most e-mail systems allow just about anything for an alias, but the format is usually determined largely by corporate culture and standards.

When Exchange is implemented, you might adopt a format for generating an alias as well as a plan for ensuring uniqueness. However, aliases are not absolutely necessary, because users don't actually require them. In fact, many companies do not use alias names; they use Display Names exclusively. You will probably spend a fair amount of time helping to establish consistency, especially if your organization has more than one site.

> **NOTE**
>
> Microsoft's solution to avoid ambiguous aliases is to use the first name plus as much of the last name as needed for uniqueness. People with the shortest aliases are either early hires or have uncommon first names.
>
> For example, billg is Bill Gates. Assuming someone named Bill Green was hired later, he would be billgr. Bill Graham, coming later still, would be billgra, and so on. On the other hand, you probably wouldn't have to worry much about ambiguity with someone named Xanthus Jones.

E-Mail Addresses

In addition to an alias, if an e-mail system is connected to the outside world, each mailbox owner usually has an *e-mail address*. Unlike an alias, this is for external use because it identifies the mailbox owner to a foreign e-mail system such as the Internet. This is the address a mailbox owner gives publicly so an outsider can send him e-mail. Once again, an appropriate connector (gateway) must exist to receive messages from a foreign e-mail system.

Fortunately, widely used messaging standards enforce a certain level of consistency in e-mail addresses. The following two are the most commonly encountered address standards, and they are discussed in more detail in the later section "Messaging Standards":

- *Simple Mail Transfer Protocol (SMTP).* SMTP defines the message transfer protocol and address format of Internet mail. The format of an SMTP address is simple: `recipient@domain`. `domain` is the entity's registered Internet domain name—for example, `bmc.com`. If desired, a business could add a site name to the domain as well, for example `houston.bmc.com`.

  The `recipient` portion of the address is formed much like an alias. Ideally, you use the same format. For example, Greg Todd might be `gregt` on the Exchange system and `gregt@bmc.com` on the Internet. If you choose not to use aliases internally, keep in mind that spaces are not allowed in Internet address. You must omit the spaces or use a dash or underscore as a replacement. Therefore, Greg Todd becomes `greg-todd@bmc.com` or `gregtodd@bmc.com`.

- *X.400.* X.400 is another standard message transfer protocol and e-mail address format. Before the Internet explosion, X.400 was the most widely implemented and used standard. Wide usage of X.400 is, for the most part, on the decline. But X.400 addresses are still encountered on the host-based e-mail systems common in large corporations.

  If Internet addresses represent simplicity, then X.400 addresses certainly represent complexity. The *minimum* address for BMC Software's Greg Todd is

  ```
  g=Greg;s=Todd;o=BMC Software;a=Headquarters;c=US;
  ```

  This is certainly not the easiest thing to include on a business card!

The SMTP Internet address format is quickly becoming a globally accepted standard, **Standards** although there are many other messaging standards in addition to SMTP and X.400. Of course, that's the nice thing about standards—there are so many to choose from! Thankfully, most e-mail systems can handle either SMTP or X.400, or both. Exchange 5.0 supports these and several more. See Chapter 9, "Exchange Server and the Internet," for more details.

Message Stores

Every messaging system has to have a place to store all the messages it handles. For Exchange, this storage is called a *message store.*

Physically, a message store is one or more files located on a disk drive accessible to Exchange server. In Exchange and in most other e-mail systems, server-based storage is logically organized into at least two main categories.

- *Private message store.* Private storage is reserved for individual mailboxes. Access is limited to the mailbox owner and to others for whom the owner grants permission.
- *Public message store.* This is shared space used by public folders. Public folders support a wide range of permissions. The public folder owner(s) are generally the only ones with full access, although by default all others have read access. For example, to facilitate group sharing of information, access is generally granted to any mailbox owner in the group.

Messaging technology has an interesting way of staying in step with disk drive technology. Back when messages were mostly simple text, drives were small. Now that gigabyte drives are commonplace, so are megabyte messages. It seems like no matter how big the drives are, they still aren't big enough. For this and other reasons, Exchange supports letting users take personal control of message storage.

In a *personal message store*, messages are transferred from the server-controlled message store into files controlled by the mailbox owner. This action is generally initiated by the mailbox owner. Usually, a personal message store is physically located on the local drive of the mailbox owner's personal computer. Although this can be a beneficial way of reducing the amount of storage required on the server, after a message is transferred to a personal store, it is no longer directly accessible by the server.

This lack of access can cause problems for some users. For example, if a user signs onto the e-mail system remotely from another computer outside the office, messages stored in the personal store won't be accessible. However, if you happen to carry your laptop with you that contains your personal message store, you've always got access to your e-mail. I find that using a personal message store is a huge benefit and a real convenience.

> **NOTE**
>
> The message store terminology used in Exchange is confusing on two counts. First, Exchange uses the terms "store," "message store," "information store," and "folders" interchangeably. For example, the personal message store is also called the "personal information store" and "personal folders." Please be aware that the usage varies in the printed documentation, in the online documentation, and in the user interface.
>
> Also, we generally think of the word "personal" as a synonym for "private," but Exchange uses these terms to distinguish between a user's messages stored centrally on the server (private message store) and individually by the client (personal message store). However, you can think of it this way: Private folders can be shared by granting permissions to others. So they are private to the owner and to whomever has been granted permissions. On the other hand, personal folders cannot be shared with anyone; they are strictly personal.

Messaging Standards

Standards   Communication between server and client (and server and server) is handled by interface components called *messaging protocols* and *Application Program Interfaces (APIs)*. A wide range of public messaging standards have been developed to promote open communications between e-mail systems. These standards simplify the job of interconnecting e-mail systems and give users greater control at the desktop.

Fortunately or not, the practical implementation of these ideas is sufficiently complicated and messy enough to support huge businesses and legions of programmers.

Support of published messaging standards has become critically important as acceptance and dependence upon e-mail has grown. Standards have made it possible to interconnect a wide range of private and publicly maintained e-mail systems in an increasingly effective global network. Improved standards have even made it possible to build an messaging infrastructure from a mix of server and client components provided by different manufacturers.

Messaging standards operate at a range of levels.

On the simplest level, protocols define formats for addresses and messages that permit uniform data transfer between e-mail systems. Implementation details are left to the creator of the software.

At a more complex level, APIs support tight functional integration between messaging components and messaging-aware applications. An API exposes software functionality directly to other programs.

Think of a protocol as something like the operating voltage specification for a table lamp. Think of an API as one of the many physical definitions that make it possible to plug the lamp into the socket, flick a switch, and have light.

Despite the obvious benefits of messaging standards, in theory at least, their practical implementation is replete with problems. There are many different standards efforts conducted by alternately cooperating and competing academics, standards organizations, industry committees, and e-mail software manufacturers. As a result, standards often overlap. Various groups adopt chunks of competing specs in an effort to claim the title of "most complete" or "most compatible." Well-intentioned efforts take a baseline specification and enhance it in mutually incompatible directions.

As a result of all this activity, most messaging standards are now enormously huge and enormously complex. As administrator, you can't avoid exposure to these things if you want your e-mail system to connect to the outside world. Exchange Server's connector software does a reasonable job of hiding complexity, but there are still several unavoidable implementation details you will have to take care of.

Don't panic though. This book will help you wade through all this stuff as it pertains to Exchange Server. Also, there are many resources out there that discuss particular aspects of standards and messaging in great detail. The information is there if you want to go dig it out.

To get started with the digging, the following sections provide a quick summary of some core messaging protocols and APIs you will likely encounter.

Protocols

Most of the protocols you will encounter with respect to Exchange pertain to the Internet. In fact, wide support of these very protocols is a major focus of Exchange 5.0. There are several, and they are covered in even more detail later on in Chapter 9.

The SMTP Protocol

The Internet—in the beginning, at least—was largely a creation of academics: research scientists, graduate students, and professors. Therefore, the original standards have been proposed and driven by the academic community.

As such, the hallmark of the Internet is simplicity. It's not that academics don't love complexity—it's just that they usually get stuck with a hodgepodge of secondhand equipment. So a lowest-common-denominator approach demands simplicity.

Simplicity and the exploding interest in the Internet driven by the World Wide Web have positioned SMTP as the *de facto* standard for addressing and sending text-based messages.

Internet mail access is required for most businesses, and this is likely to be the first Exchange connector (gateway) you set up. The following are a few important Internet-related acronyms:

- *MIME—Multipurpose Internet Mail Extensions.* MIME expands the SMTP protocol to handle message attachments and non-ASCII data. SMTP is designed for single messages containing English text (7-bit characters). If your message consists of multiple files or includes 8-bit data (characters with accent marks), you are out of luck without MIME. Fortunately, Exchange and most other e-mail systems now support MIME.

- *UUENCODE.* Like MIME, UUENCODE is another method of encoding a message that contains 8-bit data. Exchange supports UUENCODE.

- *POP3—Post Office Protocol v3.* POP3 defines the operational protocol for Internet mail servers. Version 3 is the widely used standard. SMTP defines the protocol for sending a message. A POP3-compliant server, client, or gateway is needed to receive the message. As the name implies, there have been several versions. POP3 is generally used between clients and servers, not between servers.

- *DNS—Domain Name Service.* DNS is the name service that makes the entire Internet work. Internet service providers operate DNS servers, which translate domain names (the stuff after the @) into an Internet Protocol (IP) address. The IP address is a number that locates the specified SMTP server on the Internet so that an outgoing message gets routed to the right place. DNS is also used together with Uniform Resource Locator (URL) identifiers to specify the absolute location files and other resources on the Internet.

There are certainly many other important Internet-related protocols. This having been said, there are a couple of points worth noting:

- The Internet does not provide a central directory of recipients. You must know the address before you send the message. There is no way to request a list of potential recipients or even to resolve the doubtful spelling of a name. If you don't know the domain name, you can look it up with a bit of effort. (Note that some places run a separate service, called Finger, that identifies recipient addresses in the domain. There are also companies that maintain directories of Internet entities, but these are neither universal nor comprehensive.)

- A uniform method of finding recipient addresses is sorely needed. As you will see, other messaging standards have proposed solutions to this problem.

The X.400 Protocol

Whereas the Internet was born out of the world of academia, X.400 was born out of the world of standards organizations. One such organization is the ISO—International Standards Organization—which is a worldwide federation of national standards bodies from nearly 100 countries. Another is the CCITT—a French acronym that stands for International Consultative Committee for Telegraphy and Telephony—based in Geneva.

The X.400 series of protocols was jointly developed by ISO and CCITT, and X.400 is the CCITT version of the joint standard.

As you can imagine, getting more than 100 different countries to agree on anything is a challenge. The X.400 address format is an example of the issues of design by committee. Here are some other ISO messaging standards that you are likely to encounter:

■ *MHS—Message Handling System.* X.400 is the first of a series of specifications that define a complete e-mail system called MHS. There have been a number of enhancements and revisions to the MHS specification; the current draft version is called MHS(94).

■ *X.500 and LDAP.* This is a standard for e-mail and telephony directory services proposed by the International Telegraph Union working through ISO. Since it was first proposed, e-mail directory services have become a small part of the scope of this specification, which is designed to standardize the location of data resources in general. X.500 is an ambitious specification that includes universal directory structures and naming conventions. In fact, the size and complexity of X.500 has limited its acceptance. However, LDAP—Lightweight Directory Access Protocol—which is based on X.500, shows some promise. And LDAP is supported by Exchange 5.0.

APIs

The messaging standards discussed so far are protocols rather than APIs. APIs provide the muscle of a commercial implementation that gives movement to the skeleton of a messaging specification. With a defined API in place, software manufacturers can build products to support a standard interface. Individual e-mail systems can interoperate, and server and client components can be plugged together to build complete systems.

Common Messaging Calls API

Recognizing the need for API-level support, several groups formed to define APIs to wrap around the various pieces of the ISO MHS specifications. The best of these efforts produced the *Common Messaging Calls (CMC)* API. CMC was created by the X.400 API Association (XAPIA), a consortium of leading mail-system manufacturers, telecommunications companies, and large-end users.

CMC has been expanded to include direct support for SMTP/MIME as well as X.400. There are actually two CMC APIs: Simple CMC and Full CMC. Simple CMC is designed to support mail-enabled applications. Full CMC is designed to support an entire e-mail system. Simple CMC support is available today in several products, including Microsoft Mail. In addition, Lotus and Novell selected Full CMC implementation as the primary messaging API in their next-generation, client-server e-mail systems (Notes 4.0 and Groupwise XTD, respectively).

CMC is developing largely in parallel to Microsoft's Messaging API, or MAPI, which is covered in detail in the next section. Even though Microsoft has been a key participant in the XAPIA, CMC has taken on the flavor of an "everybody else against Microsoft" effort.

Microsoft's Messaging API

Microsoft chose to lead the definition of a new messaging standard and develop the API to support it. Called MAPI, it is certainly an integral part of Exchange, and it is also an integrating component of the various Windows applications, such as those in Microsoft Office.

Interestingly, Microsoft was originally a strong supporter of CMC, and participated in developing the original specification. But as Microsoft engineers began to develop the specification for Exchange, they found that CMC could not provide the desired degree of operating system integration. Thus, MAPI was born.

The key to MAPI is support at the operating system level. Because Microsoft provides the operating system for more than 90 percent of the desktop clients, they can provide a fundamentally greater degree of integration with a MAPI-compliant messaging system such as Exchange Server.

Like CMC, MAPI exists in two versions. The first, called *Simple MAPI*, is nearly identical to Simple CMC. This is the result of Microsoft's early support for CMC. In fact, Microsoft defined support for CMC version 1.0 as an integral part of Simple MAPI.

The second version, called *Extended MAPI*, is much more than a protocol for communication between different manufacturers' e-mail systems. In fact, about the only thing the simple and extended versions have in common are the name MAPI.

With Extended MAPI (or simply "MAPI" from here on), Microsoft has created an entirely new messaging architecture to support Exchange and other e-mail systems. Exchange itself is possible because of MAPI. Discussed in detail in Chapter 4, "Exchange Client Components," the MAPI architecture provides a structure that gives all e-mail systems equal treatment.

As an Exchange user, you are committing to MAPI and open Internet protocols, such as SMTP, POP3, NNTP, LDAP, and IMAP4 in the near future. In fact, this is the direction Microsoft as a whole is headed for its products.

Network Issues

Enough about protocols and APIs. As an Exchange administrator, these are an important part of your job. But let's talk about some network issues, which are another important part of your job. After all, the biggest difference between e-mail and snail mail is the data network.

Networks connect client to server, server to server, site to site, and site to outside services such as the Internet. Here is a quick review of some important network issues and terms to start you thinking as you read the rest of the book.

Capacity

You will need to estimate capacity requirements in order to size your organization's local and wide area networks for all sites and clients. Here are some issues you need to consider:

- *Bandwidth.* Bandwidth is a measure of the rate at which data can be transmitted through a given connection. Measured in kilobits per second (Kbps), bandwidth determines the absolute capacity of a network connection. Note that the term is bits, not bytes. In general, the bigger the bandwidth, the bigger the cost. Also, you cannot always expect to actually use 100 percent of the bandwidth. For example, 10BaseT ethernet provides 10 megabits per second (Mbps) bandwidth. But realistically, you can get only about 70 percent of that before packet collisions start degrading network performance to the point of being unusable.

- *Traffic.* Traffic is a measurement of the total volume of data transmitted on the system over time, and it helps determine the average capacity of the network. The amount of traffic your network can handle is obviously a function of network bandwidth. Problem is, measuring the total volume can be complicated because traffic comes in peaks and valleys. For example, people often check messages at the beginning of the day, but they perform little network activity during lunch. Because peak traffic determines the total bandwidth you need, smoothing out the size of the peaks and valleys reduces total cost. There are techniques you can apply to help, such as scheduling site-to-site connections for non-peak hours and placing high bandwidth users on their own network segment.

Connections

The point-to-point data connections that make up a wide area network are usually supplied by telephone companies. Physical connections are made through a hardware device that connects the organization's data network on one side to phone lines on the other. The hardware device can be a conventional analog modem, an ISDN (Integrated Service Digital Network) modem, or a more specialized device. There are two kinds of connections:

- *Dial-up connection.* An temporary network connection made like a phone call. Dial-up connections use analog or ISDN telephone lines. Analog lines provide bandwidth up to about 33 Kbps, ISDN lines up to about 128 Kbps. Many modems have built-in data compression that can effectively double or triple these rates.

- *Dedicated connection.* A permanent network connection made on a leased telephone line. Phone companies supply leased lines in a variety of capacities and configurations ranging from 56 Kbps up to 1.54 Mbps on a T1 line, or more if needed. These types of connections require specialized network hardware and they are usually expensive.

Communications Protocols

You will likely encounter several communications protocols. The following are a few common ones relevant to an Exchange installation:

- *Serial Line IP, Point-to-Point Protocol.* SLIP and PPP are protocols for dial-up connections to the Internet. PPP is newer and is replacing SLIP. These protocols make it possible for remote users to connect to the organization through a dial-up Internet service provider such as CompuServe or America Online.

- *X.25.* X.25 is a standard telecommunications protocol used on certain types of leased lines. It is quite popular in Europe, but its performance suffers due to overhead.

- *Dial-Up Networking—DUN.* Referred to as RAS (Remote Access Services) in Windows NT 3.*x*, DUN is communications software built into the Windows operating system family. DUN lets one Windows computer connect to another and operate it remotely. You can use DUN to interconnect sites via dial-up connections. DUN supports SLIP, PPP, and X.25 network protocols.

Replication and Synchronization

With multiple servers, all directories and message stores must be updated when changes are made on individual servers. For example, if a new recipient is added to the Seattle office, directories on servers in the Houston and Tampa offices must show the change as well. Of course, the speed at which information is updated between sites depends on the configuration of the organization's wide area network.

There are two basic kinds of update strategies:

- *Replication.* This is the process of duplicating a master directory or message store on secondary servers. The master copy is always right. The secondary copies are replaced entirely.

- *Synchronization.* In some cases, there is no "master copy." Changes can be made independently on two or more sources of information. Synchronization identifies the changes made to each source and then updates all sources equally.

Summary

This chapter provided an overview of the general terminology and key concepts of messaging systems. Armed with an understanding of the terminology, it is time to look at the specifics of how Exchange is a complete client-server messaging system. In Chapter 3, "Exchange Server Components," and Chapter 4, "Exchange Client Components," you will learn about the architecture of Exchange, and you are introduced to the various pieces of software that provide core system functionality.

Exchange Server Components

by Greg Todd

IN THIS CHAPTER

CHAPTER 3

Microsoft Exchange Server 5.0 is the second major release of Microsoft's successful BackOffice messaging product. The goal of this major release is to be a world-class Internet protocol server and an integrated part of the Active Server development platform. In addition, it builds on version 4.0's goal to provide the best messaging capabilities and features anywhere.

New to Version 5.0

Exchange Server supports the popular electronic mail and Internet protocols—X.400, SMTP, NNTP, LDAP, and POP3—in addition to the native Microsoft messaging API, MAPI.

Exchange was first released as two products: the Exchange client that came with Windows 95, which was shipped well in advance of Exchange Server 4.0, and Exchange Server 4.0 itself. This caused considerable confusion when talking about Exchange, because it was unclear which product was being referenced. Furthermore, the original Exchange client with Windows 95 did not directly support connecting to Exchange Server 4.0; it had to be upgraded with the Exchange 4.0 client.

Since then, things have become clearer. To resolve some of the confusion, Microsoft has re-named the messaging software delivered with its operating system products. Specifically, the Windows 95 and Windows NT 4.0 e-mail client are now called Windows Messaging. And there are other MAPI clients available that will work directly with Exchange Server, such as Outlook, which is a part of Office 97. By the time this goes to press, Microsoft will have re-leased Exchange Server 5.0, and it will support even more client connectivity, including POP3 mail clients and NNTP news readers.

Exchange Server in total is composed of client software and server software. In this chapter, you're going to take a look at the components that comprise the server portion of Exchange. As you might imagine, the server is quite a complex piece of work, and a good understanding of the basic architecture will help you grasp the concepts presented throughout this book. After finishing this chapter, I recommend you read about the client portion in the next chapter, "Exchange Client Components." So let's get started!

Exchange Architecture Overview

Exchange Server has been in development literally for several years. The resulting product represents the collective effort of not only the Microsoft Exchange team, but also hundreds of beta testers. Extensive feedback from these testers has helped Microsoft build a product that in many ways was designed for the industry by the industry.

Microsoft is the first of the mainstream PC software developers to offer a messaging product that is designed from the ground up based on a client/server model. Other popular electronic mail programs, such as Lotus cc:Mail and Microsoft Mail, are based on a shared file system concept rather than client-server architecture.

Client-Server Versus Shared File

The Exchange server has been implemented as a series of NT services built on an industrial-strength, fault-tolerant, relational database. Exchange implements the electronic messaging architectural components defined by the Comite' Consultatif International Telegraphique et Telephonic (CCITT) to build a high-performance, extensible multithreaded messaging server. The CCITT, known in English as the International Telegraph and Telephone Consultative Committee, defines the following major components in an X.400 Message Handling System: User Agent (UA), Message Transfer Agent (MTA), and Message Store (MS). And because industry standard protocols are used, connectivity to other compliant electronic mail systems is much more easily implemented.

In contrast, Microsoft Mail, still one of the most widely used e-mail systems on the market, is based on a series of shared files and directories located on a file server's hard disk. Although the simplicity and network operating system independence of the implementation made the program popular, the implementation is based on a passive file structure located on a simple file server. The client software controls all interaction and movement of mail. MS Mail is a single post office solution that does not support delivery of e-mail outside its post office. To deliver mail outside the post office requires the addition of an external process, typically running on a separate machine. Large MS Mail (and cc:Mail) installations have not only the post offices to manage, but also the machines that run support applications such as External and Dispatch to keep the post offices and directories synchronized.

Exchange has been designed to take advantage of NT Server's architecture by running the MTA processes as services, called connectors. Using this connector architecture, Exchange can support communications between organizations, sites, and servers from a single machine. The architecture also helps minimize hardware requirements and points of failure in an implementation, and it greatly increases the scalability of the Exchange server.

Messaging between the Exchange servers and client is handled by remote procedure calls (RPC). When the server is operating in an NT domain, it uses NT security to validate access to the user's mailbox. This minimizes the need for the user to remember multiple passwords. RPCs enable Exchange to function over multiple protocols such as NWLINK (IPX/SPX), TCP/IP, and NetBEUI.

Exchange's directory is based on an X.500-compliant directory structure and support for X.400 addressing. Exchange conforms to the 1984 and 1988 X.400 specification, which is an ISO standard for electronic mail addressing. It is integral to Exchange, and it is used for all internal and external addressing.

The X.400 Model

The X.400 protocol model itself is composed of three components: the message transfer agent (MTA), the user agent (UA), and the message store (MS), as shown in Figure 3.1. The Microsoft Exchange Server architecture supports all of the components shown in the figure.

FIGURE 3.1.

*A basic X.400 message
handling system is a
collection of components
that work together to
transfer messages.*

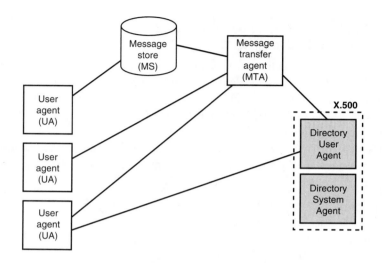

The message transfer agent portion of the model can be represented by multiple components in Exchange. One example is Exchange's internal MTA, which is used to communicate with another Exchange server's MTA. Other examples include the X.400 Connector and the Site Connector.

The message store portion of the model—called an information store (IS) in Exchange—is composed of two distinct units, the public information store and the private information store. More about these later in the chapter in the section "Information Store."

The user agent portion of the model is represented by MAPI clients, which are used to access the information store. A new concept to Microsoft messaging is Exchange's capability of supporting any MAPI-based client that supports the published API set. As mentioned earlier, Microsoft Outlook is a great example. In fact, I personally use Outlook, and I really like it.

The Directory User Agent and Directory System Agent portions of the figure are not strictly a part of the X.400 specification. However, they are specified as a part of X.500, which is a separate specification that covers how a directory works internally. There is some natural integration between the two, as shown in the figure.

Administration and Organizational Structure

Exchange adheres to an organizational structure based around a central administration model. The largest administrative unit in this model is the *organization*, which includes all servers in the messaging infrastructure, both local and remote. Typically, this organization equates to the company or organization name.

Servers in an Exchange organization are grouped by *site*. A site is a group of servers that share the same directory information and communicate over high-speed, permanent, and synchronous connections. Directory changes and updates in a site are automatically replicated to all servers, thus permitting the sharing of a single organizational directory based on a merge of all the sites' directory information.

You perform administration tasks for the Exchange organization from a single interface, the Exchange Administrator program, which can be installed on the same computer as the Exchange Server or on a separate computer. The Administrator is shown in Figure 3.2.

FIGURE 3.2.

The Exchange Administrator program can be run from either the server or a separate Windows NT computer.

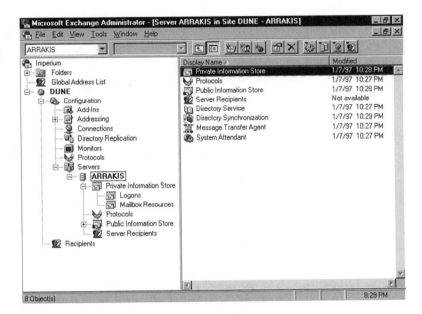

Exchange—The Server

You must install the Exchange Server in a Microsoft Windows NT domain. After it is installed, a portion of the Exchange Administrator is integrated into User Manager for Domains, as in Figure 3.3. When new NT accounts are created with User Manager for Domains, you are prompted to create an associated Exchange mailbox along with the new account.

> **NOTE**
>
> The Exchange Server takes advantage of the underlying NT domain architecture for user authentication. A single password can be used to access both the NT domain and the Exchange Server. This integration with the NT domain alleviates the need to provide a separate password to access a user's mailbox, but it requires that the Exchange server be installed in an NT domain.
>
> *continues*

continued

To some, this single login feature appears to be a problem, but Exchange Server actually uses the NT security model to ensure that the correct user is accessing the mailbox.

If more than one user uses a workstation, you can configure the client to prompt for the user name, password, and domain. To do this, select Tools | Services, and then Microsoft Exchange Server. Click Properties and the Advanced tab. Uncheck the Use network security during logon box.

Integrating with Exchange is not a problem because it becomes impossible to "spoof" Exchange and open up someone else's mail. Because authentication occurs behind the scenes, a rogue user cannot get inside the security to defeat it. When a mailbox is created, it is tied to an NT domain account, and only that individual (or someone he has explicitly assigned permissions to) can access that mailbox.

FIGURE 3.3.

After installing Exchange Server, the Exchange administrative menu is integrated with User Manager for Domains.

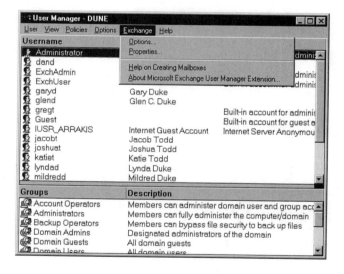

Conversely, the Exchange Administrator can create the NT domain accounts when a new Exchange user is created, then specify it directly in the Primary Windows NT Account button. This method is typically used to add a single new user, as shown in Figure 3.4, although groups of users can be added using the import option.

NOTE

Although Exchange must be installed on a computer running Windows NT Server, this does not preclude the use of Exchange in a Novell NetWare network. When installed in this environment, just configure NT Server to support IPX/SPX and Gateway Services for NetWare.

FIGURE 3.4.

When creating a new Exchange mailbox, you can specify a primary Windows NT account that will own the mailbox.

Server Components

Exchange Server is comprised of a series of NT services, databases, and log files, which can be divided into core and optional components. Each of the core components is installed and configured during the installation process. All core components are configured to start automatically. These components provide the primary messaging services: message transfer, delivery, and storage, as well as the Exchange directory services. Optional components, such as connectors and advanced security, are also NT services.

The following lists the core Exchange services with their NT service names in italics:

- Directory Services—*MSExchangeDS*
- Information Store—*MSExchangeIS*
- Message Transfer Agent (MTA)—*MSExchangeMTA*
- System Attendant—*MSExchangeSA*

As described earlier, there are other options that can be installed, such as MS Mail Directory Synchronization, cc:Mail Connector, and Key Management Service, each of which is its own NT service. As with any NT service, you use the NT Services applet in the Control Panel to manage them. See Figure 3.5.

You can configure Exchange-specific features of each service via the Exchange Administrator. The default location for the Administrator program is in the Exchange executable directory \EXCHSRVR\BIN. When started, the Administrator presents a graphical view into the Exchange organization, as in Figure 3.2.

3

EXCHANGE SERVER COMPONENTS

FIGURE 3.5.

Exchange Server services are managed with the NT Services applet.

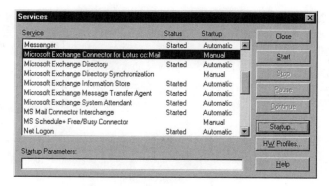

FIGURE 3.6.

The Exchange Administrator is organized using the familiar tree structure.

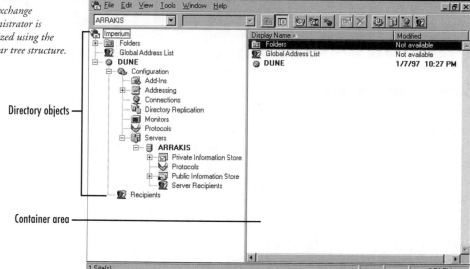

Directory objects

Container area

NOTE

Other than the client, the Exchange Administration program is the only Exchange component that does not require NT Server to run. The current version will run on NT Workstation and NT Server, but it will not run on either Windows 95 or Windows for Workgroups. Installing the Administrator component on a separate NT workstation enables the Exchange server organization to be managed from a designated administrative console.

The format of the display is hierarchical, showing all objects, users, and resources in the organization. The display is split into two areas. The directory objects are on the left. They represent all components in the organization. The container area is on the right. This area displays the current selected object. To view detailed information about an object in the container area, highlight each object. You can view the properties of each object from the File menu, or you can press Alt+Enter while the object is highlighted. The interface itself resembles Windows Explorer.

Directory Services

A key element of the Exchange architecture is the directory. It maintains all information about the organization's resources and users. It also supports mailboxes, custom recipients, public and private folders, distribution lists, servers, connectors, and any other add-ons to the Exchange server. Other components of the server use the directory to complete their jobs. The server supports OSI protocols for internal messaging. A native X.400 address is created for all new objects that are added to the database. Internally, Exchange stores the definitions for these objects in an X.500-like structure.

When users are created, at least four associated addresses are created: cc:Mail, MS Mail, SMTP, and X.400. Figure 3.7 shows an example of the addresses.

FIGURE 3.7.

There are at least four e-mail addresses associated with each user in Exchange.

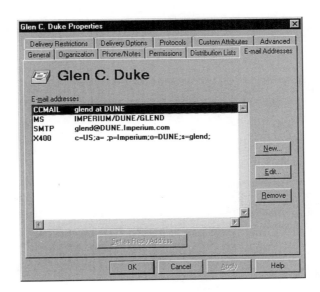

> **TIP**
>
> To change the default *root* component of the Exchange e-mail recipients, open the Site Addressing object from the Configuration component of the Exchange site (in this case, Dune). Then select the Site Addressing tab, and edit the e-mail addresses for each e-mail type, as shown in Figure 3.8.
>
> Changing the default Site Addressing can effectively hide the existence of the Exchange servers and support a uniform addressing organization address for the entire organization. This is normally done with UNIX Sendmail and the sendmail.cf file, but with Exchange, the process is quite simple.
>
> Changing the default site addressing offers a way to secure the Exchange server and NT user accounts from intruders and create user-friendly names for the recipients.

FIGURE 3.8.

The default e-mail addresses can be changed from the Site Addressing property sheet.

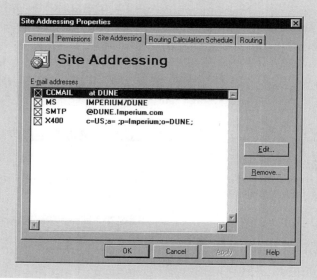

Microsoft Exchange uses objects to describe the structure of the organization. All items in the Exchange hierarchy are considered objects. This includes recipients, distribution lists, servers, and the messaging infrastructure itself.

The directory also supports special objects called *containers*. A container is an object that contains other objects and containers. The objects or recipients within the organization are addressable and maintain entries in the directory database. If there are multiple sites within the organization, the information about these recipients is replicated to the directory database on each server. This is how the global address book is built.

The Exchange directory is comprised of two key elements: the directory database and the directory service. The directory database is located by default in \EXCHSRVR\DSADATA \DIR.EDB.

CAUTION

Although the underlying database is built around a version of the Microsoft Jet database, there is a misconception that it is based on Microsoft Access. Do not confuse it with the Access Jet database—*they are not the same.*

There are two Jet databases, one that became Access and the other that was incorporated into Exchange. In reality, the underlying database in Exchange is more akin to SQL Server than to Access.

So, although Microsoft Exchange uses a relational database structure, you cannot use conventional tools to manipulate or view these tables. If you want to view this information, use Crystal Report Writer for Exchange or a tool designed specifically to access the database.

The Directory Service (DS) is a Windows NT service that manages information in the directory database and handles requests from users, services, and applications.

Users and administrators can access and manipulate directory services. The Exchange administrator is responsible for creating, deleting, and changing directory objects, as well as for populating the address book. When a new object—for example, a recipient—is added to the server, an entry is created in the server address book. This, in turn, is propagated to the site and then to the global address book, where it is available to all users in the organization. It is the responsibility of the DS to manage this process and to ensure that the integrity of the directory and its structure is maintained.

Users access the directory through the Exchange server address book. Although users cannot modify the global address book, they can create custom subsets of entries of the address book as well as create new entries in their own personal address book (PAB).

An Access Control List (ACL) controls access to Exchange Server directory objects. The objects are assigned permissions when roles are established in the Administrator program for each user or service. To view the dialog box that displays the roles, select Tools | Options. Then select the Permissions tab from the Administrator menu and check Display rights for roles on Permission Page.

After roles have been defined, the roles for directory services are displayed in the Directory Service dialog box, as in Figure 3.9. You do not always need to add permissions to every object within the Exchange architecture, because permissions can be inherited from objects higher up in the hierarchy.

3

EXCHANGE SERVER COMPONENTS

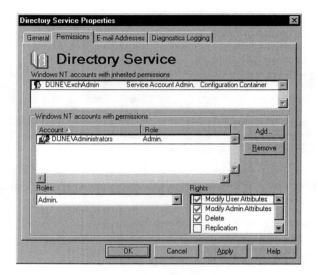

FIGURE 3.9.

Directory services permissions can be changed in the Directory Service Permissions property sheet.

Objects within the Exchange directory structure are divided into distinct groups with distinct properties, such as organization, site, and configuration, shown in Figure 3.10. This grouping permits permissions to be set based upon the group characteristics. Just as with the NT Server permissions, permissions are propagated downward in the tree. This concept is known as *inheritance*. Because of inheritance, you must consider the consequences of changing a role when you set permissions. You need to understand the following rules before setting permissions in your organization:

■   *Organization object.* When you set permissions at this level, it enables you to change the displayed organization name only. These permissions are *not* propagated downward.

NOTE

Although the Exchange Server enables you to change the organization name, as with NT Server, this does not change the underlying name. The organization name is tied to each object within the Exchange server. Changing the organization name effectively invalidates all of the underlying objects. If you must change the name, the correct procedure to follow is to reinstall the Exchange Server.

■   *Site object.* Users with permissions at this level can modify site objects and all recipients within the site.

An organizational administrator who assigns permissions for a user at this level can delegate administration. This assigns administrative permissions to the user for that site only, unless explicitly assigned.

■ *Configuration object.* Users with these permissions can configure routing, replication, and other Exchange processes.

FIGURE 3.10.

The Exchange Administrator structure is organized into distinct groups.

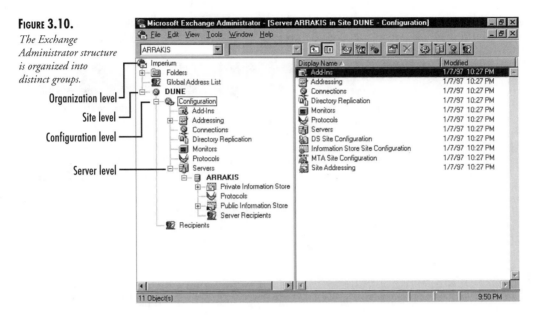

Being able to dynamically assign permissions in Microsoft Exchange closely follows those same capabilities within NT Server, but they should not be confused with NT Server. An Exchange administrator does not have to be an NT Server domain administrator. However, a person who supports both functions obviously has an administrative advantage. When assigning permissions to a user, remember that when new accounts are created, it is the responsibility of either the Exchange administrator or the NT Server domain administrator to create the accounts. To ensure no problems occur, assign appropriate permissions ahead of time.

Information Store

The Microsoft Exchange Information Store (IS) serves as the repository for all messages in an Exchange server. You can install a private information store, a public information store, or both on the server. The default is for both to be installed on the server. Each has a 16GB storage limit. Use the traffic and usage requirements of your specific situation to determine whether to install one or both types of IS.

NOTE

The Information Store is also responsible for delivering mail to users on the same server as the sender, and forwarding mail to the MTA for delivery to users who are not on the same server.

The Exchange Server information stores are actually database files. They are based on a fault-tolerant relational architecture, with transaction logs used to increase performance and to support recovery in the case of system failures. Transactions are written to the transaction logs and kept there, even after the transaction has been committed to the database. This permits the data in the transaction logs to be used to reconstruct data.

> **CAUTION**
>
> Although the underlying database is built around a version of the Microsoft Jet database, there is a misconception that it is based on Microsoft Access. Do not confuse it with the Access Jet database—*they are not the same.*
>
> There are two Jet databases, one that became Access, and the other that was incorporated into Exchange. In reality, the underlying database in Exchange is more akin to SQL Server than to Access.
>
> So, although Microsoft Exchange uses a relational database structure, you cannot use conventional tools to manipulate or view these tables. If you want to view this information, use Crystal Report Writer for Exchange or a tool designed specifically to access the database.

Architecture   The concept of *single-instance store* has also been introduced with Exchange Server. In a single-instance store, a single copy of a message sent to multiple recipients is stored only once within the information store. Each user has a pointer to the location of the message within the database. This technique yields huge benefits, for example, when a message is huge or when there is a very sizeable attachment with an e-mail.

> **NOTE**
>
> Because Exchange Server uses single-instance store, the entire server is restored when the default NT Backup utility is used to recover a single mailbox. This is not a bug, but a result of the benefit of single-instance store. As an alternative, you can use brick backup to back up individual mailboxes. However, using brick backup can increase the storage requirements for backup by 50 percent or more. Several vendors are currently working on brick-backup capability.
>
> When you install Exchange Server, the default NT Backup is replaced with a custom version that is designed to support backing up the Exchange database and supporting files without having to bring down the server. Other vendors have products that also provide this capability.

Common Information Store Features

Many features are common between private and public information stores. Let's explore a few of them:

- *Rules.* These can be used to modify how messages are processed in both the private and public store. These rules are stored as properties in the folders. There are three classifications of rules: Inbox, Out of Office, and Folder Assistants.

  All rules in Exchange are server-based. Even though rules are managed on the client, they are executed on the server. This ensures that the rules will execute even if the client is not actively logged into the server, provided there is no need to check client permissions and the rules do not reference a personal store (.pst) file. If this is the case, the rules will not execute until the Exchange client user interface is active and the client has accessed his mailbox.

  The Folder Assistant is a special case of rules that applies to public folders. Rules placed on public folders permit special processing of messages sent to these objects.

  The Out of Office Assistant is another special case. It provides a mechanism to support the execution of rules when a user is out of the office. For instance, if you would like a reply sent informing senders that you are out of the office, this is the feature to use. Although these rules can be executed from the Inbox Assistant, they are better managed in the Out of Office Assistant.

- *Views.* The Exchange client can view the contents of folders in a number of formats. The view can be either a folder or a personal view. A view defines the fields displayed when the folder is first opened. When a pubic folder is created, the owner has the option of using the default view or defining a new view for users who access the folder. The view information is stored as properties in the folder.

  A folder's default view is modified from the Exchange client and can only be changed by the owner or a user with the necessary permissions.

- *Forms.* Forms are used to define the format in which data is either displayed or created in a folder. Most messages are created using a standard form, but custom forms can be created using the Electronic Forms Designer (EFD). EFD ships with Exchange, and it is a subset of Visual Basic. It extends the standard forms capability of the Exchange client and can be used to create a send custom form and a request custom form. For more information on EFD, read Chapter 30, "The Exchange Electronic Forms Designer."

- *Folders.* Exchange uses the metaphor of folders to present and store messages within the information stores. Folders in Exchange function similarly to the folders first introduced in Windows 95.

■ *Permissions.* Each information store and folder within the information store has permissions. The permissions for the information store can be assigned only from the Exchange Administration program, as shown in Figure 3.11. These permissions can be set at the site configuration level, in the Information Store Site Configuration, and at the server level.

FIGURE 3.11.

Private information store permissions can be assigned only from the Exchange Administrator.

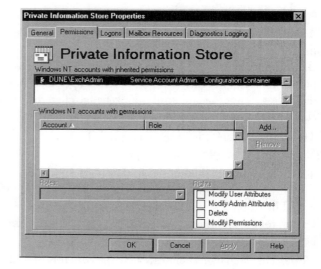

■ *Aging.* Information saved to folders on the Exchange server can be managed according to its age. For example, an item that is older than a specified number of days can be marked for deletion. This can be done for a single folder, for multiple folders, or for all folders within a site.

■ *Use of Resources.* Resource management is an important part of administrating the server. For example, the administrator can view the amount of disk storage a folder in a public information store is using, as shown in Figure 3.12.

Private Store

The private information store is one of two databases on the server where messages are stored. It contains the mailboxes for all users on the server. Each Exchange server that supports mailboxes has at least one private store. When a new user is added, the user's mailbox is created in the private store. Information about this new mailbox is passed to the directory service, and the global directory is updated. Global settings for the private information store, such as aging, storage limits, permissions, and use by mailbox, are set from the Private Information Properties page in the Exchange Administrator, shown in Figure 3.13.

FIGURE 3.12.
Public folder resources are viewed at the server level.

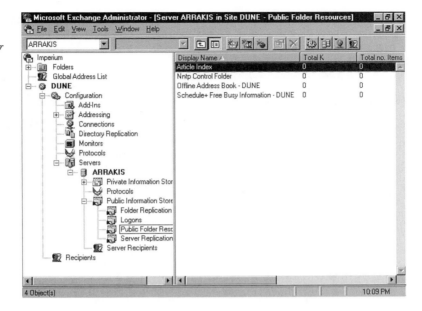

FIGURE 3.13.
The Private Information Store property sheet allows you to configure storage limits on all mailboxes.

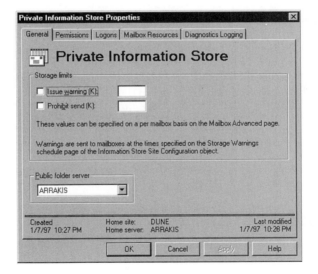

A default installation of the Exchange Server uses the private store to store messages. In Exchange Server 4.0 and 5.0, a 16GB size limit exists for both the public and the private information stores.

Although this limitation can cause problems in some instances, its severity is reduced by the single instance store, which I mentioned earlier. Users can also move their messages into personal folders, PST files located either on their local hard disks or in a designated area on the file server. The choice of personal folders should be left to the requirements of each organization.

> **NOTE**
>
> The Exchange Server has a 16GB limit per information store. This places a 16GB limit on each of the public and private IS databases. You can create additional private information stores on a server, but this is not recommended because administration can become unwieldy.
>
> You can use personal storage (PST) files to save mail messages and bypass the limitations of the information store. Because you lose administrative control using PST files, it is up to the user to manage and back up the files unless they are saved in directories on the server, which are backed up by the administrator.
>
> The 16GB IS limit will be removed in a release subsequent to Exchange 5.0.

Future Directions

In addition to user mailboxes, the private information store also contains other addressable recipients, such as distribution lists and custom recipients. A *custom recipient* is any object with an e-mail address that does not reside within the Exchange organization.

Public Store

The public store is the other IS database on the Exchange server where information can be stored. The primary difference between the public store and the private store is how the data is saved and used. In other words, the public store is not used for user mailboxes. Rather, it is used for publicly accessible information stored on the server. There are more options available for configuring the public information store than the private. Options, in addition to those already discussed, include the following:

- Logons
- General
- Replication schedule
- Folder replication status
- Age limits
- Permissions
- Diagnostic logging
- Server replication status
- Instances

A unique feature of the public store is replication. The public store supports replication of its folders among Exchange servers. For more on replication and public folders, check out Chapter 24, "Public Folders."

Message Transfer Agent

A message transfer agent (MTA) is a standard component of an electronic mail system that handles the routing, conversion, address mapping, and message transfer between servers. In Exchange, the MTA handles the routing of messages between Exchange servers; between the Information Store and the Directory; and between Exchange, the MS Mail Connector, and the MS Mail DirSync service. The MTA is a vital part of the Exchange architecture.

The Exchange MTA is configured at the server level of the Exchange Administration program, as shown in Figure 3.14.

FIGURE 3.14.

The Exchange MTA property page is used to configure the MTA.

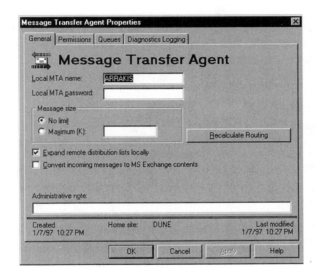

The Microsoft Exchange Server MTA can also be used to connect to X.400 MTAs that comply with the CCITT 1984 and 1988 recommendations. As with other core components of the Exchange Server, the MTA is implemented as an NT service.

The MTA is not used to connect to third-party connectors or to the Internet Mail Service. Those connectors interface directly with the Information Store.

The MTA must have an accurate routing table in order to transfer mail between systems. Normally, the routing table is rebuilt once per day. This parameter is configurable and can be done manually from the Message Transfer Agent Property page. It is a good idea to manually generate this new routing table when changes to any Exchange routing component are made during business hours. This forces the new routing information to be immediately propagated to other servers within the site.

3

EXCHANGE SERVER
COMPONENTS

System Attendant

The system attendant's (SA's) role is to support the maintenance of the Exchange server. Without it, the other Exchange services do not run.

The SA checks the directory consistency on each server in the site and performs updates as required. It also reclaims space from deleted directory objects. If monitoring tools are created, the SA gathers information about the services being monitored and delivers it to the tools. Additionally, the SA monitors the state of the messaging connections between servers and responds to link monitor mail. The SA can act as an agent for other applications to support message tracking and accounting.

At preset times each day, the SA rebuilds the site routing table and generates foreign e-mail addresses such as X.400, Internet Mail, for new recipients. You set configuration parameters for the system attendant from its property page in the Exchange Administrator program. This page is in the container area of each server in a site, as shown in Figure 3.15.

FIGURE 3.15.

The Exchange System Attendant property page is used to configure the system attendant.

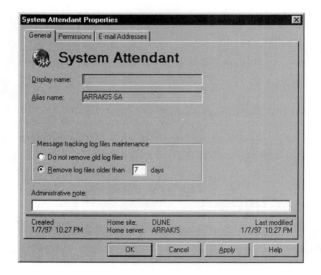

As new users are added to the site, it is the system attendant's responsibility to create the e-mail addresses.

Directory Synchronization

Directory synchronization is an optional Exchange service installed as an NT Server service. It is used to synchronize the directories between systems using the Microsoft Mail DirSync protocols, such as Microsoft Mail 3.*x* and AppleTalk Mail. It interfaces directly with the Exchange MTA and Directory Service.

The purpose of the directory synchronization protocol is to synchronize the directories on all post offices in an MS Mail network. Servers participating in this process can be either directory server post offices or directory requester post offices. One post office in the Exchange organization must be designated as directory server.

The directory server collects the directory address update information from the servers participating in the directory synchronization process. It compiles them and issues new global address list (GAL) updates to all requester post offices.

The DirSync process is a scheduled process controlled by the Microsoft Mail Dispatch and External programs.

The Exchange server can function as either the requester or server but not both. Your own requirements should determine how it is used.

When directory synchronization is configured, the administrator must specify an import and an export container. The import container stores imported Microsoft Mail addresses. The export container holds the Microsoft Exchange recipients to export to Microsoft Mail.

> **NOTE**
>
> You can control what addresses are exported to MS Mail by setting trust levels for all recipients. The only recipients that are exported are those with trust levels equal to or lower than the trust level configured in the connector.

For more about directory synchronization, check out Chapter 20, "Directory Synchronization with Microsoft Mail."

Key Management

The Key Management (KM) server is installed as a separate server within the Exchange Server organization. It supports advanced security features such as digital signature and data encryption. Install this optional Exchange Server component to manage security information used to digitally sign and encrypt messages that are sent between users within a Microsoft Exchange Server organization.

Data encryption is the process of encoding data to ensure that only the person to whom it is sent can read it. Both encryption and decryption must be supported. The KM server provides these advanced security features and supports the following services:

- Certifies public signatures and encryption keys
- Creates both public and private encryption keys
- Maintains backups of private encryption keys and public keys

■ Generates tokens

■ Maintains the original copy of the revocation list

For more information on the KM server and security in Exchange Server, check out Chapter 21, "Exchange Messaging Security with Key Management Server."

Connectors

Connectors are used to transfer messages between sites, organizations, and foreign systems. An organization with a single server requires no connectors unless it is connected to other messaging transports. However, if you have more than one server in your environment, or if you need connectivity to the Internet, for example, you will need a connector. Microsoft Exchange Server offers a number of connectors to assist in building enterprise class networks, including the following:

■ *Microsoft Mail Connector (PC).* It is used to connect the Exchange server to existing Microsoft Mail for PC networks. The MS Mail connector consists of three components: the Microsoft Mail connector interchange, the Microsoft Mail connector post office, and the Microsoft Mail connector (PC) MTA.

The Microsoft Mail connector interchange is an NT service that is installed with the Microsoft Mail connector. Its purpose is to route and transfer messages destined for a Microsoft Mail user between the Exchange server and the Microsoft Mail connector post office. It also converts the message to and from MS Mail format for delivery.

The Microsoft Mail connector post office (also, shadow or gateway post office) acts as an intermediary between the MS Mail network and the Exchange server. It is sort of a fake post office that, to the MS Mail network, looks exactly like an external MS Mail post office.

> **NOTE**
>
> The shadow post office does not support mailboxes or MS Mail clients—it is strictly an intermediary. To support MS Mail users in an Exchange environment, either use the Exchange client or install an MS Mail post office.

The Microsoft Mail connector (PC) MTA is an NT service that connects to and transfers messages between the Microsoft Mail connector post office and one or more MS Mail post offices.

> **TIP**
>
> The MS Mail External program is not required to talk to LAN-connected MS Mail post offices. The MS Mail connector performs all functions of the External program. When

connecting to MS Mail post offices over X.25 service, the External program is required to complete the connection at the remote end.

The Microsoft Mail connector combines the functions of the Microsoft External program with that of a gateway post office. In most cases, it can perform the functions of the MMTA and External programs. It can, in many cases, replace the Microsoft External program, but it does not support Microsoft Mail clients.

■ *Microsoft Mail Connector (AppleTalk).* This connector is used to support connectivity between the MS Mail for AppleTalk networks and the Exchange server. Unlike the Microsoft Mail (PC), the AppleTalk product uses a client-server system to store and transfer messages. An MS Mail AppleTalk gateway server is required to support this connector.

The Microsoft Mail connector converts Exchange messages to and from MS Mail format and transfers messages to the MS Mail post office.

The Microsoft Exchange connection is the gateway program for the MS Mail connector (AppleTalk). It runs on the MS Mail (AppleTalk) server and acts as a hub to route messages to and from the Exchange server.

■ *Internet Mail Service.* Formerly called the Internet Mail Connector (IMC), the IMS permits the Exchange server to send and receive SMTP mail. If you must support a connection to the Internet, the IMS is the connector to use.

The IMS supports messages that are sent using both MIME, which supports RTF (rich text format), and UUENCODE formats. Configuration parameters are set to control how the IMS will process outgoing messages.

TIP

When you are integrating the Exchange Server in an MS Mail environment that sends to MS Mail users via SMTP, turn off MIME encoding to avoid garbage at the end of user messages.

The Internet Mail Service complies with IETF RFCs 821, 822, 1123, 1521, and 1522.

Standards

You can configure the IMS to send e-mail attachments using either UUENCODE or MIME. In addition, the IMS can be configured to send RTF data. By default, the server is configured to send RTF data only if it is specified by the Exchange user. This can be set so that RTF data is never sent or always sent, thus overriding any configuration the client might select.

3

EXCHANGE SERVER
COMPONENTS

As with any SMTP host, an entry must be defined in the Domain Name Services (DNS) server database to support routing e-mail to the IMS. Information on how to do this is in the vendor's DNS Server documentation.

- *X.400 Connector.* This connector can be used to support connectivity to existing external X.400 backbones and public network X.400 systems. In an Exchange-only context, it can be used to connect two Exchange servers in two different Exchange sites (although the Site Connector is recommended, if possible).

  The X.400 connector supports communications with systems that conform to the CCITT 1984 and 1988 recommendations. These recommendations specify the structure and method used to transfer messages between X.400 systems.

  As with the other connectors, the X.400 connector is installed as a Windows NT service. It transmits messages to remote systems using TP0/X.25, TP4/CLNP, or TCP/IP.

  Internally, Exchange uses an X.500 directory structure so all internal addressing is in X.400 format. This eases the need to establish X.400 addresses when you use this connector to communicate between Exchange sites, because the required addresses are automatically created by the system attendant when new users are added.

  The X.400 connector can function as an X.400-relay MTA, as well as a Private Management Domain (PRMD). PRMD MTA supports X.400 backboning and, in effect, bypasses the need to subscribe to a public X.400 provider such as MCI and AT&T to transfer messages. This is sort of like an individual telephone number subscription being received by a household.

- *Schedule+ Free/Busy Connector.* This connector supports the distribution of Schedule+ Free/Busy times between Exchange clients. Free/Busy information is readily distributed between servers and a user only has to access his home server to obtain this information.

- *Site Connector.* This connector is the preferred way to connect Exchange sites within an Exchange organization. Site connectors are used to provide the most effective connection between sites. They are used when connectivity between sites is over reliable, high-speed (128 Kbps or higher) LAN or WAN connections.

  Connection between sites is managed via a *target server* list on each server. This list contains the names of all available servers in the remote site. A natural fault-tolerant condition can be created using the target server list. If an attempt to connect to the remote site using one of the servers in the target server list fails, the site connector attempts all other servers until a connection is established.

A site connector can also have a *bridgehead server.* This is a server designated in the local site that handles all communications between the two sites.

■ *Dynamic RAS Connector.* You use this connector when you are providing connectivity between Microsoft Exchange sites with no permanent connection. The Dynamic RAS Connector provides a low-cost, scheduled method of supporting locations with low volumes of message traffic. It uses a dial-up connection to establish connectivity and to send and receive electronic mail messages.

Connectors are optional. An Exchange site with a single server has little need for connectors unless it requires access to resources outside the site, such as the Internet. After you add another site, however, you must add a connector to support communications between the sites.

Microsoft offers Exchange Server in two editions: the Standard Edition, which has no connectors, and the Enterprise Edition, which ships with all connectors. You can also purchase connectors separately. To determine which edition of Exchange to install, examine the cost trade-offs between buying the Standard Edition plus the required connectors and the Enterprise Edition with all connectors.

> **NOTE**
>
> The Microsoft pricing model requires that when you are configuring a multiserver organization supporting connectors, the connectors or licenses must be for each server.

Schedule+

Schedule+ can function as a stand-alone product. However, when it is used with the Microsoft Exchange Server, it extends the concept of group scheduling. The product is tightly integrated with the Exchange Client and with the Exchange Server. It has a hidden public folder, Schedule+ Free Busy, which supports replication of user scheduling among Exchange servers. This facilitates scheduling group meetings and managing static resources, such as conference rooms, audio/visual equipment, and vehicles.

The Exchange Server administrator needs to do very little to support Schedule+. The Schedule+ Free Busy folder is at the organization level of the Exchange hierarchy in the Folders | System Folders tree, as shown in Figure 3.16.

To display configurable parameters for Schedule+, highlight the displayed Schedule+ object and select File | Properties from the Administrator menu.

By default, the replication schedule for Schedule+ conforms to the schedule configured for the information store, every 15 minutes. You can change this from the displayed property sheet.

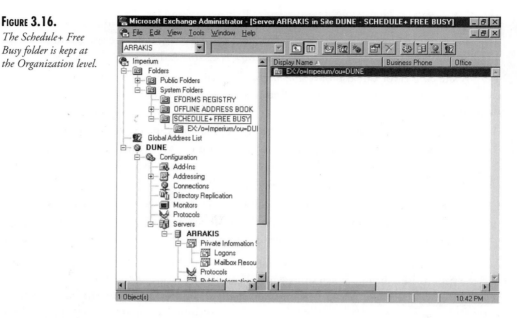

Exchange Forms Designer

The Exchange Forms Designer (EFD) is an optional component of the Microsoft Exchange client. You use EFD to create and manage custom electronic forms. Its purpose is to improve workgroup productivity by automating the distribution of repetitive information and paper forms. When used in conjunction with public folders, electronic forms are an easily implemented method of supporting shared applications such as Help Desk, Discussion Groups, and Employee documentation.

EFD is a self-contained application based on Microsoft Visual Basic 4.0. It uses an interface similar to VB4.0 to support the development of custom forms but has custom object types available to add to the forms. A VB4.0 project file is created when the application is saved, which enables the forms developer to extend the capabilities of the generated code with VB4.0. This permits the developer to add functionality not normally available in EFD by incorporating ActiveX controls to perform functions not supported in EFD.

Although EFD is considered a part of Exchange Server, it is installed on a client workstation. The components installed on the client fall into three categories:

Form Design Tools

- *Forms Designer.* This tool is incorporated into the client user agent and launches the EFD program.
- *Forms Template Wizard.* This wizard is started from the Forms Designer menu. It is designed to lead the user through the development of the correct interface for a form.

The default properties for the form are added before beginning the designer customization process.

■ *Forms Templates.* These are a set of predefined templates that can be used as the basis for customizing forms applications.

Folder Design Tools

■ *Exchange client.* The client is an integral part of the design process. Because EFD is a messaging application, testing and installing the application is done from the client.

■ *Folder Design Cue Cards.* These cue cards provide a step-by-step guide to designing applications with Electronic Forms Design.

Sample Applications

The Exchange CDs contain a set of sample applications that describe the use of public folders and custom applications in Exchange. These sample applications can be used as guidelines to assist in constructing applications for deployment in the organization.

> **CAUTION**
>
> Although the sample applications appear complete, they were designed for demonstration only. Using them in a production environment is not suggested. However, these applications can be installed in the client and used as a starting point to construct production applications.

When the Client is installed, the folder design tools are installed. The folder design tools permit users to customize any folders they may create, either private or public.

The folder design tools are installed from a share area on the Exchange server. The installation process adds the custom edition of Visual Basic 4.0 for Exchange to the end user's desktop.

For more detailed information on the Exchange Forms Designer, check out Chapter 30, "The Exchange Electronic Forms Designer."

Summary

This chapter discussed the components of the Exchange Server and how they interact.

Exchange Server has been considered among the most complex products Microsoft has developed. This chapter attempts to shed some light on this complexity by presenting an overview of each of the components that it includes.

Unlike its predecessor, MS Mail, the Exchange Server is built around industry standard architecture and protocols. The Server takes advantage of the strengths and security of the NT Domain by providing single logon to the domain and the user mailboxes. The internal services that

3

EXCHANGE SERVER
COMPONENTS

comprise Exchange Server, such as the Private and Public Information Store and the Directory Service, were also discussed.

Connectors, which provide gateway support as well as routing in the Exchange Server, were also reviewed.

The Exchange Server provides a lucrative development environment with its built-in forms capability.

The information provided in this chapter can be used to provide the basis for a detailed understanding of the Exchange Server and the capabilities it offers.

Exchange Client Components

by Greg Todd

IN THIS CHAPTER

CHAPTER 4

If you have looked at the Microsoft Exchange client software, you have seen that it is an extensive piece of work—there is a lot you can do with it. Microsoft has done a great job of packing in features and functions that users will find useful. And now, with Exchange 5.0 and Office 97, there is a new client for you to use—Outlook.

Although detailed coverage is outside the scope of this chapter, Outlook is a perfect example of Exchange's open architecture at work. Outlook is a MAPI client that provides a host of features in addition to providing connectivity to your Exchange server.

In this chapter, you are going to take a quick tour of the major architectural features of the Microsoft Exchange client software. We will focus only on the native Exchange client that is included with Exchange Server. Fortunately, regardless of which version of the client you use, they generally function the same. And if you use the Windows-based versions—Windows 95, Windows NT, or Windows 3.*x*—they look practically identical.

> **NOTE**
>
> The Microsoft Exchange client software supports several different operating systems. Currently, there exists a version for Windows NT, Windows 95, Windows 3.*x*, Macintosh, and MS-DOS. For simplicity, I refer to the MS Exchange client simply as the *client*, regardless of the operating system. However, if there is something specific to a particular version of the client, I point it out explicitly.

This chapter covers the following items about the Exchange client:

- Overview of features
- General architecture
- Modularity
- MAPI
- Information services
- Profiles
- Microsoft Schedule+

First, you look at the features found in the client. Although this chapter doesn't go into detail about every one listed, it will be a good way to be introduced to the main features available in the client.

Next, you learn general architecture. This section goes over the general structure of the client and looks at how it is put together. This is a high-level, comprehensive look. From there the subject is broken down into subset components of the architecture.

Following the general architecture, you learn about the major components of the client architecture—namely, the modular design of the client, the implementation of MAPI, information services, and profiles.

Finally, the chapter concludes with an overview of Microsoft Schedule+, the integrated scheduling package included with Exchange.

After you read this chapter, you should have a good foundation for understanding the client and its capabilities. And although it is not an exhaustive look at all the client features, it will be something to build upon in Chapter 15, "Configuring Microsoft Exchange Clients."

Overview of Features

Microsoft Exchange is, among other things, positioned as the successor and replacement for legacy e-mail systems. It is a huge step forward in functionality, power, and ease of use, and the client software is where many of those benefits are the most visible. The following are several features that help take that step forward:

- Modularity and extensibility
- Remote user support via Remote Access Services (RAS), Dial-Up Networking, or Point to Point Protocol (PPP)
- Offline folders for occasionally connected (that is, mobile) users
- Independence from transport, store, and name service
- Rich text message content
- Compliance with OLE 2.0
- Extensive drag-and-drop implementation
- Rules-based message processing
- View formatting (for example, outlining, sorting, columns, and filters)
- Powerful, customizable forms support
- Access to information sharing and collaboration features

> **NOTE**
>
> Some of these features are covered in this chapter. Others are covered in Chapter 14, "Installing Microsoft Exchange Clients."

In addition, the client currently provides support for the following platforms:

Cross-
Platform

- Microsoft Windows NT
- Microsoft Windows 95
- Microsoft Windows 3.*x*
- MS-DOS
- Macintosh

4

EXCHANGE CLIENT
COMPONENTS

NOTE

The MS Exchange client—in fact, the entire MS Exchange product—represents a radical departure from the MS Mail architecture. MS Mail is based on a *file sharing* architecture, whereas MS Exchange Server is a *client-server* architecture. This brings many benefits to Exchange, as highlighted throughout this book, including some of the features just mentioned. Certainly, MS Mail has some of those features in its Windows-based client, such as rich message content, drag-and-drop support, and electronic forms support. However, many more features exist in the Exchange client, such as offline folders, transport and store independence, view formatting, rules-based message processing, and more. Some are a direct result of the client-server architecture. Some are simply new features designed into the client. Regardless, these useful new features make the Exchange client a flexible, powerful environment in which to work.

The idea is to provide a consistent user interface, regardless of the operating system you are running. That way, you have to learn the general principles of the Exchange client only once, and it will apply across all the platforms.

Architecture

Architecture   You might have heard the Microsoft Exchange client dubbed the "Universal Inbox." In fact, the Windows Messaging icon in Windows 95 and Windows NT is labeled Inbox. Even after you upgrade the default Windows Messaging client with the full Exchange client, it is still labeled Inbox.

As it turns out, this is an appropriate moniker to assign the client; it really is designed as a means of managing all kinds of information, regardless of the type and source. Most systems provide plain electronic mail storage, but Exchange goes beyond that and literally acts as a universal inbox to contain all kinds of information. E-mail is just one type. It could hold information such as

- Exchange mail data
- MS Mail data
- Voice data
- Documents
- Faxes
- Internet mail
- Other electronic mail

Although the client itself does not necessarily store all these types of information, it does provide the means to *manage* the information. In fact, whether the information is stored locally, on an Exchange server, or on some other source of information, it can all be managed through the client interface.

To illustrate how this looks from an architectural standpoint, Figures 4.1, 4.2, and 4.3 show how some of the previously listed information might be accessed by the client.

FIGURE 4.1.

In its most common use, the Exchange client provides connectivity to an Exchange server and provides personal storage and address-book capabilities.

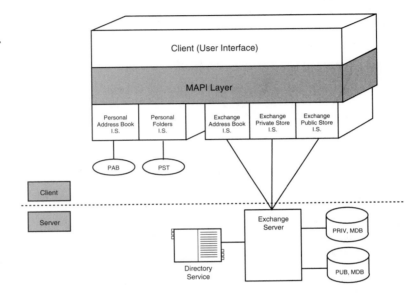

In Figure 4.2, see how the Exchange client provides connectivity to an Exchange server via three main information services, such as the Exchange Private Store Information Service (also called a *service provider*, or just *provider*). Note there are also two other IS entities—Personal Address Book (PAB) and Personal Store (PST)—that are used by the client and are stored on your local hard disk. These are available for storing local copies of messages from outside information sources. See Chapter 15 for more details on these elements.

In Figure 4.3, see how things on the server side change to an MS Mail Post Office. Also, the information services on the client side change to provide connectivity to the post office via the LAN Message Store and Remote Message Store IS components. Connectivity to the MS Mail address list is provided by the MS Mail 3.*x* Address Book IS component. The Spooler and Message Transport IS components are part of MAPI and are transparent portions of the client connectivity to the MS Mail Post Office.

The main thing to glean from these figures is that the client is consistent, no matter to which data source it is connected—whether that is an Exchange server, an MS Mail Post Office, or another source of data.

Also, in the case of connecting to other data sources, there can even be user-interface modifications to customize the client for accessing a particular type of data. For example, if you access voice data, you might want play, stop, and pause buttons on the toolbar. You might also want additional information specific to voice data in the menu items or property pages.

FIGURE 4.2.

To maintain compatibility with MS Mail 3.x, the Exchange client provides connectivity to MS Mail 3.x post offices and provides personal storage and address book capabilities.

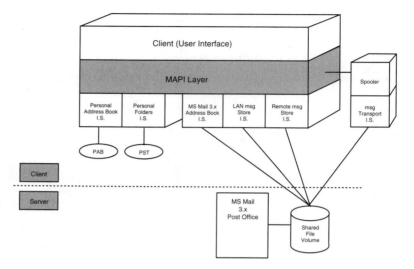

FIGURE 4.3.

Demonstrating the Exchange client's flexibility, connectivity can be provided to a variety of other data sources by implementing the proper information services.

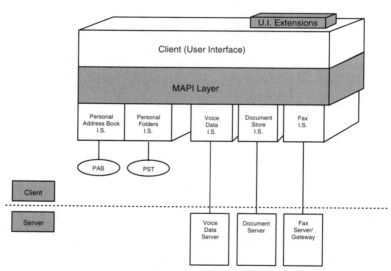

One other point about consistency. Notice how the Personal Address Book and Personal Store are common to every scenario. This implies that you can move data around and put it into a personal (local) storage medium for later use. This is a great feature, especially if you need to archive data or take it with you when you are not connected to the network.

Your interest should be piqued as to how the client works, so let's look into it a bit deeper. To understand how the client can handle messages and data of all types, you should understand a bit more about its features and design.

Modularity

The engineers at Microsoft took a modular approach to solving the problem of providing a storage medium for various—and often dissimilar—types of message data.

Figure 4.4 illustrates the modular design of the client.

FIGURE 4.4.

The Exchange client has a modular architecture that provides for flexible connections to Exchange Server.

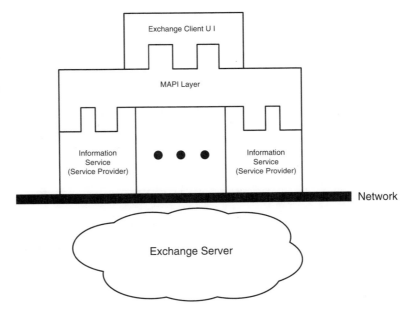

The Exchange client has a modular architecture that gives you flexible connections to Exchange Server. Following is a description of the components represented in Figure 4.4:

- The Microsoft Exchange client user interface (UI) represents the actual user interface presented to the person using the client. It displays all the messages and controls available to the user.

- The MAPI layer is an important element. It is the software that actually performs the task of interpreting the user's actions that take place in the client interface in the layer above. The MAPI layer is then responsible for converting those user actions into commands understood by the information service(s) below.

- An information service processes actions from the MAPI layer above it and communicates them to the desired messaging service. In this diagram, the messaging service is Exchange Server, but it could be anything. Here is the key to the modularity: There can be more than one information service configured to run with the client. Therefore, a single client can access multiple data sources with ease.

The really great thing about this design is that it provides extensibility—other vendors besides Microsoft can create their own "bolt-on" software for the client.

Figure 4.5 illustrates the bolt-on nature of the client.

FIGURE 4.5.

Information services, also called service providers, can easily "bolt on" to the Exchange client for access to messaging services such as Exchange Server.

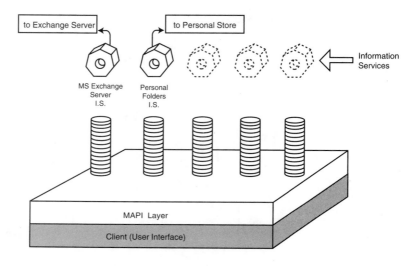

With this approach, if you need to access a certain type of information, it's just a matter of writing an information service to connect the client to the desired messaging service. In addition, parts of the actual user interface can be extended and customized. The following lists these parts:

- Menus and menu items
- Event handlers
- Toolbars
- Property pages

For example, the original Exchange client might not have a menu for a specific feature, so you might need to add a new menu item germane to the feature. Likewise, for convenience, the function provided by the new menu item might be handy to have on the toolbar; you can extend the toolbar to included the new function. Similarly, you can add event handlers and property pages where needed.

Microsoft provides a MAPI Software Developer's Kit (SDK) to provide guidance in accomplishing these extensions.

This design also provides independence from transport, store, and address services. You are relieved from worrying about whether the client is running TCP/IP, NetBEUI, IPX/SPX, or whatever. Also, it does not matter whether the messages or address information are stored locally, on a server, or somewhere else. Likewise, it does not matter where addressing information is obtained—you could use the MS Mail Post Office Address List or the Exchange Directory without worrying about the source. Theoretically, these just bolt on as well.

With this design, the client doesn't need to have any knowledge about the destination of its data, be it an Exchange Server or something else. Conversely, any messaging service—whatever it is—does not require any knowledge about sending its data to an Exchange client.

This approach truly enables the client to be applied across information types—a universal inbox.

MAPI

A key component to the modular architecture of the client is MAPI. Basically, you can list three different categories of messaging applications, all of which are supported by MAPI:

- Messaging-aware
- Messaging-enabled
- Messaging-based

You should also know that there are three subsets of the MAPI interface that roughly correspond to the preceding three types of applications:

- Common message calls (CMC)
- Simple MAPI
- Extended MAPI

Let's look at these to give you an idea of what's what.

Messaging-aware applications are the most rudimentary applications. The application's main function is not centered around messaging, but it can perform simple messaging tasks as an added feature. An example of this type of application is Microsoft Word. There might be a Send or a Post to Exchange Folder command on the File menu to provide some basic messaging, but the main purpose of Word is not messaging.

Messaging-enabled applications are slightly more complex. Their general purpose is to provide some sort of messaging functionality to the user. A good example of a messaging-enabled application is Microsoft Mail. The main function of MS Mail is to provide e-mail services, but like messaging-aware applications such as Microsoft Word, MS Mail relies on a messaging information service to perform the work of packaging, storing, retrieving, and sending messages.

Messaging-based applications are the most complex of the three types of applications. They are designed to operate over a network—many times, typically in a client-server type of environment. Of course, applications based on Exchange represent a good example of messaging-based applications; the Exchange client itself could even be included in this classification. More general examples, however, are applications built on Exchange, such as workflow, fax management, and group collaboration applications.

Information Services

As mentioned before, an information service—sometimes referred to as a *service provider*, or just *provider*—is how the connection to an external information source is bolted onto the client. The creator of the provider must follow the guidelines in the Microsoft MAPI SDK to write to MAPI.

MAPI defines interfaces for three basic types of information services, illustrated in Figure 4.6:

- Address book
- Message store
- Message transport

FIGURE 4.6.

There are three main types of information services (or providers) in MAPI. An information service can contain any or all of them.

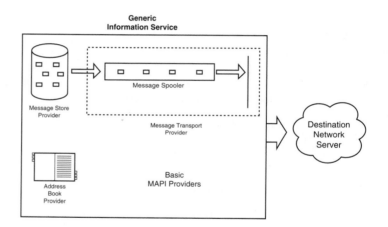

These three information services, or providers, serve as building blocks for messaging applications or other information services, which can contain any or all of them.

An *address book provider* allows access to the database that contains information on all the users, distribution lists, public folders, and so on contained in the system. In short, this provider gives the client access to the central directory service.

> **NOTE**
>
> A special form of the generic address book is the Personal Address Book (PAB). This provides a container for recipient information obtained from other address books. It is good for easy retrieval of common recipients, especially while offline. It can also maintain entries for recipients not in the main address book. These entries are called *personal one-off* addresses, and they are for recipients in foreign e-mail systems.

Note that the PAB is *not* intended for entries contained in the main address book. If you need access to address entries while you are not connected to the Exchange server, use the Off-Line Address Book provided with the Exchange client. You can find more information on the Off-Line Address Book in Chapter 14.

A *message store provider* supplies storage, organization, and retrieval facilities for messages in the system. If the message store is MAPI-compliant, it is organized into a hierarchical arrangement of folders, messages, and attachments to make things easier to find and store. You could think of it as the warehouse for your messages. This type is the most common and visible type of provider.

Two good examples of message store providers commonly used in the client are the *Microsoft Exchange Server* and the *Personal Folders* providers. Refer to Figure 4.5 to see how these bolt on to the client. The former provides connectivity, through MAPI, to an Exchange server; the latter provides connectivity, also through MAPI, to the Personal Store on your local hard drive.

The following is the general hierarchy of a message store provider:

- *Folders* are the primary organizational element. They are always at the top level of the message store hierarchy, and they can contain other folders and messages.

- *Messages* are the actual pieces of information that users of the system send each other. A message could also be a received fax, e-mail, or other information tidbit.

- *Attachments* are contained inside messages. An attachment can hold a file, an embedded OLE object, or another message. If the attachment contains a message, the embedded message can have additional attachments, which in turn can hold embedded messages, and so on.

Finally, a *message transport provider* supplies message transport services. Working in conjunction with the message spooler, which is the process responsible for actually moving a message, it is the entity that is responsible for transporting a message from the local MAPI message system to the network server. You could think of the message transport provider as a delivery truck for your messages.

Microsoft provides basic versions of these three information services with the MAPI subsystem in Windows. They can be used as is, or they can be replaced with enhanced versions created by Microsoft or by other software vendors. Together, they work to form a complete messaging system for the user.

Profiles

It's easy to add new providers by using the bolt-on architecture. However, the more you add, the more difficult it becomes to keep track of them—which one is in use in a particular situation, how it is configured, and so on.

Enter Exchange client *profiles*. Profiles are an optional service of MAPI employed to keep track of the user configuration of the information services on a client.

If you are familiar with Microsoft Mail, you know that user-specific information is kept in a file called MSMAIL.INI. Items such as the server name and mailbox name are kept there. You can think of a client profile as a service that contains multiple MSMAIL.INI files. And in Windows NT and Windows 95, they are stored in the Registry.

Profiles provide one of the client's most flexible options. They are a collection of messaging services that enable a MAPI application, such as the Exchange client, to start all the proper storage, address book, and transport providers required to connect to the desired data sources.

For example, a single user can have many profiles on a single workstation. Therefore, if you use a laptop both at work and at home, you can have a profile tailored for the way you use Exchange in both places.

As another example, many users can have their own separate profiles on a single workstation. If a certain client machine is shared by several users, each user can have a personal profile tailored to the specific and varying configuration needs of that person.

Figure 4.7 illustrates how profiles might be used.

Figure 4.7.
Profiles provide flexibility in maintaining Exchange client configurations.

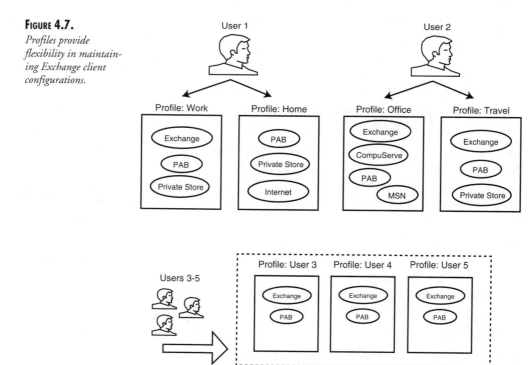

Using Figure 4.7 as an example, User 1 has a computer for work and a separate computer for home. The work computer has a profile named Work, which contains work-related information services. Likewise, the home computer has a profile named Home, which contains home-related information services.

User 2 has a single computer for both office use and travel use. So when User 2 is in the office, he selects the Office profile when Exchange starts. Likewise, when he's on the road, he selects the Travel profile.

Finally, Users 3, 4, and 5 all share a computer. They have the same information services, but because they don't use identical client settings (they each have different mailboxes, for example), each user can select a personalized profile when Exchange starts. Assuming you have the Exchange client configured properly, when the program starts, the user simply selects the profile to be used for that session.

Microsoft Schedule+

Microsoft Schedule+ (pronounced *Schedule Plus*) is included with Exchange Server. The software enables individuals or users in a group to manage schedules, calendars, tasks, and communication. It is tightly integrated with the client to provide unified functionality.

Schedule+ can be launched either from a separate icon in the Microsoft Exchange program group or from within the client. It can operate in two modes:

- Stand-alone mode
- Group-enabled mode

Stand-alone mode is available to any user, regardless of whether the user is network-connected or not. In this way, it basically becomes a personal calendar and scheduling package for use on a personal system, regardless of network connectivity.

If the Exchange client is not set up with mail, Schedule+ always runs stand-alone. If the client is set up with mail, Schedule+ will prompt the user at startup to select whether to work stand-alone or group-enabled. In stand-alone mode, all the features of Schedule+ are available, but the information cannot be shared with other users. In group-enabled mode, the same features are available, but all the information can be shared with other users in the workgroup.

Group-enabled mode is available only if the client is connected to one of the following mail systems:

- *Microsoft Exchange Server*: The primary focus for Schedule+. It is designed to integrate tightly with the Exchange Client, and therefore with the Exchange Server.
- *Other MAPI 1.0 Server*: MS Mail 3.*x* is one example of a mail server that provides MAPI 1.0 drivers. Any third party that provides a MAPI 1.0 e-mail server compatible with MS Mail must also provide drivers to support Schedule+.

4

EXCHANGE CLIENT
COMPONENTS

- *MS Mail 3.x Post Office*: The full-blown MS Mail package with which the Windows 95 Exchange client is compatible.
- *Workgroup Post Office*: The workgroup-only version of MS Mail that is included with Windows for Workgroups, Windows 95, and Windows NT. Both the original Windows 95 Inbox and the Windows 95 version of the Exchange client are compatible with a Workgroup Post Office.

Summary

This chapter gave an overview of the Microsoft Exchange client, its features, its main architectural design, and its components.

First, you looked at the features found in the client. The chapter didn't go into detail about every feature listed, but it was a useful way to get introduced to the main features available in the client.

Next, you learned general client architecture. You explored the general structure of the client and looked at how it is put together. This was a high-level, comprehensive look, a springboard into discussing the various subsets of the architecture.

Following the general architecture, you learned about the major client components, namely its modular design, implementation of MAPI, information services, and profiles.

Finally, the chapter concluded with an overview of Microsoft Schedule+, the integrated scheduling package included with Exchange.

At this point, you should have a good foundation for understanding the client and its capabilities. This chapter was not intended as an exhaustive look at all the client features, but it forms a basis to build upon later in Chapter 14.

Now that you have been introduced to the client and the server, it's time to move into a discussion of some administrative concepts that are useful for Exchange. This is the subject of the next chapter, and it should help you get a feel for what is ahead as an administrator.

Administrative Concepts

by Ron Sontagg and Ray Sundstrom
Revised by Greg Todd

IN THIS CHAPTER

CHAPTER 5

The *Microsoft Administrator's Guide* is a fairly large set of detailed descriptions of functions mostly accessible through the Microsoft Exchange Server Administrator program. Although this reference might functionally address the specific actions required to manage an enterprise Exchange installation, wading through it is quite intimidating. It discourages the beneficial approach of using forethought and planning in even modestly sized Exchange rollouts.

In this chapter, you learn concepts beyond simply using the Exchange Server or its administration program. The issues approach the installation of Exchange as a full-fledged enterprise-wide project.

For purposes of this chapter, administration of Microsoft Exchange Server and clients (the Exchange environment) is the process of identifying and organizing the human resources, information, and equipment required to install and maintain the system. The Exchange environment touches on all aspects of an organization's computer system infrastructure, including the following:

- Network topology
- Transport protocols
- Workstation configuration
- Server configuration
- NT domains and trust relationships
- NT user accounts and groups
- Connectivity to foreign systems
- Security
- Workflow automation
- Employee training

Because many of the preceding areas can be exceedingly complex, especially in large national or global enterprises, let's use the model shown in Figure 5.1 as the context within which you can address each item. The modeled enterprise can be characterized as a small-to-medium business with about 300 employees. In this example, we will use multiple Exchange servers and include one remote site.

In Figure 5.1, the main features presented are two domains (AMERICA and MEXICO), three sites (TENNESSEE and KENTUCKY on a local LAN and TEXAS at a remote location), three Exchange Servers, (two of which also serve as Primary Domain Controllers, or PDCs: MEMPHIS and ALAMO) and one Backup Domain Controller (or BDC: BOONEVILLE), one site connector on a LAN-speed network, and one dynamic RAS site connector.

The following sections present approaches to defining administrator roles, creating a task overview, meeting users' needs, establishing policies and procedures, and implementing disaster recovery. In all cases, the sections do not present an exhaustive list of administrator program functions, but rather an ordering and presentation of those tasks and functions that you will most likely need to address to ensure a successful Exchange implementation for an organization like Davy Crockett.

FIGURE 5.1.

Sample Davy Crockett organizational model.

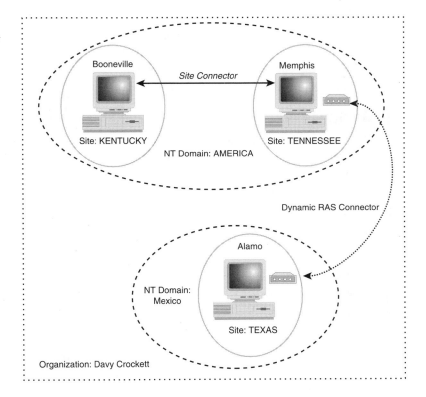

Administrator Roles

The Exchange environment must be managed through two stages (installation and maintenance) and from two administrative perspectives (site and enterprise). Depending on the size of the enterprise, further role definitions might be needed within each perspective. In the sample enterprise model shown in Figure 5.1, the significant system features to consider for an Exchange implementation are as follows:

- How many users will each site need to support?
- Where should public folders be kept and should they be shared among all sites?
- What domain trust relationships need to be established to permit administration of the TEXAS site from the KENTUCKY or TENNESSEE sites?
- How do you make TEXAS recipients automatically visible to KENTUCKY and TENNESSEE users and vice versa?

- What is the quickest way to establish a connector between Exchange Servers MEM-PHIS and ALAMO using RAS?
- What training issues can be expected for users migrating from MS Mail?
- How should the Davy Crockett organization approach backups and disaster recovery?

These questions are just a sampling of the most obvious issues facing administrators attempting to implement the Exchange environment for the Davy Crockett organization. In the following sections, you examine these questions in more detail from each administrative perspective.

Site Administrator

The *site administrator* is the person concerned with managing installation and maintenance of Exchange servers and clients at a physical location. Although many areas of responsibility overlap with those of the enterprise administrator, the following are some clear-cut areas where the site administrator should focus:

- Workstation configuration
- Server configuration
- NT user accounts and groups
- Security
- Workflow automation
- Employee training

Each of these items, which has certain tasks associated with it, is explained in the following sections. The Davy Crockett organization has two site administrators: Davy Crockett has administrator security on the KENTUCKY and TENNESSEE sites, and Administrator has administrator security at the TEXAS site.

Enterprise Administrator

The *enterprise administrator* is concerned with global issues. How a particular workstation or server is configured is not important, as long as that configuration does not interfere with global communications and enterprise standards. Although many of the enterprise administrator tasks overlap the site administrator tasks, the perspective is from a vision encompassing multiple sites and external connectivity. The following are the areas where the enterprise administrator should focus:

- Network topology
- Transport protocols
- NT domains and trust relationships
- NT user accounts and groups
- Connectivity to foreign systems

■ Security

■ Workflow automation

Because many of these areas overlap the areas of concern for the site administrator, one of the primary tasks of the enterprise administrator is to meet regularly with site administrators to coordinate issues that are in common between sites and to resolve conflicting requirements.

Task Overview

The following sections present specific tasks associated with the planning, implementation, user management, and ongoing maintenance of Exchange. The Davy Crockett organization is used as the sample Exchange environment; it was actually implemented as shown in Figure 5.1. The tasks expand, where appropriate, on the areas of concern listed earlier from the enterprise and site perspectives.

Enterprise-Wide Planning

An enterprise implementation of Exchange affects nearly every aspect of an enterprise's information environment. A significant undertaking, it has an impact on the users, the network environment, security, support, and maintenance. In all but the most trivial cases, such implementation requires a significant commitment of resources and potentially a lot of money.

As with any project, management approval and buy-in are two of the most important success factors. Aside from that, the most important thing is using a project management approach that incorporates up-front planning before taking any action. The following sections present some significant enterprise-wide planning tasks.

Network Topology

You must examine and understand the current enterprise network environment from the standpoint of *accessibility* and *traffic volumes*. Figure 5.1 serves to identify the major components of the network. Next, you should indicate the kind of connections between servers. If they are on a LAN, then indicate the speed (for example, 10Mbits/s or 100Mbits/s). If BOONEVILLE and MEMPHIS were actually connected over a network bridge or router, the effective communication speed might be only 56Kbits/s. Finally, you need to specify access requirements. An Exchange site connector works, for example, only if the router connecting BOONEVILLE and MEMPHIS permits the required packets to be exchanged between the two LANs.

Performance

Here is how network topology can influence where public folders are kept, or whether public folders should be replicated to a distant site. In the Davy Crockett organization, if the KENTUCKY site has 125 users, the TENNESSEE site has 125 users, and the TEXAS site has 50 users, you would need to consider topology in the following ways:

■ If both KENTUCKY and TENNESSEE users frequently access public folders for daily work, but their work environments are separate from each other, you would set up public folders in each site. You would not use public folder replication because of the high network traffic required between sites.

5

ADMINISTRATIVE
CONCEPTS

- On the other hand, if KENTUCKY and TENNESSEE users need to collaborate frequently, you would use public folder replication, which could have an impact on the speed (and cost) of any bridge or router needed to connect the two sites.

- Another option might be to place all public folders on the BOONEVILLE Exchange server and all mail folders on the MEMPHIS Exchange server. Because these choices depend heavily on usage patterns, network traffic analysis might be required to determine which method would work best.

- Finally, the TEXAS site would most likely use *public folder affinity* to provide access to all the public folder activity going on in the AMERICA domain. You would not use public folder replication because the dial-up dynamic RAS connector would be too slow to allow replication of all the public folder information. Of course, if the dynamic RAS connector is capable, in future releases, of using a cable modem operating at 10Mbits/s, for example, replication might turn out to be the best way to go after all.

You can apply the following general principles when planning the configuration of multiple Exchange Servers within a site.

Performance To ensure the best possible response times, do the following:

- Put the mailboxes of users who frequently send mail to each other on the same Exchange Server. This approach takes advantage of two processes: Exchange uses local delivery for the messages, so almost no network traffic will occur. And when a message is sent to multiple recipients, Exchange Server uses "single-instance" messaging to store the message. Only one copy of the message body or attachment, therefore, is stored on the server. Recipients receive a "pointer" to the stored data.

- Locate Exchange clients on the same network segment as their default (home) Exchange server. Because users tend to demand very fast response times, it is more important to ensure high network bandwidth between the users and their Exchange server than between Exchange servers.

To provide the highest possible fault tolerance, do the following:

- Locate important public folders and mailboxes on separate Exchange servers. The Sales Leads public folder, for example, might be located on BOONEVILLE, and the Help Desk public folder might be located on MEMPHIS.

- Place mission-critical folders, mailboxes, and connectors on fault-tolerant servers—that is, a server with RAID Level 1 or Level 5 hard drives and error-correcting RAM.

Transport Protocols

Because Exchange runs on the NT Server platform, the most common transports available are NetBEUI, TCP/IP, and NWLink IPX/SPX. Although NT is capable of using all three of these protocols, many Exchange services require a specific protocol. Table 5.1 lists some of these required protocols and services. Note that connecting two Exchange servers within the same site requires only a LAN connection. That is, if the NT servers can see each other, the Exchange servers can also see each other and automatically perform directory replication.

If two Exchange servers are in different Exchange sites, however, such as BOONEVILLE and MEMPHIS, you must use a site connector to provide directory replication. In all cases, replication between sites involves the transfer of Exchange messages. This provides the flexibility to use a messaging transport to connect two sites. The messaging transport can use the Internet, dial-up asynchronous connections, public X.400, or even X.25. In all cases, the success of providing directory replication between sites can be determined by the success of being able to send an Exchange message from one site to another.

Table 5.1. Exchange services and their required network transport protocols.

Exchange Service	*Required Protocols or Service*
Internet gateways/connectors	TCP/IP, SMTP, DNS
X.400 site connector	X.25, TCP/IP, TP4/CLNP
MS Mail connector	LAN, Async, X.25
cc:Mail connector	LAN, Async, X.25
Directory Replication	LAN, Dynamic RAS, Internet site connector, X.400 site connector
X.400 Gateway	X.25, TCP/IP, TP4/CLNP

NT Domains and Trust Relationships

Using the NT nomenclature, the *trusted* domain contains users, and the *trusting* domain contains resources (printers, files, applications, and so on). In the Davy Crockett organization, a two-way trust has been established between the AMERICA and MEXICO domains. The reason that you need a two-way trust might not be immediately obvious. Technically, users in the AMERICA domain do not need to log in to the TEXAS Exchange site, because the TEXAS site is being *replicated* through the dynamic RAS connector. Likewise, users in the MEXICO domain are logging in to the TEXAS site only because the TENNESSEE and KENTUCKY sites have also been replicated through the dynamic RAS connector. The trust needs to be two-way, because the service accounts for each site need to log in to each other's Exchange servers.

Security

> **TIP**
>
> All Exchange servers within the same site use the same *service account*. After you configure the first Exchange server for that site, the service account is created and used for subsequent Exchange server installations within that site.

Figures 5.2 and 5.3 show that in the installation of the TENNESSEE site's first (and only) Exchange server, the account *crockett* in the AMERICA domain was granted Log On As A Service and Restore Files and Directories rights on the TENNESSEE site.

5

ADMINISTRATIVE
CONCEPTS

FIGURE 5.2.

Exchange Server Setup screen showing that this server is the first to be installed at the TENNESSEE site.

FIGURE 5.3.

Information message confirming that the currently logged-in account has also been set up as an Exchange service account.

A similar sequence of screens and dialog boxes appeared during installation of Exchange Server at the TEXAS site, except that the Exchange service account name was *administrator*. Because the KENTUCKY site is within the same domain (AMERICA) as the TENNESSEE site, the same Exchange service account for that Exchange server installation can be designated as for the TENNESSEE site, namely *crockett*. Figure 5.4 shows that this is the case by displaying the permissions from the Permissions tab of the Kentucky Properties dialog box.

FIGURE 5.4.

Exchange service account permission associated with the AMERICA\crockett account. The other two accounts are not germane to this discussion.

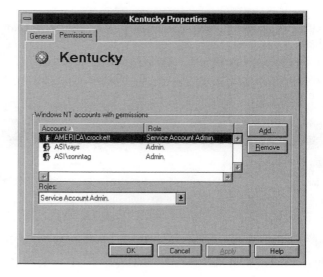

NT User Accounts and Groups

For the most part, adding Exchange to an enterprise running NT does not change the way in which users have been assigned accounts and groups, because people's work habits and work assignments dictate their needs for access to information stores and application programs.

Exchange Server, however, does impose an additional information management structure in the same sense as a database server environment such as SQL Server does. More mechanisms simply are available for managing information within Exchange than are provided for within the NT operating system. Exchange, for example, utilizes the concept of a *Manager* user account, which in a real sense has certain authorities over a group of Exchange mailboxes.

> **TIP**
>
> NT accounts, such as the Administrator, are sometimes used throughout Exchange and specifically listed in the Permissions tab of Exchange container objects. Because of possible security problems, I recommend designating another account, such as ExchAdmin, as the main Exchange Administrator and services account.
>
> One other idea: If an employee who has complex and essential security permissions leaves the company, do not delete his or her NT account. Instead, simply change the name of the account and any other descriptive personal information to that of a new employee. The reason for this approach is that under NT, when you delete an account, the account's Security ID (SID) is permanently lost. This loss invalidates all the security entries you might have created with that SID. Changing the account name, however, does not change the SID.

Security

Individual accounts can be grouped together into local or global groups. A *local group* is a list of selected accounts from the local domain, plus any accounts from a trusted domain, plus any global groups from the local or trusted domains. It cannot contain any other local groups. A *global group* is a list of selected accounts from within the local domain. It cannot contain any accounts outside its domain.

By using NT local and global groups, the enterprise administrator can more easily assign different levels of security access to groups of users. One of the more common examples of assigning group permissions is to give certain groups access to specific Exchange public folders. All users in the Accounting department, for example, belong to the global group *Accounting*, so the Exchange public folder *Accounting Notes* has permissions granted to the *Accounting* group. You need to define only one permission versus having to enter each user's account individually.

5

ADMINISTRATIVE CONCEPTS

> **CAUTION**
>
> The account designated as the *Exchange services account* can access any folder or user mailbox. This account is specified during the Exchange installation. If security of individuals' mailbox content is important, make sure that this service account is given a secure password and that the individual entrusted with this account is aware of the responsibility of protecting users' privacy.

Connectivity to Foreign Systems

Planning for connection to foreign systems involves the following:

- Identifying the native format of the foreign system—for example, MS Mail, X.400, or Internet SMTP.

- Determining the nature of the connectivity you would like to implement. Do you want to receive mail from that system? Do you want to route certain types of mail messages to the foreign system? Do you want your users to see the accounts in the foreign system?

- Checking to see whether the addressing will be compatible between the two systems if you have a currently implemented Exchange environment.

By far, the most common foreign connection is an Internet mail gateway using SMTP.

New to Version 5.0

Exchange version 5.0 adds POP3 connectivity. With this capability, you can use Exchange as a general SMTP/POP3 Internet Gateway so you can use a third-party product, such as Eudora, as your main Internet mail application.

To implement the Internet Mail Connector successfully, you must first establish a TCP/IP connection to an Internet Service Provider (ISP). In most cases, having the ISP provide you with a Domain Name Service (DNS) is easiest. You also must establish an Internet Domain Name with the InterNIC that will be associated with the TCP/IP address of your Exchange server running the Internet Mail Connector.

> **THE ADVANTAGES OF AN ON-SITE DNS SERVER**
>
> The DNS server is the Internet device that allows a particular host on the Internet to be referred to by a descriptive name rather than its TCP/IP address. The TCP/IP address for Microsoft's home Web page, for example, is 198.105.232.7. You refer to it when using your Web browser, however, as www.microsoft.com. The DNS server performs the task of associating a name request with a specific TCP/IP address.
>
> Many enterprises are hosting Web, Gopher, and FTP sites, as well as publishing information internally in an *intranet*. The DNS allows the network administrator to create a logical group of domain names so that users can easily locate needed information. If the DNS is

being provided by an outside IP, the process of updating the DNS name and address entries may become quite awkward. Fortunately, Windows NT Server 4.0 includes a DNS, so making the choice to implement your own DNS will be considerably easier. Bear in mind, however, that DNSs are a cooperative group, and you will need to consult with your ISP to determine the proper way to integrate your in-house DNS with the worldwide Internet crowd.

The other most likely foreign system connection would be through a public X.400 gateway. Here the key is in defining the address spaces correctly using the X.400 addressing conventions, which are described in more detail in Chapters 16, "Connecting to Other Mail Systems," and 18, "Connecting to Other Exchange Sites."

The next most likely foreign connection is with the MS Mail Gateway to provide connectivity to an existing Microsoft Mail environment. I think that unless you have a compelling reason to retain MS Mail, migrating to Exchange is far better. The migration process is straightforward, and the Exchange clients are available for DOS, Windows, Windows 95, and NT.

Security

You can analyze security from the following perspectives:

- *Enterprise security.* This type of security is concerned with WAN access and vulnerability of core systems that are used by all system components and users within the enterprise.

- *Site security.* This level focuses on LAN access and what usually corresponds to an NT domain.

- *User security.* Individual files, directories, accounts, mailboxes, and folders associated with a single user are managed at this level.

Enterprise Security

If the enterprise network (WAN) is not connected physically to any other outside information network, either by direct wire links or through dial-up modems, the enterprise could be considered secure. Most corporate environments, however, include the possibility of individual workstations having modems and, more recently, having direct connections to the Internet.

Modem connections can breach security in several ways:

- A user downloading software from a bulletin board or dial-up Web site can inadvertently introduce a virus.

Security

5

ADMINISTRATIVE
CONCEPTS

CAUTION

Even though NT is rated as the only C2-secure certified operating system, viruses that can be harmful in the NT environment do exist. Namely, many DOS viruses are capable of doing harm while running under the NT DOS emulation window. Boot sector viruses, although not strictly capable of running under NT, may still damage the hard disk boot sector to the point that NT may not be able to start up. You can find information on the latest NT viruses and virus scan products by performing a Web search on the Internet using InfoSeek, Lycos, Magellan, Yahoo!, or any other search engine and entering the keywords nt virus.

■ An NT or Windows 95 workstation left with a RAS Server running can enable a caller to connect to the network. If the GUEST account defaults have been overlooked, the caller can gain access to important files.

■ A user browsing Web sites that use Java or similar Web-based script languages can unknowingly initiate the transfer of malicious code to his or her workstation. From there, the code could proceed to do further damage, under the guise of the user's login security.

Workflow Automation

Full Web integration is now a prominent feature of Exchange 5.0. The challenge for the enterprise administrator and for corporate management will be to broaden their vision to include the worldwide scope of possibilities and to take the necessary time to map out a strategy.

You can use many Exchange Server components to assist you in the development of a workflow automation strategy for the enterprise. The Internet Connector enables you to send and retrieve messages worldwide. Exchange forms provide the means to specify standard methods of communication regarding specific business functions. The Exchange API permits design of custom applications that can interface directly with the directory and information stores. The following are a few simple examples of workflow automation:

■ A manager receives timesheets from employees via e-mail. Each employee fills out his or her timesheet by creating an e-mail message using the public timesheets form. When the employee's mail arrives at the manager's mailbox, it is automatically routed to a folder for that employee. The manager approves each timesheet by opening up the message and checking an OK box on the form. He or she then clicks on the Submit button, which is now active, and the employee time information is automatically entered into the corporate SQL Server database.

- A work-order form is used to initiate a customer request for a new phone line. The form is e-mailed to several recipients who are located throughout this national enterprise. One recipient who is in finance then opens a Job Order Number in his or her accounting system. Another recipient who is in field operations schedules the work to be performed.

- A medical transcription company has many employees working from home. These employees take transcriptions, in Word, which get embedded into an Exchange form. At the end of the day, the employees connect to the main office using RAS and send all messages that contain the transcription documents. At the main office, each message is routed to its appropriate folder for further processing by automated programs that route these transcriptions back to the appropriate doctors' offices.

Chapter 31, "Workflow with Exchange: Keyfile's Keyflow," provides more detail on the subject of workflow with Exchange Server.

Site-Specific Planning

Exchange sites usually consist of a group of Exchange servers located on the same LAN segment. This setup also usually means that the servers and user workstations are physically located within a close geographic area. Exchange permits easy and efficient automatic replication of Exchange servers located within the same site without any user intervention.

Consequently, site planning, which also involves the site administrator, is mostly concerned with local issues revolving around hardware, user needs, and administration. The following sections present these areas of concern for the site administrator.

Workstation Configuration

The most common question asked among administrators and management seems to be: "Well, what kind of PC do you think I need to get to run this stuff?" To "gear-heads," the obvious answer is the most blown-out machine money can buy. To management and the chief financial officer, the answer is the least expensive PC that can still do useful work, because they have to buy a bunch of them.

Unfortunately, I cannot provide *the* answer in this book because that answer depends on some magic financial analysis that includes information such as cost of maintenance, amortization, risks and benefits, productivity gains, and so on. I can make a straightforward recommendation, however, based on knowledge of the applications out there, Exchange client requirements, and what users will be doing on their PCs.

Table 5.2 presents some recommended workstation configurations, given a type of usage pattern. These recommendations are based on my opinions and are not based on any rigorous Windows benchmarks. Also, I do not believe in buying employees "minimum required" workstations. Not only are you doing your employees a big disfavor, but you also set yourself up for a horrible depreciation scenario.

5

ADMINISTRATIVE
CONCEPTS

Table 5.2. Sample workstation configurations to support a specific mix of work.

Work Mix	Workstation Configuration
Administrative; front office. Use Exchange, MS Office	Pentium/90 MHz or better, 16MB RAM or more, 1GB hard disk
Technical support; uses custom application	Pentium/133 MHz or better, 32MB RAM or more, 2GB hard disk
Developer; has numerous compilers and tools	Pentium/200 MHz or better, 64MB RAM, 4GB hard disk

Server Configuration

The Exchange Server configuration is driven by the number of users it supports and, to some extent, by the number of ancillary tasks it may perform in addition to the regular mail deliveries and public folder management. An Exchange Server, for example, may act as a *bridgehead* for several other Exchange Servers. Or it may be the principal Internet Mail Gateway. Each of these Exchange roles or functions requires additional system resources in accordance to the demand placed on them. The Microsoft Internet Exchange Gateways, for example, currently handle over a million Internet messages per day. Microsoft's internal Exchange Servers are processing over three million messages per day. This work requires some serious horsepower.

Because so many parameters can affect the selection of hardware, it is probably best to consider a minimum configuration requirement and to target that for the small- to medium-sized business environment that this book is geared toward. For the Davy Crockett organization, the following features would define a minimal starting point for any of the site servers in the AMERICA domain:

- Pentium/90 MHz or better processor
- 32MB RAM or better
- 2GB hard disk with a fast SCSI-2 controller

If the servers are performing any additional tasks, such as providing general file services or hosting an Internet Information Server Service, the list should be altered to the following minimum features:

- Dual Pentium/90 MHz or better processors. (Dual processors are especially important to take advantage of multiple threads when trying to service Exchange processes and general file access and program execution simultaneously.)
- 40 to 64MB RAM.

■ Two 2GB hard disks, each on a separate fast SCSI-2 controller. (Having two hard disks provides concurrent SCSI channel access, which prevents contention between multiple threads accessing multiple drives simultaneously.)

You can accomplish more specific tuning by using the various performance monitors described later in this book in Chapter 27, "Monitoring and Preventing Problems." Chapter 6, "Planning for Optimal Server Performance," provides good insight into this subject.

Performance

NOTE

The PCs actually used for setting up the Davy Crockett organization examples were two 100 MHz 486s with 32MB RAM each and one dual Pentium 90 MHz with 40MB RAM. The two 486s were the machines in the AMERICA domain. Also note that I first attempted to set up with only 16MB RAM on the 486s. This did not work. The disk thrashing was unmistakable and would have caused Exchange to fail under a real installation with several hundred users.

NT User Accounts and Groups

Identifying groups within an Exchange site is almost identical to establishing groups within an NT domain. You should establish your NT groups according to functional areas of the organization, such as accounting, sales, marketing, development, support, manufacturing, Q&A, and so on. You might also want to distinguish between management levels so that managers have access to more information across functional divisions.

Make sure that a site administrator account is defined, if it is different from the NT domain administrator, and that it is entered at the site and configuration levels of the Exchange object hierarchy, as shown in Figure 5.4, where Davy Crockett has the Exchange service account permission at the site level.

One of the most common uses for user account groups is to provide different levels of access to Exchange public folders. A folder hierarchy or a group of folders can be dedicated to the Sales group, for example. You might use another group of folders for customer support or tracking individual calls and responses.

The actual creation and assignment of permissions is a bit convoluted in Exchange. A folder can be created only by an Exchange client; it cannot be created by the Exchange administrator program. On the other hand, only the Exchange administrator program can set up the replication schedule for that folder.

Because folders are such a powerful and useful Exchange feature, the section titled "One-Time Implementation Tasks," later in this chapter, walks you through setting up the Sales public folder on the TENNESSEE site and how it is replicated through to the KENTUCKY site.

Site and User Security

Site security carries the same cautions regarding network and modem access as you learned for enterprise security. In addition, you should take the following steps:

- Place the Exchange servers in a physically separate room or enclosure that can be locked.
- Either encrypt all site backups or store backup tapes in a separate location that can be securely locked (a bank safe deposit box works nicely).
- Implement the Exchange *Key Management* component to provide authentication and message encryption security.

Probably the most important aspect of Exchange security is the deliberate attention paid to establishing good passwords and limiting the number of individuals entrusted with them. Chapter 21, "Exchange Messaging Security with Key Management Server," provides more details on implementing Exchange messaging security.

User-level security is not much different from the security needed for NT user accounts. The policies that have been established for users at the NT domain levels will probably be used as is. Exchange does provide for new areas where individual users may be given administrative control, or a group of users may be formed in support of certain Exchange functions.

A user, for example, might be given the responsibility of overseeing the Sales public folder (you create this public folder later in this chapter). In this case, the Exchange administrator could set up that user with Owner rights to the folder to enable him or her to add, modify, and delete any message, or to create subfolders and move messages between folders. All other users whose job functions include sales support could be made part of the NT Sales group. This group could then be given Author permission to the Sales folder, which would enable the group to create, modify, and delete its own postings to that folder, but it could not modify or delete each other's messages.

The Exchange Key Management service may be implemented and used by the user clients. The important aspect of using the security keys is in providing the users with their *security tokens*, which are essentially unique passwords that permit messages from one user to be encrypted and/or authenticated as originating from that user. The Exchange Administrator obtains this token, and it is only as secure as the method used to transmit it to the user.

Workflow Automation

Workflow automation at the site level is usually just a more detailed view of workflow automation for the enterprise, as described previously. Depending on the organization, sites can have well-defined functional areas that are distinct from other sites. If this is the case, it makes the most sense to give each site the authority and mission to develop its own automation methods. After all, usually the people who are doing the actual work can best tell you what they need to make their work easier and more productive.

Again, the key Exchange features that permit development of workflow aids are forms design and management, custom field attributes, public folders, and the Exchange API.

Employee Training

Probably the most common mistake management makes when "rolling out" a new enterprise standard is never involving the employees in the process. It really is amazing how often a new "productivity" application is given to employees who then provide the immediate feedback that their lives were simpler before this newfangled tool was foisted upon them. It is also probably true that the new tool really is better than what they had, but because of lack of involvement in the rollout process, they cannot appreciate how it is supposed to fit into their work environment.

The following shows the steps in which employees should be involved for "rolling out" a new office tool:

1. Establish the need.
2. Determine the method used to fulfill the need.
3. Present (market) these options to the employees to obtain their buy-in.
4. Establish a training schedule to prepare employees for implementation of the new method.
5. Coordinate the implementation of the method.
6. Follow up to determine success in fulfilling the needs identified.

Looks like the entire life cycle of the tool, doesn't it?

Implementing Exchange should involve users at every step. If you are converting from an existing MS Mail environment, most of their training will center around the new Exchange features, such as public folders or Internet Mail connectivity. If this is a first-time e-mail implementation, you should conduct some internal seminars on corporate e-mail. Some of the more obvious areas to cover include the following basic topics:

- What are recipients?
- What is the difference between the global and private address books?
- What constitutes a good Subject line?
- What does it mean to cc: or forward e-mail?
- How is security used by the client?
- What standards can be implemented for Subject lines to allow incoming messages to be placed in appropriate folders?
- What constitutes good and bad e-mail etiquette?
- How can Word and Excel documents be included in an e-mail message?
- How can public folders be used to help a group of employees working together?
- How are forms used in this company?

This list is not exhaustive, but each of the items in the list can become quite complex, depending on the environment and the kind of work the employees are doing. A development group, for example, could use public folders and a structured Subject line to implement a bug-tracking system. Forwarding mail can be used to inform someone, or it can be part of a strict review process.

The great thing about e-mail is that its use is infinitely varied. What is placed in a message is only limited by the imagination of the participants. Good and thorough training is the key to unlocking this potential within each employee.

One-Time Implementation Tasks

The following list summarizes the most common one-time implementation tasks for setting up an Exchange organization. Most of the items are taken from the Davy Crockett organization example:

1. Design your enterprise domain and network strategy indicating what Exchange Servers will be used and in what NT domains they will be placed (refer to Figure 5.1).

2. Install or update to NT Server 4.0 on all PCs to receive Exchange Server. Make sure that all needed services (such as RAS) and protocols (such as TCP/IP) are available. If you will use Active Server Pages, install Service Pack 2 or later.

3. Establish the necessary domain trust relationships.

4. Establish the necessary administrative and Exchange services accounts.

5. Install Exchange Servers at each physical site. Verify that the organization and site names are correct for each server.

6. Create the user mailboxes for each site. Test that messages can be sent between mailboxes within each site.

7. Create the public folder hierarchy for each site or for the organization.

8. Establish the directory replication scheme between sites. First test that messages can be sent to recipients between sites. Then implement the directory replication services.

9. Confirm that all recipients are visible between replicated sites (see "Directory Replication over Dynamic RAS," later in this chapter).

10. Establish the public folder replication scheme (see "Folder Creation and Replication," later in this chapter).

11. Establish the Off-Line Address Book.

12. Implement the Exchange Key Management Server if advanced security is required.

13. Set up foreign system connectors, such as the Internet Mail Connector. This step also requires the establishment and use of name spaces.

14. Make the Exchange client available on the network from a shared NT network drive (also called an *install point*).

The following sections provide some actual examples for more complicated steps, using the Davy Crockett organization.

Directory Replication over Dynamic RAS

In the Davy Crockett example, the TEXAS site users need to be able to send and receive messages from the KENTUCKY and TENNESSEE sites. Because the only connection available to TEXAS is via modem, a Dynamic RAS Connector had to be used to enable directory replication. The following sequence shows how this connector was set up at the TENNESSEE site on the MEMPHIS server. The same steps were then followed at the TEXAS site on the ALAMO Server. To follow along, complete these steps:

1. You need to install a RAS MTA transport stack. Choose File | New Other | MTA Transport stack. You must install and configure RAS on this server before you can install the RAS MTA transport stack. Figure 5.5 shows the available transport stacks that you can install. For this example, choose RAS MTA. The server shown in the figure is BOONEVILLE, but the RAS MTA transport was actually installed on MEMPHIS. Figure 5.6 shows the added Server object representing the RAS connector on MEMPHIS. Figures 5.7 and 5.8 show the configuration screen. Note that the Connectors tab of the Properties dialog box, shown in Figure 5.8, is empty when the RAS MTA is first installed because no connectors have been defined yet.

FIGURE 5.5.

Available choices when installing a new MTA transport stack.

Figure 5.6.

The highlighted object in the right window pane shows the newly added RAS MTA transport stack for the MEMPHIS server.

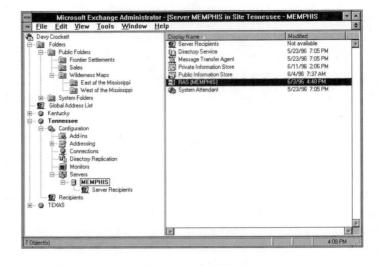

Figure 5.7.

The General tab of the RAS MTA transport stack configuration.

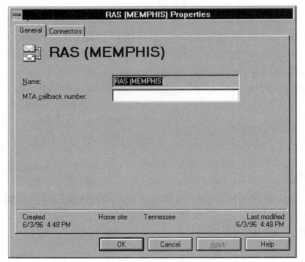

2. Now you can install a Dynamic RAS Connector. If you try to install the Dynamic RAS Connector *before* installing the RAS MTA transport stack, you get the error message shown in Figure 5.9.

   Getting this message is not a big deal. Simply go back to step 1. To install the Dynamic RAS Connector, select the Connections object and then choose File | New Other | Dynamic RAS Connector. You then see the configuration dialog boxes shown in Figures 5.10 through 5.16.

FIGURE 5.8.

The Connectors tab of the RAS MTA transport stack configuration.

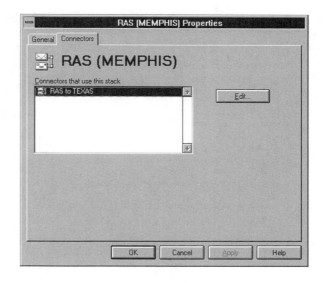

FIGURE 5.9.

Error message that results when you attempt to install the Dynamic RAS Connector before the RAS MTA transport stack has been installed.

FIGURE 5.10.

The General tab of the Dynamic RAS Connector on the MEMPHIS computer. Note that the Phone book entry, RONHP, is a prior defined RAS entry that contains the phone number of the TEXAS site ALAMO server modem.

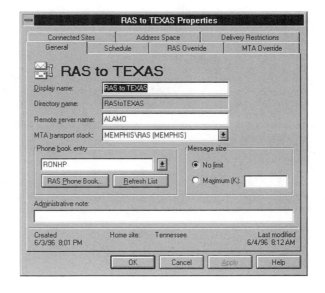

Figure 5.11.

The RAS Override tab of the Dynamic RAS Connector on the MEMPHIS computer. The Connect as fields are specified because the default Exchange services account is different at the TEXAS site than at the TENNESSEE site.

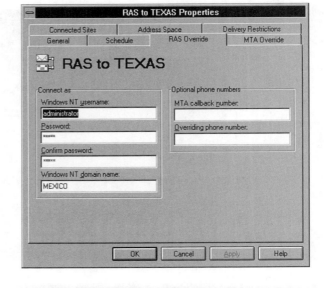

Figure 5.12.

The Connected Sites tab of the Dynamic RAS Connector on the MEMPHIS computer. This tab explicitly lists the external sites that are connected to this computer (the MEMPHIS server).

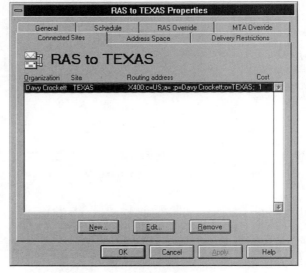

FIGURE 5.13.

The General tab of the TEXAS site, viewed by clicking the Edit button shown in Figure 5.12.

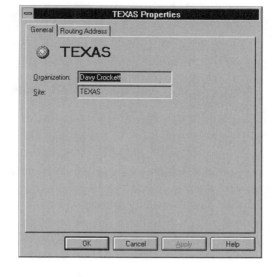

FIGURE 5.14.

The Routing Address tab of the TEXAS site, viewed by clicking the Edit button shown in Figure 5.12.

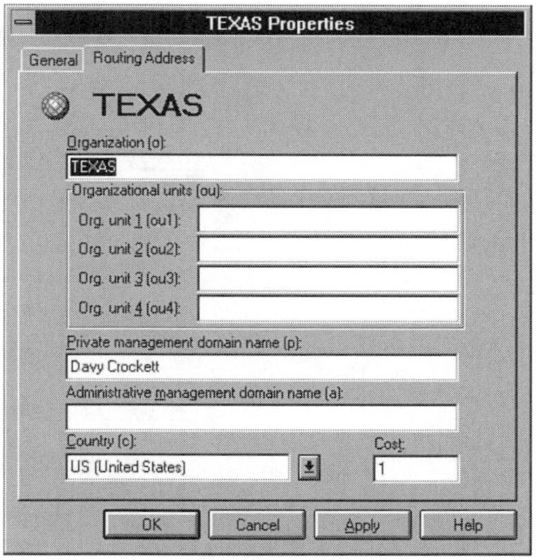

FIGURE 5.15.

The Address Space tab of the Dynamic RAS Connector on the MEMPHIS server.

FIGURE 5.16.

The General tab for configuring an X.400 address space, viewed by clicking the Edit button shown in Figure 5.15.

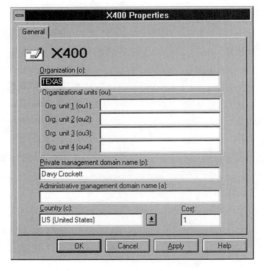

These figures show what it took to successfully configure a dynamic RAS connection between the TENNESSEE and TEXAS sites (assuming that the same set of configurations were performed on the ALAMO server). Some questions, however, remain as to the difference between the Connected Sites Routing Address and the Address Space entries and their configurations.

3. At this point, you should test the dynamic RAS connection before attempting to configure directory replication. Sending a message from TENNESSEE to a valid recipient at the TEXAS site accomplishes this test. Because the sites have not been replicated, no valid TEXAS site recipient exists at the TENNESSEE site. How do you tell the system to send a message to, say, Daniel Boon? Use the X.400 addressing method to specify Boon's mail address. In this case, enter the following into the To: field of the e-mail message:

```
x400:g=Daniel;s=Boon;o=TEXAS;p=Davy Crockett;a= ;c=us
```

Sending this message causes the Dynamic RAS Connector to dial out, connecting to the ALAMO server via modem, and then, if everything is configured as above, deliver the message to Daniel Boon.

4. Now configure the Directory Replication Connector by selecting the Directory Replication container and choosing File | New Other | Directory Replication. Figure 5.17 shows the Directory Replication container with two configured connectors. Figures 5.18 and 5.19 show the various property tabs associated with the Directory Replication Connector on the MEMPHIS server, configured to replicate with the TEXAS site.

FIGURE 5.17.

The contents of the Directory Replication container on the MEMPHIS server. Two Directory Replication Connectors are configured, one to replicate to the KENTUCKY site and one to replicate to the TEXAS site.

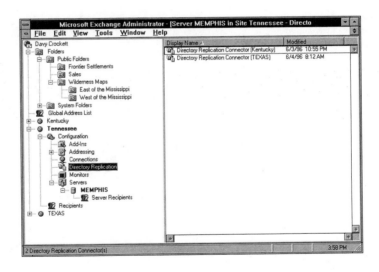

Setting up directory replication between sites on the same LAN, as between KENTUCKY and TENNESSEE, is similar to the preceding steps, but much simpler because all the configurations for RAS aren't needed. After you configure all the directory replicators, simply wait 15 to 30 minutes, and all the Exchange directory information, as shown in Figure 5.17, will become visible at all servers at all sites.

5

ADMINISTRATIVE CONCEPTS

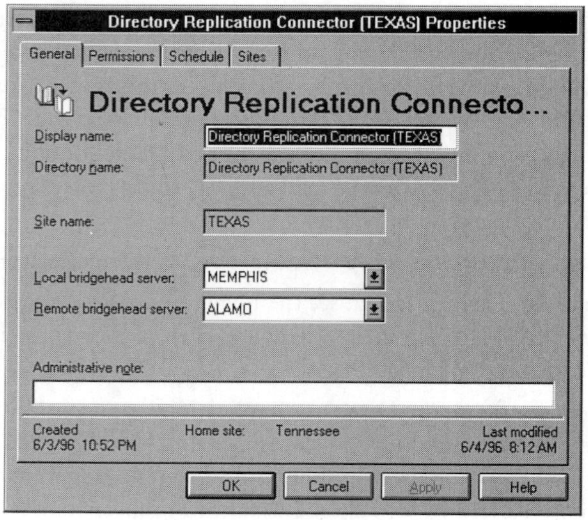

FIGURE 5.18.

The General tab of the TEXAS site Directory Replication Connector. Note that MEMPHIS and ALAMO are also functioning as bridgehead servers.

FIGURE 5.19.

The Sites tab of the TEXAS site Directory Replication Connector. TEXAS is the inbound site from the TENNES-SEE site's perspective.

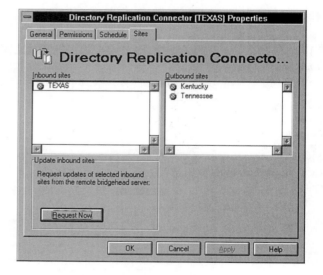

Folder Creation and Replication

The following principles govern the creation and use of public Exchange folders:

- Public folders are created by the Exchange client on the home server for that user.
- The user running the client must have permission to create public folders.
- The user who creates the folder is, by default, the owner of that folder with full permissions.

■ Other users are granted Author permission, by default, which permits them to create, modify, and delete any messages that they originate but not to modify or delete messages written by others. The site administrator or owner of the folder can change this permission.

■ Public folders should be set up with size and aging limits for their contents to maintain control over the space required by their messages.

Setting up a public folder hierarchy is probably something you want to spend some time thinking about. You need to consider enterprise-wide and site-specific issues. Even in a small organization, public folders can be used to contain information about transitory events, such as projects. Think about creating a folder hierarchy that provides some stability at the highest levels but allows a manager the freedom to create additional folders at the lower levels as needed. You do so by giving certain users (managers) permission to create folder hierarchies.

The following steps were used to create the Sales public folder on the TENNESSEE site and replicate it to the KENTUCKY site. Here's how you can set up a folder like the one in the example:

1. Using the Exchange client, create a folder at the TENNESSEE site on the MEMPHIS Server by choosing File | New Folder (see Figure 5.20). When you press OK, the Sales Properties dialog box appears with the General tab information visible (see Figure 5.21).

FIGURE 5.20.

The New Folder dialog box shown creating the public folder Sales.

2. Add groups and/or user accounts to the Permissions list of the Sales public folder. In the case shown in Figure 5.22, Fess Parker, a BOONEVILLE user in the KENTUCKY site, is given Author permission.

3. Create a message as a *posting* to the Sales folder using the Exchange client in the TENNESSEE site, as shown in Figure 5.23.

FIGURE 5.21.

Part of the dialog box sequence for creating the public folder Sales. The General tab is at the forefront.

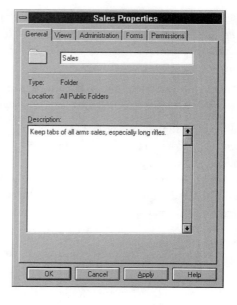

FIGURE 5.22.

Part of the Sales Properties dialog box showing the information on the Permissions Tab.

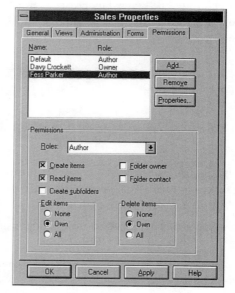

4. Figure 5.24 shows how the public folder hierarchy appears in the KENTUCKY site on the BOONEVILLE server. The directory store shows the folder, but the information store does not yet contain the posted message because the folder has not been replicated, as indicated by the message in Figure 5.25.

FIGURE 5.23.

Message posted to the Exchange public folder called Sales on the MEMPHIS server.

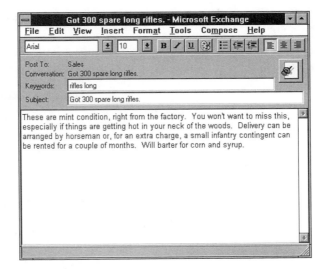

FIGURE 5.24.

KENTUCKY Exchange site object hierarchy. Note that the public folder Sales is visible.

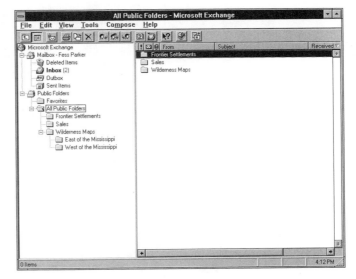

FIGURE 5.25.

Error message that appeared when user Fess Parker double-clicked on the public folder Sales using the Exchange client.

5. To replicate the Sales public folder properly, add the BOONEVILLE server in the KENTUCKY site to the Sales folder Replicate folders to list, as shown in Figure 5.26. Note that you must do this from an Exchange Administrator program connected to the TENNESSEE site and with appropriate user access permissions.

FIGURE 5.26.

The entry
Kentucky\BOONEVILLE
shows that the Sales folder will be replicated to that site. The MEMPHIS *entry was provided as a default when the folder was created.*

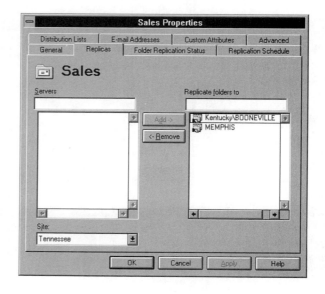

6. Figures 5.27 and 5.28 show that the message, originally posted on the MEMPHIS server, is replicated across the site connector to the BOONEVILLE server.

FIGURE 5.27.

This time the Exchange client for Fess Parker shows a posting in the Sales public folder.

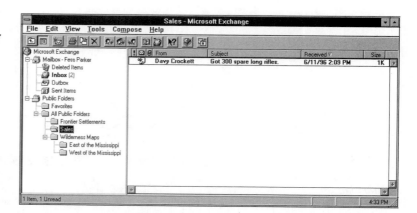

The preceding sequence of steps is fundamental to the creation of any public folder hierarchy that includes public folder replication to another site. In fact, each public folder must be configured individually, in terms of its replication to other sites. This is both a plus and a minus. It is a plus because Microsoft has provided complete flexibility for every aspect of public folder management. The minus is that setting up a large number of public folders can be quite tedious. A more complete description of the public folder configuration options is given in Chapters 13, "Configuring Basic Server Operations," and 24, "Public Folders."

FIGURE 5.28.

Double-clicking on the posting from Davy Crockett shows the details of the posting. They really had great service in those days!

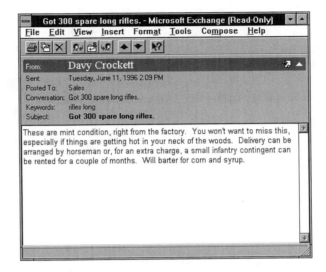

TIP

When you configure public folder replication between sites, make sure that you wait long enough for replication to take place. The shortest time frame for replication is when you choose Always on the Replication Schedule tab of the Sales Folder Properties dialog box. Replication usually requires about 15 minutes. If you check for postings before replication takes place, you might think that it didn't work. To be sure, check the Folder Replication Status tab to see when the last replication to your site actually happened. In Figure 5.29, the Folder Replication Status tab shows that information was replicated to this folder from the MEMPHIS server on 6/11/96 at 4:20 PM.

Ongoing Maintenance-Related Tasks

For the small- to medium-sized installation, maintenance should be fairly minimal. Feedback from users indicates whether performance is within the expected boundaries. The primary maintenance tasks you should be concerned with are as follows:

- Making ongoing backups
- Ensuring disk space availability
- Managing public folders
- Ensuring continuous connection to foreign systems
- Monitoring system events

- Running consistency checks on the data stores
- Running the Key Management Server
- Managing address spaces and user mailboxes

Some of these issues are explored in more detail in Chapters 27 and 28, "Diagnosing the Cause of a Problem."

FIGURE 5.29.

Replication status is shown in the Folder Replication Status tab of the Properties dialog box for the Sales folder in the KENTUCKY site.

Meeting Users' Needs

The Exchange client is a much simpler tool than any of the components associated with Exchange Server administration. Most of the issues surrounding Exchange clients include the following:

- Setting up and configuring the client on a computer
- Setting up and configuring the client for remote or telecommuting use
- Managing distribution lists
- Creating and managing folders
- Inserting objects in messages
- Sending messages to foreign systems (Internet)
- Using Schedule+ and the components that integrate with Exchange

If users are migrating from Microsoft Mail, your training effort should be minimal. Otherwise, be prepared to address each of the preceding issues in detail, or designate some network support people to meet the need.

Most importantly, you should be responsive to the inevitable frustrations expressed by these first-time users. Remember when you had to figure out the correct parameters to use with the DOS backup command? Well, you now have several dozen more parameters than before. You may not run into them for 80 percent of all e-mail traffic, but with 50 or more employees, someone somewhere will be trying to send a MIME-encoded Word document to a system that recognizes only UUENCODE. Or someone might be trying to send a 1600×1200×64KB color bitmap of some beautiful scenery to a friend down the hall who is running Windows 3.1 on a 4MB machine. And that person may wonder why every time he or she clicks on this mail message, the PC crashes.

Establishing Policies and Procedures

Exchange has the potential for participating in so many facets of a business that it is not possible to enumerate all policies and procedures that could be implemented. The areas discussed in the following sections are most likely to benefit from the creation of some standards.

E-Mail Subject Lines

Exchange enables you to apply rules to any incoming message. These rules may operate on many components of a message, as shown in Figure 5.30.

FIGURE 5.30.

The Exchange Inbox Assistant. Shown are the various filters and actions that you can impose on an incoming message.

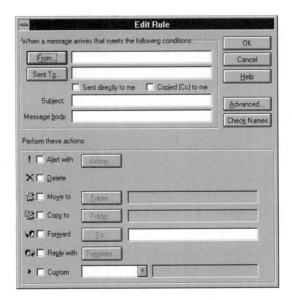

By specifying, for example, a policy that all e-mail messages for the consulting project "Acme Nose Tweezers" begin with "Acme Nose Tweezers:," a user could create a message folder into which all messages pertaining to the Acme Nose Tweezers project get placed. Similarly, in a *matrix* organization, an employee can have all e-mail messages from his or her various "bosses" placed in their respective folders by defining a routing rule based on the message originator's name.

Because all elements of the e-mail message are open to rule application, no limits are placed on how an organization might structure e-mail messages to take advantage of this automatic message processing.

Public Folders

As mentioned previously, public folders provide one of the most powerful means of establishing common communication forums within an organization. The policies and procedures governing public folders are established by the purpose of those folders. A bug-tracking folder might be managed by the testing manager, who establishes the format of subject lines and maybe even establishes a public form for reporting bugs. Another public folder may simply store all Internet Provider-related messages for read-only access.

E-Mail Attachments

With e-mail attachments, the subject gets a bit more sticky. One of the primary benefits of Exchange is its capability of using Microsoft's ActiveX technology for including in the message body objects such as Word documents, Excel spreadsheets, and any other native format application documents that adhere to the ActiveX standard. This is great for the users, but it can give the administrators a headache. For example, a user can easily include the latest images from the Hubble Space Telescope in a message. But an administrator may start to wonder where he will get the disk space to store these messages that were forwarded to all 300 of the company's employees!

Here, the initial parameters for the information store come into play. You can set limits for the size of any message and for the total disk space occupied by any mailbox. Establishing these standards requires a careful review of employee work habits and matching work-related information-sharing requirements with available and affordable hardware. Chapter 13 presents examples on how you can specify these file size limits for the message store and public folders.

E-Mail Etiquette

You can find quite a few books and Web references on the topic of e-mail etiquette. The following list summarizes some main points:

- Don't put anything in an e-mail message that you would be embarrassed to discuss face-to-face.
- Don't use ALL CAPS to make a point. ALL CAPS comes across as shouting. ALL CAPS is appropriate for indicating a verbatim input such as "type CANCEL."
- Spell check your e-mail. Just because it is on a computer doesn't mean it shouldn't be spelled correctly.

- Find out the format for sending binary attachments before sending the e-mail. In some cases, you may actually disrupt your recipients' e-mail systems by sending large binary attachments.

- If you want your e-mail to be private, encrypt it. The legal status of e-mail marked PRIVATE is still under debate.

In general, treat e-mail just as you would treat a letter delivered on your company's stationery.

Disaster Recovery

As with any mission-critical resource, the key to disaster recovery is having both a procedure for creating reliable offline backup of important information and a procedure for accessing and restoring it when needed. How often should you create backups? The answer is simple: as often as it takes you to reduce the risk of nonrecoverable data loss to an acceptable level.

How do you determine what is acceptable? Here is one example: You work at a consulting company with 50 employees who bill out at $125 per hour. You think you can skimp on backup hardware and the cost of tapes, so you run full backups just once a week, on Friday. The main company development server fails when the disk head decides it's time to dig trenches on one of the disk platters. At 6,000 rpm, the magnetic head meets the oxide layer at about 62 mph. The resulting wreckage damages the rest of the disk so that no information is recoverable. So what does your loss cost the company? A whole week of billing is gone: 50 people working 8 hours per day for 4 days. That's about $200,000 of lost billing—all because someone didn't want to pay maybe $5,000 more for tapes and equipment that could perform backups on a daily basis. Let me put it another way. You must create frequent tape (or other reliable offline storage medium) backups of all important databases. Otherwise, you're living life on the edge, if you know what I mean.

I hope the preceding scenario will raise the hairs on the backs of some necks and get people asking themselves when *exactly* was the last system backup run. Is the preceding scenario the worst case? Not even close. Depending on the size of your business, losses due to poor backup procedures can easily exceed millions of dollars.

To protect against data losses, go ahead and spend the money for an offline tape backup system that will ensure recoverability under all circumstances. This system includes being prepared for the following:

- Occasional user requests to recover lost or corrupted development code from a day ago to a month ago.

- Full recoverability of all files on all servers to the nearest day of the current month, even if the entire office burns down. This is accomplished by creating two backups at once and storing one copy off-site in a safe deposit box.

- Full recoverability of all files on all servers for any given month, going back for one full year.

5

ADMINISTRATIVE CONCEPTS

■ Full recoverability of certain "archived" files for the shelf-life of the tape (about five years). You can extend this lifetime by restoring and re-archiving the tape contents.

The preceding capabilities are applicable to all system software and data components. The method you use may vary because of certain application-specific requirements. Microsoft SQL and Exchange Servers, for example, need to use a special backup program to back up live database files. Having a special backup program, however, does not change the fact that you need a procedure in place to run these backup jobs.

Although this book is not intended to be a backup primer, the following concepts may aid in the discussion of how backups and disaster recovery in general are handled with Exchange:

Archive Bit. This special flag is part of the directory entry associated with all files in most operating systems. The flag is used to indicate whether a file has been modified since the last time it was backed up.

Full or Normal Backup. Copies all files from the source machines to the backup medium and then marks them as having been *archived*.

Copy. Copies all files from the source machines to the backup medium but does not mark them as having been archived. This read-only operation does not disturb any of the file states.

Differential Backup. Copies all files from the source machines that have been changed since the last normal backup to the backup medium but does not mark them as having been archived. Thus, differential backups have a tendency to grow in size as more and more files get changed.

Incremental Backup. Copies all files from the source machines that have been changed since the last normal or incremental backup, and then those files are marked as having been archived.

Software Compression. This process is like PKZip for backups. The information on disk is read and then compressed by the backup software before being written to tape.

Hardware Compression. Works just like software compression except that the backup hardware performs the data compression.

A WARNING ABOUT COMPRESSION

Most backup software presents users with a choice of selection: No Compression, Software Compression, or Hardware Compression. Although compression is advantageous because it allows more information to fit on a given tape format (usually about a 2:1 factor), you may run into some pitfalls.

Think about the fact that a disaster recovery plan will be in place for years and that the procedures and equipment to support it will need to be effective over many years. If you use software compression, your backup data can be read only by the software that created it. If you use hardware compression, your data can be read only by the hardware that created it. For example, the 8mm tape backup unit you bought two years ago failed, and you have to restore some important client database information today. That particular drive is no longer manufactured. You can get other 8mm drives, but because you used hardware compression, which was proprietary to your drive, you won't be able to read the information with any of the new 8mm replacement units. If you had used software compression, or no compression, you would be able to restore your data.

Finally, with regard to performing tape backups, whatever hardware or software system you use, it must be reliable and simple to use. If the tape backup software requires an engineer to run it, don't buy it. If it is not easy to use, people will avoid using it.

Exchange Server Backups

This section gives a brief overview of the Exchange backup and recovery environment. You can find more specific details in Chapter 25, "Backup and Recovery."

Exchange Server uses a fully relational transaction database as its information store. Microsoft has implemented a *transaction logging* feature that records all information store or directory events and transactions in special transaction log files. If the system performs an abnormal shutdown—for example, a power failure or system blue screen—Exchange detects it and, when the system is restarted, attempts to recover the database from the log files. The log files essentially serve as a record of all the transactions and events related to the directory and information stores.

The following is a breakdown of the important components of each backup type as it pertains to Exchange:

> *Full backup.* The directory and information stores are backed up. All log files are backed up and then purged. The Exchange files are now at a known "marker" state, which provides a context for subsequent incremental or differential backups.

> *Copy.* The directory and information stores are backed up. All log files are backed up. Files are not marked or changed in any way.

> *Incremental backup.* The log files are backed up and then purged.

> *Differential backup.* The log files are backed up but not changed in any other way since the last full backup.

The reason for Incremental and Differential backups is that the Exchange information store can be very large. Rather than be forced to back up the entire database during daily backups (as most traditional backups would require), just the changes, as recorded in the log files, are backed up.

5

ADMINISTRATIVE CONCEPTS

These backups and restores are accomplished by a special version of the NT Backup software, which is installed during the Exchange Server installation process. In fact, this version has been designed to be able to recognize all Exchange Server sites and to be able to back up and restore to them remotely. Figure 5.31 shows the organizational hierarchy when selecting the Exchange Organization window.

FIGURE 5.31.

The Microsoft Exchange window available from the special version of Backup that is installed with Exchange. This view was obtained from running Backup on the BOONEVILLE server.

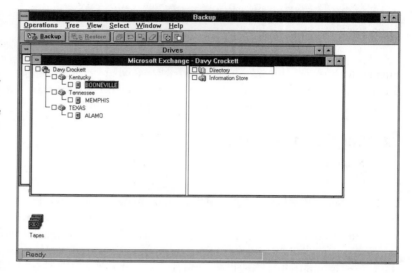

Notice that all three sites in the Davy Crockett organization show up in this window as possible backup options. The specific site selected also indicates that the directory and information store are available to be selected for an operation.

CAUTION

The Microsoft Exchange Reference indicates that incremental and differential backups cannot be run when circular logging is enabled. This is not strictly true. As Figure 5.32 shows, you can run an incremental backup.

Microsoft is really saying that you *shouldn't* run incremental or differential backups when using circular logging (which is the default). The reason is that circular logging overwrites the log files periodically. If you are relying on incremental or differential backups for recovery, you could potentially find yourself without recourse because circular logging just overwrote the last week's worth of changes to the information stores. Just be sure to uncheck the boxes shown in Figure 5.33 if you plan to use incremental or differential backups as part of your regular backup cycles.

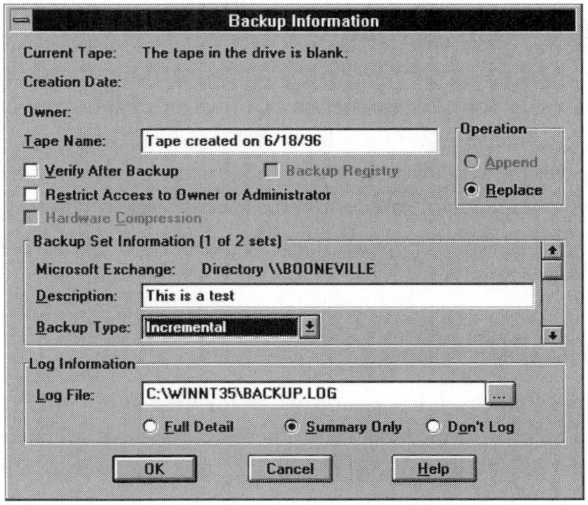

FIGURE 5.32.

This window shows that an incremental backup is about to be run even though circular logging is currently enabled.

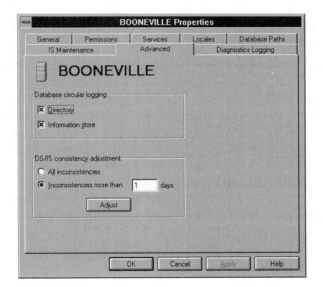

FIGURE 5.33.

The Advanced tab under the BOONEVILLE Properties showing that circular logging is the default.

Safety Through Replication

At least some of Exchange's information may be protected through replication to another server or site. Public folders, for example, are prime candidates for safety through redundancy. Microsoft's reference states that when a replicated server is brought back online, its information is updated from the current information on the replication servers.

Having a Written Plan

Many more aspects are involved in being prepared for disaster and recovery than just using the tape backups. None of these measures, however, will do any good if the methods and procedures used for recovery are stored in one individual's brain. Include the Exchange backup plan, general server backup plans, and all other business-related aspects of disaster recovery, such as insurance, emergency phone numbers and contacts, financial systems records, client notification procedures, and so on, in a written disaster recovery plan that is kept both on-site and in a secure location (such as a safety deposit box) off-site.

Summary

This chapter has provided a framework for organizing an Exchange Server implementation strategy. The most important fact to keep in mind is that Exchange is a tool that will be used by people. That is why some of this chapter has been devoted to organizational principles surrounding people. The installation and maintenance tasks are presented from the perspective of the enterprise administrator and the site administrator. These tasks touch on networking, workstation and server configuration, managing user accounts, connectivity to foreign systems, security, workflow automation, and training.

The examples use the Davy Crockett organization (refer to Figure 5.1) as a typical small- to medium-sized business with a few hundred employees. You explored specific cases for configuring the Exchange Servers and the domains and trusts needed for proper messaging and replication, and the creation of public folder and public folder replication. You learned what to expect in terms of performance, security, and remote connection through dynamic RAS. Thus, the scope covered was large and necessarily at a high level. The remainder of this book revisits each of the concepts presented in this chapter from a more detailed and functional view. In most cases, the initial installation of Exchange Server may very well require only the information presented in this chapter. However, to truly use the rich feature set incorporated into Exchange Server in the best way possible for your organization, read on and enjoy!

IN THIS PART

Planning

II

PART

Planning for Optimal Server Performance

by Greg Todd

IN THIS CHAPTER

CHAPTER 6

Performance This entire section of the book pertains to the planning process for rolling out Microsoft Exchange Server. In addition, the process is given good coverage in the *Installation Guide* and the *Concepts and Planning Guide*, which are part of the Exchange Server documentation. You should definitely refer to those manuals for other suggestions regarding the planning process. As I point out in other chapters, this book is intended to complement rather than replace the Exchange documentation. So perhaps, after reading this book, you will have even more insight into what it takes to plan a rollout of Exchange Server.

The planning process is a multifaceted exercise that can sometimes take a while to complete, depending upon the complexity of your undertaking. It generally consists of topics such as understanding the Exchange Server software, determining exactly what you want Exchange to do for you, anticipating the security aspects, planning how both Windows NT Server and Exchange Server will fit with your enterprise's structure, setting expectations for performance, determining what hardware to use—the list goes on.

For some people, the thought of planning alone is enough to cause pain. For others who are less planning-averse, the idea brings happy thoughts of an orderly, structured world where things always go according to plan. Whatever your personal response, one of the most important parts of the planning process is to get an accurate understanding of the system requirements for your Exchange server. This includes both setting an expectation of how the system should perform and deciding exactly what hardware to choose for your server. And because planning certainly is an important part of a successful Exchange rollout—especially in larger, more complex scenarios—you should spend some time doing it. You knew I was going to say that, right?

Bear in mind that it is impossible to tell you exactly which hardware you need for your specific environment. Even if I tried, it would probably be wrong. However, what I can do is provide guidelines and concepts you can use to fit your situation. This chapter offers information that will help you make an informed decision about your own server system requirements. Along with that, it discusses a couple of tools that will help you refine your requirements and give you hard data to back it up—or to justify changes. These tools come with Microsoft Exchange Server right out of the box, or they are readily available for free, so there's no need to go tool hunting or to buy anything else.

The following are the topics you'll look at in the context of system requirements:

- The number of users per server
- Choosing the right processor, disk, and RAM
- Microsoft Exchange Optimizer utility
- Windows NT Performance Monitor counters
- Simulating a user load with LoadSim

First, this chapter handles the question to which everyone wants an answer: How many users will Microsoft Exchange Server support? Unfortunately, there is not a straightforward answer to this question. However, this chapter will give you some insight into the issues surrounding the question so that you can answer it for your specific installation. After all, that's the one you care the most about.

Next, you learn concepts related to planning the components in the main subsystems of your server: CPU, disk, and RAM. These are the most crucial components to Exchange, and they deserve the most attention. Some would argue that the network should be included in this list. But assuming your server sits on a network that runs at LAN speeds—10–100 Mbits/s—you will likely need to be concerned first with your server's CPU, disk, and RAM.

After that, you will get an advanced peek at the Microsoft Exchange Optimizer. This utility plays an important role in getting Microsoft Exchange Server parameters configured properly on the hardware you've selected. You'll get a feel for some of the questions it will ask you and for some of the parameters it configures—before you start the Exchange Server setup process.

Finally, the chapter wraps up with a discussion of two tools helpful to understanding Exchange Server performance: Microsoft Exchange Server objects and counters found in Windows NT Performance Monitor, and Microsoft's load simulator utility for Exchange, LoadSim. These are useful tools in helping you understand your own system requirements. Because determining precise hardware requirements can be an ongoing thing, with these you should be able to refine your requirements over time.

After you read this chapter, you should understand foundational concepts about performance and how it relates to your server hardware requirements. There are several roles an Exchange server can play, but here I will focus on the performance when using it as a messaging server. That will serve as a good starting place to understanding overall server performance characteristics.

Also, you will have a jump on things, because you will have general ideas about how to set up both your server hardware and the Exchange software for good performance *before* the installation process begins. Finally, you will know how to apply NT Performance Monitor and LoadSim to the task of understanding Exchange performance.

You might be familiar with some of the topics I plan to cover here, or you might never have thought about them. Regardless, it's worth your while to take a few minutes and read through this chapter. And when your boss wonders how you knew so much about this stuff, you can just smile. So grab a comfortable chair and something to drink, and let's dive in.

> **NOTE**
>
> In this chapter, the terms Exchange Server, Exchange, and server are used somewhat interchangeably. Because Microsoft Exchange Server really connotes the entire product—client, server, connectors, and so forth—in the context of performance, I am referring strictly to the server portion of the entire Exchange Server package.

Number of Users per Server

If you think about it, the number of users per server—or server capacity—is one of the key issues driving the entire system-requirements process. The first question out of people's mouths is usually, "How many users can Exchange Server support?" More to the point, the number of users you need to support is a main issue when deciding how much hardware to throw at Exchange.

There's good news and bad news. The good news: This is the question everyone else is asking, so you're asking a valid question. The bad news: There is no simple answer to the question. The answer depends upon what the users will be doing with Exchange. Put simply, the usage profile of your users has a direct impact on how many users your Exchange server will support for a given hardware configuration. Of course, there are other factors that influence server capacity, but the main factor is user profile.

Suppose your users are pretty new to messaging. They have never really tried the brave new frontier of electronic communication via computer, so they are going to get their chance by using Exchange Server. Chances are good this type of user will have light usage patterns and consequently won't place much load on the system. Performance-wise, a single Exchange server can handle many users with this type of usage profile; a thousand would be no problem.

> **NOTE**
>
> Incidentally, when you look at LoadSim later in this chapter, you learn about using it to simulate users with a certain usage profile. LoadSim has three default user profiles—Low, Medium, and Heavy—which are good for modeling performance for different classes of users.

On the other hand, maybe you have more sophisticated users who have significantly higher expectations of their messaging system. In contrast to the neophytes described above, their usage patterns are quite heavy; these are advanced users who send and receive lots of e-mail. They require connectivity to many other e-mail users, quite possibly all over the world. They probably use the Internet. They may even need Web or news server support. In short, electronic messaging is a basic part of daily life. As a result, these users will demand more of their server and will place a higher load on Exchange. In this case, you will be able to support fewer users on the same hardware platform—maybe half, give or take some.

Make sense so far?

Now, a single Exchange server can handle varying numbers of users—from very small installations of 25, for example, up to huge installations in the thousands. Naturally, this user scaling depends on the hardware and the user load. With modest hardware, such as a 486/66 with 32MB RAM and a single disk, you can expect to handle 100 or less light (or "Low," in LoadSim terminology) users who are only using e-mail. At the other end of the spectrum—for example, with four Pentium Pro/200 processors, 1GB RAM, and a couple of huge hardware-disk arrays—you can realistically expect to approach a couple thousand simultaneous users (roughly, depending on the exact user profile and how the hardware is configured).

However, bear in mind that two thousand users could have only 8MB each of single-instance mailbox storage, because, at the time of this writing, Exchange 4.0 and 5.0 have a 16GB limit on the information store. For most installations, mailbox size is something to consider. The 16GB limit is supposed to be removed in a release subsequent to Exchange 5.0.

Future Directions

> **NOTE**
>
> In this context, when I talk about numbers of users, I am referring to simultaneous active users, not total users configured on the server or in the Exchange directory. So don't confuse number of users with how many users have mailboxes on the Exchange server itself. For example, suppose you have four servers in a site with a total of 2,000 user mailboxes in the Exchange directory—that's 500 users per server. If there are only 200 users active on a single server at any one time, plan the hardware for each server around the 200 active users. But if you think all 500 will be active, plan around that instead.

Of course, one other important factor to consider is what is acceptable in terms of response time. How fast do your users require the system to respond? Generally, the rule of thumb is to keep response times at a second or less. If you can live with slower response times, you can support more users on a given hardware configuration. For example, some folks use three seconds as the maximum response time, so they should be able to support more users on the same hardware configuration than those who require one-second response time. Regardless, the response time requirement has a definite impact on the planning process.

Arguably, the most common range for Exchange server installations is 200–500 concurrent users per server. This can be supported by a single Pentium/133 with a 2MB level 2 cache, 128MB RAM, and two fast disk volumes. You learn about these implementation details later in this chapter in the sections about configuring the server: "Choosing the Right Processor," "Choosing the Right Disk Subsystem," and "Choosing the Right Amount of RAM."

To summarize, Table 6.1 provides some basic guidelines for hardware requirements using Exchange strictly as an e-mail server. These are intended only as guidelines, not as absolute performance data, but they will get you in the ballpark for setting up your server.

Table 6.1. Basic Exchange server hardware requirements.

# Users	Processor(s)	RAM	# of Disk Volumes & Type
Up to 100	486/66	32MB	1 Fast SCSI-2
100–200	Pentium/100	64MB	2 Fast SCSI-2
200–500	Pentium/133	128MB	2 stripe sets or disk arrays
500–1000	2 Pentium/166	256MB	2 hardware disk arrays; 1 Fast Wide SCSI-2
Over 1000	2 Pentium Pro/166	512MB	2 hardware disk arrays; 1 Fast Wide SCSI-2

Technically, according to the product documentation, Exchange Server requires an absolute minimum of 24MB RAM. The software will certainly run with this, but Microsoft *recommends* at least 32MB RAM. Personally, I would not roll out an Exchange Server in a production environment with less than 32MB RAM. For non-Intel based computers, increase these minimums by 16MB.

At the other end of the spectrum, things start to get fuzzy when you start trying to plan for over a thousand users per server, because the exact hardware requirements depend on what the users are doing. Plus, this level of server can really get into a lot of money, so it necessitates some planning. Furthermore, given the 16GB store limit in Exchange 4.0 and 5.0 at the time of this writing, two thousand users would have only 8MB each of single-instance storage space.

Assuming your users are light users, these estimates should produce reasonable response times and support your users well enough that you don't have to worry whether you've either underallocated or overallocated hardware for the server. If they're more intense, you'll need to bump up the hardware a bit more.

The recommendations in the # of Disk Volumes & Type column might not make sense right now, but you learn more details later in this chapter in the section, "Choosing the Right Disk Subsystem." In fact, after reading this chapter, you will have a better idea where all these recommendations come from.

With that said, take a few minutes and look more closely at selecting the right hardware. For Microsoft Exchange Server, the processor, RAM, and disk subsystems are the most crucial hardware components in the computer, so they should receive the most attention. The following three sections go into more detail about the issues surrounding the selection of each.

ABOUT EXCHANGE WITH LANS AND WANS

Here are a few thoughts on running Exchange on local area networks and wide area networks.

You've probably noticed that the discussion of LAN adapters has been conspicuously absent from this chapter. There are two main reasons. First, I don't want to get into a discussion about designing a network infrastructure—that could take up an entire book by itself. Second, a LAN is rarely the bottleneck in an Exchange Server configuration anyway. Exchange Server is very much a client-server system, and its communication mechanisms have been optimized so that they approach theoretical minimums.

With that in mind—and given that client-server applications are less network-intensive anyway—you will be best served by a high-performance network adapter, such as a PCI or EISA bus master card. These types of adapters rarely become a bottleneck, presuming you will be running at least a 10Mbits/s Ethernet network. If you are running Token Ring, 16Mbits/s is preferable. Again, choose a PCI or EISA bus master card. Of course, if you can run a 100Mbits/s network, that's great; the chances are even less that your LAN will be the source of a bottleneck.

Now, things change a bit when running Exchange Server on a WAN. There are a couple of considerations here. If you're using Remote Access Services (or Dialup Networking in Windows 95), you should naturally use the fastest modem available. In virtually all cases, that will be the main bottleneck in the system. The main exception is if you have many remote users pounding on an Exchange Server equipped with very modest hardware. Still, Exchange is surprisingly fast over a modem using RAS, especially at 33,600 bps under Windows NT or Windows 95.

The other WAN consideration is how your LANs are connected if you have a geographically dispersed organization. If you have a fast link such as a T1 or T3 between remote locations, that is a perfect way to split your servers into two Exchange Sites joined by the T1. Because the T1 is considered a fast link, you can use the Exchange Site Connector to connect your two sites and maximize the performance of interserver and intersite traffic. Again, this type of link could technically be a "bottleneck," but I use the term loosely here because performance between two geographically distant locations is likely not to be as good as on a LAN anyway—at least not yet.

Choosing the Right Processor

The first thing to realize about Microsoft Exchange Server is that among disk, RAM, and CPU, Exchange tends to consume CPU resources the most. That is to say, as load increases, Exchange Server will typically bottleneck on the CPU before the disk or the RAM.

NOTE

When I speak of "CPU" or "processor," I'm not limiting it to a single CPU. These days, it is not uncommon for a server's CPU subsystem to be comprised of one, two, or more physical

continues

continued

processor chips. I'm actually referring to *CPU resource*, regardless of whether there is one or more physical processors present. Of course, the more processors in the system, the more CPU resource Exchange Server has at its disposal because of Windows NT's capability to make use of multiple processors. And Exchange Server does a great job of taking advantage of this Windows NT benefit. As of this writing, Exchange generally does well up to four CPUs in a symmetric multiprocessor (SMP) system. Exactly how well it does depends on many things, such as the architecture of the computer and what types of tasks Exchange Server is performing. However, I would reserve three and four CPU configurations for very large enterprise Exchange servers with complex configurations supporting many hundreds of simultaneous users.

Effect of the Processor on System Performance

The effect the processor has on system performance is twofold.

First, it speeds up the response time for the user. Making the system run as fast as it possibly can speed up the execution of Exchange's many server processes. That makes things snappy for the user, which makes the users happy, which makes you happy—especially if your boss is one of the users.

Second, the processor provides user scalability. That is, it gives the server the capability of handling an increasing number of users without compromising response time. This is especially true of multiprocessor systems. If you consider the architecture of the Exchange server itself, you will find that it is multiprocess and multithreaded. The Microsoft engineers designed Exchange's server components with modern multiprocessor systems in mind, so the design lends itself well to that.

A benefit from this multiprocessor-aware design is that when the processor becomes the bottleneck, you can relieve it by adding another processor to the system. This is no small accomplishment. In fact, it is something the personal computer industry has been waiting a number of years for. And now we have Microsoft Exchange Server as a real-world application, which was created to leverage this technology.

Guidelines for Selecting the Processor

With these ideas in mind, the following are some general guidelines for selecting the right CPU for the job. They are especially applicable for sites supporting hundreds of users per server or more. Some guidelines might seem intuitively obvious. That's good; you're in the right mindset. However, it is worth listing them anyway. Maybe it will jog some other ideas in your mind:

- If you purchase a single CPU system (that is, one not capable of supporting multiple processors), get the absolute fastest CPU you can. This will extend the usability of the server as long as possible by preventing the CPU from becoming a bottleneck as user load increases. If you expect to support a smaller, static number of users, this approach will help provide the fastest response time possible.

■ If you purchase a multiprocessor-capable system, consider the guidelines given in Table 6.1. You might be able to get away with a single, fast CPU for now, especially because the server has the capability of supporting more than one CPU. This will help as user loads increase, because it will extend the usability of the server by adding additional processors.

■ Look for a large level 2 (L2) cache, whether you use multiple processors or not. A large L2 cache provides benefit in multithreaded applications such as Exchange Server. In single-processor systems, at least 512KB is preferred. However, larger L2 caches—2MB, for example—will produce even better performance with Exchange Server. You should look for large L2 caches when you plan to run multiple processors, because a large L2 cache helps relieve host bus congestion that can occur in multiprocessor systems.

■ Bear in mind that all multiprocessor computer systems are not created equal. Some multiprocessor implementations are rather limited for one reason or another. Maybe they have a shared processor cache architecture, or maybe they just suffer from a poor overall design. Although you might still get some extra kick out of multiple processors in these machines, you won't get as much performance as other better (and probably more expensive) implementations. The better implementations usually provide dedicated, large L2 processor caches and superior host bus and memory designs. The result is quite a boost when you add that second processor. Or third. Or fourth. If you're plunking down big bucks for those processor components, you definitely want your hardware design to be able to keep up.

■ Finally, remember that if the system is not CPU-bound, adding additional CPUs will probably not help things. A common misconception is that you can add more processors and continue to get significant benefits from doing so—not so if the disk, for example, is a bottleneck in the system. If anything, it will just exaggerate the problem where the bottleneck lies. It might help a little, but your efforts (and your money) will be better spent toward finding and removing the real bottleneck first.

You can also read more about CPU optimization, bottlenecks, and more in the Windows NT Resource Kit. It is an excellent guide for learning about general performance under Windows NT, and that information will be directly applicable to Exchange Server.

Choosing the Right Disk Subsystem

There is much to be said on the subject of the disk subsystem in Exchange. Basically, there are three main areas to understand:

■ The Exchange buffer cache
■ Configuring your disks for Exchange Server
■ The benefit of disk arrays

Regarding the third item, I will especially note the benefit hardware array controllers. One other subject pertaining to disk arrays that will be addressed is *fault tolerance*. Disk fault tolerance is a key component of making a reliable Exchange server. And that's what we all want, right?

Exchange Buffer Cache and Disk I/O

The first thing to know with Exchange is that the amount of RAM and the amount of physical disk I/O are related. That is, more RAM in the system helps to minimize disk I/O—to a point. This is because RAM is allocated to Exchange's database buffers, also called the *buffer cache*.

> **NOTE**
>
> The buffer cache is not to be confused with NT's System Cache. Although it serves a similar purpose, it is completely separate. In fact, Exchange doesn't even use the NT System Cache for disk I/O. Instead, it builds and maintains its own buffer cache, using the RAM you have installed in the system. The net effect is that the NT System Cache has very little to do aside from caching network activity, so it is allocated minimal RAM, usually around 5MB or less.

A large buffer cache will result in more cache hits, meaning fewer trips to the physical hard drives to read or write data. Naturally, there is a point of diminishing returns limit to this. You can't just keep adding RAM until there is no more disk I/O, but you can use this approach to help relieve a potential bottleneck on an otherwise moderately performing disk subsystem.

Figure 6.1 depicts a hypothetical example of this idea, just to give you a feel for what I am talking about. The actual cache hit rates your Exchange server experiences will vary based on several variables, including number of users, size of database, and type of usage profile.

Configuring Your Disks for Exchange Server

This section is especially important if you are using Exchange to host a large number of users—in the hundreds or more.

First, you must know that under the covers, Exchange is actually run by a full-fledged relational database engine complete with a database store and a transaction log. This engine is not unlike a commercial database system such as Oracle or MS SQL Server. Therefore, it is beneficial to apply similar performance techniques to the Exchange server computer.

The basic idea is to separate the drive where the transaction logs are kept from the drive where the database store is kept. Figure 6.2 shows how this should be done.

The reason for doing this is that the log is constantly written to and rarely read from, and those writes are all sequential writes. Exchange is just logging all the transactions as they happen—sequentially—in the log file. For optimal performance, the system should be configured so this sequential writing is not interrupted, and placing the logs on their own dedicated volume is the best way to accomplish this.

FIGURE 6.1.

As the Exchange server database buffer cache increases by adding more memory, the result is beneficial to a point of diminishing returns.

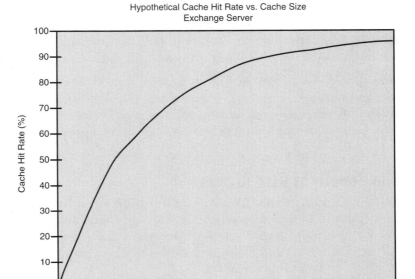

FIGURE 6.2.

Split the Exchange Server logs and store between two separate disks.

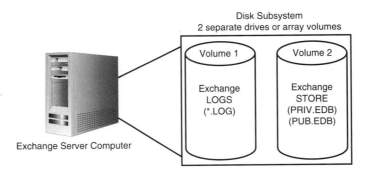

TIP

It is always best to configure your Exchange logs on a fault-tolerant volume. The database logs are your lifeline to re-creating the database store should something get hosed in the store. Therefore, it is extremely important to consider a fault-tolerant volume for the logs; it can make your life easier by minimizing the chance of losing valuable data on your Exchange Server machine. I recommend a mirrored (RAID-1) volume for the logs. It provides the best fault tolerance coupled with good sequential write performance. RAID volumes are covered in better detail in the next section, "The Benefit of Disk Arrays."

As for the store, in contrast to the logs, its disk I/O is very random. Data is constantly being read from or written to various places in the database, which makes the I/O patterns unpredictable. At any given time, you don't know whether Exchange will request a read or write or whether it will be at the beginning of the database, the end, or somewhere in the middle.

If you placed the store and the logs on the same physical drive, the nice sequential writing to the logs would be repeatedly interrupted by the random I/O to the store. In a large Exchange server with many users, this scenario will hinder performance and potentially cause the disk subsystem to become a bottleneck before it should. So, simply splitting the logs and store solves the problem.

The Benefit of Disk Arrays

You might already be familiar with the concept of disk arrays, commonly referred to as Redundant Array of Inexpensive Disks (RAID). If so, that's fine. You already know the performance benefits. You may also know that RAID sets can be implemented in software and hardware. Software RAID is a feature built into Windows NT Server. Hardware RAID controllers can be purchased from third-party vendors.

If you don't know much about RAID, here's an overview of basic concepts and how they apply to Exchange server performance. The fundamental idea is that more total disk I/O can occur if multiple disks are performing I/O simultaneously. This additive performance effect can really show dramatic improvements in overall disk I/O, but there are some things you need to know about.

First, understand a few common RAID configurations:

- *RAID level 0,* referred to as a *stripe set* in Windows NT Server. With RAID-0, data is distributed across multiple disk drives and accessed simultaneously from the drives in the set. In this way, the data can be accessed much faster than with a single drive. RAID-0 has no fault tolerance—that is, if one drive in the set fails, you lose all data in the stripe set.

  Of the three configurations listed here, RAID-0 provides the best overall read and write performance, especially for random I/O. There is no I/O overhead introduced due to fault tolerance, so the drives in the array are totally dedicated to I/O.

  You also will not lose any space in this configuration to fault tolerance. For example, if you have four 2GB drives in RAID-0, the volume size will be 8GB.

  You must have at least two drives to set up RAID-0.

- *RAID level 1,* referred to as a *mirror* in Windows NT Server. This is just what the name implies—one disk, which is a mirror of another disk. This arrangement is fault-tolerant because if one disk fails, the system can use the mirror. When the faulty disk is replaced, the drive is rebuilt from its mirror.

Planning for Optimal Server Performance

CHAPTER 6

125

6

PLANNING FOR
OPTIMAL SERVER
PERFORMANCE

With Windows NT Server, you configure a disk volume as a mirror of another disk volume. Typically, that means you will have only one physical disk mirrored with another physical disk for purposes of fault tolerance. There cannot be any striping in each mirror, because NT does not enable stripe sets to be mirrored.

However, with a good hardware array controller you can mirror stripe sets. For example, if you have six drives, the array controller will mirror the first three drives with the other three drives. Furthermore, depending upon the manufacturer's array controller, the three drives in each mirror will be configured as a RAID-0 set of three drives.

Performance of an NT Server mirror set should theoretically be the same as with a single disk, although there is some overhead for write I/O and for managing the mirror. With a hardware array controller, RAID-1 write performance will typically be better than RAID-5 on the same controller, but not as good as RAID-0. RAID-1 read performance will be equivalent to a RAID-0 array of half the number of disks. For example, if you have three drives mirrored with three drives, RAID-1 read performance would roughly equal read performance of a three-drive RAID-0 array.

You will sacrifice half your total disk space in this configuration for the benefit of fault tolerance and good performance. For example, if you have four 2GB drives in RAID-1, the volume size will be 4GB.

You must have at least two drives to set up RAID-1. Windows NT Server supports mirroring a maximum of two volumes. Hardware array controllers typically support many more.

■ *RAID level 5,* referred to as a *stripe set with parity* in Windows NT Server. This functions in much the same way as RAID-0, except that parity information has to be calculated and written to the stripe set along with the data. The parity information is distributed among the drives and interleaved with the data. This has some overhead in terms of volume size and I/O performance, but the benefit is fault tolerance. If any drive in the set fails, the data can be reconstructed from the remaining drives in the set after the faulty drive is replaced. If two drives fail at the same time, however, all data in the set is lost.

As a tradeoff, overall performance will not be as good as with a RAID-0 set. Specifically, during disk writes the parity information has to be calculated "on the fly," and the parity information has to be written in addition to the actual data. That means a potentially significant performance penalty in disk writes. Disk reads should perform somewhere close to RAID-0.

You will sacrifice a portion of your total disk space in this configuration for the benefit of fault tolerance. The volume size is an *n–1* calculation. For example, if you have four 2GB drives in RAID-5, the volume size will be 6GB, that is $(4-1) \times 2GB = 6GB$.

You must have at least three drives to set up RAID-5.

Using a Hardware Array Controller

If your Exchange server is going to be heavily used, you'll want to get all the performance possible out of the disk subsystem. Consider using a hardware drive array controller, which will provide all the same benefits from software striping as described earlier. However, there will be the additional performance advantage, because it is implemented in hardware. And there may well be additional configuration options, too. This way, you won't have to bother with configuring NT Server's software striping support—one less thing to worry about when you install NT. Simply configure the controller itself for the RAID configuration you want and let it do the work. To NT, a RAID set on an array controller will just look like any other single disk volume.

What features should you look for? An array controller should have its own on-board processor dedicated to handling the RAID sets. The server's processor and operating system should not incur the overhead of managing the RAID set, and they can be left alone to do their job of serving your Exchange users. Also, the controller should be available in an EISA or PCI version for optimal performance.

An array controller should enable mirroring of more than two drives. With this approach, you get the performance benefits of RAID-0 striping combined with the fault-tolerance benefits of mirroring. For example, you could install six drives in your system, three mirrored with three. Both sets of three would be striped for performance and mirrored for fault tolerance. Although it requires more drives to achieve the same disk space as RAID-0 or RAID-5, it is the best overall performing fault-tolerant scheme, especially for write-intensive applications.

An array controller should have some on-board cache. This fast memory cache is located right on the array controller itself, and accessing cached data from it will be extremely fast—much faster than using NT's System Cache. The controller uses its cache transparent to the operating system, and it is managed by the controller rather than by NT. All this adds up to less overhead on the operating system and the server resources.

Finally, although you're using an array controller, you should still set up two separate logical volumes so you can split the logs and the store, as described earlier in the section "Configuring Your Disks for Exchange Server." The effect of doing this is you will get the benefit of array fault tolerance and performance on both log I/O and database store I/O. Don't forget to set up your logs on a fault-tolerant volume such as RAID-1.

Choosing the Right Amount of RAM

Microsoft Exchange Server can use any amount of RAM you throw at it—anywhere from the recommended minimum of 32MB up to 512MB, 1GB, or whatever your server hardware can support. This is in part because of the design of Exchange itself, and in part a benefit of running under Windows NT Server.

RAM is used for several things in a Microsoft Exchange Server system, and it will be allocated in various ways by the operating system.

Planning for Optimal Server Performance

CHAPTER 6

127

6

PLANNING FOR
OPTIMAL SERVER
PERFORMANCE

> **NOTE**
>
> In this section, I use the terms "RAM" and "memory" interchangeably. They are intended to mean the same thing.

Windows NT Server Needs Memory

Windows NT needs a certain minimum amount of RAM for itself—usually in the neighborhood of 16MB for Windows NT Server. This 16MB is made up of the different Windows NT system-level processes such as CSRSS, LLSSRV, LOCATOR, LSASS, RPCSS, SERVICES, SMSS, SPOOLSS, SYSTEM, and WINLOGON.

Included in this 16MB minimum will be some memory allocated to the NT System Cache. Exchange Server doesn't actually use the NT System Cache for disk I/O because it has its own. And even though the network-caching aspect of the System Cache is useful, it is not nearly as beneficial to the system as the Exchange server database buffers. Naturally, you want more memory allocated to the buffers, not the System Cache.

You can minimize the NT System Cache size by selecting Maximize Throughput for Network Applications. With this setting, NT will page memory used by the System Cache before it will page memory used by applications such as Exchange Server.

> **TIP**
>
> Windows NT Server automatically chooses Maximize Throughput for File Sharing when it is first installed. However, the Exchange Server Setup program automatically changes it to Maximize Throughput for Network Applications for you.

You find the Maximize Throughput for Network Applications setting in the Control Panel, as illustrated in Figure 6.3.

From the Control Panel, start the Network applet. Click the Services tab. Then select the Network Service called Server, and click the Properties button. A dialog box appears that gives you some radio button options; click Maximize Throughput for Network Applications.

Selecting this option helps NT make decisions when choosing which process's memory to page to disk when NT needs memory. When you choose this setting, if NT needs to page, it will tend toward leaving system and application processes, such as those that comprise Exchange, in memory, and it will page the NT System Cache first. That's what you want because Exchange Server doesn't use the System Cache much.

Of course, if the system is really running low on memory, even the Exchange processes will have their memory paged. That is one of the first signs that you need to add more RAM to the server. It is also something that will cause server performance to degrade, because every time a required process needs memory that must be paged in from disk, there is a big performance hit. You can monitor the paging activity using NT Performance Monitor's Process and Memory objects, covered later in this chapter in the section called "Windows NT Performance Monitor Counters."

FIGURE 6.3.

You can adjust overall system performance optimization in the Control Panel's Network applet.

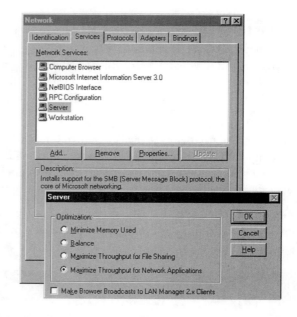

Exchange Server Needs Memory

There are four main processes that comprise Microsoft Exchange Server. Depending on the configuration of your Exchange Server software, there may be more, but these four are the basic components that all Exchange Servers will have. They run as Windows NT services, and the following list gives the service name followed by the description:

- MSExchangeIS—The Information Store
- MSExchangeMTA—The Message Transfer Agent
- MSExchangeDS—The Directory Service
- MSExchangeSA—The System Attendant

These services all require some amount of memory at startup time—usually 15–20MB total just to get going. Furthermore, as the system runs and is put under more stress, they will tend to use more memory depending on what is happening in the system. This is especially true of the Information Store. If you have adequate memory in your system, it is not uncommon to see the Store's working set jump to 50MB with a couple hundred users. Fortunately, you can monitor the memory usage for all these processes with the Process object in Windows NT

Planning for Optimal Server Performance

CHAPTER 6

129

6

PLANNING FOR
OPTIMAL SERVER
PERFORMANCE

Performance Monitor. That way, you can get an exact picture of how much memory each service has in its working set in your specific installation. For a listing of some useful Performance Monitor counters, including working set, see the section, later in this chapter, "Windows NT Objects and Counters in Performance Monitor."

There might also be services running for other Exchange Server options you have installed, such as Internet Mail Connector, cc:Mail Connector, Key Management Service, MS Mail Connector, or Directory Synchronization (DXA). These require memory too—at least 1-5MB each.

The Exchange Server Database Buffers Need Memory

The Exchange Server buffer cache is comprised of a number of 4KB database buffers. As you learned in the earlier section, "Exchange Buffer Cache and Disk I/O," physical disk I/O and the amount of memory in your machine are related. This is definitely a key aspect of performance, and it will figure into your decision of how much memory to put in the system.

Look at an example of how additional memory might be allocated to the various parts of the system, especially the database buffers. As you add memory to the computer, the following two tables illustrate how the Exchange Optimizer allocates memory.

For example, say you want to support 200 simultaneous users on your server. They will use private and public stores, and there are 800 total users in the organization. Based on recommendations from Microsoft Exchange Optimizer, Table 6.2 gives an idea of how memory might be allocated to the three main consumers of memory in Microsoft Exchange Server: the NT Server and Exchange system processes, the Exchange Server database buffers, and the Exchange Server directory buffers.

Table 6.2. An example of Exchange Server memory usage.

Memory	System Processes	Database Buffers	Directory Buffers
32MB	29MB	2.5MB	0.5MB
64MB	47MB	14MB	3MB
128MB	71MB	53MB	4MB
256MB	119MB	133MB	4MB

Although the exact mix changes somewhat depending on your Exchange Server configuration—the number of users supported, whether you use private and public stores, and so on—Exchange makes good use of the RAM you give it. For example, if you have 256MB of memory for your server, or more, Exchange will put it to work.

To illustrate this, take the example one step further. Say you want to support 600 simultaneous users per server, using public and private stores, and there are 5,000 total users in the organization. Table 6.3 shows how the memory allocation might change to accommodate these changes. Again, this is based on recommendations made by the Exchange Optimizer.

Table 6.3. An example of Exchange Server memory usage supporting more users.

Memory	System Processes	Database Buffers	Directory Buffers
32MB	31MB	0.8MB	0.2MB
64MB	56MB	7MB	1MB
128MB	81MB	39MB	8MB
256MB	128MB	106MB	22MB

See how memory is shifted to system processes when there is less system memory? And as you increase system memory, Exchange Server puts it to work in the buffers and in the system processes to prevent paging. Plus, with more total users in the organization, the directory buffers get additional memory. In contrast, shown earlier in Table 6.2, with fewer users the directory buffers peak at 4MB. Perhaps this simple example helps demonstrate the importance of memory to the Exchange buffer cache and to the NT system processes.

TIP

To properly optimize the usage of your server's memory, use the Microsoft Exchange Optimizer, called PerfWiz for short because that is the name of the executable: PERFWIZ.EXE. This invaluable utility examines your server's resources and makes decisions about how to allocate memory, disk, system threads, and so on. For more detail about PerfWiz, read the next major section in this chapter, "Microsoft Exchange Optimizer."

Anything Else You Run Needs Memory

The title of this section is an obvious statement, but you'd be surprised how many folks just skip right over this idea without thinking about it.

For example, if your Microsoft Exchange Server functions as a Domain Controller—either Backup or Primary—it will have to use a certain amount of memory to support that function. The NT Server Security Account Manager (SAM) and its database will take up some memory as well. Also, if you are logged in to the NT Console of your Exchange server, that will take some extra memory. Each console command prompt requires memory. Any console application you might run, such as NT Performance Monitor, also requires memory and imposes CPU overhead. Finally, other applications you've installed that run as NT services require memory, and possibly CPU resource.

Bottom line: You want to stay off the server console if possible, and be mindful of the services running on the system. I usually don't even log on; just let Windows NT Server boot and sit at the logon prompt. The Exchange processes will start automatically and without any intervention on your part. In fact, with servers handling hundreds of users, you should consider dedicating the machine explicitly to Exchange Server. For most functions that an Exchange server performs, there isn't really a need to logon anyway—just let it serve.

Microsoft Exchange Optimizer

One area into which Microsoft has put a lot of effort is optimizing Exchange server performance. Microsoft Exchange Server is an intricate piece of software with many features and capabilities. However, along with that goes an unavoidable degree of complexity when attempting to configure it for the best performance. Wouldn't it be great to have a tool that can examine your system's resources, know what parameters in Exchange need to be tweaked, and then set those parameters for you automatically?

Enter Exchange Optimizer, or PerfWiz for short. (The two terms can be used interchangeably, so I'll reference both.) The engineers at Microsoft have invested a significant amount of research and development into creating a tool that will do precisely that—and with a minimum of user intervention. In the spirit of wizards found in other Microsoft applications, PerfWiz asks a few key questions, runs some tests on your hardware, and then makes recommendations based on what you told it and what it found.

Typically, you run PerfWiz after the Exchange Server Setup program has finished; Setup prompts you to run it at the end of the installation process. You can also invoke PerfWiz on its own at any time. This is an especially good idea if you have just upgraded or changed any hardware in the system or added lots of new users. Any time you add (or remove) RAM, upgrade the processor, or reconfigure the disk drives, be sure to run PerfWiz.

This section takes a peek at PerfWiz to see what it looks like. Sometimes it's good to know what's coming with a utility like this, so you can be prepared ahead of time for the kinds of questions PerfWiz will ask. In the process, you can get a feel for PerfWiz, for the information you need to give it, and for the information it will give you.

> **TIP**
>
> Run PerfWiz with a -v parameter for verbose mode. You can run it from the command line, or you can simply modify the Target in the shortcut for Microsoft Exchange Performance Optimizer, as shown in Figure 6.4.
>
> The verbose mode provides more detailed information during the PerfWiz run about how buffers and threads will be allocated, disk drive performance, and so on.

FIGURE 6.4.

Here, Exchange Optimizer is configured to run in verbose mode.

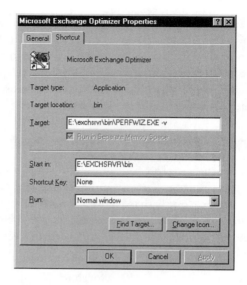

A Sample Session with Exchange Optimizer

I would like to take a minute and go through a PerfWiz session. This will give you a feel for what the utility looks like and for what will happen when you run it. You will also be better able to provide the information PerfWiz asks for.

Figure 6.5 shows the opening screen for PerfWiz.

FIGURE 6.5.

After this opening screen, Exchange Optimizer will shut down your Exchange Server services for optimization.

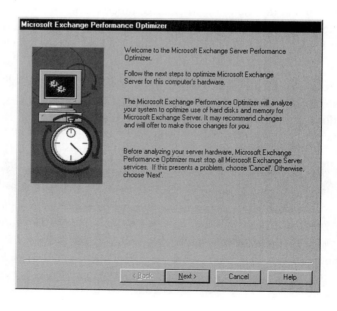

CAUTION

It is not obvious in Figure 6.5, but notice the last paragraph. When you click the Next button, PerfWiz will shut down all your Microsoft Exchange Server services. This has to happen to alter the Exchange Server system parameters—just be aware of it if your server happens to be up and running with people using it.

The next PerfWiz screen requests some information about how your server will be used.

Suppose that you have 800 total Exchange users in your organization who will use both e-mail and public folders. You plan to divide the users over four servers supporting 200 users each. Also, each of the four servers is dedicated to Exchange Server—that is, no other tasks such as file sharing, print sharing, or other applications are required of the server. Figure 6.6 depicts how the selections should look.

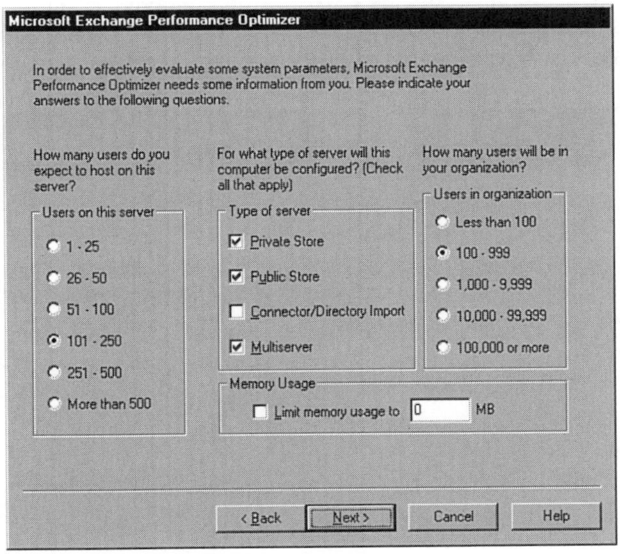

FIGURE 6.6.

Optimizer needs some information about how your server will be used.

The information that Optimizer needs is basically broken down into four categories:

- *Users on this server.* This is how you specify how many concurrent users you want this particular Exchange Server to support. As in the example, you want this server to support up to 200 users.

- *Type of server.* Here, you specify the way the server will be configured. As in the example, you need e-mail (Private Store) and public folder (Public Store) support. In addition, you know this server will be communicating with the other three servers in the organization, so leave the Multiserver option checked. This server will not be serving as a backbone connecting servers together, so the Connector/Directory Import option should not be checked. However, if you are configuring this server with a Site Connector, check this option.

■ *Users in organization.* This is how you specify the total number of users in your organization. In other words, this is all the users that will appear in your Exchange Directory. There are 800 total users in the example, so check the 100-999 option.

■ *Memory usage.* This determines how much of your server's RAM Exchange can use. It directly affects the amount of RAM PerfWiz will use for its calculations and parameter settings. This server is a dedicated Exchange server, and you don't want to limit the amount of system memory for PerWiz's analysis, so leave the Limit memory usage box unchecked. In other words, all the server's RAM is to be available for Exchange, so you want PerfWiz to perform its analysis based on using all available RAM.

The next screen, as shown in Figure 6.7, lists the disk drives in your system and whether they will be considered for storing Exchange Server files. You can exclude any drive automatically by double-clicking on the drive in the list. Also, if there is not enough space on a drive to make it usable, it will be excluded from the list automatically.

NOTE

The screen in Figure 6.7 appears only if you are running PerfWiz in verbose mode.

Figure 6.7.
Drives D: and E: are ready to be analyzed by Optimizer.

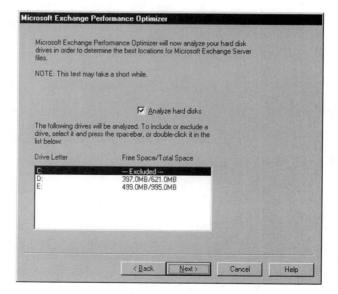

After you click Next, the drives are tested using a mix of sequential and random disk I/O. Then PerfWiz will show its performance results for the Random Access (RA) and Sequential (Seq) disk tests, as in Figure 6.8. The numbers are in milliseconds, so lower numbers indicate better drive performance for this test.

> **NOTE**
>
> The screen in Figure 6.8 appears only if you are running PerfWiz in verbose mode.

FIGURE 6.8.

Drives D: and E: have been analyzed by Optimizer.

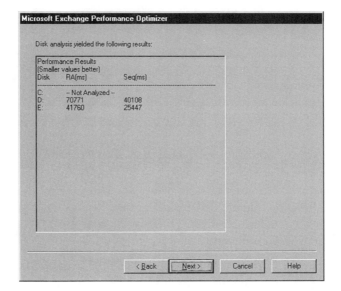

> **CAUTION**
>
> When you run PerfWiz in verbose mode, the disk test will report a table of numbers for Random I/O and Sequential I/O as in Figure 6.8. PerfWiz uses these to help determine which drives should contain the database store, the database logs, the directory, and so on. However, these numbers should not be construed as an indicator of absolute disk performance. Therefore, for example, don't panic if PerfWiz says your huge disk array is only one percent faster on Random I/O than your single, nonarray disk drive. The performance numbers produced by PerfWiz are not designed to be interpreted by themselves as a definitive performance measurement of your disk subsystem. They are there to help PerfWiz make decisions about the best place to locate your database files and log files.

On the next screen, as shown in Figure 6.9, Optimizer makes recommendations about which drives should contain which files.

FIGURE 6.9.

Optimizer makes its recommendations about where to place Exchange Server files.

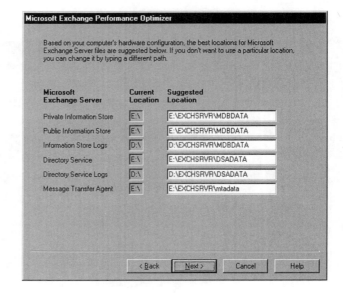

In Figure 6.9, Microsoft Exchange Server was originally installed on drive E:, as shown in the Current Location column. PerfWiz is suggesting to move the Store and Directory logs to drive D: and leave the database Store, Directory Service, and MTA on drive E:, as shown in the Suggested Location column.

PerfWiz makes these determinations based on three main things. First and foremost, PerfWiz tries to split the logs and the store onto separate drives if at all possible. Second, PerfWiz tends to place the database store on the drive with the best random I/O (RA) score. Third, PerfWiz tries to place the logs on the drive with the best Sequential I/O (Seq) score. In this case, the first and second rules held, but the third one was overridden by the more important option of splitting the logs and store.

There are other variables that factor in the decision, such as drive size and available space, but the three I listed are the most important. Bear these in mind when you are designing a server for Exchange.

> **TIP**
>
> An array of disk drives, such as one configured with a hardware disk controller, will provide much better *random* I/O performance than a single drive. On the other hand, an

array will not necessarily provide better *sequential* I/O than a single drive. This makes a good case for a volume consisting of one drive mirrored with an identical drive for the logs and another volume consisting of a RAID array for the store.

You're almost finished with PerfWiz. On the screen that follows (not shown here) you can allow the system to automatically move the files for you in accordance with the recommendations in Figure 6.9. This is usually a good idea so that all files are sure to be located properly.

The final series of screens deals with the meat of PerfWiz—the Microsoft Exchange Server parameters. There are six screens of system parameters, shown in Figures 6.10 through 6.15.

NOTE

The screens in Figures 6.10 through 6.15 appear only if you are running PerfWiz in verbose mode.

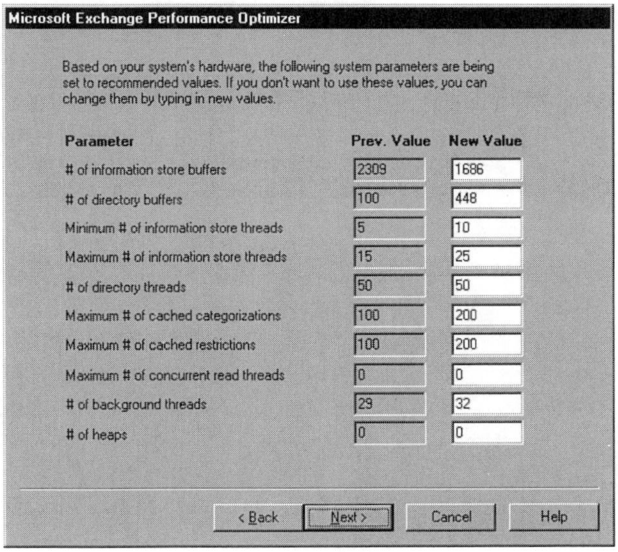

FIGURE 6.10.
The first screen of Exchange Server system parameters.

Microsoft Exchange Performance Optimizer

Based on your system's hardware, the following system parameters are being set to recommended values. If you don't want to use these values, you can change them by typing in new values.

Parameter	Prev. Value	New Value
# of information store buffers	2309	1686
# of directory buffers	100	448
Minimum # of information store threads	5	10
Maximum # of information store threads	15	25
# of directory threads	50	50
Maximum # of cached categorizations	100	200
Maximum # of cached restrictions	100	200
Maximum # of concurrent read threads	0	0
# of background threads	29	32
# of heaps	0	0

< Back   Next >   Cancel   Help

The Exchange Server system parameters shown in Figure 6.14 and the PerfWiz parameters shown in Figure 6.15 are new to version 5.0.

New to Version 5.0

FIGURE 6.11.

*The second screen of
Exchange Server system
parameters.*

FIGURE 6.11.

*The second screen of
Exchange Server system
parameters.*

Microsoft Exchange Performance Optimizer

Based on your system's hardware, the following system parameters are being
set to recommended values. If you don't want to use these values, you can
change them by typing in new values.

Parameter	Prev. Value	New Value
# of private information store send threads	2	2
# of private information store delivery threads	2	2
# of public information store send threads	2	2
# of public information store delivery threads	2	2
# of information store gateway in threads	2	2
# of information store gateway out threads	2	2

< Back   Next >   Cancel   Help

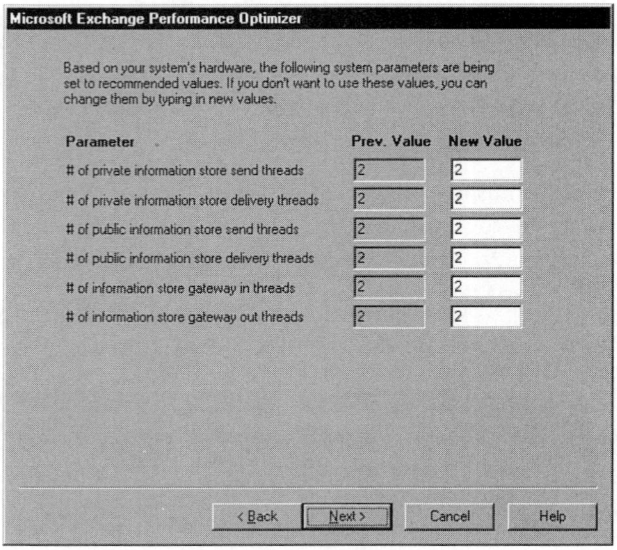

FIGURE 6.12.

*The third screen of
Exchange Server system
parameters.*

Microsoft Exchange Performance Optimizer

Based on your system's hardware, the following system parameters are being
set to recommended values. If you don't want to use these values, you can
change them by typing in new values.

Parameter	Prev. Value	New Value
# of information store users	100	250
# of concurrent connections to LAN-MTAs	40	40
# of concurrent connections to RAS LAN-MTAs	10	10
# of LAN-MTAs	20	20
# of X.400 gateways	20	20
# of XAPI MA threads	2	2
# of XAPI MA queue threads	2	2
# of XAPI MT threads	2	2
# of XAPI MT queue threads	2	2
ds_read cache latency (secs)	60	60

< Back   Next >   Cancel   Help

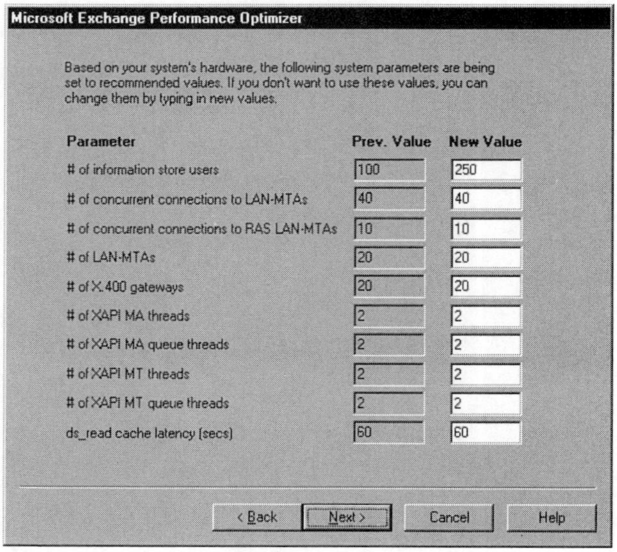

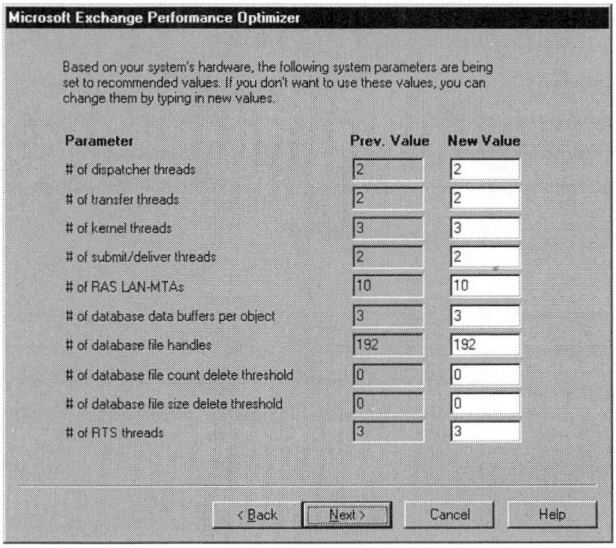

FIGURE 6.13.

The fourth screen of Exchange Server system parameters.

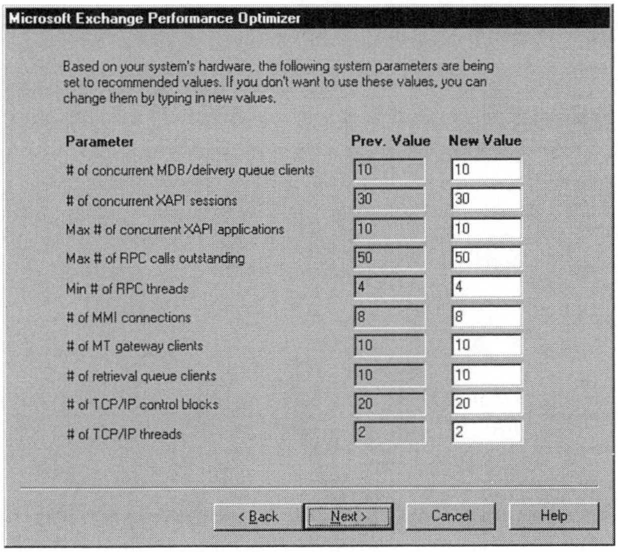

FIGURE 6.14.

The fifth screen of Exchange Server system parameters.

FIGURE 6.15.

The final screen of Exchange Server system parameters.

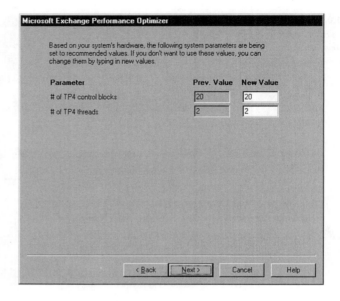

As you can see, there are several parameters. Some of them may be altered a lot—such as `# information store buffers` on the first screen—some of them not at all. You can change PerfWiz's suggestions, but I do not recommend it. Microsoft has spent a lot of time tweaking and testing these parameters to get the right mix. And you can really mess up your server performance if you aren't careful. That's why PerfWiz exists.

I hadn't planned to explain the purpose of every parameter shown in Figures 6.10 through 6.15, but I do want to point out two important ones: `# of information store buffers` and `# of directory buffers`. These are arguably two of the most important Exchange parameters. Having them sized properly for the amount of RAM in the server will significantly help optimize performance. Conversely, size them improperly, and your performance will immediately go down the tubes. Too large, and the server will start paging excessively and thrash itself to death. Too small, and Store I/O will be choked off and your system will become disk-I/O constrained. Again, this same idea applies to all the other parameters, too. So if you decide to play around, be careful!

Both the buffer parameters represent a quantity of 4KB buffers. In the case of the `# of information store buffers` parameter, these buffers are used to hold information being read from or written to the private or public database. It actually performs the function of a disk cache that is dedicated to the database. So here the Information Store—that is, the private and public databases—will have 1,686 buffers allocated for it. That figures to 6,744KB of buffers, or just under 7MB of system RAM.

The same concept applies to the `# of directory buffers` parameter.

Planning for Optimal Server Performance

CHAPTER 6

141

6

PLANNING FOR
OPTIMAL SERVER
PERFORMANCE

Now you're finished, ready for PerfWiz to save the changes to the Registry and restart Exchange. Figure 6.16 shows the final screen of PerfWiz.

FIGURE 6.16.

*PerfWiz is finished and
ready to restart the
Exchange services.*

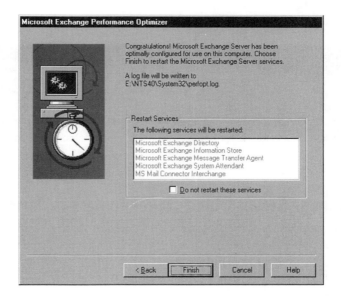

At this point, if PerfWiz stopped your Exchange services at the beginning, it will restart them for you. If you ran PerfWiz with the Exchange services already stopped, it will not restart them for you.

One final note: The activity during the PerfWiz session is logged in a file called PERFOPT.LOG, stored in your SYSTEM32 directory. This is a cumulative log, so every PerfWiz run is documented automatically.

Windows NT Performance Monitor Counters

If you have been around Windows NT for any length of time, you have probably played around with—or actually used—Windows NT Performance Monitor (PerfMon). There are many performance counters contained in PerfMon, and these counters can provide you detailed information on how various systems within Windows NT are performing.

To help you wade through the myriad of counters, this section suggests a few good ones that will get you started. These counters should prove useful when you are monitoring the usage and performance of Microsoft Exchange Server. The exact counters you use will vary some with your exact implementation; for example, you might not use NetBEUI, so NetBEUI-specific counters won't be useful to you. Regardless, the general principle is the same—and you can use these counters to begin some exploration on your own.

In this section you find two groups of counters: the Exchange-specific counters, which are installed when Exchange Server is installed, and the generic counters, which are installed as a part of Windows NT Server.

Although these are only a few of the many counters available, this list should get you started exploring the PerfMon counters for yourself. There is a wealth of information to be gathered.

TIP

Don't forget to run `diskperf -y` from a command prompt to activate the PerfMon disk counters before trying to use the Logical Disk (and Physical Disk) object. You can also activate the disk counters via the Devices applet in the Control Panel. Find Diskperf in the list and set its Startup Type to BOOT. With either method, you must restart your machine for the change to take effect.

Exchange Server Objects and Counters in Performance Monitor

Some applications have their own performance objects—containers for the performance counters. These make life much easier when you are tracking performance or system behavior, because they provide specific performance information on components within Windows NT. Table 6.4 lists the Exchange-specific objects that are automatically installed in Performance Monitor during setup.

Table 6.4. Exchange objects installed in Performance Monitor.

Object Name	Description
MSExchange Internet Protocols	Contains counters pertaining to supported Internet protocols, such as LDAP, NNTP, and POP3
MSExchangeCCMC	Contains counters pertaining to the cc:Mail Connector
MSExchangeDB	Contains counters pertaining to the Exchange Server database engine (DB)
MSExchangeDS	Contains counters pertaining to the Exchange Directory Service (DS)

Object Name	Description
MSExchangeIS	Contains general counters for the Exchange Server Information Store (IS)
MSExchangeISPrivate	Contains counters pertaining to the Exchange Private Information Store
MSExchangeISPublic	Contains counters pertaining to the Exchange Public Information Store
MSExchangeMSMI	Contains counters pertaining to the MS Mail Connector Interchange
MSExchangeMTA	Contains counters pertaining to the Exchange Mail Transfer Agent (MTA)
MSExchangeMTA Connections	Contains counters pertaining to connections to the MTA
MSExchangePCMTA	Contains counters pertaining to the MS Mail Connector (PC) MTA
MSExchangeWEB	Contains counters pertaining to the Exchange Web Connector

There are dozens of Exchange Server counters included in these objects. Table 6.5 contains some useful counters to get you going.

Table 6.5. Useful Exchange Server counters.

Object Name	Counter	Description
MSExchangeDB	% Buffer Available	(Instance=Information Store) The percentage of the database buffer cache that is available for use. This counter and the following one help monitor the effectiveness of your database buffer cache.
MSExchangeDB	% Buffer Cache Hit	(Instance=Information Store) The percentage of requests for store data that were satisfied from the database buffer cache.
MSExchangeIS	User Count	The number of users connected to the store.

continues

Table 6.5. continued

Object Name	Counter	Description
MSExchangeISPrivate	Messages Submitted/min	The rate messages are being submitted by clients. A rate consistently higher than `Messages Delivered/min` could indicate the server can't keep up with delivery load.
MSExchangeISPrivate	Messages Delivered/min	The rate messages are delivered to all recipients. A rate consistently lower than `Messages Submitted/min` could indicate the server can't keep up with delivery load.
MSExchangeISPrivate	Send Queue Size	The number of messages in the send queue. Another counter that can indicate when the server is overloaded.
MSExchangeISPublic	(same counters as MSExchangeISPrivate)	

Windows NT Objects and Counters in Performance Monitor

Following are some of what I call generic counters that are installed as a part of Windows NT. Table 6.6 contains a list of some objects and counters that I have found useful when keeping an eye on Windows NT.

Table 6.6. Generic objects performance monitor.

Object Name	Description
Cache	Contains counters pertaining to the NT System Cache
Logical Disk	Contains counters pertaining to the logical disk drives in the system (you must enable these counters with `diskperf -y` and reboot)
Memory	Contains counters pertaining to memory usage in the operating system
Paging File	Contains counters pertaining to the status of the NT page file
Process	Contains counters pertaining to every process running under NT
Processor	Contains counters pertaining to the system processor(s)
Server	Contains general counters pertaining to the server service of the system
System	Contains general counters pertaining to the operating system itself

Again, there are dozens of counters included in these objects. Table 6.7 contains some useful counters to get you going.

Table 6.7. Useful generic counters.

Object Name	Counter	Description
Cache	Data Map Hits %	The percentage of successful references to the in-memory system data cache.
Logical Disk	% Disk Time	The percentage of time the disk is busy servicing I/O requests.
Logical Disk	Avg. Disk sec/Transfer	The average amount of seconds it takes the disk to satisfy a disk transfer (read or write).
Logical Disk	Disk Bytes/sec	The rate at which data is transferred to or from the disk during I/O operations.
Memory	Available Bytes	The amount of virtual memory in the system available for use.
Memory	Cache Bytes	Size of the NT System Cache. Note that the system cache is for both disk and LAN.
Memory	Pages/sec	Indicates overall paging activity—the rate at which memory pages are written to or read from the disk.
Paging File	% Usage	Shows what percentage of the page file is in use. Could indicate whether you need to increase your page file size.
Processor	% Processor Time	Amount of time the processor is busy doing work. This is User and Privileged time combined.
Process	Working Set	Shows the number of bytes in the working set of the selected process (Instance). A working set of memory is memory that was recently used by threads in the process—that is, the set of memory with which the process is currently working.
Process	Page Faults/sec	Shows the rate of page faults by all threads executing in the selected process. Can indicate there is memory pressure in the system. If Memory: Pages/sec is also getting activity, there could be a memory shortage in the server.

continues

Table 6.7. continued

Object Name	Counter	Description
Server	Bytes Total/sec	The rate at which the server is sending data to and receiving data from the network.
System	Processor Queue Length	The number of threads waiting in the processor queue. Values consistently above 2 can indicate processor congestion. (You must also monitor at least one thread from the Thread object for this counter to be nonzero.)

Simulating a User Load with LoadSim

This entire chapter focuses on subjects surrounding server requirements for running Exchange and optimal server performance. In this section, I want to introduce you to Microsoft Exchange Server Load Simulator (LoadSim), a tool that can assist in analyzing and optimizing server performance.

One way to effectively go about addressing the issues of server performance is to have a method for placing a predictable, reliable, repeatable load on an Exchange server so its performance can be measured. LoadSim is a tool that provides a method to do precisely that.

A lot of attention has been paid to the development of LoadSim, and it has proven itself a valuable tool both in testing Exchange as a product and in validating server configurations. For example, a single Pentium-based Windows NT machine could simulate 100 users, all simultaneously performing e-mail, public folder, and Schedule+ tasks against the same Exchange server. LoadSim logs data about the activities of its simulated clients that you can use to analyze the performance of a server.

Figure 6.17 shows an example of a LoadSim screen during a test run. In this case, LoadSim is simulating 100 simultaneous Exchange users with a single Windows NT Workstation computer.

Chapter 29, "Understanding and Using LoadSim," covers the implementation and use of this utility in detail. There is also a white paper available from Microsoft on the subject. If you plan to use LoadSim, I highly recommend reading both Chapter 29 and the Microsoft document. When you know how to use it, LoadSim is a powerful tool to have at your disposal.

Planning for Optimal Server Performance

CHAPTER 6

147

6

PLANNING FOR
OPTIMAL SERVER
PERFORMANCE

FIGURE 6.17.

*LoadSim is simulating
100 Exchange users
with a single NT
Workstation computer.*

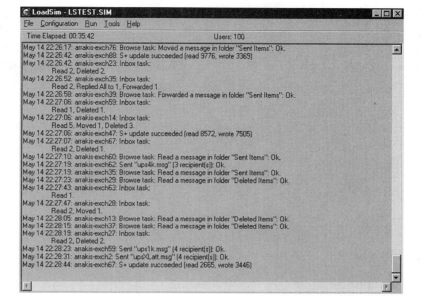

Summary

Performance and system requirements are always interesting subjects to talk about. It's even fun to debate it with colleagues from time to time. And perhaps there are some items in this chapter that you would want to debate with me. No problem. At least I got you thinking about it, and that's part of the goal.

Either way, the topics in this chapter are crucial to grasp if you have responsibility for deploying Exchange servers, especially if each server is to support a few hundred users or more. Topics such as server capacity, the proper CPU types, the benefits of multiple CPUs, disk subsystem configuration, fault tolerance, the proper amount of RAM, interpretation of PerfMon counters, and application of LoadSim are all important considerations during the process of planning your server rollout.

Most of the discussion assumes each Exchange server must support a number of users in the hundreds. In fact, many of the performance and optimization techniques in this chapter don't really matter that much if you have a very small—say, 25 users or less—installation. However, some ideas, such as disk fault tolerance and CPU selection, are relevant no matter what size installation you have.

By now, you should understand general implications of performance on your Exchange server's hardware requirements. Also, you should have some general ideas about how to set up Exchange for good performance *before* the installation process begins. Finally, you should have a better idea of how to apply Performance Monitor and LoadSim to the task of understanding Exchange performance.

The next chapter examines some other aspects of planning your installation. And when you are considering things such as multiple servers and single- and multiple-site installations, the concepts presented in this chapter will prove useful.

CHAPTER 7

Considerations for a Successful Rollout

by Ken Ewert

IN THIS CHAPTER

Now that you've decided to install Microsoft Exchange Server, the fun starts; you need to develop an implementation plan. You shouldn't undertake any project without developing an implementation plan, and Exchange is no exception.

> **NOTE**
>
> To help you develop this plan, Microsoft has released a set of templates outlining the basic steps required to implement Exchange Server. You can find this template on the Microsoft Back Office Deployment Templates CD, Part #098-63461, available from Microsoft Inside Sales.

An automated design tool is also available on the Microsoft Exchange Server Technical Resource CD: the Microsoft Exchange Server Modeling Tool. This tool will help you define the Exchange organization structure and the components required to support it.

When you develop a deployment plan, you must consider in detail the environment that will be supported. Exchange is designed to operate in most existing electronic mail environments, but you must be careful when you design the support infrastructure.

Consider both the client and the server and determine where a specific service will be supported and how it will be supported. If a particular connector is not available from Microsoft, you need to identify sources of connectors and service providers. These third-party products must be not only identified, but tested for functionality.

> **TIP**
>
> Microsoft maintains a database of third-party connectors and service providers at its Web site:
>
> `http://www.microsoft.com/Exchange/EXISV`

You should consider the following in planning the rollout:

- Physical considerations
- Naming conventions
- Exchange Sites
- Linking Sites
- User Considerations

Physical Considerations

Your Exchange system is going to be made up of physical servers put into logical groupings connected by networks with various characteristics. To ensure a successful rollout, you need to have a fundamental understanding of the requirements of the network and servers you will be using.

Windows NT Domains

Windows NT Domains are logical groupings of one or more Windows NT Server computers structured to be managed and used as a single unit. This unit provides the foundation for the Windows NT Server directory services. A single logon is supported for the domain; users need to log on only once to the domain, not separately to each server within the Domain. The Exchange server takes advantage of this structure and, by default, uses the logon security information provided by the NT Domain to validate users. This is the reason an NT Domain is required for Exchange Server, regardless of the underlying network operating system (NOS).

NOTE

There is no requirement for the Exchange Server to run on the Domain controller, but there is a requirement that it be installed only on a Windows NT Server.

There are four NT Domain models; each supports different numbers of users. Each can support a Microsoft Exchange server organization based on the model:

- *Single domain model.* A single PDC, a BDC, and member servers support the entire enterprise. This model provides easy administration and no trust relationships.
- *Single domains with trusts (also known as Complete Trust Model).* A two-way trust exists with every other domain in the enterprise. The total number of trust relationships that must be set up is equal to $N*(N1)$, where N is the number of domains. This model makes it possible for an administrator in any domain to manage users and resources in any other domain. This domain model is difficult to support and best suited for small businesses.
- *Single master domain.* A master domain is trusted by one or more other domains; however, these are one-way trust relationships. The master domain administrators can administer the entire enterprise, but local administrators are allowed to manage the users and resources only of their own domain.
- *Multiple master domains.* This is a hybrid of the second and third models. The master domains are linked in two-way trusts; each trusts an upstream and a downstream domain, forming a loop.

> **TIP**
>
> In certain environments, such as with roving users, it may be appropriate to request login credential information to be used specifically in accessing an Exchange mailbox. Such cases include when the Windows NT account that is currently logged into the computer does not have access to a specific Exchange mailbox. In these cases, an option is available from the Exchange client to disable network security via the Tools | Services | Exchange Server | Advanced menu item.

The first phase of the Microsoft Exchange Server design is reviewing the NT Domain architecture. If one does not exist, all efforts should be focused on establishing one before you proceed. If one exists, review the architecture to be sure that it can support the Exchange server organization structure and that the architecture will meet the organizational needs.

When installing Exchange in a Novell NetWare environment, you must install an NT Domain. The sole purpose of this domain is to provide Exchange server logon and security validation. To the individual Exchange user, this functions just as the current Microsoft Mail product does today. A separate logon and password are required before a connection to the Exchange server can take place, but in this case the logon is an NT logon and the password is the password for that NT user account.

> **NOTE**
>
> The Exchange server can run either IPX/SPX or TCP/IP network protocols, making it simple to roll out in Novell-centric environments.

Primary Domain Controller (PDC)

Every NT Domain has a primary Domain controller (PDC). A given Windows NT server can assume one of three roles in the domain; Domain controller, backup Domain controller, or member server. In this architecture, there is a single primary Domain controller (PDC), which maintains the master copy of the security account manager (SAM) database; only one PDC is allowed per domain.

Depending on the size of the domain, the PDC can reside on the same machine as the Exchange server. This will reduce the physical number of servers required in the domain. When working in a Novell environment, this could be very useful.

Be sure to size the server to meet the needs of the domain. When sizing a PDC, consider the following information:

- The number of NT users accounts to be supported by the Domain controller.
- Storage capacity of the server. The SAM stores three record types: user, machine, and group accounts. Storage must be allocated for each user (1KB) and Machine (.5KB) account created. In addition, although there will be relatively few group accounts (4KB), they have to be considered as well.

It is recommended that the SAM not grow to be more than 40MB in size, because these records must be loaded into RAM on the PDC or BDC machines:

- Processor speed of the Server
- Server memory
- Backup Domain Controller (BDC)

Windows NT Domains can also have a backup to the PDC—the Backup Domain Controller (BDC). It also maintains a copy of the master SAM, which allows it to help authenticate users (that is, load sharing with the PDC) and can be promoted to a PDC role in case of PDC failure. There can be multiple BDCs in a given Windows NT Domain; however, none are required.

The BDC is the primary authentication tool. In all cases, when a BDC is available it will validate the users. Although none is required, it is very highly recommended; in the case of a PDC failure, no users can be authenticated by the domain.

The number of user accounts is a good guide for deciding how many BDCs to implement. The number of user accounts in the domain dictates the number of BDCs to use. A good estimate is approximately one BDC for every 2,000 users. You also may want to use physical location in your calculation of how many BDCs and where to implement them, because you will want to make sure that in large LANs, MANs, and WANs, a BDC is close to large groups of users.

A final class of server exists in Windows NT Domains: the Domain server (or resource server). This functions as a file and print, application, or communications server and does not explicitly authenticate users for access to the Windows NT Domain. The Exchange server must run on the Windows NT server platform and can function in any of these roles. In large installations, it is suggested that the Exchange server be installed as a stand-alone server (Domain server) to minimize the amount of login services running. If this is not feasible, it can be installed on either a PDC or BDC.

Network Considerations

In order for the Microsoft Exchange Server to function, it must have at least one physical connection to the network. This statement might prove to be misleading, but without a network connection there can be no client access (except for a client locally installed on the server). The Exchange Server can have multiple network adapter cards, 32-bit adapter cards, and/or PCI adapter cards. You can maximize network throughput by using multiple, high-speed network cards. SCSI disk subsystems and multiple adapters should be a major consideration for reducing I/O bottlenecks and optimizing overall server performance.

E-mail could be new to the existing network structure. In many cases it is the first application that must be shared among multiple locations and systems. A typical network installation has grown over months and sometimes years, often without much planning; when installing the Exchange Server, you need to plan the connectivity between these systems. The Exchange Server design requires careful planning to determine how best to incorporate these locations. Not all solutions will work; to support this effort and better understand the network requirements, a number of key factors must be reviewed:

- Transmission speed requirements
- Distance of the link
- Amount of internetwork traffic
- Network traffic patterns
- Budget

Newer, faster, and more affordable methods for linking LANs, WANs, and MANs are being providing by carriers. Dedicated links are replacing dial-up connections and other types of services; however, there are still hurdles in making these connections. LANs are optimized for data transmission; WANs are not. Data throughput drops when you transmit LAN data over a WAN, because WANs do not typically have the same bandwidth.

Network Bandwidth

Network bandwidth is the amount of data per second that can be transmitted over a communication link. Carefully examine the underlying physical network to ensure that the existing network connections are adequate for deployment of the solution. It is crucial to take into account not only the size of your links but the proposed utilization as well. Too often, all efforts are geared toward sizing for the current opportunity; this is a serious mistake. The focus should instead be placed on the plans for the links over a period of time for all applications.

The Exchange Server can represent a small portion of the utilization of bandwidth. Other applications will also be using these links. Interaction between these applications and the Exchange Server should be considered, as well as the impact of the added Exchange traffic on the links.

Performance   Overall bandwidth and response times will be affected by the selected site connector. Consider the impact on the existing applications. There may be very large, fast connections between the sites, but they could already be inundated with other network traffic, which impedes overall performance of the network link. It might be necessary to increase bandwidth in areas of heavy network traffic, such as locations where large amounts of graphic, audio, and video data are being transmitted. Exchange performance can be simulated using the LoadSim utility that ships with the server. Chapter 29, "Understanding and Using LoadSim," provides a detailed discussion.

When you are looking at the network links, you also should consider traffic bursts. *Traffic bursts* occur when a majority of the bandwidth is utilized for short periods of time. Characteristic of this traffic is the appearance of low overall utilization, but with bursts of traffic during certain periods, which severely impact overall link and server performance. When working with these types of connections, there are two possible solutions: increasing the bandwidth or selecting a connector that will support more granular control of the connections. This will permit scheduling of connections and better utilization of the bandwidth.

Define site boundaries so that sites are joined to each other by data connections that "stretch" and "shrink" on demand. Three types of data connections provide this flexibility:

- Packet-switch services such as the Internet
- Circuit-switched services
- Leased lines

Transport Protocols

The Exchange Server can use a number of transport protocols to connect to other Exchange Servers. Native to the implementation are TCP/IP, IPX/SPX, and NetBEUI; however, Exchange will support other transports for wide-area connectivity. Each of these transport protocols installs its own MTA for messaging. An overview of the supported Transports follows:

- *X.25.* This protocol requires the use of the Eicon Technologies port adapter. Note that Exchange 5.0 supports only the Eicon adapter, because it is the only one on the Hardware Compatibility List.
- *Dynamic RAS.* Using this transport, a system will support ISDN, Asynchronous communications, and X.25 protocols.
- *TCP/IP.* This standard protocol also serves as a transport for some services, such as X.400.
- *OSI.* This communications transport requires TP4 networking support.

Server Hardware Design

Microsoft provides some guidelines for deciding the actual hardware requirements for the server. Consider these when the Exchange server is being used only for e-mail, and no other functions are being supported. As additional functions are supported on the system, memory requirements will increase. You should consider the following:

- The number of users to be supported on the server
- The types of Information Stores to be housed on the server (private, public, or both) and the amount of required disk space each will need
- The number of connectors (if any) to be supported on the server
- The amount of disk and memory available to use (Exchange may not be the only application running on the Windows NT Server)

When you are installing the Exchange server, make every attempt to use more than a single disk. Exchange will take advantage of a multiple disk configuration, spreading the system files across the disks and optimizing reads and writes.

The following chart, from the Exchange Server Concepts and Planning Guide, provides some server configuration guidelines. These figures should be used only as guidelines because actual implementations of the Exchange organization are based upon the actual implementation:

Server Type	Processors	RAM	Disk	Users
Low-end	1 Pentium	32MB	2GB	100–300+
Middle	1 Pentium	64MB	2–5GB	250–600+
High-end	3 Pentium	256MB, 2–8GB	500–1,000+	

Plan your systems for growth. Never size the server for today's needs; provide hardware that will permit growth in memory and disk, with a minimum of disruption to the organization. Also consider processors that can be upgraded. If this is not feasible, consider installing multiple servers to support projected growth. When you are sizing the servers, consider the following:

- *The Disk I/O System.* Allocate enough disk storage for growth. Use high-speed caching SCSI controllers for better performance

- *Memory.* Exchange will take as much memory as it needs to run. Run the Performance Optimizer to establish the required memory cache for the server. Adjust the memory to restrict Exchange from using all available memory.

Using Multiprocessor Machines

- *Using separate disks for the transaction logs.* Use the FAT system to store the transaction logs. FAT drives are better optimized for sequential data writing, which is precisely the type of I/O used for Exchange transaction logs. This is also the recommendation in all white papers on Exchange performance produced by Microsoft.

- *Disk usage for the Information Store, size of the mailboxes, messages, public folders, and aging limits.* Review these over a period of time and adjust as appropriate.

Naming Conventions

Critical to the deployment of Exchange is the establishment of a naming convention. Conventions need to be established for the following Exchange objects:

- Organization name
- Sites
- Servers
- Mailboxes
- E-mail aliases

You must carefully assign the names, because they collectively will be used to identify the Exchange server and recipients. As stated throughout this chapter, Exchange assigns both a display name and a directory name to each object in the Information Store. The display name can be easily changed, but the underlying directory is never changed. This is especially true of the first three of these objects; once named, they can not be changed without reinstalling the server.

Organization Name

Exchange uses the organization name at the top of the hierarchy to define the overall name for all sites and servers under its control. The Exchange organization tree starts at this point. The name for the organization is usually the company installing Exchange Server (for example, SAMS or NCR). The organization name does not have to be a single word (you can use spaces); however, Exchange uses the organization directory name to generate default e-mail addresses, so it must be unique. This is an X.500-like directory structure; the entries created are populating a database.

> **NOTE**
>
> All Exchange Sites that you intend to connect together with any of the available site connectors must have a common organization name.

Site Names

Site names must also be unique. A good choice for the site name is the site's geographic or physical location (for example, Philadelphia or Denver). If at all possible, the site name should be meaningful to the casual viewer. This will help not only the administrator but also the end user in identifying people and locations.

Server Names

The server name is, by default, the Windows NT computer name. Plan these names carefully; once you establish them, they cannot be changed unless you reinstall the Exchange server.

The naming of servers has always been subjective; corporate policies can dictate machine names. When you are connecting to the Internet, though, be careful when you are naming a machine; assume it will be visible to the outside world. Naming the machine "accounting," for example, is asking for trouble. Also, never use a name that defines the machine's role or location (for example, garage, sauna, or finance)—you never know when you might have to move it.

> **NOTE**
>
> RFC 1178, "Choosing a Name for your Computer," provides some guidelines for naming a computer.

Mailbox (Recipient Names)

A mailbox is assigned to every object in the Exchange server. Default addresses are created based on the alias names created when the NT account is added in the case of a user, or using the scheme defined in the autonaming tab of the Exchange Administrator Tools | Options dialog box.

> **TIP**
>
> When you are adding a large number of user accounts, use the header utility provided in the Exchange Technical Resource Kit to create the header file for a .csv (comma-delimited) file. When this is done, import the headers into Excel and add the appropriate fields. You can then import this .csv file with the Exchange Administration program to import the users and create mailboxes.

Often, an organization has several users who are not Exchange users. These users need to be accessed by existing Exchange users. The easiest way to do this is to add these users to the Exchange Global Address List. You do this by using custom recipients. A custom recipient is a reference to a mail recipient located outside the Exchange organization (for example, Internet users).

You should also create mailbox names with ease of identification in mind. Coordinate the naming scheme with the NT account names or previous e-mail addresses. Several names are created when a mailbox is created:

First Name	The user's first name.
Last Name	The user's last name.
Alias Name	The alias is the default name for the users directory. It is generated by the Exchange Server based on an algorithm defined by the administrator when setting the Exchange autonaming options.
Display Name	This entry is used for display in the address book and Administrator Window. The default is also defined from the Administrator autonaming options.
Directory Name	This name defaults to the first alias name, but it can be changed. Once defined, it cannot be changed.

> **TIP**
>
> Multiple recipient containers can be created (and even nested within recipients containers) in the Exchange Site; properly named, this hierarchical structure will resemble the depart-

mental structure of many organizations. This creates an easy-to-use directory for users to access other addresses, inside and external.

These components define an addressing structure that builds the recipient addressing scheme. This is your most vulnerable point in the assignment of names. Exchange uses names in a number of ways—aliases, display names, and proxies are a few. When the Exchange server is installed in a Windows NT Domain and users are added to the existing domain, an Exchange user is also created. The alias for that user is the NT account name. A "friendly name" must be created based on display information the administrator provides. The method to be used should be determined before you start to add users (see Figure 7.1). After you determine the method, set the auto-naming option of the Exchange Server Administrator program to reflect the choice for all users added to the Exchange Server Site. This parameter is configured by choosing Tools | Options from the Exchange Administrator menu and then selecting the AutoNaming tab.

FIGURE 7.1.

Assigning Exchange default naming conventions.

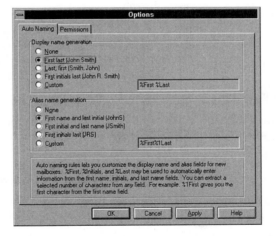

The alias name is used to define the Exchange mailbox, so by default this name conforms to the NT user; however, this is not always true, especially in the case of a custom recipient where there is no NT user account.

E-Mail Addresses

Two types of addresses exist within Exchange: custom recipients (addresses of users outside the Exchange organization) and Exchange mailboxes (recipients defined within the Exchange organization). When you configure the Exchange 4.0 server, three default e-mail addresses are created for each object. These default addresses are created based on the directory name and site information of the object. They are critical for the operations of Exchange and should not be deleted; however, they can be modified (see Figure 7.2). You access the Site Addressing Object from the Exchange Administrator by selecting the Configuration Container in the Exchange Organization Site.

WARNING

Deleting any of the default recipient addresses in Exchange could cause the server to stop functioning.

FIGURE 7.2.

The Site Addressing property page showing the three default addresses.

The following are the three default addresses when installing Exchange 4.0:

- Microsoft Mail, which is used to communicate via the Shadow Postoffice to the Microsoft Mail Servers
- SMTP, which is used for communications over the IMC
- X.400, which is used for internal communications as well as connecting X.400 providers

When installing Exchange 5.0 or upgrading to 5.0 from 4.0, you will get the same three, plus one additional default address type: CC Mail, which is used to communicate with connected cc:Mail installations.

The root address for these protocols can be changed from the Site | Configuration | Site Addressing dialog box in the Exchange Administrator (see Figure 7.3); if recipients have been created, their addresses will be automatically updated.

These address types are provided as defaults; you can add additional addresses as needed. Adding third-party connectors to other mail systems usually will include installing additional address types. You can also create custom address types to support unique internal addressing requirements.

FIGURE 7.3.

Site Addressing Properties page.

When you use the Internet Mail Connect (IMC), you must consider several issues, among them domain addressing and security. The first issue, domain addressing, has traditionally been relegated to UNIX servers and sendmail. Exchange provides some rudimentary domain-address resolution. This support makes it quite easy to use the domain name as the root for all user addresses, and leaves the resolution of the name to the appropriate server to Exchange. Instead of an Internet address such as `username@servername.org.com`, the addressable name can be `username@org.com`. This also hides the actual server name from the outside world. This change in root SMTP addressing is done at each site through the Site | Configuration | Site Addressing dialog box.

If your installation requires multiple addresses for a given address type, Exchange supports multiple entries for any address type. You can add an additional address (called a *proxy*) for any address type by going to the user's Email Addresses Tab and pressing the NEW button. When multiple addresses (proxies) of any address types created, only one can be used as a Reply address. This is the address the connector uses when sending mail out to the other mail system. To choose which proxy address is the Default Reply Address, select the address and press the Set as Default button. As currently implemented, there is no limit to the number of addresses that can be added to a recipient. Prudence is the only deterrent.

NOTE

To enhance security further, consider changing the default username for SMTP mail to a friendlier name, such as *firstname.lastname*, rather than the alias. In the case of John Jones, who has a mailbox on server zeus in the bozo domain, the SMTP address would be (assume the alias name is `jjones`) `jjones@zeus.bozo.com`. When this address is sent to the outside world, it advertises the user's NT account name and the Exchange Server on which

continues

continued

the user's mailbox resides. Creating an alternative SMTP address and assigning it as Reply Address provides a much more secure architecture. To the Exchange organization, messages to John.Jones@bozo.com will be routed to jjones regardless of where the server for his mailbox resides. This ensures security to the organization.

TIP

The Exchange Server can be made to support multiple Internet domains with the add-on imcext.dll that is provided with the Exchange Server Technical Resource Kit.

Individual installations may require support for common addresses—postmaster, webmaster, support and so on. Exchange provides a number of methods to create these. The method you choose depends on your organizational needs.

Creating a new mailbox for these accounts ensures that they will appear in the Global Address book. An alternate recipient can be associated with this mailbox, and mail will be routed automatically to the appropriate destination. This works well if there is one person handling all support issues; however, if it is a support address, multiple people typically are associated with this address. This can be accomplished by defining an alternative recipient as a distribution list or making the support mailbox itself the distribution list. Either way, a custom recipient is created that will support the required needs.

Custom recipients can also be defined to support special circumstances. These recipients do not have a presence in the organization, and only provide a placeholder for receipt of mail. When you choose this method, the requirements are to provide a central location for the receipt of support queries—for example, in an organization in which multiple mail systems exist and the address being created supports the entire organization and all mail systems.

Distribution Lists

As the Exchange server deployment begins, related groups within the organization will want to broadcast messages among themselves. The method to support this is *distribution lists (DLs)*. The distribution list contains the names of all people within the department or group to be supported. The members of distribution lists can be hidden to ensure privacy (see Figure 7.4). The administrator can create a new distribution list by selecting File | New Distribution List from the Exchange Administrator menu. Naming DLs with descriptively clear names by logical function or other obvious naming conventions will make it easier for users to find the specific DL they are trying to send to.

Distribution lists can also be created by individuals. These are called Personal Distribution Lists (PDLs), are stored in the users Personal Address book, and are available only to the single user. DLs created in the Administration program are made available to the entire Exchange organization.

FIGURE 7.4.

Distribution List properties.

NOTE

You can also use distribution lists to propagate permissions. Rather than assign permissions to individuals, assign them to a distribution list. Any person added to that distribution list will then inherit any permissions assigned to that distribution list.

TIP

A distribution list can contain other distribution lists as members.

Exchange Sites

Exchange sites are the logical units by which servers within an Exchange organization are grouped. Most default configurations are done on a per-site level, with the options to override these defaults at both the server and user levels as required. This enables a simple administration model in the general case, with the flexibility to set detailed or custom configurations to tailor your Exchange system to your specific needs.

Assumptions for Exchange Sites

The main assumption for an Exchange Site is uninterrupted, high-bandwidth, connectivity between all servers within a single site. These assumptions allow Exchange to simplify the configuration of communication between Exchange servers within a site, thereby allowing message routing as well as directory replication to appear to work right out of the box. All message routing and directory replication is point-to-point within a site, because each server has a direct connection available to any other server within that same site.

Single Versus Multiple Sites

In planning your rollout, you will find yourself asking what the benefits are of single versus multiple sites. Essentially, the trade-offs are complexity versus ease of administration and granular control of connectivity issues between Exchange Servers.

Because most administration configurations can be defaulted at the site level, the fewer sites your Exchange organization has, the fewer site level-specific configurations you need to configure and maintain. This makes adding a new server into an existing site as simple as pointing the install process to an existing Exchange server in the site you want to join. The setup process will then automatically bring the server into the site and configure messaging and directory replication to take place automatically. No additional configuration is needed, and the server is ready for users to be put on it.

By using multiple sites, you do gain the ability to tightly control the directory replication and message routing that will occur between servers in separate sites. This is a big win for controlling the utilization of links due to either bandwidth or availability constraints on those networking links. By using site connectors, administrators have the ability to batch up replication and messaging traffic in groups so that efficient use of the link is carried out. The downside to this is that you need to set up individual site connectors between these sites that explicitly configure these routing and replication connectivity settings. The more sites you need to connect, the more connectors you need to install and configure and the larger the directory replication process becomes.

In many cases, the need to install multiple sites is based on geographic and sometimes divisional criteria. As previously mentioned, the determining criteria could also be administrative.

When you are designing the Exchange organization, use common sense to minimize the traffic between servers in a site and reduce network bandwidth requirements. Consider the following:

- Group users who communicate among themselves on the same server. This will isolate traffic to a single Directory Store and take advantage of the Exchange server Single-Instance Store architecture.
- Use fault-tolerant servers wherever possible to support critical sites.

- Replicate public folders to ensure that information is always available regardless of server failure.

- Distribute administrative workstations and client installation points within the organization.

Administration of Sites

Microsoft Exchange is administered from a single administrative view, which contains all servers within the organization broken out by site. To administer a particular site requires that the administrator connect to a server in the remote site (see Figure 7.5). This is easily done from the Exchange Administrator. This dialog box is automatically displayed when the Exchange Administrator is started and no default server has been chosen. To connect to a different server when the Administrator has been started, choose File | Connect to Server from the menu.

FIGURE 7.5.

Connect to a different server in the organization.

Sites and NT Domains

The Microsoft Exchange Server architecture uses the NT Domain architecture extensively, relying on the NT Domain for administration and security support. A key criticism of LAN-based, e-mail programs has been the need to maintain a separate user ID and password. Exchange, because of the integration with the NT Domain, does not require a second logon when using NT as the primary operating system.

Architecture

There is no requirement to coordinate the installation of sites with the domain, but efforts should be made to make the installation as simple as possible to maintain. In fact, Microsoft Exchange Server supports four domain models within the NT Domain architecture:

- *Multiple sites within a domain.* Multiple Microsoft Exchange sites can exist with a single Windows NT Server Domain. By supporting separate sites, each site can be configured to allow custom configuration of intersite connections. This provides a great deal of flexibility in routing. This model will be the second most used architecture. Use of this model most closely parallels a multisite NT Domain.

- *Multiple domains within a site.* Microsoft Exchange sites can span Windows NT Server Domains; however, a two-way trust must exist between the domains. The site servers assume they're using the same service ID; the service account for every Microsoft Exchange server computer, by default, is specified when the servers are installed. When this is set up, an administrator can log on to the network once and administrate all of the Exchange server computers. The user accounts should also be maintained in a single Windows NT server Domain, for ease of administration. The complexity of this model requires a great deal of planning to implement and support.

- *Single domain/site topology.* This is used when the implementation is small enough to warrant only a single NT domain and a single Exchange site. This Microsoft Exchange architecture model is the easiest and most effective; the domain and site topologies are the same. This model is highly effective in small and single-location networks. This model can be used when supporting a single site NT Domain. The majority of small organizations will base their architecture on this model.

- *Users and servers in separate domains.* In this model, users are in a separate domain from the servers; the server domain must trust the user domain. This model can be used when an organization has been broken up into Resource and Administrative Domains. Be careful when you are building the Exchange user base, and define trusts between the domains.

Connecting Exchange Sites

Site connectors are used to connect multiple locations. Although there is a site connector, this is not the only means of connecting sites. Both the X.400 and the Internet Mail Service (IMS) can be used as site connectors. Depending on the requirements of the locations, one connector may be more appropriate than another:

- *Site connector.* This is the easiest connector to use. It has low overhead and provides automatic load balancing and fault tolerance. When configuring a local connector, the remote is automatically done; however, the connector traffic cannot be scheduled, and the connector will attempt to use all available bandwidth.

- *X.400 connector.* Use this to support an existing X.400 backbone. It can also be used as a connector between Exchange server sites. It provides more control than the site connector and will permit scheduling of connections, control of the message size, and support for TCP/IP, TP4, and X.25. Traffic is routed via a bridgehead server, which could be a bottleneck. This is also a good choice if you choose not to or are unable to implement NT trust relationships between domains.

- *Internet Mail connector.* If there is an existing SMTP backbone in place, SMTP becomes very attractive. Message sizes can be set, and the connector can be configured to support inbound, outbound, or both. No scheduling of the connection is possible; message format conversion is required.

- *Dynamic RAS connector.* The dynamic RAS connector is used when no permanent connection exists between sites. Scheduling is supported, as well as support for asynchronous, dial-up connections.

As part of the planning process, review the organization requirements and consider the following:

- Are redundant connections between sites a requirement?
- Will a failure in the bridgehead server cause sufficient grief to warrant additional connections?

■ Is enough bandwidth available on the backbone to support multiple connections between sites?

■ What type of traffic can I expect between the sites? Does it warrant direct connections between the servers?

Linking Sites

After you define the Windows NT Domain architecture and the Exchange Server architecture, you might need to link geographically separate sites. Sites can be configured to exchange directory information, public folders, and messages. The following sections discuss what you need to do when you connect these sites. It is critical to plan the number of sites and their boundaries carefully. After sites have been created, it is difficult to split or move them.

There are several factors that determine where to draw site boundaries. Some are necessary conditions that all Microsoft Exchange Server computers must satisfy in order to be placed in the same site. Others should be considered when you are planning site boundaries. These include administration, cost, security, network bandwidth, performance, link availability, and link reliability. There are also less tangible organizational issues that you should consider, such as grouping users who should work together in a single site.

One or more connections can be configured between sites. This redundant routing strategy offers load balancing between sites and across the organization. With each route, costs can be assigned; the Exchange Server connectors uses these costs to route information. The connectors will load balance routing over the remaining connections based on these assigned costs. These redundant routes can be used to reroute messages if the primary routes become unavailable; this ensures that messages will continue to flow between sites and the outside world in a manner that is fault-tolerant.

Connectors

The traditional method of connecting mail systems has been through gateways, a program, or hardware that supports translation from one protocol to another. Microsoft Exchange offers another method: the connector, a program that not only does protocol translation, but supports routing between mail systems as well. Exchange uses connectors in a number of ways—to connect sites as well as to support foreign mail systems, such as Microsoft Mail, SMTP, and X.400. The architecture designed by Microsoft provides an open structure for the extension of the Exchange Server by supporting the development of connectors by Microsoft as well as third-party developers. The following sections describe the currently available connectors.

Site Connector

The site connector is the most efficient way to connect two sites, because it uses RPC for site-to-site communication. Site connectors require permanent connections with higher bandwidths (more than 128KB) than the other connectors. However, they are easy to configure (see Figure

7.6). No network transport has to be configured, because it uses RPC. Messages are routed in their native format with this connector; no translation is required. A new site connector is created from the Exchange Administrator by selecting File | New Other | Site Connector.

FIGURE 7.6.

Creating a new site connector.

Site connectors are point-to-point; each connection from a local server is to a remote server in the distant site. This implies that the connection is between known servers in the site, and this is true—the Site connector maintains a target server list for the remote site. It uses this list to establish the connection. By using the target server list, the Exchange Server is less likely to encounter blocked connections because of server outages, and it can balance the messaging load among servers within the remote site.

If more control is required, bridgehead servers can be created within each site and targeted as the single source for the transfer of messages.

The simplicity of the site connector is not without its shortcomings; when active, the site connector will attempt to use all available bandwidth, and the message size cannot be controlled.

X.400 Connector

X.400 is used with TP0/X.25, TP4/CLNP, or TCP/IP. It is a more robust method of connecting sites, because it offers more control over the connection.

When it is used, the administrator can control the message size (which cannot be done with the site connector), providing a more effective use of network bandwidth. If there is an existing X.400 backbone or if you want to access a public X.400 system, this connector provides the best functionality.

Dynamic RAS Connector

The dynamic RAS connector (DRAS) is a dial-up site connector. It uses the NT Server Remote Access Service asynchronous communications instead of a permanent network connection between sites. This connector supports dial-up connections over slow, nonpermanent lines, and it provides an inexpensive method of providing electronic-mail services to small remote locations. The RAS connector can be configured to connect at prescribed times (see Figure 7.7); after the configuration is set, the Microsoft Exchange Server will make the connection as required. To set up a new Dynamic RAS Connector, you must first create a new RAS MTA by selecting File | New Other | New MTA Transport Stack | RAS MTA Transport Stack; then select the server on which stack is to run. When this is created, select File | New Other | Dynamic RAS Connector.

FIGURE 7.7.

Schedule for DRAS connections.

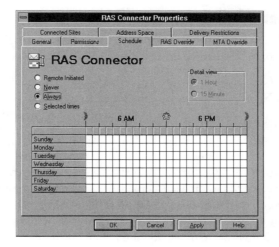

Internet Mail Service (IMS)

Standards

The Internet Mail Service, known as the Internet Mail Connector (IMC) in Exchange 4.0, was renamed to the Internet Mail Service (IMS) when it became a core component of the Exchange 5.0 Server and no longer was an add-on connector. It is used to communicate between the Exchange Server and other messaging systems supporting the SMTP protocol. The IMS conforms to the following Internet Engineering Task Force (IETF) Requests for Comments:

RFC	Description
821	Simple Mail Transport Protocol
823	Standard for the format of ARPA Internet text messages
1123	Internet Host Requirements
1521,1522	Multipurpose Internet Mail Extensions (MIME)

The Internet Mail Service can be configured to support inbound mail, outbound mail, or both. It provides a highly configurable interface to Internet mail. When used in conjunction with DNS Services, the IMS can route messages to servers within the Exchange organization. It will support the generation of friendly names for messages destined for the Internet.

NOTE

The Exchange IMS will not start if the DNS server is unavailable. Multiple DNS servers will minimize the need to restart the IMS.

Microsoft Mail Connector (PC)

The Mail Connector (PC) MTA is responsible for exchanging mail between Exchange users and Mail for PC Networks users.

The Mail Connector (PC) MTA is an MTA process for PC Mail post offices that runs as a Windows NT service and is designed to replace existing MS-DOS EXTERNAL.EXE MTAs and OS/2 and Windows NT MMTAs. The Mail Connector (PC) MTA provides the same functionality as the existing MS-DOS, OS/2, and Windows NT MTAs but is also Exchange-aware.

The Microsoft Mail Connector consists of three components: the Microsoft Mail Connector Interchange, the Microsoft Mail Connector Postoffice, and the Microsoft Mail Connector MTA. The Microsoft Mail Connector Postoffice (also known as the Shadow Postoffice), provides an entry point for mail originating in the Microsoft Mail Network. Because it is a Microsoft Mail Postoffice, it is visible to other Microsoft Mail Postoffices in the network and can be addressed by them. Including this post office in the DirSync process enables messages and directory information to be traded between the two systems.

The Shadow Postoffice does not support users, so it cannot be used in place of an existing Microsoft Mail Postoffice.

Sites with users running Microsoft Mail can configure synchronization of the directories to ensure the most current addressing information. Exchange participates in the current Microsoft Mail DirSync process. This can cause extra load to be placed on the individual server(s) where this is configured. Doing directory synchronization in off-peak hours should minimize the impact on those servers.

Microsoft Mail Connector (AppleTalk)

The Microsoft Mail Connector (AppleTalk) provides connectivity between the Exchange Server and the Star Nine Mail product for AppleTalk (previously Microsoft Mail for AppleTalk). It consists of two components: the Microsoft Mail Connector, a component to convert messages to Microsoft Mail format and provide connectivity to the Microsoft Mail Postoffice; and the Microsoft Exchange Connector, a gateway program for messages destined between the Exchange Server and the Microsoft Mail (AppleTalk) server.

CCMail Connector

The CCMail Connector provides both a messaging and directory replication connection to installations of Lotus's cc:Mail product. The current support is for CCMail DB6 database formats.

Other Mail Systems

Connectivity to other messaging systems is a capability inherent in the Exchange Server; Microsoft has designed the Exchange Server to support existing Microsoft Mail server gateways in addition to native support for three connectivity options: a 1984 and 1988 X.400 MTA; the Microsoft Mail connector for communications between Microsoft Mail users and the Exchange Server; and the Internet mail connector, which connects Microsoft Exchange Server users to the Internet. Chapter 16, "Connecting to Other Mail Systems," contains additional information.

The scalability of Microsoft Exchange provides a robust client-server messaging system that offers multiple methods for connecting to other systems. In addition to the connector technology, the gateway components of Microsoft Mail can be used while migrating. Some MS Mail installations may have an existing investment in gateway connectivity to outside systems. These gateways can be utilized by Exchange Sever to extend this external connectivity to Exchange users. The following Microsoft Mail gateway services are just some of the connectors that can be used with the Exchange Server to support connectivity to other mail systems:

- Microsoft Mail for PC networks
- Microsoft Mail for AppleTalk and compatible networks
- Fax Gateways
- X.400
- SMTP
- SNADS
- PROFS
- MHS

As part of the planning process, a view of the organization must be provided that includes the following:

- *Projected traffic volumes.* Traffic projections can only be estimated at this point, but routing of messages between the Exchange organization and remote sites and mail systems will increase the load. Tools are available within Exchange to monitor the increased traffic volumes. LoadSim and the custom performance monitor views also should be used occasionally to help determine system performance.

- *Impact of use of bridgehead servers.* A single point of connectivity is established with the bridgehead server. Will connectivity require additional resources to be allocated to support the new communications requirements?

- *Support for legacy systems and gateways.* With any organization, existing gateways and services must be supported. What are the support requirements for these services, can these be supported with the current configuration installed, or do hardware and software need to be modified or added to support the connectivity?

- *Connector requirements.* What types of connectors are required to support connectivity to these messaging systems? Are connectors available from Microsoft to support this messaging protocol? What are the administrative issues associated with supporting the proposed connectors?

■ *Other needs.* Are third-party connectors required to support the organization's needs? Is there another method of supporting this functionality?

Most external mail systems can be supported by the existing Microsoft Exchange connectors, or MS Mail gateways. Review the communications requirements for the remote e-mail system to help narrow the connectivity requirements.

User Considerations

When you are planning the installation of Exchange Server, there are choices for individual users that need to be taken into consideration. All administrators want to save themselves time; with Exchange, careful planning before the installation will greatly minimize the amount of running around that will be required .

Setup Issues

A key to installing these users is to define a standard installation method and consistency in client installation. Exchange ships with a Setup Editor to customize the installation scripts, setup program options, and user options (see Figure 7.8).

FIGURE 7.8.

The Exchange Setup Editor.

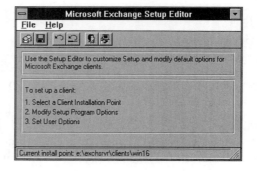

The Setup Editor generates a default.prf file, which provides a set of defaults to the Exchange setup program. The administrator has the option of creating a custom version for each user or each operating system or a single profile that can be customized as needed. In either case, the Setup Editor will provide answers to some of the questions asked during installation of the client software.

Exchange supports both Services Providers and Connectors—Service Providers on the clients and Connectors on the server. When you are designing the system, review the support requirements for each platform to identify the appropriate location in which to install the service.

One service to consider is the Exchange Server Service itself; configuration information and total client count must be available to assist in determining server requirements.

A Microsoft Mail provider can be installed as either a client or server service. Determine the requirements for access to Microsoft Mail. If you do a trial installation, consider installing the service on the client. As additional clients are added, and a full migration is undertaken, it might be more appropriate to use the Microsoft Mail Connector on the Exchange servers. Consider also the Microsoft Mail gateways that will remain in the site after the migration is underway.

Implementing Exchange Server into an existing Microsoft Mail network requires some thought. Is the Exchange Server meant to replace Microsoft Mail? If so, how will the migration be done?

Consider a phased approach. Install the Microsoft Mail service provider and the Exchange client to support the Microsoft Mail post offices as users are migrated to the Exchange Server.

Key issues to consider when using this approach include the following:

- Number of Microsoft Mail mailboxes to support
- Number of Servers to support
- Transport being used
- Timetable for migration of the users to Exchange Server

Windows Messaging (formerly the Exchange client), the inherent messaging client for both Windows 95 and Windows NT 4.0, is currently the only client that ships with the Internet Service Provider. The Exchange client—the version that ships with the Exchange Server—does not need an Internet Service Provider; all Internet access is provided at the server through the Internet Mail Connector. As part of the planning process, think about the types of clients that will be supported and where Internet Services must be supported.

Currently, the choice between Internet Service Provider and Internet Connector is restricted to Windows 95. Soon Windows NT 4.0 will be added. When you need to support other platforms, the choice is clear: use the Internet Mail Connector on the Exchange server.

You can also use the Internet Service while you are migrating existing users to the Exchange server. One advantage of the Internet Service with Windows 95 is its capability of accessing POP3 servers. With POP3 support installed, existing UNIX post offices can continue to be supported for the receipt of mail until the migration is complete.

The Windows Messaging clients also support access to SMTP servers to send Internet mail. They do not accept SMTP connections, so incoming Internet mail must be routed to a POP3 server.

Cross-Platform

While the migration is in progress, these clients can be supported with a standard SMTP and POP3 server installation on a UNIX platform; you must have expertise with UNIX and, specifically, sendmail to assure that the entries in the DNS database permit the correct routing of mail to the appropriate destination. As Exchange is deployed, the sendmail database support required to keep routing accurate becomes less of a problem; Exchange can provide message routing both within and without the organization.

Storage Considerations

Configuring an Exchange organization is no easy effort. This is not because it is necessarily complex, but because of the many options available to the designer. For example, there are two possible message stores in an Exchange Server:

- Private Store
- Public Store

Each of these stores has a 16GB limitation, which can limit the Exchange Server to a maximum of 32GB of total storage per server. These limits are not as restrictive as they might seem, because they apply only to messages stored in the server message stores. When you are designing the Exchange server, you must understand these limitations and user requirements to implement an effective design. The following represent some things you must consider when you design the Exchange server:

- The amount of server storage used by each user
- Storage quotas (if employed)
- Aging limitations on folders
- Single-instance storage
- The use of personal folders
- The number of rules, views, and finders defined by users on the server
- The use of public folders

As an administrator, concerns range from restricting server storage to enabling the users to manage their own storage (and possibly increasing administrative support requirements). Each of these has its advantages and disadvantages. Weigh the circumstances to determine what is appropriate for the organization.

Server-Based Storage

If you choose server-based storage, remember that the maximum size of the private message store is 16GB. As the administrator, review the current e-mail storage requirements for the installed base. By looking at the size of the current user-message store, determining an average, and then performing some quick calculations, it should be relatively easy to determine the number of users that can be supported from a single server.

An easy way to determine Exchange Server user storage requirements is to determine the average mailbox size for each user and divide that by the maximum size of the Information Store (16GB). Using this method will yield the maximum number of users an Exchange Server can. For example, if users have a 20MB Message Store (mailbox), 16GB/20MB = 800 users/server.

NOTE

There are two Information Stores managed by the Exchange Server: the Private and Public Information Stores. The Private Information Store also maintains information other than just mail messages—user rules and forms are also stored there. These calculations will provide only preliminary storage requirements. Other factors will affect server storage requirements as well.

Aging is described as the amount of time messages reside in the Information Store. If a message is retained beyond a prescribed period of time, should it be deleted? What policies should be put in place to support management of mail messages? What type of age limit should be placed on the message Store?

Aging is a concern; how long should a user maintain archive mail? When is it appropriate to delete old mail? Aging is manageable with Exchange. You need to establish a plan for managing this process.

For those users who never purge their deleted mail, the administrator has the tools to force a purge. Be sure that the activation of this capability is included in the rollout plan.

Mailbox storage is not the only place mail can be delivered in Exchange. You can also use personal folders to store mail. Saving mail to personal folders will bypass the 16GB limitation of the private Message Store. In effect, a single Exchange server can now manage more users. The downside is that the management of user space is now relegated to the user.

When you use personal folders, .pst files, consider where they will be stored. Some corporate strategies are to put these files up on file servers so that they are accessible anywhere on the network and are available for corporate initiated backup schemes. In contrast, some strategies call for users to maintain their personal folders on their local computers. When this method is chosen, individual workstation storage requirements are the concern, and there is less need to reserve storage on the Exchange Server. It then becomes the user's responsibility to back up messages.

NOTE

Putting personal folder .pst files on a network server can increase overall network utilization. Messages coming down from the Exchange server must first travel over the network to the client and then back over the same network to the personal folder .pst file being kept on a file server. Best performance and network utilization will be achieved by having personal folder .pst files kept locally on user's machines.

TIP

Personal folders (.pst files) can be an ideal way to store messages, but they can become unwieldy. To archive messages when using .pst files, select Tools | Service | Add | Personal Folder from the Exchange client main menu. Rename the new personal folder archive (or some other meaningful name). Move all the messages to be archived to this personal folder. When you have finished, remove the folder from the inbox and copy it to backup media. A suggested practice is to create an archive for each month.

The archive does not have to be removed from the client, and you can maintain it as a separate Information Store on a continuous basis.

You also need to think about instances of multiple users sharing a single workstation. When this occurs, some of the inherent security designed into the Exchange client may be bypassed.

By default, the Exchange client uses NT network security to check the user ID and connect to the appropriate mailbox. It is not evident to the user, but NT Security validates the user based on the security credentials created by the logon process. These credentials are used internally by NT and have now been extended to support this application. When using this method, access to the mailbox occurs without further validation from the logged-on user. When a user is accessing Exchange servers located in other domains, accessing mailboxes when logged in as a different person, or on a Novell network, additional validation is required. Network logon validation must be disabled to support these environments. When this is done, instead of the mailbox automatically opening, a dialog box appears asking for logon information.

Even more important, because logon security is disabled, profile configuration procedures should be reviewed. Profiles need to be created on each workstation a user accesses, or establish support for "roving users."

Roving user configuration setup differs depending on the operating system. Registry entries are used to point to the client-configuration information in Windows 95 and Windows NT; Windows 3.*x* uses an .INI file.

Client E-Mail Editors

The Exchange client uses a built-in editor to read and send mail. organizations that use the Microsoft Office 95 or Office 97 suite (and specifically Microsoft Word) have another editor option: WordMail. New installations of Microsoft Word offer an option to install WordMail. When it is installed, it becomes the default editor for Exchange. If messaging is internal, this is an excellent option to use; however, be careful when you send Rich Text to other mail systems and the Internet. Rich Text Format (RTF) is a standard advocated by Microsoft as a vendor-independent method of sharing data between word processing systems. It preserves all formatting code and is understood by any word processor that understands RTF.

Exchange by default sends data in RTF. This preserves the formatting characters of the message; however, few electronic mail systems understand RTF data. When an Exchange RTF message is sent to a system that does not understand RTF, the received message has an attached file, winmail.dat, which contains all the formatting. When you send mail to the Internet, you should not send Rich Text formatted messages. An option is available on the properties page of the Internet Mail Connector to turn this off.

If WordMail is installed and becomes the default editor, the default editor can be changed back to the Exchange default editor from the Exchange Inbox. This does not remove WordMail as an editor, so either editor can be used to compose, read, or send mail. If you want to remove WordMail entirely, you can do so from the Office Setup program.

Remote Users

How will remote users be supported in the Microsoft Exchange environment? There are a number of new considerations to be made here as well.

Exchange Remote Mail users require remote access; remote users of Microsoft Mail access the Microsoft Mail Server through a personal computer running the Microsoft Mail Eternal program. The added capabilities available with a Point-to-Point Protocol (PPP) connection, and Remote Access Services will appear to be both cumbersome and overkill to many veteran Microsoft Mail administrators.

Many administrators feel the use of RAS Service is not warranted to support the delivery of remote mail; however, from a maintenance point of view, there are fewer hardware components to support. Although RAS provides a reliable method of remotely receiving the mail, it also supports connectivity to the LAN. Consequently, more overhead is required to support this added functionality. In reality, when you use the Microsoft Exchange Server Remote client, there is little difference between the functionality it provides and that supported by Microsoft Mail Remote.

When you are migrating from a Microsoft Mail Remote to Microsoft Exchange Remote with PPP, you know the traffic volumes, because there is no change in the number of users supported, only in the method of access. No additional modems need to be added.

Expect to monitor the remote access connections as traffic increases for remote users. Also keep in mind that these lines will be used by users accessing other services on the LAN. When you install new RAS Services, sizing becomes more difficult and will require some experimentation and monitoring.

As communications expertise grows, there will be more demand for ISDN, Frame Relay, and X.25 services. Remote access for large corporations can be provided by any of these services; RAS configuration for other than default dial-up connections is beyond the scope of this book. If support for these telecommunications services is a consideration, consult your network provider for information on the adapters and software required to support this connectivity.

The Exchange Configuration editor provides great control over the installation of remote user software. The Editor is designed to build default client configurations that include supported Information Service Providers and also permit the modification of the binding order for the client protocol stack; this is critical to Exchange connectivity both for remote and local users and will speed loading time for the client software when done correctly. Be sure it is understood what protocols will be used to support Exchange in the organization before you make any changes to the protocol stack or binding order.

If the binding order must be changed after the client is installed, you must do so with the Registry Editor in Windows 95 and Windows NT. In Windows 3.1 and Windows for WorkGroups, the binding order is an entry in the System.ini file.

Remote users are users who access the Exchange Server from a dial-up connection. Exchange also supports mobile users. For both categories of users, you must define how they will be using their workstations.

A remote user has a dial-up connection to the Exchange server and will always use a dial-up connection. A remote user should maintain messages in personal folders to make sure that archived messages are readily available. The user can compose messages offline and upload them to the Exchange Server at designated times set by parameters in the client software.

A mobile user is occasionally on the road and maintains a permanent connection via the LAN to the Exchange Server when he or she is back in the office. This user should be set up with an offline storage (.ost) file for sending and receiving messages. When using .ost files, the administrative team should configure the remote client before allowing the mobile user access to the software. Use of .ost files permits a user to compose messages offline and send and receive mail as needed. When the user returns to the office, the laptop will synchronize the user's mailbox with the laptop. This is an ideal method of ensuring consistency between workstations while traveling.

Summary

This chapter should be used merely as a guideline for the successful installation of Microsoft Exchange Server. Some activities must be performed so that a successful installation can occur.

NT and Exchange can be tightly coupled. In an NT Domain installation, NT Logon Security can be used to eliminate a secondary logon. Additionally, the Exchange Server organization model can, but does not have to, mimic the NT Domain model. Exchange organizational models exist that complement the NT Domain models.

Take the time to develop a concise implementation plan that includes a well-thought-out naming convention. A standard convention cannot be established for everyone and must be determined based on a number of factors, including corporate standards as well as previously implemented conventions.

Sites are locations that support Exchange Servers. An Exchange site was designed to support multiple servers, and the Exchange organization was designed to support multiple sites. This hierarchy provides a flexible structure for the expansion of the Exchange organization—not only internally, but also externally with the use of connectors.

The Exchange Server can be installed in either a single-site or multisite environment. The design of the Exchange organization, the supporting communications links, and administrative requirements will determine which will be used.

Exchange Server is a constantly evolving product and offers a great deal of flexibility in design and implementation. As additional components are developed to support the server, the methods described here will be replaced by newer ones. To keep abreast of the latest capabilities of the Server, a number of sources are available; these include the following:

- The Microsoft support newsgroups at `msnews.microsoft.com`. The following Exchange-related newsgroups are available:

  `microsoft.public.exchange.admin`

  `microsoft.public.exchange.applications`

  `microsoft.public.exchange.clients`

  `microsoft.public.exchange.connectivity`

  `microsoft.public.exchange.misc`

  `microsoft.public.exchange.setup`

- The Microsoft Exchange Web page at

  `http://www.microsoft.com/Exchange`

- There is also an Exchange ListServer at

  `msexchange-request@insite.co.uk`

  To subscribe, send a mail message with the single word SUBSCRIBE in the body of the message.

- The Exchange Community Site at

  `www.exchangeserver.com`

Exchange Server 4.0 to 5.0: Migration and Coexistence

by Eric Lockard

IN THIS CHAPTER

Upgrading your Microsoft Exchange Server organization from Exchange Server 4.0 to 5.0 is an easy and straightforward process. Microsoft has done a fairly good job of allowing you to independently migrate different portions of your organization at your own pace. Servers can be updated independently of one another over time, and clients can be independent of server versions, either before or after their servers have been updated. In short, you have about as much flexibility as you could ask for in upgrading your Exchange Server organization at the pace most appropriate for your resources and topology.

There are, however, several considerations you should be aware of when migrating from 4.0 to 5.0. This chapter covers these in detail and presents several server and client upgrade strategies.

Benefits of Upgrading to Microsoft Exchange Server Version 5.0

New to
Version 5.0

There are many feature and functionality improvements provided by Microsoft Exchange Server 5.0, many of which were introduced in Chapter 1, "Overview of Microsoft Exchange Server 5.0." These include the following:

■ Support for Internet standard e-mail, news, and directory service clients via the POP3, SMTP, NNTP, and LDAP Internet protocols

■ HTTP Web client browser access for mailboxes, public folders, and directory data

■ The ability to author active Web pages using Active Server Script and the Exchange Server Active Messaging COM interfaces

■ The Microsoft Outlook client

■ Numerous other end-user and administrative features and enhancements

However, in addition to the many feature upgrades provided by Exchange Server 5.0, there are also thousands of bug fixes, usability enhancements, and performance improvements above and beyond Exchange Server 4.0. Even if you don't plan to take advantage of the new features, you should consider upgrading to version 5.0. As of the time of this writing, Microsoft was not charging an upgrade fee for Exchange clients (even to use the Outlook client), so the expense to upgrade your Exchange Server software to version 5.0 software should be fairly minimal.

In short, there are many reasons to upgrade to Exchange Server version 5.0 and very few reasons not to. Do it today!

Compatibility

Versions 4.0 and 5.0 Coexistence

Larger organizations may have hundreds of Microsoft Exchange servers in many sites spread geographically over the globe. Servers may be located in remote branch offices with little or no local IT personnel on site. It would therefore be quite unreasonable for Microsoft to expect Exchange Server customers to upgrade all the Exchange servers in an organization, or even within a single site, simultaneously.

Similarly, many Exchange Server organizations may want to upgrade clients on a separate schedule from servers, rolling out 5.0 servers throughout the organization before introducing 5.0 clients or supporting the Microsoft Outlook client (which also ships as part of Microsoft Office 97) before the Exchange servers are upgraded. It would therefore also be quite unreasonable for Microsoft to expect Exchange Server customers to upgrade Exchange servers in lockstep with Exchange clients.

Luckily, Microsoft addressed both these concerns with version 5.0. Microsoft Exchange Server versions 4.0 and 5.0 servers can coexist quite nicely together within the same Exchange Server organization or site for indefinite periods. Servers can be upgraded one at a time over an extended period.

Exchange Server version 5.0 also supports 4.0-level clients and vice versa. Clients and servers can therefore be upgraded and rolled out independently of one another over an extended period of time.

Before You Begin

As with most things, it is beneficial to put together a plan that covers your upgrade to Exchange Server 5.0. The plan should cover the following:

- Steps to take before *any* Exchange servers are upgraded to version 5.0. This should include upgrading the Windows NT Server Operating System (including service packs) and ensuring that all Exchange Server 4.0 servers are running the latest Exchange Server 4.0 service pack.
- Steps to take before each individual server is upgraded, such as making a backup of the Exchange Server Information Store and Directory Service database(s).
- The order and timetable for server upgrades. Which servers will you upgrade first and when?
- The order and timetable for upgrading clients. Which client populations will you upgrade first? Are you allowing clients to upgrade independently of servers? What about users using the version of Outlook that comes with Office 97?
- A checklist covering things to consider during each server upgrade.

Upgrading Your Windows NT Server Operating System

At a minimum, Microsoft Exchange Server 5.0 requires one of the following:

- Microsoft Windows NT Server version 3.51 with Windows NT Server service pack #5 or greater
- Microsoft Windows NT Server version 4.0 with Windows NT Server service pack #2 or greater

However, Microsoft Windows NT Server version 4.0 with service pack #3 is strongly recommended. Additionally, certain components of Microsoft Exchange Server version 5.0 (specifically, the Active Server components) require Windows NT 4.0 and will not install on Windows NT 3.51.

Windows NT Server version 4.0 provides increased performance benefits over Windows NT Server version 3.51. Microsoft has indicated that Exchange servers can realize up to 30 percent performance gains simply by upgrading the underlying Windows NT Server Operating System to Windows NT Server version 4.0. Thus, even though the core components of Exchange Server 5.0 work well and are supported on Windows NT Server version 3.51, it is beneficial for you to upgrade all your Exchange servers to Windows NT version 4.0 with the latest service pack, even if you don't immediately plan to take advantage of the new features.

The Windows NT Server operating system on each Exchange server must be at one of these levels prior to upgrading an Exchange Server 4.0 machine to Microsoft Exchange Server 5.0 or installing 5.0 on a fresh machine. The Exchange Server Setup program will refuse to install Exchange Server 5.0 otherwise.

Additionally, the Windows NT Server Primary Domain Controllers for each NT security domain in which Exchange servers are located should also be upgraded to the latest Windows NT Server service pack.

TIP

A *service pack* is a relatively small, free product upgrade, available from Microsoft on the Internet or CD-ROM, which contains bug fixes (also known as "hot fixes") for problems encountered by customers since that version of the product was released on compact disc. Hot fixes are individual fixes for specific problems and are sometimes released individually. In general, a service pack includes all the hot fixes released for a specific version since the product version was released, including any fixes distributed in previous service packs for that version. Service packs may also occasionally contain new features or functionality. In general, installing the latest service pack for a product provides all the bug fixes included in all previous service packs for that product version. Except in special circumstances, there is no need to install each service pack individually or to install individual hot fixes unless you encounter a specific problem addressed by a recent hot fix that has not yet been incorporated into a service pack. Just install the most recent service pack and you get all the bug fixes up to that point.

At the time of this writing, the latest service packs and hot fixes for Microsoft Windows NT Server can be accessed on the World Wide Web at http://www.microsoft.com/ntserver or via anonymous FTP at ftp://ftp.microsoft.com/bussys/winnt/winnt-public/fixes, or you can order the latest service pack on compact disc by calling the Microsoft Order Desk at (800) 360-7561 between 6:30 a.m. and 5:30 p.m. Pacific Standard Time.

You can easily determine which Windows NT Server version and service pack you have installed by selecting Help | About Windows NT from any Windows NT system window or the Windows NT Explorer (see Figure 8.1).

FIGURE 8.1.
Determining which Windows NT Server service pack you have installed.

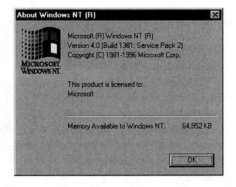

In general, it is a good idea to install and run the latest service pack for each of your server operating system(s) and server applications. Service packs are thoroughly tested by Microsoft and supported (and often required) by Microsoft Product Support.

MIPS and PowerPC Machines

Unlike Microsoft Exchange Server 4.0, Exchange Server 5.0 discontinues support for machines with MIPS or PowerPC CPUs. Microsoft found that the number of **New to Version 5.0** customers utilizing these types of machines did not justify the effort involved in developing, maintaining, and supporting products for these platforms. Future versions of Microsoft Windows NT Server will most likely discontinue support for machines with these CPUs as well. If you have MIPS or PowerPC machines running Exchange Server 4.0 in your organization, you can upgrade them to the latest Windows NT Server and Exchange Server 4.0 service packs and continue to run Exchange Server 4.0 on these machines during your upgrade. However, you should probably plan to replace them with Intel Pentium or DEC Alpha (or compatible) machines in the near future.

Exchange Server 4.0 Service Packs

As discussed previously, Exchange Server 5.0 provides additional features and capabilities above and beyond those provided by the 4.0 version. To support these additional features, version 5.0 supplies enhancements to the underlying replicated directory service schema in the form of additional attributes and object classes. When you install the first 5.0 version Exchange Server in an Exchange Server site, the directory service schema for that site is upgraded to include these additional object classes and attributes. This enhanced schema is, in turn, replicated around to the other Exchange servers in the site, including version 4.0 Exchange servers.

8

EXCHANGE SERVER
4.0 TO 5.0

This is all fine and dandy if you have only a single site, but what happens when you (or the system) start to use these 5.0 specific objects and attributes and you have other sites in your organization that are still using the old 4.0 schema? Can the old 4.0 version Exchange servers handle the new 5.0 level schema?

Compatibility   Microsoft anticipated this situation and actually included the most critical portions of the version 5.0 directory service schema in service pack #2 for Exchange Server 4.0, along with the capability for the directory service of reloading the schema without needing to be restarted.

For these reasons, it is essential that all Exchange Server 4.0 servers in your entire organization be running Exchange Server version 4.0 service pack #2 (or greater) before you upgrade or install the first 5.0 version Exchange Server anywhere in your Exchange organization. You can determine the version of a Microsoft Exchange server by viewing the properties of the server object in the Exchange Server Administrator window (see Figure 8.2).

WARNING

All Exchange Server version 4.0 servers in your Exchange organization must be running Exchange Server 4.0 service pack #2 (or greater) before you upgrade or install the first 5.0 version Exchange Server anywhere in your Exchange organization, or directory replication problems could occur. You can determine the version of a Microsoft Exchange server by viewing the properties of the server object in the Exchange Server Administrator window (see Figure 8.2).

FIGURE 8.2.

Determining which Microsoft Exchange Server service pack you have installed.

NOTE

The Exchange Server version 5.0 setup should detect whether any 4.0 version Exchange servers within your organization are not running at least service pack #2 level and will warn you if this is the case.

TIP

At the time of this writing, the latest service packs and hot fixes for Microsoft Exchange Server 4.0 can be accessed on the World Wide Web at `http://www.microsoft.com.exchange` or via anonymous FTP at `ftp://ftp.microsoft.com/bussys/exchange/exchange-public/fixes`, or you can order the latest service pack on compact disc by calling the Microsoft Order Desk at (800) 360-7561 between 6:30 a.m. and 5:30 p.m. Pacific Standard Time.

There are a few exceptions to this rule. If you have only a single 4.0 Exchange server in your organization, there is no need to install any Exchange Server service packs before upgrading it to Exchange Server version 5.0. The 5.0 version of Setup is capable of upgrading any and all version 4.0 servers independent of service pack level.

Similarly, if you plan on upgrading all Exchange servers in your organization simultaneously (or within a very short time period, such as all in the same day), you do not need to install 4.0 service packs before upgrading directly to 5.0.

The only thing to watch out for is a situation where 5.0 version Exchange servers and 4.0 version Exchange servers that are not running service pack #2 (or greater) are allowed to exist in the same organization for extended periods of time. The new 5.0 version directory schema information can cause pre-service pack #2 4.0 version servers to crash or to stop replicating directory information. If you happen to get into this situation, upgrading your version 4.0 Exchange servers to version 5.0 or installing service pack #2 (or greater) will address the issue.

To be on the safe side, its best to simply make sure all version 4.0 Exchange servers in your organization are running at service pack #2 level (or greater) before introducing the first 5.0 version Exchange server into your organization.

NOTE

Exchange Server service pack #3 for version 4.0 "breaks the rules" for service packs. It does not include the bug fixes and functionality released in previous Exchange Server 4.0 service packs. There are two reasons for this. First, because of the issues with the Exchange

continues

continued

Server version 5.0 directory service schema and 4.0 version coexistence, Microsoft actually silently updated the 4.0 version retail product discs to include service pack #2 functionality. All Exchange Server version 4.0 products purchased after about August 1, 1996, come with service pack #2 pre-installed. The second reason is that Exchange Server service pack #2 was quite large, weighing in at around 10MB. Because the primary way to get service packs is to download them from Microsoft over the Internet, size counts. Microsoft made the decision to start fresh with service pack #3 for Exchange Server version 4.0 so that it would be small and easily downloadable. This made a lot of sense, because many of the retail product boxes are already at service pack #2 level. Thus, if you attempt to install Exchange Server version 4.0 service pack #3, you may get a warning that indicates that you must first install service pack #2 if you purchased your Exchange Server before August 1, 1996, and have not yet installed service pack #2. You can determine the version of a Microsoft Exchange Server by viewing the properties of the server object in the Exchange Server Administrator window.

Upgrading Bridgehead Servers

The documentation for Microsoft Exchange Server version 5.0 discusses a procedure for upgrading to version 5.0 without updating all version 4.0 Exchange servers to service pack #2 (or greater). The procedure involves upgrading all directory replication bridgehead servers to version 5.0 and then restarting the version 4.0 servers so that the new, version 5.0 directory service schema is reloaded.

This procedure is not recommended. A much better approach is to simply ensure that all Exchange servers in the organization are running at least service pack #2 and then upgrade Exchange servers to version 5.0 at your own pace. By taking this route, servers can be upgraded in whatever order you want, and there is no need for any servers to be restarted.

Upgrade Approaches

There are several approaches to upgrading your organization to Microsoft Exchange Server version 5.0:

- Upgrade servers initially, clients later
- Upgrade clients initially, servers later
- Upgrade servers and clients together

The 5.0 version of Exchange Client includes several new features that work only with 5.0 level Exchange servers. These features will be unavailable on version 5.0 clients that are not operating against 5.0 version servers, and any applicable menu items will appear disabled. All version 4.0 level functionality will continue to work just fine.

For this reason, there is a slight preference to upgrading servers before upgrading clients, but this is not a strict requirement. Exchange Server 5.0 provides sufficient flexibility in this area for you to upgrade clients and servers completely independently.

Although not officially supported by Microsoft, there is a neat little trick for making users aware of new versions of Exchange Client. Each time Exchange Client is started, it looks under the local Registry key HKEY_LOCAL_MACHINE\Software\Microsoft\Exchange\Client for the string value UpgradePath. If this value contains a file share pathname (for example, \\Exchange\clients\win95), the client will access that file share before starting up to see whether a newer version of the client software is available. It does this by opening the exchng.stf file at that install point and reading the version number from the "App Version" string on the second line of the file. If the version is greater than that of the local exchng.stf file, the Exchange client will offer to run the setup.exe from that share and upgrade the client right then and there. If not, or if the file server is unavailable, the client will start without the user being aware of the check.

This is great, but how does that Registry value get set in the first place? Well, you can configure the Exchange Client installation to put it there! For the Windows NT and Windows 95 client installs, simply add a line like the following to the end of the exchng.stf file for each of your Exchange client install shares:

```
<line number>  AddRegData    """LOCAL"","Software\Microsoft\Exchange\Client"",
➥""UpgradePath"", ""\\Exchange\clients\win95"""
```

where `<line number>` is the number of the next line in the file. This instructs the Exchange Client Setup program to add the Registry value to the Registry on the client computer.

For Windows 3.1 Exchange clients, the upgrade path is stored in the local exchng.ini file under the "Microsoft Exchange" section. The line to add this value to the Windows 3.1 Exchange Client exchng.ini file looks something like this:

```
<line number>  AddIniLine    """exchng.ini"", ""Microsoft Exchange"",
➥""UpgradePath"", ""\\Exchange\clients\win16"""
```

Similarly, the version of Microsoft Outlook supplied with Exchange Server version 5.0 can also be configured to add the proper Registry value by adding a line like the following to the outlook.srg file in the \Program files\Microsoft Office\Office directory on an Outlook install share:

```
[HKEY_LOCAL_MACHINE\software\microsoft\office\8.0\outlook\upgradepath]
➥"serverpath" = "<\\\\exchange\\clients\\outlookr>"
```

You can use this capability of upgrading clients to a newer version of the Exchange Client software or even for forcing an upgrade yourself by incrementing the "App Version" of the install share. This can be handy if you change a default client setting, such as deleting the Deleted Items folder on exit or the RPC binding order, and want to disseminate this change to your Exchange users.

There are number of limitations with these features, including the lack of any ability to provide this automatic upgrading for DOS or Macintosh Exchange clients. For more information, see Microsoft Exchange Knowledge Base article #Q145743.

Scheduling Server Upgrades

The low-level database format of the Exchange Server Information Store was enhanced and modified in version 5.0 to support the new version 5.0 functionality. When upgrading a version 4.0 Exchange Server to 5.0, the Exchange Server Information Store will automatically upgrade the Information Store database to the new format. This can take quite a long time, and your server will be unavailable during this interval.

Although the time it takes to upgrade the database is dependent upon your Exchange Server hardware configuration, a good rule of thumb is to allow 1 hour per GB of Information Store database for the upgrade process. Thus, the upgrade could conceivably take up to 32 hours if you have a full 16GB of private and another 16GB of public storage. (This is a worse case estimate. In practice, it will likely take considerably less time to upgrade even a server with this much data.)

WARNING

Once you upgrade a server to version 5.0 and the Information Store database is converted to the version 5.0 format, it cannot be converted back to the 4.0 format. It is strongly suggested, and is also just good practice, to make a backup of your Information Store and directory service databases prior to upgrading your version 4.0 server. This way you are covered if something goes wrong during the upgrade.

NOTE

The Information Store database upgrade is a fault-tolerant process. That is, if the power fails or some other interruption occurs during the upgrade, the version 5.0 Exchange Server Information Store will pick up where it left off once the power comes back on. The upgrade process utilizes the same, fault-tolerant transaction logging mechanisms as the Exchange Server Information Store employs during normal operation and thus should be immune to most interruptions or faults that don't cause physical disk media damage.

Upgrading Servers

Once you have upgraded all your Exchange Server version 4.0 servers to service pack #2 (or greater) and have upgraded your Windows NT Server operating system to the latest service pack, you are ready to upgrade your servers to Exchange Server version 5.0 according to the schedule you have defined.

After backing up your Exchange Information Store database, the next step is to ensure that any Exchange server monitors for the server are shut down. Server monitors can be configured to restart the Exchange Server services in the event that any of the Exchange Server services stop for some reason. Obviously, you don't want this to happen while you are performing the upgrade, so it's a good idea to ensure that any server monitors for the server are stopped during the upgrade period. Alternatively, you can use the Maintenance Status property page in the Administrator program to put the server monitor into maintenance mode.

The next thing is to ensure that all remote Windows NT Performance Monitors (PerfMons) monitoring the server are shut down. The Windows NT PerfMon application will hold certain Exchange Server files open on the Exchange server even when running remotely from another server. In order for the version 5.0 Exchange Server Setup program to update these files, all PerfMons running with counters for this server must be stopped.

Now comes the fun part: Put the Exchange Server 5.0 compact disc in the CD-ROM drive and run setup.exe from the appropriate directory under Setup/ *<platform>*, or alternatively run setup.exe from a network share where you've copied the appropriate directory from the compact disc.

Setup will search for installed components and should offer to upgrade your version 4.0 Exchange Server if you are upgrading a version 4.0 machine (see Figure 8.3).

Chapter 12, "Installing Microsoft Exchange Server," covers the installation process for installing a brand new version 5.0 Exchange Server.

FIGURE 8.3.

The version 5.0 Setup program detects your Exchange Server version 4.0 server and offers to upgrade the Exchange Server software.

After warning you that the database upgrade could take a few minutes, Setup will ask you for your Product ID, which can be found on the label of your Exchange Server version 5.0 compact disc. After you type in the Product ID code and press OK, Setup looks to see whether this is the first version 5.0 Exchange Server to be installed in the site (see Figure 8.4). If it is, Setup tells you the directory schema will be updated to the 5.0 version and points you to the README file on the CD for information on installing subsequent version 4.0 servers (see the section "Installing Version 4.0 Servers After Upgrading to Version 5.0," later in this chapter).

FIGURE 8.4.

The version 5.0 Setup program detects this is the first version 5.0 server to be installed in the existing 4.0 site.

Setup then copies over the version 5.0 files and begins converting the Information Store database to the version 5.0 format. Here is where things can take a while, depending upon the size of your database.

The rest of Setup is easy and is the same as that for new servers. Setup adds information to the NT Registry and directory service, grants the service account any needed permissions, and starts the Exchange Server services. Congratulations! You just upgraded your server to version 5.0.

Running the Performance Optimizer

Performance

Microsoft has made several changes to the Exchange Server Performance Optimizer in version 5.0, some visible, some not. Many of these changes relate to performance enhancements Microsoft has made in the product since the 4.0 version.

Your next step after installing version 5.0 or upgrading a version 4.0 server to 5.0 should be to run the version 5.0 Performance Optimizer. The version 5.0 Performance Optimizer should be run on every 5.0 server, regardless of whether it is a new Exchange server or one you have upgraded from version 4.0.

When upgrading a version 4.0 server to 5.0, the Exchange Server Setup program will not offer to run the Performance Optimizer (Setup offers this only on new server installations). You will need to run the program from its icon in the Microsoft Exchange Windows folder.

> **NOTE**
>
> It is a good idea to rerun the Exchange Server Performance Optimizer whenever any software or hardware change is made to the Exchange Server machine, particularly when memory is added or removed or when new Exchange Server software (including service packs) is installed.

A new option in the Performance Optimizer is the POP3 only checkbox under Type of server (see Figure 8.5).

FIGURE 8.5.

The version 5.0 Performance Optimizer provides a new POP3 only option for servers hosting primarily POP3 clients.

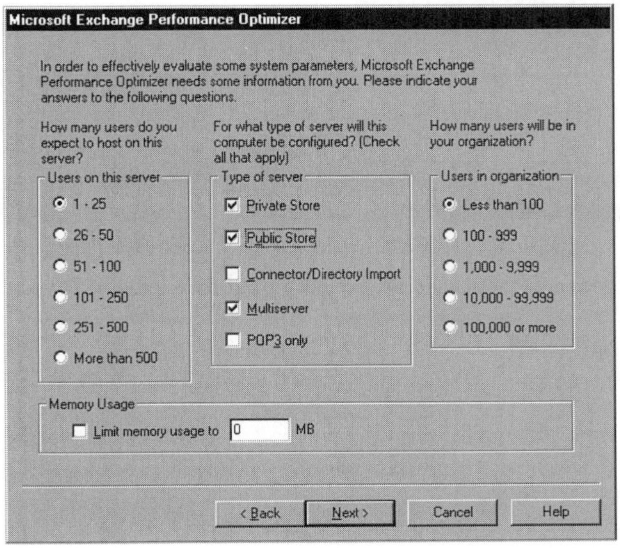

If you plan to host primarily POP3 clients on this server, you should check this option. **Performance** Note that any choices you make in the Performance Optimizer are only hints to the Exchange Server software about how you plan to use this machine. The Performance Optimizer does not disable any capabilities based upon the choices you make. Instead, it simply modifies system settings, such as memory cache sizes and thread pools, to best optimize the software for the use you specify. Therefore, even if you check the POP3 only checkbox, users can still use Microsoft Outlook, the Exchange client, or other types of MAPI or Internet client applications. The server will simply be tuned for a user population consisting primarily of POP3 clients and may not offer the best performance if the server is instead used to host a large number of other client application types.

Similarly, choosing to leave the POP3 only checkbox unchecked does not prevent users from using POP3 client applications against their mailboxes, provided POP3 protocol access is enabled in the Exchange Server Administrator program.

Upgrading the Key Management Server

Upgrading the KM server is an easy, painless experience. See Chapter 21, "Exchange Messaging Security with Key Management Server."

Installing Version 4.0 Servers After Upgrading to Version 5.0

Many organizations have decentralized IT departments. Commonly, one IT group within the company may begin upgrading its Exchange servers to version 5.0 while another group is still installing new version 4.0 Exchange servers at another location.

> **WARNING**
>
> Due to the extensive directory service schema modifications made by the version 5.0 Exchange Server Setup program to support the new 5.0 functionality, the version 4.0 Exchange Server Setup program will no longer work properly once a version 5.0 Exchange server has been added to the site.

Compatibility If for some reason you need to continue to install version 4.0 servers into an Exchange Server site after you have introduced a version 5.0 server, you need to create your own special version 4.0 Exchange Server setup network file share. The setup.exe file that came on the version 4.0 CD should be replaced with the version provided in the Support\Exch40*<platform>* directory on the Exchange Server 5.0 CD. Because CD-ROMs are, obviously, read-only, you need to copy the contents of the Setup*<platform>* directory from the version 4.0 CD to a file server share. Next, replace the setup.exe file with the one from the proper location in the Support directory on the version 5.0 compact disc, and either install subsequent version 4.0 Exchange Servers directly from that file server or burn yourself a new version 4.0 compact disc.

Summary

This chapter covered upgrading your version 4.0 Exchange Server organization to version 5.0. You learned that although not a strict requirement, it is recommended that you first upgrade all your Exchange Server machines to Windows NT Server version 4.0 with service pack #3 before you begin.

The most important point this chapter made is that you should make sure that all your existing version 4.0 Exchange servers have been updated to at least Exchange Server service pack #2 level before you upgrade the first 4.0 server to version 5.0. Otherwise, problems could occur.

After this, you can proceed with updating servers and clients to version 5.0 independently and at your own pace. Be sure, however, to make backups of your server databases before you upgrade, just in case. Also, remember that once you upgrade a server to version 5.0, there is no going back.

Lastly, you learned that you must use a new setup.exe provided with version 5.0 for installing version 4.0 servers if you want to continue to install version 4.0 servers after you've added even one version 5.0 server to an Exchange Server site.

Microsoft Exchange Server version 5.0 is a powerful and functional upgrade to version 4.0. Upgrading to version 5.0 should be a relatively simple and painless operation if you pay attention to the small number of gotchas discussed in this chapter.

Exchange Server and the Internet

by Paul Garner

IN THIS CHAPTER

CHAPTER 9

People, including people inside Microsoft, often say that the Internet took Microsoft by surprise. The release of Exchange Server 5.0 is one example of the fact that once the company had quickly recovered from its state of surprise, it took support for the Internet completely to heart. The new generation Exchange Server talks to the Internet as a native.

New to Version 5.0

The new Internet protocol support is the most significant set of changes between Exchange 4.0 and 5.0. Whether you are new to Exchange or have been running an existing 4.0 system and are upgrading to 5.0, you can now think of it as the center of a communications infrastructure that extends beyond the limits of your organization. This chapter will help you understand these new capabilities and plan to deploy them effectively.

This chapter does not go into detail on the protocols themselves; you can get that information from reading specialist books or the relevant Internet RFCs (Requests For Comments), which are the documents describing the standards for the Internet protocols and content formats. Table 9.2 (at the end of this chapter) provides references for these RFCs. By the time you reach that table, you will be able to plan to deploy these new features and understand the following:

- The caveats and issues associated with each protocol
- How to use Exchange Internet protocols internally
- How to use Exchange to communicate with Internet users
- How to use Exchange to communicate across the Internet with other organizations

Why Is Internet Support So Darned Important?

When you think about it, the main goal of Exchange Server is to enable communication between individuals and groups. Over the last two to three years, the main electronic one-to-one, one-to-many, or group communications mechanism outside of business organizations has become the Internet. Of course it has been around a lot longer than that—since the '70s in fact—but it is only with the creation of the World Wide Web and the ability to access visually exciting high-quality information over the Internet and publish that information easily that its usage has grown dramatically. Other factors have played a significant part. Government-sponsored and private-sector investment in the primary communications infrastructure on which the Internet runs has multiplied. At the same time, the cost of effective bandwidth to the end-user has dropped dramatically—both equipment costs and connection costs. The net (no pun intended) effect is that the number of people connected to the Internet and using it as a primary source of communication has rocketed upwards. At the end of 1996, there were in the region of 500,000 registered domain names on the Internet and an estimated more than 25 million people using it. With this critical mass, no organization can afford to ignore the benefits of being connected, and in order for that connection to be effective, it can't ignore the need for the tools that it uses internally to be seamlessly integrated.

So, you could say that it's obvious that the ability to talk Internet protocols and handle the prevalent content formats used on the Internet is essential for anyone planning to deploy an electronic communications infrastructure. Without that ability, communication with the majority of people outside their organizations is essentially cut off, and the flexibility of access within them is greatly limited. Simply put, it was essential for Microsoft to change Exchange Server into a system that natively supports Internet standards.

It takes more than external communications to make Internet protocol support important, though. As people develop other applications, whether they target people who are directly connected to the Internet or applications within organizations, their communications are likely to be based on Internet protocols. So, Internet protocol support is not only important for communication with people outside the organization over the Internet network, but it is also important inside the organization to give you the flexibility to support other standards-based communication applications. Good examples are intranet Web applications. These are applications built using Web servers and accessed with Web browser clients. They have some advantages over more traditional networked applications, because they can be more straightforward to develop and concentrate their code on the server. For the most part, therefore, they are easier to manage. Because of the new Web support in Exchange 5.0, you can now build Web applications that make use of information stored in Exchange Server and update it dynamically.

Many of the categories of electronic communication that Exchange has made available to business users also have their parallels in the world of Internet communications. By making Exchange natively support the Internet protocols and content formats on which those same classes of application rely out on the Internet, Microsoft has enabled seamless communication of information between users of those applications—internally and externally. My use of the term "natively" is important here. I mean that the server itself supports those protocols and formats directly. You do not need to configure, manage, and support gateways, the separate applications that convert the native protocol and format into the equivalent on the Internet.

Let's be specific: What are the categories of communication I am talking about here? The following sections present this list.

E-Mail

The main application in Exchange Server 4.0 was messaging. Its goal in life was to be a great messaging server for business use, and this was—and still is—the reason most people deploy it.

On the Internet, the SMTP protocol is the standard for message transfer between computers, and POP3 is the protocol that client applications now use to retrieve messages from mailboxes. Exchange has always provided an Internet Mail Connector that enables it to interact with SMTP systems. Now in Exchange 5.0, it adds native POP3 support so the same clients that you use to retrieve mail from Internet mailboxes can be used against mailboxes on an Exchange server. The SMTP support has also been redesigned so it is part of the core set of Exchange services, providing greater performance and flexibility.

Discussion

On the Internet, a number of technologies for group discussion have evolved. The primary one is now Usenet, which is supported by a protocol called NNTP. Again, Exchange Server 4.0 provided good group discussion capabilities in public folders. People could set up discussion folders in Exchange and read and post items to those shared folders, but there was no way of integrating those discussion groups with those out on the Internet. You had to treat them completely separately.

Exchange 5.0 now provides an NNTP newsfeed facility, which allows postings in public folder discussions to be replicated to the Internet and vice versa. You can post a message from your Exchange client into a folder, and it will appear in the corresponding newsgroup on the Internet. You can also use NNTP newsreaders to access discussions held in Exchange.

In addition to this, the Web support in Exchange 5.0 allows you to interact with those same discussions from your Web browser and incorporate them as part of a Web site.

Directory Lookup

The Internet has no single directory of users—if it did, it would be a big one. Rather, a model is developing where individual organizations can publish their directory to the Net and you can query those directories with a client that supports the LDAP protocol. Exchange Server has always provided a directory in which, among other things, the users of the system are registered. Its support for the LDAP protocol means that you can publish that directory to the Internet if you want, or use LDAP-compliant clients inside your network.

Calendaring–Group Scheduling

The other key area where Exchange has always been a market leader in terms of functionality is group scheduling. Exchange makes it very easy for people to schedule their time in a group, arrange meetings, and organize resources. There are currently no Internet standards for scheduling protocols or information formats, but Microsoft is actively working with the Internet key standards body—the IETF (Internet Engineering Task Force)—and other vendors to create the standard scheduling protocol of the future.

Later in the chapter, you will go into more depth on each of these and see how you can make use of the integration in Exchange 5.0. I've included the relevant Internet standards documentation references at the end of the chapter so you can get details of exactly how each of them works.

Planning to Use Internet Protocols

As with any other aspect of deploying Exchange for messaging and information sharing in your organization, the use of the native Internet protocol support requires some planning and preparation. Your chances of successfully building a robust, secure system that meets the requirements that your users put on it improve if you decide what you want to do beforehand and work out the steps to get there. If you are planning to use the Internet protocol support in Exchange, you will need to do the following:

1. If you are not already running TCP/IP on your network, establish where you will need it in order to do what you want and deploy it. It is required to run this set of protocols. If you are just going to need SMTP connectivity, the only place you'll need to worry about it is on the server connecting with SMTP to the Internet. If all people in the organization need to connect to their mailboxes using POP3, you need it just about everywhere.

2. You'll probably want to establish a policy for what kinds of information in your system is going to be accessible using which protocols and where it will be accessible from: internally only or from out on the Internet. This will help guide your plan.

3. Decide what protocols will be used for what and by whom. Each protocol can be enabled or disabled, not only across an Exchange site, or for particular servers, but for individual users as well.

4. If you do not already have an Internet connection, work out how you'll need to be connected to meet your requirements.

5. Decide for each protocol (except POP3, where it doesn't make sense) whether to allow anonymous access.

Authentication and Anonymous Access

The concept of anonymous access is new in Exchange Server 5.0, and it is critical to its use on the Internet. Normally, in order to use Exchange, you have to be known to the system and logged on to a Windows NT account that is associated with your Exchange identity. Your Exchange identity is your entry in the Exchange directory. Using this mechanism, Exchange can check your rights to access individual mailboxes and folders in the system.

This doesn't work well, though, if you want to make information in your Exchange system available to people out on the Internet. First, you don't necessarily know who they are, and they are not all in your directory. Second, they have no way of logging on to a Windows NT account in order to be authenticated with an identity. You still want to be able to grant them access to selected resources in your system though, which you do by granting permissions to the built-in Anonymous account (see Figure 9.1).

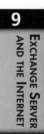

An *anonymous user* is simply someone whose identity the Exchange server doesn't know. Either they have no identity in the system, or they are not authenticated with a particular identity. When a nonauthenticated request comes into an Exchange server with one of the Internet protocols, the server checks the permissions of the anonymous account on the requested resource before making it available.

The LDAP, HTTP, and NNTP protocols supported in Exchange 5.0 allow controlled access by anonymous users.

FIGURE 9.1.

Permissions on a folder can be granted to an identity called Anonymous.

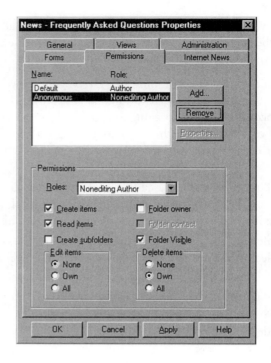

These protocols also allow users to be authenticated with the system. This allows users who have mailboxes on the system to be authenticated and given access to the same resources that they would have with the Exchange clients through their browser or news reader. It also allows you to provide other users on your network who don't have mailboxes controlled access to information in the system. You can create a custom recipient object for all those who need access. This gives them an identity with Exchange, and they can be given explicit permissions to access folders and to access the directory with LDAP. In order to allow them to be authenticated on the system, you need to associate their NT account with the custom recipient object in the directory that represents them. Once you have done this, you can explicitly control which protocols they can use (see Figure 9.2).

FIGURE 9.2.

The Protocols property page on a Custom recipient object.

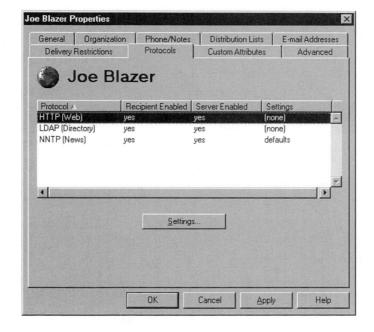

Support for Internet Standards in Exchange Server 5.0

Standards

In addition to supporting the same set of protocols as Exchange Server version 4.0, Exchange 5.0 adds support for all the significant Internet standards used for those application classes that were mentioned previously. It also adds some enhancements to the original set of protocols (see Figure 9.3):

- POP3
- NNTP
- HTTP
- SSL
- LDAP
- MIME

FIGURE 9.3.
Exchange protocol support architecture.

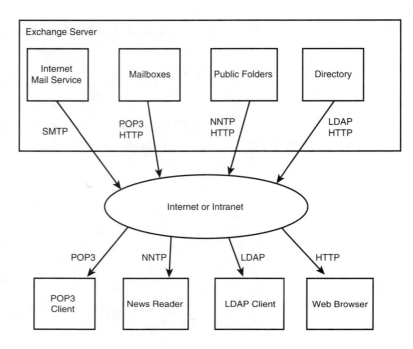

Using POP3 to Access Mailboxes

POP3 (Post Office Protocol 3) is the current Internet protocol that provides users with access to messages stored in their mailboxes. Most mailboxes on the Internet itself are POP3 mailboxes. If you get a personal Internet account with an ISP (Internet Service Provider), the mailbox that your ISP will provide for you will likely be on a POP3 server, and you'll use a POP3 client to access it.

Now, with Exchange 5.0 onward, you can log on to your Exchange mailbox and retrieve messages using any POP3 client, provided that POP3 access has been enabled for your mailbox on the server.

This is extremely useful in a number of situations. However, if you or your users are going to use this feature, you should be sure that you (and they) understand what you get out of it and what you don't. By the time you've read this section, you should have a clear picture of the situations where it is particularly appropriate and what the trade-offs are. Have a hit list of the things to plan in order for POP3 to work well.

Why Use POP3?

Here are a few of the scenarios in which POP3 access is particularly useful:

- You want to support remote or traveling users.
- There are users in your organization who can't run full Exchange clients.
- You want to provide mailboxes for users outside your organization.

POP3 conveniently adds another option for providing remote users with access to mail. A remote user could be someone who is simply traveling or someone who works in a remote location—a regional account rep for instance. You can always support direct dial-up access using RAS, but using POP3 allows you to avoid long distance telephone call costs by providing a local ISP connection for users. They then use the Internet to connect to their mailbox with a local call.

> **NOTE**
>
> There are other opportunities for remote users to connect to Exchange via the Internet:
> - Using PPTP
> - Connecting Exchange clients directly as if they are on a local network
>
> Windows NT 4.0 makes available the option of using PPTP (Point-To-Point Tunneling Protocol) to connect using dial-up to a local Internet access point and then across the Internet to the corporate network. PPTP provides a secure remote connection to your network across the Internet. Users can dial into an ISP that supports PPTP, and their connection is securely tunneled to a server behind the firewall on the corporate LAN. Remote users then get the benefits of full RAS use with a local call to their ISP, rather than a costly direct long distance connection.
>
> You can also, of course, connect an Exchange or Outlook client directly across the Internet to an Exchange server. Many companies however, won't want to place their Exchange servers unprotected on the Internet (see the section later on in this chapter titled "Connecting Exchange Server to the Internet") and will put them behind a firewall. This causes a problem, because while an Exchange client connects to the server via RPC on port 135, the client's connections to the Store and Directory service are made through dynamically assigned ports after the initial port 135 connection is made. Because the firewall needs to be configured to expose particular ports, randomly assigned ports don't work across the firewall. There is a article in the Knowledge Base on `Microsoft.com` that explains how to set values in the NT Registry to force Exchange to use known ports for the clients' store and directory service connections.

In the second scenario, POP3 provides users who can't run Exchange clients with access to Exchange mailboxes. These users may be running UNIX workstations or X terminals, for which there is no native Exchange client. You would likely have to supply these users with a separate PC just for access to mail (although that might be desirable for other application standardization reasons) or maintain a separate mail system for them with a gateway into Exchange.

Finally, a common situation is one in which people inside your organization need to work closely with people externally, and they want to be able to send them mail. If they don't have their own mail system, you can provide them with an internal mailbox and allow them to connect over the Internet using POP3.

Understanding the Trade-Offs

Most good POP3 clients allow you to download messages to the client for filing in storage on the client machine. POP3 doesn't support the manipulation of message storage on the server, so you are limited to dealing with the messages in the Inbox folder on your Exchange mailbox. You can't access other folders in your mailbox, and you can't move messages between folders on the server. This is probably not much of an issue if you use a POP3 client all the time—you just manage your mail folders on your client machine. If you mix your client usage (running Outlook on your desktop while in the office and running the Internet Explorer mail or Netscape's POP3 client on your laptop machine to access your mailbox while you are out of the office), you have to be careful that you don't lose track of where your mail is. Most POP3 clients, certainly Microsoft's Internet Explorer mail client and Netscape Navigator, allow you to leave messages on the server rather than deleting them when you download them. It's advisable to make use of this option to make sure that messages are still available to your desktop client when you are back in the office.

Conversely, consider carefully the use of rules for managing your inbox if you are going to do this. If you set up Inbox Assistant rules in your Exchange client to move messages to folders in your server mailbox, remember that you won't then be able to access those messages that have been moved from your POP3 client.

Before Deploying POP3

When planning your POP3 service as an administrator of the system, there are some things you should consider before you set it up. These will allow you to both maintain a secure environment and make sure that users can make the most effective use of the system:

- Which users need POP3 access?
- How will they authenticate with Exchange?
- Which IMCs will they connect to for outgoing mail?
- How will you handle account and mailbox naming?
- What are the message format support requirements?

With Exchange, you can enable POP3 access for everyone who has a mailbox in your site, or you can restrict access to specific mailboxes (see Figure 9.4). Clearly, if keeping the tightest possible security is a concern, it is good to limit POP3 access to just those users that need it. There are two ways of doing this. The first option makes a lot of sense if you have specific users at a particular location who need to get at their mailboxes using POP3. You can concentrate those users on a particular server and enable POP3 access to all the mailboxes on just that server, leaving it disabled on all other servers. If you create a mailbox on the POP3-enabled server, it will be automatically accessible to POP3 clients. This means that it is easy to manage who has POP3 access and who doesn't. Of course, you can switch POP3 access to any individual mailbox on and off from the protocols tab on the mailbox property sheet in the Exchange Administrator Program if you want finer granularity of control.

FIGURE 9.4.

A POP3 client connected to an Exchange Server mailbox.

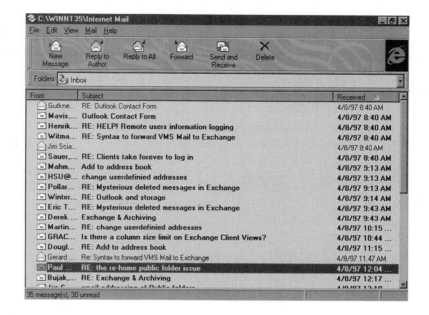

When it comes to deciding what authentication mechanism to use, you have two options. If your users will be connecting from machines that are logged on to their NT domain, you can specify that NT challenge/response authentication is to be used, and Basic Authentication will not be accepted. This is more secure because you don't have clear text-user credentials flying around the network—although, in most cases, it is only suitable for access within your intranet. For other situations—when the user is connecting over the Internet, or from an operating system that can't participate in the NT authentication mechanism—you need to enable Basic Authentication. Both authentication schemes can be made more secure by using SSL to encrypt the data that is traversing the net. **Security**

There are two caveats to this. The first is that not all POP3 clients support SSL. In fact, at the time of this writing, few do. You need to check, and be specific about which clients you will support if you are going to do this. The second is that in order to provide SSL, you need to set up Microsoft Internet Information Server on the Exchange server machine to manage the keys. There is considerable effort involved in acquiring, installing, and managing certificates for any significant number of users.

Configuring the Exchange server containing the mailboxes to interact with POP3 clients is just half the story. POP3 clients read mail from a mailbox using POP3, but to send outgoing mail, they connect to an SMTP server. So, in order for your POP3 users to be able to send mail, you configure at least one IMS. (IMS, or Internet Mail Service, is the name for the new version of the Internet Mail Connector, IMC, in Exchange 5.0). You need at least one of these for each physical network on which you have POP3-accessible mailboxes. For the sake of simplicity here, let's assume just one IMS, although the principles are the same as you scale up.

9

EXCHANGE SERVER AND THE INTERNET

The IMS that you use for POP3 client access can be either your main IMS for general traffic to and from the Internet or a separate one configured for POP3 usage. Whichever you choose, it clearly has to be available to the locations from which POP3 users will be connecting.

An IMS can be configured to reroute messages that are submitted to it with SMTP back out again. This is its default configuration. You can switch this off to reduce the risk of spoofing. Incoming SMTP messages can then be routed only to Exchange mailboxes. However, it must be on if the POP3 clients that connect to it are to be able to send mail to recipients across the Internet (see Figure 9.5).

FIGURE 9.5.

A POP3 client connects to IMS to submit messages.

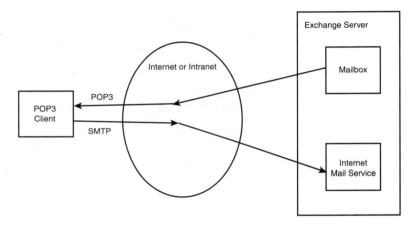

Compatibility

Next, consider your naming conventions carefully. One of the main reasons that it is important to plan for POP3 access before deploying your Exchange system is the relationship between NT account names and mailbox names. Many POP3 clients require these names to be the same. The Microsoft Internet Explorer mail client, for instance, requires that the mailbox name is the same as the NT account name if NT challenge/response authentication is being used. The Eudora POP3 client always requires them to be the same. This clearly limits the flexibility you have in mailbox naming or the choice of POP3 clients you can allow to connect to the system.

Finally, you need to think about the content formats and character sets you will support. In most cases, the decision over the defaults is easy, especially if you have a policy for which POP3 clients you will support and if you are operating in a single country. In most cases, you can select your default content type support for the Exchange site and there will be few exceptions. The exceptions can be dealt with by overriding the site defaults in the mailbox property sheet in the Exchange administrator program.

After POP3

Over the next year or two, POP3 will be superseded by a new, richer Internet protocol for mailbox access called IMAP4. However, for now, POP3 has the job.

Using NNTP for Discussion Groups

New to
Version 5.0

NNTP (Network News Transport Protocol) is the protocol that supports group discussion. *Newsgroups* are the places where these discussions take place. They are commonly referred to as *USENET newsgroups* on the Internet, where they have proliferated; there are currently more than 10,000 of them. They are used for discussions on everything from Shakespeare (`humanities.lit.authors.shakespear`), to investing in the Far East (`misc.invest.stocks`), to cookie making (`alt.cooking-chat`). Between these, there are many useful, relevant topics where there is fruitful discussion. To be clear about the terminology, in common use, the term *Usenet* refers to the set of public newsgroups that are maintained on the Internet. From here on, I'm going to refer to them as just *newsgroups*—partly for brevity, and partly because I want to include newsgroups that you can set up in your own organization or place on the Internet outside of the Usenet name space.

By the time you have read this section of the chapter, you should have a clear understanding of the support that Exchange 5.0 has for newsreader clients and for newsfeeds to and from news servers across the Internet.

NNTP Basics

Figure 9.6 shows how NNTP works. You can interact with a newsgroup by connecting a client application called a *newsreader* across the network to a *news server* that hosts a set of newsgroups. Once you have a newsreader, in order to be able to access a newsgroup all you need to know is the name of a news server on which it is hosted. You must be able to connect to that news server and have permissions to access it.

FIGURE 9.6.

Client access using NNTP.

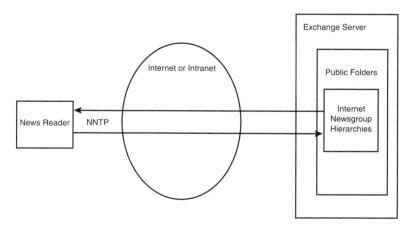

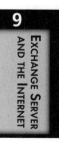

9

EXCHANGE SERVER
AND THE INTERNET

Newsgroups are often replicated between news servers using a process known as a *newsfeed*. This means that popular Usenet newsgroups can be hosted by many servers, in many places on the Internet. This distributes the load and may provide users with access to a local server, which in turn may reduce noticeable network latency.

This mechanism is particularly useful to organizations that set up news servers that serve a particular user constituency, a group with common interest. In addition to hosting their own newsgroups, they can replicate other relevant newsgroups in a single place, and their users need to access only a single server to be involved in any of the discussions. For instance, an organization serving the pharmaceutical industry may set up a news server that takes a newsfeed from other servers on the Internet, replicating in all the relevant discussions on pharmaceutical research. Their users know that they just have to connect to that one server to get all of the newsgroups they want.

NOTE

News as referred to here has nothing to do with today's headlines that you might get from a service, such as Knight-Ridder, or Web sites, such as MSNBC or CNN Online. A service such as Reuters, Knight-Ridder, or the services provided by companies such as Desktop Data provide published news rather than serve up discussions. The newsfeeds referred to here are NNTP newsfeeds and are used to distribute the contents of discussions from one server to another. The NNTP protocol, Usenet, and its associated terminology originated at Duke University in 1979, where it was used by faculty, staff, and students to publish information, post announcements, and so forth.

Once you've connected to a news server with your newsreader and obtained the list of newsgroups on that server, you can subscribe to any of the newsgroups that you have permissions to access. (Most of the public newsgroups don't restrict access, but many special interest or company-specific newsgroups may do so.) If you've subscribed, your newsreader will store away a pointer to that newsgroup for quick reference. When you connect to the newsgroup, your newsreader will download and display the headers of the messages that are in that group. Then each subsequent time you connect to the group, it will download headers of any new postings. Typically, the content of the posting remains on the server until you request it. If you select a message to read, the newsreader will download the content of the message and cache it on your computer. A typical newsreader also tracks for you which messages you have read and can show you just those that you haven't yet read.

The common newsreader clients present discussions in a threaded format. The first message in a thread is displayed, and below it, usually in a collapsible tree, are the messages that people have posted in response. Any newsreader worth its salt will display the threads sorted by the time of the last response in the thread (see Figure 9.7).

In order to keep the size of newsgroups manageable, news servers typically allow you to set an expiration time on a newsgroup. Posts that are made to the newsgroup are kept on the server for the designated expiration period and then deleted. Busy newsgroups can grow in size rapidly, and without this feature, people subscribing to the newsgroup would be faced with a long download of lots of old headers when they first join. The expiration time should be set according to the level of activity in the newsgroup and the extent to which information is relevant.

If users download headers from the server with their newsreaders and then leave them for a while, when they select an item to read they may be presented with a message saying that the posting is no longer on the server.

FIGURE 9.7.

A newsreader connected to an Exchange server.

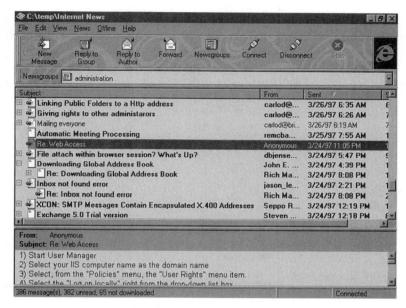

So that, in a nutshell, is the interaction between the newsreader client and the news server. To complete the NNTP story though, you should learn how the news servers communicate among each other to replicate the contents of the discussion among them.

Pull Newsfeeds and Push Newsfeeds

News servers provide the storage for newsgroups and can distribute the postings to other servers. This is done using a replication mechanism known as a *newsfeed*.

There are two kinds of newsfeed: You can set up a *pull newsfeed* on a server to monitor a newsgroup on another server. When a new post is made to the newsgroup on the monitored server, the first server picks it up during its next poll. Hence the term *pull*. Likewise, when a post is made to the server on which the newsfeed is configured, it will in turn post the item to the newsgroup on the other server (see Figure 9.8).

Push newsfeeds are typically more efficient. They don't require one server to poll the other server to find out whether there are new items to download. They do however, take more coordination to configure, as they have to be set up on both servers. In this case, the only action that the newsfeed carries out is when a new posting is made to a newsgroup on that server. The newsfeed picks it up and posts it to the other servers it is feeding (see Figure 9.9).

9

EXCHANGE SERVER
AND THE INTERNET

FIGURE **9.8.**

A pull newsfeed.

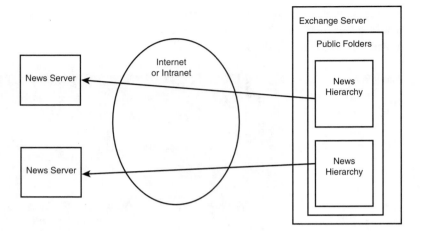

FIGURE **9.9.**

A push newsfeed.

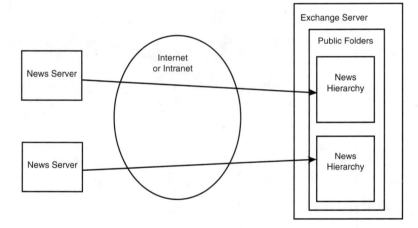

Which newsfeed mechanism you choose will depend greatly on what you are doing. Here are some rough guidelines:

■ If you want to bring in copies of Usenet newsgroups and host them in Exchange for your users, you can make an arrangement with an ISP who has instances of those groups on a server to set up a push feed from their server.

■ If, on the other hand, you just want a small number of newsfeeds replicated from specific servers on the Internet, you can set up a pull newsfeed on your server to do all the work. You might want to do this, for instance, to pull down Exchange specific newsgroups from the server `msnews.microsoft.com`.

■ For internal use, for distributing discussion content that originates within your organization to different locations, it is much easier to use public folder replication if you are using Exchange server in each location.

A wizard in the Exchange Administrator program helps with configuring newsfeeds. The wizard can be invoked from the File | New Other menu (see Figure 9.10).

FIGURE 9.10.

The Exchange Administrator Newsfeed configuration wizard.

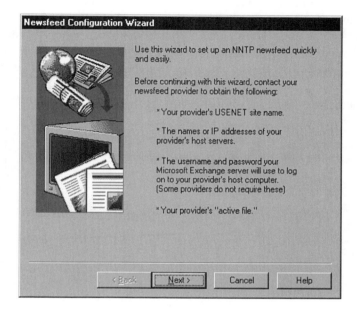

Running Exchange Server 5.0 as a News Server

You can deploy news capabilities using Exchange in a number of ways. It's worth going through them in some detail so you have a grasp of what is possible. Let's do that first, and then look at the key things you have to consider when planning to deploy newsreader access to Exchange.

The first approach is simply to say hey, I have all these other mechanisms to access information using Exchange, why do I need NNTP news as well? If that's the case, you can probably skip to the next section without much harm. Before you do, though, you might want to read the first part of this section, which talks about some of the things you can do. It may pique some interest.

On the other hand, you may wish to consider the following scenarios:

Accessing Usenet:

Employees inside your organization can make good use of Usenet newsgroups on topics related to their work. Pharmaceutical researchers, for instance, may gain benefit from access to a newsgroup such as sci.bio.microbiology for discussions on bacterial growth patterns. Rather than provide them with unrestricted access to the Internet from your corporate network, you take a newsfeed from those groups that are relevant into folders in Exchange. Your users can then access those newsgroups, using their Exchange or Outlook clients (see Figure 9.11) or NNTP newsreaders inside your network. They can make postings, which in turn can be replicated out to the Internet copy of the newsgroup if the Exchange server is so configured. Because the news items are fed into folders, the owner of the newsgroup folder has the opportunity to control who has access to the information internally and whether they can post items into the newsgroup. Internet fans are well known for their opinions on freedom of access, so to many Internet purists this kind of control would be abhorrent. However, if this kind of selective access facility allows users to make use of Internet newsgroups that company policy would otherwise exclude them from, it can be argued that it is a good thing.

FIGURE 9.11.

An NNTP newsfeed from the Internet accessed by Exchange clients.

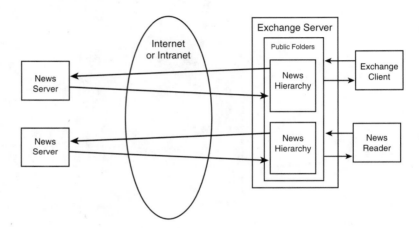

Of course, in addition to using access control on the folder to restrict users from posting to newsgroups, it is also possible to configure the newsfeed to be an incoming-only newsfeed. By setting up the news service this way, you can allow internal users to comment on the information coming in from the newsgroup among themselves in the same folder, and the postings will not be propagated out to the Internet.

So, taking newsfeeds from out on the Internet is one possibility. Another is to use NNTP as a publishing mechanism.

During migration:

Often if you are migrating your organization from one or more other messaging systems to Exchange, there will likely be some period of time during which some users are not using Exchange. Those users who haven't yet been migrated to Exchange can't participate in Exchange-based discussions. You may have people in your organization who are not Exchange users and will not be any time soon. Perhaps you have users running on UNIX workstations, for instance, for which there is no native Exchange client. You can provide them with access to discussions using NNTP. If those users have a newsreader configured on their workstation, however, they can connect to the server containing the published discussions and participate in those discussions.

Interacting with people outside your organization:

Suppose you want to provide your customers with an opportunity to interact with each other. Your goal is to enable them to help each other to use your products effectively, and at the same time reduce the support burden on your staff. One way of doing this is to put a product-specific newsgroup on the Internet, hosted on your Exchange servers, and allow people to use it to converse. It is easy for your staff to monitor and contribute to the newsgroup, but you get the benefit of enabling peer support among your customers (see Figure 9.12).

FIGURE 9.12.

A customer peer support scenario using Exchange Server's NNTP support.

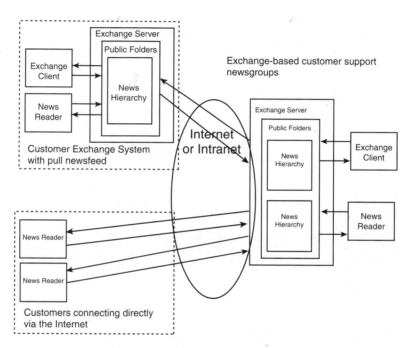

Not possible with NNTP today is publishing the content created by Exchange or Outlook custom forms. There is a fixed set of fields handled by NNTP, so the additional properties that are on the items created by the custom forms are not displayed to newsreader users.

Planning an NNTP Deployment

Exchange Server gives you a lot of control over deployment of NNTP newsgroups. You need to plan for the following:

- Which folders are accessible as newsgroups?
- On which servers are they accessible?
- Who owns the folders and controls access to them?
- Who can access individual newsgroups?

- How will you handle moderation of specific newsgroups?
- Will newsfeeds replicate both in and out of your folders, or just inbound?

Responsibility for the configuration of NNTP access is split between the Exchange administrator and the owners of the folders hosting the newsgroups. As an administrator, you get to select which servers can serve the NNTP protocol to newsreaders and which trees in their public folder hierarchy are accessible to newsreaders. Once you have specified a particular folder tree as an Internet News tree, you can delegate ownership of folders in the tree to other people in your organization.

The owners of folders within the Internet news hierarchies you have created can control, from the folders' property pages in the Exchange or Outlook clients, whether an individual folder within the hierarchy is exposed to NNTP newsreaders and who has permissions to access it. They can grant permissions to individuals, groups, or anonymous users to read from or post to the folder.

As the owner of a folder, being used as a newsgroup, if users want to exercise editorial control over the content of the discussion, they can set up the folder that hosts the discussion as a moderated folder. They simply set the moderation configuration in the property sheet on the folder and assign one or more moderators to select the postings that get published to other participants in the newsgroup. See Chapter 24, "Public Folders," for details of how to configure public folders.

> **NOTE**
>
> An Exchange server that is being used to provide NNTP access to newsreaders has to have a replica of each folder that it offers in its public store. If you create a folder in a tree that is designated an Internet News hierarchy, it will be created on the home public server of the user that created it, not necessarily on the server on which the root of the Internet news hierarchy was created. It will be accessible only if the server that it is created on has NNTP access enabled, or if a replica is created on a news server by an administrator. It is worth planning this carefully, because it can lead to confusion if people create folders in an Internet News hierarchy and expect them to be published without regard to which server they are located on physically.

HTTP—The Exchange Web Client

Now, this is where things really start to heat up in terms of new features in Exchange 5.0 for Internet protocol support. One of the major innovations in Exchange 5.0 is integration with the World Wide Web. The Web has really been the driving force behind the huge growth in the use of the Internet over the last few years. Its key feature, and the main reason for this growth in usage, is the flexible graphical user interface it allows you to present across many different client platforms.

Exchange Server 5.0's Web support provides the following features:

■ Users can access their mailboxes from their Web browser. They can browse their personal folders, read their mail, and send mail and responses. They can access public folders to read and post items, and they can browse the directory.

■ External users who don't have Exchange mailboxes can have authenticated access to public folders and the directory from a Web browser.

■ Anonymous users can have access to some public folders and can search for entries in the directory.

■ You can set up a Web site that hosts discussions using Exchange public folders to host them, or you can use Exchange to enable dynamic interactive Web content to be managed easily. See Chapter 32, "Exchange Server as Part of the Active Server Platform," for details of this.

By way of comparison with the other Internet protocols, the HTTP support in Exchange allows you to access the same features on your Exchange Server as the combination of a POP3 client, a newsreader, and an LDAP directory client—all from your Web browser (see Figure 9.13). It provides access to mailboxes, public folders, and the directory and also provides access to schedule information in the next release. You can use your browser to send mail and post messages to discussions in folders, or you can look up details in the directory.

FIGURE 9.13.

An Exchange mailbox accessed using a Web browser.

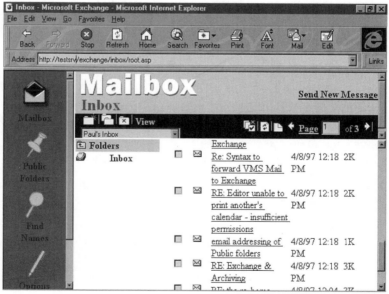

As with the other protocols you, the administrator, are in control of whether, and how, clients can access your system with HTTP. And as with NNTP and LDAP, you can restrict access to authenticated users who must log on with their user identity in order to get at any information in Exchange, or you can provide anonymous users with access to some information in the Exchange directory and public folders.

How HTTP Support in Exchange Works

Very briefly, let's look at the important concepts in HTTP and the related technologies that make up the Web.

The combination of two related standards makes the Web work—the HTTP protocol and the HTML standard for content format. (These acronyms stand for HyperText Transfer Protocol and HyperText Markup Language, respectively.) A Web server, such as Microsoft's Internet Information Server, sitting on the Internet or on your intranet, serves up the HTML content to the client browser using the HTTP protocol.

An HTTP request from a browser will typically reference the Web page that it wants the server to return in the response. The response that the server sends back contains the HTML content that the browser displays. The HTML contains the format information that the browser uses to create the page, plus references to other files containing graphics or HTML pages that the browser then requests from the server separately. The references to the HTML pages and graphics files in the requests use a format called *Uniform Resource Locator (URL)*.

Your Web browser is the most likely place you will use URLs. You use them all the time to reference locations on the Internet or your intranet. A URL to the Exchange logon will likely look something like the following:

```
{HYPERLINK http://AcctsSvr/Exchange/pf/
peerfldr.asp?obj=000000007A5765F76A59B053900F14D663 }
```

The URL specifies the Web server that contains the Exchange Active Server Components that are in a virtual root called Exchange. When a user traverses through the folder hierarchy to a particular folder, the URL to the page that displays it will look something like this:

```
{HYPERLINK http://AcctsSvr/Exchange/pf/
peerfldr.asp?obj=000000007A5765F76A59B053900F14D663 }
```

Users can bookmark URLs to specific folders in their browser and use them to go straight to the folder they want.

The HTML pages that are referenced by URLs in requests from the browser can also contain scripts and references to executable objects. These scripts and objects can either be executed on the server when the page is requested, to generate the HTML that gets sent back to the client dynamically, or they can be sent to the browser as part of the response and executed by the browser.

The Exchange Web service is made up of a set of scripts that control the connection between IIS and the Exchange server using the Exchange Active Server Component objects and generate the HTML that is sent to the browser (see Figure 9.14).

FIGURE 9.14.

HTTP enables browsers to retrieve HTML from a server.

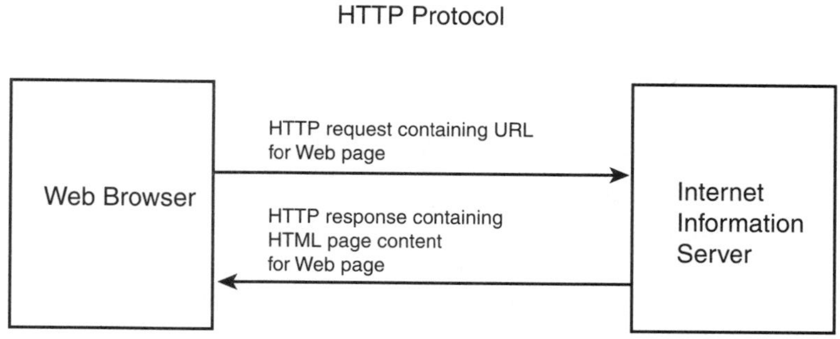

HTTP Protocol

Web Browser

HTTP request containing URL
for Web page

HTTP response containing
HTML page content
for Web page

Internet
Information
Server

Exchange on the Web—Active Server Components

New to
Version 5.0

Although the other Internet protocols that Exchange Server supports are handled directly by the Exchange server processes, primarily the store and the directory service, the HTTP support is handled by Microsoft Internet Information Server (IIS). Rather than serve the protocol directly, Exchange interfaces to IIS through a set of scripts and executable objects that run as part of IIS. These scripts and the object libraries that they use are known as the Exchange Active Server Components. (In the Exchange Server 5.0 beta, this feature was called the Exchange Web Connector. It was changed for the final release to reflect the flexibility of the integration with IIS).

> **TIP**
>
> The scripts are stored in the Exchsrvr\webdata directory on the server—either the Exchange server itself or on the IIS server where you installed the Exchange Active Server Components.

The Exchange user interface that is displayed in the browser is made up of a combination of static HTML, dynamic HTML generated by the scripts on the server, and JavaScript functions that run in the browser to carry out operations such as launching a new browser window when you read a message (see Figure 9.15).

FIGURE 9.15.

The Exchange Active Server components.

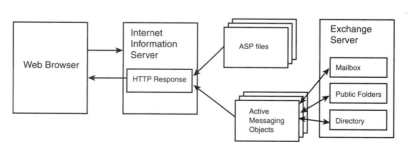

9

EXCHANGE SERVER AND THE INTERNET

When a browser connects to IIS and requests a page that is part of the Exchange Web user interface by specifying its URL in the request, the server runs the script in the requested page. In summary, this is what happens:

1. The script checks the security credentials of the user's browser, and if necessary, a login request is displayed.

2. It connects to Exchange by calling the functions in the Active Messaging library. Remember from the previous discussion on authentication and security that it can either connect to a specific mailbox, or it can connect anonymously and just display the contents of public folders and the directory.

3. The scripts and the Active Messaging object library dynamically create the HTML that shows the content of the mailbox, folder, or message, which is sent back to the browser to be displayed to the user.

NOTE

The fact that the Exchange Web client that you view with your Web browser is essentially a set of scripts that form an Active Server application means that it is incredibly flexible. You change the HTML that it dynamically generates very easily by modifying the scripts, writing new ones, or configuring Web sites using Web development tools such as FrontPage. This means you can use Exchange as the foundation for truly interactive Web sites. To understand the details of this and the things that it enables you to do on the Web, read Chapter 32 after you understand the basics described in this chapter.

Planning Access to Exchange from the Web

Here are the things that you need to consider in order to successfully plan Web access to your Exchange System:

- Which browsers do your users need?
- Which servers should be HTTP servers?
- How will you handle authentication and anonymous access?

To use this service, browsers that support JavaScript 1.1 and frames are needed. Both Microsoft Internet Explorer 3.0a and Netscape Navigator 3.0 or later versions meet the requirements.

Because Exchange uses Internet Information Server to do its HTTP protocol handling, you can use a completely separate machine from your Exchange server to do this work for you. You can choose to locate both Exchange Server and IIS on the same machine or install them on separate machines. When you run Exchange setup, you can elect to install the Exchange Active Server Components. These are the objects and scripts that allow IIS to talk to Exchange and provide HTTP access to Exchange. If you want to co-locate IIS and Exchange, install IIS and run Exchange setup, making sure that you install the Exchange Active Server Components. If you want to use a separate IIS machine, run Exchange setup again on the IIS machine and just install the Active Server Components. The setup process is described in detail in Chapter 12, "Installing Microsoft Exchange Server."

Each of the other Internet protocols can be enabled or disabled at either a site, server, or individual user level in the Exchange administrator program, but because Web access can be run on a separate server to Exchange, there is no capability of manipulating the HTTP protocol configuration at the server level from within the Exchange administrator program. You need to use Internet Information Server Manager to do any configuration tasks for the HTTP protocol at the server level.

> **NOTE**
>
> You'll use NT Server 4.0 with at least Service Pack 2 (SP2) and IIS 3.0 to run the Exchange Web Service. The Exchange server installation procedure checks the version when you run setup and will prompt you if it finds that the required software isn't installed.

For mailbox access from the Web, as opposed to reading public folders or querying the directory only, browser access to the service should be authenticated. At the time of this writing, you can only use Basic Authentication for this, requiring users to enter their logon credentials separately. The credentials are transmitted in clear text unless you set up SSL and specify in the Exchange Administrator that SSL sessions are required.

Later versions of the browsers will solve this problem. You will be able to use NTLM authentication, enabling a Windows client to authenticate in the background using an encrypted NT token obtained from the client machines current NT session. Of course, this will work only if the browsers you are using are running on Windows machines in your NT network. If you need people to be able to connect across the Internet or from machines that are not part of your NT network, you need to keep Basic Authentication enabled as well.

LDAP for Access to the Directory

New to Version 5.0

The Lightweight Directory Access Protocol (LDAP) is the Internet standard protocol for accessing directory information. Because Exchange Server 5.0 now supports access to its directory service using LDAP, you can allow people with LDAP clients to search your organization directory.

Today, a few POP3 clients provide support for querying directories with LDAP, and there are a number of separate LDAP clients that allow you to query a directory for e-mail addresses or telephone numbers.

Without access to your directory in order to be able to send someone in your organization e-mail, people externally have to know their e-mail address beforehand. How many times have you heard things like "What's your e-mail address?" or "I'm calling because I need to send Carol some e-mail and I need to know her e-mail address."

9

EXCHANGE SERVER
AND THE INTERNET

LDAP enables you to do two things: First, if you have users that are running POP3 clients internally rather than Exchange or Outlook clients, it enables those people to be able to access the Exchange directory, which they can't do otherwise. Second, you can publish your directory outside your organization on the Internet so that external people who want to send e-mail to contacts inside your organization can find out the relevant e-mail addresses on their own.

It also has other uses. If you allow them to, people with clients that support LDAP can look up telephone numbers or extensions from your directory or their physical location (see Figure 9.16). Exchange Server 5.0 doesn't support updating the directory using LDAP, although this is planned for an upcoming version.

FIGURE 9.16.

An LDAP client connected to an Exchange Server.

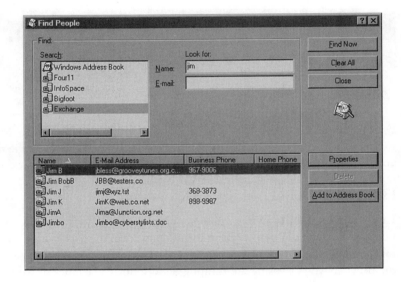

Considerations when Planning to Use LDAP

Clearly, there are many issues to consider when making internal information about your organization more available, and there is planning to do from a technical perspective. Here are the main things to consider when planning to use LDAP for access to your corporate directory:

- Which directory attributes should you publish?
- Do you want to make information public or restrict access to certain known users?
- Which servers on your network will provide the LDAP protocol support?

Each entry in the Exchange directory has a number of attributes associated with it. The name of the individual or entity that the entry represents is one of them; that entity's e-mail address and phone number, office location, and so forth are all likely to be stored as attributes in the directory. Some of this information you'll likely want to make publicly available, and some you won't for security or commercial reasons. In the Exchange Administrator program, you can configure which directory attributes are made available to people browsing or searching the directory anonymously and which attributes are available to authenticated users.

Like the NNTP and HTTP support in Exchange, you can enable non-authenticated users to gain access to the directory. The Enable Anonymous checkbox in the LDAP protocol property page allows you to switch anonymous access on and off. If you enable anonymous access, LDAP clients connecting to the server without authenticating will be able to search the directory on the set of attributes that you have made available to anonymous users (see Figure 9.17).

FIGURE 9.17.

Directory attribute selection in the Exchange Administrator program.

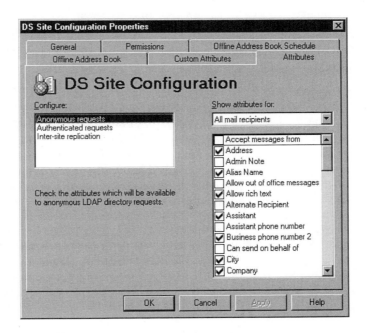

Finally, you can select which servers in your Exchange system will serve the LDAP protocol. Each server has a replica of the complete directory, so any server can make queries against the directory and respond to LDAP requests. How many servers and which ones in particular you'll want to use depends, of course, on what you are doing. If a large percentage of your users use POP3 clients full-time to access their mailboxes and want LDAP access to the directory, you'll probably enable it on all servers. If your primary use of LDAP, on the other hand, is to allow people on the Internet to get in touch with your sales force, you will probably need to have LDAP enabled on only a server that is connected to the Internet.

From a security standpoint, it is good practice to enable LDAP only on the servers that require it.

SSL–Encrypted Connections

SSL stands for Secure Sockets Layer. Sockets is the term for the access points that the high-level Internet protocols, such as POP3 and LDAP, use to manage their connection over the underlying TCP/IP protocol. SSL is used in conjunction with the higher-level protocols to provide them with an encrypted channel over which to transfer their data. This prevents what

9

EXCHANGE SERVER AND THE INTERNET

Security

Security

would otherwise be clear text content from traversing the network and being picked up and viewed by people for whom it isn't intended.

Instead of using their usual IP ports, an alternate SSL port is assigned to each protocol. When they are running on their SSL ports, the protocols work in exactly the same way; they just operate over the secured channel provided by the alternate port. When a protocol makes a socket level connection between a client and a server using its SSL port, a connection is set up so that the client and server can encrypt and decrypt data that is sent across the link. The protocol itself, and the application using the protocol, doesn't see any difference, except that the connection may be marginally slower to set up.

Under the covers, the SSL code does the work. On the client, it generates a random encryption key with which to encrypt the data it sends to the server. It then has to transmit that key to the server so that the server can successfully decrypt the data when it arrives and use the same key to encrypt information it is retuning to the client. In order to do this without compromising the key, the client obtains the server's public key and uses it to encrypt the encryption key it generated. It then transmits the encrypted key to the server. The server is the only machine that can decrypt the key, using the private half of its public/private keypair. Once it has done this, both parties in the connection, the client and the server, are then safely in possession of the key that is used to encrypt and decrypt the session.

The main advantage to application implementers is that SSL is transparent to the application protocol and provides a common encryption mechanism for all the higher-level protocols. The primary use of SSL so far is on the Web to encrypt data to and from secure Web sites. It is, however, also used by some POP3 clients for encrypting the protocol stream containing mailbox data as it traverses the network.

The biggest issue for a protocol using SSL, at least on the Internet rather than your internal network, is how it can trust the server to which it is sending its encryption key. How does it know that the server that it is sending that encrypted data to is the one that is supposed to get it? Before it uses the server's public key to encrypt and send the key, it checks the certificate associated with that key. On the Internet, a *Certificate Authority,* such as VeriSign, should have issued the certificate. If the client has been configured to trust certificates issued by that particular certificate authority, it treats the server as authenticated and trusts its public key.

This means that if you are going to connect your Exchange server to the Internet and use SSL for public access using any of the Internet protocols, you should get a certificate for the server from an Internet certificate authority.

Using SSL with Exchange

Exchange provides a mechanism with which you can use SSL encryption with any of the Internet protocols. You can switch it on and off on a per-protocol basis from each protocol's property page. If you are going to enforce the use of SSL, rather than allow it as an option, you are going to greatly limit the types of client that people can use to access your system. Today, for that very reason, it isn't much use with NNTP. It is of some use with POP3, because there are a few POP3 clients that can use SSL. Its main use will be with HTTP and LDAP, however.

If you want to use SSL with any of the protocols, not just with HTTP, you need to have IIS installed on your server. Exchange makes use of the SSL and key management facilities in IIS. The protocols you will most likely be interested in using SSL with will be HTTP to encrypt the data sent to browsers, POP3 (some POP3 clients do support it), and LDAP. The main reason that you will likely want to use SSL isn't necessarily to encrypt the information sent from Exchange across the network, but to encrypt the plaintext passwords that get transmitted when Basic Authentication is used instead of NTLM. In the case of LDAP, because NTLM authentication is not an option, it is especially important to configure SSL to protect the integrity of the password if you are going to allow authenticated access.

The first time you configure a protocol to use SSL, go into the Key Manager dialog box in the Internet Information Server Manager program, create a key for the server, and associate it with the protocol or protocols for which you want to use it. If you are going to use the protocol for public access on the Internet, you can use the program to request a certificate from a Certificate Authority. Then, once you receive the certificate from the certificate authority, use the Key Manager to install the certificate so that client programs accessing your server know that they can trust it (see Figure 9.18).

FIGURE 9.18.

The Internet Information Server Key Manager.

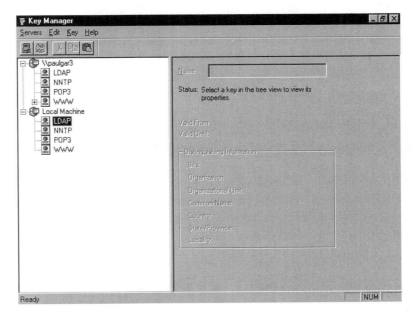

Alternate Ports Used for SSL

If you are going to use SSL to connect to your Exchange system from out on the Internet, and if you have a firewall, you are going to need to know which ports to open. Table 9.1 lists the alternate ports used for SSL.

9

EXCHANGE SERVER
AND THE INTERNET

Table 9.1. Port references.

Protocol	Normal Port	Alternate Port for Use with SSL
POP3	110	995
SMTP	25	465 (Exchange doesn't use Port 465 for secure SMTP, but negotiates SSL sessions on Port 25)
NNTP	119	563
HTTP	80	443
LDAP	389	636

Note that these are the registered port numbers for these protocols over SSL, and registration doesn't necessarily guarantee that all implementations will use them.

Connecting Exchange Server to the Internet

In many ways, the Internet support available in Exchange Server 5.0 is useful just within an organization. It allows people to access information using their Web browser and provides them with the ability to use a variety of different client programs. As I've tried to point out in this chapter, though, Exchange really comes into its own when connected to the Internet. It becomes a conduit for information between your organization and the external world—for messaging, for discussion groups and other public applications, and through the directory access provided by LDAP and the Web client. Moreover, it provides a mechanism for people in your organization to stay in touch from beyond the reach of your own network.

There are two possible situations that you're likely to find yourself in at this point: In the first, your network is already connected to the Internet, and you have an Internet firewall in place. Your focus here will be on how to get the right Exchange traffic through the firewall. In the second, you are not connected to the Internet at all, and you want to get there.

Now, wouldn't it be great if all you had to do was take a cable from your network and plug it into a conveniently placed socket on your machine room wall, the one with a label on it that says "Internet." Unfortunately, connecting to the Internet isn't quite that straightforward, both from a planning perspective and operationally. There are a number of issues to consider up front, plus the ongoing task of making sure that your Internet connection is functioning correctly without compromising the security of your information.

This section of the chapter is intended to give you a feel for the main things to consider when planning to make that connection—and some tips for how to do it. Discussion of how to build effective connections between corporate networks and the Internet is sufficient for a book in itself—probably several. So this section is going to briefly focus on the key issues that you'll want to think about in planning for Exchange.

Dial-Up Connections

You can use a dial-up connection to an ISP that will provide you with an Internet connection for SMTP mail delivery and for access to Usenet newsgroups. This can be your primary connection to the Internet if your mail traffic is light enough, or you can use it as a backup to cover for the case when a permanent connection is out of service.

It used to be difficult to configure this in Exchange Server version 4.0, and it wasn't as reliable as it could be. Fortunately, it has been improved considerably in the 5.0 version and tightly integrated into the Remote Access Service (RAS) in Windows NT that controls the connection. You can configure it all from the New Internet Mail Service Wizard or, for an existing IMS, from its property page in the Exchange Administrator Connections container.

> **NOTE**
>
> Many people ask whether they can connect Exchange Server to their POP3 mailboxes at their ISP—"Since Exchange supports POP3, this should work, right?" Sometimes they want to do this because they don't understand the difference between POP3 and SMTP, and sometimes they ask because it appears to be more cost-effective than getting an SMTP connection. Often, though, it is simply because they want to keep the same e-mail addresses in their new environment.
>
> POP3 is a client protocol for connecting clients to mailboxes, not a server-to-server mail transfer protocol. That is the purpose of SMTP. So there is no mechanism in POP3 for connecting two server mailboxes together and pulling mail from one to the other.
>
> If you want your users to keep their existing mail addresses at your ISP when they move to Exchange, you can do one of two things:
>
> - It is often possible that you can have your mail account at your ISP configured to forward all incoming mail to your Exchange mailbox. People then keep their Internet mailboxes, but only use their Exchange mailboxes to manipulate their messages.
>
> - An alternative, that will work if your ISP was providing you with a domain name for your organization and mailboxes addressed with that domain name, is to have the ISP point that domain name at your Exchange system, instead of the mailboxes that it holds on its servers for you. This is usually a matter of simply reconfiguring its DNS (Domain Name Service) or perhaps changing the routing information in its mail host.

In the same way, you can configure a newsfeed service using the New Newsfeed wizard, or you can reconfigure an existing newsfeed to be dial-up from its Exchange Administrator property page in the connections container.

Security and Firewalls

If, in addition to sending messages to and from the Internet, you are going to provide your users with access to information held in Exchange from locations out on the Internet, and you are not already among them, you are going to need to join that rapidly growing number of permanently connected organizations.

An Internet *firewall* is essentially a device that filters traffic flowing between the Internet and your corporate network. You can configure a firewall to restrict traffic to flow only between particular network addresses, or ranges of addresses, and only for particular service protocols. This reduces the risk of an attack on your systems and information from someone on the Internet by restricting what they can see and access.

A firewall may also carry out other functions, such as mapping the IP addresses on your network to IP addresses on the Internet. The IP addresses of machines on your network are not then visible to people externally, which reduces the threat of a successful attack on your computers. This also allows you to assign IP addresses inside your network independently of the constraints of the addressing range of your subnet on the Internet.

When building a secured connection to the Internet, it is a good policy, though harder work of course, to allow access only to devices that need to be accessed from the Internet restricted to just the protocols that are required.

Before you configure your Internet firewall for your Exchange system you need to consider the following:

- Which protocols are going to be exposed to the Internet from Exchange?
- Which of these will use SSL?
- On which servers do they need to be supported?

This will tell you which ports at which addresses need to be accessible through the firewall. If you have a single-server Exchange system, things become a lot easier. You just need to decide which services, and therefore which protocols, you are going to make available on the Internet. The following sections are primarily intended to help you make decisions about how you might want to arrange your system if you have more than one server.

SMTP

SMTP connectivity is often the first priority, because this will allow people to send and receive e-mail across the Internet. You will likely have one, two, or at maximum a few servers routing mail to and from the Internet depending on the size of your organization. You can restrict access to just those servers from the Internet.

POP3

POP3 is a little more complex. If you want people to be able to access their mailboxes from outside the firewall using POP3 clients, any server containing a mailbox that needs to be accessed using POP3 should be made available through the firewall. If there are particular users who require POP3 access, you might be able to concentrate them on a single server so you can expose just that server through the firewall.

NNTP

For NNTP access there are two things to consider: First, if you need to take newsfeeds in from the Internet, you need to expose the servers on which the newsfeed connector is running. Then, in order to provide access to users with newsreaders coming in from the Internet, you provide access to the Exchange servers that are your news servers, have the protocol enabled, and contain replicas of the newsgroup public folders.

LDAP

You can pick one or more servers to deal with LDAP requests from the Internet. Because all the Exchange servers in your organization store a replica of the directory, you can use any of them to provide LDAP support. You will probably pick just one server, and likely use one that is your main Internet Mail Service.

HTTP

Because Exchange's Web service is provided by Internet Information Server, which can be located on a machine with the Exchange Active Server Components installed on it separate from the Exchange server itself, you can select one or more IIS machines that will provide access to Web browsers from outside on the Internet. This reduces the risk of the Exchange Servers themselves being compromised.

SSL

Each protocol uses an alternate port for connections using SSL. So, if you have SSL enabled for any of the protocols you are using, and you want it to be utilized by people connecting their clients from the Internet, you open the appropriate alternate ports for the protocol's SSL connection through the firewall (see Figure 9.19). Check the table in the previous SSL section to see which ports you will need to configure on your firewall.

Some firewall arrangements are of the type that provides a network segment that sits between the Internet and your internal network—accessible from both, but preventing connections coming from the Internet into your internal system. In this case, a good approach might be to put an Exchange server on that segment exposing the Internet protocols you want to use on the Internet and put only the mailboxes and folders on it that need to be there. If you are just using it to support NNTP clients on the Internet accessing your public discussion groups, the only folders that have replicas on that system are those that are supporting those groups. You should be aware, though, that any Exchange server will contain a copy of your directory, and like any other system, no matter how secure, there are risks associated with connecting it directly to the Internet.

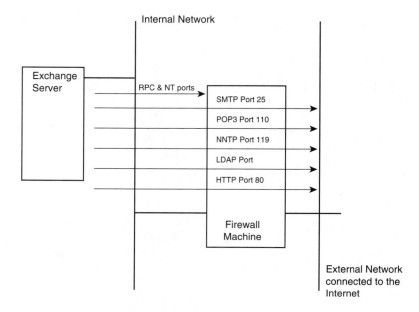

FIGURE 9.19.

An example of an Exchange system connected to the Internet.

Do I Have to Have a Firewall?

Not every organization has or even needs a firewall. I wouldn't want to be caught recommending not having one, but clearly for some people the risks don't justify the expense of creating and maintaining this kind of configuration. What if you don't have a firewall? There are a couple of steps you can take to make things more secure if you want to use Exchange internet protocols on the Internet.

The idea is to expose only the service protocols you want people to use to the Internet, but not the rest of the available protocols on the machine. In this way, you can prevent people from gaining access to your NT system or to the RPC ports that Exchange uses.

First, install a separate network adapter and connect that to a segment connected to the Internet (see Figure 9.20). Leave the first adapter connected to your internal network. Through that adapter, internal people can access the system normally, and Exchange can communicate with the other Exchange servers in your system.

You then configure the second card so that none of the NT network services are bound to it.

People accessing Exchange from the Internet can connect using Internet protocols, but the server won't answer on any of the other ports.

FIGURE 9.20.

Connecting Exchange to the Internet with a separate network adapter.

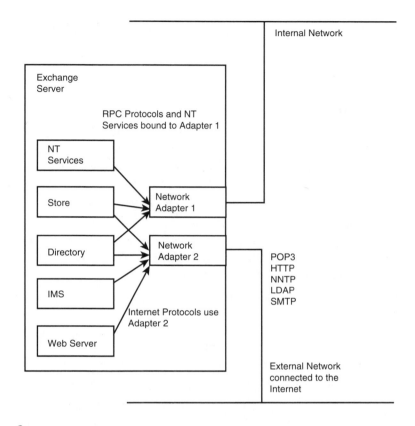

Internet References

Table 9.2 lists the relevent major RFCs documenting the protocols I've talked about here. These documents are the ones that are used by the protocol implementers, so they are very detailed and are often written in a technical style that doesn't make them easy for everyone to understand. However, they are the definitive specifications for the protocols and may therefore be useful. I've included just the main RFC documents in the table; in many cases, there are others that cover specific aspects of the protocol or revisions to it.

Table 9.2. RFC References.

Protocol	Main RFC
POP3	RFC 1725
SMTP	RFC 821
NNTP	RFC 977
HTTP	RFC 1945 / 2068 (HTTP 1.1)
LDAP	RFC 1777

If you want to read the RFCs or find out about other RFCs, a good starting point is on the Web at

```
http:/www.isi.edu/rfc-editor
```

Summary

This chapter describes the new Internet features in Exchange Server 5.0. You should now have an understanding of the possibilities and be able to draw up a plan for how to make use of the protocols in your environment. Whether or not you've already got an Internet Connection into your Exchange system for sending and receiving e-mail, you should consider taking advantage of the new Internet protocol support in Exchange 5.0.

You can make use of NNTP support either to connect to the Internet to pull Usenet newsgroup discussions into your network so that they are easily accessible in a controlled way, or to host discussion groups in your network and enable people to connect to them from the Internet in order to engage in discussions with your users.

Users in your organization can now use different POP3 mail clients to get mail from their mailboxes or to send mail out, and they can use those clients either internally in your network or to connect in from the Internet if they are working remotely. You have the opportunity to configure the system to do either, which will provide greater flexibility and potentially save on telecommunications charges by doing so. You can also give POP3 users access to the directory using LDAP, which means that they don't lose out on directory lookup functionality.

Another possibility is to use the integration with Microsoft Internet Information Server to enable people to get at information in Exchange using their Web browsers. If they have a mailbox on the system, users treat their browsers like a mail client and send and receive mail with it. They can also access information in public folders and browse the directory.

Finally, the ability to set up and control anonymous access for NNTP newsreaders, LDAP, and access to folders and the directory from the Web adds a whole new dimension to interaction with people outside your organization.

CHAPTER 10

Migrating from Lotus cc:Mail

by Brian Murphy

IN THIS CHAPTER

The transition from one messaging system to another rarely occurs without some bumps and jitters along the way. However, much of the potential for these problems can be removed by a clear understanding of what the migration and coexistence tools will and won't do and some planning based on the unique needs of your environment. Migrating from Lotus cc:Mail to Microsoft Exchange is no exception to this rule. Once you are familiar with the tools and some guidelines for their use, you'll find that you can build, test, and execute your migration plan in a very short period of time.

Configuring messaging connectivity and directory synchronization between cc:Mail and Exchange is easy to accomplish. Migrating users can be more involved, because there are some limitations with local data files that you may need to work around. The cc:Mail Connector and the migration wizard work closely together to provide seamless conversion of Exchange Custom Recipients, representing cc:Mail users, into Exchange Mailboxes. Moving Bulletin Board data from cc:Mail to Exchange Public Folders is straightforward, but does require some additional work to recreate access control lists in the Exchange Administrator program.

Planning for a Smooth Migration

Effective planning is the key to any successful migration and coexistence story. There are many different tools and ways of using them, but without the right process and knowledge of their limitations you can find your migration stalled by unforeseen problems.

Constructing a migration plan helps you identify tasks and highlight problems as well as document solutions and workarounds. A planning document is also the ideal way to pass on that knowledge to others in your organization in a structured way. I recommend creating an Exchange Public Folder and posting your migration plan and any additional documentation there as a reference.

Once you've built your migration plan, you need to test it. Resist the temptation to skip this step. Work through the steps outlined in your plan in a test lab or a confined section of your system and validate your decisions. It's very likely that you'll refine your plan considerably as a result of this testing. Remember, planning equals success.

Some baseline goals are a useful starting point in the planning process. Your list may have some additional goals, but typically the goals of messaging system migration are the following:

- Minimum user disruption
- Minimum downtime during transition
- High message fidelity during coexistence
- High data fidelity during migration
- Migrated messages that allow replies

Single-Phase Versus Multi-Phase Migration

The most fundamental decision you will make in migrating your cc:Mail infrastructure to your Exchange Server topology is whether to move everything in one single step, or in multiple steps over time. This decision is dependent on the amount of time and resources that are available, as well as the existing cc:Mail topology and your current cc:Mail administration model. For large installations or organizations where there are links to other external cc:Mail systems, there is often a prolonged period of coexistence. The decision refines down to evaluating how much inertia there is in the cc:Mail infrastructure and how strong the drive is to complete the migration to Exchange Server.

Single-Phase or "Big Bang" Migration

A "Big Bang," or single-phase, migration involves moving all cc:Mail clients and post offices to Exchange or Outlook clients in a single step. This approach has the benefit of being fast and reducing coexistence overhead, but can require a large staff to coordinate and execute.

For smaller and centrally located cc:Mail installations with little data to migrate and a small number of users, this can be a practical option because it eliminates the need to maintain and manage long term coexistence between the two systems. Remember that all user machines need to have the new clients installed and ready to run.

For larger, geographically distributed cc:Mail networks with more shared and user data, the resources and level of coordination needed to achieve a single-phase migration in a short time frame can make this approach impractical. This can be a significant problem when you consider the coordination needed between international sites and the impact that the differing time zones can have on a tight cutover schedule.

The following are the advantages:

- Very fast cutover to Exchange Server
- Greatly simplified planning
- Minimal coexistence overhead
- Reduction of nondelivered messages

Here are the disadvantages:

- Considerable coordination required
- Possible necessity of a large staff
- Need for users' training before cutover

Multi-Phase Migration

A multi-phase migration moves cc:Mail users and Bulletin Boards to Exchange in multiple phases over a period of weeks or months. This gradual method allows you to segment your migration and move data to Exchange, based on either the users' geographical location or their department in your organization.

This method is useful in the "mirror" scenario, where the old cc:Mail system is hub-based and geographically distributed, and the Exchange site topology maps closely to the old cc:Mail hub backbone. The cc:Mail hub post office in each area can be connected via the cc:Mail Connector, allowing hub administrators to manage their own connectivity and directory synchronization and migrate users according to a timetable that suits their departments.

A multi-phase migration strategy requires more planning and a much greater focus on the coexistence elements than a single-phase strategy. At the same time, it provides greater freedom in distributing tasks. There is greater scheduling flexibility in multi-phase migrations, because the tasks can be performed independent of the coordination required for single-phase migrations.

The following are the advantages:

- Fine-tuning of migration plan possible over time
- Greater scheduling flexibility
- More manageability of staffing needs
- User training possible "just-in-time" for each area being migrated
- Significantly less risk than "Big Bang" method

Here are the disadvantages:

- Slower transition to Exchange
- Planning is more complex
- Significant coexistence overhead
- Increased chance (because of Partial Post Office migrations) of nondelivered messages

Capacity Planning

When specifying hard disk space on your Exchange Server, make sure that you have ample capacity for the temporary files generated by the Migration Wizard and the Exchange Server Information Store. Both the cc:Mail database and the Exchange Server Information Store support single-instance storage. This means that messages and attachments are stored in the database once, and each recipient has pointers to a single copy of each item.

When migrating data from systems such as cc:Mail, it's not possible to preserve single-instance storage. As a result, if you have a message with a 1MB attachment sent to 10 users, and all 10 of these users are migrated to Exchange, there will be 10 copies of the message and attachment in the migration data files and the Exchange Server Information Store. There is no solid rule on how much space you should allocate for migrated data, because it varies with the content that your users send and the number of recipients to whom they send it. The best method is to do a test migration from a production post office and from this extrapolate the size of the migration files and the growth of the Exchange Server Private Information Store (PRIV.EDB in the \exchsrvr\mdbdata\ directory). Don't forget that Bulletin Boards are migrated to the Exchange Server Public Information Store (PUB.EDB in the \exchsrvr\mdbdata\ directory) and will need to be tested also.

User Naming Conventions

During migration, it is possible to modify the format of user names coming from cc:Mail before they are used to create Exchange Mailboxes and Windows NT Accounts.

The common naming standard for cc:Mail post office users is "Last, First." However, there are no discrete First and Last name fields in the cc:Mail directory. When cc:Mail users with the "Last, First" name format are propagated to the Exchange Directory via directory synchronization, the name string is parsed and the First and Last name fields in the Exchange custom recipient are populated. As a result, the Exchange Administrator auto-naming rules are used, and an alias name is assembled from the First and Last name elements (see Admin | Tools | Options | Auto-naming). cc:Mail user names in the "First, Last" format are not parsed in this way, and the "First, Last" name is used to populate the Display and Alias name fields.

If you are currently using the "Last, First" format, I recommend that you let directory synchronization do this work for you.

Messaging and Directory Synchronization

You should decide how many cc:Mail Connectors will be needed to handle message traffic and directory synchronization in your organization. This is where metrics on the current message traffic between post offices can be invaluable. A small cc:Mail site that is consolidating its post offices onto one Exchange server will be able to have one cc:Mail Connector to a hub post office. Larger cc:Mail sites will need to consider message traffic more carefully and give more thought to future migration before deciding on only one cc:Mail Connector.

In the simplest case, cc:Mail and Exchange can be connected by a single cc:Mail Connector service. This can become a problem in cases where there are multiple Exchange sites to which users are being migrated. One feature the Migration Wizard offers is the ability to convert custom recipients created by directory synchronization or Exchange Administrator Import into mailboxes. Directory synchronization creates all the cc:Mail users as custom recipients in the home site for the cc:Mail Connector. When you attempt to migrate users to an adjacent connected site, the custom recipient conversion will fail because the Migration Wizard cannot delete the custom recipient. The custom recipient can be deleted only in the site in which it was created.

When users are being migrated to different Exchange sites and custom recipient conversion is being used in your migration, the best approach is to establish a cc:Mail Connector for the group of post offices that will be migrated into that site.

E-Mail or "Proxy" Addresses

For each connector installed on an Exchange server, there is an e-mail address assigned to all
recipient objects, which represents them outside of Exchange. Recipient objects include
Exchange mailboxes, custom recipients, public folders, and distribution lists. For example, a
user on an Exchange server with cc:Mail, MS Mail, Internet, and X.400 connectivity installed,
will display e-mail addresses for each connector.

It's possible to have multiple e-mail addresses in a single address type. This is an important
coexistence feature. The primary e-mail address is displayed in bold font and is the address that
is displayed on outbound messages. The secondary e-mail address is shown in normal font and
is used as an inbound address only. (See Figure 10.1.) Messages to either address will be routed
to the same Exchange mailbox.

FIGURE 10.1.

*Exchange mailbox
e-mail addresses.*

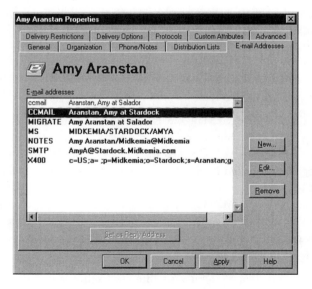

A cc:Mail user who is migrated to Exchange will receive a new cc:Mail e-mail address based on
the site addressing information for cc:Mail. This user's old cc:Mail address is imported as a
secondary proxy, allowing messages addressed to both the old and new addresses to be routed
to the correct Exchange mailbox.

CAUTION

You need to install at least one MS Exchange Server v5.0 in every site where Exchange users will communicate with cc:Mail users. This is required so that users in the Exchange site can have cc:Mail Proxy addresses generated for them. If you don't install an Exchange version 5.0 server in a site where users are sending mail to cc:Mail users, replies from cc:Mail users to Exchange users will not be able to be routed.

TIP

In Figure 10.2, the cc:Mail proxy addresses generated for users in your Exchange site can be changed by updating the Site Addressing tab on the Site addressing object in the site's configuration container.

FIGURE 10.2.

Exchange Administrator Site Addressing.

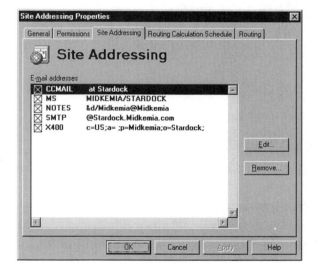

Groups and Distribution Lists

Managing distribution lists on both cc:Mail and Exchange is a considerable administrative burden. It some cases, it can make sense to maintain groups or distribution lists in both systems. In most cases, it will be much simpler to move distribution list management to Exchange. The Import and Export facilities provided by the Exchange Administrator allow bulk creation, deletion, and update of distribution lists.

Which Client?

You decide which Microsoft messaging client your organization will use. Microsoft Outlook handles messages and calendaring in one application and offers many personal information management features. Outlook is tightly integrated with Office 97, but it is supported only on the 32-bit Windows platform. Microsoft Exchange and Schedule+ are two separate applications focused on core messaging and calendaring, respectively, without the additional Personal Information Manager features that Outlook delivers. Exchange and Schedule+ clients are available for the 16-bit Windows and Apple Macintosh platforms, and both Outlook and Schedule+ clients have options to import Lotus Organizer v1.x/2.x calendar information.

Compatibility   Outlook supports a very useful "message recall" feature that allows users to recall a message that they have sent in error. The Exchange client does not support this feature. If you need to have a mixed environment with both Outlook and Exchange clients, your Exchange clients will not be able to recall messages and will see the special Outlook Recall message as a new message in their client.

Using MAPI Providers

Messaging API providers for both the Outlook and Exchange clients are available from Transend Corporation. These MAPI providers allow Exchange and Outlook to exchange messages with cc:Mail DB6 and DB8 post offices. If you are considering performing an operating system upgrade, it can make sense to update users to the new client software at the same time. Using the MAPI providers for cc:Mail, you can leave the cc:Mail post offices in place until the operating system upgrade is completed.

cc:Mail Mobile Users

If you have existing cc:Mail Mobile users, you provide Windows NT RAS (Remote Access Services) to allow Microsoft messaging clients similar dial-up capabilities. Until the RAS infrastructure can be put in place, have all cc:Mail Mobile clients use your existing dial-in facilities.

Using the cc:Mail Router for Windows NT (Release 8), cc:Mail Mobile users can connect to the network via Windows NT RAS and make a TCP/IP connection to their cc:Mail post office. This allows you to consolidate all your remote client access—whether they are cc:Mail Mobile, Microsoft Outlook, or Exchange users—onto a Windows NT RAS configuration and remove your existing cc:Mail-centric dial-up access facility. Consolidating these services will help reduce support and operational costs.

Tools of the Trade

There are several tools and resources that you should explore prior to commencing your transition to Exchange Server. If you have a very simple scenario, the Exchange Connector for cc:Mail, Exchange Migration Wizard, and Exchange Administrator programs may be all you'll ever need to use. The Exchange Resource Kit, part of the BackOffice Resource Kit, is growing constantly with value-add tools that have been built either by Microsoft or by people implementing Exchange in their own organization. Additionally, several information resources available on the World Wide Web are listed for your reference.

Exchange Connector for cc:Mail

New to
Version 5.0

With Exchange Server version 5.0, Microsoft provides you with a cc:Mail Connector for messaging and directory synchronization. The cc:Mail Connector is installed at server setup time and can also be removed via the setup program. The cc:Mail Import/Export interface is used to move messages and attachments between cc:Mail and Exchange.

You should ensure that you have the right version of Import/Export on the machine for the post office version to which you are connecting. My experience has shown that incorrect Import/Export versions are the most common problem in a mixed cc:Mail DB6 and DB8 post office environment.

Although message and attachment fidelity is good, there are some limitations. cc:Mail rich text information, such as font color, is not preserved. Also, the connector doesn't replicate information between cc:Mail bulletin boards and Exchange public folders. Better news is that although Exchange doesn't handle forwarding in the same way that cc:Mail does, it can preserve the cc:Mail forwarding history on messages inbound to Exchange.

Performance of the cc:Mail connector is affected by several factors. The hardware configuration of the server running the service, the other processes being run on the machine, and the Performance Wizard settings all affect throughput to some degree. Throughput figures of around 4,000 messages an hour are possible, but there can be a significant fall-off in performance over time under load. This is a result of fragmentation inside the post office and can be solved by running the normal cc:Mail maintenance procedures specific to your version of the cc:Mail database.

Performance

Directory synchronization offers some useful filtering ability when importing cc:Mail directory entries to Exchange. Particular address formats can be defined, and addresses matching the format are included or excluded. You can also control whether Exchange directory information will be propagated past the bridgehead cc:Mail post office. Most importantly, there is a Run DirSync Now option on the cc:Mail Connector Import Container tab. This is invaluable for forcing directory synchronization after the initial installation or when significant changes have been made on either side that need to be propagated immediately.

To begin configuring the Connector, open the Connector for cc:Mail object in the Exchange Administrator, Connection container. Select an existing Exchange mailbox for the Administrator's mailbox and enter the post office path, name, and password information as shown in Figure 10.3. Ensure that you select the correct Import/Export version for the post office you're connecting to and that the files are available on the system path.

FIGURE 10.3.

cc:Mail Connector Post Office options.

If you need to restrict the size of messages being sent across the Connector, this can be configured on the General page as shown in Figure 10.4.

FIGURE 10.4.

Configuring message size limitation.

You configure the cc:Mail address space on the Address Space property page by selecting New General and entering CCMAIL in the Type field, as shown in Figure 10.5. Without this address space configured, no cc:Mail messages will be moved across the Connector.

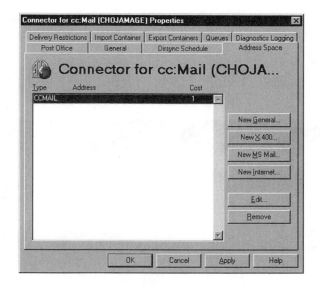

FIGURE 10.5.
Setting up the cc:Mail Address Space.

Figure 10.6 shows the schedule for directory synchronization. Choose whether you want the directory updated always or only at specific times of day. Directory synchronization for cc:Mail systems with large numbers of address entries places a noticeable load on the server and may require directory synchronization to run in non-business hours.

FIGURE 10.6.
Scheduling directory synchronization.

Figure 10.7 shows how you can select the container in which cc:Mail directory information will be created. The simplest approach is to use the existing recipients container; however, you

can specify a separate container as I've done in this example. This is helpful when you also have addresses from other messaging systems to manage and store each type in custom recipient containers.

Use the include and exclude address formats options to provide more granular control over which directory entries are shown in the Exchange directory.

> **NOTE**
>
> If you select the Always option for running directory synchronization, directory synchronization updates will occur every 15 minutes.

FIGURE 10.7.

Setting import options.

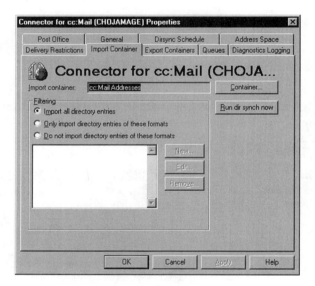

You can select multiple recipient containers to be exported to cc:Mail. Figure 10.8 shows a single container configuration.

Troubleshooting As a troubleshooting aid, there is some basic diagnostic logging available, as shown in Figure 10.9. Cranking up this logging can provide some interesting information, but it does place an additional load on the connector and can fill up the Windows NT Application log in no time. For best performance, leave the logging level set to None so that only exceptions are recorded in the Windows NT Event log. You can enable higher diagnostic logging when you are troubleshooting a specific problem.

As shown in Figure 10.10, Inbound and Outbound Exchange queues can be monitored, and bad messages can be deleted if required.

FIGURE 10.8.

Configuring the export container.

FIGURE 10.9.

Setting diagnostic logging.

NOTE

If the Exchange Information Store is not running, this information will not be available until the Information Store is restarted.

FIGURE 10.10.

Checking the cc:Mail connector message queues.

Performance   Performance counters are another valuable monitoring and troubleshooting tool. It's a good idea to run Performance Monitor on your cc:Mail Connector machine, at least initially, to keep an eye on its health. Here is a list of the available counters that you can examine:

- Microsoft Exchange MTS-IN
- Microsoft Exchange MTS-OUT
- Messages sent to Lotus cc:Mail
- Messages sent to Lotus cc:Mail/hr
- Messages sent to Microsoft Exchange
- Messages sent to Microsoft Exchange/hr
- DirSync to Lotus cc:Mail
- DirSync to Microsoft Exchange
- NDRs to Lotus cc:Mail
- NDRs to Microsoft Exchange

NOTE

An *NDR* is a nondelivery report notification.

Exchange Migration Wizard

The Exchange Migration Wizard supports migrating user mailboxes, messages, attachments, and public bulletin board data from cc:Mail v5.x (DB6) post offices to the Exchange server.

Windows NT accounts can be created at the same time as the mailbox. If you select not to create Windows NT accounts, the Migration Wizard will use the current auto-naming rules configured in the Exchange Administrator to try to match an existing Windows NT account to the new Exchange mailbox.

The wizard won't migrate any of the mail lists (public or private), post office address books, post office remote address lists, or propagation lists. The content of a user's Archive files should be copied onto the user's mailbox on the cc:Mail post office for this data to be migrated.

> **TIP**
>
> Large numbers of users copying archive data to the cc:Mail post office can adversely affect performance for other cc:Mail users. Also, there may not be room up on the production post office for the archive data. One way around these problems is to use a temporary migration post office that supports migrating users only. Users who are about to be migrated can be moved to this post office and copy their archive data up to the post office without impacting other users.

> **CAUTION**
>
> You must stop the cc:Mail connector prior to migrating users. When cc:Mail accounts are migrated to Exchange, they can be deleted from cc:Mail by the directory synchronization process. Check that the users were migrated successfully and then restart the cc:Mail connector.

> **TIP**
>
> If you need to migrate users from a cc:Mail DB8 post office, you can achieve this by moving the DB8 users to a DB6 post office with Import/Export Full User Move and using the Migration Wizard to migrate them from cc:Mail DB6 to Exchange Server.

Microsoft has indicated that direct migration of data from cc:Mail DB8 post offices to the Exchange Information Store will be possible in an upcoming release of Microsoft Exchange Server.   **Future Directions**

One-Step Migration

One-step migration extracts the user and shared data from the cc:Mail post office into a set of temporary migration files and imports it to Exchange in one cycle. If you don't need to modify any user directory naming information, or add additional proxy addresses, this is the easiest choice.

10

MIGRATING FROM LOTUS CC:MAIL

Two-Step Migration

Two-step migration extracts the user and shared data from the cc:Mail post office into a set of migration files that can then be modified and imported to the Exchange server at a later time using the Import from Migration Files option, as shown in Figure 10.11.

FIGURE 10.11.

Importing migration files as part of a two-step migration.

Partial Versus Complete Post Office Migration

You can select all users on a post office to be migrated, or select any combination of individual users. I recommend that you migrate entire cc:Mail post offices wherever possible to simplify your coexistence and prevent splitting groups in your organization across the two systems. Where a partial migration is necessary, try to move users who exchange e-mail and use Organizer to book meetings most frequently.

Running a cc:Mail Migration

Start the Migration Wizard from the Windows NT program start menu underneath the Microsoft Exchange group and select the cc:Mail option, shown in Figure 10.12.

FIGURE 10.12.

Select the cc:Mail migration option.

At the cc:Mail information screen, shown in Figure 10.13, check the following:

- Have you configured and run the connector and completed directory synchronization?
- Have you stopped the cc:Mail connector while you are performing the migration?
- Have you prevented all cc:Mail agents, routers, administration programs, and clients from accessing the database during the migration?

FIGURE 10.13.

cc:Mail Migration reminder screen.

As shown in Figure 10.14, enter the information about the post office from which users are to be migrated.

FIGURE 10.14.

Enter the post office name, path, and password to be migrated.

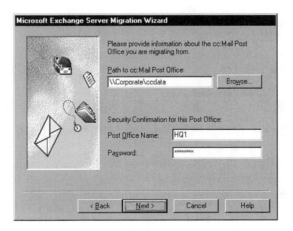

As Figure 10.15 shows, select a one-step if you don't need to modify any of the extracted user information before it is imported to Exchange, and indicate the location to which temporary migration files should be written.

FIGURE 10.15.

Select one- or two-step migration.

Figure 10.16 illustrates that you can choose whether you want to create mailboxes, migrate to an existing mailbox, or convert a custom recipient to a mailbox. Select whether personal e-mail and bulletin board data will be migrated.

TIP

Deselect the Information to Create Mailboxes option if you have already created mailboxes during a previous run of the Migration Wizard, or are converting custom recipients into Exchange Mailboxes. Converting from a custom recipient to a mailbox will preserve the existing template details and proxy address information.

If you deselect this option and there is no existing mailbox, the Migration Wizard will produce an error. If you select this box and there is already an existing mailbox or custom recipient, the Migration Wizard will produce an error.

CAUTION

Creating mailboxes manually via the Exchange Administrator program can cause migration errors. When the Migration Wizard creates mailboxes, it adds a unique identifier for the mailbox as a secondary proxy. This MIGRATE proxy allows the Migration Wizard to correctly identify the recipients of migrated messages. Mailboxes created manually via the Exchange Administrator program do no have this MIGRATE proxy address and will fail to find the user mailbox for the migration.

If you need to create Exchange Mailboxes and Windows NT user accounts in advance of data migration, run the Migration Wizard with the Information to Create Mailboxes option selected and the Personal e-mail and Bulletin Board Information options deselected. This will generate migration files that create Exchange mailboxes and Windows NT Accounts only.

FIGURE 10.16.

Select the information to be migrated.

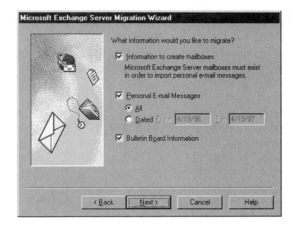

Select which users you are migrating, as shown in Figure 10.17.

FIGURE 10.17.

Select the users to migrate.

Enter the name of the Exchange server to which the user and shared data will be migrated, as shown in Figure 10.18.

> **CAUTION**
>
> If you are converting custom recipients to mailboxes, remember that the custom recipients must have been originally created in the site to which the users are being migrated.

If you are migrating bulletin board data, set the default permissions for the new Exchange Public Folders. Setting this to No access, as shown in Figure 10.19, can be changed in the Exchange Administrator program after the migration has been completed.

FIGURE 10.18.

Select the server where the users are to be migrated.

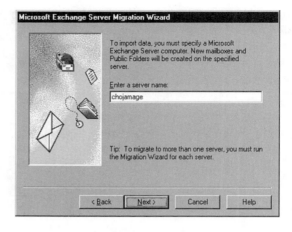

FIGURE 10.19.

Configure the default permissions on new public folders.

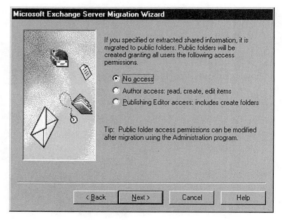

An owner must be nominated for the new public folders that are created, and it is configured as shown in Figure 10.20.

FIGURE 10.20.

Select the owner of new public folders.

Choose in which recipient container migrated users will be created (see Figure 10.21). You can also specify a mailbox as a template to create other mailboxes.

FIGURE 10.21.

Choose the target recipient container and optional mailbox template.

If you specify not to create Windows NT Accounts, the Migration Wizard will use the Exchange Administrator auto-naming rules to try and assign the correct Windows NT account to the Exchange mailbox. To check or configure the auto-naming rules that will be used, open the Exchange Administrator program and select Tools|Options|Auto Naming. Configure Windows NT Account preferences as shown in Figure 10.22.

FIGURE 10.22.

Select whether Windows NT accounts are required and specify the home Windows NT Domain.

Figure 10.23 shows the status screen that is displayed at the end of migration. Error conditions reported on this screen should be investigated using the Event log. Warnings are non-critical, but the administrator should understand the cause of any warning events.

10

MIGRATING FROM
LOTUS CC:MAIL

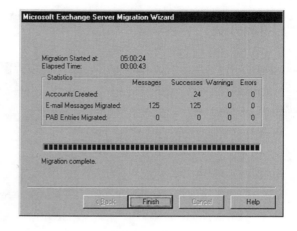

FIGURE 10.23.

Status screen at the end of migration.

Migration Performance

Performance

For best performance when migrating cc:Mail, ensure that you use an Intel CPU machine for the extract phase. Because the extraction for cc:Mail uses some 16-bit code, it runs in x86 emulation mode on RISC machines, which is an order of magnitude slower than on Intel CPU machines.

Other Tools

Here is a list of other tools that you should be aware of when planning and executing your migration:

- Use the Microsoft Exchange Administrator program interactively and via the batch Import and Export functions to create and maintain distribution lists. Import and Export in Exchange Server are quite powerful and merit some close study.

- Investigate the tools delivered in the BackOffice Resource Kit. You can download the Exchange Server component of the BackOffice Resource Kit from Microsoft's Web site at http://www.microsoft.com/exchange/reskit.htm.

- If you are performing an operating system upgrade and installing the new Exchange or Outlook client in advance of migrating your cc:Mail post offices to Exchange Server, using MAPI providers from Transend Corporation allows you to leave your cc:Mail back-end in place using the new clients. You can find out more at http://www.transend.com.

NOTE

If you have a license for Microsoft Office 97 and are using Microsoft Outlook, you can use the Transend Corporation ConnectorWare for cc:Mail that is provided on the Office 97 CD-ROM to connect to the cc:Mail post office.

Other Resources

There is a considerable store of Microsoft Exchange information and tools being accumulated by users and administrators. The World Wide Web makes these normally invisible resources available and accessible. If you have a concern about your cc:Mail migration, chances are that someone has already found it, and there is some received wisdom that you can benefit from. Here is a short list of places to look on the Web:

■ *Exchange Mailing List.* Experience counts, so it makes sense to talk to people who have walked the road ahead of you. Many cc:Mail customers participate in this Internet forum and have valuable observations to share. To access more information about the Exchange Mailing List, including content, rules and how to subscribe, look at `http://www.msexchange.org`. There are also links to Exchange Frequently Asked Questions and other Exchange-related sites.

■ *Exchange Community Site.* Microsoft hosts an Exchange Community Site that includes peer discussion areas on migration issues, links to tools, and other sites, as well as a store of reference materials and recent Exchange-focused news items. Take a look at `http://www.exchangeserver.com`.

■ *Slipstick Systems.* Slipstick Systems run an Exchange-focused site that has several Frequently Asked Question lists for Exchange and Outlook, many client and server tools, and handy links to resources on Microsoft's Web site. Check out this site at `http://www.slipstick.com`.

Sample Roadmap for cc:Mail Migration

> **TIP**
>
> Before you migrate a cc:Mail post office, ask users to clean out any information that they don't need to be migrated and perform post office maintenance operations.

These are the steps for a typical cc:Mail migration:

1. Set up and configure the Exchange Connector for cc:Mail.
2. Run directory synchronization and verify that all cc:Mail users are created in Exchange as custom recipients and all Exchange users exit as external addresses in cc:Mail.
3. Test messaging connectivity and attachment fidelity.
4. Install clients for your test population.
5. Migrate the test users' mailboxes to Exchange Server.
6. Run both systems in parallel to verify acceptable coexistence with your test population.

10

MIGRATING FROM
LOTUS CC:MAIL

7. Deploy the Exchange Internet Mail Service and test.

8. Retire the cc:Mail Link to SMTP and reroute inbound and outbound SMTP mail for both cc:Mail and Exchange users through the Exchange Server Internet Mail Service.

9. Identify the groups of production users who most actively share Organizer data.

10. Hold client training sessions for these users.

11. Send an advisory e-mail to users about to be migrated, explaining what steps they need to take in the migration process, including instructions for moving messages from cc:Mail Archive files up to the cc:Mail database before the migration.

12. Migrate these Organizer users' mailboxes to Exchange Server at the same time to avoid the difficulty of Organizer and Exchange users being unable to view or access each other's calendars.

    Users cut over to the Exchange or Outlook client and the old cc:Mail client can be removed from the user's machine.

There are some common tasks, such as group or distribution list consolidation on Exchange Server, that I have not included in this roadmap because they can be completed independently of this sequence.

Summary

A good migration project is one where the job gets done on schedule. The essence of a great migration project is one where the job gets done on schedule and you're never surprised by a single thing that happens. In the real world, there is a limit to the amount of time we can spend on planning and testing, so these perfect cases are understandably rare.

In this chapter, you learned about having clear goals for your migration and setting realistic user and management expectations of what you'll be able to achieve, and in what time frame. You've navigated the planning and testing of a migration and explored the tools that you'll use to deliver your cc:Mail users and shared resources to Exchange Server.

Some words of advice for you before you begin: Spend some time doing research using some of the resources I've mentioned. Read the Exchange List Server and talk to your peers there; they're bound to have helpful hints that will save you time and effort. Finally, be ready to perform course corrections on your migration at any time—they are an expected part of the process.

Migrating from Microsoft Mail

by Robert Henriksen

IN THIS CHAPTER

CHAPTER 11

As you might expect, the migration path from Microsoft Mail is quite painless—with one or two exceptions, notably in (not) sharing Schedule+ data between pre- and post-migration users. Microsoft has been very aggressive in gaining market share by developing migration tools to facilitate defections from rivals' products, and when the source product is their last-generation version, the migration tools are about as seamless as can be. The actual steps of migrating mailboxes, MTA duties, and directory synchronization duties are quite straightforward. There can be user impact during the actual migration in several areas, however, and it's important to have a strong understanding of the implications of the changes you will be effecting. There are also different administrative loads to the different possible migration strategies that will be of interest to *you*.

This chapter will start with information on the impact of a crash conversion versus a staged migration. You will then learn the steps to transferring the MS Mail postoffice list(s) entries to the Exchange Global Address List (GAL) and setting up message transfer between an Exchange site and a Microsoft Mail network. Then, I will walk you through using Exchange's Internet Mail Connector to service the legacy MS Mail postoffices—you can have a party to burn that Microsoft SMTP Gateway system! Finally, you will explore the interoperability potholes that do exist in a Microsoft Mail-to-Exchange migration and what you can do to minimize their impact.

Crash Conversion Versus Staged Migration

Your migration strategy will be driven by the number of mail users your system supports, the degree of handholding they require, your own staffing level, the degree to which Schedule+ is used in your organization, and how twitchy the users are about change! The benefits of gradual conversion are as follows:

- There is less risk. There is a better chance of discovering glitches and streamlining processes over time.
- You can convert enthusiastic, technical users first and allow positive word of mouth to spread.
- It is less demanding on support staff.

The benefits of crash conversion are as follows:

- There are no interoperability issues—everyone can continue to access each other's calendar data.
- There is less chance of bounced mail.
- There is less user confusion. Everyone's got the same client software.

Compatibility ## Technical Problems with the Migration Procedure

The two major technical issues in a staged migration are bounced mail and the loss of access to shared calendars. I'm not harping on the negative sides of the process gratuitously; it's important to bring out the downside of this process right away so you know what you're trying to avoid during the design of your migration strategy.

Bounced mail occurs when MS Mail user A sends a message to the old MS Mail address of user B, who has already moved over to an Exchange mailbox. This can happen for several reasons:

■ DirSync may not have yet occurred between MS Mail and Exchange, so the old MS Mail address for user B is still being displayed in the MS Mail GAL. You will learn how to manually initiate a DirSync cycle in Chapter 20, "Directory Synchronization with Microsoft Mail." Manual DirSync frees you up to migrate mailboxes at any time, rather than in the evenings just prior to scheduled DirSync, to avoid the bounce problem.

■ User A may be replying to an old message in his inbox from user B, sent by B while she was still using MS Mail. This one is hard to avoid or prevent, other than through user education.

■ Lastly, the Microsoft Mail client has an unfortunate feature of copying and saving GAL entries to the user's personal address book whenever a message is sent to a GAL address. Compounding this behavior, the client resolves names typed into the To: field of a new message against the personal address book *first*, and the GAL *second*, by default. You can ask your users to configure their mail clients to check the GAL first, then the PAB.

So, as users get migrated, more and more personal address book entries will become inaccurate, yielding misaddressed messages. You can send preemptive warning/educational messages to your users to expect this problem, but you should still expect calls to the help desk. I've found the most effective thing to tell users is not what they shouldn't do, or why the problem exists, but rather to give them a single, universal rule for what they *should* do to ensure they don't experience the problem. For instance, always address internal e-mail by selecting from the GAL, rather than typing names into the To: field.

Access to other users' shared calendar data is the other sticky issue when conducting the migration. The only interoperability between the Schedule+ 1.0 format and both OutLook & Schedule+ 7.0, is Free/Busy information that can be exchanged between Microsoft Mail and an Exchange site. Also, meeting invitations sent between MS Mail and Exchange to a resource account won't be automatically accepted—the auto-accept invitations feature only works between two Exchange accounts. This is because the algorithm for auto-accepting invitations for a Schedule+ 7.0 resource account only looks in the BCC: field of the invitation, which MS Mail doesn't support.

Compatibility

There really isn't any technical solution to these calendar interoperability issues; your only option is to plan the user/mailbox migration around calendar usage patterns. Determine which users need access to each other's calendars and batch those users into groups when migrating mailboxes. If you have a resource account that is accessed by everyone in the organization, such as a master calendar of events, you should consider moving it to Exchange in the early part of the migration. It will create a demand to get migrated, rather than resistance, (although you can court backlash with this technique!). You can manually do an export of the appointments and import them into a mirror resource account on the MS Mail network, so users still on MS Mail can also view the entries.

If your present MS Mail installation is small—anywhere up to a few dozen users, for example— it can be feasible to do a crash conversion. The steps to prepare for such a conversion will be covered later; more commonly, though, a gradual migration will be called for, and the bulk of space in this chapter will be devoted to the issues involved in this slower route.

Migration Strategy

The larger your organization, the less likely that a crash conversion will work for you, and the more you will have to face up to living with the problems during a gradual migration.

The following is a very common scenario:

1. Set up Exchange's MS Mail Connector and MS Mail directory synchronization with the MS Mail network. If you have a physically dispersed MS Mail network, with WAN links, you should consider deploying Exchange servers at each site and backboning MS Mail message traffic and DirSync operations with Exchange servers. (This is discussed further in Chapter 20.)

2. Distribute Exchange client to your test users.

3. Migrate the test users' mailboxes to Exchange.

4. Run in coexistence mode with this handful of guinea pig users for a few weeks.

5. Deploy the Exchange Internet Mail Service and test.

6. Retire the Microsoft SMTP Gateway for MS Mail and reroute inbound and outbound SMTP mail for both MS Mail and Exchange mailboxes through Exchange's Internet Mail Service.

7. Identify the groups of users who most actively share Schedule+ data.

8. Hold training sessions for these users.

9. Install the Exchange client on their workstations alongside the existing MS Mail client in preparation for the mailbox migration.

10. Migrate these user mailboxes to Exchange together to avoid breaking their access to each others' calendar data.

The users can then begin using the Exchange client in lieu of Microsoft Mail.

An interesting question is whether to have the users begin using the Exchange client to access their MS Mail accounts, even before their mailbox is migrated to Exchange. The decision of whether to do that depends largely upon whether you plan on having the users keep their mail on the Exchange server or in a Personal Folder (.pst) file on their C: drive or a home directory.

The Exchange client can be used to access a Microsoft Mail account, but it cannot keep using the .mmf file on the postoffice. It instead has to transfer the new incoming mail to a .pst file. If you want to access the contents of the legacy data in an .mmf, you must first move the .mmf from the postoffice to the C: drive, then import the contents into the .pst.

The significance of this is that when you do migrate the user's mailbox to Exchange server, the Exchange client will have the ability to use a server-based mail store again, and you then have to move all the messages in the user's .pst file back up to the server. In a sophisticated user environment, this can be left to the user; often, you can get stuck with the job. After a handful of users, you will be wishing for an easier way.

My preference is to deploy the Exchange client and leave it dormant—unused—until after the mailbox migration occurs. The Migration Wizard program you run will bring over the full contents of the user's .mmf file and personal address book entries from the MS Mail postoffice directly into the Exchange server-based store. The next morning, when users fire up their new Exchange client, they see exactly the same message store contents as they saw the day before in the MS Mail client.

Another advantage to sticking with the dichotomy of MS Mail account/MS Mail client and Exchange account/Exchange client is simplicity. Users know where they stand by looking at their screens—it's an either/or world. Their mailbox has been migrated or it hasn't. You don't want to deploy Exchange clients against MS Mail mailboxes and find yourself doing training on the Exchange GUI and feature set, saying, "Here's another really great feature—oops, but you don't get to use that one until after your *mailbox* has been migrated." There's a *lot* to be said for avoiding all that!

Crash Conversion: Directory Export/Import

A crash conversion requires that you at least populate the Exchange GAL with mailboxes equivalent to the MS Mail postoffice. The Exchange Migration Wizard will be your tool of choice for this. You have two basic options when using the Migration Wizard, or MigWiz: one- and two-step. One-step creates the directory entries in Exchange for the inbound mailboxes, creates NT domain accounts if desired, and can bring across as much or as little of the mailbox data as desired. Two-step migration extracts a user list from the MS Mail postoffice directory to a .csv file first. This gives you a chance to open that file, make changes to display names, and add additional fields for the extended directory information available in Exchange (phone, address, and so forth). When finished with the .csv file, you run MigWiz again and indicate the .csv file. It migrates the indicated accounts in that file, adds any additional information supplied in the .csv, and again draws over as much or as little legacy mailbox data as desired.

Launch MigWiz from the Start menu or the Program Manager, as shown in Figure 11.1.

Select the second option, Migrate from MS Mail for PC Networks, as shown in Figure 11.2.

FIGURE 11.1.

Launching Migration Wizard.

FIGURE 11.2.

Select the MS Mail option.

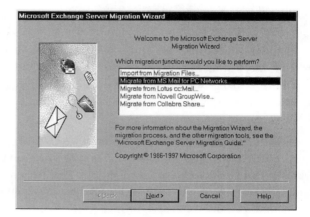

In Figure 11.3, you get a warning about coexistence issues and Exchange client rollout. As discussed previously, you will want to ensure you've installed the Exchange client on the affected users' machines and conducted training before this step. Because this section is oriented toward a crash conversion, don't be worried about coexistence issues. They will be discussed later in this chapter, along with the staged migration procedures.

FIGURE 11.3.

MigWiz coexistence and client rollout warning.

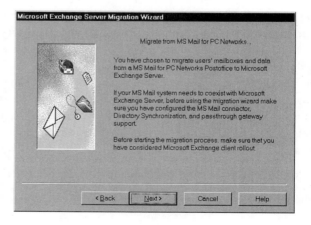

Enter the UNC path to your postoffice and your MS Mail admin username and password, as shown in Figure 11.4. A common error here is that the postoffice is read-only. This is caused by an MS Mail client that has locked open the \maildata\glb\master.glb file. You can use File Manager to open the file's properties, click the Open By button, and disconnect the user.

FIGURE 11.4.

Enter the postoffice and admin information.

Next, select whether you will be doing a one- or two-step migration (see Figure 11.5). Let's look at a two-step; the one-step is identical—just a few less steps.

FIGURE 11.5.

Select a one- or two-step migration.

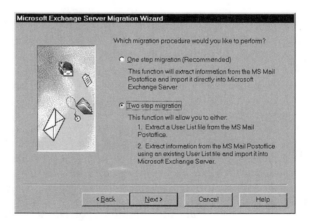

Enter the filepath for your target extraction file—where you want the user data saved to. This will be a filename ending in .csv, as shown in Figure 11.6.

Now, MigWiz will read the postoffice directory and display the name list, as shown in Figure 11.7. You can select one entry or hold down the Ctrl key and click on several names. You can also select a contiguous block by clicking the first name, holding down the Shift key, and then clicking the last name. To select almost all entries, use the Select All button, then use Ctrl+clicking to deselect a few entries. The .csv file will be built with just the selected names.

FIGURE 11.6.

Specifying a filepath for the extraction file.

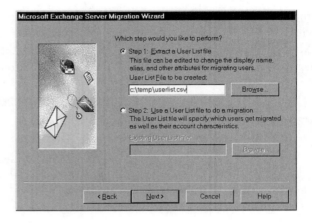

FIGURE 11.7.

Selecting mailboxes for export and migration.

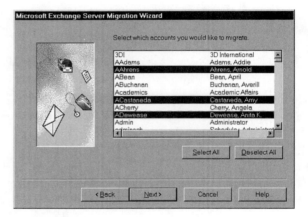

When you click the Next button for the last time, as shown in Figure 11.7, MigWiz pours the data into your specified export file and displays a last page in the Wizard with the results. Click the Finish button to close MigWiz (see Figure 11.8). You are shown a misleading dialog (see Figure 11.9)—the migration isn't complete. You've simply completed the first of two steps, creating the user list file.

You can now open your extraction file in Excel, another spreadsheet, or even a text editor. Modify the current data as desired and add columns if you wish. You need to ensure that the column headers you add match the Exchange schema (see Figure 11.10). A complete listing of mailbox field names should be found in some sample *.csv files on the Exchange Server CD-ROM. Note that it's not necessary to insert columns in any particular order—you just have to ensure there's a match between the column header and the Exchange schema.

FIGURE 11.8.

Completion of the first step of the Migration Wizard.

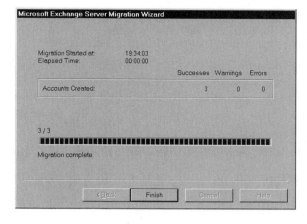

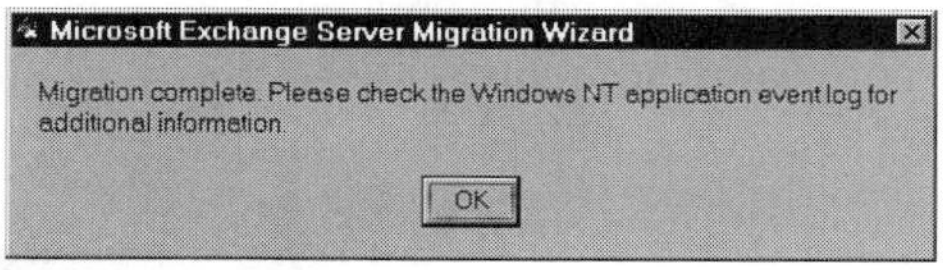

FIGURE 11.9.

Misleading MigWiz completion dialog box.

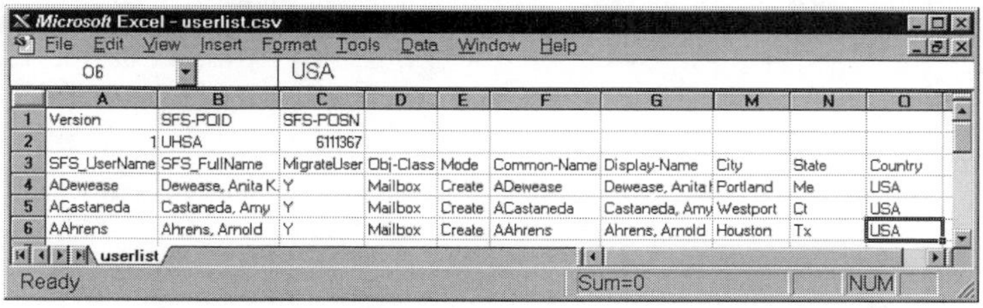

FIGURE 11.10.

Modifying the MigWiz export file.

TIP

The MS Mail directory yields only a display name Smith, John and mailbox name Jsmith by default. There aren't fields in its directory for First Name and Last Name. This can cause functional issues, because Exchange's name resolution of strings typed into the To: field of new messages searches the last name field (along with display name and alias). You can extract the first and last name values from the display name using Excel and import these separate names into the Exchange directory. Microsoft's knowledge base article Q148500, found at http://www.microsoft.com/kb/, gives the steps required.

One of the big advantages to using this two-step process is that you can perform data updates and additions more efficiently. Another is that you can delegate the work to others without having to give them Exchange Admin access permissions. I highly recommend that in order to protect the integrity of your data, you use Excel's ability to protect cells from modification. Highlight the cell range(s) you want someone to be *able* to modify, select Format | Cell from the menu, and clear the Locked checkbox on the Protection property page. Then, select Tools | Protection | Protect Sheet and enter a password. Save the file in Excel format to preserve this cell protection formatting. You can now pass this file to another person for data entry work without fear of jeopardizing the original data from your postoffice directory. You need to save the file back into .csv format before performing the second step of MigWiz, of course.

When you have the .csv file ready, relaunch MigWiz and move through the pages to the same step as displayed in Figure 11.6. Select Step 2 and enter the filepath for your modified .csv file.

You are given the chance to specify what mailbox and schedule data will be pulled across (see Figure 11.11). One of the nice features here is the ability to bring only recent mail—in whatever date range you like. This is a great opportunity to clean house. You should warn users that only mail newer than X date will be migrated, and give them instructions on using the MS Mail client's export feature to archive any messages they want to retain before you migrate their accounts.

FIGURE 11.11.

Parameters for the migration of mailbox data.

If you check Personal Address Books, MigWiz will extract the personal address book entries from each mailbox's .mmf file into an Exchange .pab file format. Each mailbox will receive an e-mail with its .pab file attached. The message will contain instructions to the user on saving the attachment and using the File | Import command in the MAPI client to draw the entries into their own .pab file.

Specify a server name. MigWiz will go to that server and extract the recipient container list for you to select a target container (see Figures 11.12 and 11.13). Note that if you want the MS Mail mailboxes to be migrated into different containers, or to different servers, you need to run MigWiz once for each server/container combination.

Note that you can specify an Exchange mailbox to be used as a template, as shown in Figure 11.13. This is slightly cumbersome; the mailbox cannot be hidden, so it will appear in the GAL unless you just unhide it for MigWiz sessions. It's also not as flexible as editing a .csv file—a template will make *all* mailboxes show the same value for a given field. But it has its place in the scheme of things—fields like company name, for instance. To create a template mailbox, simply create an Exchange mailbox and fill in only the field you want to populate across all maiboxes. Save the mailbox without specifying a primary Windows NT account, then select it in the MigWiz previous page.

FIGURE 11.12.

Select the target server for the migrated mailboxes.

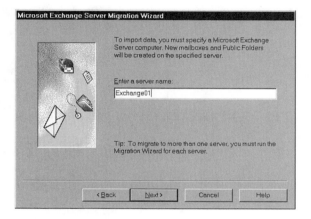

FIGURE 11.13.

Select a recipient container for the mailboxes.

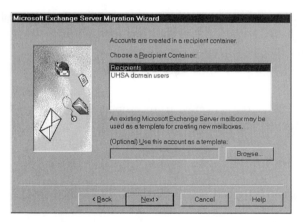

You can specify how MigWiz will handle assigning ownership of these new mailboxes to NT domain accounts (see Figure 11.14). If there is a direct match between a new mailbox's alias and the username of a domain account in the specified domain, that domain account will automatically be given Primary Owner permissions. If there is no exact match, the rule you select below will apply. The first two options have a nice fringe benefit: the display name for the mailbox will be used for the Full Name field in the domain account information. Also, the username and passwords of the newly created domain accounts are saved into the file \exchsrvr\bin\account.password. Random password generation effectively prevents use of the domain account and mailbox until you reset the password for the domain or distribute the values found in the account.password file. Using the second option lets users immediately start using their new accounts without any additional labor on your part, but it is less secure. If you know that matching domain accounts already exist, or if you want to create the domain accounts in a separate process (perhaps to make use of a domain template account), select the third option.

Figure 11.14.

Rules for creating NT domain accounts for new mailboxes.

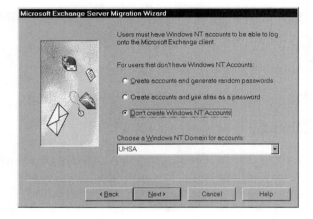

This is an area where the mailbox/account creation process could be improved upon. You are given a chance to specify a mailbox template, but here, where a domain account can be created, there's no way to use a domain account template. It would be quite tedious to manually specify home directories, group memberships, and profile paths for all newly created domain accounts.

Lastly, the Wizard will begin the process of creating Exchange mailboxes for the indicated users and copying their .mmf file contents to Exchange. You will have a dialog box to track the progress (see Figure 11.15), and each mailbox created will have a corresponding entry in the NT Event Log.

Figure 11.15.

Mailbox migration progress dialog box.

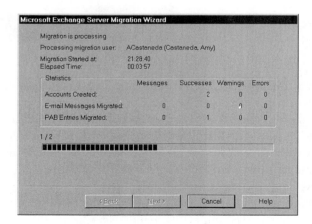

> **WARNING**
>
> The MS Mail mailboxes being migrated must not have clients logged in those mailboxes while the Migration Wizard is working! The migration of those mailboxes will fail, and the Wizard is none too specific about that fact—it just tells you to check the Event Log for more information about the migration session. The MS Mail client locks its associated .mmf file open, which prevents the Wizard from accessing the contents. Because the usual procedure is to migrate the mailbox, delete the mailbox, then DirSync the directories, this problem can have unpleasant consequences.
>
> If you're running the MigWiz against a handful of mailboxes, you can use Server Manager to ensure that the affected users don't have their .mmf files open. If you're migrating an entire postoffice, the safest thing is to stop sharing the \maildata directory and then reshare it with access only to the account under which you're running MigWiz. This will disconnect all MS Mail clients.

The migration of an entire postoffice mailbox can take some time. A 700MB, 500-mailbox postoffice took 12 hours to migrate to Exchange, where the MigWiz was running directly on the Exchange server with one Pentium 90, 80MB RAM, and two mirrored disk volumes. I didn't employ the date filter on the mailbox contents, however, to filter down the quantity of messages.

When the MigWiz finishes its work, it refers you to the Event Log to check for more information. You should definitely scan this for any red stop symbols, to ensure that none of the mailboxes were orphaned on the postoffice. You can also keep the postoffice \maildata directory archived on the server for a few weeks as a fallback, in case someone needs access to the original .mmf files for whatever reason.

Message Transfer: Microsoft Mail Connector

Setting up message transfer between an Exchange server and a Microsoft Mail postoffice is a pleasantly simple thing. If you have multiple postoffices and already have the MS Mail MTA External deployed, you will want to take some time to plan how to integrate the two mail networks during the migration.

The Exchange Microsoft Mail Connector is almost a complete replacement for External. It will perform message transfer over LAN, dial-up connections, and X.25; the only thing it can't do is support Microsoft Mail Remote dial-in clients. If you have remote users deployed with MS Mail Remote, you need to keep at least one instance of External running.

Because Exchange was designed with a shadow MS Mail postoffice, you have the flexibility of using either Exchange's MS Mail Connector or an instance of External. The Exchange MTA will move outbound messages from the information store to the shadow postoffice, shared as

\\exchangeserver\maildat$. From there, it can be picked up and transferred by External or the MS Mail Connector. Because of the greatly increased robustness of the Exchange code, the message tracking capability, the logging built in to Exchange, and the monitoring functions, you will probably want to retire your instances of External and begin using the MS Mail Connector instead.

Integration with Existing Postoffice(s)

If you have a number of postoffices, you can set up the MS Mail Connector with a single MTA acting as a hub for all the postoffices (see Figure 11.16).

Figure 11.16.

Configuration possibility for the MS Mail Connector: single MTA hub.

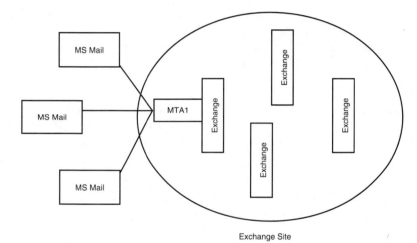

Exchange Site

Alternately, you can install several MTAs under the Connector to service different groups of them, as shown in Figure 11.17. This approach is recommended when you have different connectivity, such as servicing all modem-linked postoffices with one MTA and the LAN postoffices with another.

Figure 11.18 shows a large organization with numerous physical sites, using an Exchange Server at each site to localize both the message transfer and directory synchronization traffic. The connections between the different Exchange servers over the WAN links provide the backbone functionality for the MS Mail postoffices.

Last, if you chose to use your existing MS Mail MTAs for message transfer, your network would look like Figure 11.19.

FIGURE 11.17.
*Configuration
possibility for the MS
Mail Connector:
multiple MTAs.*

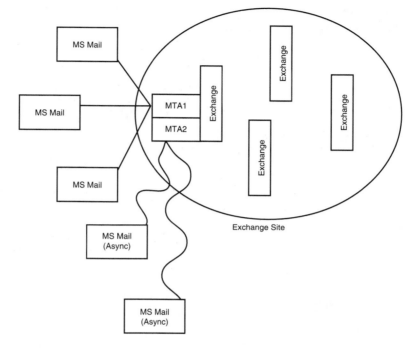

FIGURE 11.18.
*Configuration
possibility for the MS
Mail Connector:
backboning MS Mail
traffic over Exchange.*

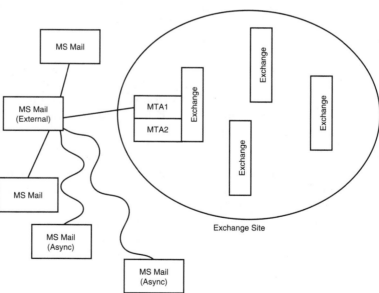

FIGURE 11.19.

*Configuration where
existing MS Mail
External MTAs are
used.*

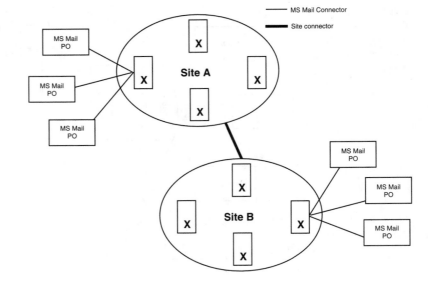

Configuration

The overview of setting up message transfer between Exchange and MS Mail is as follows:

1. Ensure that the MS Mail Connector is installed on your Exchange server.

2. Configure entries in Exchange for all the MS Mail postoffices it needs to be aware of so it can build a routing table with all the postoffice entries.

3. Configure all your MS Mail postoffices with an External Postoffice defined for Exchange.

4. Either create one or more Connector MTAs to run on your Exchange server or configure your existing MS Mail External program(s) to service the shadow postoffice on the Exchange server.

First, ensure the MS Mail Connector is presently installed on your Exchange server! If you've purchased the Enterprise Edition of Exchange, it should be listed in the Admin program under Site | Connections. If not, rerun the Exchange Server Setup program, click the Add/Remove button, click the Change Option button for Microsoft Exchange Server, and check the box for the MS Mail Connector. Performing this addition does not require that you reboot the machine or even stop and restart the Exchange services. If you originally purchased the Standard Edition of Exchange Server, the MS Mail Connector isn't included—you need to purchase the Connector seperately.

Next, launch the Exchange Admin and change to the Site | Connections container, as shown in Figure 11.20. Double-click the MS Mail Connector object, and you will have the MS Mail Connector Properties dialog box, Interchange page, as shown in Figure 11.21.

FIGURE 11.20.

Location of the MS Mail Connector object.

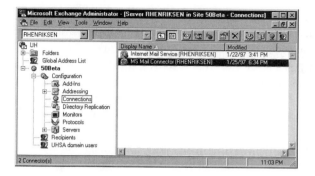

FIGURE 11.21.

MS Mail Connector Properties dialog, Interchange page.

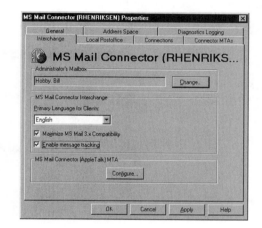

First, specify an Administrator's Mailbox. You can set up a separate mailbox that will serve as the location for notifications from the Internet Mail Service, MS Mail Connector, and so forth, or simply specify your own. I prefer to select my own account until the entire Exchange installation is established. You can then go back and modify this assignment—changing this value later isn't a problem.

The Maximize MS Mail 3.*x* compatibility checkbox means that messages with embedded attachments sent from Exchange clients will be converted to OLE 1.0 objects. It's important to leave this checked if MS Mail clients need to be able to receive embedded data. Note that this does apply to a simple attached file from an Exchange client. It applies only when the OLE 2.0 capabilities of Exchange are used—to paste a range of spreadsheet cells into a message, for instance. Note also that leaving this feature enabled does have a downside: The total message size for each message so converted is increased. The other setting on this page, Enable message tracking, is well worth turning on. You can cap the number of days of tracking logs maintained by the system, and you can't anticipate when you will need access to this information. So there are definitely benefits to employing this feature and little or no downside.

Compatibility

The next property page, Local Postoffice, displayed in Figure 11.22, is usually a read-only page for you. This page gives the network name and postoffice name for the shadow postoffice on the Exchange server. You refer to the network name and postoffice name when configuring directory synchronization and setting up the External postoffice names on your MS Mail postoffices. These values are taken from your Organization name and site name, and they are by far the safest values for you to use. It doesn't hurt anything to have several network names in use in your MS Mail system. If you want to change this value, it's better to do this early. Changing this value is akin to changing the site addressing values, but probably worse—in addition to using the Regenerate button to change the MS Mail addresses for all objects in the site, you need to change all your MS Mail postoffices to point to this new postoffice name. There will be plenty of potential for bounced mail if you change these values after mail starts flowing through your organization.

FIGURE 11.22.

Postoffice properties for the "shadow" postoffice on the Exchange Server.

The next two property pages, Connections (see Figure 11.23) and Connector MTAs, can be somewhat confusing at first. The first page is similar to defining External postoffices for an MS Mail postoffice—letting Exchange know what MS Mail postoffices exist and whether they're direct or indirect. The next property page, Connector MTAs, enables you to create and configure one or more MTA services. You definitely need to make at least one entry in the Connections page, but if that link to a postoffice will be serviced by an instance of MS Mail's External program, no configuration in the Connector MTA page is required. Use of Exchange's MTA is recommended over the MS Mail External program.

On the Connections page, click the Create button to get the Create Connection dialog box, shown in Figure 11.24. This is also a bit confusing—rather than fill in the network name and postoffice name, you give it the UNC path to the postoffice share, and it will extract the necessary information itself.

FIGURE 11.23.

MS Mail Connector dialog, Connections page.

FIGURE 11.24.

Defining an external MS Mail postoffice to Exchange.

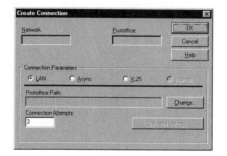

Click the Change button in the Connection Parameters section of this dialog and enter the UNC path into the resulting dialog box, as shown in Figure 11.25.

FIGURE 11.25.

Entering the UNC path to the external postoffice.

If the Exchange service account does not have share or file/directory permissions on the postoffice in question, you can use the Connect As and Password fields to supply a different domain account, just as you use the Connect As field in Explorer when mapping a drive letter. Be sure to use a format of *domain\username* in the Connect As field. If the service account already has access to the maildata share, leave Connect As fields blank. When you click OK, you should return to the Create Connection dialog box, now filled in with the network name and postoffice name.

11

MIGRATING FROM
MICROSOFT MAIL

The Upload Routing button in this dialog is used to extract the information about all the External postoffices known to this first postoffice. You want to use this only in the event that you want MS Mail's External program to handle most of the MTA traffic. You would define one connection between Exchange and a sample MS Mail postoffice and then extract information about all the other postoffices through that beachhead postoffice. That information is used to build the routing table for your Exchange site. It lets all the Exchange servers in the site know that if a message needs to go to any of the MS Mail network\postoffice names discovered as downstream of the beachhead PO, the message needs to be placed in the outbox of your Exchange server's shadow postoffice. From there, an instance of MS Mail External will pick it up and deliver it to the appropriate mailbox.

> **NOTE**
>
> In addition to defining the MS Mail postoffice to Exchange, be sure to add the Exchange shadow postoffice's network/postoffice name in the list of External postoffices at each MS Mail postoffice.

If you're using a hub-style messaging topology, as modeled in Figure 11.13, you definitely do not want to use the Upload Routing capability. Instead, repeat this Create Connection procedure to define all the postoffices that will be serviced by the Exchange MTA. If this is a postoffice accessible over your LAN or WAN, click OK to return to the MS Mail Connector dialog box—you've finished defining this postoffice. If this postoffice is accessible only via modem or X.25, select the appropriate radio button in the Connection Parameters section of this dialog and fill in the remaining fields.

If you're using MS Mail External MTAs and using the Upload Routing command to define indirect postoffices, the Connections property page will look like Figure 11.26. There will be one postoffice directly under your server icon, and the remaining postoffices will be indented below the first. For each hop required, the postoffices will be indented a column further over. With the Exchange-as-hub routing, your Connections page will look like Figure 11.27—all of the postoffices you define will be serviced by Exchange MTAs, and they will be indented a single level below the Exchange server.

Now that you've defined the postoffice(s) that your Exchange site and organization will be communicating with, you will want to create message transfer agents (MTAs) to perform the actual movement of messages out to the MS Mail postoffices and retrieve inbound messages from their outboxes. Change to the Connector MTAs property page (see Figure 11.28).

Click the New button and type in a name for this MTA in the resulting dialog box (see Figure 11.29). I prefer to use a format of MTA-*whatever*. The lack of spaces means you don't have to encase the name in quotes if you use batch files to manipulate the service, and the prefix of MTA- puts it in directly after the MSExchange service entries in the Service list for the server.

FIGURE 11.26.

MS Mail Connector,
Connections page using
MS Mail External for
message transfer.

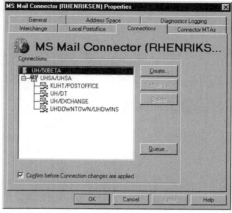

FIGURE 11.27.

MS Mail Connector,
Connections page using
Exchange MTA(s) as a
routing hub.

FIGURE 11.28.

MS Mail Connector,
Connector MTAs page.

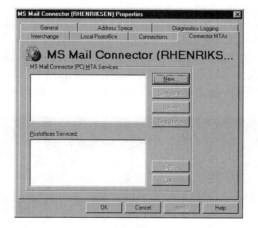

FIGURE 11.29.

*Creating a new
Exchange-to-MS Mail
MTA.*

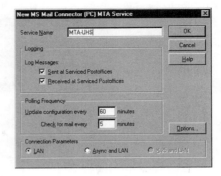

Unlike most of the other logging parameters for the functions in Exchange, MTA logging switches are buried in the property page for each MTA instance. Click OK to return to the Connector MTA page (refer to Figure 11.28). Now that you've created an MTA, you have to list what postoffices this MTA should service. To ensure that the new MTA is highlighted in the upper list of this dialog box, click the List button by the lower list window. You will see a screen like Figure 11.30, listing all the postoffices that are known from the Connections page. Double-click each PO name you want serviced by this MTA, to move them over to the Serviced LAN Postoffices column. Click OK when finished.

FIGURE 11.30.

*Defining the postoffices
serviced by a new MS
Mail Connector MTA.*

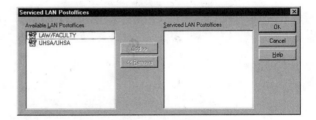

If you move to the Address Space property page, you will see that the entries have all been filled in appropriately for the Connections and MTAs that you've established. Note that there are costs associated with each route. This gives you the opportunity to do such things as set up a primary MTA and route for a connection to a remote postoffice over a WAN link with a cost of 1; then define a backup MTA that would use a modem over an async connection, with a cost of 100 (only used when no other option is available).

TIP

A reminder about cost values in Exchange: When applied to connectors and MTAs, values from 1 to 100 are used. The values of 1 and 100 have special significance. A route of 1 is used exclusively, unless and until that link has failed. Only then will other routes be used. A route with a cost of 100 will never be used until all other connection possibilities have failed. When your routes are all between 2 and 99 (that is, no 1 paths exist) they are all used, but the distribution of traffic is weighted towards the lower-cost routes.

Exchange also uses the total cost of a route—the sum of costs of each link, or hop. In other words, Exchange will distribute more traffic over a single-hop link with a cost of 3 than a two-hop link with costs of 2 and 2 (2+2=4, 4>3).

Monitoring

Monitoring the MS Mail Connector comes back to the same tools as most Exchange components: event logging, performance monitor screens, and e-mail notifications.

The event logging levels can be set in two places: in the MS Mail Connector properties dialog box, Diagnostic Logging page; and within the property page for the server itself). There are three diagnostic categories for this connector (see Table 11.1).

Table 11.1. MS Mail Connector diagnostic logging categories.

Category	Description
MSExchangeMSMI	Microsoft Mail Interchange—activity between Exchange and the shadow postoffice
MSExchangePCMTA	PC Message Transfer Agent—message transfer activity between the shadow postoffice and External MS Mail postoffices
MSExchangeATMTA	AppleTalk Message Transfer Agent—message transfer activity between the shadow postoffice and MS Mail for AppleTalk Network postoffices

As with all Exchange logging, you probably don't want to crank the levels up to medium or maximum except for very short focused periods while you're reproducing a problem. You can very quickly drown under a flood of event log entries.

The Performance Monitor has the usual overwhelming flood of objects and counters to pick from. I keep several different instances of PerfMon running as my wallpaper, to keep any one instance from getting too cluttered with lines. A good counter to add to your "first alert" window is the counter Work Queue Length in the MSExchangeMTA object. It shows whether messages are stacking up. Because the MTA is a core Exchange server component, its work queue reflects all the MTA flow through that server, not exclusively for the MS Mail Connector. There are two other PerfMon objects that deal specifically with MS Mail:

Performance

- MSExchangeMSMI (Microsoft Mail Interchange)
- MSExchangePCMTA (Microsoft Mail for PC Networks Message Transfer Agent(s))

The MSMI object has counters for showing only the quantity of traffic, not for specifically indicating a problem. Unless you have a very steady, constant flow of traffic between Exchange and MS Mail so that a drop in activity would be telling, this object can't give you any warning indications.

The PCMTA object lets you select any of its counters against individual Connector MTAs or measure its values across all the MTAs. There are two counters that give you some warning signs of problems: LAN/WAN Failed Connections and X.25/Asynch Failed Connections. These, in conjunction with the Work queue length, give you a good start on some real-time monitoring. A server monitor and link monitor will round out the picture, but implementation of those will be covered in Chapter 27, "Monitoring and Preventing Problems."

Directory Synchronization

The nuts and bolts of implementing directory synchronization between Exchange and a Microsoft Mail network are left to the next chapter. Here is the overview:

- You can make one Exchange server within your site the DirSync Server for your MS Mail network or make one server a requestor against an existing MS Mail DirSync server.

- You can leave an existing Dispatch process running on the MS Mail side or use a batch file running directory on the Exchange server to perform the same function.

- In order to be able to perform a manual DirSync cycle, you must make a small registry modification to the MSExchange Directory Synchronization service and restart that service. Manual DirSync is extremely useful during a staged migration—you can migrate mailboxes during a workday and immediately update the MS Mail GAL to reflect the new addresses of the migrated mailboxes.

Retiring the MS Mail SMTP Gateway

Here's one of the best parts about deploying an Exchange server—getting to deep-six that old Microsoft SMTP Gateway for Microsoft Mail! You can shift all inbound and outbound Internet message traffic for all the existing MS Mail postoffices over to the Internet Mail Service (IMS) on an Exchange server, and no one's address has to change. The users should never know anything's happened—except that they won't be calling you anymore asking whether the gateway is down. They also won't be calling you anymore asking what the 10,000 lines of hash at the bottom of a message are (an attached file that didn't get decoded).

Here are the steps to take:

1. Install, configure, and test the IMS on your Exchange server, using the procedures outlined in Part III, "Implementation."

2. Deploy directory synchronization between Exchange and MS Mail. Without this, Exchange won't have any knowledge of the MS Mail mailboxes. There has to be a custom recipient in the Exchange GAL for each MS Mail account.

3. Use the migsmtp.exe utility in the Exchange Resource Kit to add a second SMTP address for each custom recipient.

4. Update your organization's DNS; have the host name of your old SMTP Gateway aliased against the Exchange SMTP site address.

5. Insert the SMTP Gateway installation diskette in your SMTP Gateway computer and run INSTALL -R to remove the gateway. Reconfigure the postoffice as a downsteam postoffice so it will still handle outbound SMTP mail correctly for the MS Mail clients (forwarding it to Exchange's shadow postoffice).

In step two, you can either use DirSync to populate the Exchange GAL with custom recipients for the MS Mail mailboxes or perform a one-time directory import/export. I strongly recommend using DirSync, however. If you run the batch file included on the Exchange Unleashed CD-ROM, you avoid some of the hassle of maintaining separate dispatch computers (in MS Mail 3.2 or older) or the configuration complexities in setting up the Dispatch service on an NT box (MS Mail 3.5).

Migsmtp is a wonderful utility. It will let you run through every mailbox and custom recipient in a server's directory and add a second SMTP address. That extra SMTP address can be made the default replyto address, or kept strictly secondary. For instance, let's say you've selected an Exchange SMTP site address of @foobar.com. You have two MS Mail postoffices serviced by an MS Mail SMTP Gateway, and the gateway maps the two postoffices to addresses of @mail1.foobar.com and @mail2.foobar.com.

All the custom recipients you've created via DirSync for the MS Mail users now show one SMTP address in the Exchange GAL, @foobar.com. Even if you reconfigured your DNS to route @mail1.foobar.com mail to the Exchange server computer, it would be rejected by the Exchange IMS; Fred@mail1.foobar.com doesn't exist—Exchange knows only about Fred@foobar.com. Run migsmtp and add a second SMTP address to Fred's mailbox, @mail1.foobar.com. Now Exchange knows to accept that message for Fred, and because the MS Mail address for Fred's custom recipient entry is the legacy postoffice, the Exchange MTA knows to direct the message to the MS Mail Connector for transfer to Fred's mailbox on the old postoffice.

Now that you've got Exchange ready to accept and properly route inbound SMTP mail for the MS Mail mailboxes, you can reconfigure your DNS. Before, the hostnames mail1.foobar.com and mail2.foobar.com both resolved to the IP address of the old SMTP gateway. Now, have these two names aliased to the hostname of the Exchange server. That should take care of the inbound mail. Besides being infinitely more reliable, MS Mail users will now enjoy properly decoded attachments whether they're sent in UUENCODE, BinHex, or MIME. The old gateway only supported UUENCODE.

Lastly, you will want the outbound mail handled by the Exchange IMS also. Run the install program for the SMTP Gateway with an -R switch, on the gateway computer. It will remove the gateway software from the postoffice and ask you whether you would like to reconfigure this postoffice to be downstream postoffice. This is exactly what you want—give it the network name and postoffice names for the *shadow* postoffice on the Exchange server. Use the disk for the Gateway Access Component to ensure that any and all other postoffices are aware that the upstream PO is now the shadow postoffice as well.

Summary

In this chapter, you reviewed the different strategies for migration (crash versus staged), keeping in mind the complications behind conducting a staged migration. You explored the mechanics of directory export/import and use of the Migration Wizard, as well as the planning, configuration, and monitoring of the MS Mail Connector.

You looked at an overview of Directory Synchronization to prepare you for Chapter 20, because DirSync is an important part of retiring the SMTP Gateway. Finally, you learned the steps required to retire the old SMTP Gateway for Microsoft Mail and service all inbound and outbound MS Mail via the Exchange Internet Mail Service.

PART

III

IN THIS PART

Implementation

Installing Microsoft Exchange Server

by Greg Todd

IN THIS CHAPTER

CHAPTER

12

Now that you've finished the preparation and planning phases, you are ready to install the actual Exchange Server software.

This chapter is straightforward, covering the following main topics specific to Exchange Server 5.0:

- Items to consider before running Setup
- An overview of the general installation process
- An introduction to Microsoft Exchange Optimizer
- An overview of the Exchange Server icons, including the Performance Monitor workspaces

This chapter steps you through the process of installing the Exchange server. There are multiple screen shots throughout to clarify the information presented and to show that the Exchange Server Setup is a simple matter. After you read this chapter, you should have a clear understanding of the Exchange Server installation process.

Before You Run Setup

Compatibility   The following is a list of tasks you should complete before you run the Setup program for Exchange Server 5.0:

- If your Exchange server will be on a Windows NT 3.51 Server computer, be sure Service Pack 5 (or later) is installed.

  You absolutely must have Service Pack 5 installed before you set up Exchange. If not, you will get a warning screen like Figure 12.1 when you run Setup, and Exchange will not install.

- If your Exchange server will be on a Windows NT 4.0 Server computer, no service pack is required. However, if you want to use Active Server components, be sure Service Pack 2 (or later) is installed.

  You can read more about how Exchange Server 5.0 integrates with the Active Server technology in Chapter 32, "Exchange Server as Part of the Active Server Platform."

- Designate an account to use as the Exchange *services account*.

  You need to have an account prepared so you can allow Setup to grant it advanced user rights, which have to be in place for Setup to configure the proper context in which to install and run Microsoft Exchange Server. See the Tip if you want to know more about setting or examining the user rights.

FIGURE 12.1.

Exchange Setup will not proceed with NT Server 3.51 if you do not have at least Service Pack 5 installed.

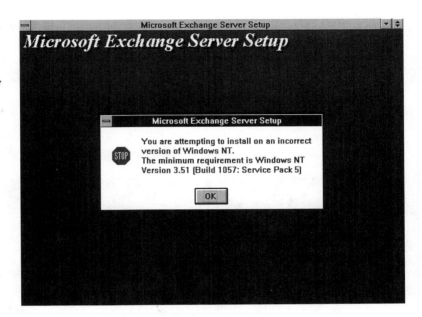

TIP

I do not recommend using the built-in Administrator account as the services account. This is inherently insecure, and you should create a new Domain Administrator account expressly for the purpose of serving as the Exchange services account.

Security

■ Be sure the Primary Domain Controller (PDC) or the Backup Domain Controller (BDC) in your NT domain is up and running.

The domain's PDC or BDC must be up and running to have a successful installation. Additionally, you can install Microsoft Exchange Server on a PDC, a BDC, or any server participating in a domain. If you expect your Exchange Server usage to be light and you want to minimize the number of machines used, install it on your PDC. If you expect your Exchange Server usage to be heavy, consider installing it on a stand-alone server in the domain so Exchange doesn't have to authenticate users in the domain.

■ Know whether this server is the first server in an Exchange site or an additional server in an existing site.

You need to know whether this is your first server in a site or an additional server in an existing site as Setup asks you. Refer to Chapter 7, "Considerations for a Successful Rollout," for more information about configuring sites.

■ Ensure that TCP/IP is installed and configured if you plan to install the Internet Mail Service.

The Exchange Internet Mail Service uses TCP/IP to connect to the Internet or other SMTP-based e-mail services, so you must have TCP/IP installed and configured before using it.

■ Close any MAPI-based applications before starting Setup.

Be sure there are no applications open that use MAPI, such as Microsoft Word or Microsoft Mail. The best thing is to have nothing else running at all during Setup.

SETTING A USER RIGHT IN WINDOWS NT SERVER

Here's how to manually configure or examine an account for any user right. In this example, you check to ensure that the DUNE\ExchAdmin account has the Log on as a service user right:

1. Run the User Manager for Domains program, which is usually found in the Administrative Tools folder.

2. Select Policies | User Rights to bring up the User Rights Policy dialog box.

3. Check the Show Advanced User Rights checkbox; search down the Right: list box and select Log on as a service. The Grant To: list box should be empty.

4. Click the Add button to bring up the Add Users and Groups dialog box. Click the Show Users button and find the domain account you want to grant the right to log on as a service. Click the Add button and the name appears in the Add Names box at the bottom of the dialog. Click OK to close the dialog box and return to the User Rights Policy dialog box.

5. The Grant To: list box should now contain the domain account you selected. Figure 12.2 shows how this might look. Click OK to finish.

6. Close the User Manager for Domains program.

Again, Microsoft Exchange Server Setup does all this for you—all you need to do is tell it which account should be granted the special user rights that Exchange needs. But in case you ever need to set or examine specific user rights, now you know how.

Running Setup

To run Setup, find the appropriate Setup program, SETUP.EXE, on your Microsoft Exchange Server CD-ROM. It is in a directory that matches the computer type you have. For example, if you are running an Intel-based machine, you will run Setup from the \Setup\I386 directory.

FIGURE 12.2.
*The DUNE\
ExchAdmin account
has been granted the
user right to Log on as a
service.*

The Welcome Screen

After you find the appropriate version of Setup and run it, you see a screen that looks like Figure 12.3.

FIGURE 12.3.
*The Microsoft
Exchange Server Setup
opening screen.*

You might want to click the Help button to get some additional information about Setup.

The Opening Screen

After you click OK, you're presented with another screen like Figure 12.4.

There are three setup options in Figure 12.4:

- *Typical* installs the Microsoft Exchange Server software and the Administrator program. No client software, connectors, or online documentation (EXCHDOC.HLP) is installed. If you need a basic server installation, you probably want to choose this option. However, if this is your first server, you might want to select Complete/Custom.

- *Complete/Custom*, as the name implies, enables you to choose what to install from the available options, including online documentation, client software, and connectors.

■ *Minimum* installs only the Microsoft Exchange Server software. Choose this option if you already have other Exchange servers installed and don't need all the extras—the Administrator program, connectors, or help files—on this server.

You can also change the destination directory where the Exchange files will be installed. Setup automatically selects the first drive it finds with enough disk space to accommodate a minimum installation, but you might want to change it if you want the files somewhere else.

Custom Installation

If you choose the Complete/Custom option, you are presented with a screen like Figure 12.5. If you choose one of the other options, you skip this screen.

From this screen, you can pick and choose which options to install. The first option, Microsoft Exchange Server, has options within it that can be selected or deselected. Click the Change Option button to see them.

A complete installation takes almost 150MB of disk space. This includes the server software, MS Mail Connector, cc:Mail Connector, X.400 Connector, sample applications, Microsoft Exchange Administrator program, Active Server components, and the online documentation. If you don't need some of these, especially the connectors and sample applications, uncheck them now so they aren't installed.

A minimum installation, consisting of just the Microsoft Exchange Server program, takes about 90MB of disk space.

FIGURE 12.5.
This shows custom installation with all available options selected.

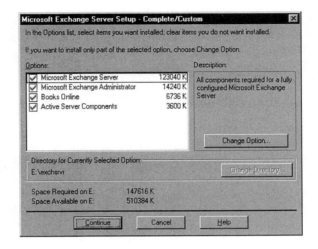

Web Service

Before the installation proceeds, the World Wide Web Publishing Service needs to be stopped, as shown in Figure 12.6. It will be started again automatically when Setup is finished.

New to
Version 5.0

FIGURE 12.6.
The World Wide Web Publishing Service needs to be stopped.

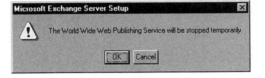

Licensing Mode

After you select the type of installation, Setup asks you to specify the client licensing mode, Per Server or Per Seat, as shown in Figure 12.7.

The two licensing options, and adding and removing licenses, are explained in the online help. Press the Help button to read about them.

Organization and Site

In the next screen, you specify the Exchange organization and site information for this server. If this is the first server in a new site, Figure 12.8 shows how the screen should look.

Note that the Create a new site radio button is selected by default. Also, the Organization Name and Site Name fields are automatically filled in with the company name you specified when you originally installed Windows NT Server and with the NT Server domain name, respectively. Both these fields must have a value.

FIGURE 12.7.

This screen is where you specify the client licensing mode for Microsoft Exchange Server.

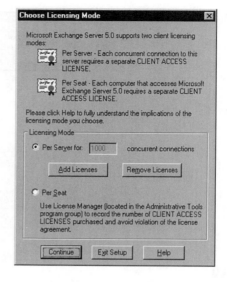

FIGURE 12.8.

This is the screen where the organization and site information is specified.

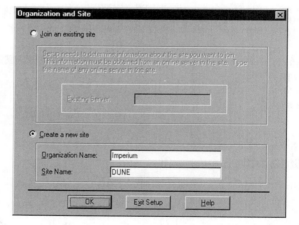

Sometimes you might be installing an additional Exchange server in an existing site. If this is the case, click the Join an existing site radio button. You must then specify the name of an existing server in the site, as in Figure 12.9. The Exchange server you specify must be up and running, because Setup proceeds to poll it for site-specific information to be used in your new server.

Services Account

At this point, Setup is almost ready to start copying files to the server. However, you need to designate a special account as a services account. Figure 12.10 shows how Setup prompts you for the account. Use the Browse button to find the desired account and fill in the box. You must have the password for this account, and it must be a Domain Administrator account.

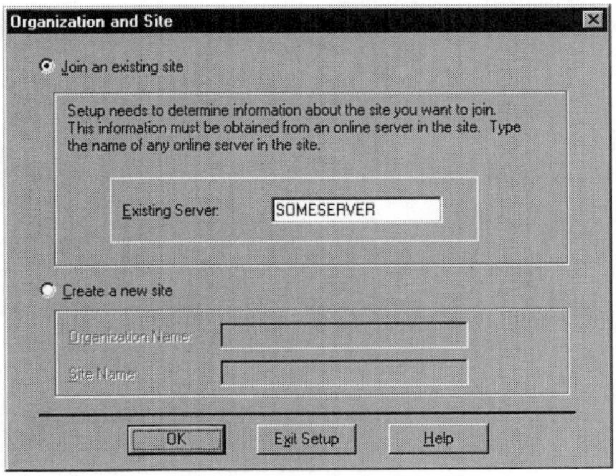

FIGURE 12.9.

Your new server will join the existing Exchange site of which SOMESERVER is a member.

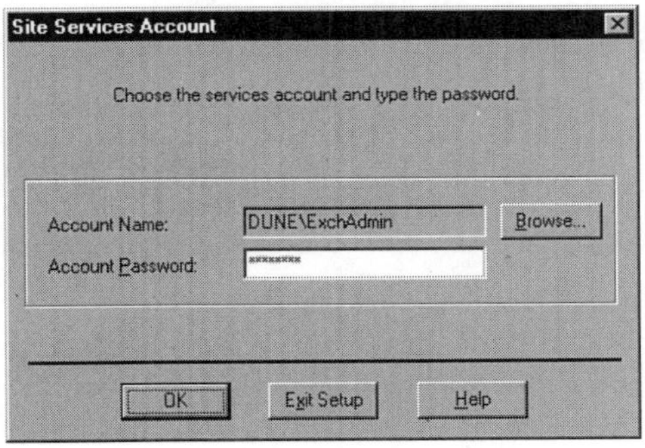

FIGURE 12.10.

ExchAdmin is the services account designated in the domain DUNE.

The services account has to be in place for several reasons. First, the core of Exchange Server is actually a collection of multiple NT services for the information store, the directory, and so on. These services are started and run by the services account.

Security

Also, all additional Exchange servers in the same site use this same services account to start and run their services. Furthermore, all Exchange servers in a site communicate with each other using this account for a security context. If one server needs to send another server a message, the services account is one of the basic elements that enables them to talk to each other.

So, if you're installing two servers in the same site, you need to specify the same services account for both of them. If you don't, they won't be able to communicate with each other.

> **NOTE**
>
> There's one other twist on this: Exchange servers in the same site don't have to be in the same NT domain, provided there is a trust relationship established between the domains. However, although they're in different domains, they still must use the same services account.

If your designated services account does not already have the appropriate rights, Setup will do it for you. (See Figure 12.11.)

FIGURE 12.11.
*The services account
was granted the
appropriate advanced
user rights by Setup.*

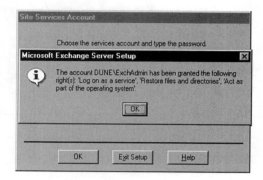

The Log on as a service user right is granted to the services account so the Exchange Server processes can register with Windows NT as a service. When the services attempt to start, they must log on to NT using the security context of the services account. And if the services account is not given this right, the Exchange Server services will not start.

The Restore files and directories user right is also granted to the services account. This means just what it says; files and directories can be restored regardless of file and directory permissions already in place. In a domain, this right applies to the Primary and Backup Domain Controllers. On a nondomain controller server, this right applies only to that computer. Although this right is already granted to the Domain Administrators group, Setup wants to ensure it is granted to the specific services account.

Finally, the Act as part of the operating system user right is granted to the services account. This right allows a process within Windows NT to perform as a secure, trusted part of the operating system. Some subsystems within Windows NT are granted this right by default. Likewise, the Exchange Server services must be provided the right to act as a part of the operating system because they are also considered a trusted component of NT.

Performance

Finishing Setup—Microsoft Exchange Optimizer

At this point of the process, Setup will ensure everything is ready to go, and it will start copying files.

After Setup successfully finishes its job of copying, modifying the Registry, and installing services, you get the opportunity to run the Microsoft Exchange Optimizer as shown in Figure 12.12. The Optimizer is covered in detail in Chapter 6, "Planning for Optimal Server Performance."

FIGURE 12.12.

After Setup completes,
it automatically
prompts you to run the
Microsoft Exchange
Server Optimizer.

Typically, you run the Optimizer utility so that the internal Exchange Server parameters can be set according to your system resources. Exchange Server's default internal parameters are likely not to be configured correctly for your system, so it's a good idea to run Optimizer when you finish Setup.

TIP

My usual practice is to exit Setup at this point without running Optimizer and modify the Target in the Shortcut property of the Microsoft Exchange Optimizer icon to pass -v (verbose) as a parameter to PERFWIZ.EXE, as shown in Figure 12.13. Then I run the Optimizer program. This way, I get more detailed information on exactly what parameters are altered in the system. Optimizer's verbose mode is covered in Chapter 6.

FIGURE 12.13.

You can modify
Microsoft Exchange
Optimizer properties so
it runs in verbose mode.

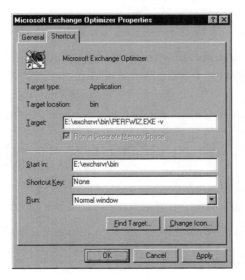

The engineers at Microsoft have spent a great deal of time and effort to make Optimizer as smart as possible about the configuration decisions it makes. If you run in verbose mode, it becomes apparent just how many different server parameters there are. And from my experience, Optimizer does a fine job of setting them correctly.

Microsoft Exchange Server Icons

Now you are finished with the Microsoft Exchange Server Setup program. If the setup is successful, it will have created a common folder named Microsoft Exchange that contains some icons, similar to Figure 12.14.

FIGURE 12.14.

Microsoft Exchange Server Setup automatically installs several icons in a common folder.

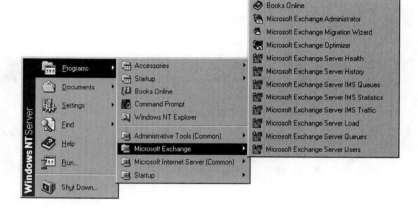

There are several icons here, so let's take a look at them.

First, if you installed online documentation, you will see the Books Online icon. This is a help file that contains an electronic copy of the Microsoft Exchange Server documentation. This is an excellent resource for reference—it is an electronic version of the hard copy manuals.

After the Books Online comes the Microsoft Exchange Administrator program icon. The function of this program is covered in more detail in Chapter 13, "Configuring Basic Server Operations," and in Chapter 22, "User Management with Exchange."

Following the Administrator icon is the Microsoft Exchange Server Migration Wizard. This tool helps you migrate from Lotus cc:Mail or Microsoft Mail. More on this in Chapter 10, "Migrating from Lotus cc:Mail," and in Chapter 11, "Migrating from Microsoft Mail."

After the Migration Wizard icon is the Optimizer icon. You might have already modified the properties for this one as described in the previous section, so you're familiar with it. Microsoft Exchange Optimizer is covered in Chapter 6.

Finally, the next icons represent Windows NT Server Performance Monitor workspaces. These workspaces are ready-made views of various Exchange Server performance counters to help get you started monitoring performance of the server. Each one represents a .PMW file, and they are located in the BIN subdirectory where you installed Exchange Server—for example, C:\EXCHSRVR\BIN. Here's an overview of what each icon represents and why you use it:

- *Microsoft Exchange Server Health* represents a summary of your Exchange Server's state of being. It is mainly a CPU utilization chart that shows counters for overall CPU utilization and for how the main processes within Exchange Server are using the CPU. Paging is also included because it is a useful counter to help detect potential performance problems in the server.

  You use this to get an up-to-date look at your server's status. This is a great workspace to add other relevant counters, such as Memory:Available Bytes or System:Processor Queue Length. The update interval is very small, so you get a very close look at server health.

  If you use the System:Processor Queue Length counter, don't forget you also have to monitor a counter in the Thread object to activate it. Any thread counter will do; just pick one.

> **TIP**
>
> When you open these Performance Monitor workspaces, there is no menu bar. Double-click in the graph area (or press Enter) to make it appear. Then you can maximize or do whatever to the window.

- *Microsoft Exchange Server History* is designed to give you a good long look at what your server has been doing over the past 100 minutes. This mainly shows message activity in the public and private stores, along with the user count, MTA work queue length, and amount of paging.

  This is a good graph to keep open so you can glance at it periodically. The Work Queue Length of the MTA is very useful to watch if you have multiple Exchange servers sending mail to each other. Also, the counters are excellent ones to monitor on a more frequent basis if you need finer granularity than 60-second intervals. I regularly watch MSExchangeIS:User Count, MSExchangeMTA:Work Queue Length, and Memory:Pages/sec.

> **NOTE**
>
> Although installed by Setup, the following three IMS-related workspaces will not show any data if the Internet Mail Service has not been installed. These workspaces get their data from the counters in the MSExchangeIMC PerfMon object, which is installed only along with the IMS.

- *Microsoft Exchange Server IMS Queues* is a bar chart that shows the status of four main Internet Mail Service (IMS or MSExchangeIMC) queues. These queues are important to exchanging messages with the Internet or other SMTP mail services.

  This chart is updated every second to give you a very current look at each queue. For example, if messages are not making it out of Exchange onto the Internet, or from the Internet into Exchange mailboxes, these queues might provide a clue as to why.

- *Microsoft Exchange Server IMS Statistics* is a simple graph that shows the total number of inbound and outbound messages that have been passed by the Internet Mail Service during the past 50 minutes.

  If you are interested in monitoring how many messages the server's Internet Mail Service has handled over time, this is a good graph to monitor. The counters are cumulative over time.

- *Microsoft Exchange Server IMS Traffic* is a graph that depicts traffic through the Internet Mail Service and the number of inbound and outbound connections.

  This graph is updated every second to provide a real-time view of the traffic being handled by the MSExchangeIMC. This is a good one to fire up if you are concerned that the traffic on your server may be getting too heavy, or if the data from another chart suggests there may be a problem in the IMS.

- *Microsoft Exchange Server Load* is slightly different than Server Health. Although the load on your server ultimately can affect its health, the Load workspace gives insight into how much traffic your server is managing.

  This workspace only scratches the surface of showing how much load is on your server—there are many more counters to look at, such as those related to Logical Disk, CPU, and Network Interface. Use this as a quick view into generic server load. The update interval is a bit longer, so you get a bigger picture of what the server's load is doing over the last 16–17 minutes.

- *Microsoft Exchange Server Queues* shows the status, in bar chart format, of five major queues that exist in Microsoft Exchange Server. These queues are critical to maintaining good system performance, and if any of them start to become backlogged you will notice a delay in message delivery. It also probably indicates a bottleneck somewhere in the system.

  The queues are (left to right):

```
MSExchangeMTA:Work Queue Length
MSExchangeIS Private:Send Queue Size
MSExchangeIS Public: Send Queue Size
MSExchangeIS Private:Receive Queue Size
MSExchangeIS Public:Receive Queue Size
```

This workspace is a good one to open periodically to get a current check on the status of the main system queues, updated every 10 seconds. Although the window itself doesn't show what queue each bar represents, if you enlarge the window, you will see the legend at the bottom. If any of these starts growing or stays above 10, you should start investigating why.

■ *Microsoft Exchange Server Users* is a very simple PerfMon chart that shows the number of physical machines (users) connected over the network to Exchange Server. This workspace is also in bar graph format. If you look in the Chart Options, you will see that the Histogram radio button is selected rather than Graph.

This graph is useful to have sitting in the corner of the screen to give a quick visual indicator of how many users are on the server at any given time. The refresh interval is 10 seconds—you might want to vary it.

There are three other workspace files, in case you are using the Internet Mail Service (IMS). These three basically show the flow of messages through the IMS and associated counters. If you haven't installed the IMS, the MSExchangeIMC object is not installed, so these counters don't function.

NOTE

Note that although the Internet Mail Connector from Exchange 4.0 is referred to as the Internet Mail Service in Exchange 5.0, the PerfMon counter is still MSExchangeIMC.

Summary

As I said in the beginning, this chapter is straightforward, and you now should have detailed insight into the Setup process:

■ Items to consider before running Setup
■ An overview of the general installation process
■ An introduction to Microsoft Exchange Optimizer
■ An overview of the Exchange Server icons, including the Performance Monitor workspaces

First and foremost, the objective in this chapter is to provide you with a step-by-step guide through Exchange Server 5.0 Setup exactly as you might encounter it yourself.

Another objective is to provide a checklist of last-minute items to check before running Setup, such as having the proper NT Service Pack installed, having a services account ready, and other things.

You have been introduced to Exchange Optimizer so you can see how important it is and how it fits into the Setup process. Refer to Chapter 6 for more details about how the Optimizer works, what it does for you, and why you use it.

Finally, the chapter covered a summary of the icons installed for Microsoft Exchange Server 5.0 and gave some suggestions about how, when, and where to use them. Most of these represent components of Exchange Server that are covered in more detail elsewhere in this book.

Configuring Basic Server Operations

by Ron Sonntag and Ray Sundstrom
Revised by Greg Todd

IN THIS CHAPTER

Exchange Server is the engine of Microsoft's client-server messaging system. It manages the tasks required for information interchange: messaging, information storage and organization, information sharing, scheduling, and security.

Exchange is designed to run on an NT Server computer, and it shares some of NT's features, such as centralized management using graphical tools, integrated security, and network communications.

To use Exchange, you must install and configure the appropriate services. During installation, Exchange installs and configures services necessary for basic operation. After installation, Exchange is ready to support clients, send and receive e-mail, support creation of public and private folders, and support group scheduling with Schedule+.

This chapter covers the steps that maintain the basic Exchange services. You are introduced to the Exchange Administrator, shown in Figure 13.1, and its role in maintaining Exchange.

FIGURE 13.1.

The Exchange Administrator, connected to an Exchange Server.

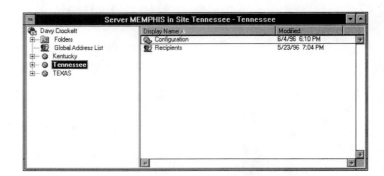

With Exchange Administrator you will be able to

- Set display options for various components within the Exchange Administrator.

- Set security options, enabling different user accounts to have access to various administrative functions within Exchange.

- Manage Exchange object deletion. Setting values that control when an object that is marked for deletion is actually purged from Exchange.

- Configure where and how often an Offline Address Book is generated and control what recipients are included.

- Administer the General Message Store. This includes controlling public folder storage, the storage of users' messages, support for rules and views, enforcement of storage size and age limits, direct delivery of messages addressed to users on the same server as the sender, and forwarding messages addressed to users on other servers and systems to the message transfer agent.

- Configure the Message Transfer Agent. Setting various messaging default, timeout, and retry values; configuring maximum message size and controlling message routing; and enabling diagnostics logging.
- Configure the System Attendant. Enabling and controlling message tracking logs.

Exchange Administrator Program Overview

The Microsoft Exchange Administrator is the graphical tool that allows management of Exchange Servers. It enables you to configure and maintain an organization, its sites, and servers from a single location. You can run the Administrator from an NT Server or workstation.

After initial Exchange setup, you can manage nearly all aspects of the Exchange Server using the Exchange Administrator, on which you find more detail later in this chapter.

Basic Server Operations Overview

The Exchange Server maintains information in a variety of ways. The two main repositories are the *directory* and the *information store*.

The directory holds information about recipients, servers, and messaging configurations. Other Exchange components and third-party applications that work with Exchange use the directory to route messages.

The information store has two components: a repository for data and a collection of services that enable users to send e-mail and use folders.

General Directory Settings

Nearly every component of the Exchange messaging infrastructure is represented as an object and is managed in some manner by the directory. The following are some of the major objects:

- *Organization.* The root object, which contains all other objects. It is represented as the name of your organization.
- *Site.* A group of one or more Exchange Servers, all on the same local area network (LAN).
- *Server.* An NT Server running Exchange Server.
- *Connectors.* A variety of communication protocols that connect an Exchange Server to other messaging systems (either Exchange or non-Exchange). Connectors are available for Exchange, Microsoft Mail (PC and AppleTalk), X.400 systems, and the Internet (SMTP).

  Other connectors may be available, from Microsoft or third-party suppliers, for communication with other messaging systems.

- *Public folders.* Users can share public folders and send messages to them.

- *Recipients.* An object that can receive messages and information. Recipients may be mailboxes, distribution lists, and public folders.

- *Global address list.* A list of all recipients in an organization.

- *Directory.* A repository that stores all the information about an organization's messaging infrastructure.

- *Public information store.* A repository that holds all public folders on a server.

- *Message transfer agent (MTA).* The Service responsible for routing messages to and from an Exchange Server.

- *System attendant.* A service that provides maintenance and support for other Exchange services. The system attendant is responsible for monitoring, logging, checking data consistency, routing table maintenance, and generating e-mail addresses.

You set the Directory's configurable options by selecting DS Site Configuration from the Exchange Administrator window, as shown in Figure 13.2.

FIGURE 13.2.

Selecting the DS Site Configuration container.

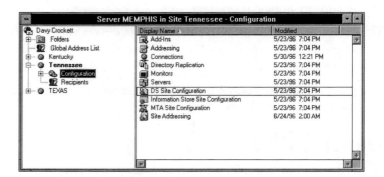

Each setting is displayed on one of the property pages (tabs) in the Exchange Administrator window. The DS Site Configuration property pages are General, Permissions, Offline Address Book Schedule, Offline Address Book, and Custom Attributes.

On the General property page, shown in Figure 13.3, you can do the following:

- Edit the configuration container Display name. It is the name for the DS Site Configuration container, which appears in the Exchange Administrator window. The default name is DS Site Configuration (and need not be changed).

- Manage object deletion. Objects deleted from the directory are managed by two time values: Tombstone Lifetime and the Garbage Collection Interval.

The Tombstone Lifetime (Days) value controls the amount of time you want to keep information about a deleted object. When you delete a user's mailbox, for example, the name is deleted from the server where the deletion takes place, but Exchange keeps a marker (a tombstone). The tombstone is replicated to other servers, and the mailbox entry is deleted from their directories.

The default setting for the Tombstone Lifetime is 30 days. When you change this value, consider how long it takes for directory information to replicate. Further, consider how long a server that participates in replication might be out of service. Set the Tombstone Lifetime long enough so that every server can be notified before the tombstone is removed.

The Garbage Collection Interval (Hours) is the number of hours Exchange waits between removing garbage from the system. After you delete a user's mailbox, for example, and the tombstone lifetime has been reached, the tombstone can be removed at the next garbage collection.

The default setting for the Garbage Collection Interval is 12 hours.

FIGURE 13.3.

The DS Site Configuration General property page.

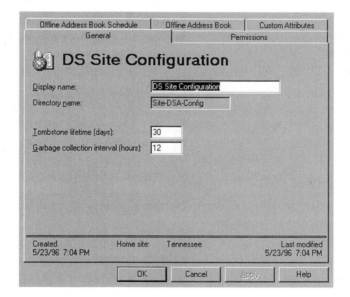

On the Permissions property page, shown in Figure 13.4, you can do the following:

- Specify the rights that users or groups have on the DS Site Configuration object. The default is User Rights. The security roles you set here are inherited by objects in the site's Configuration Container.

FIGURE 13.4.

The DS Site Configu-
ration Permissions
property page.

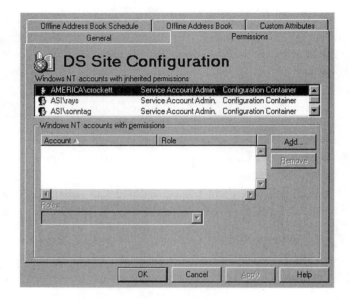

On the Offline Address Book Schedule property page, shown in Figure 13.5, you can do the following:

■ Schedule when the offline address book is created. This tab has two option buttons: Selected Times and Always.

When the Selected Times option is enabled, a calendar that enables you to select the times to generate the offline address book is active. The default is 3:00 a.m. every day.

If your recipients change often, you may choose to generate an offline address book more frequently. When you change the schedule, bear in mind that a large address book may take hours to generate.

When the Always option is enabled, Exchange attempts to generate the offline address book every 15 minutes.

The Offline Address Book property page controls the attributes of the offline address book. The offline address book enables remote users to have information about other users when the remote users are disconnected from their Exchange Server. For the offline address book, you can select which Exchange Server generates it and which recipients are in it.

Figure 13.5.

The DS Site Configuration Offline Address Book Schedule property page.

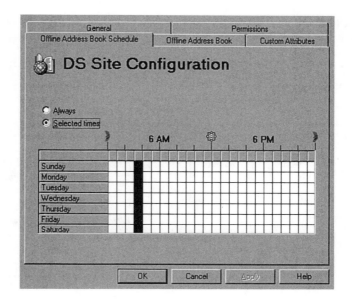

On the DS Site Configuration Offline Address Book property page, shown in Figure 13.6, you can do the following:

- Select a server to be the Offline Address Book server. One of the servers in a site generates the offline address book, which is written to a hidden public folder on that server. You select the server from the list box.

- Select the recipients that are to be included in the offline address book. The default is the recipients for the site. Other options may be the global address list or any custom recipients container you have created.

    To choose which recipient container to use, click the Modify button below the control labeled Generate Data Files from the Address Book Container. A dialog box guides you through selecting the recipient container of your choice.

- Select the Generate Offline Address Book Now button. This control enables you to generate an offline address book manually rather than wait for one to be generated on the set schedule.

If you want to store special information about recipients, Exchange enables you to define up to 10 custom attributes in the Custom Attributes property page, which is shown in Figure 13.7. You can define a field, for example, for an employee badge number.

FIGURE 13.6.
*The DS Site Configu-
ration Offline Address
Book property page.*

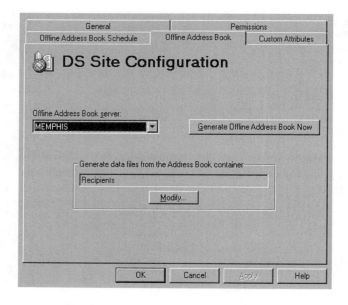

FIGURE 13.7.
*The DS Site Configu-
ration Custom
Attributes property
page.*

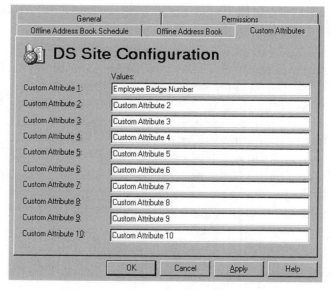

Custom attributes apply to all recipients for a site.

To create a custom attribute, select the Custom Attributes tab. The DS Site Configuration page has 10 entries for custom attributes. Simply enter the label for the custom attribute that you want to create. After you create it, you can enter the custom attribute value on the Custom Attributes property page of each recipient object.

General Message Store Settings

The information store enables users to send and receive e-mail and to store information in both public and private folders. Information stored in public folders can be shared with other Exchange users.

The information store functions include the following:

- Storage of public folders
- Storage of users' messages (in the private information store)
- Support for rules and views
- Enforcement of storage size and age limits
- Direct delivery of messages addressed to users on the same server as the sender
- Forwarding of messages addressed to users on other servers and systems to the message transfer agent

You can maintain the configuration of the information store by selecting Information Store Site Configuration from the Exchange Administrator window, as shown in Figure 13.8.

13

CONFIGURING
BASIC SERVER
OPERATIONS

FIGURE 13.8.

Selecting the Information Store Site Configuration container.

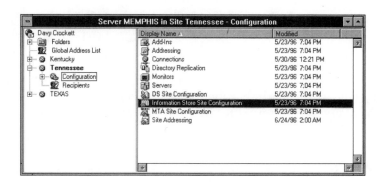

The Information Store Site Configuration includes several property pages: General, Permissions, Top Level Folder Creation, Storage Warnings, and Public Folder Affinity.

On the General property page, shown in Figure 13.9, you can do the following:

- Modify the display name (the name that appears in the Administrator window). The default is Information Store Site Configuration.

■ Set the location of the public folder container. This control enables you to set the container where all new public folders for the site will appear. By default, public folders appear in the recipients container.

You can, for example, create a container named Public Folders. Putting all public folders into this container makes it easier for users to find a specific folder in their address books.

■ Enable message tracking for messages processed by the information store. This option activates daily logging of message routing information. The Message Tracking Center uses these log files to track routing information.

FIGURE 13.9.

The Information Store Site Configuration General property page.

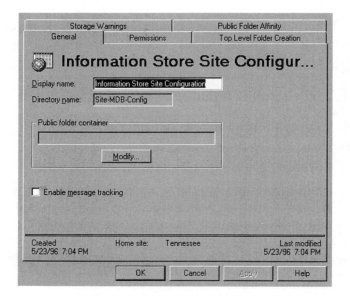

On the Permissions property page, shown in Figure 13.10, you can specify the rights that users or groups have on the Information Store Site Configuration object. The default is User Rights. The security roles are inherited from the site's configuration object. You also can assign users new security roles by using the Windows NT accounts with Permissions dialog at the bottom of this page.

On the Storage Warnings property page, shown in Figure 13.11, you can set the schedule on which messages are sent to mailbox owners or public folder contacts who have exceeded the maximum amount of space allocated for their mailboxes or public folders.

FIGURE 13.10.

The Information Store Site Configuration Permissions property page.

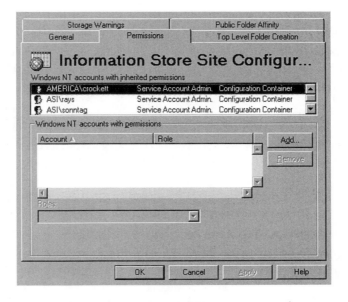

FIGURE 13.11.

The Information Store Site Configuration Storage Warnings property page.

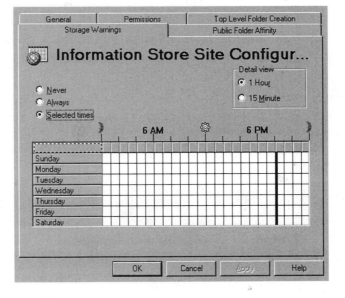

On the Top Level Folder Creation property page, shown in Figure 13.12, you can set which users have the right to create top-level public folders using the Microsoft Exchange Client. Top-level public folders are the highest tier of the public folder hierarchy. The owner of that folder can set permissions to enable other users to create folders below the top-level folder.

FIGURE 13.12.

The Information Store Site Configuration Top Level Folder Creation property page.

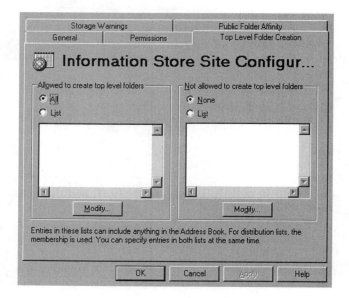

On the Public Folder Affinity property page, shown in Figure 13.13, you can configure Microsoft Exchange so that clients in your site can connect to public folders in other sites. Doing so can reduce the need to replicate public folders to all sites that may need access to them. If a public folder replica is available at multiple sites, a cost can be associated with access by site; Exchange then connects the user to the least costly site.

> **NOTE**
>
> In order to use Public Folder Affinity to connect to public folders at other sites, users must have a network connection to that site. The network connection must be capable of supporting remote procedure calls.
>
> Examples of the type of connection required are direct network connections (via Ethernet, for example) or a remote network connection using Microsoft's Remote Access Services for Windows.

FIGURE 13.13.

The Information Store Site Configuration Public Folder Affinity property page.

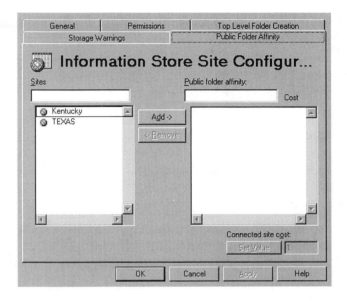

Public Folders

A *public folder* holds information that can be shared by a group of users. Public folders can provide services such as message forums and electronic bulletin boards. You can set up a public folder, for example, to hold employee classified advertisements. Company press releases and annual reports could be held in folders contained within a company communications folder.

You create public folders using the Exchange client. Folders you create are either top-level folders (at the top of the public folder hierarchy) or subfolders (folders created within folders). Who can create top-level folders is controlled by settings in the Top Level Folder Creation property page of the Information Store Site Configuration container. Settings in the parent folder control who can create subfolders.

A *folder* is a special type of recipient and, like other recipients (for example, mail boxes), can receive mail.

After you can create a folder, its properties can be maintained either with the Exchange client (to a limited extent) or the Exchange administrator; see Figure 13.14.

To maintain a public folder's properties with the Exchange administrator, select the folder in the Administrator window and then choose File | Properties. There are several property pages: General, Replicas, Folder Replication Status, Replication Schedule, Distribution Lists, E-mail Addresses, Custom Attributes, and Advanced.

FIGURE 13.14.

The Public Folders container.

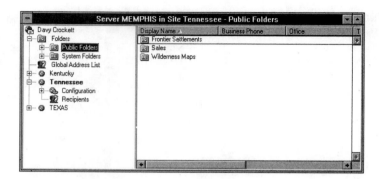

On the General property page, shown in Figure 13.15, you can do the following:

- Modify the folder name. It is the name that appears in the public folder hierarchy.

- Modify the address book display name. This name appears in the address book. The name can either be the same as the folder name or changed to something else.

- Create an alias name. You can use this name in the To box when sending mail to the folder.

- Set the age limit for all replicas of the folder. A public folder may have replicas (that is, copies of itself on other servers). The age limit determines the amount of time messages can remain in all replicas of the public folder before they expire and are removed.

  Age limits set here take effect on any replica that does not have an age limit set at either the information store or individual replica level.

- Set client permissions. Client permissions are initially set in the Exchange client when the folder is created. You can view or modify them here.

- Enter a note about the folder. This information then appears in the address book.

On the Replicas property page, shown in Figure 13.16, you can set up copies (replicas) of folders on other servers in your site. You can select servers that receive copies of a folder from the Servers list box and add them to the Replicate Folders To list box on the site you select in the Site list box. From the Replicate Folders To list box, you can remove servers that are to no longer receive replication of the folder.

Information about the condition of the copies of a folder is displayed on the Folder Replication Status page, which is shown in Figure 13.17. You can find the following information: the server name, last received time, average transmission time in seconds, and replication status (whether the copy is in sync with the original).

FIGURE 13.15.
The Public Folders General property page.

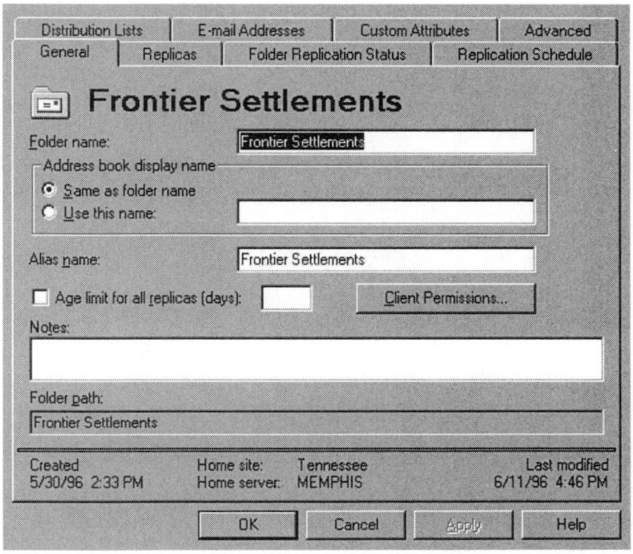

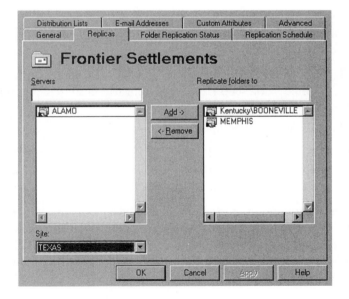

FIGURE 13.16.
The Public Folders Replicas property page.

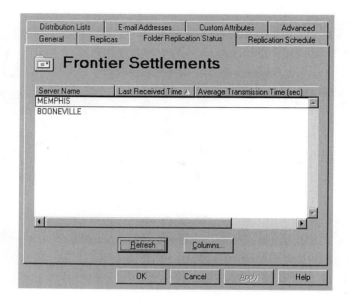

The Replication Schedule property page, shown in Figure 13.18, controls when the folder will be copied. The options are to use the information store schedule, never, always, or selected times:

- Selecting the Use Information Store Schedule option copies the folder using the same schedule that is set on the public information store Replication Schedule property page.

- Selecting the Never option prevents the folder from replicating.

- Selecting the Always option causes the folder to replicate every 15 minutes.

- Selecting the Selected times option activates a weekly calendar that enables you to select specific times for folder replication in 15-minute increments.

On the Distribution Lists property page, shown in Figure 13.19, you can specify which distribution lists this folder belongs to. This way, the folder can receive messages addressed to the distribution list. The Distribution List Membership box shows all the distribution lists the folder belongs to. Clicking the Modify button opens a dialog box, shown in Figure 13.20, that enables you to assign the folder to distribution lists.

FIGURE 13.18.
The Public Folders Replication Schedule property page.

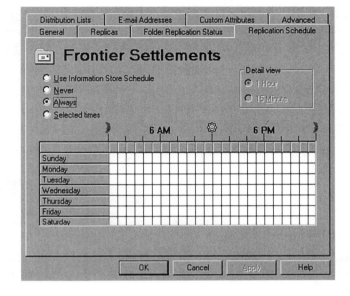

FIGURE 13.19.
The Public Folders Distribution Lists property page.

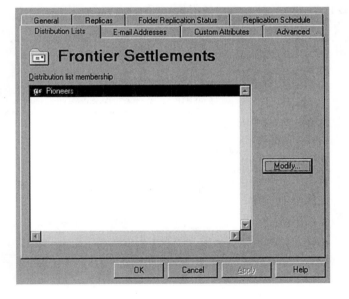

13
CONFIGURING
BASIC SERVER
OPERATIONS

Figure 13.20.
*The Public Folders
Distribution Lists
Modify dialog box.*

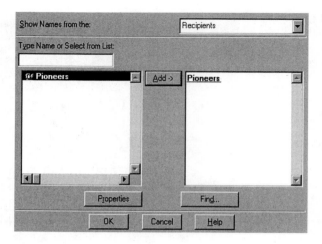

Public folders are recipients and have e-mail addresses. On the E-mail Addresses property page, shown in Figure 13.21, you can view, edit, remove, and create them.

Figure 13.21.
*The Public Folders
E-mail Addresses
property page.*

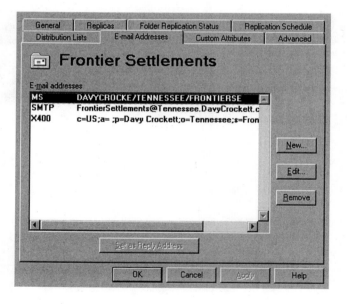

On the Custom Attributes property page, shown in Figure 13.22, you can enter values for the custom attributes assigned to all recipients using the DS Site Configuration property page.

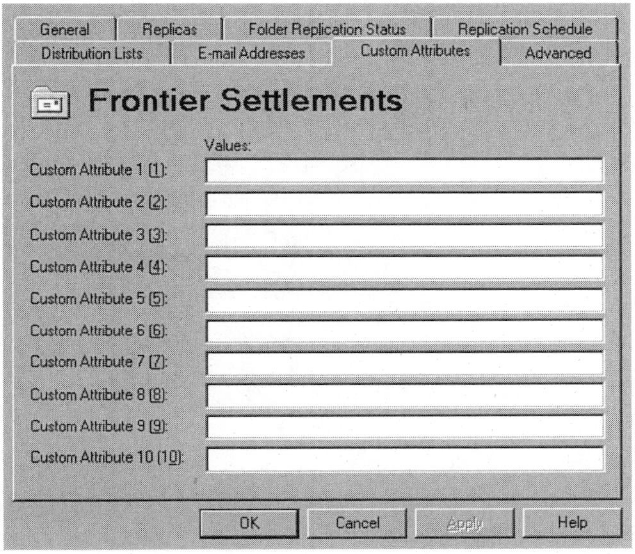

FIGURE 13.22.

The Public Folders Custom Attributes property page.

On the Advanced property page, shown in Figure 13.23, you can do the following:

- Set up a simple display name, which is used by systems that cannot display the normal display name for the folder.
- Set public folder storage limits. Use the global default values set in the Public Folders General property page by checking Use Information Store Defaults. A warning can be issued to the owner of a public folder when the folder has reached a storage limit if you check Issue Warning(K) and enter a storage limit value (in kilobytes).
- View the directory name. This name helps distinguish between directories that have the same display name but are in different parts of the directory hierarchy.
- Set the Trust level. The trust level controls whether information about the folder is replicated to a specific recipient. If the trust level set for the folder exceeds the trust level of the recipient, the information is not replicated.
- Choose a setting in the Replication msg importance list box. This control sets the priority for replication, with higher priority messages being sent first.

- Check Hide from address book if you do not want this public folder to appear in the address book. You can still send messages to a folder hidden from the address book, but you need to know the folder's full name.

- View the container name where the folder is stored.

- Create an administrative note, which can be any text, up to 1,024 characters. This information is visible only in the Exchange Administrator.

FIGURE 13.23.

The Public Folder Advanced property page.

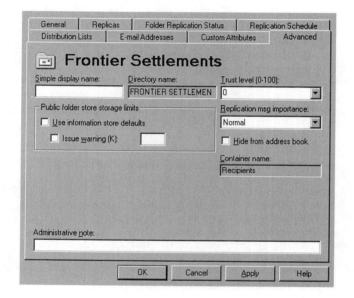

Configuring the Message Transfer Agent

The Exchange Message Transfer Agent (MTA) is responsible for delivering messages to other Microsoft Exchange message transfer agents, information stores, connectors, and third-party gateways.

The MTA is configured in the site configuration container and in the server configuration container. You configure the MTA in the site container by selecting MTA Site Configuration in the Exchange Administrator window, as shown in Figure 13.24. The property pages for the site's MTA configuration are General, Permissions, and Messaging Defaults.

FIGURE 13.24.

*Selecting the MTA Site
Configuration
container.*

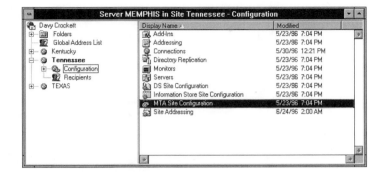

On the General property page, shown in Figure 13.25, you can do the following:

■ Modify the display name (the name that appears in the Administrator window). The default is MTA Site Configuration.

■ Enable message tracking for messages processed by the site MTA. This option activates daily logging of message routing information. The Message Tracking Center uses these log files to track routing information.

FIGURE 13.25.

*The MTA Site
Configuration General
property page.*

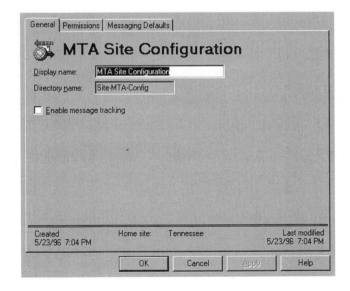

13

CONFIGURING
BASIC SERVER
OPERATIONS

On the Permissions property page, shown in Figure 13.26, you can do the following:

- Specify the rights that users or groups have on the MTA Site Configuration object. The default is User Rights. The security roles are inherited from the site's configuration object.

FIGURE 13.26.

The MTA Site Configuration Permissions property page.

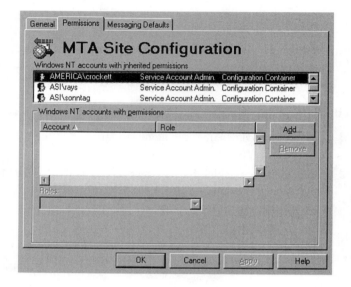

The Messaging Defaults properties control values that affect the transmission of messages. These parameters include timeouts for connecting to other systems, message retries, and nondelivery notification. On the Messaging Defaults property page, shown in Figure 13.27, you can do the following:

- Set Request To Send (RTS) values. These values determine how often you want to verify delivery as messages are being sent, how long you want to wait after an error to restart, and how often you want a verification that another system has received your transfer.

  Checkpoint size (K). Sets the amount of data to be sent before a checkpoint is requested. Errors in transmission cause the data from the last checkpoint to be re-sent. Large checkpoint values slightly increase transmission speed but cause larger data packets to be sent again in the case of an error. A value of zero turns checkpointing off.

  Recovery timeout (sec). Sets the amount of time that the MTA waits for a reconnection after an error occurs before restarting the transfer from the beginning.

Window size. Sets the number of checkpoints that can be inserted before the MTA waits for acknowledgment. The larger the window size, the faster the transmission, but the greater the resource utilization.

■ Set association parameters. Associations are communication channels between Exchange and other systems, and are used to transfer messages to a system. You can have multiple associations in each connection.

Lifetime (sec). Sets the amount of time to keep an association open to a remote system after a message is sent. Higher values are useful if the association services frequent message traffic.

Disconnect (sec). Sets the amount of time to wait for a response to a disconnect request before terminating the connection.

Threshold (msgs). Sets the maximum number of messages waiting to be sent. When the threshold is exceeded, the MTA establishes another association.

■ Set connection retry values. Connection retry values determine how many times you want to try to open a connection, reopen a connection, or resend a message after an error. If the connection can't be opened and the message sent, Exchange sends a nondelivery report to the originator of the message.

Max open retries. Sets the number of times the system tries to open a connection before it fails.

Max transfer retries. Sets the maximum number of times the system tries to transfer a message.

Open interval (sec). Sets the amount of time, in seconds, to wait before trying to reestablish a connection after a communications error.

Transfer interval (sec). Sets the amount of time, in seconds, to wait before retransmitting a message across an open connection after an error.

■ Set transfer timeouts. Messages can have different priorities and require different handling. An urgent message, for example, is expected to be processed more quickly than a non-urgent message. If a transfer fails, you must determine how quickly to send a nondelivery report to the originator. You can assign a different amount of time for each message priority.

Urgent. Sets the time, in milliseconds, to delay before sending a nondelivery report for an urgent message.

Normal. Sets the time, in milliseconds, to delay before sending a nondelivery report for a normal message.

Non-urgent. Sets the time, in milliseconds, to delay before sending a nondelivery report for a non-urgent message.

FIGURE **13.27.**
*The MTA Site
Configuration
Messaging Defaults
property page.*

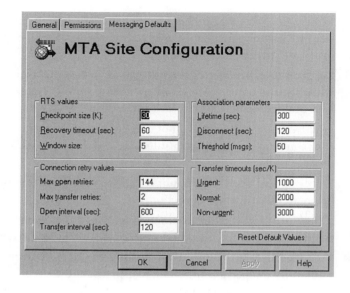

The property pages for the server's MTA are configured in the server configuration container (see Figure 13.28), using the Message Transfer Agent property pages. The property pages that configure the server's MTA are General and Diagnostics Logging.

FIGURE **13.28.**
*The Server Configura-
tion container.*

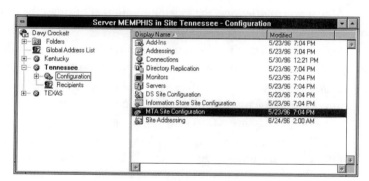

On the General property page, shown in Figure 13.29, you can do the following:

- Set the local MTA name. This name is used to identify the MTA to foreign systems. The default is the server name and is set during installation.

- Set the local MTA password. This password is used by foreign system when connecting to the MTA. The default is no password.

■ Set the maximum message size (in kilobytes) that the MTA can receive. All messages that exceed the maximum are returned to the originator. Selecting the No Limit option allows the MTA to accept messages of any size.

■ Select the Recalculate Routing button to rebuild the routing table manually. The routing table contains the information that the MTA needs to determine how to route messages. When connections are added or changed, recalculation may be necessary.

■ Select Expand remote distribution lists locally. A remote distribution list is created on a server in another site. Remote distribution lists are distributed by directory replication. If a user sends a message to a remote distribution list, and the distribution list is expanded on the server to which he or she is currently connected, Exchange can determine the best routing for the message. Checking this box guarantees the most efficient message handling; however, expanding large distribution lists can have an impact on server performance.

■ Select Convert incoming messages to MS Exchange contents. This selection applies proper character translation for inbound German, Swedish, and Norwegian messages. See Exchange documentation for more details.

■ Create an administrative note. You can enter up to 1,024 characters. This information is visible only in the Exchange Administrator.

FIGURE 13.29.

The Server Configuration MTA General property page.

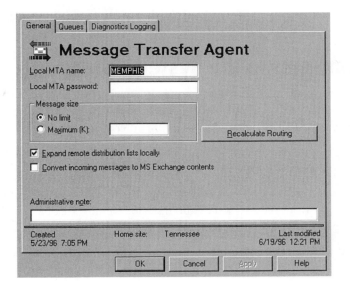

13

CONFIGURING
BASIC SERVER
OPERATIONS

The settings on the Diagnostics Logging property page, shown in Figure 13.30, control the amount of information written to the NT Event Log for the activities related to the MTA. Generally, you leave diagnostics logging at the default settings (none) unless you are performance-tuning or troubleshooting an Exchange Server.

FIGURE 13.30.

The Server Configuration MTA Diagnostics Logging property page.

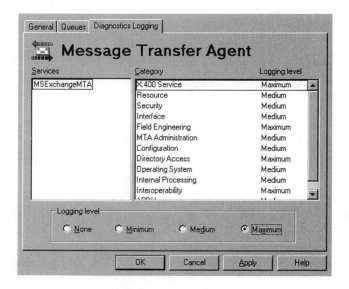

Configuring the System Attendant

The system attendant provides a group of "helper" functions for Exchange. It generates e-mail addresses for new recipients, maintains the message tracking log, and monitors the connection status between Exchange Servers, among other tasks.

If message tracking is enabled, the system attendant writes logging information that is used by the message tracking center.

You configure the system attendant in the server configuration container by selecting System Attendant from the Exchange Administrator window (see Figure 13.31). The System Attendant property pages are General and E-mail Addresses.

On the General property page, shown in Figure 13.32, you can do the following:

FIGURE 13.31.

Selecting the System Attendant configuration.

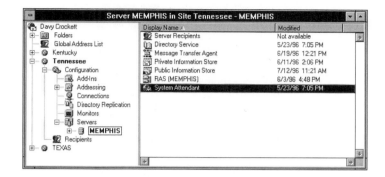

■ Maintain the message tracking log files. New log files are created daily for message tracking. You can select Do Not Remove Old Log Files if you want a permanent record of message delivery, or Remove Log Files Older Than (*Number*) Days if you want to limit the amount of space used by logging. *Number* can be any value from 1 to 99.

■ Create an administrative note of up to 1,024 characters.

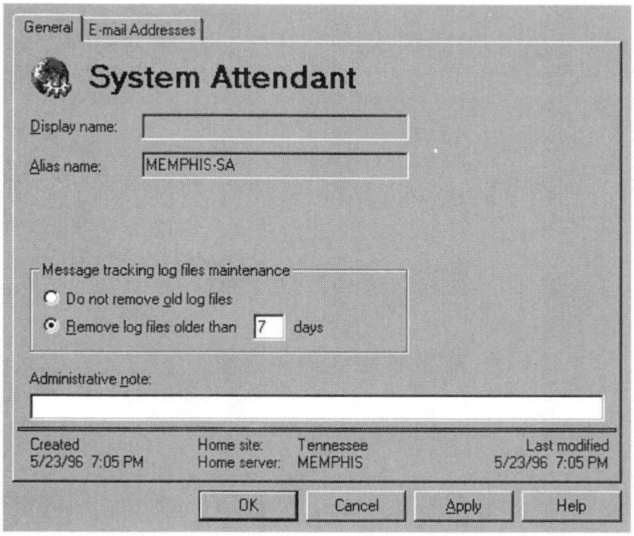

FIGURE 13.32.

The System Attendant General property page.

Summary

Exchange is a powerful and flexible messaging engine. A great number of the aspects of tuning and maintenance are handled automatically by Exchange itself. There are, however, many features that can be configured to customize Exchange for your particular organization.

Administrative tasks can be distributed among several people by setting configuration permissions. You can display information that can be useful for your users, such as recipient custom attributes. You can control the amount of storage that Exchange needs by configuring message size, private information store size, and public folder size. You can balance loads between servers in a large organization by replicating heavily used information. You can influence the amount of processor time Exchange consumes by setting how often replication occurs for public folders and the offline address book. If you configure logging functions, you can have valuable tools for monitoring performance, diagnosing problems, and tracking message delivery.

Carefully administrating Exchange will ensure a smooth-running messaging environment.

Installing Microsoft Exchange Clients

by Greg Todd

IN THIS CHAPTER

CHAPTER 14

New to Version 5.0

With Exchange Server 5.0, there are a few new ways clients can access an Exchange server. In addition to the Exchange client included with the product, you can use a Web browser or any POP3, Network News (NNTP) and LDAP client. You can even use Outlook, the new personal information manager client included with Office 97.

Covering the installation of all these different clients is outside the scope of this book. However, there are great resources available for the various clients that cover the topics in better detail. For example, the Outlook client is given great coverage in the Sams book, *Teach Yourself Microsoft Outlook in 24 Hours*. With that in mind, this chapter will stick to the versions of the Exchange client that ship with Exchange Server.

Cross-Platform

Setting up the Exchange client software is a simple matter because Microsoft has created a very easy process for installing it regardless of the operating system you are running. The Exchange client software runs on Windows NT, Windows 95, Windows for Workgroups 3.11, and MS-DOS 6.2.

This chapter covers the following topics:

- Items to consider before running Setup
- An overview of the Setup process for each supported operating system
- A look at the Exchange Setup Editor

First, this chapter identifies items to consider before installing the Exchange client. These items are basic but they're worth mentioning.

Next, this chapter steps through the process of installing the client software with screen shots from each operating system.

Finally, this chapter examines the Exchange Setup Editor, a program that selects defaults for the setup process to make it even easier.

After you read this chapter, you should have a clear understanding of the Microsoft Exchange Client installation process and the Exchange Setup Editor.

Before Running Setup

Here are a few items to be aware of when getting ready to run the Setup program:

1. Decide which version of the Exchange client you need to install.
2. Be sure you are connected to the computer that runs Exchange Server.
3. Close any MAPI-based applications, shared files, or system files before starting Setup.
4. Be sure you have an account on the Exchange Server.

The first decision you need to make is which version of the Exchange client software to install. This is usually based upon the type of operating system you will use, but there can be other reasons for selecting a particular version, such as limited disk space.

As stated earlier in this chapter, the Exchange client runs under Windows NT, Windows 95, Windows for Workgroups 3.11, and MS-DOS 6.2. There are slight differences in the user interface of each Windows version. Of course, the DOS client is quite different, because it's not running under Windows. However, you will find that each version functions basically the same, even the DOS version.

You must consider disk space when you are selecting which version to install. The Windows NT version takes around 15MB if you install just the bare essentials—almost 27MB if you install Schedule+, all the help files, information services, and other stuff. The Windows 95 and Windows 3.*x* versions take approximately the same amount of space as the Windows NT version, give or take a few megabytes.

In contrast, the DOS version takes only 2.5MB. And it provides the basic functionality of the Windows versions. If you're in a situation in which disk space is limited and you don't care about the nice Windows interface, this is a good option. And it actually works!

Next, be sure the machine on which you're installing the client is properly connected to the network and to the Exchange server. This is usually a foregone conclusion, but if you think you are connected to the network and you're not, it can be very frustrating when you try to run Exchange for the first time. And it sort of makes you feel dumb when you figure it out.

If you want to be sure, check with your network administrator. If you happen to be the network administrator, there are utilities such as Ping—if you're running TCP/IP—and RPC Ping—if you're running any supported protocol—that can help determine whether your client and server are talking over the network. RPC Ping is a very useful utility, and it is covered in Chapter 28, "Diagnosing the Cause of a Problem."

Troubleshooting

Of course, if you intend to install the client software when the machine on which you're installing is disconnected from the network, that's another matter. Maybe you want to use only Personal Folders. Or maybe you intend to use the client via a modem connection instead of over the network. It's not a problem—in fact, Setup is designed to allow precisely this. You just won't be able to connect to the Exchange Server machine over the network.

Next, close any MAPI-based applications that are running. This includes applications such as Microsoft Mail. If you are installing under Windows 3.*x*, be sure all shared and system files are closed, because Windows cannot update them if they are open.

Finally, if you intend to get up and running immediately after finishing Setup, be sure you have an account on the Exchange server to which you plan to connect.

Running Setup

To run Setup, find the appropriate Setup program, Setup.exe, on your Microsoft Exchange Client Software CD. It is in a directory that matches the language and operating system and computer type you have. For example, if you are running English Windows NT on an Intel-based machine, you will run Setup from the \Eng\WinNT\I386 directory.

14

INSTALLING
MICROSOFT
EXCHANGE CLIENTS

The Windows NT Client

The Windows NT Client for Microsoft Exchange requires Windows NT version 3.5 or higher. This requirement is different from the Exchange Server itself, which requires at least Windows NT 3.51 with Service Pack 5. Naturally, the Windows NT version of the Exchange client is a full 32-bit implementation of the software.

If you are using an Intel-based machine, the Setup program will be in the \Eng\WinNT\I386 directory.

After you find the appropriate version of Setup and run it, you should see a screen that looks like Figure 14.1.

FIGURE 14.1.

The Microsoft Exchange Client for Windows NT Setup opening screen.

After this screen, fill in your name and the name of your company, if applicable. If it isn't in the system already, this information is stored in the registry key:

```
HKEY_CURRENT_USER\Software\Microsoft\MS Setup (ACME)\User Info
```

Next, select the destination folder in which the main application files will be installed (see Figure 14.2). You can change the destination folder in which you will install Exchange.

You are then presented with three installation options as shown in Figure 14.2.

Typical installs the software necessary for normal operation of the Microsoft Exchange Client. Schedule+ is also installed. The main difference between this and the Complete install is this one does not include all the information service options.

Complete/Custom, as the name implies, enables you to choose which options to install from all options available. This includes online documentation, Schedule+ software, and information services.

FIGURE 14.2.

The Microsoft Exchange Client for Windows NT will be installed in C:\EXCHANGE.

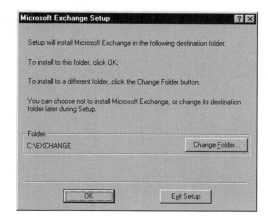

Minimum installs only the bare minimum software to get Microsoft Exchange and Schedule+ up and running. Choose this option if you have limited disk space.

If everything goes OK, you see the files start to copy. At the end of this process, Microsoft Exchange and Microsoft Schedule+ icons are installed in the All Users Programs folder of the Start menu, as shown in Figure 14.3.

FIGURE 14.3.

The Microsoft Exchange and Microsoft Schedule+ icons are installed in the Start menu.

Also, in Control Panel you see an additional icon called Mail, as in Figure 14.4. This applet is how Exchange profiles are managed. More on this can be found in Chapter 15, "Configuring Microsoft Exchange Clients."

NOTE

If you installed Windows Messaging with NT, there will already be a Mail icon present in the Control Panel. After installing the client, the icon will remain, but its applet will be upgraded to work with the newly installed Exchange client.

Compatibility

FIGURE 14.4.

The Mail icon is installed in Control Panel by Setup.

At this point you are ready to run Exchange. When you run it for the first time, you are prompted for some information so Exchange can create your profile. You learn more about profiles in Chapter 14. All profiles are stored in

```
HKEY_CURRENT_USER\Software\Microsoft\WindowsNT\CurrentVersion\
➥Windows Messaging Subsystem\Profiles.
```

There are also some related keys kept in

```
HKEY_LOCAL_MACHINE\SOFTWARE\Microsoft\Exchange
```

and in

```
HKEY_CURRENT_USER\Software\Microsoft\Exchange
```

You probably won't need to modify any of these, but they're still good to know about.

The MS-DOS Client

The MS-DOS Client for Microsoft Exchange requires MS-DOS version 5.0 or higher. I recommend MS-DOS 6.2. This version of the Exchange client is a 16-bit DOS application. It does, however, run under a Windows NT command prompt.

The Setup program will be in the \Eng\DOS directory. After you find the appropriate version of Setup and run it, you see a screen that looks like Figure 14.5.

FIGURE 14.5.

The Microsoft Exchange Client for MS-DOS Setup opening screen.

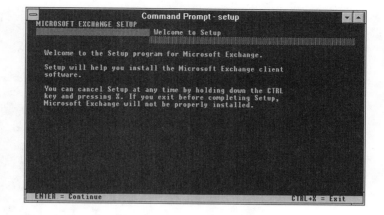

Next, you must choose one of the three install types, as shown in Figure 14.6.

FIGURE 14.6.

Local is the default type of installation for the MS-DOS Exchange client.

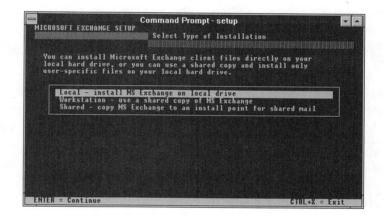

The Local option installs a copy of Exchange right on your local hard drive.

The Workstation option copies the necessary files from the shared installation point (put there previously by an administrator using the Shared option) to your local hard drive.

The Shared option copies the required files to a directory that is shared on the network so other users can perform a Workstation installation of the MS-DOS client.

After you select the option, select the destination directory in which you want to install the Exchange client software. Then select the local time zone and the language from the next two screens. Following that, an Installation Options screen appears, as in Figure 14.7.

FIGURE 14.7.
*Select which compo-
nents to install for the
MS-DOS client.*

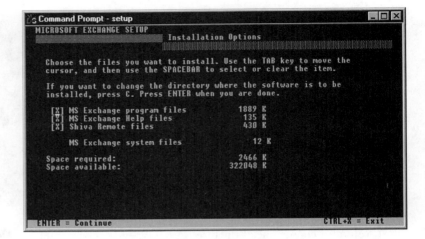

MS Exchange Program files installs the main Exchange client files. You have to select this option to get up and running.

MS Exchange Help files installs the help files so they are available when you run the MS-DOS client.

Shiva Remote files installs software that enables you to establish a remote PPP (Point to Point) connection with the network that contains the Exchange Server. It provides similar functionality to RAS (Remote Access Services), and it supports IPX, TCP/IP, and NetBEUI.

After this screen, the files are copied and Setup is finished. You are ready to run Exchange for the first time. See Chapter 14 for more detail.

The Windows 95 Client

The Windows 95 Client for Microsoft Exchange requires the original version of Microsoft Windows 95 or later. On a typical Windows 95 system, there is likely software installed called Microsoft Exchange for Windows 95 version 4—that's what the splash screen says when you open the Inbox icon on the Windows 95 desktop. The Exchange client is perfectly functional, but it needs to be upgraded to the full Exchange client to provide the ability to connect to Exchange Server 4.0 or 5.0.

> **NOTE**
>
> There is some understandable confusion with the nomenclature here. If you open the original Inbox installed with Windows 95, it runs software called Microsoft Exchange for Windows 95 version 4. And what you are now installing is also called Microsoft Exchange. The difference is that the original Windows 95 Microsoft Exchange client is not capable of providing access to Exchange Server—it only provides access to MS Mail 3.x or

Workgroup Postoffices, Microsoft Fax, MSN, and Internet Mail. The new Exchange client included with Exchange Server does provide the capability of accessing an Exchange server. Because Windows 95 was originally released much earlier than Exchange Server 4.0, its bundled Exchange client has caused a slight mixup. And since you're most likely installing Exchange 5.0, you should upgrade to the version 5 client anyway.

Not to worry. The upgraded version of the Exchange client is a full 32-bit implementation, and it provides access to an Exchange server. And, like the Windows 95 Exchange client, it retains the capability of accessing MS Mail and Workgroup post offices, and all the other information services you need.

The Setup program is in the \Eng\Win95 directory on the client CD.

After you find the appropriate version of Setup and run it, you see the generic opening screen that resembles Figure 14.1 from earlier in this chapter.

The opening Setup screen for the Windows 95 client looks much the same as the other Windows versions of Exchange. Again, evidence that Microsoft has tried to make the installation of Exchange as similar as possible across platforms.

After this screen, fill in your name and the name of your company, if applicable. If it isn't in the system already, this information is stored in the registry key

`HKEY_CURRENT_USER\Software\Microsoft\MS Setup (ACME)\User Info`

Setup then searches for any existing Exchange client software. Assuming that the old Exchange client software was originally installed with Windows 95, Setup finds it and presents a screen something like Figure 14.8.

FIGURE 14.8.

Setup finds the existing older version of Exchange originally installed with Windows 95.

14

INSTALLING MICROSOFT EXCHANGE CLIENTS

Presumably, you want to upgrade over the existing version of Exchange, because it's probably not doing you much good unless you use MS Mail or the built-in fax capability. You can select the destination folder where the main application files will be installed or click OK and move on.

Next, you are presented with the three installation options as shown in Figure 14.9. Also, you can change the destination folder where you will install Exchange.

FIGURE 14.9.

The Microsoft Exchange 5.0 Client for Windows 95 will be installed in C:\Program Files\Microsoft Exchange.

Typical installs the software necessary for normal operation of the Microsoft Exchange Client. Schedule+ is also installed. The main difference between this and the Custom install is that this install does not include all the Information Service options.

Custom, as the name implies, enables you to choose which options to install from all options available. This includes online documentation, Schedule+ software, and Information Services.

Laptop installs only the bare minimum software to get Microsoft Exchange and Schedule+ up and running. Choose this option if you have limited disk space.

If everything goes OK, the files start to copy. If this is the first time you've installed the new Exchange client, you must restart Windows 95 when Setup finishes, as shown in Figure 14.10.

NOTE

The requirement to restart is different from the Windows NT client installation, which does not require a restart.

FIGURE 14.10.

*You must restart
Windows 95 after the
installation of the
Exchange client.*

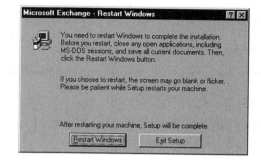

In this example, I have chosen the Typical installation. Microsoft Exchange and Schedule+ icons are added to the menus, as shown in Figure 14.11.

FIGURE 14.11.

*The Microsoft
Exchange and
Schedule+ icons are
added to the menu.*

In Control Panel, the icon called Mail still exists, as in Figure 14.12. As I mentioned in the section "The Windows NT Client," this is how Exchange profiles are managed. However, with your new version of the Windows 95 Exchange client, now you have the capability to configure a profile that connects to Microsoft Exchange Server. More on this in Chapter 14.

FIGURE 14.12.

*You use the Mail icon
in the Control Panel to
configure Exchange
profiles.*

14

INSTALLING
MICROSOFT
EXCHANGE CLIENTS

At this point, you are ready to run Exchange. When you run it for the first time, you are prompted for some information so Exchange can create your profile. You learn more about profiles in Chapter 14. All profiles are stored in

```
HKEY_CURRENT_USER\Software\Microsoft\Windows Messaging Subsystem
```

There are also some keys kept in

```
HKEY_LOCAL_MACHINE\SOFTWARE\Microsoft\Exchange
```

and in

```
HKEY_CURRENT_USER\Software\Microsoft\Exchange
```

The Windows 3.x Client

The Windows 3.x Client for Microsoft Exchange requires a 16-bit networked version of Windows 3.x, preferably Windows for Workgroups (WfW) 3.11.

This version of the Exchange client is a 16-bit implementation of the software, and it provides access to a Microsoft Exchange Server.

The Setup program is in the \Eng\Win16 directory.

After you find the appropriate version of Setup and run it, you see a screen that looks very similar to the other Windows versions of Exchange. Again, Microsoft has done a good job at making the installation of Exchange as similar as possible across platforms.

After this screen, fill in your name and the name of your company, if applicable.

Then, Setup searches for any existing Exchange client software. Presumably this is your first install under Windows 3.x, so it doesn't find anything. A screen with a default folder name appears. You can change it at this point, or click OK to continue.

Next, you are presented with the three installation options, as shown in Figure 14.13. Here, also, you can change the destination folder in which you will install Exchange.

Typical installs the software necessary for normal operation of the Microsoft Exchange Client. Schedule+ is also installed. The main difference between this and the Custom install is that this one does not include all the Information Service options.

Custom, as the name implies, enables you to choose which options to install from all the options available. This includes online documentation, Schedule+ software, and Information Services.

Laptop installs only the bare minimum software to get Microsoft Exchange and Schedule+ up and running. Choose this option if you have limited disk space.

FIGURE 14.13.
The Microsoft Exchange Client for Windows 3.x will be installed in C:\EXCHANGE.W16.

If everything goes OK, the files start to copy. When they are finished copying, you are asked for your time zone.

In this example, I have chosen the Typical install. A Microsoft Exchange group is added to the Program Manager, and the Exchange icons are placed there, as in Figure 14.14.

FIGURE 14.14.
The Exchange client icons are placed in a Microsoft Exchange program group.

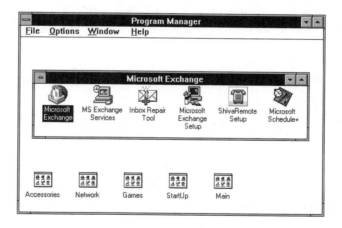

14

The changes to the Control Panel are slightly different from the other versions of the Exchange client. There are two additional icons in Control Panel rather than one. One icon is called Mail and the other icon is called Fax, as in Figure 14.15. Select the Mail icon to manage Exchange profiles. Select the Fax icon to set up fax modems.

FIGURE 14.15.
Use the Mail icon in Control Panel to configure Exchange profiles, and use the Fax icon to set up fax modems.

Now you are ready to run Exchange. When you run it for the first time, you are prompted for some information so the client can create your profile. You can also create your profile by running the Mail applet from the Control panel.

Profiles in the Windows 3.x Client

As you learned earlier in the chapter, the Windows 95 and Windows NT clients store their profile information in the Registry. Because Windows 3.x does not have a Registry, profile information is stored the old-fashioned way—in .INI files.

After you install the Windows 3.x client, you should find some new .INI files in your Windows directory. Also, there should be a couple of new directories. Finally, your WIN.INI file is modified to contain information relating to the Exchange client. The following are the new INI files:

- EXCHNG.INI
- MSMAIL.INI (assuming you installed the MS Mail provider)
- COMPOBJ.INI
- SCHDPLUS.INI (assuming you installed Schedule+)

The main file of interest is EXCHNG.INI. It contains general application-specific settings for the client itself. However, the user profile information is not stored in this file; profiles are stored in other .INI files kept in the MAPI directory.

There are two new directories created during setup: MAPI and FORMS. User profile information is stored in the MAPI directory in a series of .INI files. There is one main file—PROFILES.INI—which acts as an index to the .INI files that actually contain the profile information. In turn, the real profile information is stored in .INI files with names such as F16E0A00.INI and F26E0A00.INI, for example. The names won't necessarily be these, but they will be something similar—machine-generated filenames that are assured to be unique. If you have only one profile on your machine, you will have two files in the MAPI directory: PROFILES.INI and F16E0A00.INI. If you add another profile, F26E0A00.INI will contain the new profile, and there will be a total of three files.

Exchange Setup Editor

After running through the Exchange client setup routine, you might start to wonder how all the defaults came to be the way they are for the Setup program and for the client itself—settings such as the default installation directory, which default Exchange server to connect to, and the default Program Manager Group for the client icons. This section describes more about how the defaults are determined.

Setup Editor basically controls the default settings for the following:

- The Exchange client Setup program
- The user settings in the Exchange client

A Tool for the Administrator

Setup Editor is intended as a tool for the administrator to help make things more consistent for installing Exchange clients.

For example, you are an administrator who always wants your users to install the client software to the same directory on their hard drives. Using Setup Editor is a way to accomplish that. When you specify the directory name you prefer, it will be used rather than the default. As a result, you will have an easier time managing many users because there is an additional degree of standardization among the client installations.

> **NOTE**
>
> Unlike Exchange 4.0, the Setup program for Exchange 5.0 does not install a shortcut for Setup Editor. The program does reside in the \exchsrvr\bin folder.
>
> Setup Editor can be used only for Windows NT, Windows 95, and Windows 3.x clients.

New to Version 5.0

14

INSTALLING MICROSOFT EXCHANGE CLIENTS

Figure 14.16 shows the main screen of Setup Editor for Windows NT, STFEDTR.EXE. There is also a STFEDT16.EXE, which you won't need unless you're using WfW 3.11.

FIGURE 14.16.

Setup Editor has EXCHNG.STF opened on the Intel-based Windows NT client install point.

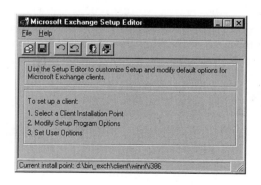

Setup Editor has the three main steps for setting up a client. From the opening screen, you can do the following:

1. Select a Client Installation Point. This is the location in which you will find the Setup program and associated files that you want to modify. This is explained more in the following section "Selecting a Client Installation Point."

2. Modify Setup Program Options. These are parameters that control how the Setup program functions. This is explained more in the later section "Setting Defaults for the Setup Program."

3. Set User Options. These are parameters that control how some aspects of the Exchange client operate. This is explained more in the later section "Setting Client Defaults for the User."

> **NOTE**
>
> You cannot use Setup Editor on installation files that reside on a CD-ROM or a network volume to which you do not have write access. This is because Setup Editor needs to modify and create files during the process. It is mainly intended to customize shared areas where multiple users run Setup to install their client software.

Selecting a Client Installation Point

The *client installation point* is where you keep the client files. Sometimes it's shared over the network to allow easy access to authorized users. So when you select the client installation point, you are really finding where the Setup program and its associated files are located for the particular operating system you want.

By selecting a client installation point, you are actually opening the file called EXCHNG.STF. This is an ASCII file that contains important information about the setup process for the client and for the configuration of the client itself.

When you first start Setup Editor, there are no other features active until you open the .STF file. After you open the .STF file, you can modify the defaults for the Setup program and modify client defaults for the user. From the File menu, click Select Client Installation Point. Navigate the directories until you find where the setup files reside for the client software you want to configure. You can also invoke this by clicking the little icon on the toolbar with two envelopes on it.

Setting Defaults for the Setup Program

Now that you've found the client installation point you want to configure, things get a little more interesting. First, look at the process of modifying defaults for the client Setup program. Figures 14.17 through 14.20 show the four tabs of the Setup Program Options property sheet that appears when you select File | Modify Setup Program Options. You can also invoke this by clicking the little screen icon on the right side of the toolbar.

FIGURE 14.17.

The General tab of modifying the Setup Program Options.

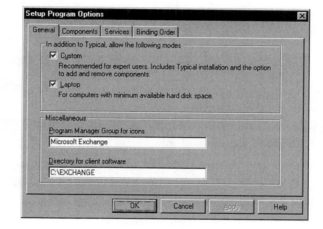

FIGURE 14.18.

The Components tab of modifying the Setup Program Options.

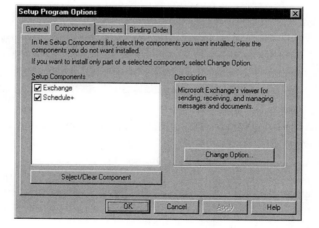

FIGURE 14.19.

The Services tab of modifying the Setup Program Options.

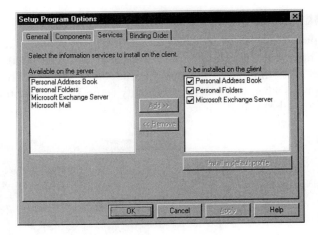

FIGURE 14.20.

The Binding Order tab of modifying the Setup Program Options.

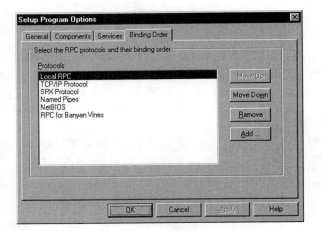

You can modify several aspects of the Setup program's defaults, such as the destination directory, the name of the Program Manager group to use, whether Custom and Laptop configurations are available options, which components and services to install, and the binding order of the RPC protocols. The Binding Order tab in Figure 14.20 is probably least intuitive, but quite important nonetheless. This tab sets the order in which the client tries various protocols in an attempt to establish an RPC connection with an Exchange server. The protocols are explained in the section "A Description of the Protocols," later in this chapter.

The best way to understand the purpose of the tabs represented in Figures 14.17 through 14.20 is with a couple of examples.

Example 1

Suppose you want to standardize the Setup procedure for your users. They are strictly desktop users and not very sophisticated. So you want them to have only the Typical installation option available, not Custom or Laptop. You want the default Program Manager group to be Microsoft Exchange and the default directory to be C:\EXCHANGE. You want your clients to have Exchange and Schedule+. And because you're migrating from MS Mail, they should also have the capability of connecting to an MS Mail post office. Finally, the network is small, so the protocol will remain NetBIOS over NetBEUI.

To accomplish this, the tabs depicted in Figures 14.17 through 14.20 should be modified as follows:

- In Figure 14.17, uncheck Custom and Laptop so those installation options do not appear to the user. Leave the items under Miscellaneous as they are.
- In Figure 14.18, nothing should change.
- In Figure 14.19, select Microsoft Mail and click Add. That will cause the MS Mail information service to be installed on the client.
- In Figure 14.20, move the NetBIOS protocol to the top and move Named Pipes below it. The others can be removed if you know those protocols will not be used in your network environment.

TIP

With the NetBIOS selection, all the NetBIOS interfaces on the computer are tried in the order of their LANA number. If you have only one network card, this is not an issue. But if you have multiple network cards, make sure the one you want to use for connecting to Exchange Server is configured as LANA 0. Otherwise, there will be a delay while trying to connect as the timeout period expires.

CAUTION

Make sure your desired protocol is at the top of the Protocol list; the order is **Performance** important. This list represents the binding order for the client; that is, the order each protocol will be tried when attempting a connection to an Exchange server. If you don't get the protocols in the correct order, the client will incur a long delay before it connects to the server, because the client must wait for each protocol to timeout before getting to a protocol that will support an RPC connection to the server. And unless the client is running on the same machine as the Exchange server, always ensure Local RPC is *not* at the top.

Example 2

Suppose you want to standardize the Setup procedure for your users. They are desktop and laptop users, mostly experienced. You want them to have all three installation options, Typical, Custom, and Laptop. You still want the default Program Manager group to be Microsoft Exchange and the default directory to be C:\EXCHANGE. You want your clients to have Exchange and Schedule+. You're rolling out Exchange Server initially, rather than migrating, so there needs to be connectivity only to an Exchange server. This is a pretty large network, so you've chosen TCP/IP as the protocol.

To accomplish this, the tabs depicted in Figures 14.17 through 14.20 should be modified as follows:

- In Figure 14.17, nothing should change.
- In Figure 14.18, nothing should change.
- In Figure 14.19, nothing should change.
- In Figure 14.20, simply remove the Local RPC protocol from the list, making TCP/IP Protocol the top entry. As in Example 1, you can remove the other protocols if you know they will not be used in your network environment.

A Description of the Protocols

Following is a brief description of the protocols listed in Figure 14.20, which a client uses to establish an RPC session with the Exchange server computer. These apply to Intel-based computers:

- `Local RPC`: Local RPC (LRPC) is used when both the client and the server are running on the same computer. (This RPC method does not generate any network activity.)
- `TCP/IP Protocol`: The RPCs are using TCP/IP via Windows Sockets.
- `SPX Protocol`: The RPCs are using SPX via Windows Sockets.
- `Named Pipes`: The RPCs are using Named Pipes.
- `NetBIOS`: The RPCs can use any protocol that supports NetBIOS. For example, all the protocols included with Windows NT will work: NetBIOS over TCP/IP, NetBIOS over IPX, and NetBIOS over NetBEUI. The NetBIOS interfaces are tried in the order of their LANA number.
- `RPC for Banyan Vines`: The RPCs are using Vines SPP.

Setting Client Defaults for the User

The group of settings I will explain in this section provides a way to set defaults for the Exchange client that will be active after the client is installed. This is another useful way of maintaining consistency across multiple installations, because you can set some standards for how defaults will be set in the client when it is installed. If you select the File menu and click Set User Options, the User Options property page appears, similar to Figure 14.21. You can also invoke this by clicking on the little person icon on the toolbar. Figures 14.21 through 14.25 show the five tabs of the User Options property page.

FIGURE 14.21.

The General tab of the User Options property page.

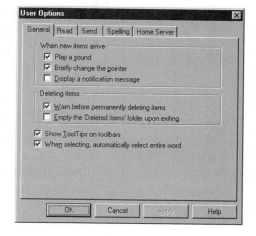

FIGURE 14.22.

The Read tab of the User Options property page.

FIGURE 14.23.
*The Send tab of the
User Options property
page.*

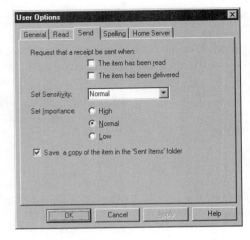

FIGURE 14.24.
*The Spelling tab of the
User Options property
page.*

FIGURE 14.25.
*The Home Server tab
of the User Options
property page.*

These screens are also mostly self-explanatory; they reflect default settings the user will see in the Tools | Options property page in the Exchange client after it is installed and running.

However, Figure 14.25, which shows the Home Server tab, needs clarification. It is blank in this example, but if you enter a server name in the Home Server text box, that Exchange server will be the default server the client attempts to connect with when it is initially run. The checkbox labeled Use network security to logon to Microsoft Exchange tells the client to use NT authentication features when trying to connect to an Exchange server. You want to keep this checked under normal circumstances, because it will provide a way for a client to connect to an Exchange server that does not reside in that client's NT domain. If you uncheck it, your NT user account must be in the same NT domain as the Exchange server. Finally, the Offline Address Book Path is the default path to where the client's offline Address Book will be stored.

Again, these settings are only defaults; they can be changed by the client after installation. But setting them to the defaults you want before installation makes things much more consistent across multiple users' installations.

Putting Things Back

When you first select a client installation point, you might notice a BAK subdirectory that wasn't there before. This is where Setup Editor places unmodified copies of the files it is opening. When you want to cancel the changes or revert to the original settings, these files are used.

There are two levels of reverting to old settings. First, if you want to revert to how things were when you started the current session of Setup Editor, select File | Undo All Changes. This selection puts the settings back they were at the beginning of the Setup Editor session. Another way to accomplish this is to click the curved arrow without the line under it.

Second, if you want to revert to how things were before any changes were ever made by Setup Editor, select File | Restore Defaults. This selection puts the settings back where they were before you made any changes with Setup Editor, regardless of whether you saved the changes along the way. Another way to accomplish this is to click the curved arrow with the line under it.

Saving Your Work

When you are finished making your changes, be sure to save them with the File | Save menu item. You can also use Ctrl+S or click the little diskette icon in the toolbar.

Summary

This chapter is straightforward in its objectives and provides a detailed insight into the Setup process by including the following:

- A list of items to consider before running Setup
- An overview of the Setup process for each supported operating system
- A summary of the Exchange Setup Editor

Initially, the chapter provided a checklist of last-minute items to check before running Setup. Some of these are fairly intuitive, but it's good to point them out anyway. This chapter mainly provides a guide through the Exchange Client Setup as you might encounter it yourself in the various supporting operating systems. Finally, the chapter covers a summary of the Exchange Setup Editor and how it affects the installation process.

## CHAPTER 15

Configuring Microsoft Exchange Clients

by Greg Todd

IN THIS CHAPTER

Chapter 4, "Exchange Client Components," introduced the Microsoft Exchange client software and explained its architecture and its major features and functions.

In this chapter, I'd like to take that a bit further and actually delve into the client itself and look at things in more detail. This should serve two purposes. First, it will provide an understanding of the various Exchange client features and how and why you would want to use them. Second, it will help you know what to do and where to start when you need to configure your own Exchange client.

There will be some overlap between the two chapters, but if you haven't read Chapter 4, go ahead and skim over it now. It's fairly short and shouldn't take too long. Plus, there are some foundational client concepts explained there that might help this chapter make more sense.

New to Version 5.0

Exchange 5.0 introduces features that provide the capability of accessing the server with several different types of clients, such as POP3, NNTP, LDAP, and Web browsers. Although there is value in each of these, this chapter will specifically focus on the Exchange client itself. To learn more about the specific Internet-related features of Exchange, check out Chapter 9, "Exchange Server and the Internet."

> **NOTE**
>
>
>
> As mentioned in Chapter 4, there are several versions of the Microsoft Exchange client software. Currently, there exists a version for Windows NT, Windows 95, Windows 3.x, MS-DOS, and Macintosh. For simplicity, I refer to any of these simply as the client, regardless of operating system version. The examples used in this chapter are based on the Windows NT 4.0 client. The Windows NT 3.51, Windows 95, and Windows 3.x clients are very similar. However, although similar in operating principle, the DOS client is somewhat different in several places. Check the Exchange documentation for details.

There is a list of items that should be covered in order to provide a good overview of the client. In this chapter you learn about the following:

- Architecture review
- Profiles and information services
- Folders
- RAS and working offline
- Address books
- Other user options

It's probably a good idea to begin with a review of the client architecture. This section reiterates some of the ideas brought out in Chapter 4.

After that you can dive right into one of the key aspects of the client—user profiles and information services and how they interrelate. This is an area where the client gets much of its power and versatility.

Following that you learn about folders, which are another key aspect of the client. Folders work together to form a powerful feature of the software, and you should find them quite natural to use (as I have).

For those who either work remotely or in an occasionally connected environment, it makes sense to discuss the client's capabilities in that area. Exchange uses RAS/PPP and offline folders to accomplish this, and it is arguably one of the handiest features in the program.

Next, a discussion of Exchange Address Books is in order. Here, you learn about the different kinds of address books and how and why you would want to use them.

Wrapping up the client, you look at some of the remaining user options. There are many configurable options, but this section discusses the most general ones and picks up some that were not covered in the previous sections. Things such as rules-based mail processing, custom views, and searching are included.

After reading this chapter, you should have a good grasp of how the Exchange client works, of its architecture, of its major features, and why you would want to use them. You should see the similarities between the clients on all operating systems and get some idea of where the DOS client differs. And although it covers a lot of ground, this chapter is intended to supplement, not replace, the documentation that comes with Exchange. The Exchange manuals are well done, so use them!

Finally, although this chapter does not explicitly cover the new Outlook 97 client, the general concepts covered in this chapter still apply to Outlook. For example, the concepts of client architecture, profiles, information services, folders, working offline, and address books all are relevant and applicable to Outlook. Certainly, Outlook has many more useful features than the generic Exchange client—and some features are implemented in slightly different ways—but if you understand the information in this chapter, you will have a better grasp of topics that pertain to Outlook.

New to Version 5.0

Architecture Review

Architecture

As covered in Chapter 4, there is a key aspect to the Exchange client architecture: modularity. This approach to the design enables the client to lend itself well to playing the role of "universal inbox." Figure 15.1 illustrates this.

It is clear that at an architectural level the client really is designed to be a means of managing all kinds of information, regardless of the type and source. Whereas many systems provide plain old electronic-mail storage, Exchange goes beyond that and literally acts as a universal inbox to contain all kinds of information. So rather than being the central focus of the product, e-mail

15

CONFIGURING EXCHANGE CLIENTS

is relegated to existing as one of many types of information the client can manage. In fact, the client can connect to a variety of data sources simply by implementing the proper information services.

FIGURE 15.1.

The Exchange client derives its flexibility and extensibility from its modular architecture.

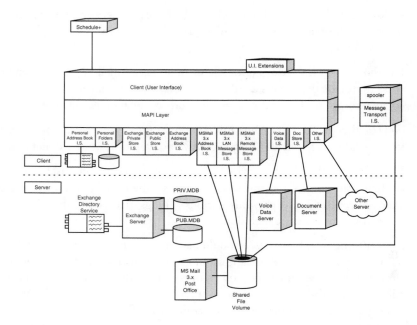

Modularity and Consistency

An important thing to remember is that the client is consistent no matter what data source it is connected to. Therefore, whether you are connecting to an Exchange server, an MS Mail post office, or another source of data, the basic user interface and functionality remain the same. It's just a matter of adding the right information service to get to the information you need.

Another aspect of consistency as a result of modularity is that the client is freed from constraints imposed by network transports or storage mediums. These are abstracted from the interface the user sees, so the client does not change whether you are running TCP/IP or IPX/SPX, looking at e-mail, or listening to voice mail. When sending information, the client does not need any knowledge of the destination. Conversely, when the client is receiving information, it does not need any knowledge of where it came from. It's just sort of one big information blob out there, and you see it through the Exchange client with a consistent interface.

One other point about consistency. The personal address book and personal store are always available regardless of the type of external data the client is connected to. That implies that you can move data around and put it in a personal (local) storage medium for later use. This is a great feature, especially if you need to archive data or take it with you when you are not connected to the network.

Extensibility

An important byproduct of the client's modular design is extensibility. That is, the architecture supports "bolting on" additional pieces to the client where necessary. That way, no one has to wait on Microsoft to develop all the pieces that anyone anywhere might need. Using the MAPI SDK, third parties can develop their own information services to fill whatever need might arise.

Using this design approach also extends the life of Exchange beyond what a bunch of marketing types—or engineer types—sitting in a room can dream up. And that's good, because none of us likes having to throw away something like a messaging system after making such a huge investment to get it up and running.

Going back to the user interface for a minute, there's an additional goody in the case of connecting to other data sources. There can be user-interface modifications, or extensions, to customize the client for accessing a particular type of data. If you look back at Figure 15.1, you will notice a U.I. Extensions box on the top of the user interface. The types of client extensions include the following:

- Menus and menu items
- Event handlers
- Toolbars
- Property pages

For example, if you access voice data, you might want play, stop, and pause buttons on the toolbar. You might also want additional information specific to voice data in the menu items or property pages.

That about does it for the review of the client architecture. Now let's move into some details of the client itself. This is where the really good stuff starts.

Profiles and Information Services

Information services and profiles are a part of MAPI. The two are related, and understanding how they work together is important to understanding how the client works.

An *information service*—sometimes referred to a *service provider*, or simply a *provider*—is the way the client connects to an external information source. This is a modular component that bolts on to the client to provide access to whatever information is needed.

A *profile* is a collection of information services. If you think of an information service as being like an .INI file that specifies a type of connection and its associated preferences, you can think of a profile as a container for multiple .INI files.

Let's look closer at information services first, then profiles. After that, you should see the relationship between the two more clearly.

Information Services

MAPI defines interfaces for three main types of information services:

- Address book
- Message store
- Message transport

These three information services serve as building blocks for messaging applications or other information services, which can contain any or all of them.

In reality, an information service is just a DLL. In the simplest and most common case, a DLL contains one information service. Sometimes, a DLL can contain more than one information service, or an information service can be composed of more than one DLL.

If you open the Mail applet in the Control Panel and click the Add button, the available information services will appear, as shown in Figure 15.2.

FIGURE 15.2.

The available information services are shown when you try to add a service to a profile.

There are five main information services that come with the Exchange client:

- Internet Mail
- Microsoft Exchange server
- Microsoft Mail
- Personal Address Book
- Personal Folders

There are also several related DLL files:

- MINET32.DLL—MAPI 1.0 Service Provider for Internet Mail
- EMSABP32.DLL—Microsoft Exchange Address Book Provider
- EMSMDB32.DLL—Microsoft Exchange Server Information Store Service Provider
- EMSUI32.DLL—Microsoft Exchange Configuration Library
- EMSUIX32.DLL—Microsoft Exchange Extensions DLL
- MSFS32.DLL—MAPI 1.0 Service Provider for Microsoft Mail
- MSPST32.DLL—Microsoft Personal Folder/Address Book Service Provider

> **NOTE**
>
> In the 32-bit operating systems—Windows NT (shown here) and Windows 95—the 32-bit client is used, so the DLLs just listed have a "32" appended to them. In the 16-bit versions they have nothing appended—for example, EMSABP32.DLL is EMSABP.DLL.

The Microsoft Exchange Server information service is composed of EMSABP32.DLL, EMSMDB32.DLL, and EMSUI32.DLL. This is an example of an information service made up of multiple DLLs.

The Microsoft Mail information service is composed of MSFS32.DLL. This is an example of an information service in a single DLL.

Both the Personal Address Book and the Personal Folders information services are contained in MSPST32.DLL. This is an example of a single DLL containing two information services.

Profiles

With the client's modular extensible architecture, it is easy to add new information services. However, at some point it gets difficult to keep track of all the services. That is where profiles come into the picture.

Profiles are used to keep track of the user's configuration of various information services on a client, and they provide one of the client's most flexible features. When you start the Exchange client, the profile tells the client what information services to start.

In Windows NT and Windows 95 clients, the profiles are all stored in the Registry. In Windows 3.x and MS-DOS clients, they are stored in files on the disk.

For example, a single user can have multiple profiles on a single workstation. If you use a laptop both at work and at home, you can have a profile tailored for the way you use Exchange in both places.

As another example, many users can have a profile on a single workstation. If several users share a certain client machine, each one can have a personal profile tailored to the specific and varying configuration needs of that person.

Figure 15.3 illustrates how profiles might be used.

Using Figure 15.3 as an example, User 1 has a computer for work and a separate computer for home. The work computer has a profile named Work, which contains work-related information services. Likewise, the home computer has a profile named Home, which contains home-related information services.

User 2 has a single computer for both office use and travel use. When User 2 is in the office, he selects the Office profile when Exchange starts. Likewise, when he's on the road, he selects the Travel profile.

15

CONFIGURING EXCHANGE CLIENTS

Figure 15.3.
Profiles provide flexibility in maintaining Exchange client configurations.

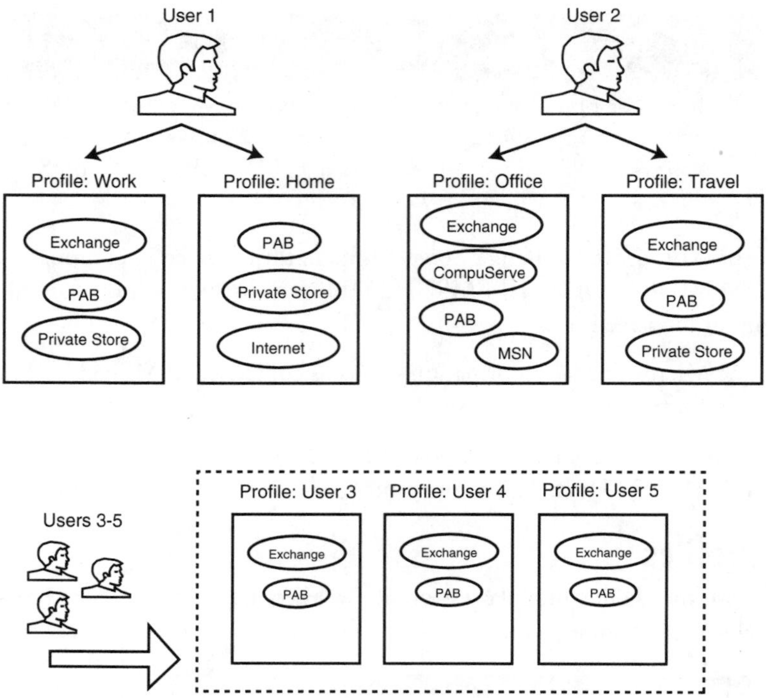

Finally, Users 3, 4, and 5 all share a computer. They have the same information services, but because they don't use identical client settings (they each have different mailboxes, for example) each user can select a personalized profile when Exchange starts.

Accessing Profiles in the Client

There are two completely different ways to get to the profiles (I found this confusing at first, but after you get the idea that both approaches are doing the same thing, it's easy to understand):

- Via the Mail applet in the Control Panel
- Via the Tools | Services menu in the client

The first way to access client profiles is through the Mail applet. Although both methods are similar, this is the more flexible way of managing profiles. When you activate the applet, it shows the current default Exchange profile, as shown in Figure 15.4.

> **NOTE**
>
> Note that with the Windows 3.x client, you can accomplish the same thing by opening the MS Exchange Services icon, which was installed in the Microsoft Exchange group during client setup. This just runs Control Panel and opens the Mail applet in one step.

FIGURE 15.4.

One way to access the client profiles is by using the Mail applet in the Control Panel.

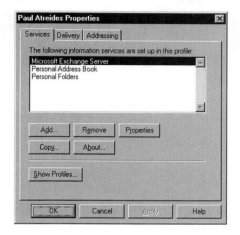

The second way to access client profiles is through the Exchange client itself. This will show the currently-in-use profile when Exchange is opened. And unless you configure the client to enable selecting another profile at startup, this will be the default profile.

Open the Tools menu, and select the Services menu item to bring up the Services dialog box as shown in Figure 15.5.

NOTE

If you notice a slight response delay in opening the Tools menu immediately after the client has been started, don't be alarmed. You are seeing an artifact of certain optimizations built into the client. It is designed to present a usable message viewer as quickly as possible while still instantiating the menus for a few seconds after the client starts and the viewer appears.

Performance

FIGURE 15.5.

Another way to access the client profiles is by using the Services entry in the Tools menu of the client.

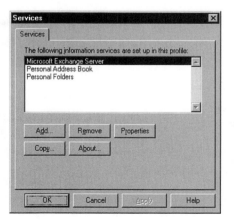

15

CONFIGURING EXCHANGE CLIENTS

> **NOTE**
>
> Here again, you can accomplish the same thing by opening the Tools menu, selecting Options, and selecting the Services tab. This is identical to using the Tools | Services menu.
>
> I suppose if you're counting, this actually makes *four* distinct ways to configure profiles.

Notice the slight difference between the information shown in Figure 15.4 and Figure 15.5. Don't let this confuse things—both are accessing exactly the same profile information. In reality, Figure 15.5 is a subset of Figure 15.4, so it makes sense that they both show the same things.

However, there are a few differences that make the Mail applet a slightly more flexible way to manage profiles than the client's Tools | Services menu.

Figure 15.4 is entitled `Paul Atreides Properties`; Figure 15.5 is entitled simply `Services`. The title of Figure 15.4 will change depending on which profile is set as the default. For example, if Duke Leto is the name of the default profile, the title will read `Duke Leto Properties` rather than `Paul Atreides Properties`. The title of Figure 15.5 does not change.

Also, Figure 15.4 has two extra tabs that Figure 15.5 does not. They give additional profile configuration, such as specifying a folder where new mail is sent, which address books are used, and the order in which the address books are searched.

Finally, Figure 15.4 has a Show Profiles button. This shows all the profiles available on the client machine, as depicted in Figure 15.6. From here, you can configure the information services in any of the displayed profiles. You can also set which profile will be the default when the Exchange client starts on this computer.

FIGURE 15.6.

Using the Mail applet, you can manage any profile available on the client machine.

Usually, you would use the Mail applet if you want to make changes to any profile that exists on the client machine. It is also the way to create new profiles. For example, if you maintain multiple profiles on the same machine—say, one for work and one for home—you could easily configure the profiles this way.

Similarly, if you currently have the client open and just need to add a new information service (or remove an old one) from your active profile, then using the Tools | Services method would be the way to go.

That should do it for profiles and information services. You should now have a better idea of what they both are, how they relate to the client, and when and why you would use them. Let's move on to the next key element of the client: folders.

Folders

If you're like me, you sometimes have a hard time trying to keep things organized. I find myself putting papers and letters and bills and whatever into piles everywhere, especially when I'm in a hurry.

Fortunately, one day I discovered manila folders. These are great, and now instead of piling things up everywhere I can put stuff in folders, label the folders, and put them in a drawer or filing cabinet. What a concept, right?

It just so happened that the engineers at Microsoft figured the folder metaphor was a good one to use for the Exchange client, too. This makes it much easier to organize all that information you'll undoubtedly get in your universal inbox. And unlike real-world folders (or at least the ones I use), Exchange client folders can contain other folders as well as messages. So if one level of hierarchy isn't enough, making more is a simple matter. All in all, client folders are quite natural to use.

There are three categories of folders in the client:

- Private
- Personal
- Public

A *private* folder is a server-based folder that is part of a user's mailbox. *Inbox* and *Outbox* are examples of private folders. Private folders are stored in the private-information store on an Exchange Server, and they are displayed under the Mailbox object in the client.

A *personal* folder is a client-based folder that contains any kind of information the user wants to store off the server. You must create your own personal folders after installing the Personal Folders information service. Personal folders are usually stored on the user's local hard drive, and they are displayed under the Personal Folders object in the client.

A *public* folder is a server-based folder that is available to all users of Exchange, much like a bulletin board. It can contain various types of information including e-mail, spreadsheets, graphics, and voice mail. Public folders are stored in the public-information store on an Exchange Server, and they are displayed under the Public Folders object in the client.

Figure 15.7 shows a view of the client with all three types of folders installed and expanded so you can see them.

FIGURE 15.7.

The Exchange client is configured with private, personal, and public folders.

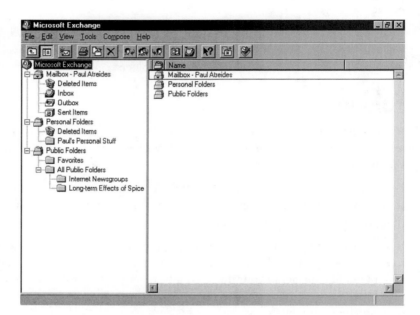

The next three sections take a closer look at the different types of folders.

Private Folders

Private folders are your mailbox folders. When you install the Microsoft Exchange Server information service, the client is given access to private folders. Look at Figure 15.8, which depicts an open mailbox with all the private folders in it.

You can see in this figure that there are three messages in the Inbox. One of the messages, at the top, is bold because it is unread; the other two have been read. Also, notice on the left side the highlighted Inbox icon has a [1] to the right of it. That indicates the number of unread messages in the Inbox—in this case, 1. This makes it easy to see at a glance how many unread messages you have.

There are several things you can do with private folders. (Actually, these actions pertain to all folders to some degree.) You can open and close them, create and delete them, move and copy them, rename them, and look at their properties. These particular actions are accessed via the File menu or via a right mouse button click.

FIGURE 15.8.

The Mailbox contains all the user's private folders, including the Inbox.

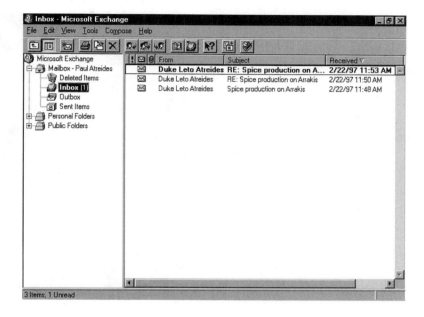

You can do most actions with the mouse as well as with the menus—and many times it is more intuitive to use the mouse. For example, moving a folder is a matter of dragging and dropping. Opening is just a double-click, and clicking the right mouse button on a folder (or any object in the client) will pop up a menu of actions appropriate for the object. Very simple.

Most of these actions—move, rename, and so on—are self-explanatory, but let's look at the properties for a moment. Figure 15.9 shows the properties for the Inbox private folder.

Notice here that in the General tab you can type in a new name for the Inbox. That's right, you can actually rename the Inbox if you want to. So, if you don't like the plain old Inbox name, you could call it something more flashy, such as Universal Inbox.

There are other tabs on the properties sheet you should know about.

NOTE

The tabs on the properties sheet, or a subset of them, are available to all three types of folders. The exact function of each is generally the same, but the details can vary depending on the folder type and whether the tab contents apply to that folder.

You use the Views tab to create custom views of your information. You learn more on this later in the chapter, in the section "Other User Options."

The Administration tab is mostly for public folders, but in the context of private folders, it defines which view is the default when a user is opening the folder.

15

CONFIGURING
EXCHANGE
CLIENTS

FIGURE 15.9.

You can access the properties for any folder via the File menu, by pressing Alt+Enter on the highlighted folder, or by clicking the right mouse button on the folder and selecting Properties.

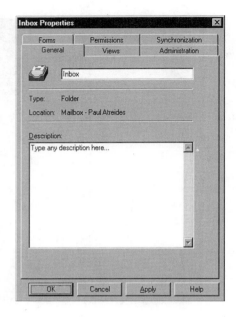

You use the Forms tab to install custom forms into the folder. You learn more on this in Chapter 30, "The Exchange Electronic Forms Designer."

The Permissions tab controls who, other than the folder's owner, has permission to use the folder.

Finally, in the Synchronization tab you configure the folder to function as an offline folder—an extremely useful feature. You learn more about this in the section, "RAS and Working Offline."

One more thing about private folders. The four default private folders—Inbox, Outbox, Deleted Items, and Sent Items—cannot be moved or deleted.

Personal Folders

Personal folders are your own folders, which you use to contain whatever you want. Functionally, they are quite similar to private folders.

If you want to keep e-mail in your personal folders, that's fine. If you want to copy public folders or other things into them, that's fine too. The basic idea is that you can have your own personal folders—usually stored on your own hard drive or a file server—that you can do with whatever you want. So wherever your computer goes, your personal folders go, too.

For those of you familiar with MS Mail, personal folders are analogous to MS Mail .MMF files. In Exchange, a personal folder—also called a *personal store*—is kept in a .PST file. When you install the Personal Folders information service, the client is given access to personal folders. Figure 15.10 shows personal folders being added to the client's profile.

FIGURE 15.10.

Personal folders are stored in .PST files. Access to them is added to the client profile with the Personal Folders information service.

You must select a path and .PST filename for the personal store. Also, you can rename the folder to something else if you want. You choose the type of encryption here, and you can enter a password if you want to password-protect your personal folders.

CAUTION

If you forget the password for your personal folders, there is no way to remove it or to get it back. The information in there will be inaccessible.

Of the six Property tabs that show up on private folders, only four of them appear on personal folders: General, Views, Administration, and Forms. However, these four function identically for personal folders and for private folders.

TIP

After you have created a .PST file, you can remove the Personal Folders information service without deleting the .PST file. Then, if you want to add the service again later—or move the .PST to another client and use it there—you can reuse the .PST, and all the information that was in it before will still be there.

Public Folders

Public folders are a bit different from private or personal folders. Although from a folder perspective they function similarly, their purpose is quite unlike private and personal folders.

Public folders form the foundation of Exchange's group-collaboration features. They provide the ability for information to be posted on an Exchange Server in such a way that anyone who uses the server can view, modify, and add to the information contained in the folders. And all this information is presented in a seamless, consistent way with the client.

Figure 15.11 shows a public folder with three postings in it.

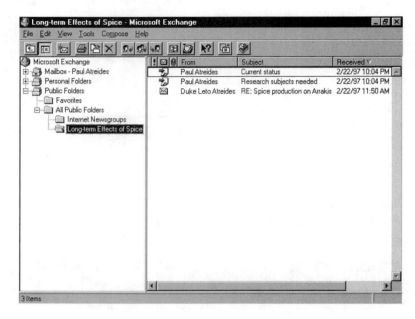

FIGURE 15.11.

Public folders provide an easy way to disseminate information to many Exchange users at once.

It isn't necessary to install an information service to make public folders available—they are in the client folder list by default.

If you are familiar with MS Mail, Exchange public folders loosely correspond to MS Mail public folders. I say "loosely" because Exchange public folders have been dramatically overhauled and given immensely more power with features such as replication.

A posting in a public folder looks much the same as an e-mail message, which makes sense given Microsoft's dedication to consistency in the client user interface. The main difference is semantic: typically, messages are posted to a public folder rather than sent and received as with e-mail.

As for Property tabs, of the six that show up on private folders, only five appear on personal folders: General, Views, Administration, Forms, and Permission. However, these five function identically for public folders as for private folders with one exception. The Administration tab includes some extra features such as access permissions and rules-based processing for new additions to the folder.

New Folders

With all this talk of folders, you probably have this unstoppable urge to create a bunch of folders and get organized. Well, maybe not. But at some time you will need to create new folders.

Creating a new folder is simple; you use the File | New Folder menu item. After you select this—assuming you have proper permissions to create folders—all you do is give the folder a name and you're ready to use it. This procedure works the same for private, public, and personal folders.

Naturally, you can display an icon for this process on the toolbar for convenience. This is configured using the Tools | Customize Toolbar menu. Then all you have to do is click the icon to create a new folder.

> **NOTE**
>
> You configure the client toolbar using the Tools | Customize Toolbar menu item. Any action that has a menu entry can be configured with an icon on the toolbar.

Folders and Messages

Before you move on, you need to learn about one last aspect of folders—which is, how does one put things in folders in the first place?

You can receive e-mail in your private folders, and you can view postings in public folders, but how do they get there originally? This might be obvious to most, but it's worth covering.

Composing new e-mail or a new posting is all contained in one main place: the Compose menu. And for convenience, there are two alternative ways to get at the same functions: by using the toolbar and by clicking the right mouse button on an existing message.

You usually put new messages in a private folder by sending an e-mail message using Compose | New Message.

You usually put new messages in a public folder by posting them using Compose | New Post in This Folder. You can also click the right mouse button on an existing message to display a menu of available options; among them will be a post action.

This is where a picture is worth a thousand words. Look at Figure 15.12, which shows the Compose menu opened while an e-mail is highlighted in the Inbox.

There are a variety of actions available that you can use to act upon an e-mail message. For example, if you highlight a posting in a folder, Reply to All would be grayed out. But highlighting an e-mail message in a folder looks just like Figure 15.12. If you have a custom application, this is one area where you might want to consider extending the user interface to include the appropriate action.

If you want to see all the options relevant for an object, click the right mouse button on it. Figure 15.13 shows what this looks like for a public-folder posting.

15

CONFIGURING EXCHANGE CLIENTS

FIGURE 15.12.

There are several actions that can be carried out on an e-mail message. The menu is context-sensitive, and it shows appropriate actions depending on what is highlighted.

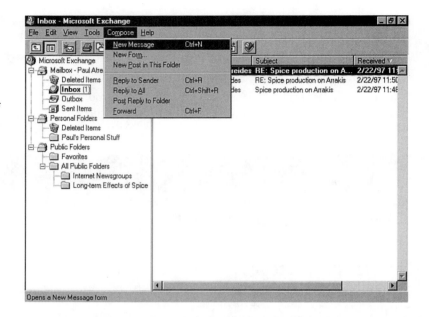

FIGURE 15.13.

These are the actions for a posting, which are very similar to actions for a message.

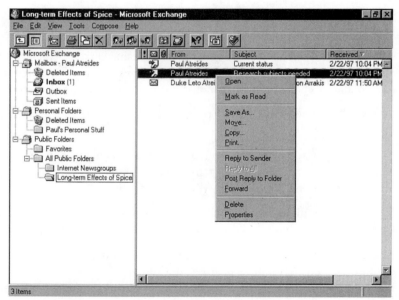

You can also place icons on the toolbar that perform the same actions as those shown in the menu. Again, use Tools | Configure Toolbar.

That's all you need to know about folders to get started using them. The next section explains another neat aspect of the client: working remotely and offline.

RAS and Working Offline

Arguably one of the most valuable features of the client is the ability it provides the user to work remotely and offline. This section investigates these features, shows how they are related, and explains why you would want to use them.

Begin by learning the definitions of these two terms.

Working *remotely* is using the client while you are actually connected to the Exchange server's network via a modem. In effect, you are online with the server using your remote connection.

Working *offline* is using the client while you are not connected to an Exchange server. However, you still have the ability to use server-based folders—for example, private folders—that have been configured for offline use.

These two are related because you can configure folders to be used offline—that is, while you are not connected to the network. Then you can use RAS to dial in to your network to work remotely or synchronize your offline folders, for example. Sound useful? Let's look at this a little more.

Working Remotely

Working remotely involves using a dial-up service, such as Remote Access Services (RAS), Dial-Up Networking (DUN) or Point to Point Protocol (PPP). All of these are supported with the client, depending on which operating system you are using:

- Windows NT 3.51 and 4.0 use RAS.
- Windows 95 use DUN.
- Windows 3.*x* and DOS each use third-party PPP software included with Exchange called ShivaRemote.

For purposes of this discussion, I refer to RAS as it works with the Windows NT 4.0 client, but the principles apply across the board to all the clients using RAS, DUN, and PPP.

> **NOTE**
>
> In Windows NT 4.0, Remote Access Services is now referred to as Dial-Up Networking. This is mainly a part of the effort to be consistent with the look and terminology of Windows 95. Underneath, it's still much the same RAS from NT 3.51, but with some new features added on.

For example, suppose you have a computer at work and a computer at home. Normally, you process your e-mail while at work, but sometimes you like to check it while you're home. Working remotely, all you have to do is connect to the office network using RAS and log in to your Exchange Server using your home-based client. Then you can operate in Exchange as though you were at the office, albeit not as fast.

15
CONFIGURING EXCHANGE CLIENTS

Performance When you work remotely, you are actually connected to the Exchange server network with your modem instead of with a network card. Everything works the same, just slower. The speed is directly proportional to the speed of your connection. I recommend no less than a 14.4Kbps modem; a 28.8Kbps modem is much better. If you have something faster, that's better still!

Assume you have configured RAS for a dial-up connection to a RAS server on your Exchange Server network. From there, it's simple to enable the client for remote usage (in three steps):

1. Modify the Microsoft Exchange Server Information Service Properties in your profile to set the type of connection you want when the client starts.

2. Modify the Microsoft Exchange Server Information Service Properties in your profile to include your RAS information.

3. Modify the Microsoft Exchange Server Information Service Properties in your profile to configure Remote Mail.

When you are finished with these, connect to the network with RAS and use the client as usual to connect to the Exchange Server.

Fortunately, you can configure the three configuration steps in a single place. Figure 15.14 shows the property sheet for the Microsoft Exchange Server information service.

FIGURE 15.14.

The configuration for using the client remotely is done in the Microsoft Exchange Server Information Services Properties.

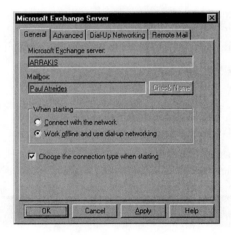

The first item is configured in the General tab. This is a handy feature because you can have the client ask you which way you'd like to work whenever it loads.

The second item is configured in the Dial-Up Networking tab. This basically leverages the existing RAS setup. Whatever is configured in RAS will apply to this.

The third item is configured in the Remote Mail tab. See the following sidebar for more information on Remote Mail.

REMOTE MAIL

The client contains a feature called Remote Mail. When you enable the client for remote use, the Remote Mail menu item is available in the Tools menu. You use Remote Mail to connect to Exchange Server to retrieve headers of your e-mail and to send e-mail you have composed while offline. Then you actually work with the e-mail, using the main client interface—the Viewer.

You might ask, why would anyone use Remote Mail instead of always synchronizing an offline Inbox (described in the next section "Working Offline")? Some people will never use Remote Mail; others will use it extensively. The main advantage of using Remote Mail is you can select which e-mail headers to download. With an offline Inbox, the only option is to synchronize the Inbox with the one on the server. For example, if you have 50 new e-mails, but you care about only a few of them, Remote Mail lets you select only the ones you want for downloading. Otherwise, you would have to download all 50 e-mails to synchronize the Inbox.

Here is one other point. You can use Remote Mail two ways: with an offline folder and without an offline folder. In the first case, if you use Remote Mail with an offline folder, the downloaded e-mail lands in the offline folder. In the second case, if you use it without an offline folder, you must have a personal folder available for the e-mail to land in.

The online help in the client is useful for configuring for Remote Mail.

To this point, you've learned how to work when you are connected to the Exchange Server—even when the connection is a remote one. Next, you learn the notion of working with a folder while you aren't connected to the Exchange Server.

Working Offline

Working offline is an Exchange term. It refers to specific folders—such as the Inbox, Outbox, Sent Items, and Delete Items—which are configured to function whether the client is connected to the network or not.

This is an excellent feature for what I'll call the "occasionally connected" user. In other words, if you are the type of user who is connected to the network only sometimes, that qualifies for occasionally connected.

For example, say you work in the office part of the time, at home part of the time, and on the road part of the time. Aside from the fact that you work too much, you don't want multiple computers floating around—you just want to use your laptop wherever you are. While in the office, you plug your laptop into the docking bay, which provides a network connection. No problem. While at home, you use RAS to work remotely. No problem. But while on the road (or on a plane), you can't very well connect to the server to read those 300 new e-mails you have in your Inbox.

Offline folders solve this. You can read and reply to your e-mail while you work offline. Then, when you get back in the office, you can synchronize the offline folders to get new e-mail and send the ones to which you replied.

In our example, the first thing to do is configure the Inbox and the Outbox as offline folders. This is simple: just modify the folder properties to make it an offline folder. Click on the Inbox, and choose File | Properties. Then click the Synchronization tab and select When offline or online. Figure 15.15 shows the dialog box.

FIGURE 15.15.

Configuring a folder for offline operation is a matter of modifying the folder properties.

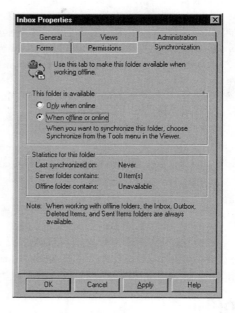

> **NOTE**
>
> You can configure any private folder and the Favorites public folders as offline. No other public folders can be configured for offline use.

From here, just click OK. If this is the first folder you have configured for offline use, a dialog box appears advising that an offline folder file—an .OST file—must be created. After you select where to keep the file, Exchange initializes the .OST file.

Notice that when you configure the Inbox for offline use, the Deleted Items, Outbox, and Sent Items folders are also configured the same way. However, the Mailbox parent folder itself does not follow suit. That is because when you work with offline folders, your main e-mail folders—the Inbox, Outbox, Deleted Items, and Sent Items folders—are always available.

The final step is to synchronize the folders. You do this using the Tools | Synchronize menu, as shown in Figure 15.16.

FIGURE 15.16.

Any time you want to synchronize an offline folder with a server-based folder, such as the Inbox shown here, use the Synchronize command.

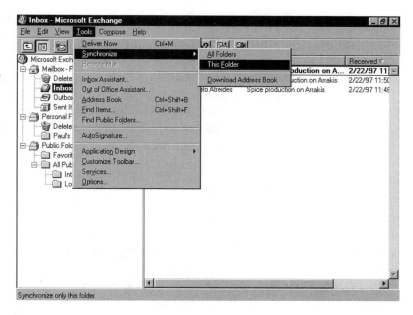

You can choose to synchronize either all offline folders or just the one that is highlighted. If you have multiple offline folders with a lot of information in them, this could take a little time. If you need to re-sync only one folder, then do only that one. While the synchronization takes place, as shown in Figure 15.17, Exchange lets you know the progress of the operation.

FIGURE 15.17.

Exchange presents a progress bar showing how much of the offline folder synchronization has been completed.

Now you're ready to work offline with your mailbox. You can read your unread mail, compose replies, and compose new mail—all while not connected to the Exchange server. When you get back to the office, all you have to do is connect to the server; an offline folder synchronization will occur to send and receive your e-mail. Of course, you can connect to the server using either a LAN connection or a RAS connection; the synchronization will still happen. If you ask me, that is a powerful feature. It makes life much easier if you are out of the office for any amount of time.

About Working Offline

Before you move on, there are a few things that need to be pointed out about working offline.

15

CONFIGURING
EXCHANGE
CLIENTS

First, when you have an unsent e-mail, the Outbox icon turns red. That shows there is at least one message there that has not been sent, and it is a visual cue to synchronize your folder when you are reconnected to the server.

Second, when you are composing e-mail offline, you do not have access to the Global Address List. How are you going to address e-mail unless you have a list of available e-mail addresses? I'm glad you asked that. The next section, where you learn about address books, covers that in more detail. The quick answer is that you have to either use a personal address book or use an offline version of the Global Address List. With the latter, it is just a matter of synchronizing it like you do other offline folders. Keep reading, and I promise I will get to it in a minute.

Third, if you plan to often alternate between working online and working offline, configure your profile to prompt you each time Exchange starts whether you want to work online or offline. Just edit your profile as shown in Figure 15.18.

FIGURE 15.18.

Sometimes, it is more convenient to configure your profile to prompt for the connection type when you start Exchange.

One way to get to this dialog box is via the Tools | Services menu from the client. From the Services property sheet that appears, open the Properties of the Microsoft Exchange Server service. Then the dialog similar to Figure 15.18 will appear. Check the box titled Choose the connection type when starting. Then, every time you start the client, you will be prompted to choose whether you want to work offline or connect to a server.

OK, enough of that. As promised, the next section explains address books.

Address Books

In Exchange, an address book is a directory of e-mail addresses you use with the client. It contains one or more lists of recipients.

This section covers the various aspects of Exchange address books and talks a little about addressing.

Address Book Types

There are typically two types of address books you have access to in the Exchange client:

- Global Address Book (or Global Address List)
- Personal Address Book

The Global Address Book contains a list of names of all recipients in the Exchange organization. Remember, recipients include directory entities such as users, mailboxes, distribution lists, and public folders. In other words, the Global Address Book is a directory listing.

The Personal Address Book is a user address book stored locally in a .PAB file. Like the Global Address Book, it contains recipients as well, but just the ones the user puts in there.

One important addition to these two is the offline Address Book. It is basically a copy of all or part of the Global Address Book, and it is handled just like the offline folders covered in the last section. You learn more on this later in this chapter, in the section "Offline Address Book."

You can get to the address books via the Viewer menu. Choose Tools | Address Book. You can also press Ctrl+Shift+B or click the address-book icon on the toolbar. Doing so brings up a window similar to Figure 15.19.

FIGURE 15.19.

The Address Book is a separate window in the client, invoked by menu, key combination, or toolbar icon.

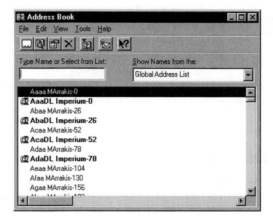

Within these two address books, there are three main types of addresses that can appear:

- Regular addresses
- Gateway addresses
- Custom addresses (or one-off addresses)

The regular addresses are self-explanatory. They are made up of the normal recipients present in the Exchange Directory, such as other Exchange users, folders, distribution lists, and so on. They can exist in either the Global Address Book or a Personal Address Book.

Gateway addresses are addresses of users in e-mail systems outside the Exchange organization. These users are reached via a gateway, which is simply a software component that connects the Exchange system to the outside e-mail system. If these addresses are created by an Exchange administrator, they will appear in the Global Address Book. For example, if you use the Internet Mail Connector (IMC), which is a gateway to SMTP mail, you will likely have gateway addresses in the Global Address Book.

Custom addresses are really gateway addresses used to address a recipient in a foreign e-mail system. When they are created by a user and stored in a Personal Address Book they are referred to as *one-off addresses*. There are localized templates available on the Exchange Server, which the client uses for creating one-off addresses, including Internet (SMTP), MacMail, Microsoft Mail, cc:Mail, and X.400.

When you create a custom address, the proper format to use is

`[AddressType:Address]`

You must include the brackets—for example,

`[smtp:PaulA@Dune.Imperium.com]`

The following are some valid `AddressType` entries:

SMTP	FAX	MHS
MCI	X400	X500
MSA	MS	MSPEER
PROFS	SNADS	COMPUSERVE
3COM	ATT	TELEX
CCMAIL		

Configuring the Address Book

If you click the drop-down list box called Show Names from the: in Figure 15.19, you will see entries in addition to Global Address List such as Personal Address Book, the organization name, and so on. This determines which addresses you're looking at.

You can configure which of these shows up as the default using the Tools | Options menu. Select the Addressing tab as shown in Figure 15.20.

In this example, the Global Address List will show up when the address book is opened. Personal addresses are kept in the Personal Address Book, and it is searched for matching names before the Global Address Book is. That makes sense, especially when a user is working offline and the Global Address Book might not be available. Besides, any strange addresses you might have will likely be stored in the Personal Address Book.

FIGURE 15.20.

The Address Book options can be easily configured.

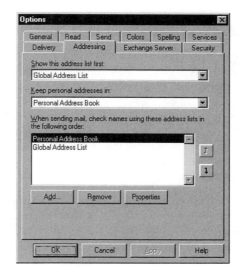

Offline Address Book

As mentioned earlier, the offline Address Book is basically a local copy of all or part of the Global Address Book, and it is handled just like the offline folders covered in the last section.

The purpose for the offline Address Book is simple. When you work offline, there isn't any way to address e-mail, because you are not connected to an Exchange server. Unless you have all the addresses you need stored in your Personal Address Book, you should create an offline Address Book.

You create the offline Address Book by selecting Tools | Synchronize | Download Address Book.

Before you create the offline Address Book, you are presented with two options, as shown in Figure 15.21. You can download either the entire Global Address Book and all the details, or you can skip the details. The latter option downloads faster and takes less space. If you plan to use encryption, you must download details. Having a copy of the main address book is invaluable if you spend time working in Exchange while not connected to a server. Obviously, this process must be done while online and connected to the Exchange server.

Performance

FIGURE 15.21.

When creating an offline Address Book, you can opt to not download the address details if you want to save room and synchronize faster.

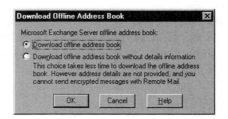

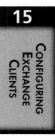

15

CONFIGURING EXCHANGE CLIENTS

Other User Options

As you've probably noticed by now, there are many options available in the client—maybe even some you won't ever use. Besides the ones covered up to this point, there are several other user options available.

Some are intuitive and obvious, such as saving a file, opening a file, setting general options, and so on. I won't bother talking about those. However, there are three other main ones I want to mention that serve to round out the client features.

Views

Views enable you to group your messages in ways to better organize and manage them.

The client Viewer has some default views built into it, and you can select them using the View | Personal Views or View | Folder Views menus. But if you don't like those, you can build your own.

Choose View | Define Views to bring up the Define Views dialog box as shown in Figure 15.22. Just click New to build a new view.

FIGURE 15.22.

You can design your own Folder views and Personal views using the Define Views dialog box.

Folder views are available only to the specific folders in which they are created. For example, if you had some data that was specific to a particular folder, that would be a good place for a folder view. It wouldn't apply to all folders, just the one for which it was created.

Personal views are available to all folders. For example, if you have a personal preference for the way fields are presented when you look at your Inbox, you could create a personal view for it. That view would also apply to other folders you open.

Simply select the type of view you want to create—Folder or Personal—and click New. From there, just name your view, select the columns, groupings, sorting, and filter, and you're finished. The client online help provides more details.

The Assistants

There are two client assistants found in the Tools menu: the Inbox Assistant and the Out of Office Assistant, shown in Figures 15.23 and 15.24, respectively.

FIGURE 15.23.

The Inbox Assistant lets you apply rules to process the incoming e-mail.

FIGURE 15.24.

The Out of Office Assistant automates your mailbox while you are out of the office.

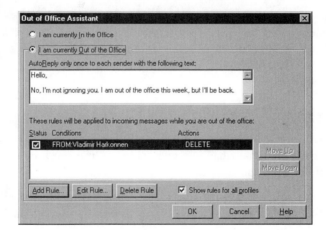

The functions of these two assistants are somewhat related in that they both provide automated processing for your incoming e-mail.

The Inbox Assistant is simply there to process your incoming e-mail and hopefully make life a little easier for you. By applying rules to each incoming message, the Inbox Assistant can decide whether to keep it, move it, trash it, and so on, depending on how you configure the rules.

For example, say you want to delete all mail that comes from someone named Vladimir Harkonnen. Just configure the rule to look for e-mail from Vlad, and select the Delete action. The Inbox Assistant takes care of it from there. If you decide to start keeping Vlad's e-mail for some reason, just delete the rule.

The Out of Office Assistant is there to manage your mailbox for you when you aren't there to manage it personally. It performs the same function as the Inbox Assistant, with one addition: it will automatically respond to incoming e-mail with a message you give it.

15

CONFIGURING
EXCHANGE
CLIENTS

For example, say you will be out of the office for a week, and you don't plan to take a computer with you to work remotely. And because you're so popular, you just know your mailbox will fill up while you are gone. Plus, you really don't want to deal with people thinking you are just slacking off and ignoring them by not answering their e-mail. In addition, you still want to trash all e-mails from our friend Vladimir Harkonnen. Just configure the Out of Office Assistant as shown in Figure 15.24, and you're set.

Both Assistants' rules are server-based. That is, as long as the rule does not reference a personal folder (PST), they will be applied any time. You do not have to be logged in for the rules to take effect.

These features are quite useful. I recommend you play around with them and see for yourself how they work.

> **NOTE**
>
> Don't confuse these assistants with the Office Assistants, which are included as a feature of Office 97. These cute little animations are part of the Office 97 online help suite—a completely separate thing.

Searching

The client provides another useful tool: the ability to search any of your folders to find something. This is especially handy if you're like me and you keep tons of old e-mail. I can never remember where I put stuff after a couple months.

You activate the search applet in the Tools | Find menu. I call it an applet because it is actually a separate window from the main Exchange client Viewer—much like the Address Book is a separate window.

Figure 15.25 shows what the Find applet looks like.

For example, while we're talking about your pesky e-mail–sending colleague, Vladimir Harkonnen, suppose you got some e-mail from him at one time in the past that you decided to keep. You know you moved it to a personal folder somewhere, but you aren't sure how many messages there are and what they said. Just configure a search to look for all messages from Vladimir Harkonnen, and the Find applet will locate them for you.

The Find applet is not limited to a personal store. You can also use it on the Inbox or wherever you have messages stored. It's quite a powerful and flexible tool.

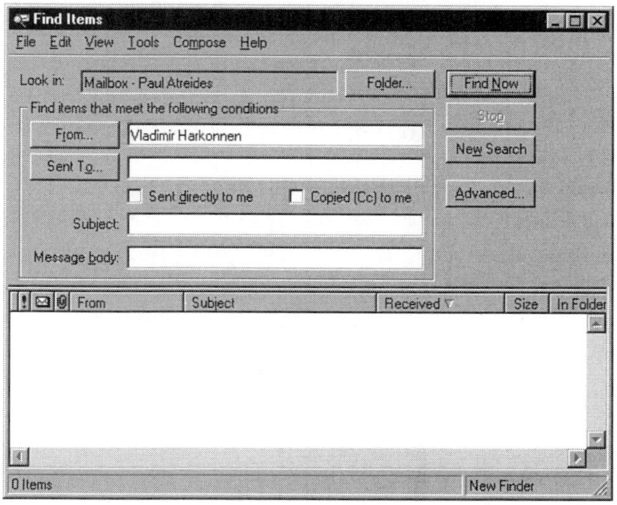

FIGURE 15.25.

The Find applet gives you the capability of searching your folders for messages.

Summary

Whew! This chapter covered a lot of client topics:

- Architecture review
- Profiles and information services
- Folders
- RAS and working offline
- Address books
- Other user options

As you can see, the Exchange client has much to offer in features and functionality. I find it to be very useful, and everyone I talk to that uses it says they like it, too.

> **TIP**
>
> If you like the Exchange client, as I do, you should try Outlook 97. I use Outlook every day, and I like it even better than the Exchange client. Outlook contains all the features of the Exchange client, plus some powerful personal organization features. There are several books available on the subject. One I can recommend is *Teach Yourself Microsoft Outlook in 24 Hours* by Sams Publishing.

If you've never used the client before, you might like the looks of the Exchange client after reading this chapter. If you are already somewhat acquainted with it, then you probably have your opinions formed. Perhaps, though, this chapter has helped fill the gaps in your knowledge so you can get more out of using it than you were before.

15

CONFIGURING
EXCHANGE
CLIENTS

Summary

Connecting to Other Mail Systems

by Robert Henriksen
Revised by Kevin Kaufmann

IN THIS CHAPTER

Users will be delighted at the new client capabilities in Exchange, but connectors are one of the main areas that are going to make the administrator's heart go pitter-pat. Under Microsoft Mail, the gateway products could be the source of a lot of heartburn. It's difficult to emphasize just how much better life is now with Exchange, so I'm just going to dive in.

Exchange ships with four *connectors,* the new term for what were called *gateways* in Microsoft Mail. Like everything else in Exchange Server, they are implemented as services. In this chapter, you will focus on the MSMail and X.400 Connector; the cc:Mail and Internet Mail Service are covered in Chapters 10, "Migrating from Lotus cc:Mail," and 17, "The Internet Mail Service," respectively.

It is strongly advisable to run Exchange and your existing MSMail post office(s) concurrently during your configuration/testing and migration period, instead of performing a crash conversion. To do this, you must first install and configure the MSMail Connector to get message transfer (MTA) running between Exchange and your existing Microsoft Mail post offices. Then enable directory synchronization between Exchange and the Mail post office(s), as covered in Chapter 20, "Directory Synchronization with Microsoft Mail." In the setup examples to follow, I assume you have a fairly straightforward environment—a few MSMail post offices, all on a single LAN/WAN, and no X.25 or dial-up async connections between post offices.

The Internet Mail Service is a very robust product as well—albeit with a couple of missing links, which you'll review. The most common source of problems in implementing the Internet Mail Service is overconfiguration. It takes only a few settings to get it up and running, and I'll show you when to leave well enough alone.

The X.400 Connector isn't likely to see a tremendous amount of use in smaller installations. X.400 is generally used by large corporations that have existing X.400 mail systems they need to interoperate with or that use a public X.400 service provider. This chapter gives you a real-world perspective on just what X.400 is and where you might find it applicable.

In Exchange 5.0, Microsoft added the cc:Mail Connector to provide message transfer and directory synchronization with Exchange. The connector uses the cc:Mail Import/Export program to get and put mail into the cc:Mail PostOffice database.

Finally, it is possible to connect an Exchange Server with the following:

- PROFS
- DEC All-In-1
- AT&T Mail
- MCI Mail
- OfficeVision
- MHS
- 3+Mail

These are all currently available via legacy gateway products—messaging gateways that were created for use with Microsoft Mail 3.*x.* You can employ them in an Exchange Server environment by first configuring Exchange-to-Microsoft Mail connectivity, and then from Microsoft Mail to the third-party mail system via one of these legacy gateway products. Third-party Exchange Connectors are being written for a variety of the just-mentioned mail systems, so you should definitely look into their availability if you need these connections. Using the Microsoft Mail-era gateways would be reintroducing a lesser grade of software and a weak link in the chain.

The following companies have either announced or are shipping companion products for Exchange Server:

Wireless connections	Ardis
	Inmarsat
	Integra
	Ericsson
Fax	OmTool
	FacSys
	Fenestrae
	Active Voice (include voicemail)
Family of products	C2C

For a full list of current gateways that are available for Microsoft Exchange, look at `www.microsoft.com/exchange/exisv`.

Microsoft Mail Connector

Compatibility

I suggest taking advantage of the MTA included in Exchange's MSMail Connector and retiring the Microsoft Mail EXTERNAL program. The reporting, logging, and monitoring functions in Exchange are far superior to MSMail and can also be completely administered remotely. You don't have to make an either/or decision; it is possible to mix and match which post offices are serviced by Exchange's MTA and External. If you already have a complex network of post offices linked with one or more instances of External, you can leave that running and gradually phase the Exchange MTA into the mix. In smaller environments, it's safe to configure the MSMail Connector MTA to take over—it's simple to toggle back to the External MTA if the need arises. Like the Internet Mail Service, you can get yourself into trouble by tweaking more settings in the MSMail Connector than you need.

How It Works

MSMail Connector actually consists of three components, as shown in Figure 16.1.

- MSMail Connector Interchange Service
- MSMail Connector Postoffice (\\exchange_server\maildat$)
- MSMail Connector MTA (Message Transfer Agent)

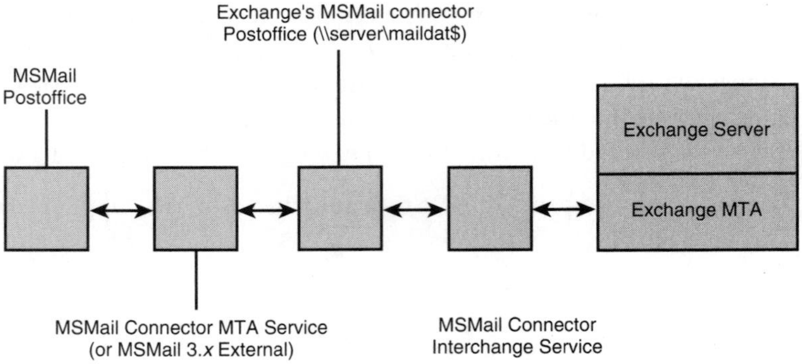

FIGURE 16.1.
Two different services handle, store, and forward at the Exchange server when sending mail between Exchange and MSMail.

Exchange's MSMail connector
Postoffice (\\server\maildat$)

MSMail
Postoffice

Exchange Server

Exchange MTA

MSMail Connector MTA Service
(or MSMail 3.*x* External)

MSMail Connector
Interchange Service

The MSMail Connector Interchange Service performs the conversion from the native Exchange message format to MSMail's message format. It then places the outbound message into the Connector Postoffice \\exchange_server\maildat$. At this point, the transfer from the Connector Postoffice to the target Microsoft Mail post office can be performed by either Exchange's MSMail Connector MTA or a traditional Mail External program. The Interchange Service could have been written to perform both the translation and the MTA, but then you would have been locked into using Exchange's MTA. Using an intermediate PO gives you the flexibility of using the older External program if desired.

Note that the Connector Postoffice is strictly used for MTA; it does not contain any mail accounts of its own. Also, if you use one of the Microsoft Mail gateway products in conjunction with Exchange, you need to install the gateway access component on the Connector Postoffice for the Exchange users to access the Mail 3.*x* gateway.

Configuration Choices

You can structure your MTA one of three ways:

Use Exchange's MSMail Connector MTA to route messages with a single PO (instead of MSMail's External program). This is recommended for single post offices. (See Figure 16.2.)

FIGURE 16.2.
The MSMail Connector MTA handles message transfer between Exchange and a single post office.

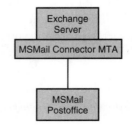

Exchange
Server

MSMail Connector MTA

MSMail
Postoffice

Make Exchange's MSMail Connector MTA the hub for all the post offices, as shown in Figure 16.3 (recommended for multiple post offices).

FIGURE 16.3.

All mail to and from Exchange, and between the post offices, is routed by the MSMail Connector MTA.

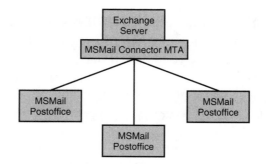

Define all but one post office to Exchange as "downstream" and allow the existing External program(s) to handle distribution of mail within the MSMail network (see Figure 16.4). This latter option is advisable if you have a large, far-flung MSMail network with a variety of WAN links, async dial-up, and so on.

FIGURE 16.4.

All Exchange MS Mail is funneled through a single connection point into the Microsoft Mail network. The message transfer is performed by an instance of MSMail 3.x External.

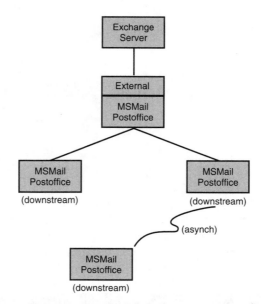

TIP

If you are rolling out an Exchange server at each physical site, you can use Exchange site connectors as your backbone between different groups of MSMail post offices.

Implementing Your Configuration Decision

If you ran the standard Exchange installation, your Site\Connections container should show the MSMail Connector object inside. If you don't see it, rerun the Exchange setup program off the CD-ROM, select Add/Remove Components, click the Details button for Exchange Server, and check the MSMail Connector option.

Double-click on the MSMail Connector in the Connections container to view its Properties dialog box, as shown in Figure 16.5.

FIGURE 16.5.

*The Interchange Page
of the MSMail
Connector Properties.*

The MSMail Connector Properties dialog box will default to displaying the Interchange Page and insist you enter an Administrator's Mailbox before moving on. I suggest using your own mailbox for all these various Exchange components until you have everything up and running smoothly. You can always delegate responsibility (and the receipt of error messages) to someone else later.

TIP

Another way to handle assignment of administrative duties is to create a Mailbox called PostMaster. Give yourself permissions on this mailbox, in addition to your usual mailbox. Then configure the Exchange Server service properties in your profile to open this second mailbox in addition to your own. That way, you can still monitor any error/status messages and originate messages as coming from PostMaster. You can also give several network-support people access to the PostMaster mailbox, for redundancy.

16

Maximize MS Mail 3.*x* Compatibility determines how OLE objects are handled.   **Performance**
Because MSMail 3.*x* clients can handle only OLE 1.0 objects, you activate this
flag for the connector to convert OLE 2.0 objects within messages down to 1.0 format for
MSMail recipients. Note that this will roughly double the size of the message, because both
versions of the object will be included.

Enable Message Tracking is well worth activating. This data is written to log files in the
\exchsrvr\tracking.log directory, as opposed to the Event Viewer's Application Log. Each day's
data is a separate file, named with the format *YYYYMMDD*.log. You can select the number
of days' worth of logs to retain in the property page Admin\Site\Configuration
\Server\servername\System Attendant. By the time you learn there's a missing message, it's too
late to go back and turn on message tracking. For this reason, and because you can limit the
quantity of logging data retained, I recommend activating this feature—there's no downside
except for the small amount of disk space it will use.

The Local Postoffice page (see Figure 16.6) gives you the properties of the MSMail Connector
Postoffice. You'll need to know this post office's name when configuring directory synchronization with MSMail post offices. The Regenerate button is used if, for some reason, you want
to change the name of the Connector Postoffice. All the existing Exchange mailboxes would
have to be updated with the new MSMail address to reflect the post office name change. Unless you have some compelling reason to tinker here, I'd leave things well enough alone. In my
site, the existing post offices were named LAW/Faculty and LAW/Students. The Connector
Postoffice's default name of UH/Central (Exchange organization/site) caused no problems in
MTA between these two different network names.

FIGURE 16.6.

*The Exchange
Connector Postoffice
properties.*

The Connections page is used to specify which post offices, and hence which MSMail addresses, the Exchange MTA can reach. After you add the various post office names here, you configure the Connector MTA to service some or all of them. You should initially see an empty Connections list except for the MSMail Connector Postoffice (see Figure 16.7).

Click the Create button in the Connections page to add an entry for your first MSMail post office. You'll be shown the Create Connection property page, as in Figure 16.8. This is a confusing area; in the Create Connection dialog box, you don't enter information directly into the provided fields.

FIGURE 16.8.

Creating a connection from Exchange Connector to the MSMail post office.

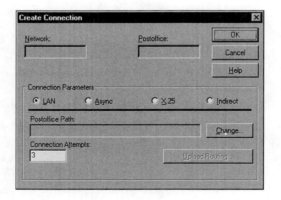

Use the Change button to display Figure 16.9, enter a UNC path to the post office, and click OK.

FIGURE 16.9.

Entering the UNC path to the post office.

Exchange will extract the network and post office name for you, as shown in Figure 16.10. If you are defining a post office that is connecting over an Async connection, select the connection parameter Async. This dialog box will expand to display the necessary modem-configuration options. Ignore the Upload Routing button for now and click OK.

FIGURE 16.10.

The network and post office names are extracted by Exchange automatically.

You should now see an entry for your first post office, similar to that shown in Figure 16.11.

FIGURE 16.11.

The completed connection entry for a Microsoft Mail post office, as described in Figure 16.2.

To configure Exchange to service multiple post offices, as in configuration option B (from Figure 16.3), click the Create button again and repeat the preceding process for the next post office. Repeat as many times as necessary until you wind up with something like Figure 16.12. The single indent for all the post office names indicates the desired hub configuration—all the post offices are serviced by the Exchange message transfer agent.

FIGURE 16.12.

The Exchange Hub MTA routing, as described in Figure 16.3.

To configure Exchange for configuration option C, you first create a single entry in the Connections page for the post office that will serve as the gateway into the Microsoft Mail network. Open this post office connection with the Modify button, click upload routing, and then click OK. You'll see something similar to Figure 16.13. All the other post offices currently being serviced by your existing Microsoft Mail network should appear indented below the primary post office.

In Figure 16.13, an MTA (either MSMail's External or the Exchange MSMail Connector MTA) will handle message transfer between the Exchange site and Law/Faculty. Messages destined for Law/Students and UH/Central will then be transferred from Law/Faculty to the appropriate downstream post office by an instance of MSMail External.

> **CAUTION**
>
> Defining the downstream post offices for Exchange ensures that Exchange knows that it can send mail to all the MSMail users—but it doesn't automatically provide an MTA! In option C, be sure to include the Exchange Connector PO (\\server\maildat$) in the external.ini for your instance of External. This will ensure that downstream MSMail users can successfully send to Exchange mailboxes.

FIGURE 16.13.

The downstream MTA routing, as described in Figure 16.4.

Next, you'll create one or more message transfer agents (MTAs) to service the post offices defined under Connections and specify which (or all) of these MSMail post offices each MTA will be responsible for handling. If all your post offices are a single LAN, simply configure them all under a single MTA. In the Connector MTAs property page (see Figure 16.14), click the New button to create an MTA.

FIGURE 16.14.

The MSMail Connector MTA property page.

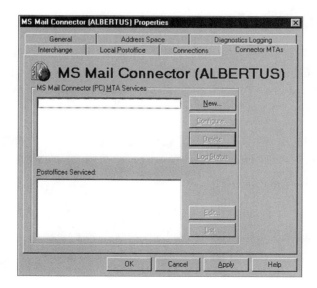

You'll see Figure 16.15. Enter a name for the MTA. A naming scheme of MTA - *name* is useful because it leaves no confusion about its function when seen in the Control Panel | Services list, and it places it directly below all the Microsoft Exchange entries in the Services list.

FIGURE 16.15.

*Defining a new
Connector MTA.*

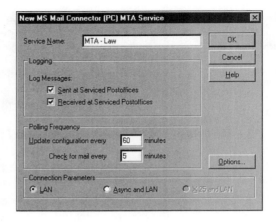

Leave the message Logging and Polling Frequency as is for now, and click OK to return to the
Connector MTAs page (refer to Figure 16.14).

> **TIP**
>
> An Exchange MSMail Connector MTA can handle asynchronous connections between it
> and an instance of External at a remote site. When you select LAN and Async from the
> MTA properties page in Figure 16.15, the dialog box will expand to include the COM port
> selection. The modem must be dedicated to the Async MTA; it cannot be shared with
> Remote Access Service.

Here's where you specify the post offices serviced by this MTA. Click the List button to see
Figure 16.16. Highlight the desired post offices, and use the Add>> button to transfer them to
the Serviced LAN Postoffices list. Click OK when finished, and you should see a Connector
MTAs property page similar to Figure 16.17.

FIGURE 16.16.

*Selecting post offices for
the MSMail Connector
MTA.*

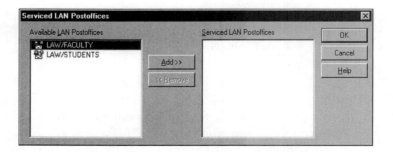

Connecting to Other Mail Systems

CHAPTER 16

397

16

CONNECTING TO
OTHER MAIL
SYSTEMS

FIGURE 16.17.

*MSMail Connector
MTA configuration for
MTA hub-style
configuration, per
Figure 16.3.*

At this point, you can close the MS Mail Connector Properties dialog box; you've finished the configuration on Exchange Server. You need to manually start the MSMail Connector Interchange service in the Control Panel before MTA will begin. You should also ensure that this service is set for Automatic startup.

Finally, configure your MSMail post offices to recognize the existence of the Exchange Connector Postoffice. This procedure is explained in the *MSMail 3.5 Administrator's Guide,* Chapter 7, "External Postoffice Administrative Tasks." Assuming all your post offices are on the same LAN (no modem links or X.25), refer to the section "Adding Direct Route Postoffices."

Testing Message Transfer

I'm going to use the sample account Admin on post office LAW\Faculty for this description. To run this test, make sure that the following are true:

- The MSMail Connector Interchange service is started in the Control Panel | Services.
- Either the MSMail Connector MTA you've configured or your existing External is running.
- Your MTA is temporarily configured to poll for new mail every 1 minute (not required, but a timesaver). Polling frequency for the MSMail Connector MTA is set in the Exchange Admin at Site | Connections | MSMail Connector, using the Configure button on the Connector MTA page. Remember to set the polling frequency back to 5 minutes when you are finished with your tests to conserve the server's resources! (See Figure 16.18.)

FIGURE 16.18.

Shorten the polling frequency of the MTA during testing.

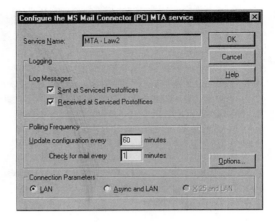

Because each mail server doesn't yet have directory information about the other(s), you have to manually address the test message. It's simplest to do this from Exchange and then reply to that test message from Microsoft Mail.

Open your Exchange mailbox and compose a new message. Click the To: button to get the Exchange directory dialog box and select the New button (see Figure 16.19). Select the type Microsoft Mail Address, select In this message only, and then click OK.

FIGURE 16.19.

Addressing e-mail to a foreign address.

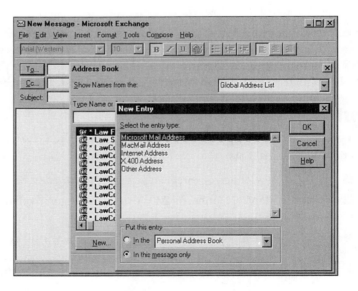

Fill in the display name with whatever you like, then the appropriate network name, post office name, and account name, as shown in Figure 16.20. In my example, it's LAW/Faculty/ Admin. OK your way back to the message and send it. When the test message arrives in the Microsoft Mail Admin mailbox, simply use the Reply function to create an appropriately addressed test message for the Mail-to-Exchange side of the link.

FIGURE 16.20.

Manually entering a Microsoft Mail address.

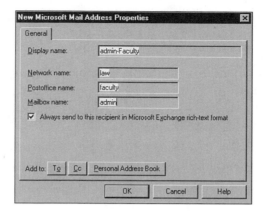

TIP

You can also type the Microsoft Mail Address into the To: field using the format [MS:*NET/ PO/MAILBOX*]. For the example above, you would type [MS:LAW/Faculty/Admin].

Lotus cc:Mail Connector

New to Version 5.0

Like the other connectors, the cc:Mail connector runs as a Windows NT service. There are three components to the connector:

- *cc:Mail service.* The Windows NT service that moves mail between Exchange and the cc:Mail post office and synchronizes the cc:Mail and Exchange directory.

- *cc:Mail store.* Set directories on the Exchange server used for temporary storage of mail and directory entries.

- *cc:Mail Import/Export.* The process that extracts and inserts mail and directory entries to the cc:Mail post office.

The cc:Mail Connector is covered in detail in Chapter 10.

Internet Mail Service (IMS)

New to Version 5.0

The Internet Mail Service (known as Internet Mail Connector in Exchange 4.0) is the replacement for Microsoft's SMTP Gateway. It is a quantum leap beyond the old gateway in reliability and ease of configuration. Noteworthy new features include the following:

- *Remote administration.* You can reconfigure and start/stop the service remotely. No more AC lamp timers to reboot the SMTP Gateway machine nightly, like some folks used to (oh, the good old days).

- *Both UUENCODE and MIME support.* The default encoding can be set at the server, but overridden by the admin for particular domains and by the user on a per-message basis.

- *NDRs.* Nondelivery reports to the Admin via e-mail for a slew of different error conditions.

- *The ability to block messages.* You can block, at the server, Out of Office and Automatic Reply messages to the Internet.

- *Prioritization of outbound mail handling.* If 75 percent of your SMTP mail is to @BigCustomer.com, you can set priority for handling e-mail to this address. Not that anyone in your organization would use company e-mail for personal correspondence, but…

- *The ability to restrict use.* You can restrict use of the Internet Mail Service by your users, by mailbox and/or distribution list membership.

- *Blacklist ability.* You can blacklist certain hostnames from sending mail into your site—great for filtering those get-rich-on-the-Internet solicitations.

- *Size restrictions on messages.* Protection against mail bombing or simply against clogging your site's slow WAN link to the Internet.

- *Choice of using a relay host.* You can choose a relay host for all mail, direct delivery using DNS, or a combination of both.

- *Dynamic dial-up connection to ISPs.* In other words, you do not need a dedicated line to the Internet (T-1, ISDN, switched 56, or nailed-up modem connection). By popular demand, this feature was added to Exchange in service pack 2.

How It Works

The Exchange MTA uses the MTS-In and MTS-Out folders in the Exchange Information store as the store-and-forward location for Internet mail. The IMS service polls the MTS-Out folder for mail and transfers it into the \Exchsrvr\IMSData\Out directory in preparation for handling. The IMS then converts the message format to SMTP, encodes any attachments, and attempts to send it (see Figure 16.21). If the transmission fails, the message is returned to sender with an NDR (non-delivery report). You have extensive control over configuration of delivery retries and message timeout intervals.

When a remote host attempts to connect to the Exchange IMS to send a message, the IMS first checks against the blacklist of hostnames. If the sending computer isn't on the blacklist, the connection and subsequent message is accepted by the IMS and placed into the \Exchsrvr\IMSData\In directory. The IMS then checks for a match between the message's addressee and the Exchange GAL. If a match is found, the message is converted into the Exchange message format and dropped into the MTS-In folder for handling by the Exchange MTA (see Figure 16.21).

FIGURE 16.21.

The structure of IMS message handling.

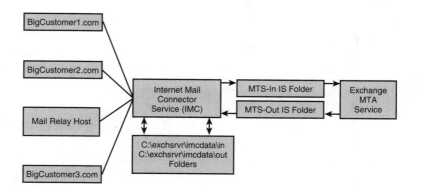

The Internet Mail Service is covered in detail in Chapter 17, "The Internet Mail Service."

X.400 Connector

Cross-
Platform

X.400's most common applications are for

- Large, multinational corporate e-mail systems, particularly in a heterogeneous environment of PCs, minicomputers, and mainframes
- Corresponding with U.S. government systems
- Use in the European community

X.400 was developed to solve a problem which the Internet (or more accurately, the Internet and the SMTP mail format) has since solved—linking proprietary e-mail systems. Development on the X.400 standard began back in the early 1980s, long before the Internet had emerged from its closed NSF and educational environment. X.400 and SMTP can be fairly described as another Beta-versus-VHS standards tussle. X.400 is inarguably the more feature-rich (and complex), but the ubiquity of the Internet and simplicity of SMTP addressing has made it the huge favorite for the majority of e-mail.

X.400's sophistication in handling multilingual environments, support for return receipts, and other features has earned it a place in large multinational corporations. The mix of languages in the European Community has also meant a somewhat greater acceptance of X.400 there than in America. The U.S. government also requires X.400 compatibility for use in its installations. This government requirement alone guarantees the continued inclusion of X.400 capabilities into messaging products for years to come, no matter how little mainstream use of the standard exists, compared to SMTP.

The biggest handicap of X.400 is the cumbersome addressing scheme. Compare the SMTP address

```
Rhenriksen@uh.edu
```

to

```
c=US;a=;p=UH;o=Central;ou=OquinnLawLibrary;ou=MIS;s=Henriksen;g=Robert
```

It gets much worse when there are often, by necessity, additional components in the address to handle company divisions, branches, departments, offices, and so on. When X.400 was first released in 1984, there was no directory standard specified to ease some of the pain of working with these addresses. The X.500 directory specification was released in 1988, but is sufficiently cumbersome itself that it has failed to erase the stigma that has held X.400 back from widespread deployment.

A very useful characterization of X.400 is that it is a set of tools, not a product. It was never intended that the guts of X.400 addressing be exposed to the end user; instead, they form the underlying foundation of new mail systems. In the rush to market in the mid-80s, however, the new X.400-based products were immature and failed to hide the addressing scheme from the users. The ugliness of raw X.400 has been the standard's bane ever since.

You might find yourself using the X.400 Connector in performing an import of a large client's e-mail directory as custom recipients into a separate recipient container for your Exchange site. Ideally, you should then be able to exclude that separate recipient container from integration into your Exchange Global Address List. Unfortunately, that's not the case in this release of Exchange Server. So, you could have a GAL of 10,300 entries—300 mailboxes for your users, and an additional 10,000 custom recipients. A workaround for this would be to implement the X.400 connectivity for your site, and then your users would manually add individual X.400 entries into their personal address books for those contacts they need in the remote organizations.

How It Works

The Message Transfer Agent (MTA), in addition to transferring mail messages between Exchange servers, also acts as the X.400 gateway between other X.400 systems (such as Retix and HP Open Mail) and Exchange. There are two configuration objects that must be configured for MTA transfer messages to/from an X.400 system:

- MTA Transport Stack
- X.400 Connector

The MTA transport stack must be created first from the Exchange Admin program by selecting File | New Other | MTA Transport Stack. You will then be given the option to create any of the following stacks:

- Eicon X.25
- RAS
- TCP/IP
- TP4

The following assumes you are installing the TCP/IP stack—the Exchange Admin program will allow you to install the stack only if you have installed the TCP/IP (or the transport you are using) onto your Windows NT server that is running Exchange (see Figure 16.22).

FIGURE 16.22.

TCP/IP Transport stack.

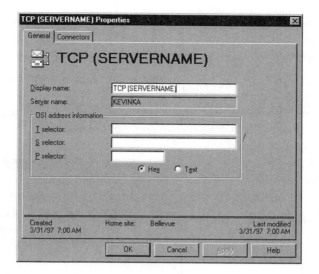

The Transport stack is used by the MTA to determine the Exchange transport settings. The T, S, and P Selectors (which stand for Transport, Session, and Presentation, respectively) can be text or hex and should only be configured if the other X.400 system is configured to send the selector when making a connection to the Exchange Server.

It is possible to associate multiple X.400 connectors to the same transport stacks, which are on the Connectors property page.

TIP

When setting up the X.400 connector for the first time, you should try to simplify the configuration as much as possible and not use any of the selectors on either side. After you get it working, define the selectors as required.

The X.400 connector is next. To create the X.400 connector select File | New Other | X.400 Connector from the Admin program and then select the transport stack that you have previously created. Without exception, the X.400 connector object is the most complex and has the most options. It is useful to keep in mind that only a small subset of all of the options, listed as the following, are required to be set:

■ Display and Directory Name
■ Remote MTA
■ Stack Address
■ Address Space

The Remote MTA name is used by the Exchange MTA when binding the remote X.400 MTA; the name and password are used to verify that the remote MTA is allowed to connect to the Exchange server.

The Stack Address is different, depending on which transport stack you are connecting over. For TCP/IP, the stack depicted in Figure 16.23 allows you to enter the remote IP address or hostname. You should verify the IP address or hostname by using the PING utility from the Exchange server that will be transferring the mail message.

FIGURE 16.23.

TCP/IP Stack property page.

Also note that you can configure the incoming and outgoing T, S, and P selectors. It is a very common mistake to forget to enter one of these values or mistype the value; these must match exactly with the selector from your remote X.400 system.

The Address Space must be set so the Exchange MTA knows which mail messages to route through this connector. Figure 16.24 shows an example of an X.400 address space; when you first set up the connector—or during testing—it is a good idea to make the address space as encompassing as possible, and after it works, scale it down to more accurately reflect the addresses to which you will be sending.

Standards Finally, it is important to note that most commercial X.400 systems, especially legacy X.400 systems, are 1984-compliant. Exchange supports 1984 and 1988. If you will be connecting to a 1984 system, you must change the MTA conformance option on the Advance property page, as displayed in Figure 16.25.

Further detail on the use of the X.400 Connector is beyond the scope of this book. You can find more information on the standard in your Exchange documentation and at

```
http://www.microsoft.com/exchange/x400.htm
```

FIGURE 16.24.

FIGURE 16.24.

Address Space.

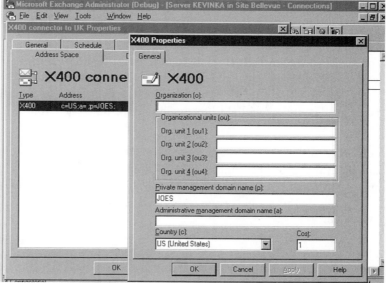

FIGURE 16.25.

TCP/IP Stack property page.

Summary

In this chapter, you learned the capabilities (and limitations) of the three Exchange connectors, the basic configuration of the MSMail Connector and IMS, and an overview of the X.400 Connector. Although Exchange's connectors do not allow the kind of ultimate flexibility that

UNIX and other third-party mail products can offer, they are tightly focused products that offer robust functionality, excellent reporting and management features, ease of use, and a healthy assortment of configuration options.

You should definitely look at the Exchange Server Resource Kit for a number of valuable extensions to the management and configuration controls provided in the base product. The code is available for download from http://www.microsoft.com/exchange and is included with TechNet. The full kit with documentation can be purchased from Microsoft Sales, 800/426-9400.

Performance   Administrators of existing Microsoft Mail installations will find little or no risk in immediately taking advantage of Exchange's MSMail Connector and quantum improvements in performance and reliability. Exchange's Internet Mail Service will make it feasible (both financially and technically) to connect your LAN to the Internet mail system, if you were not already connected.

The Internet Mail Service

by Douglas Strauss

CHAPTER

17

New to
Version 5.0
This section of the book pertains to the IMS, Internet Mail Service (formerly called the Internet Mail Connector) for Exchange 5.0. The IMS is an integrated part of both the Enterprise and Standard editions of Exchange Server editions. The IMS is based on the SMTP protocol, Simple Mail Transfer Protocol, which is used on the Internet to transfer mail between mail servers, as well as allowing POP (Post Office Protocol) or IMAP (Internet Message Access Protocol) clients to send mail. The IMAP and POP protocols only define how to download mail from a mail server and rely on SMTP for all sending. The IMS supports many of the Internet standards and recommendations found in the RFCs (Requests for Comments) in regard to electronic mail. Following is a partial list of mail-transfer–related RFCs that are supported by Exchange Server 5.0 out of the box (these are discussed in detail in the section "What's New in Exchange 5.0?," later in this chapter).

Standards   Standards and other documented information on the Internet are referred to as RFCs. Not all RFCs are actual standards; many are informational, experimental or never quite were agreed upon and accepted. Mail related RFCs can be found on the Web at HTTP:// WWW.IMC.ORG. The following are descriptions of the standards:

- RFC 821   Simple Mail Transfer Protocol (SMTP). Defines the basic SMTP interaction between the SMTP server and client for the transfer of message envelope properties.

- RFC 1123   Requirements for Internet Hosts—Application and Support (Sections pertaining to SMTP Mailers). Suggests how hosts on the Internet should work under certain situations. SMTP is just a small part of the overall RFC.

- RFC 974   Mail routing and the Domain system (DNS). Suggests how Mail hosts should interact with Domain Name System. See the section "Domain Name Service (DNS) and SMTP," later in this chapter.

- RFC 1869   SMTP Service Extensions (ESMTP). Defines how SMTP hosts advertise and request the extended features supported. See the section "ESMTP," later in this chapter.

- RFC 1870   SMTP Service Extension for Message Size Declaration (SIZE). Defines how SMTP hosts can advertise the maximum message size they will accept or state the size of a message before it is delivered to a server. See the section "What's New in Exchange 5.0?," later in this chapter.

- RFC 1891   SMTP Service Extension for Delivery Status Notifications (DSN). Defines how SMTP hosts can relay Message IDs and tell receiving hosts what sort of notification the sender would like about the delivery. See the section "What's New in Exchange 5.0?," later in this chapter.

- RFC 1895 SMTP   Service Extension for Remote Message Queue Starting (ETRN). Defines a method for SMTP servers to queue up mail for hosts without full-time Net connections and how they can trigger mail delivery when they are connected. See the section "What's New in Exchange 5.0?," later in this chapter.

NOTE

ETRN support was introduced in Service Pack 1 (SP1) for Exchange 5.0. You will need to upgrade to at least Service Pack 1 for Exchange 5.0. You can tell whether you need to upgrade by the Dial-up Connections tab of the IMS; if you see a box to enter a command instead of the Mail Retrieval button, you need to upgrade.

In addition to these mail transfer protocols, Exchange supports RFCs that cover the message content. Following are some of the RFCs that are supported: **Standards**

- RFC 822   Basic SMTP message format. Defines the format for all message headers and limitations for the width of messages. It does not cover attachment or character-set issues.

- RFC 1521   MIME (1) Multipurpose Internet Mail Extensions, MIME message format.

- RFC 1522   MIME (2) MIME encoding for headers.

  RFCs 1521 and 1522   are extensions to the basic RFC 822. They cover how to encode content to preserve 8-bit data, character sets, and information about the type of data used.

- RFC 1945   HTML Markup for electronic MIME mail messages. Covers the basic aspects for HTML rich text support in MIME body parts.

- RFC 1154   Automatic UUENCODING/UUDECODING of message content including both non-MIME and encoded BLOBS within MIME body parts.

- RFC 1154   Binhex encoding and decoding of Macintosh message content. RFC 1154 is a widely used RFC, but it has never been officially accepted. It is the basis for encoding 8-bit data for non-MIME message bodies.

These features take the IMS to the cutting edge of Internet mail technology by supporting many of the newer standards in addition to the basic SMTP requirements. Some of the features are unprecedented in other mail products, such as the PerRecipient Content encoding options (see the section "What's New in Exchange 5.0?," later in this chapter) as well as full MAPI support to allow transmitting of inline attachments using the Rich Text feature. Also, the integration of the dial-up and rich scheduling features make Microsoft Exchange a great addition to the small office as well as the large office requiring the DNS and scalability of the IMS along with the rest of Exchange.

Internet and IMS Terminology

As mentioned previously, mail transfer on the Internet is usually referred to as SMTP. In the SMTP world, there is a concept of SMTP servers and SMTP clients in regard to mail delivery. Almost every host on the Internet can act in either of these roles. POP and IMAP clients support only the client side of the SMTP protocol, because they do not receive messages via SMTP.

This is similar to the regular postal system, where the person sending the mail, the client, puts the contents into an envelope and hands this to the postal worker. The postal worker, or server in this case, will route the mail as needed to its final destination.

As with the postal service, the SMTP Client is the one to initiate a call to the SMTP Server's port 25, which is reserved for mail delivery.

Troubleshooting A common question people have about SMTP is whether the server is up and responding. The quick and fairly easy way to see whether your server is up and running is to mimic an SMTP client and connect into port 25 or your SMTP server.

Run Telnet, which is included with all versions, with the following command:

```
TELNET MYHOST.MYDOMAIN.NET 25
```

The 25 at the end of your host's address tells Telnet to connect to port 25 instead of the default port for logging into a machine. You will get back a line starting off with the following:

```
220 dougefresh.imc.wspu.net Microsoft Exchange Internet Mail Service 5.0.1457.9
```

The 220 tells you that the host positively acknowledged your connection and awaits a request. At this point, you can either type QUIT or mimic an SMTP client more by typing EHLO, which will return a list of the ESMTP features supported on the server:

```
EHLO
250-dougefresh.imc.wspu.net supports the following extensions:
250-XAUTH
250-XEXCH50
250-HELP
250-VRFY
250-SIZE 0
250-ETRN
250 DSN
```

From here, there are a number of things you can do; the best place to see your other options is in the RFCs listed previously for 821 and the ESMTP protocols (see Figure 17.1).

During the SMTP conversation, each command from the client is replied to using a numeric response from the server. The following list from RFC 821 shows the meanings of the different levels of response codes:

- 1yz   Positive Preliminary reply. SMTP does not have any commands that allow this type of reply.
- 2yz   Positive Completion reply. The requested action has been successfully completed. A new request may be initiated.
- 3yz   Positive Intermediate reply. The command has been accepted, but the requested action is being held in abeyance, pending receipt of further information. The SMTP sender should send another command specifying this information. This reply is used in command sequence groups.

■ 4yz Transient Negative Completion reply. The command was not accepted and the requested action did not occur. However, the error condition is temporary and the action may be requested again. The sender should return to the beginning of the command sequence (if any).

■ 5yz Permanent Negative Completion reply. The command was not accepted, and the requested action did not occur. The sender-SMTP is discouraged from repeating the exact request (in the same sequence). This will usually result in a non-delivery report when the recipient's address on the envelope is not a valid account on the server.

FIGURE 17.1.

Sample conversation between an SMTP client and an SMTP server.

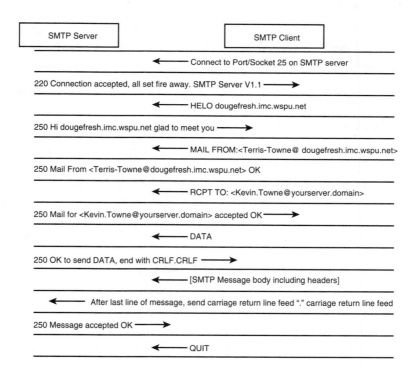

SMTP Server	SMTP Client
	◄──── Connect to Port/Socket 25 on SMTP server
220 Connection accepted, all set fire away. SMTP Server V1.1 ────►	
	◄──── HELO dougefresh.imc.wspu.net
250 Hi dougefresh.imc.wspu.net glad to meet you ────►	
	◄──── MAIL FROM:<Terris-Towne@ dougefresh.imc.wspu.net>
250 Mail From <Terris-Towne@dougefresh.imc.wspu.net> OK	
	◄──── RCPT TO: <Kevin.Towne@yourserver.domain>
250 Mail for <Kevin.Towne@yourserver.domain> accepted OK ────►	
	◄──── DATA
250 OK to send DATA, end with CRLF.CRLF ────►	
	◄──── [SMTP Message body including headers]
	◄──── After last line of message, send carriage return line feed "." carriage return line feed
250 Message accepted OK ────►	
	◄──── QUIT

The second digit (y) encodes responses in specific categories. The third digit (z) gives a finer gradation of meaning in each category specified by the second digit.

These codes normally are used along with text information stating the problem and are included in Exchange Non-Delivery reports when failures are encountered. For more information about these codes, the full text, and examples, see RFC 821.

During the DATA section, no response is returned until the CRLF.CRLF is seen by the server. Some servers will send LF.LF instead, which is not standard but will work fine with 4.0a and above of Exchange.

Domain Name Service (DNS) and SMTP

The SMTP RFCs allow any mail server on the Internet to deliver electronic mail messages to just about any other server on the Internet. Usually, SMTP servers make direct connections from the originating SMTP domain's mail server to the destination's mail server. At other times, there may be servers that handle mail for that domain or relay messages for a domain.

In order for this to be possible, there are some basic requirements that must also be met to enable the SMTP servers to figure out how to connect to the remote domain or relay server. The Internet has a hierarchical database of SMTP domains and the associated hosts that will handle mail for them.

There is also a mapping for each of these hosts to an IP (Internet Protocol) address that uniquely identifies this host on the Internet. The name of this huge "database" is DNS or Domain Name System, as shown in Figure 17.2.

FIGURE 17.2.

Simple hierarchical diagram of the DNS.

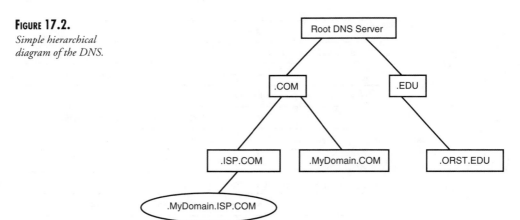

In the figure, each box shows a DNS Server and the domain it is responsible for. When a request comes in from a user or another DNS server, the server will handle the request using either stored information or cached information, or relay the request to the appropriate DNS server node in charge of the subdomain. The DNS server to relay this request to is found by doing a query to the top-level servers. These servers are referred to as Root Name servers, which maintain the master lists for the top-level domain portions of the Internet and are maintained by the Internet Engineering Task Force (IETF) using the registered information they are in charge of. Once the information is found, it is both cached based on the TTL value and returned to the calling program. TTL is discussed in the section, "DNS Resource Records."

It is important to note that the DNS is hierarchical; any given DNS server contains only information about the domains assigned to it or any information it has managed to queue up from previous queries. When you register your domain name (also referred to as *name space*) with the IETF, you must also provide the location of a DNS server, which will maintain your name space and any hosts or subdomains that you want to be a part of your domain. This also means that somebody else can't become part of your domain without your permission.

> **NOTE**
>
> Although DNS is considered to be globally the same, in NT you will notice the option to put in the address of multiple DNS servers. The secondary server, as well as the rest of the list, is considered backup for the original. This means that if a DNS lookup for an address results in a host not found, the next server in the list is not used. All servers are considered to handle the same information. If you want to have both an external and internal DNS, you need to have your DNS handle both the intranet and Internet address spaces.

EXAMPLE: Reserving a DNS Domain

You want to get your company with Internet mail and you have a dedicated link to the Internet. Your company is called STRAUSS Inc., and on the Internet you want to be known as STRAUSS.COM. This means you need to register STRAUSS.COM as the domain name space to be in charge of. You first register it with the IETF; if the name is not already taken, it's yours— once you pay, of course.

Along with obtaining the domain, you must supply the location of DNS servers that will service this domain space. This information is stored on the root name servers on the Internet to allow other DNS servers to find and query your DNS server.

Along with registering, you maintain full control of all hosts that append STRAUSS.COM to their addresses, as well as any subdomains you want to create. Once you own it, you can create almost any subdomain you want, such as ALICIA.STRAUSS.COM, and have machines that are in that domain. HOST1.ALICIA.STRAUSS.COM is an example of this, where HOST1 is a server residing in the ALICIA.STRAUSS.COM domain.

DNS Resource Records

The DNS database is mostly made up of the following types of database records. These handle the most common requests that occur on the Internet:

- *A Record.* Associates the host and domain name to an assigned IP address. Because the IP address is pretty hard to remember for every location you may want to visit, this makes it easy:

```
dougefresh.imc.wspu.net.    IN    A    157.55.16.239
```

NOTE

It is normal practice to always create an MX record for any A Record entry that is going to be used as a mail host. If the mail domain is the same as the A Record information on the Net, it is still done to speed up the delivery of SMTP mail. All servers will do a DNS query for the MX record first. If this fails, they then try the A Record before reverting to other methods, such as host files. Most DNSs, upon returning the MX information, also return the A Record. Because of these two occurrences, it is much quicker to look up an address where the MX Record exists. It also means one less call by the system to resolve the address.

■ *MX Record.* Associates the "mailing" domain to one or more A Records. Because the mail server may not always be guaranteed to be running, most larger companies have two or more servers to allow the main mail server to be serviced. Another feature of the MX record is load balancing among servers in a domain. If two records have the same cost, the remote host will randomly choose one of the hosts to connect and deliver mail to:

```
WSPU.NET.  IN    MX    10    dougefresh.imc.wspu.net
WSPU.NET.  IN    MX    10    equal2.imc.wspu.net.
WSPU.NET.  IN    MX    20    MYISPBackup.ISP.NET.
```

NOTE

Multiple entries for a domain allow load balancing, queuing, or host-down situations.

When the records are of equal weights, the sending host will randomly select an equally weighted host from the list.

When the host is not reachable on the network, down for maintenance, or has a dial-up connection, the host that has the next highest weight is tried for delivery until the list of possible hosts is depleted or a circular route is found pointing back to the sending host.

As a caveat of the host-down situation, it is common that there may be two MX records where the lower weight is a dial-up connection, and the higher cost is the domain's ISP that will hold mail until the domain dials up to retrieve its mail.

Thus, the MX record is providing all other hosts which mail address domain(s) it will service as well as allowing for redundancy if you have multiple hosts.

■ *CNAME Record.* Allows for aliasing of a domain or hostname. When a domain goes through a name change, creating this record is a quick method to handle the mail traffic and other connectivity issues. These are meant to be temporary while people get used to the new naming convention:

```
OLD-DOUG.WSPU.NET. IN    CNAME   DOUGEFRESH.IMC.WSPU.NET.
```

■ *FQDN.* A common term associated with a DNS, it stands for Fully Qualified Domain Name. All it really means is that the name provided is complete with hostname and domain that it is in—as well as being in a valid DNS.

The most common mistake when creating DNS entries is to not make addresses fully qualified. Each DNS file has a domain that it contains the entries for by default. If the domain listing does not have a period (.) at the end of the address, it is assumed to be a part of the local domain and will have the domain automatically appended.

Troubleshooting

NOTE

If you have the following two entries in your DNS file, they would have completely different results when you queried for the information:

```
DNS file for MYDOMAIN.NET

MYHOST1.MYDOMAIN.NET     IN  A    111.22.33.44

MYHOST2.MYDOMAIN.NET.    IN  A    111.22.33.45
```

If you query the DNS for MYHOST1 and MYHOST2, you will get back the following responses:

```
MYHOST1.MYDOMAIN.NET.MYDOMAIN.NET

MYHOST2.MYDOMAIN.NET
```

where MYHOST1 won't be reachable since it does not exist as you would expect. This causes mail to not be delivered and users to be unable to connect to WEB, MAIL, or FTP servers.

■ *PTR.* Called a Reverse Lookup record, it is another type of host-to-IP mapping, but in the reverse. DNS allows you to type in an IP address to get back the host and domain name associates with it. This is great to use if you want to know who is really sending you mail and to clarify whether they are really who they say they are.

■ *IN-ADDR.ARPA.* Part of the PTR record; the address is entered in the database in reverse order and has this appended to the end of entry:

```
239.16.55.157.IN-ADDR.ARPA.      IN PRT  DOUGEFRESH.IMC.WSPU.NET
```

■ *TTL.* Stands for Time to Live. Every entry in DNS has a life span to allow for changes to be made to hostnames and addresses. Most addresses will be valid for at least a few days, based on the TTL time length associated with it. This allows DNS servers that query each other to save time by requesting the same data only the first time it is requested during a short period of time. Subsequent requests by the client are handled with cached data, and the TTL value is set on a Per Domain basis in the DNS headers for each domain file the server is in charge of.

NOTE

With the Reverse Lookup, it is possible to tell whether people sending you mail are really who they say they are, although it is not proper SMTP etiquette. The mail is not rejected because a reverse lookup fails or is inconsistent with the data on the HELO or EHLO command line.

You may be wondering where the hierarchical part of all this comes into play. Remember that the DNS is considered global for the whole Internet, and having one server contain all the data would require massive processing power and storage space. To alleviate this, all around the Internet are many DNS Servers that handle requests from both hosts. These servers are in the domain that is serviced and controlled by the server, as well as other DNS servers that may need to provide an IP address for one of their clients to connect into a different domain than their own. DNS is not only used by SMTP Mail, but for WEB, FTP, and Telnet, as well as almost any Internet-enabled application. Most of these will only use the A Records and CNAMES; the MX Records are really limited for SMTP mail usage.

ESMTP

In addition to SMTP, there is an extended version called ESMTP that adds some additional features that are supported by the default SMTP protocol, as well as allowing it to be extended even farther. The supported ESMTP protocols in the IMS 5.0 are covered in the section "What's New in Exchange 5.0?," later in this chapter.

Rich Text and Transport Neutral Encoding Format (TNEF)

A common acronym that is associated with Microsoft Mail and Microsoft Exchange is TNEF or Transport Neutral Encoding Format. This format is defined in the MAPI 1.0 spec and allows MAPI 1.0 and, to some extent, MAPI0 clients, to send rich text over the Internet. Rich text consists of all the formatting that can be done within an Exchange message, such as color, indentation, OLE attachments, regular attachments including placement within the message, and custom forms.

NOTE

When sending TNEF messages out, any attachments, such as spreadsheets or any other items, are embedded into the TNEF as one large body part. When using UUENCODE, each attachment is encoded separately. If you send a TNEF message to a MIME and UUENCODE recipient, the MIME recipient will receive one encoded blob whereas the UUENCODED recipient will get two—one for the TNEF and one for the attachment itself.

When connecting two Exchange servers over a site connector, all messages are automatically TNEFed to preserve all the MAPI properties between servers.

Compatibility

What Is the IMS and How Is It Different from IMC?

New to Version 5.0

In the 5.0 release of Microsoft Exchange, the Internet Mail Connector went through a name change and emerged as the Internet Mail Service. From the user perspective, there is little difference in functionality. Internally, lots of changes occurred so that message handling is much better, and there is a great deal of resource sharing for content conversion between different Exchange components.

What's New in Exchange 5.0?

In the 5.0 release of Exchange Internet Mail Service, there were a number of Extended SMTP features added and many changes in basic functionality to better share functionality among components.

IMAIL

Cross-Platform

As mentioned previously, a large portion of the original IMC code was moved into the Exchange server and is now shared among multiple exchange components. The name for this component is IMAIL and it is shared between NNTP, IMS, and POP3.

The following are some of the key features of IMAIL:

■ *Better handling of common malformed MIME errors for inbound.* The conversion component is much more tolerant of errors in basic MIME or non-MIME messages. When errors are encountered, the conversion stream is rewound and conversion retried. A best attempt is made to display the information.

■ *Full fidelity of Internet messages.* Messages that are traversing the Exchange system to POP3 clients will retain the original format; there is no header loss between what comes into Exchange and what the end client downloads from the server.

■ *HTML Message support.* Outbound messages can maintain much of the basic formatting using the HTML language, and clients, such as the Internet Explorer, that support it will display most of the formatting that is available in the Exchange client.

■ *Fixed font support.* For inbound messages, it is settable from the Internet Mail tab of the IMS Admin page. Messages that originate on the Internet and don't have font information inbedded with TNEF or HTML will be tagged using a fixed font to retain any lists created outside of Exchange.

■ *Support of NT NLS (National Language Support).* This extends the number of character sets in which the Server can send and receive mail. Settable from the Internet Mail tab, it is used as a default suggestion for MIME and forced for both inbound and outbound non-MIME messages. If the settings between non-MIME SMTP servers are not correct, you will end up with unexpected character translations. For MIME messages outbound, the character set is extracted from the message body.

Troubleshooting   In some languages where many POP clients are not localized, it is common for the U.S. mail clients to be used. With this, the message contents may be MIME and tagged incorrectly as US-ASCII or ISO-8859-1, but they really contain the local language.

> **NOTE**
>
> The Registry setting to control this is found at the following:
>
> ```
> HKEY_LOCAL_MACHINE\System\CurrentControlSet\Services\MSExchangeIS\
> ➥ParametersSystem\InternetContent\ISO-8859-1
> ```
>
> which is a DWORD value. The value is defaulted to 0. When set to 1, the non-MIME character setting is used for any 8-bit characters found in the message body.

DIAL-UP

Dial-up is integration with NT RAS, supporting a rich scheduling mechanism as well as a mechanism to run any local program or batch file once a connection is established to an ISP.

ESMTP

Extended SMTP support is used to advertise and use extensions for the SMTP protocols.

DSN

Delivery Status Notification (DSN) is an ESMTP extension that allows hosts to relay a user's request for Delivery, Non-Delivery, or No notification if the message is successful or failed. It also allows control of the content of a report, such as getting back just the message headers or the full message. Finally, it can be used to relay information such as a Message ID so a report that comes back to a sending host or client can associate the two.

SIZE

This ESMTP extension allows a receive host to advertise the maximum message size in KB it will accept. This tells the sending host not to send messages that are over this size or attempt delivery into a system. It is very useful for any type of slow link where you may want to limit message sizes to under a megabyte or two. This is configured on the IMS Admin page under the General tab. The Max message size controls both inbound and outbound mail delivery restrictions.

XEXCH50

This is a custom ESMTP extension that allows two Exchange 5.0 servers to transfer additional information stored on the message envelope. This will work only between two IMSs talking to one another's directory over the Internet, where Rich Text is turned on or the IMS is being used as a site connector.

XAUTH

This is a custom ESMTP extension that enables NTLM Security between two IMSs connected directly over the Internet. Once the connection has been authenticated, everything that goes over the wire will be encrypted. This makes it virtually impossible for intruders on the Internet to sniff message content or any other part of the message when traversing the Internet. In general, messages going over the Internet are not considered to be secure and are accessible to anyone running a network sniffer. The XAUTH is configured on the IMS Admin Security page and is invoked only on outbound connections where XAUTH is supported. If XAUTH is turned on and the remote host does not support the option, mail will not be delivered.

ETRN

For the SP1 release of Exchange 5.0, the IMS added ETRN support for both SMTP Server and Client. *Server* refers to the IMS that has mail queued up for a remote domain and awaits the ETRN command to commence delivery. *Client* refers to the remote server that dials in and issues the ETRN to trigger mail delivery from the Server once it is connected to the network. ETRN on the client side is triggered only during RAS dial-up, but on the Server side it is always available but hardly needed, because most mail will succeed on the first attempt at delivery.

Message Rerouting

By default, a newly installed 5.0 IMS will accept mail for any domain and inspect the envelope recipients to determine whether it should be submitted into Exchange or routed back out to the Internet. This is mostly an added feature for POP and IMAP clients so they can easily use the IMS as their SMTP routing host when sending outbound mail. The POP Rerouter also allows rewriting the envelope domain address to easily migrate users from one domain name to another. If upgrading from 4.0, this feature can be configured and turned on under the IMS Admin routing tab. This feature is also referred to as POP Rerouting.

Client Address Resolution

For the Exchange client, typing in the SMTP addresses of users that have valid entries in the Exchange DS will be auto-resolved to their DN names. This reduces the chance for looping messages out the IMS and speeding delivery for users that want to use SMTP addresses when sending to other Exchange users.

PerRecipient Message Format

In version 5.0, additional support was added in the Personal Address Book, Exchange Directory, and all the clients to allow clients (or admins using Custom Recipients) to set the message format on a PerRecipient basis. Once an address is resolved in the client's TO/CC/BCC line, right-clicking on the address will bring up the PerRecipient dialog (see Figure 17.3).

17

THE INTERNET
MAIL SERVICE

New to
Version 5.0

FIGURE 17.3.

Accessing the Recipient Address properties.

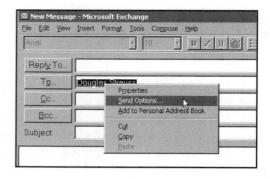

Once selected, using the right mouse button, the pop-up menu in Figure 17.4 appears. Use Alt+K to resolve names or the menu option when typing an SMTP address directly to the message header. Note that Exchange auto-detects SMTP addresses containing both the "at sign" (@) and at least one period (.).

FIGURE 17.4.

PerRecipient Send Options dialog.

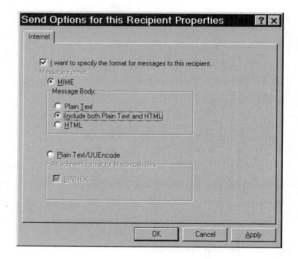

In Exchange 4.0, getting properties for a recipient allowed you to trigger Rich Text (TNEF) on or off at a PerRecipient basis and set message format properties only on a Per Message basis. As shown in Figure 17.4, this has been extended in 5.0 to a PerRecipient basis. You can tell the IMS to send to a user using MIME+PLAIN TEXT, MIME+HTML, MIME+HTML+PLAIN TEXT, NON-MIME, or NON-MIME MAC. Note that the HTML and Rich Text cannot be used at the same time and will default to Rich Text, because it can preserve all the HTML information as well as attachment placement and OLE for delivery to MAPI-enabled clients.

All these options for the Recipients are also settable in the Exchange Admin when creating new accounts or by setting the properties on the Address proxies for recipients.

IMS Architecture

The IMS was designed using the Exchange Developer's Kit (EDK). The EDK provides a mechanism for connectors to access outbound folders (MTS-OUT) and submit messages into Exchange (MTS-IN), much like a typical client would use its OUTBOX and INBOX.

In addition to the queues provided by the EDK, the IMS also maintains a couple of queues on disk. The IMCDATA\IN directory is used for inbound messages awaiting conversion to MAPI properties and submission to the MTS-IN. The IMCDATA\OUT directory is used for outbound messages awaiting deliver to an SMTP Server. Messages in all queues, with the exception of the MTS-IN, are monitored in the IMCDATA\QUEUE.DAT file. Each are explained a bit more in the following sections.

Function of the IMCDATA\IN Directory

Messages from the Internet are written into this directory as they come off the wire and then are locked down to disk. Any required conversions or rerouting is done after the message is fully received. From here, they are placed into the OUT directory if the domain is not an Exchange domain. If addressed to an Exchange recipient, the message is passed off to IMAIL conversion for MAPI properties and submitted into the MTS-IN for delivery.

Function of the MTS-IN Folder

Once the message is submitted into MTS-IN (also referred to as the *Information Store* or *MDB*), it is either delivered directly to the user's mailbox on the server or passed over to the MTA for routing.

Function of the MTS-OUT Folder

Any messages that are routed to the IMS based on the Address Routing tab settings end up in the MTS-OUT. When they arrive in this folder, the IMS is notified and will pick up the message and determine what renderings are required for each recipient of the message. This is referred to as *bucketing* and will generate Internet message content, grouping recipients together based on the MIME, Rich Text, and Character set settings.

Function of the IMCDATA\OUT Directory

Once the desired format recipients are rendered, the file is placed into the OUT directory pending delivery to the SMTP server. Until all the recipients for a rendered file are delivered, the file will remain in the OUT directory.

QUEUE.DAT

Queue.dat is used mostly to keep track of all the messages pending delivery in either direction for the IN and OUT directories, as well as messages found in the MTS-OUT folder. The MTS-IN files are no longer in the file, because the responsibility for delivery is placed into the hands of the Information Store.

For every recipient pending delivery in the OUT directory, an entry exists in the queue.dat file detailing the current status. This consists of whether the recipient was successfully delivered to, a non-delivery report was generated for this user, or delivery is going to be retried at a later time. These entries are kept around as long as the message file exists in the OUT directory.

> **NOTE**
>
> If the IMS is stopped and the queue.dat file deleted, every recipient in the OUT message files will be retried delivery as if the message just arrived in the queue. This will most likely result in duplicate delivery of mail messages and reports. If there is a need to delete the queue.dat file, the IMS should first be run in FLUSH mode (described in the section "Common Questions and Issues," later in this chapter) to force the disk queues to empty.

Design Philosophy

The main philosophy for the IMS was to be a reliable SMTP client-server as well as being fast. For the 5.0 version, there was much more emphasis dealing with malformed messages that normally came in from the Internet. Many times in 4.0, MIME messages came in missing boundaries or just malformed; these ended up as message.txt files at the client. In 5.0, much work has been done to work around many of the common occurring problems that may still occur. Alas, it will never be one hundred percent, but most of the messages should be rendered correct. In addition to the enhancement of the content handling, another big change in 5.0 is full fidelity of message content so messages will come into and go out from Exchange maintaining their complete original structure.

For multilingual support, there are many more language formats supported out of the box in 5.0 when compared to 4.0. Gone are the TRN translation files, replaced by the built-in NT NLS support.

Using the IMS—Connectivity Scenarios

When you are thinking about how to set up the IMS, it is important to know how the users will need to use the system. If you will have POP or IMAP users who will use the IMS as their SMTP rerouter, you need to make sure POP Rerouting is turned on (see Figure 17.5).

If your company wants to connect to both the Internet and an intranet, you must decide whether the IMS will be on a dual-homed machine. That is, it has two Net cards and will be on both the Internet and the corporate backbone. This can be a large security issue for some, but it solves the problem quickly. On the other hand, you can set up the Address space to route intranet mail to one IMS in the site and Internet mail to another. This can be controlled with the weighting of the address spaces.

FIGURE 17.5.

The POP Rerouting page for the IMS.

NOTE

The weighting of address spaces can be misleading. Setting one connection high and another low for overlapping address spaces does not mean all mail in the overlapping areas will go with the lowest route. The mail delivery will be balanced based on the weights, so some mail could always end up going out to an IMS you didn't expect.

One thing to note about the address space: it was based on X.400, so the address matching goes from general to specific as you read from left to right. For SMTP, it is the reverse for the data after the @ sign; it goes from specific, such as your hostname, to general, such as the COM or NET domains.

This provides you with a way around this load balancing act, where you can change the SMTP address space so it does not overlap when it matches up an address with a route. To do this, leave the SMTP address space blank for Internet mail. All SMTP mail will match this address implicitly so you will have normal mail flow. Then enter an address space for your intranet, such as *DOUGEFRESH.WSPU.NET. All mail within the DOUGEFRESH.WSPU.NET domain will be an explicit match—and thus a better match than the implicit match—and it will always be used first.

Other methods may consist of having a firewall server between the Exchange IMS and the Internet or a combination of RAS and an intranet DNS for the internal company only. Only mail going outside the company would head out over RAS.

In general, there is never a clear answer as to what the best solution will be for a particular company. It all comes down to cost economics. You have to decide how money is best spent and reusable for other purposes, such as a proxy server in addition to a mail server—the cost of a dedicated T1 compared to the slowness of dial-up connection that is intermittent or dedicated.

The Exchange IMS can be used to connect to the Internet or intranet in two ways: over the network using TCP/IP or over RAS with any of the supported features. If you are working within an organization trying to integrate your different mail systems over SMTP, you're pretty much going to be using the TCP/IP option.

If you want to be able to send and receive mail over the Internet, however, you need to either get a dedicated connection or make use of a local ISP that will queue up your inbound mail while handling your DNS address space for you. The cost of the dedicated connection for many smaller companies would not be feasible.

Determining Which Method to Use

The big question is whether to use an ISP and dial-up to retrieve and send mail or get some sort of dedicated connection. The answer is really up to the needs of the company and its employees.

If you are planning to host your own Web site, have very active users connecting out to Web sites and sending or receiving large volumes of mail, the periodic RAS connection may not be enough. You should be able to share the connection between your Web server, users requiring Internet connectivity, and your SMTP mail flow.

The main benefit of the direct connection is speed. If you and your customer are both using dedicated connections, mail transfer will probably be less than a minute. If either of you is using RAS, it could be as fast as a minute if you hit it just right, but most likely it will be between 30 minutes to an hour or so. It really depends on how often your site dials up to deliver mail and how often the customer site dials up to download mail.

Dial-Up Connection Benefits

The number one benefit is cost, both for the connection and for administrative hassles. When you set up using Dial-up Connections, it is strongly recommended to not set the IMS to make direct connections to hosts on the Internet (use DNS option on the Internet Mail page). It is much better to be configured to forward all mail to your ISP, which can better service remote hosts on the Internet. This will reduce your actual connection times to the ISP and thus may reduce costs. It means more work for the ISP for delivery handling, but much less time for you to be connected over the modem.

When using RAS, it is important to also remember to forward all mail to the ISP directly, or much of your time trying to deliver mail may be spent resolving address routes and making timely connections to remote hosts over the Internet. There may also be some cases where you are not connected to your ISP and messages queuing up from users will NDR, because the message will time-out before being delivered in a timely manner.

NOTE

A common reason for this would be the remote host's not always being reachable on the Internet or over a very slow connection such as 2400 baud. This will drastically increase your connect times to deliver mail to some locations.

The IMS has a variety of dial-up settings that can be configured by the administrator (see Figure 17.6). Each has special benefits over the others, depending on your company's mail usage requirements.

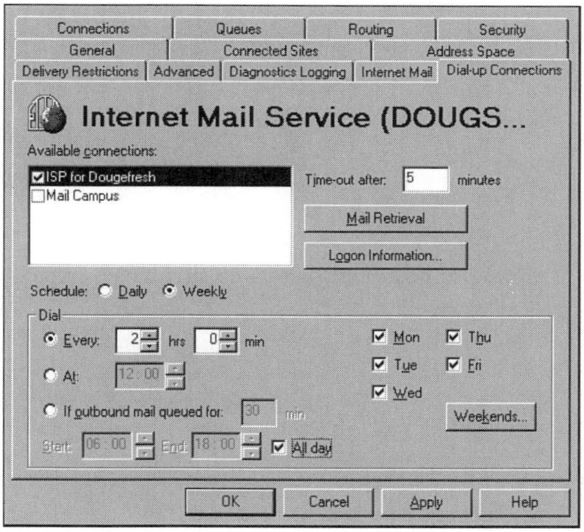

FIGURE 17.6.

IMS Dial-up Connections page.

In the diagram, notice there are three basic dial-up connection schedules that can be configured:

- ■ *Every.* This option will dial approximately every X hours and Y minutes. The base time is when the IMS first comes up, and it will continue dialing until it is restarted. If hours of the day are limited, it will initiate at the starting time and calculate from there. For a site where lots of inbound mail is expected, this may be the best option, because it allows inbound delivery each time the IMS dials up. Because some ISPs may try mail delivery at the same time ever hour, it is also a great solution for these scenarios.

- ■ *At.* This option will only dial the ISP at most once a day. For offices in which there is very little mail traffic, both in- and outbound, this may be the best option. Also, if the ISP's pricing structure is based on how often you connect or are connected, this option may help reduce the total time needed by dealing with all the day's mail once during the day.

17

THE INTERNET
MAIL SERVICE

- *If outbound mail queued for.* This option is a little misleading as to the actual functionality involved. For sites that have lots of outbound mail, this option allows the admin to instruct the IMS to connect after no connections have been made in the last Y minutes. Thus the option really means "connect no more often than Y minutes."

Choosing the right option depends on the requirements of both your company's mail usage and the capabilities of your ISP. The IMS will also make use of connections made by other applications running on the same NT server. Whenever the associated RAS connection is activated, the IMS may notice this and try mail delivery over this connection. Other services may try the same, but must remain aware that the connection can be pulled out from underneath them at any time (see Figure 17.7).

FIGURE 17.7.

ETRN configuration page using custom and explicit and wildcard domain listing.

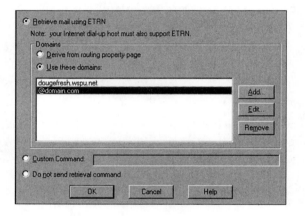

In the SP1 update for Exchange 5.0, additional support was added for ETRN. As you can see in Figure 17.7, there is a button for Mail Retrieval. This option allows the administrator to select a method compatible with the ISP:

- Send an ETRN command using the information from the POP Rerouting page.
- Send a custom ETRN with the data entered by the administrator. The information is as follows:

DOMAIN.COM	Tells the server to deliver mail destined for DOMAIN.COM only.
@DOMAIN.COM	Tells the server to deliver mail destined for DOMAIN.COM and any subdomain as well; thus, mail to SUB.DOMAIN.COM would also be delivered.
#QUEUENAME	If the ISP supports queues, they may allow you to kick-start your personal queue and deliver any mail that is destined for your site. This would need to be configured by your ISP in conjunction to your request.

The IMS does not support #QUEUENAME when it is running as the SMTP server.

- Run a local program or batch file to trigger the ISP to start mail delivery. Because many ISPs may have homegrown solutions, such as pinging the server or Telnet to a special port, the IMS provides a quick method to run batch files that can perform this functionality. But admins should be careful, because this will run every time the IMS connects up to the ISP and is much like running a program manually.

- Do not send retrieval command. This does nothing special when a connection is made to the ISP. If the ISP tries mail delivery every 15 minutes or so, this may be the option of choice, assuming you configure the IMS to stay connected for 15 minutes.

> **NOTE**
>
> A limitation of the ETRN RFC is the requirement for PPP or SLIP connections to have dedicated IP addresses. Not all ISPs may want to divvy these out, because they may be in short supply and then need every IP they can get for dial-up users that may need Web or POP access. The requirement is based on how ETRN works. Unlike the original TURN that would allow a SMTP client-server to switch roles and thus the direction of mail transfer, ETRN is considered more secure because it will rely on the DNS or some other information for mail delivery, making it harder for people to connect as your company and steal all your mail. Because ETRN most likely will need a defined route, a dedicated IP address may be required.
>
> One workaround for this is to have an ISP that may use a DHCP server that links into the DNS, but this could open up some timing gaps if new mail comes in after you disconnect and another client connecting up right after you uses the same IP address.
>
> Option two, your ISP could put up a firewall for all customers using it for mail delivery, and can then assign the IP addresses using the range of addresses reserved for intranets. Thus, the ISP doesn't need to worry about doling out expensive addresses, but it does need some extra work at its end for mail handling.
>
> Option three, you can create some other method that will work in their environment and can also work with Exchange using the ETRN or the custom batch file.

These limitations are currently under investigation while this book is being written, but there could be a complete new method some day to trigger a host to dump its queues.

Future
Directions

Dedicated Line

Performance

A common question that comes up is, "When is it time to move from dial-up to dedicated line?" The answer is not clear. The biggest issue will be how much your company must rely on Internet mail and if it can afford to wait the additional time for inbound and outbound mail delivery. Another reason to switch to a dedicated line is long connect times, because there is so much traffic to and from the Internet that you end up connected for most of the day anyway. There may also be large backlogs in the messages awaiting delivery if your ISP limits the amount of time you can be connected.

Still, it all boils down to the cost of getting a dedicated connection over modem, T1, or something faster, and what the business need is for your company. Most dedicated lines can be shared to provide Internet access to users, hosting of a Web site for the company, or other Internet-related features such as newsfeeds into Exchange or FTP access.

Finally, one resounding time to know when you should switch is when users start to really complain about poor mail delivery times. Watching out for all the previous situations should prevent this or at least allow finer tuning of the system to keep complaints to a minimum.

Internet/Intranet/Extranet

Recently, there has been much hype about Internet, intranet, and Extranet with regard to the Web and mail. For the IMS, it is all just one big TC/IP network that may or may not have access to the whole world. The intranet and/or Extranet is basically the internal LAN that your company has configured. The main differences are whether there is an internal DNS that is not associated with the Internet DNS, as well as connectivity to the Internet in general. Usually, the internal DNS names are not registered and not reachable on the Internet, so there is no need to register them with the IETF.

It is important to route mail appropriately to the machines acting as network gateways to the Internet. This can be done using the Exchange routing or using the IMS routing tab to do this over SMTP.

Installation and Configuring

The following sections cover some of the major requirements for the NT Server prior to installing the 5.0 IMS. Following this is a walk-through of some of the important setup steps and then a discussion of different approaches to getting the IMS connected to the Internet.

Requirements

Prior to installing, you should first make sure the server is correctly configured. You should also know the answers to the following, which the Setup Wizard will require:

- Fully qualified Domain name to be used for inbound mail.
- Name of the Administrator account to which you will want problem notifications in Exchange to be forwarded. The Wizard will create one for you if you want.
- Name and password for the service account that was used for the other Exchange services.
- Which server in your site you wish to install the IMS on, of course.
- IP address of one or more DNS servers that you will use to resolve hostnames.
- If you are going to use RAS, you will need to configure at least one RAS connector to be used by the IMS Service.

■ If you are using RAS, you will probably need to have a dedicated IP address from your ISP. Dynamic IPs may not work, because the DNS is based on static IP addresses.

Prior to installing the IMS, you will need to configure your TCP/IP protocol with a hostname (set by NT with your machine name by default), domain name, and IP address of your DNS server(s). It is a good idea to provide both a primary and secondary DNS server, in case the primary server is down and you won't have an interruption in outbound mail delivery.

It is also a good time to make sure there is a return path to your server by using a program called NSLOOKUP provided with Windows NT 4.0 and most UNIX hosts. Another tool called RESTEST is mentioned later for outbound mail routing issues.

Troubleshooting

17

THE INTERNET
MAIL SERVICE

TIP

To check the DNS for correct records, you can start RESTEST in a CMD window under NT. It will come up with the > prompt. Type the following:

```
> MyServer.Mydomain.com.
```

The . at the end of the address makes it an FQDN and will speed up the query. NSLOOKUP should respond with the IP address of your Exchange server.

Next type the following commands and data:

```
> Set type=mx
```

```
> Mydomain.com.
```

NSLOOKUP will respond with a list of MX records, along with their associated costs and the hosts that will handle the mail for this domain. This should be the same information as returned prior to setting the type of lookup to be MX.

If this information points to your Exchange Server, other SMTP servers should be all set to deliver mail to you.

A Walk Through the Install

Version 5.0 of Exchange includes the Internet Mail Service by default, and adding this to your existing Exchange server requires no special disk, as it did in 4.0 (see Figure 17.8).

To start the IMS Wizard within the Exchange Admin, go to the File menu and select New Other. On the right side, you will see a list of items; select Internet Mail from the list of options. This will take you through the install, requesting much of the information listed previously (see Figure 17.9).

If you did not configure the TCP/IP for the LAN or have a RAS connection defined, the installation will fail to proceed until this is properly configured. A list of available defined connections will appear, allowing you to select one from the list. In most cases, you will have only one dial-up to configure to a single ISP. If the mail server is a dial-up mail hub for different sites, additional connections and schedules can be configured after the installation is complete with the IMS Admin Dial-up Connections page.

If the DNS settings found in the Control Panel's Network extension under the TCP/IP tab are not configured, the wizard also will not allow you to continue (see Figure 17.10).

FIGURE 17.8.

Starting the installation wizard for the 5.0 IMS.

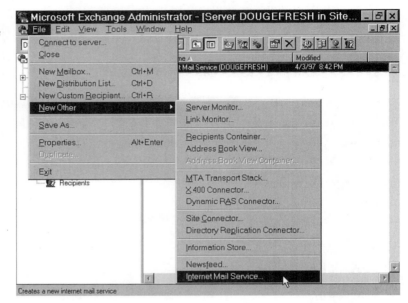

FIGURE 17.9.

Selecting a RAS Dial-up Connection to use from the wizard.

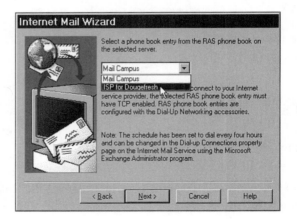

Figure 17.10.

*Setting the default
SMTP site address
domain.*

The most important page to fill out that must conform to your DNS is the Specify Site Address page of the wizard. The domain address typed in here will be propagated to all users within a site and will become their default return address for all outbound mail. This address should be registered within the DNS using an MX or A Record; if not, mail will never come into the system.

> **NOTE**
>
> If you already have the IMS installed and you need to change your default SMTP addressing for all users, it can be set from under Site Configuration and getting properties for Site Addressing. Then click on the Site Addressing tab to edit the current default address space for all users in a site.

The wizard page allows you to define a new Admin account or use an existing account. The existing account can be a public folder whose address is not hidden from the address book, or a Distribution List if you have a group of admins. The mail messages sent to the admin are notifications that are configured from the notifications page on the Internet Mail tab of the IMS admin page. These can range from duplicate aliases that may have been accidentally created in a multiple server site to just bad custom recipient addresses defined on the system.

> **NOTE**
>
> Inbound mail addressed to the Postmaster at the default domain will automatically be accepted inbound by the IMS and delivered to the address specified under IMS Admin unless an account is specifically created that has this address as one of its SMTP proxy addresses.
>
> Accounts that are configured to receive the Admin notifications must reside on Exchange. Mail cannot be routed out an IMS, because this can easily create loops in mail delivery.

Troubleshooting # Common Questions and Issues

The following troubleshooting questions are more than likely to come up both when you're setting up the IMS and when you encounter problems with connectivity. The most common problem is correctly setting up the DNS for most organizations, resulting in mail going out but never making it into the mail system. This is usually related to the DNS or other configuration problems that can be more easily determined using the information in this section.

What Sort of Logging Will the IMS Create?

The IMS contains a few settable levels of logging that are controlled within the the IMS admin module under the Diagnostic Logging tab. It is also available, along with all other Exchange components, when opening the properties with a server object name listed within a site's Configuration and Servers container. For the IMS, there are three types of logging mechanisms:

- *Event Viewer.* Most hard errors that may occur with the IMS will be placed into NT's Event Log. Using the Event Viewer to check on the status of NT and Exchange as a whole on a regular basis is a good idea. Logging levels for the IMS can be turned up or down from the login page. Only the last two entries don't increase entries into the Event log.

  It is a good idea on your server to configure the Event Log to overwrite data after a certain number of days and increase the default limits for the logs. This will prevent events not being posted, but will also cause older ones to be lost. The logs can always be archived once you check them over, however. This option is always active to report important problems that may occur and should be the first place to look when problems arise. Additional levels of logging are controlled by all the categories except SMTP Protocol Log and Message Archival, which are discussed later in this list.

- *Message Archival.* This logging should be used only when trying to debug content issues for the IMS/IMAIL components. It will archive every message that comes in or leaves Exchange via the IMS, including all rerouted mail. This option should not be left active, in order to prevent filling up the hard disk and causing mail delivery to stop. This option is activated by the Message Archival category.

- *Protocol Logging.* This logging can be used when trying to determine connectivity problems. It will show everything that the IMS sends or receives over the wire when set to the Maximum, except for outbound message content. This is handled by a function call in NT that cannot be logged by the IMS. For inbound the content of the messages will be there. This option is activated by the SMTP Protocol Log category.

  This logging is most useful for dropped connections or possible invalid parameters reported by users or the event logs. Each log file associates to a single connection from the Advanced option on the Connections tab. If your system is set up for the 5.0 defaults of 30 inbound and 20 outbound connections maximum, you can expect to see up to 50 log files. These will grow very fast and are recommended for debugging purposes only.

Why Can I Send Mail but Can't Receive?

This question is the most common one for first-time implementers of any SMTP system. It always leads to the same answer: check the DNS to ensure that your domain and host are correctly configured. In the Support directory on the Exchange disk is a utility called RESTEST that uses the Resolver built into the IMS and can be used to check the DNS for proper mail delivery. Another tool is NSLOOKUP, which comes with NT 4.0 and is part of the DNS/Bind source for most UNIX systems.

A secondary cause may be the ISP queuing up all your mail, but never being able to deliver it to your IMS. It might not support ETRN as you thought, or the retry times might be completely out of whack with your system. If the ISP is UNIX and you can connect to a Telnet session, you can try typing `mailq` to see what is queued up and whether the mail is destined for your domain.

Run RESTEST as follows:

```
RESTEST MYDOMAIN.COM
```

You can include the `-DEBUG` option for more detail, but run this from the server or another machine that uses a DNS. This is not 100 percent, because it will also use

```
NSLOOKUP (A, MX)
```

This allows you to directly query the DNS server for information;, by default, it will be set to look up only A Records. Typing `SET TYPE=MX` will change it into Mail Exchange mode.

Typing the FQDN should show you your IMS's MX record and associated A Record information. If not, this is why you're not getting any mail.

How Do I Change the Inbound Domain Address?

To change the default domain address for a site, start Exchange Admin; then select the configuration object from the directory listing. In the right pane, you will want to get properties on the Site Addressing object. Then, going to the Site Addressing tab, you can change the default Internet addressing. For users with multiple SMTP proxies, this change affects only the default one, which is always listed in all caps.

If this value is changed, you *must* also change the DNS to reflect the changes and the IMS's routing page so the IMS knows to accept this mail as inbound to Exchange. It will also require a restart once the data is changed in the IMS Admin pages.

Can the IMS Be Set Up to Accept Only Inbound Mail or Send Outbound Mail?

This can be done from the Connections tab of the IMS Admin pages; click on the Connections tab and you can set which direction the IMS should function. If you want to have the

IMS for inbound only, it is important to remove any address space you have configured so mail does not get queued up in the Information Store waiting to be picked up by the IMS.

> **NOTE**
>
> There is a small problem in version 4.0 and 5.0, where the IMS will not start up if no address space is entered. By creating a bogus address space, you can work around this problem and allow the IMS to start up.

What Does Flush Mode Really Mean?

Flush mode, which is settable on the Connections tab, allows the IMS to clean out the temporary queues it keeps on disk. When this mode is selected, no connections are accepted and no mail is picked up from the outbound Exchange queue (MTS-OUT). Note that this does not control the flow of messages into the outbound queue. If you are removing an IMS from the enterprise, it is also important to delete the address space as well if the IMS will not be used again in the future.

Changing Timeout Values for SMTP Connections

When you run into connection problems, where connections over a modem may time-out using the default values, you can easily change these within the Windows NT Registry to extend the amount of time to wait for commands. The values used are based on the recommendations of the RFCs. The following Registry settings can be located using Regedit under the following path. The values are in hexadecimal:

```
SYSTEM\CurrentControlSet\Services\MSExchangeIMC\Parameters
```

- SMTPRecvTimeout - 0x12c (300 Seconds, hex)

   The amount of time IMS waits for packet transmission. Setting to zero means it will never time out.

- SMTPWaitForAck - 0x12c

   The time IMS will wait for an OK response to a command sent to another host.

- SMTPWaitForBanner - 0x12c

   The time the IMS will wait to receive the initial HELO banner when connecting up to a host.

- SMTPWaitForDataBlock - 0x258 (600 Seconds, hex)

   The time the IMS will wait while receiving the message body or DATA portion of the message. This is not total time, but idle time.

- SMTPWaitForDataInitiation - 0x78 (120 Seconds, hex)

   The time the IMS will wait for an SMTP Client to start delivery of the message body.

- SMTPWaitForDataTermination 0x258

  The time the IMS will wait for an SMTP Client to send the terminating code to end the data portion of a message.

- SMTPWaitForMailFrom - 0x12c

  The time the IMS will wait for the envelope MAIL FROM command to be acknowledged by the SMTP Server.

- SMTPWaitForRcpt - 0x12c

  The time the IMS will wait for the envelope RCPT TO command to be acknowledged by the SMTP Server.

Summary

The Internet Mail Service is a key connecting point between the Microsoft Exchange Server and your customers. The information provided in this chapter about general Internet concepts concerning SMTP and DNS are very important when people start to send mail into your organization. The RAS connectivity and and installation should help you decide what sort of configuration will be best suited for you. Lastly, the Common Questions and Issues should provide a good start to resolving problems as well as preventing them as you implement the IMS.

Overall, the Exchange IMS is a very integrated part of the whole Exchange server and one of the key areas of focus for most companies deploying Exchange. One of the key ideas that was kept in mind during the product's life cycle was that the IMS would most likely be running in some closet without much user intervention. For the most part this should be true, but with the ever-changing environments of the intranet and Internet, a watchful eye is a good idea. The Exchange server may not be the only one to watch; changes in DNS or the Network will quickly result in mail problems.

When using dial-up connections, there are many dialing options that can be configured to match the needs of your company. Some of the extended features for mail queuing are very dependent on the ISP involved. It is important for the ISP to allow all mail to be routed through their servers and the queuing up of messages for your domain.

Proper configuration of the DNS to help balance the load to multiple IMSs that may be on the network and allowing for failure redundancy are very important. It is always important to double-check changes in DNS to make sure that remote hosts will be able to deliver mail into your domain and have proper fallback to alternative servers if the resources exist. This is not required, however, because the remote hosts will also queue up mail and retry at a later time.

Connecting to Other Exchange Sites

by Kimmo Bergius
Revised by Kevin Kaufmann

IN THIS CHAPTER

After you decide on the placement of sites and servers in your organization, you have to start thinking about connecting your sites. If you are going to have only one site, the connections between the servers are automatic and are configured automatically during the installation of the server software. If you are going to have several sites, you have to choose a connector or connectors to connect these sites together.

Message transfer and communication between two sites differ from message transfer and communication between servers within a site. Servers in the same site communicate with each other using Remote Procedure Calls (RPCs). All communication within a site is server-to-server communication, with all the servers communicating directly with the target server. Two services on each server are responsible for communicating information to servers in the same site: the Directory Service (DS) and the Message Transfer Agent (MTA). The Directory Service is responsible for replicating the contents of the directory between the servers, and the Message Transfer Agent is responsible for transferring messages. All other Exchange services rely on these two services to transfer their information between servers. Communication within a site is also known as *intrasite communication*.

Communication between sites is called *intersite communication*. Intersite communication is handled by *connectors*. There are two different connector types: a *messaging connector* and a *directory replication connector*. A messaging connector handles all message traffic between two sites. You can use four different connectors for this task. A directory replication connector is responsible for replicating directory information between sites. The directory replication connector performs this job by placing the information to be replicated into a message and then relying on the messaging connector to transfer the information between the sites. Directory replication and directory replication connectors are discussed in detail in Chapter 19, "Configuring Directory Replication."

A connection between two sites in the same organization consists always of two similar connectors, one in the local site and one in the remote site. In some cases, you can configure both connectors at the same time, but mostly the two connectors must be configured separately in both sites. Both connectors must, however, be configured before a connection exists between the two sites.

TIP

If configuring both sites at the same time is possible, you should do this, because this makes the configuration process very simple and error-free.

> **NOTE**
>
> In this chapter, the term *local site* is used for your own site, and the term *remote site* is used for the site to which you are connecting the local site.

Different Messaging Connectors

There are four connectors that you can use as a messaging connector between two sites:

- Site Connector
- X.400 Connector
- Dynamic RAS Connector
- Internet Mail Service (IMS)

> **NOTE**
>
> In Exchange 4.0, the Internet Mail Service was called the Internet Mail Connector Service. Functionally, they are the same.

Choosing a Connector

You also can choose from four connectors to use as a messaging connector between two sites:

- Site Connector
- X.400 Connector
- Dynamic RAS Connector
- Internet Mail Service (IMS)

People have different opinions about the basic rule for choosing a connector. According to the first opinion, you should always try the site connector first if you have a connection that supports it and then switch to some other connector if the site connector doesn't work properly. The other opinion promotes the use of the X.400 connector over the site connector and suggests that you should always use the X.400 connector if the connection between the two sites is not a direct LAN-grade connection. Both of these statements contain a shade of truth. Remember that the selection of a connector between two sites is not final; you can always change the connector if the one you choose does not meet your requirements.

Performance

TIP
Here's a rule of thumb: When you choose a connector, always start with the site connector if two conditions are met:

- The connections between the sites meet the requirements for a site connector; that is, the connection is medium- to high-bandwidth and supports the use of RPCs.

- You do not want to restrict the traffic between the two sites—for example, schedule of transfer, the maximum size of messages transferred, users who are allowed to use the connector, and so on.

If the site connector takes up too much of the connection bandwidth or you want to control the traffic, then switch to the X.400 connector. Use the dynamic RAS connector only if you have no other connection to a remote site than a dial-up connection or as a backup connector, and use the Internet Mail Service only as a backup connector.

If the preceding tip gave you enough information about choosing a connector, you can go directly to the configuration instructions for your chosen connector later in this chapter. If, however, you want to know more details about choosing a connector, read on.

Before you can choose a suitable connector, you need to find out certain information. Primarily, this information has to do with the type, protocol, and available bandwidth of the connection between the sites, but you should also try to estimate how much network traffic your messaging connector will create. When you designed your Exchange environment, you probably gathered a lot of information on users and the amount of mail traffic they currently create. You can also use this information to estimate the amount of intersite traffic your users are going to create.

Network Types and Protocols

Before you can choose a connector between two sites, you have to determine the type of the connection between the sites and the protocols that the connection supports.

Network connections can be divided into three categories, depending on the bandwidth the connection offers (see Table 18.1).

Table 18.1. Network connections.

Connection	Bandwidth	Connector Possibilities
Low-speed connection	Less than 64 Kbs	
	Modem or ISDN	Dynamic RAS Connector
	X.25	X.400 Connector
	TCP/IP network connection	X.400 Connector, Internet Mail Service

Connection	Bandwidth	Connector Possibilities
Medium-speed connection	64 Kbs to 2 Mbs, Network connection supports RPCs	Site Connector
	TCP/IP network connection,	X.400 Connector, Internet Mail Service
	X.25	X.400 Connector
High-speed connection (LAN grade connection)	More than 2 Mbs, Network connection supports RPCs	Site Connector
	X.25	X.400 Connector

Available Bandwidth

You can always determine the total bandwidth of the network connection between two sites. Determining how much of this bandwidth is actually available is much more difficult. Available bandwidth means how much of the total bandwidth is left after the bandwidth used by other applications using the same connection has been deducted.

You might be using a 64Kbits/s leased line, for example, to connect two Exchange sites. Users could also be accessing a database or transferring files over the same connection. This means that the connector between the two sites would no longer have the whole 64Kbits/s to itself but would have to coexist with the other network traffic. To calculate available bandwidth, you must be aware of all other traffic using the same connection.

TIP

You can monitor the usage of your network using any network monitoring software, such as the Network Monitor included in Microsoft System Management Server. You can also use NT's Performance Monitor to monitor the amount of available bandwidth.

Bandwidth Used by Exchange

To determine whether your existing network will support Exchange, you should try to estimate how much network traffic will be created by your Exchange environment. The following factors affect the network traffic in the Exchange environment:

- Number of users and the number of messages they are going to send from site to site
- Placement of connectors to the outside world and the number of messages sent to and from the connectors—for example, if the Exchange organization is going to have just one IMS connected to the Internet
- Number of public folders and amount of replication from site to site
- Number of directory changes that need to be replicated from site to site

You can estimate many of these factors by analyzing the traffic created by users in your existing system. Ask different users to monitor their mail system usage for a few days and record the number of messages sent to the same system, to foreign systems, and to public folder usage. This information will tell you a lot about the initial requirements of your new system and will help you plan your hardware, software, and infrastructure requirements. If you are currently using a mail system based on file sharing and the system performance is adequate, the same network infrastructure will probably support migrating to an Exchange system. Keep in mind, though, that as the new system offers better performance and new capabilities, the usage of the system will increase, thus increasing your hardware and infrastructure requirements.

Multiple Connectors

You can define multiple connectors between two sites. The connectors can be all the same type or different types. You use multiple connectors for two reasons:

- Fault tolerance
- Load balancing

Fault tolerance means that you can have two or more connectors between two sites usually using different connections. Having two or more connectors ensures that if one of the connections and connectors is unavailable for some reason, the message can be sent using another connector.

Performance   *Load balancing* means dividing site-to-site message traffic between two different connectors. In load-balancing configurations, the connectors are usually the same type, and they can use the same or different connections. If you have a lot of message traffic between two sites and the connection is not the bottleneck, you can divide the processing of messages between two servers in both sites. You therefore would configure two connectors between the sites into two different servers. The cost of the connectors participating in load balancing must be the same.

Connector Cost

If multiple connectors are used between two sites, the MTA on the local server must be able to determine which one should be used to transfer the message. The MTA uses a definition called the *cost* to determine which connector should be used. The cost is defined as a number from 1 to 100. If multiple connectors are used between two sites, the one with the lowest cost associated with it is used to transfer the message.

Connector costs are cumulative, which means that if a message has to travel through multiple connectors, the cost from the source server to the target server is the cumulative cost of all the connectors handling the message. If you have three sites—for example, A, B, and C—A and B are connected using a site connector with a cost of 1. B and C are connected with a similar site connector with a cost of 1, and A and C are connected with an X.400 connector with a cost of 5 (see Figure 18.1). Messages from A to C are routed through site B because of the lower cost (1 + 1 = 2 compared to 5).

FIGURE 18.1.

Multiple routes.

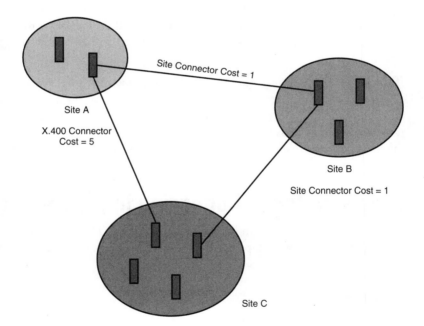

Site Connector Cost = 1

Site A

X.400 Connector
Cost = 5

Site B

Site Connector Cost = 1

Site C

What happens if a message is sent from site A to site C and the connector from site B to site C is unavailable? The MTA on the server on site A still sends the message to site B, because it cannot be aware of the status of the connector between sites B and C. Site B also calculates a route for the message, but it knows that the connector between B and C is not available, so it uses the least costly route to C, which is via A. The MTA on A again checks the routing and finds out that the cheapest way from A to C is via B, but it also sees that the route via B has already been used, so it sends the message along the cheapest available route, which is directly to C.

> **TIP**
>
> You can view all your connectors, including information about cost and address type for the entire site, by opening the Site Addressing object and viewing the Routing property page. From this page, you can view the Connector details by double-clicking the entries, and you can also manually rebuild the routing table.

How Does Exchange Select a Connector?

When you send a message that is addressed outside your home server, the MTA on your home server examines the recipient address of the message. If the message is to another server in your own site, the MTA establishes a connection directly to the MTA on the target server and transfers the message.

If the recipient of the message is not within your own site, the MTA examines the possible routes to the target server and chooses the route that has the lowest cost associated with it. The cost of a route from the local site to the remote site is the cumulative cost of all the connectors through which the message has to pass. After the MTA chooses the lowest cost route, it passes the message to the first connector in this route, and this connector is responsible for transferring the message to the next site in the route.

Property Pages Appearing in All Connectors

Some property pages are common to several connectors. These property pages are explained in the following sections. Each property page also has a list of connectors for which you can find the property page.

Address Space

Applies to: Site Connector

X.400 Connector

Dynamic RAS Connector

Internet Mail Service

(cc:Mail Connector)

(MS Mail Connector)

All connectors, whether they are used to connect two Exchange sites or an Exchange system and another mail system, have to be associated with an address space. The address space defines a set of addresses that the connector is to handle. You could define an X.400 connector, for example, to connect an Exchange site to another site in the same organization and specify the following value for the connector's address space:

X400   c=us, a= , p=*organization_name*, o=*site_name*

where *organization_name* and *site_name* are the organization and site name of the remote site, respectively. This address space defines that the X.400 connector will handle all sent messages in which the X.400 address fields c, a, p, and o match the values defined in the address space.

You define the address space by selecting the Address Space tab in the Connectors property window. The program displays the Address Space property page, shown in Figure 18.2.

FIGURE 18.2.

The Address Space property page.

An address space definition should contain the fields that are necessary to distinguish the messages that the connector should handle. You can also define multiple address spaces and even multiple address types for a single connector.

NOTE

You can use an asterisk (*) as a multicharacter wildcard and a question mark (?) as a single-character wildcard in an address space.

In an X.400 address, the Administrative domain field (ADMD, a field) cannot be left blank. If you want to define that no ADMD is needed, type a space in the field.

Connector Schedule

Applies to: X.400 Connector

Dynamic RAS Connector

You can set the X.400 connector or dynamic RAS connector to initiate a connection to the remote server at specified times by defining a *schedule*. You define the connector schedule by selecting the Schedule tab in the Connectors property window. The program displays the Schedule property page, shown in Figure 18.3.

FIGURE 18.3.

The Schedule property page.

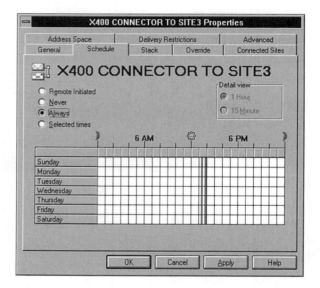

You can choose from four options to determine the schedule:

Remote Initiated   The local connector never initiates a connection to the remote site but rather waits until the corresponding connector in the remote site initiates a connection. After the remote connector finishes sending messages to the local site, the local connector sends all queued messages to the remote server. You can use this feature so one side will incur all the connection costs.

> **NOTE**
>
> You can define the Remote Initiated option in only one of the connectors participating in a connection. If the schedule in both connectors is defined as Remote Initiated, no messages are ever delivered.

Never	This option disables the connector.
Always	The connector establishes a connection to the remote site approximately every 15 minutes and sends all queued messages.
Selected times	The connector operates according to the schedule defined in the bottom of the window. You can specify the schedule using either a 1-hour or a 15-minute schedule grid.

You cannot define a schedule for the site that assumes that the network connection between the sites is permanent and always available. For the Internet Mail Service, you can configure when the server will dial up the remote side on the Dial-up Connections property page.

Delivery Restrictions

Applies to: X.400 Connector

Dynamic RAS Connector

Internet Mail Service

Delivery restriction means that you can allow or deny the right to use the connector on a user basis. You set delivery restrictions by selecting the Delivery Restrictions tab in the connector's property window. The program displays the Delivery Restrictions property page, shown in Figure 18.4.

FIGURE 18.4.
The Delivery Restrictions property page.

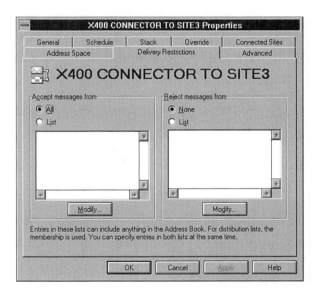

You can allow only specified users to use the connector by adding the names of these users in the Accept messages from list. Alternatively, you can deny the use of the connector from specified users by adding the names of these users in the Reject messages from list. In this case, everyone except the users listed will have access to the connector. If a user is not allowed to use a certain connector, the system informs of this restriction by sending an error message to the user.

Connected Sites Property Page

Applies to: X.400 Connector

Dynamic RAS Connector

Internet Mail Service

If the messaging connector used to connect the two sites is an X.400 connector, dynamic RAS connector, or the Internet Mail Service, you have to define the remote site in the connector's Connected Sites property page, as shown in Figure 18.5. Otherwise, the directory replication connector cannot use the messaging connector to transport the replication messages. Only the site directly in the other end of the messaging connector has to be defined on the Connected Sites page. All the other sites within the organization are defined automatically through the Routing Information Daemon (RID). You do not have to define the connected sites for the site connector because this information is configured automatically.

FIGURE 18.5.

The Connected Sites property page.

Restricting Message Size

You can restrict the size of messages delivered through an X.400, dynamic RAS, or Internet Mail Service by specifying the maximum message size in kilobytes. The specified size is the size of the total message. You cannot define a maximum size for attachments. You define the maximum message size on the Advanced property page for the X.400 connector and on the General property page for the dynamic RAS and Internet Mail Services. You cannot define the maximum message size for the site connector.

Site Connector

The following table lists the advantages and disadvantages to using the site connector:

Advantages	*Disadvantages*
Most efficient of the connectors.	Requires a fast and permanent network connection that supports RPCs.
Easiest connector to configure; both the local site and the remote site can be configured at the same time.	You have relatively little control over the operation of the connector, such as connection scheduling, maximum message size, and users allowed to use the connector.
Automatic load balancing and fault tolerance through multiple source and target servers.	The connector can saturate a link if multiple servers in the local site establish a connection to multiple servers in the remote site at the same time.

You should choose the site connector if

- You have a LAN-grade connection that supports the use of RPCs.
- You do not need to have control over when and how messages are transferred between sites or who uses the connector.
- You want to have a connector that is efficient and simple to configure.

The site connector is the most efficient of the connectors, because it does not convert messages from one format to another. Instead, the message stays in the internal Exchange format. For this reason, this connector is sometimes called the *Exchange connector*.

The site connector uses RPCs to communicate information between servers in two different sites. This is another reason for the efficiency of the site connector. RPC can run over a variety of network protocols, including:

- TCP/IP
- NetBIOS
- SPX

When you install and define the site connector or X.400 connector, no new software is installed in the system. These connectors are just a set of definitions that tell the Message Transfer Agent that it should transfer messages to the other site as well as to servers within the same site.

18

CONNECTING TO
OTHER EXCHANGE
SITES

Target Server and Bridgehead Server

A *target server* is the server in the remote site to which the server in the local site establishes a connection to deliver the message. Any server in the remote site can be a target server. A *bridgehead server* is a server in the local site that takes care of all the message traffic to the remote site. By default, no bridgehead server is defined for the local site, but instead all servers within the local site can establish a connection to all servers in the remote site. By default, all the servers within the remote site are defined as target servers.

As the administrator, you can direct message traffic to the remote site through a specific server in the local site by selecting one of the servers to act as a bridgehead server. Only the bridgehead server is therefore allowed to establish a connection to the remote site. All other servers in the local site transfer a message destined to the remote site first to the bridgehead server, which then initiates a connection to a server in the remote site and transfers the message.

You can also limit the number of servers in the remote site to which the bridgehead server (or all servers, if no bridgehead server has been defined) in the local site can establish connections. You do so by using the target server's property page. Initially, all the servers in the remote site are listed as target servers, but you can remove servers from the list and thus direct message traffic through certain target servers.

If you are defining a site connector between two sites and want to direct all traffic between one server in the local site and one server in the remote site, you should configure the connector in both sites so that a single server in the local site is selected as a bridgehead server and a single server in the remote site is defined as a target server.

All target servers are associated with a cost, which defines the selection of the target server. The cost is defined as a number from 0 to 100. The costs 0 and 100 have special meanings: 0 means that the specified target server is to be used always if it is available, and 100 means that the target server is used only if no other target servers are available. The costs 1 to 99 are used to determine the target server, using a weighted average calculation. This means that if one target server has the cost 1, and another has the cost 2, the first one is used roughly twice as much as the second one.

> **NOTE**
>
> Do not confuse the target server cost with the cost specified for a connector. The target server cost is defined as a number from 0 to 100, and the connector cost from 1 to 100. Also, the target server cost will affect only how much each target server will be used (excluding the special cost values 0 and 100), whereas the connector cost will actually determine the order in which the connectors will be used.

Figure 18.6 illustrates three different site connector configurations between two sites. Both the sites have three servers: A, B, and C. In the first example, the site connector is defined using default settings—that is, no bridgehead server in the local site and all servers in the remote site as target servers. In the second example, a bridgehead server has been selected in the local site, but all the servers in the remote site are still target servers. The third example shows how message traffic between the two sites has been directed through two servers only, where one server in both sites has been selected the bridgehead server and just one server in the remote site has been defined a target server.

FIGURE 18.6.

Different site connector configurations.

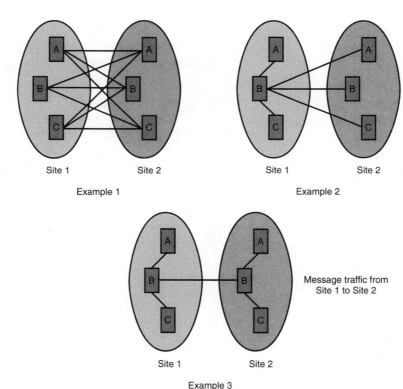

Site 1   Site 2   Site 1   Site 2

Example 1   Example 2

Message traffic from Site 1 to Site 2

Site 1   Site 2

Example 3

Site Service Account

Site connector uses RPCs to transfer the information between sites much in the same way as two servers within the same site communicate with each other. Also, the service account used to start the server MTA services affects the operation of a site connector. If the site service account used in the local site has no access rights to the remote site, the site connector does not work properly.

The easiest configuration is to have the same service account in both sites. This configuration is easy to establish if the sites are within the same NT domain. Because the site connector requires a permanent connection between the sites, it is also possible and quite feasible to set up a trust between the sites and use the same service account in both sites, if the sites are within different NT domains.

Sometimes you cannot use the same service account in both sites. For these cases, you can override the local site service account and define a different account to be used when connecting to the target site. You do so by using the Override property page, as shown in Figure 18.7. The Override feature is much the same as the File Manager Connect As feature you use when connecting to network resources in different domains when no trust exists between the domains.

Figure 18.7.

The Override property page.

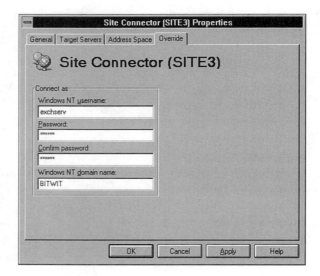

Installing and Configuring the Site Connector

The following steps include only the necessary definitions to install and configure the site connector. Additional definitions are discussed briefly after the basic installation steps.

1. Open the Exchange Administrator program and choose File | New Other | Site Connector.

> **NOTE**
>
> The program might display a message informing you that the connector cannot be installed in the current container and asking whether you want to switch to the Connections container. Click OK in the message box.

2. Type the name of a server in the remote site. The server can be any of the servers in the target site. The Site Connector Properties dialog box appears, displaying information for the remote site.

3. Click OK. The program displays a message asking whether you want to create the site connector in the remote site as well.

NOTE

You can create the site connector for both sites at the same time only if you have Admin access rights to the remote site and the selected server. Otherwise, you must create the site connector in each site separately.

4. Choose Yes if you want to create the site connector in the remote site as well. Otherwise, choose No. The Site Connector Properties dialog box appears.
5. Click OK.

If you chose to create the site connector to the target site in step 4, the sites are now connected, and you can test the connector by sending a message to a user in the remote site. Otherwise, you must configure the remote site separately before the site connector configuration is finished and you can start sending messages to the remote site and back or configure a directory replication connector between the sites.

TIP

Always test the site connector before going further by sending a message to a user in the remote site, using the user's full X.400 address.

Advanced Configuration of the Site Connector

The Site Connector property pages contain some additional settings that you can optionally use to further control the operation of the connector.

General Property Page

Apart from the name of the connector and the remote site, you can use the General property page to define a cost for the connector or a bridgehead server in the local site.

The connector cost is used to select a connector to transfer the message between two sites in a multiple connector configuration. Type the cost in the Cost field. For more information, see "Connector Cost," earlier in this chapter.

A bridgehead server enables you to direct message traffic to the remote site through a specific server in the local site. You can define a bridgehead server by selecting Specific Server and then selecting the server name from the list. For more information, see "Target Server and Bridgehead Server," earlier in this chapter.

Target Servers Property Page

On the Target Servers property page, you can define the servers in the remote site to which the servers in the local site can establish a connection. For more information, see "Target Server and Bridgehead Server," earlier in this chapter.

Address Space Property Page

The X.400 address of the target site is automatically entered in the Address Space property page. You can modify this address space or define additional address spaces using the options in this property page.

Override Property Page

A site connector uses RPCs to communicate between the two sites. This capability requires that both sites use the same site service account. If the sites do not have the same service account, however, you can define the service account of the remote site in the Override property page. This task is much the same as using the Connect As option when connecting to a resource in File Manager.

The X.400 Connector

The following table lists the advantages and disadvantages to using the X.400 connector:

Advantages	Disadvantages
Gives you a lot of control over how and when the connector is used and which users can use it.	Not as efficient as the site connector.
Messages to other Exchange sites and organizations can be transferred in the Exchange internal format, which improves efficiency.	Can create bottlenecks when a lot of traffic between two sites is routed through two machines.
Supports TCP/IP, TP0/X.25, and TP4/CLNP connections.	Relatively complicated to configure.

You should choose the X.400 connector if

- You have tried the site connector and it saturates the connection between the sites.
- You have a TCP/IP connection between the sites that is not fast enough to accommodate a site connector.
- You want to control when and how messages are transferred between sites or which users can use the connector.
- You want to connect two sites over an existing X.400 backbone.

Compared to the site connector, the X.400 connector gives you a lot more control over how and when the communication between two sites is to occur. The X.400 always uses one server in the local site (the bridgehead server) and one server in the remote site to transfer the information. This setup enables you to direct message traffic through certain servers. You can also define a schedule for the connector, as well as limit the maximum size of messages transferred over the connector, and allow or deny access to the connector on a user basis.

When you configure an X.400 connector between two sites, one server in both sites is chosen to act as the messaging bridgehead server for this connector, and the connectors are configured on these servers. This setup directs all message traffic between the two sites through these servers.

The X.400 connector enables you to connect two sites using an X.400 network as a backbone. You therefore do not need to have your own connection between two sites, but instead both sites need to have a connection only to a public X.400 network, which can be used as a backbone. You can also connect two Exchange sites directly, using an X.25 or a TCP/IP-capable network connection.

The X.400 connector supports three different protocols: TCP/IP, TP0/X.25, and TP4/CLNP. Before you can define the X.400 connector, you have to define a suitable transport stack. For most connections, using the TCP/IP transport stack is easiest. You use the TP0 stack only for connections over an X.25 network and the TP4 stack only if you are configuring a connection to a mainframe computer that supports only the TP4 protocol.

Installing and Configuring the X.400 Connector

The following steps cover the installation of the TCP/IP transport stack, which is the most common of the transport stacks. Before you can define the transport stack, you have to install TCP/IP and configure it on the server.

1. Open the Exchange Administrator program and choose File | New Other | MTA Transport Stack. The program displays a window with a list of available transport stacks.

2. Select the TCP/IP MTA Transport Stack and the server where the stack is to be installed. Then click OK.

3. The program displays the property window for the TCP/IP transport stack. On the General page, you can define a name for the transport stack (or accept the default name). You need to define the OSI address information only if multiple applications or services are using the same transport. The Connector page shows all connectors using this transport stack.

4. Click OK.

The transport stack has now been configured, and you can go on by configuring the X.400 connector. The following steps include only the necessary definitions to install and configure the X.400 connector. Additional definitions are discussed briefly after the basic installation steps.

1. Choose File | New Other | X.400 Connector. The program displays a window listing all the possible X.400 connector types. Select TCP/IP X.400 Connector and click OK. The program displays the Properties window for the X.400 connector.

> **NOTE**
>
> The program might display a message informing you that the connector cannot be installed in the current container and asking whether you want to switch to the Connections container. Click OK in the message box.

2. Type a Display and Directory name for the X.400 connector in the corresponding fields. Use names that enable you to identify the connector in the Connections container—for example, X400 CONNECTOR TO SITE3.

> **TIP**
>
> Some of the definitions within the Exchange server are case sensitive. You therefore should always choose to type all names and other definitions in either upper- or lowercase. Generally, using uppercase letters is advisable.

3. Type the Remote MTA name and password in the corresponding fields. When you are configuring an X.400 connector to another Exchange site, the Remote MTA name is the name of the remote server, if you have not defined another name on the Override page of the remote server's X.400 connector (for more information, see "Override Property Page," later in this chapter). Also, by default, the password is blank unless you have defined a password for the remote server's MTA, either in the remote server's Message Transfer Agent property window or in the X.400 connector's Override page.

4. Select the Schedule tab, and define a schedule for the connector. For more information, see "Connector Schedule" earlier in this chapter.

5. Select the stack page. Select IP Address, and type the IP address of the remote in the field.

6. Select the Address Space tab, and define an address space for the connector by clicking New X.400. The program displays a window, where you should type the following information:

Field	Type
Organization (o)	Site name of the remote site
Private management domain name (p)	Name of the Exchange organization

Field	Type
Administrative management domain name (a)	A single space
Country (c)	Select your country from the list

7. Type a cost for the connector in the Cost field (for more information, see "Connector Cost," earlier in this chapter). Then click OK. The defined address space appears in the list.

8. Select the Connected Sites tab. Select New, and type the name of the remote site in the Site field. Then click OK. The remote site then appears in the Connected Sites list. For more information on connected sites, see "Connected Sites," earlier in this chapter.

9. Click OK in the property window. The X.400 connector is now defined for the local site. For the connection to work between the sites, you have to configure the X.400 connector in the remote site by performing the same steps.

TIP

Always test the X.400 connector before going further by sending a message to a user in the remote site, using the user's full X.400 address.

X.400 Connector Advanced Configuration

You can further fine-tune the X.400 connector by using the properties explained in the following sections. Some of the property pages (Schedule, Delivery Restrictions, Connected Sites, and Address Space property pages) are also discussed earlier in this chapter.

Override Property Page

If you want to override the local MTA name and password defined in the local server's Message Transfer Agent property page, you can define connector-specific values on the Override property page. Connector-specific passwords are handy in some cases, because if you have to remove the connector for some reason, you do not have to change the passwords on all the other connectors for security reasons. The MTA name and password entered for the X.400 Connector in the remote site have to exactly match the values entered here.

You can also use the Override property page to define connector-specific connection values. Values specified here override the values specified in the Messaging Defaults property page in the MTA Site Configuration Properties window. You do not generally need to alter these values.

Advanced Property Page

On the Advanced property page, you can specify X.400 specific settings, such as the X.400 mode and link options and maximum message size. The X.400-specific options are defined by the MTA to which the X.400 connector is connected. If you are connecting two Exchange sites using an X.400 connector and a direct TCP/IP connection between the sites, you should make sure that the settings 1988 normal mode, Allow BP-15, and Allow MS Exchange contents are selected. These settings define that the X.400 connection conforms to the 1988 X.400 standard and that messages can be transferred using the Exchange internal message format (the most efficient X.400 mode).

The Two-Way Alternate setting enables you to define whether incoming messages from the remote site will be transferred during a connection established from the local site. This setting is particularly useful when the connection between the two sites is an expensive X.25 network. Thus, each site is responsible only for costs associated to message traffic initiated in the local site.

You also can use the Advanced property page to define the maximum size of messages transferred over the X.400 connector. If you want to limit the maximum messages size, select Maximum (K) and type the required size (in kilobytes) to the field.

Dynamic RAS Connector

The following table lists the advantages and disadvantages to using the dynamic RAS connector:

Advantages	Disadvantages
Gives you a lot of control over how and when the connector is used and which users can use it.	Data transfer rate is dependent on the speed of the modem or ISDN line.
	Relatively complicated to configure.
Supports asynchronous modem and ISDN connections.	Can create bottlenecks when a lot of traffic between two sites is routed through two machines.

You should choose the dynamic RAS connector if

■ The only connection to a remote site is a dial-up modem or ISDN connection.

■ You want to configure a backup connector between two sites to improve fault tolerance.

You can use the dynamic RAS connector to connect two sites much in the same way you use a site connector. The biggest difference is that this connector does not require a permanent connection to the remote site. Instead, the dynamic RAS connector can use connections defined in the NT Remote Access Service (RAS) to communicate to the target site.

With RAS, you can connect two NT server computers using a normal telephone line (modem connection), an ISDN line, or an X.25 connection. The dynamic RAS connector can use any defined RAS connection. The RAS connector is used to connect two sites if no permanent connection exists between the sites.

Before you can install and configure the dynamic RAS connector, you have to install and configure the Remote Access Service on your NT server. You do so using the Network icon in the Control Panel. You should also define a phone book entry for the remote server to which you want to connect. The RAS phone book entries are configured using the Remote Access program (which you can find in the Remote Access Service program group).

The following steps illustrate the configuration of the RAS MTA Transport Stack:

1. Choose File | New Other | MTA Transport Stack. The New MTA Transport Stack window appears.

2. Select RAS MTA Transport Stack from the Type list box and the server on which the stack is to be installed from the Server box. Click OK. The RAS Properties dialog box then appears.

3. The name of the transport stack is automatically entered in the Name field in the General property page. Optionally, you can define an MTA callback number for the local transport, which can be used to further enhance data security when using a RAS Connection. If callback is enabled, the server initiates a connection to the remote server, and after the remote server answers the connection, is terminated. The local server waits until the remote server calls back to the number defined here. The callback requires that RAS callback security be enabled in RAS.

   In the Connectors property page, you can see a list of connectors that use this transport stack.

The RAS transport stack is now configured, and you can go on configuring the dynamic RAS connector. The following steps include only the necessary definitions to install and configure the dynamic RAS connector. Additional definitions are discussed briefly after the basic installation steps.

1. Choose File | New Other | Dynamic RAS Connector. The program displays the RAS Connector Properties window.

18

CONNECTING TO
OTHER EXCHANGE
SITES

NOTE

The connector is installed in the Connections container. If you are not in this container, the program displays a dialog box asking whether you want to move to this container. Click OK.

2. In the General property page, type the display and directory names for the connector. Also type the name of the remote server and select the transport stack to be used and the RAS phone book entry. You can define a new phone book entry by selecting RAS Phone Book.

3. Select the Schedule tab. In the Schedule property page, you can define the times when the local server can initiate a connection to the remote server. For details, see "Connector Schedule," earlier in this chapter. By default, the schedule is set to Always.

4. Select the RAS Override tab. On the RAS Override property page, you should define a user account that has access rights on the target server. The account should be defined at least as a user (have at least Send As and Mailbox Owner rights) on the Servers and Configuration containers in the target server. You can also specify the site service account for the remote site. On this page, you can also override the call and callback telephone numbers.

5. Select the Address Space tab. Define an address space for the connector by clicking New X.400. The program displays a window, where you should type the following information:

Field	Type
Organization (o)	Site name of the remote site
Private management domain name (p)	Name of the Exchange organization
Administrative management domain name (a)	A single space
Country (c)	Select your country from the list

6. Type a cost for the connector in the Cost field (for more information, see "Connector Cost," earlier in this chapter). Then click OK. The defined address space appears in the list.

7. Select the Connected Sites tab. Select New and type the name of the remote site in the Site field. Then click OK. The remote site then appears in the Connected Sites list. For more information on connected sites, see "Connected Sites," earlier in this chapter.

8. Click OK in the property window. The dynamic RAS connector is now defined for the local site. For the connection to work between the sites, you have to configure the connector in the remote site by performing the same steps.

TIP

Always test the dynamic RAS connector before going further by sending a message to a user in the remote site, using the user's full X.400 address.

Dynamic RAS Connector Advanced Configuration

You can further fine-tune the Dynamic RAS Connector by using the properties explained in the following section. Some of the property pages (Schedule, Delivery Restrictions, Connected Sites, and Address Space property pages) are also discussed earlier in this chapter.

MTA Override Property Page

You can use the MTA Override property page to define connector-specific connection values. Values specified here override the values specified in the Messaging Defaults property page in the MTA Site Configuration Properties window. You do not generally need to alter these values.

Internet Mail Service

The following table lists the advantages and disadvantages to using the Internet Mail Service:

Advantages	*Disadvantages*
Gives you a lot of control over the maximum message size and which users can use it.	Messages have to be converted from the Exchange internal format to the SMTP format, which decreases performance.
Supports existing TCP/IP and SMTP backbone networks.	Can create bottlenecks when a lot of traffic between two sites is routed through two machines.
	Connections cannot be scheduled.

You should choose the Internet Mail Service if

- You want to connect two sites over an existing SMTP backbone.
- You have an existing TCP/IP connection between the sites, and you want to configure a backup connector between two sites to improve fault tolerance.

Using the Internet Mail Service, you can connect two Exchange sites within an organization and then use Directory Replication over the IMS. You can connect the sites, for example, over the Internet, but doing so is not recommended for the following reasons:

Security. Connections over the Internet, especially using the SMTP message format, are highly insecure. You can, however, use the Exchange advanced security features to minimize the risk of security violations, but you should still be aware of this risk.

Security

Bandwidth. You are sharing the Internet with thousands of other users, and you can never be sure that your connection will be reserved a sufficient amount of bandwidth.

Performance

Control. Because the Internet is a collection of networks administered by many different companies and institutions, none of which is responsible for the whole Internet, you have no control over whether the link is available.

18

CONNECTING TO OTHER EXCHANGE SITES

> **NOTE**
>
> If you have an existing permanent TCP/IP connection between two sites, in most cases you should use the X.400 connector to connect the sites. The X.400 connector supports direct TCP/IP connections as well and is much more efficient than the IMS. You should use the IMS as a connector between two sites only in cases where you want to use an existing SMTP backbone network to connect the sites.

This chapter does not provide any information on how you configure the Internet Mail Service. The procedure is essentially the same as when you use the IMS to connect your Exchange system to another SMTP system, which is discussed in detail in Chapter 16, "Connecting to Other Mail Systems." The only difference when using the IMS to connect two sites within an organization is that you have to define the remote site in the Connected Sites property page so that you can configure the Directory Replication Connector over the IMS.

Summary

Selecting a connector to connect two sites within an Exchange organization is one of the most important and difficult tasks that faces an administrator configuring an Exchange system. Take the following steps to perform the selection and configuration:

1. Assess your needs—how much message traffic there will be between the two sites and how you want to control the traffic.
2. Find out the network connections available between the two sites, if any.
3. Select the connector that will meet your needs and update the network connections if necessary.
4. Install and configure the connector.

The most important thing to remember is that you can always change the connector if it does not suit your needs. Therefore, you should always start with the Site Connector if your connection supports its use. Later you can move on and use the X.400 Connector, if necessary. The Dynamic RAS Connector and the Internet Connector should only be used as backup connectors, or in the case of the RAS Connector, if you have only a dial-up connection between the two sites.

After you have successfully installed and configured the messaging connector between the sites, you can configure the directory replication connector, which is detailed in the following chapter.

Configuring Directory Replication

by Kimmo Bergius

Revised by Kevin Kaufmann

IN THIS CHAPTER

CHAPTER 19

A Microsoft Exchange organization is a collection of servers and sites that share the same directory. A Microsoft Exchange directory is an X.500-based database that contains information about the objects within an Exchange organization. All the servers within a site and within an organization contain practically the same objects and information. All the directories are equal, with none of them being the master directory. The Exchange directory architecture is based on a multiple master directory model.

The service that maintains the directory is called the Directory Service (DS). This service is also responsible for replicating changes to other servers and sites.

In order to update and maintain all the directories within an organization at the same level, Exchange utilizes a feature called *directory replication. Replication* means that changes made to one of the directories will be replicated—that is, copied to other servers. Directory replication is done using two different methods within an Exchange organization: the first method is used within a site and the second between sites. Replication within a site is called *intrasite replication* and replication between sites is called *intersite replication.*

When you have installed a server into an existing site, directory replication to the other servers within a site is configured automatically. Directory replication between two sites has to be configured manually by the administrator after the messaging connector connecting the two sites has been configured (see Chapter 18, "Connecting to Other Exchange Sites").

Directory Replication Within a Site

The DS takes care of directory replication between servers in a single site. The DS on one server uses *remote procedure calls (RPCs)* to communicate directly with the DS on another server.

Directory replication between two servers in the same site is configured automatically when you install a new server to an existing site. The automatic configuration is done during the installation program and is based on the name of an existing server that the administrator supplies during the installation (see Figure 19.1).

FIGURE 19.1.

Entering information about the existing server.

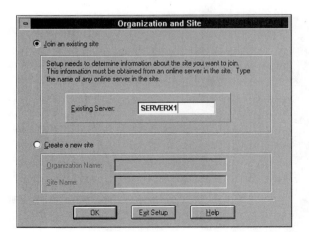

NOTE

Troubleshooting

There are two main reasons why the installation might fail:

1. The user supplies incorrect information for the Service Account. This will prevent the startup of the local Exchange services and will also prevent the DS from connecting to the existing server if you are installing a server to an existing site.

2. Server TCP/IP settings are incorrect (you have not specified the correct information in the Network program under the Control Panel) or the information contained in the DNS server is incorrect.

If setup fails, please confirm first that you have specified the correct information for the Service Account, and then that the TCP/IP settings in the local server and on the DNS server are correct.

After the installation program has finished copying the necessary files onto the server, it will start the core services. The DS on the new server connects to the DS on the existing server and adds itself to the existing server's directory. Then the DS downloads a partial copy of the contents of the directory database from the existing server. This partial copy contains all other objects except the recipients. The recipient information is not downloaded, because it can take a considerable amount of time, and the installing administrator probably would not like to wait for hours for the installation to be completed. A complete copy of the directory is replicated to the new server when it is started for the first time after installation.

Knowledge Consistency Check (KCC)

All the servers within a site maintain a list of servers that they should replicate information to (REPS-TO) and a list of servers they should receive replicated information from (REPS-FROM). Architecture These lists are used during the replication process to verify that the updated directory information is sent to all the servers within the site. All the servers should maintain an up-to-date list of the servers within a site. To check the validity of the lists, a server uses a function called Knowledge Consistency Check (KCC). There are actually two processes within the KCC: one used to check knowledge on servers in the local site (intrasite KCC) and the other to check knowledge of other sites (intersite KCC; see "Directory Replication Between Sites" later in this chapter).

During a KCC, the local server checks the lists for servers within its own site that it is aware of and then connects to the other servers one by one. After a connection to a remote server has been established, the local server checks whether its own REPS-TO and REPS-FROM lists contain the same servers as the lists on the remote server. If the lists do not match, the local server adds the new information into its own lists. Then the local server establishes a connection to the next server it is aware of and so on, until it has checked the REPS-FROM and REPS-TO lists against the lists on all other servers within the site. When the lists are up-to-date, they can be used as server lists for directory replication and thus confirm that all updates in the directory will be replicated to all servers within the site.

By default, the KCC is run once every day, but you can run it manually by selecting Check Now in the Directory Service property window under the server container (see Figure 19.2). You should run the KCC manually only if you want to speed up the process of identifying new servers within the site or if you suspect that something has gone wrong with the normal directory replication.

FIGURE 19.2.

Running the Knowledge Consistency Check manually.

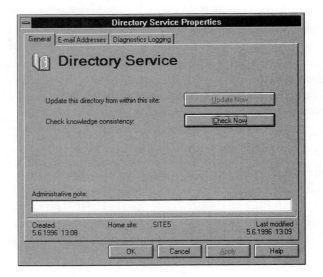

Directory Replication Within a Site

When you make a change to the directory on one server, that particular server (Server A) is responsible for replicating the change to all the other servers within the site. After the change has been committed to the directory, Server A waits for a certain period of time, called the *directory latency time,* before it starts replicating the change to the other servers. This delay will force the DS to wait for any other updates and then replicate them all at the same time. The latency time is defined in the registry and can be changed using the NT Registry Editor, but generally there is no reason to change the time. By default, the directory latency time is set to 5 minutes.

> **TIP**
>
> Because of the replication latency time, updates to a particular server will not be effective in other servers right away. You should be aware of this and allow some time for directory replication to work, before starting to wonder why replication or the system in general does not work properly. An Exchange administrator's most valuable asset is a lot of patience!

After the latency time has expired, Server A checks the REPS-TO list and establishes a connection to the first server on the list (Server B) to inform that a change has occurred in the directory on Server A. After this, Server A waits for a specified time, called the *replicator notify pause,* before informing the next server of the change to give Server B enough time to get the updates from Server A. By default, the replicator notify pause is set to 30 seconds.

When Server B is informed by Server A that a change has occurred in Server A's directory, it will check in its own directory for the latest change it has received from Server A. This check is done using *update sequence numbers (USN).* Each object in the directory has a USN, and each server also has a USN. When you change an object in the local directory, the change will set the object's USN to a number that is the server's USN + 1, and then increment the server's USN by 1. Additionally, each server in the site maintains a list of all other servers and the corresponding USNs that were valid during the last directory replication from the particular server.

When Server A informs Server B of changes in its local directory, it will also send Server B its own server USN. Server B will then compare this to the list it maintains on other servers in the site, and will request from Server A all objects that have a USN greater than the one saved in its own list (see Figure 19.3). The request is sent to Server A; the DS on Server A establishes a connection to the DS on Server B, uploads the requested information, and updates its own USN on the list on Server B. Now all objects on Server A with a USN equal to or smaller than the server USN have been replicated to Server B.

FIGURE 19.3.

Replication within a site.

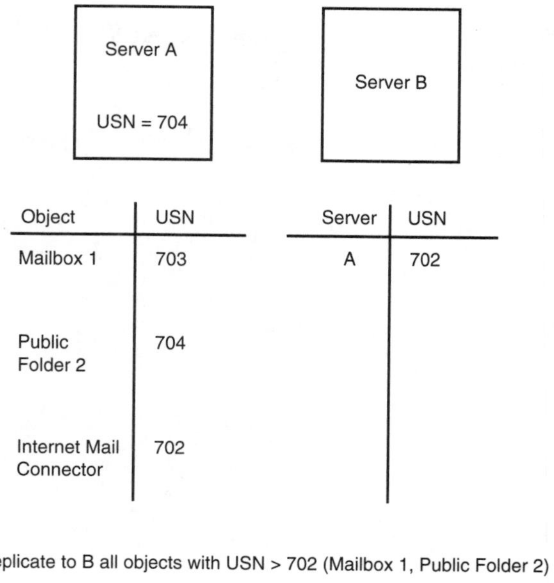

A will replicate to B all objects with USN > 702 (Mailbox 1, Public Folder 2)

Deleted Objects

When you delete an object—for example, a mailbox—from the directory, the directory marks the object as deleted; an object that is marked as deleted is referred to as a *tombstone object*. The tombstone object has a normal USN and is replicated to all the other servers just like any other object, which is how the Exchange servers learn that the object has been deleted. A tombstone object cannot be seen from the Exchange Client or the Exchange Admin program.

All these complicated functions ensure that the directories on all the servers within a site are kept up-to-date. The functions also ensure fault tolerance. When new servers are added to the site, one of the existing servers is informed about the new server, which starts directory replication immediately to the new server. Through the Knowledge Consistency Check, knowledge of the new server will be propagated to other servers within the site. Furthermore, the USNs ensure that all updates will be replicated to all servers within the site. Even if a server is down for a long period of time, it will receive all updated information as soon as it comes back up.

Directory Service Site Configuration

One of the first things you should configure after you have installed the first server into a new site is the DS Site Configuration. This object can be found under the site's Configuration container, and it contains two settings that affect directory replication: the *tombstone lifetime* and the *garbage collection interval* (see Figure 19.4).

Figure 19.4.

The DS Site Configuration Properties window.

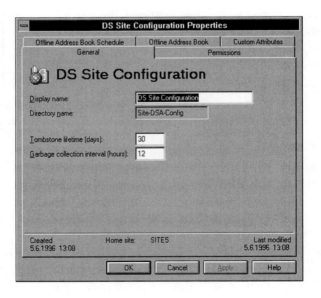

Tombstone lifetime defines the time that tombstones are kept in the directory. By default, the time is 30 days. You should define a time long enough so that the tombstone object (and thus the deletion of an object) can be replicated to all servers within the organization. When a particular tombstone object expires, it is deleted from the directory during a function called *garbage collection.*

The garbage collection interval is how often Directory Service should look for and delete expired tombstone objects from the directory.

Configuration of Directory Replication Within a Site

Even though directory replication within a site is configured and run automatically, there are a few settings affecting replication that you should be aware of. Most of these settings can't be set through the administration program, but rather are set in the NT Registry.

> **NOTE**
>
> If you are not sure how to change the settings in the NT Registry or are unsure about the effects of a particular change, do not change the settings. A faulty setting can prevent NT or one of the Exchange services from starting.

All the Registry keys that affect the Directory Service and replication are located under the following subtree (see Figure 19.5):

```
HKEY_LOCAL_MACHINE\System\CurrentControlSet\Services\MSExchangeDS\
```

FIGURE 19.5.

Directory Service parameters in the Registry.

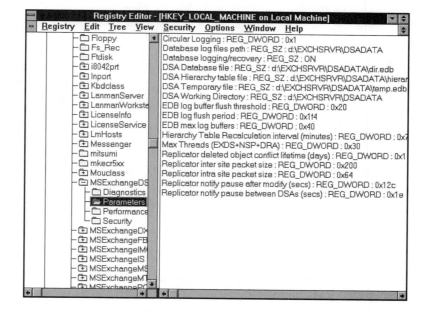

19

CONFIGURING DIRECTORY REPLICATION

In general, you do not need to change the values of the registry keys. You can, however, use them to locate the directory files and fine-tune your environment. The directory latency time (mentioned earlier in the chapter) is Replicator notify pause after modify (secs) and the replicator notify pause is Replicator notify pause between DSAs(secs).

Directory Replication Between Sites

Replication between two sites is different from replication within a single site. The Directory Service on one server does not communicate directly with the DS on another server. Instead, the replication information is passed between the sites as normal e-mail messages by a messaging connector. You need to configure a directory replication connector between two sites to take care of creating the replication messages and passing them over to the messaging connector and on to the other site. Furthermore, you can define a schedule for replication, which cannot be done for replication within a site.

> **NOTE**
>
> Before you configure a directory replication connector between two sites, you have to configure a messaging connector (see Chapter 18) and make sure that the connector works—that is, that you can send normal e-mail messages in both directions over the connector. You can check the operation of a messaging connector by sending mail to a user in the other site using the user's full X.400 address. Once the messaging connector works, you can go on to define the replication connector.

Replication Bridgehead Server

The servers within a site do not replicate their own changes to all the other servers in the other sites in the organization. When you configure the replication connector between two sites, you also select one of the servers in each of the sites to take care of replication between the sites. These servers are called *directory replication bridgehead servers*. All other servers within a site replicate the changes to objects in their directories to the bridgehead server, normally using the method for intrasite replication. The local bridgehead server is responsible for replicating the information to the specified replication bridgehead server in the remote site. Only one server in a site can be responsible for replication to another site. There can be multiple bridgehead servers within a site, if the site is connected to multiple remote sites. One server can, however, be responsible for directory replication to several different sites.

Contrary to messaging connectors, you cannot have two directory replication connectors between two sites. Furthermore, the directory replication connections are transitive, which means that you do not and cannot have two different replication paths between two sites. Consider an example of three sites: A, B, and C. You define a replication connector between A and B and A and C. After this, you cannot configure a further replication connector between sites C and B, because there already exists a replication path from B to C via A (see Figure 19.6).

FIGURE 19.6.

Directory replication links between sites.

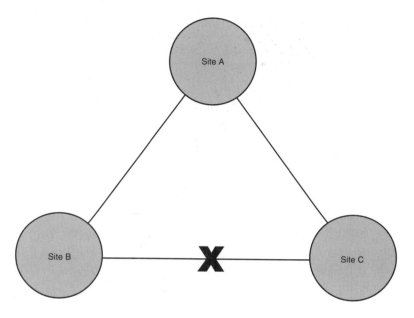

At a quick glance this would seem like a bad thing, considering fault tolerance. The replication connectors are, however, just a definition that defines which server is responsible for creating the replication messages and to which server in the remote site they are sent. The directory replication information is sent as messages using the normal messaging connectors between the sites, of which there can be several. This provides fault tolerance and on the other hand simplifies configuration, because the defined message transport paths are used for all communication between sites—even directory information. The route for a replication message is chosen exactly the same way as the route for a normal, interpersonal mail message.

Replication Connector Topology

The basic rule applied to configuring messaging connectors can also be applied to configuring directory replication connectors: you should try to minimize the amount of hops that replicated directory information has to make from any source to any destination. The directory replication connector topology in an organization does not have to be exactly the same as the messaging connector topology, but usually this makes life a lot easier. For example, you could configure a directory replication connector between two sites, even though these sites have not been directly connected using any messaging connector. This would, however, mean that the directory replication messages between these two sites (as well as normal message traffic) would travel via a third site.

Consider the following example: You have an organization with four sites, A through D (see Figure 19.7). The ideal configuration for directory replication information would be to choose one of the sites—for example site A—to act as a "hub" for directory replication. This means that you would define three directory replication connectors: A to B, A to C, and A to D. In

19

CONFIGURING
DIRECTORY
REPLICATION

this configuration, any replicated directory information would have to travel over two hops at the most.

FIGURE 19.7.

Directory replication links between four sites.

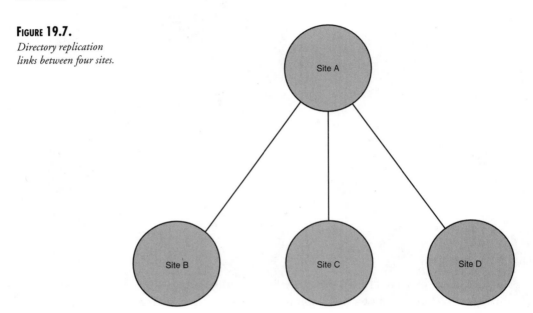

Before configuring the directory replication connectors within an organization, you should always consider the way the messaging connectors are configured. Consider again the example in Figure 19.7. What if the sites are connected to a chain using site connectors, A to B to C to D? If you configured the replication connectors in the already mentioned way (A to B, A to C, and A to D), the replication of a change in a server in site D to a server in site C would mean that the bridgehead server on site D would create a directory replication message and send it first to site A. The message would travel over three messaging connector hops. The bridgehead server on site A would then create another replication message and send it to the bridgehead server on site C, and the message would travel over a further two messaging connector hops (see Figure 19.8, example 1). Thus, the replication process would load the system unnecessarily.

If you instead defined the replication connectors similarly to the messaging connectors, A to B, B to C, and C to D (see Figure 19.8, example 2), the furthest a replication message would have to travel is three messaging connector hops (from D to A). Directory replication would not load the system as much as in example 1. The directory replication schedule for the different bridgehead servers is critical in this configuration (see "Directory Replication Connector Schedule," later in this chapter).

FIGURE 19.8.
Directory replication links and messaging connectors.

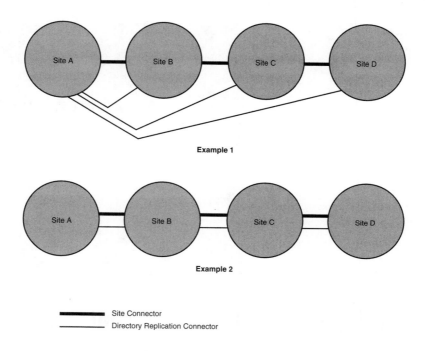

Example 1

Example 2

━━━━━ Site Connector
───── Directory Replication Connector

To summarize, there are two rules to designing a directory replication topology:

1. Minimize the amount of hops over which directory replication messages have to be transported.
2. Consider the underlying messaging-connector topology.

Connected Sites

If the messaging connector used to connect the two sites is an X.400 Connector, Dynamic RAS Connector, or the Internet Mail Service (for more details on the different connectors, see Chapter 18), you will have to define the remote site in the connector's Connected Sites property page. Otherwise, the replication connector will not be able to use the messaging connector to transport the replication messages. Only the site directly at the other end of the messaging connector has to be defined on the Connected Sites page (see Figure 19.9). The DS will get information on all other sites within the organization through the Knowledge Consistency Check. You do not have to define the connected sites for the site connector, where this information is configured automatically.

19

CONFIGURING
DIRECTORY
REPLICATION

FIGURE 19.9.

The Connected Sites property page.

Configuring the Directory Replication Connector

Configure the Directory Replication Connector between two sites with the following steps:

1. Select New Other from the File menu, and then Directory Replication Connector. If you are not in the Directory Replication container under the site configuration container, the Administrator program will ask whether you want to switch to this container. Select OK.

2. The New Directory Replication Connector window appears (see Figure 19.10). This window lists the sites for which you can configure a new directory replication connector. Type the name of the server that is to be used as the replication bridgehead server in the remote site.

FIGURE 19.10.

The New Directory Replication Connector window.

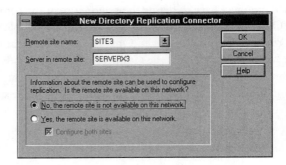

3. If you have an available network connection to the server in the remote site (for example, you are using a site connector) and you have administration rights on the remote server, you can choose to configure a replication connector to both servers at the same time. In such a case, first select Yes, the remote site is available on this network, and then configure both sites. The Directory Replication Connector Properties window appears (see Figure 19.11).

FIGURE 19.11.

The Directory Replication Connector Properties window.

4. The program will show a default directory and display name in the appropriate fields. You can change these names if you want. Use a name that will identify the remote site to which the replication connector is connected.

5. Go to the Schedule property page and change the replication schedule if necessary (see the section "Directory Replication Connector Schedule," later in this chapter). The default is that replication will occur every 3 hours.

6. Choose OK.

If you chose to configure both sites in step 3, the Directory Replication Connector is now ready for use, and directory replication between the two sites should start. If you didn't choose to configure both sites, you have to perform steps 1 through 6 in the remote site as well, before the replication connector is properly configured.

Directory Replication Connector Schedule

Unlike directory replication within a site, replication between two sites can be scheduled. The schedule is defined using the Schedule property page (see Figure 19.12) on the Directory Replication Connector property window (the Directory Replication Connector object is located in the Directory Replication container under the Site Configuration container).

19

CONFIGURING DIRECTORY REPLICATION

> **NOTE**
>
> Delivery of the replication messages is dependent on the schedule of the replication connector and the schedule of the messaging connector transporting the replication messages. In a multisite organization, the messaging connector schedules should be considered when designing the replication schedules.

FIGURE 19.12.

The Schedule property page.

You should consider the organization as a whole when defining the directory replication connector schedules. Consider the examples in Figure 19.8, example 2, an Exchange organization with four sites. If you schedule each of the directory replication connectors to replicate the information once a day, it might take three days to replicate a change to all sites within the organization. Of course, this configuration and delay in replicating the changes is perfectly OK, as long as all of the administrators are aware of the delay.

How Replication Between Sites Works

Architecture   The basis of directory replication between sites lies in the intrasite replication within a site. All information regarding the site and the servers it contains is replicated to all the servers in the site—and thus also to the replication bridgehead server responsible for replication between two sites. The bridgehead server will then replicate all changed objects on to the other site. Replication within a site must work properly so that the bridgehead server has a complete picture of the site. Then all information will be replicated to the remote site as well.

Directory replication between sites works on a pull basis. This means that the replication bridgehead server will request updated information from the remote site, based on the defined replication schedule. The replication bridgehead server in the remote site never sends updates to the local site if it has not been asked to do so. The bridgehead servers use USNs to determine which objects have been updated since the last replication, much in the same way as for intrasite replication.

During the configuration of the directory replication connector, basic information about the remote site will be added to the local directory. The Administrator program will show the name of the remote site and a Configuration container for the site. This information has to exist before any further directory replication can occur. The Configuration container for the remote site will, however, be empty and no actual configuration information for the remote site will exist at the local site.

> **NOTE**
>
> When you configure a directory replication connector, the name of the remote site should appear in the administrator program within a few minutes. Sometimes it may happen that even after some time, no other configuration information will appear under the configuration container. This generally means that the messaging connector between the two sites is not working properly. If this is the case, check the messaging connector.
>
> You can check where the directory replication messages are stuck by opening the Message Transfer Agent object under your local server name in the Administrator program and then opening the Queues page. The queue list will show all outgoing queues, including the one to the remote site. If the connector to the remote site shows items sent by the DS, the messaging connector does not work properly.

Depending on the schedule defined in the directory replication connector's Schedule property page, the local site might request all updated and new information from the remote site. The replication bridgehead server on the remote site will create a replication message containing the requested information and send it to the local bridgehead server. When the local server receives the replication message, it will be passed on to the local Directory Service, which will add the information to the server's own directory. Then the information about the remote site will be replicated on to the other servers in the local site, using the normal intrasite-replication method.

Now the local site has basically the same information as the remote site. In a multisite organization, the next step is the Knowledge Consistency Check. Recall that the KCC consists of two functions: the intrasite consistency check, which checks whether the local server knows about all the servers within its own site, and the intersite consistency check, which checks whether the information replicated from a remote site contains information about any other sites. If it finds information about a site it is not previously aware of, it updates its internal REPS-FROM list and creates the new site name container, and an empty Configuration container will appear in the Administrator program. After this, the local site will start request updates for both sites.

The KCC is run automatically only once a day, which might affect the time it takes for new sites and their information to appear in remote sites. You can force the server to run the KCC by opening the Directory Service page under the local server in the Administrator program and clicking Check Now on the General page. This will run the KCC immediately and add knowledge of all new sites so directory replication can occur.

After the local server has received the directories from the local site for the first time, normal directory replication starts. At scheduled times, the replication connector will request information from other directly connected sites and will receive information on all updated objects.

Configuration Steps in a Multiple-Site Environment

This example explains the replication configuration steps in an organization consisting of three sites: A, B, and C (see Figure 19.13). The sites have been connected so that sites A and B are connected via a site connector, and sites A and C are connected using an X.400 connector over an X.400 backbone network. Furthermore, a backup connection has been defined between all the sites using the Dynamic RAS Connector. Because the main messaging connectors are configured so that message traffic flows through site A, this site will also be used as the hub for directory replication. All messaging connectors have been configured and tested. The next task is to define two directory-replication connectors.

FIGURE 19.13.

A sample configuration.

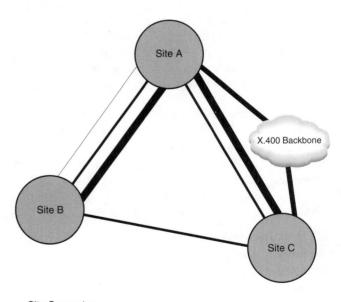

The directory replication connectors are configured by doing the following steps (all the configuration steps should be performed on the replication bridgehead server on each site):

1. Define a directory replication connector from site A to site B. Because these sites are connected using an RPC-capable link, you can configure the directory replication connector to both sites at the same time. Use the Always option in the replication connector's Schedule property page, so that replication will start immediately. When you look at the configuration on the bridgehead server on site A, it should show the name and an empty configuration container for site B and vice versa. After a few minutes, the rest of the configuration information should appear as well.

   Now site A has a full copy of site B's directory, and vice versa.

2. Next, define a directory replication connector between sites A and C. Because these sites are connected over an X.400 network, you have to configure the replication connector separately to the bridgehead server in each site. Before you add the replication connector, check that the remote site has been defined in the local site's X.400 Connectors Connected Sites property page. Again, select Always for the schedule for the replication connectors.

   After a few minutes, the remote site name and configuration container should be seen in the Administrator program. After a few more minutes (depending on the X.400 Connector's schedule), the rest of the configuration information should be replicated.

   Now site A has a full copy of site B's directory, and vice versa. The next task is to make B and C aware of each other.

3. In site C, open the Directory Service object under the bridgehead server and select Check Now on the General property page. This will run the KCC on site C. KCC will check the information received from site A and discover a new site: site B. KCC will then add the new site and a configuration container into the Administrator program and start directory replication to site B via site A. After some time, complete information about site B will appear on site C.

4. Now go back to site B and open the Directory Replication Connector object under the Directory Replication container. Open the Sites page, select site A from the Inbound Sites list, and select Request Now. A dialog box will appear asking for the request type. Select Update only new and modified items. This will request site A to send all new directory information to site B.

5. After the directory replication has occurred, open the Directory Service object under the bridgehead server on site B and select Check Now on the General property page. This will run the KCC on site B. KCC will check the information received from site A and discover a new site: site C. KCC will then add the new site and a configuration container in the Administrator program and start directory replication to site C via site A. After some time, complete information about site C will appear on site B.

Now all the sites know about each other, and normal directory replication can start. You can now change the Replication Connector Schedule to the one you want to use normally.

In the preceding steps, you used forced directory replication. Of course, you could just set the replication connector's schedule to whatever you want it to be and wait for replication to occur. Also, the KCCs on different sites will be run automatically and thus new replication links be configured. Forcing replication speeds the process and makes it easier for the administrator to verify that replication works.

Forcing Directory Replication Between Sites

Normally, directory replication between sites occurs according to a schedule specified in the Directory Replication Connector's property window. You can, however, force directory replication to occur between two sites by opening the Directory Replication Connector's property window and selecting the Sites page (see Figure 19.14). This page will show all sites from which this replication connector should receive information and the sites where replication information should be sent via this site. You can manually request an update on a certain site's information by selecting the site in the Inbound Sites list and by clicking Request Now.

> **NOTE**
>
> When forcing a manual replication with Request Now, you should always select the option to update only new and modified items. The Refresh all items in the directory option can cause a copy of all objects to be re-sent to your site and cause significant network traffic.

FIGURE 19.14.

The Sites property page.

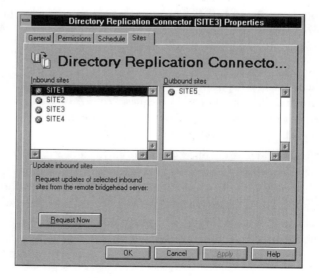

Removing a Directory Replication Connector

You might have to remove a directory replication connector if, for example, a site is deleted from the organization. The connector can be removed by simply selecting the right connector under the Directory Replication container and selecting Delete from the Edit menu (or by pressing Del).

After you have removed the connector, all information about the sites should be removed as well. This will be done automatically in time, but you can force it by running the KCC manually. If you will never replicate to that site again, you should also run the IS/DS Consistency check that can be found on the General property page in the server's property window.

> **NOTE**
>
> Running the IS/DS consistency check will re-home any public folders that were created in the remote site to your local site and remove all the mailboxes from the remote site that have any access to the public folder.

Summary

In this chapter, you learned about directory replication within a site and between sites. All servers within an Exchange organization share the same directory. In order to accomplish this, changes to the directory have to be replicated across the whole organization. This is accomplished by two functions: directory replication within a site (intrasite) and directory replication from site to site (intersite). The first function is automatic and requires no configuration from the administrator. The latter function depends on directory replication connectors configured on top of messaging connectors that are discussed in Chapter 18. Configuring a replication connector is relatively simple, and the only thing that the administrator has to consider is the path upon which the replication is done over an organization. The simple rule to accomplish efficient replication is to follow the shortest path possible, much in the same way as for a messaging connector.

The Exchange directory cannot be replicated to another system at present, and it is even impossible to replicate the directory to another Exchange organization. Eventually, the Exchange Directory will be compatible with, and ultimately replaced by, the new Windows NT Active Directory. It is, however, possible to replicate part of the directory information, the information on recipients, to a Microsoft Mail system. This can be done using a function called *directory synchronization,* which is discussed in the next chapter.

Future Directions

19

CONFIGURING DIRECTORY REPLICATION

IN THIS PART

IV
PART

Administration

Directory Synchronization with Microsoft Mail

by Robert Henriksen

IN THIS CHAPTER

CHAPTER 20

Directory synchronization is a key tool in implementing your migration from Microsoft Mail. Even if you're migrating only a single MSMail post office to Exchange, you should plan on setting up both systems to run concurrently. This allows you to roll the MSMail mailboxes over to Exchange gradually, without the Exchange mailboxes being cut off from the legacy MSMail system. Shifting a few Microsoft Mail users to Exchange for a test period helps determine whether your fundamental configuration decisions are sound for your company. If you discover, for example, that you need to go back and rename the Exchange organization and site (that is, tear down the Exchange server(s) and rebuild them), you'll have to displace only a few user mailboxes.

Electronic mail has become so crucial to everyday business that it's rarely worth the risk to do a crash conversion. Directory synchronization, combined with a message transfer agent (External or the MSMail Connector), is the tool that will enable you to conduct a controlled migration. Running MSMail and Exchange concurrently enables you to schedule the work of conducting the migration into manageable stages, rather than attempting the crushing job of reconfiguring every mail client and conducting training for all users at once. Even if you'll be doing a crash conversion of mailboxes, connecting the systems will let you perform plenty of testing in a production environment before committing the bulk of your users.

In addition to supporting testing and migration, setting up directory synchronization is necessary if you want to replace the old Microsoft SMTP Gateway with an Exchange Server running the Internet Mail Service to service your MSMail users. See Chapter 11, "Migrating from Microsoft Mail," and Chapter 17, "The Internet Mail Service."

The Exchange Server has to know what MSMail mailboxes exist, and where they are, before it can accept inbound SMTP messages for them. Populating the Exchange GAL with Custom Recipients for the MSMail mailboxes gives Exchange that information. Although you could achieve the same effect by doing an manual import of MSMail directory information into the Exchange GAL, it's safer to have directory synchronization happening automatically on a nightly basis to ensure that the two directories are accurate.

NOTE

If you are currently using the Workgroup edition of Microsoft Mail—the copy that is bundled with Windows for Workgroups, Windows95, or Windows NT—directory synchronization isn't available. You use the Migration Wizard bundled with Exchange Server to create accounts *en masse* on Exchange from your workgroup post office. See Chapter 11 for details on using Migration Wizard.

This chapter starts with an overview of the directory synchronization process (*DirSync* from here on) for the single post office administrators. There'll also be a description of leveraging Exchange's strengths in a large, far-flung MSMail deployment. From there, you'll explore the two ways Exchange can be incorporated into DirSync with Microsoft Mail post offices, then walk through the configuration of each method. You'll learn how to manually fire a DirSync cycle for testing purposes, instead of having to wait for the scheduled time. I'll outline the most common, straightforward configurations to get you up and running, and highlight the pitfalls and shortcuts along the way.

Directory Synchronization Overview

This book does not attempt to cover the exact procedure of implementing directory synchronization on the Microsoft Mail side. The *Mail 3.5 Administrator's Guide* covers DirSync in two chapters. The configuration parameters for the post offices are laid out in Chapter 9, "Global Directory Synchronization," but the configuration of the *dispatch* program, which is required for DirSync to occur, isn't explained until Chapter 14, "The Dispatch Program."

Here's what I wish the Microsoft Mail documentation had laid out up front about directory synchronization:

- Microsoft Mail post offices are simply passive shared directories on a file server. They are incapable of performing any actions whatsoever—they are not programs, or active code of any sort.

- For messages to be transferred between post offices, a program called EXTERNAL must be running at all times. External is a Message Transfer Agent (MTA). It checks the outbound directory of every PO it is responsible for on a scheduled basis (usually every five minutes). It performs the actual transfer of messages between post offices. External runs on a dedicated computer (in MSMail 3.2 and older), or alternately as a service on an NT computer (in Microsoft Mail 3.5).

- A second program must also be running continuously in order to perform the directory synchronization functions: DISPATCH. Like External, Dispatch can run on either a dedicated computer (in MSMail 3.2 and older) or as a service on an NT computer (in MSMail 3.5). Dispatch does not actually perform the procedures described in the following numbered list; Dispatch simply watches the clock and triggers a program called, simply, NSDA when scheduled to do so. NSDA, in turn, spawns the appropriate utility programs to perform the actual work of directory synchronization.

  You can think of NSDA as the general contractor of the DirSync operation. The utilities reqmain.exe, import.exe, and rebuild.exe are the subcontractors that actually do the work.

- Separate Global Address Lists (GALs) exist on each MSMail post office and Exchange server. It is possible for the different GALs to contain different information, either by design (excluding entries from the DirSync cycle) or due to DirSync problems.

For the administrators not already using MSMail DirSync, here's the big picture. DirSync is a three-step process, typically scheduled to occur automatically each evening. All participating

20

DIRECTORY SYNCHRONIZATION WITH MS MAIL

Mail post offices act as DirSync requestors. One of the POs also does double-duty as the DirSync server. (See Figure 20.1.) The three steps are referred to by Microsoft documentation as T1, T2, and T3:

T1. Each requestor post office creates a list of any changes that have occurred in its own directory. This list is e-mailed to the account $System on the DirSync server post office. This T1 event fires at each requestor post office. The scheduled time for the T1 is set on a per-post office basis.

T2. The DirSync server integrates these lists of changes into a composite list of all the changes submitted from the various requestor POs. This composite list is then e-mailed back to the mailbox address of $System at each of the requestor POs. This T2 event fires only once, at the DirSync server post office.

T3. The requestor POs each import their copy of this composite list of changes and rebuild their individual copies of the Global Address List (GAL), thus incorporating the changes that have occurred across all the post offices. This T3 event fires at each requestor post office, just like the T1.

FIGURE 20.1.

Overview of the directory synchroniza-tion process.

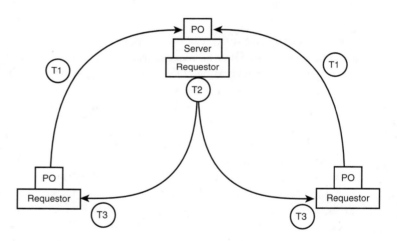

There are two choices on how to integrate Exchange Server into a Microsoft Mail DirSync routine:

■ You can make an Exchange Server the DirSync server for your MSMail network.

■ You can configure the Exchange Server to function as a DirSync requestor in an existing MSMail network.

I believe the clear winner is to make Exchange the DirSync server because of the enhanced reporting and logging functions of Exchange—not to mention the overall robustness of the product. If you have only one post office now, it's a no-brainer. If you already have DirSync in place between multiple POs, the deciding factor will be how many requestor POs you would have to reconfigure to use Exchange as the new DirSync server for the organization. Depending upon how large your installation is, you might decide to forgo the benefits of an Exchange DirSync server for ease of integration with a large existing system. Personally, even if I had as many as a few dozen Microsoft Mail post offices, I'd switch them over to use Exchange's DirSync server.

NOTE

Exchange Server does not perform all the duties of the Microsoft Mail Dispatch program. You will still need to have an instance of Dispatch running to service the MSMail side of directory synchronization (steps T1 and T3, assuming you've decided to use Exchange as your DirSync Server). Alternately, you can use a batch file running on the Exchange server to perform the same functions as Dispatch (an example batch file is included on the *Unleashed* CD-ROM).

As discussed in Chapter 11, you can use the MSMail Connector to perform MTA for all your MSMail post offices, negating the need for the MSMail External program.

The previous discussion assumed that you're integrating a single Microsoft Mail DirSync deployment with an Exchange Organization structure—one link exists between the two. It is also possible to better manage DirSync messaging traffic across WAN links between widespread MSMail post offices by backboning Microsoft Mail DirSync traffic across Exchange site connectors. There can be only one Exchange server per site participating in MSMail DirSync—as a requestor or server, it doesn't matter. However, deploying the DirSync software on a single server within each site in your organization is fine. (See Figure 20.2.)

FIGURE 20.2.

Backboning MSMail DirSync traffic over Exchange site connectors.

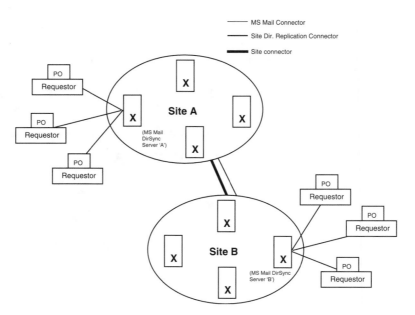

20

DIRECTORY SYNCHRONIZATION WITH MS MAIL

Using this backboning technique allows you to keep the MSMail DirSync traffic localized for the post offices in a particular Exchange Site, and the Exchange directory replication traffic between sites will include the information on each site's custom recipients for MSMail users.

Configuring Exchange as the DirSync Server

> **NOTE**
>
> To configure and begin using MSMail Directory Synchronization, you must already have installed and configured the MSMail Connector (see Chapter 11). DirSync passes the directory information between post offices via mail messages. Therefore, DirSync can't occur without functional message transfer between post offices.

Launch the Exchange Administrator Program and open the Site | Connections container (see Figure 20.3).

FIGURE 20.3.

The Exchange Administrator Connections Container.

Now, select File | New Other | DirSync Server (see Figure 20.4).

FIGURE 20.4.

Adding a DirSync server.

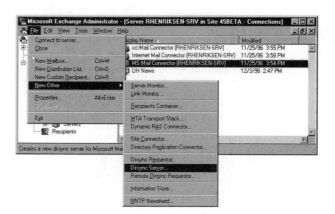

You should now have the Properties dialog box open, as shown in Figure 20.5. Type a name for this DirSync server. Because you can have only a single DirSync Server per Exchange site, I recommend using some form of the Site name (for example, DXA-Site1). Then click the DirSync Administrator button and select a mailbox for the DirSync Administrator. The simplest choice is to use yourself for all the various Administrator addresses until you get settled. Then, as needed, you can go back and reassign responsibilities for these various reporting functions to other people. There are no complications from changing the Administrator role for DirSync after the initial configuration.

FIGURE 20.5.

The Directory Server Properties dialog box, General page.

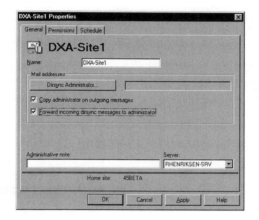

You should activate the Copy administrator on outgoing messages and Forward incoming DirSync messages to administrator flags. The latter gives you confirmation that the MSMail Dispatch program is performing step 1 of the cycle, and that those T1 requests are making it to the server (the MSMail Connector MTA is working). Copy Administrator on outgoing messages lets you know that Exchange has performed its T2 function and responded to the requestors with a composite list of directory changes.

Note that these status messages cover only steps 1 and 2—you do not receive any confirmation on whether the Mail Dispatch program has successfully performed step 3. This is still a lot more information than was delivered to you under Microsoft Mail, however. After you've settled into a routine and are comfortable that the scheduled DirSync cycles are performing properly, you can always go back and turn these flags off.

If you elect to use a scheduled batch file to fire the nightly DirSync cycle instead of using the MSMail Dispatch program, you can insert a network alert message at the end of the T3 portion of Dirsync back to your workstation, or have the batch file employ the sendmail utility (available in the BackOffice Resource Kit) to send a status message via e-mail.

TIP

If you operate in a very structured environment, you might want to have a log of each DirSync cycle. One way to do that would be to turn on a high-enough level of logging in Exchange Administrator to capture all DirSync-related activity in the Event Viewer's Application Log. A more focused method is the following:

1. Create a public folder called, for example, DirSync Log.

2. Set the permissions for this folder as Author for your account and just Reviewer for network support personnel and/or management.

3. Create an Inbox Assistant rule for your account to automatically move the DirSync status messages into this new public folder.

Now all the status messages during each evening's DirSync cycles will be dropped into this public folder. You can also create rules about the maximum age of messages retained, or maximum folder size, to keep things from getting out of hand.

Next, Select the Schedule property page (see Figure 20.6) and select the time you want the T2 function to occur.

Figure 20.6.

The Directory Server Properties dialog box, Schedule page.

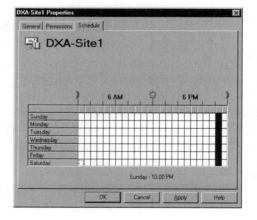

I'd suggest something simple like Table 20.1.

Table 20.1. Directory synchronization schedule.

Job	Suggested Time	Responsible Program
T1	8:00 p.m.	MSMail Dispatch program/service
T2	10:00 p.m.	Exchange DirSync server service
T3	12:00 a.m.	MSMail Dispatch program/service

It's possible to select multiple times each day for Exchange to perform the T2 function, but this is of questionable value with just a few post offices. So, highlight the 10:00 p.m. bar in the Schedule page.

This is all that's required to configure Exchange as the DirSync server. Something you will definitely want to do is enable the ability to manually fire a T2 event on the Exchange Server. Without this, you'll have to wait overnight to see whether your directory synchronization is functional. Another advantage to enabling manual DirSync cycles is that you can migrate mailboxes in the middle of the day and immediately update the Mail post office GALs so that no mail gets bounced. Finally, if you want to use a batch file in place of the Dispatch program, you must enable the manual T2 function.

This modification is an originally undocumented feature of Exchange that can be found in Microsoft's Knowledge Base, article Q146738. This will require modifying the Exchange Server's Registry, with all the usual dire warnings about what a risky business that can be.

CAUTION

Using Registry Editor incorrectly can cause serious, systemwide problems that might require you to reinstall Windows NT to correct them. No one can guarantee that any problems resulting from the use of Registry Editor can be solved. Use this tool at your own risk.

Open the Registry Editor (in Program Manager, select File | Run and enter `regedt32.exe`) and locate the following key:

`HKEY_LOCAL_MACHINE\System\CurrentControlSet\Services\MSExchangeDX`

Ensure that you've highlighted the `MSExchangeDX` key and select Edit | Add Value (see Figure 20.7). Add the values as indicated in Figures 20.8 through 20.10.

FIGURE 20.7.

Adding the Registry Key for manual T2.

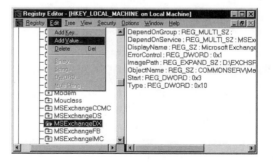

Figure 20.8.

*Enter value name and
data type as shown.*

Figure 20.9.

*Enter Data value as
shown.*

Figure 20.10.

The finished result.

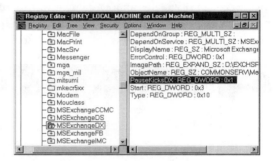

You will need to use Control Panel | Services to stop and then restart the Microsoft Exchange
Directory Synchronization service for this change to take effect. You'll use this new capability
a little later, when executing a manual DirSync cycle.

TIP

Be sure that the MSExchange Directory Synchronization Service is configured for Automatic startup, and if it is not currently running, go ahead and start it now.

Configuring MSMail DirSync Requestors

Next, you'll be either setting up anew the DirSync Requestor parameters on your MSMail post
office (if you've never used DirSync before) or reconfiguring each post office's DirSync requestor
configuration to point to the Exchange Server as its new DirSync server. The *MSMail
Administrator's Guide* walked you through this in Chapter 9, in the section "Checklist for the
Requestor Postoffice." You need to know the name of the Exchange Server Interchange PO.

To find this, go to the Exchange Administrator, Site\Connector\MSMail Connector, and look on the Local Postoffice property page (see Figure 20.11). The default is Organization name\Site name.

FIGURE 20.11.

Postoffice name for Exchange Server's MS Mail Connector PO.

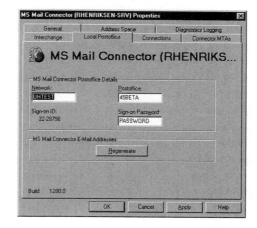

Configuring Remote DirSync Requestors

Finally, you need to tell Exchange about the MSMail requestor post office(s) that it will be hearing from every night. Go back to the Exchange Administrator and select the DirSync server you've created in the Site | Connections container. Now, select File | New Other | Remote DirSync Requestor (see Figure 20.12).

FIGURE 20.12.

Command to define a new remote DirSync requestor.

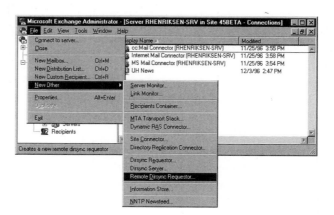

In the New Requestor dialog box (see Figure 20.13), select the desired post office. Note that you need to have already defined the Microsoft Mail post office in the MSMail Connector properties, under the Connections page. See Chapter 11 if you have not already done so.

20

DIRECTORY
SYNCHRONIZATION
WITH MS MAIL

FIGURE 20.13.

The New Requestor dialog box, selecting the post office.

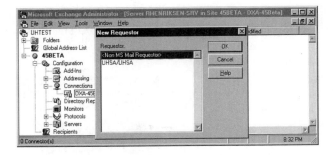

In the resulting PO Properties dialog box (see Figure 20.14), you can use the existing MSMail post office name for the Name field or a label that might be more descriptive to end users. This is something to stop and think about, because you can have this name appended to the usernames displayed in the Global Address List. This function can be useful to indicate in the GAL which mail accounts have not yet migrated to Exchange and the name of their home PO. If your post offices are serving different types of users, this could be used to label the usernames with what division they work in, for instance. It's trivial to go back and change this name (unlike some other names in Exchange), so you shouldn't let yourself come to a grinding halt over this issue.

FIGURE 20.14.

The remote DirSync Requestor Properties dialog box, General page.

You can leave Password, Requestor address type, and requestor Language well enough alone—unless you're DirSyncing with a non-English formatted post office, of course! *Do* check the Export on next cycle checkbox, to ensure that all the existing Exchange mail accounts get integrated into the MSMail GAL(s) when you run through the first DirSync cycle.

Figures 20.15 and 20.16 show the Import Container and Export Containers property pages. The Import Container page specifies which recipient container the *incoming* MSMail addresses should be added to. Because this is defined per post office requestor, this parameter enables you to separate the members of different post offices into different recipient containers, if you so want. The Export Container page specifies which containers should be included in exportation to the MSMail post office GALs. The default is to simply throw them all into the Export column, to ensure that the organization's entire GAL is exported to the MSMail system.

FIGURE 20.15.
The Import Container property page.

FIGURE 20.16.
The Export Containers property page.

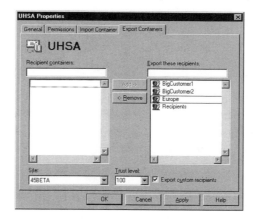

Trust levels allow a higher level of control over what recipient objects are exported during DirSync and what trust level is assigned to imported recipients—MSMail recipients have no intrinsic trust level of their own. The site-level trust value set in Figure 20.16 can be thought of as a limbo bar. For any given object within the site to be exported to the foreign mail system, it's got to get under the limbo bar. So, the trust value set at the recipient object (found in the Advanced property page of the object's Properties dialog box) must be lower than the Site-level trust value.

CAUTION

Don't remove a DirSync requestor immediately after using it to draw in MSMail custom recipients; you will instantly lose all those custom recipients if you do! The custom recipients created by directory synchronization will be lost, both from the container and from any distribution groups to which they've been added. Wait until you migrate all those users off the MSMail post office, then delete the corresponding remote DirSync requestor.

continues

20

DIRECTORY SYNCHRONIZATION WITH MS MAIL

> continued
>
> If you want to populate Exchange's GAL with just the Microsoft Mail userlist, without using regularly scheduled directory synchronization, you can use the Export/Import commands in the Exchange Admin program to manually populate the Exchange GAL. The Import function is described in Chapter 22, "User Management with Exchange."

Manual DirSync Cycle

Okay, so far you've done the following:

1. Created a DirSync server in Exchange's Site | Connections container
2. Configured the MSMail requestor post office(s) to use Exchange as their DirSync server
3. Defined the MSMail requestor post office(s) in Exchange as Remote DirSync Requestors

Now it's time to manually step through a DirSync cycle to see whether it's working properly. This can all be performed from the Exchange Server console or from an NT Workstation with an Administrator-level logon. Let's step through the T1-T2-T3 cycle for DirSync between a single MSMail post office requestor and an Exchange DirSync server:

1. Increase the frequency of the MSMail Connector MTA to every 1 minute. That way, during this DirSync testing, you won't wait long between each step. (See Figures 20.17 and 20.18.) Double-click on the MSMail Connector object in the Site | Connections container and study the figures.

FIGURE 20.17.

Connector MTAs properties. Select the appropriate MTA service and click the Configure button.

FIGURE 20.18.

Increase polling frequency (Check for Mail every) to 1 minute.

2. Open a command window and map L: to the executable share of your MSMail post office server. (NET USE L: *servername*\mailexe).

3. Map M: to the post office share *servername*\maildata.

4. Launch the MSMail admin program and do a full import and export (Admin\External-Admin\Config\Requestor\Import and \Export). This sets the stage to both populate Exchange's GAL with the contents of the Mail PO directory and draw into the Mail GAL all the current Exchange mailboxes and distribution groups. In the future, DirSync will just be swapping changes to the GAL, not each PO's entire directory. You should have already flagged the post office's remote DirSync requestor on Exchange to do a full export (refer to Figure 20.14).

5. Exit the Mail Admin program. Ensure that you're at an L:\> prompt and enter the following command:

```
reqmain -t
```

This is the T1 portion of the DirSync cycle. If you are performing these functions at a Windows NT computer, preface the command with forcedos:

```
forcedos reqmain -t
```

6. Wait a couple of minutes for the T1 e-mail message to be sent to Exchange and for Exchange to process the request. Here's a key difference between Exchange's execution of T2 and Dispatch's. As soon as the Exchange DirSync service receives a T1 message, it draws the information into the Exchange GAL. If you run an instance of Performance Monitor while testing, you can see the Exchange Server's CPU utilization spike when the T1 message hits it. So, you should see the MSMail users in the Exchange GAL within a couple of minutes of running the T1. However, Exchange does not prepare and send the response message to the requestor(s) until the scheduled time for a T2 in DirSync Server\Properties\Schedule. This is because the T2 should include the changes from *all* the post offices—so all participating post offices should send their T1 messages before the T2 fires.

20

DIRECTORY SYNCHRONIZATION WITH MS MAIL

7. Fire the T2 by pausing the MS Exchange Directory Synchronization Service. See Figures 20.19 through 20.23. Use Control Panel | Services if you're logged on locally at the Exchange Server; otherwise, use the Server Manager for Domains (Computer | Services menu) on a remote NT computer. You will receive a 2140 error upon successfully pausing the service. This error message is the reason Microsoft did not document this capability. Do not worry—this is a "good" error.

FIGURE 20.19.

Using Server Manager for Domains to remotely control Exchange's services.

FIGURE 20.20.

Select the Directory Synchronization service.

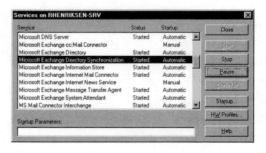

FIGURE 20.21.

Confirm the pause command.

FIGURE 20.22.

Pausing the service.

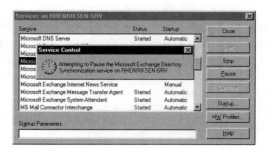

FIGURE 20.23.

The appropriate response from the service.

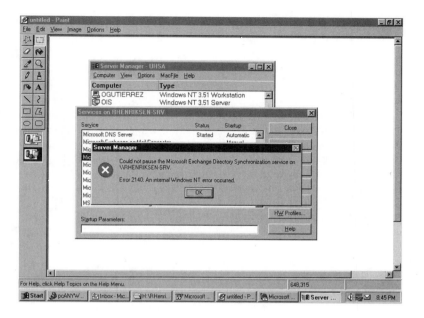

8. Wait a couple of minutes for the T2 message to be sent to the Mail PO. At this point, the message containing the composite list of all post office directory changes is sitting in the $System mailbag of the post office, waiting for the "subcontractors" of the T3 function to do their work.

   Fire the T3 by taking the following steps (9, 10, and 11) in a command-line window. The T3 consists of a set of three commands. Because the T3 has to fire for every requestor post office, that's three operations to be performed for each post office. As with the T1, preface these commands with forcedos if executing them at an NT computer.

9. L:\> reqmain -r

10. L:\> import *adminaccountname* -p*password* -q -y

WARNING

Before you perform the last step, it is important to stop and ensure that the following two files are not locked open by one of the users' mail clients: \GLB\Galindex.glb and \NME\GAL.nme. These two files are recreated during the rebuild command in step 11: rebuild.exe creates new copies named galindex.gl$ and gal.nm$, then deletes the original files and renames the new files to the original names. If a client has either of these files

continues

continued

locked open, DirSync will fail at this point. If this happens, you'll find both versions of the file on your post office, and the $ named version will have the time stamp of the last DirSync cycle.

Use File Manager to open the properties of each file (File | Properties) and then click the Open By button in the File Properties dialog box to view who, if anyone, has the file locked open. Use the Close Selected button to shut them out. If your own logon name appears here, you don't need to worry about that. In NT 4.0, you still need to use File Manager—Explorer doesn't support the Open By function!

Scheduled DirSync operations are just as vulnerable to this problem when you have users who leave their MSMail client running 24x7. You can schedule a batch file to stop sharing the \maildata share during the scheduled T3 time on the MSMail post office machine if two things are true: the post office is on an NT machine, and your DirSync T3 process is running locally on that machine. One flaw: If you have the SMTP Gateway, it'll be disconnected from the post office until you arrive in the morning. To me, this is better than not having DirSync! You can also use a lamp timer to power cycle the SMTP Gateway machine every night, just after DirSync, and before you migrate that function to an Exchange server. It's embarrassing to suggest this kind of chewing gum and string workaround, but, hey—it gets the job done.

11. `L:\> rebuild -f`

Now log into an account on this Mail post office, and admire the Exchange mailboxes that appear in the MSMail GAL.

MIXED MEMBERSHIP IN E-MAIL GROUPS

If you're currently running Microsoft Mail DirSync between multiple post offices, you've probably run across the problem of distribution groups that contain users from different post offices; that group can't participate in directory synchronization. In other words, that mixed-membership group cannot appear in the GAL of the native post office or of other post offices.

After completing the DirSync process with Exchange, just create a replacement distribution group on the Exchange server and add in all those users from the various post offices. Problem solved! An Exchange distribution group can contain native Exchange mailboxes and custom recipients—that is, MSMail accounts—from multiple post offices and still participate in DirSync. Doesn't faze it a bit. The only downside is that MSMail users cannot see the membership of that list until after their account has been migrated to Exchange.

TIP

The custom recipients created in the Exchange GAL from the Microsoft Mail directory will have only a display name and e-mail address entered. It's possible to automate the process of filling in the first name and last name fields from the display name. Microsoft has a knowledge base article Q148500, found at http://www.microsoft.com/kb/, which describes the steps required.

Configuring Exchange as a DirSync Requestor

If you've decided to configure Exchange to function as a DirSync requestor, you probably already have a functioning synchronization process in place. Open the Exchange Administrator program and select the Site | Connections container. Now select the File | New Other | DirSync Requestor command (see Figure 20.24).

FIGURE 20.24.

Creating a new DirSync requestor.

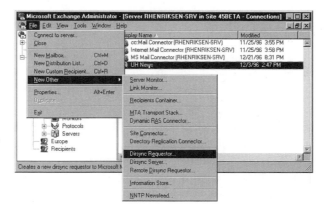

First, you need to tell Exchange which Microsoft Mail post office is the directory synchronization server. You'll be given a list of the known post offices from which to select. This list is generated from the MSMail Connector, in the Connections page (see Figure 20.25).

FIGURE 20.25.

Select the DirSync server post office.

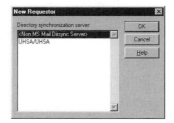

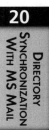

You now have the Properties dialog box for the new Exchange requestor (see Figure 20.26). Now, enter a name for this requestor. A name based on the site is a good choice—perhaps ExcSite1req. If you choose to have this requestor name appended to the usernames in the GAL, a more user-friendly name is probably called for. The Address Types section of this page specifies which types of custom recipient addresses will be included in the submissions to the DirSync server.

FIGURE 20.26.

General settings for the requestor.

The configuration decisions for the Import and Export pages are the same for using Exchange as for the DirSync server, discussed earlier in this chapter.

In the Settings page, Figure 20.27, you'll want to stick with the default settings in the Participation section. If you have added fields to the directory in MSMail, or renamed any of the ten Custom Attributes in the Exchange directory, you'll want to activate the Template Information checkboxes. Because your first DirSync cycle hasn't occurred yet, you should activate both checkboxes (Import and Export on next cycle) in the DirSync information section. This will ensure that both copies of the GAL (Exchange and MSMail) are fully populated with each other's directories.

The Schedule page is a source of some confusion, because, under MSMail, you had to specify a time for the execution of both the T1 cycle and the T3 cycle. Here, you need to specify only the time for the T1 to occur. When Exchange receives the composite list of changes from the DirSync server, the Directory Synchronization service automatically processes the information into the Exchange GAL—in other words, the T3 occurs on demand.

When you've completed your configuration of this requestor, you should see an additional entry in the Configurations container for this requestor, similar to Figure 20.28.

FIGURE 20.27.

Settings for the requestor.

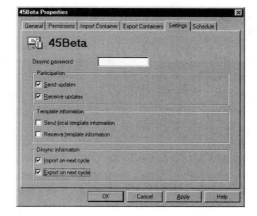

FIGURE 20.28.

The new requestor.

Manual DirSync Cycle

Okay, now run through a DirSync cycle to make sure that the Exchange server is functioning properly as a requestor. (This procedure is also described in the Microsoft Knowledge Base, article Q148309.) The following steps are required:

1. Modify the Exchanger Server's NT registry to enable a manual T1.

2. Increase diagnostic logging temporarily to capture all the information about the DirSync activities. You'll need this information only if you need troubleshooting data.

3. Step through the DirSync cycle as described later in this section.

4. Turn off diagnostic logging.

The registry modification needed is exactly as already described, in the section "Configuring Exchange as the DirSync Server," earlier in this chapter.

20

DIRECTORY
SYNCHRONIZATION
WITH MS MAIL

Troubleshooting To increase diagnostic logging, open the MSMail Connector, select the Diagnostic Logging page, and change MSExchangePCMTA to Maximum (see Figure 20.29).

FIGURE 20.29.

Diagnostic settings for Directory Synchronization.

Now, step through the manual DirSync cycle:

T1. Pause the Directory Synchronization service, exactly as described earlier. Wait a couple of minutes for the MTA to transfer these T1 messages to the DirSync server.

T2. Enter the following two commands against your Mail DirSync server. Preface the commands with forcedos if running them on an NT computer. The -d switch is needed only if you're using a drive letter other than M: for the post office data share.

```
srvmain -r -d<drive>
srvmain -t -d<drive>
```

Again, wait a couple of minutes for the DirSync messages to get back to the Exchange server.

T3. The Directory Synchronization service will automatically process the change list from the DirSync server. There is no need to manually execute a T3 for an Exchange DirSync requestor. You will see a CPU utilization spike as Exchange processes the T3 message.

Finally, be sure to go back and turn diagnostic logging for MSExchangePCMTA back down to none.

Summary

In this chapter, you learned the ways in which Exchange Server can be integrated into Microsoft Mail directory synchronization: as a DirSync server or a requestor. You also explored the procedures for configuring both. The idea of using Exchange Site Connectors as a means of backboning DirSync LAN traffic across your WAN was also introduced. You also reviewed the steps for manually stepping through a DirSync cycle. Some common pitfalls in the DirSync process were examined, and a sample batch file for automating on-demand DirSync cycles wrapped up the chapter.

Directory Synchronization between Microsoft Mail and Exchange Server is a "set it and forget it" function. You can use a sample batch file to automate things. And you can customize it to aid in the occasional manual directory synchronizations—such as when migrating user accounts during the day and, if desired, as a replacement for the MSMail Dispatch utility.

The following batch file, DIRSYNC.BAT, can also be found on the Sams Publishing Code Center Web page at

```
http://www.mcp.com/sams/codecenter.html.
```

Here is the file:

```
Dirsync.bat@echo off
REM    MSMail <--> Exchange Directory Synchronization,
REM    WITH EXCHANGE PERFORMING DIRSYNC SERVER FUNCTIONS.
REM    MODIFY THE STATEMENTS BELOW WITH SERVER NAMES & SHARE NAMES
REM    APPROPRIATE FOR YOUR INSTALLATION.

REM    This batch file must execute locally on the Exchange Server
REM    which is hosting the Exchange < - > Microsoft Mail MTA

REM    You must have the 'sleep.exe' utility from the NT Resource Kit
REM    in your %system_root%\System32 directory for this batch file

REM    If you use the NT Schedule service to fire this batch file, you must
REM    either configure the Schedule service to run with a domain account
REM    with permissions on the M: drive share, or modify the
REM    'net use m: \\server\maildata' statement to read:
REM    'net use m: \\server\maildata <password> /user:domain\<username>'
REM    Example: net use m: \\server\maildata Flippyflop /user:campus\admin
REM    Otherwise, the batch file will fail!

net use l: /d
net use l: \\<your servername here>\mailexe
l:
cd\
cls
if errorlevel == 1 Goto Fail

net use m: /d
net use m: \\<your servername here>\maildata

Echo ###
Echo ###  The T1 will fire first...
Echo ###
sleep 5

forcedos reqmain -t

Echo ###
Echo ###  Sleeping for 15 seconds after the T1...
Echo ###
sleep 15
```

```
cls
Echo ###
Echo ###   Cycling the MTA to force through the T1 msg...
Echo ###
net stop <NAME OF YOUR MTA HERE>
net start <NAME OF YOUR MTA HERE>
Echo ###
Echo ###   Sleeping for 45 seconds to allow the MTA to send the T1 msg...
Echo ###
sleep 45

cls
Echo ###
Echo ###   Pausing Exchange DirSync service to fire T2
Echo ###   An error message is normal and expected here!
Echo ###
net pause msexchangedx
sleep 5
cls
Echo ###
Echo ###   Sleeping for 60 seconds to allow the T2 time to process...
Echo ###
sleep 60

cls
Echo ###
Echo ###   Cycling the MTA to force through the T2 msg...
Echo ###
net stop <NAME OF YOUR MTA HERE>
net start <NAME OF YOUR MTA HERE>

cls
Echo ###
Echo ###   Sleeping for 60 seconds to allow the MTA to send the T2 msg...
Echo ###   The three components of the T3 are next.
Echo ###
sleep 60
forcedos reqmain -r
forcedos import admin -ppassword -q -y
forcedos rebuild -f

goto End

:Fail
Echo There is a dirsync problem; step through dirsync manually to troubleshoot
goto End

:End
cls
Echo DirSync has completed.
Sleep 5
```

Exchange Messaging Security with Key Management Server

by Jim Reitz

IN THIS CHAPTER

CHAPTER 21

Security   You have learned that Microsoft Exchange Server is a secure mail server that provides for secure logon and encrypted client-to-server and server-to-server network sessions—thanks to the inherent security features of Windows NT Server. Only authorized Windows NT Server identities can gain access to mailboxes and public folders. The traffic flowing on the network between Exchange machines is encrypted so that others on the network can't easily eavesdrop or "sniff" these packets. So why is there a need for something called *Advanced Security*?

The standard security features of Exchange Server are aimed at providing network-level, or *point-to-point* security. The Advanced Security features on the other hand, are designed to provide *end-to-end* security for e-mail messages—that is, security that works all the way from the *sender* to the *recipient*, regardless of how the mail gets routed or what type of network it travels over. For end-users, there are two primary features of Advanced Security:

- Digital signatures
- Encrypted message contents

Digital signatures provide users with the ability to verify that the message they have received is precisely the same as the one that the original sender sent them. If even one bit of the message has been tampered with since the originator signed it, the recipient will be alerted. This is called message *authenticity* and provides the user with confidence that the message is the genuine article. Additionally, a digital signature acts much like a handwritten signature on paper—it is a unique identifier that allows the recipient to verify the identity of the person who sent the message.

Encryption of an e-mail message makes the contents totally private so that only the sender and the intended recipients can read it. When you send an encrypted message to a specific user, it is encrypted *for their eyes only*. Even a top-level Exchange Permissions Administrator with full access to the mail server cannot read the contents of an encrypted message. Without the right *private key*, an encrypted message is merely an opaque blob of random data. This type of privacy is especially important as more and more of a company's mail flows over the public Internet, where connections between servers cannot be assumed to be encrypted. Additionally, an encrypted message stays encrypted at all times, whether it is stored on an Exchange Server in a mailbox folder, or whether it's stored locally in a user's PST or OST message store file. The message contents are only temporarily decrypted "in memory" while the recipient has opened the message to read it.

Exchange Server provides the administrator with a sophisticated system for managing the signing and encryption keys that enables users to use digital signatures and encryption. This system is called the *Exchange Key Management Server (KMS)*. This is an optional service that is installed on one of the Exchange Servers in an Exchange organization. The Key Management Server provides the following functions:

- Enabling and revoking users' ability to use Advanced Security
- Acting as a Certificate Authority to issue *certificates* for users
- Providing secure archive and *recovery* of users' encryption keys

The *key recovery* feature is particularly critical when message encryption is being used in a corporate environment. Exchange uses very strong encryption algorithms to encrypt message contents. This is a potent weapon, but it's very much a double-edged sword. It's important to understand that if users lose their encryption keys, there's nothing that you or anyone else can do to retrieve their encrypted mail without those keys. The encryption algorithms used have no "hidden secrets" or "back doors." The only way anyone—even Microsoft—can get at the encrypted data is either to have the right keys or try *every possible combination* of keys until one works. Even the weakest version of Exchange Advanced Security (due to U.S. government export laws, a weaker version must be shipped outside the U.S. and Canada) still has over one trillion possible keys to try for every e-mail message.

Key recovery provides a secure way to archive users' encryption keys so that only a trusted company security officer can retrieve them and give them back to the user. This feature is also useful in cases where an employee is terminated or leaves the company, but the employee has left critical encrypted data in his or her mailbox that the company needs to retrieve. Exchange KMS enables companies to recover such critical company data.

Installing Key Management Server

Before your user can begin using digital signatures or message encryption, you must first install the Key Management Server on one of your Exchange Servers. There is only a *single KMS per organization*, so you should choose to install it on a server to which your trusted security administrators will have access. The first KMS you install will become the main KMS for the entire organization. If your Exchange organization has multiple sites, you will need to configure each additional site to point to the central KMS before those sites can use Advanced Security. These additional sites require e-mail connectivity to the site containing the KMS and working directory replication with the main KMS site; they do not require direct connectivity to the KMS machine.

COMMON MISCONCEPTIONS

At first glance, it may seem like a single Key Management Server for an entire multisite organization is totally insufficient. After all, what if all of my clients can't make a network connection to this central machine? It's important to understand the following two key concepts.

First, the KMS is never involved in the day-to-day business of signing or encrypting e-mail. It simply issues and revokes keys and certificates. This happens initially when users are first security-enabled and then again about 12–18 months later when the users' certificates expire. Think of the KMS as a driver's license bureau. Users must obtain their driver's license before they can get started, but the license bureau is never involved in day-to-day driving. Users have to go back every year to get their license renewed, however.

continues

> *continued*
>
> Second, Exchange clients never need to connect to the KMS directly over the network. They simply must be able to send e-mail to and from the KMS machine. E-mail is the protocol that is used for clients to request the key and certificates and then renew them.
>
> Because of these concepts, a single KMS for an organization is usually quite sufficient. But some companies may be highly decentralized, and for management or political reasons, multiple KMS systems may be desirable. In Exchange Server 4.0 and 5.0, there is a limit of one KMS per organization. Microsoft has said they plan to allow multiple KMS machines in a future version of Exchange.

Future Directions

To install the main Key Management Server, you need the Exchange Server installation CD and a couple of blank floppy disks. Installation must be performed on the machine that will physically host the KMS:

1. Log in to the Exchange Server machine that will host KMS with an NT administrator account. This is required in order to install new server software. Make sure the Exchange Server is running.

2. Load the Exchange Server CD and change directories to \Setup\<*platform*>\Exchkm, where <*platform*> is your appropriate machine platform (for example, I386 or Alpha).

3. Run SETUP.EXE to start the KMS installation. The setup program allows you to choose where the KMS files will be located, including the private key recovery database. Note that the default setting is C:\Security, which is in a different directory than the regular Exchange Server files (C:\ExchSrvr). This is suggested deliberately. Even though the private key recovery database is encrypted for security, it's still a good idea to back it up separately. Figure 21.1 illustrates the directory settings in KM Setup.

FIGURE 21.1.

The KM Setup dialog.

CAUTION

If you are attempting to install the KMS on any French-language Windows NT Server, you will receive an error message. This is because the use of most encryption software in France—currently including Exchange Advanced Security—is prohibited by the French government. To comply with these laws, Microsoft has disabled KMS from being installable on any French-language Windows NT Server, whether you are actually in France or not.

If you are a multinational organization with offices in France, you are also prohibited from security-enabling users inside France, even if the KMS is located elsewhere. Government laws can change from time to time, so you should check with Microsoft periodically to see if these restrictions are currently in effect for Exchange. And of course this is more of a legal issue than a technical one, so your company's own legal department may be the best resource for answering questions about legal regulations and risks.

4. Setup will identify the NT account that is being used as the Exchange Service Account on this machine and prompt you for the password. You must enter the proper password for KMS to start and log on properly.

5. The setup program prompts you to select a country code, as shown in Figure 21.2. This is simply required in order for the KMS to create properly formatted X.509 certificates—but it is otherwise not important. (In most other cases, Exchange Server omits the country code from the X.500 addresses that it uses internally.)

FIGURE 21.2.

The Country code and startup floppy selections.

6. At the bottom of the dialog box in Figure 21.2 is an important choice: whether to create a KMS startup floppy disk or not. If you choose this option, you will be prompted for a blank floppy disk to contain the KMS startup password. If not, you need to be prepared to write down the startup password. Then you enter it manually every time you start the KMS service.

7. A random startup password is chosen, which is required to allow access to the encrypted private key database. If you chose the floppy disk startup method, you will be prompted to insert the disk in the A: drive (or your first removable drive, if your machine doesn't have an A: drive). If you chose the manual password option, it will be displayed for you to write down, as shown in Figure 21.3.

FIGURE 21.3.

Displaying the startup password (manual startup method).

8. Once setup has finished, you should immediately make a backup copy of your startup floppy disk, or—if you chose the manual password method—make a copy of the password. Keep these backup copies in a secure location, under lock and key. If your original floppy disk is ever lost or destroyed, you will have no other way to gain access to the private key database unless you have a backup of the password.

9. You can start the KMS service by using the Windows NT Control Panel. Select the Microsoft Exchange Key Manager service. If you chose the floppy disk startup option, make sure that your startup floppy is in the disk drive and click Start. If you chose the manual password startup option, you must type the startup password in Startup Parameters, as illustrated in Figure 21.4; then click Start.

FIGURE 21.4.

Control Panel startup, showing the optional startup password.

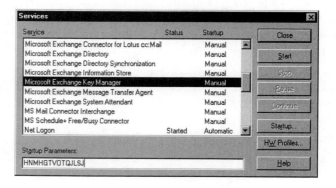

If you want, you can configure the Microsoft Exchange Key Manager service to start automatically when the system boots up, but you need to ensure that the startup floppy disk is in the drive at all times, or the service will fail to start. Because of the sensitivity of the private key database, you should use this option only when your server machine is physically secured and you are sure no untrusted users have access to the startup floppy disk. Leaving a floppy disk in the drive can cause boot problems on some Intel server machines (RISC machines generally don't boot from floppy), but fortunately, most modern servers can be configured to either not boot from floppy or boot first from the hard drive. This is usually done via the machine's CMOS setup.

WHY A KMS STARTUP PASSWORD?

Unlike most services running on your server, the KMS needs access to some particularly sensitive data—the private encryption keys for all your users. If attackers were to gain access to this data, they could potentially decrypt any user's encrypted mail. To ensure that this can't happen merely by gaining physical access to the KMS server, the database containing the private encryption keys is encrypted with a 64-bit symmetric key. This key is derived from the startup password; only those programs with access to the startup password will be able to decrypt the private key database.

Once the setup program is finished, open the Exchange Administrator program on the server where you just installed KMS. Open the Configuration container for your site. As displayed in Figure 21.5, you will see the following new objects: CA and Encryption.

FIGURE 21.5.
Exchange Administrator program, showing the CA *and* Encryption *objects.*

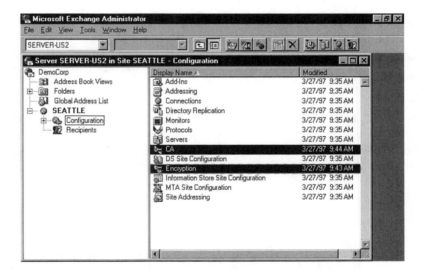

Configuring Additional Sites to Use Key Management Server

Once you have successfully installed KMS on the server in your first site, you should ensure that the new directory information (CA and Encryption objects) has been fully replicated to other sites before configuring them. For each additional site where you want to security-enable users, you must configure that site to use the original KM Server that you installed.

You configure additional sites by running KMS Setup on a server in each site. Note that this secondary setup will copy KMS files, but does not actually install a running KM Server. The main purpose of this secondary setup is to configure the `Encryption` object in the new site's directory container, so that it contains the address of the original KMS.

To configure additional sites:

1. Log in to one of the Exchange servers in the site with a Window NT administrator account. Make sure that Exchange Server is running on this machine.

2. Load the Exchange Server CD and change directories to \Setup*<platform>*\Exchkm, where *<platform>* is your appropriate machine platform (for example, I386 or Alpha).

3. Run SETUP.EXE to start the KMS installation. Setup will prompt you for the directory to hold the KMS files.

4. Setup will detect that the main KM server already exists in a different site and will skip the remainder of the setup questions. Again, the main purpose of this "secondary" setup is to create an Encryption directory object for the new site. This object contains the e-mail address of the main KM server, which allows clients in the new site to automatically send e-mail when they wish to become security-enabled.

5. Setup displays a message (see Figure 21.6) with the name of the main KM server site so the local administrator knows who to contact for KMS administration.

FIGURE 21.6.

Message showing that an additional site has been configured.

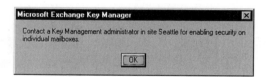

Once the main KM server is installed and your additional sites have been configured, you are ready to start security-enabling your users.

UPGRADING KMS FROM EXCHANGE 4.0 TO 5.0

Compatibility

When you upgrade your servers from Exchange Server 4.0 to version 5.0, you only need to upgrade the *primary* KM server, which is the only *actual* KM server that's running in your organization. As the previous section indicates, each of the other sites that use the KMS simply have an *encryption* object that points to the main KMS. You do not need to upgrade these "secondary" sites to 5.0.

To upgrade your primary KMS machine from 4.0 to 5.0, run the KMSetup.exe program from the Exchange Server 5.0 CD, just as you would for a new install. The KMSetup program will automatically detect your existing KMS installation and offer to upgrade it to 5.0. Your key archive database will be preserved during this process, but it's always a good idea to back up critical data before and after any upgrade procedure.

KM Server Administration

Once KM Server is installed and running, the first thing you'll want to do is change the default administrator password that ships with the system. The default KMS admin password is password, so it's a good idea to change it immediately. Because private key management and recovery is a highly sensitive security function, administration of the KMS is restricted—above and beyond normal Exchange Server administration. To perform KMS administration functions:

1. You must already have Admin permissions on your site.

2. Your Windows NT account must be listed as a valid KMS administrator.

3. You must know the special KMS administration password.

To change add/remove KMS administrator and to change the special KMS admin password:

1. Start the Exchange Administrator program and connect to the server that hosts the KMS—actually, you can connect to any server in the site, as long as you have network connectivity to the KMS machine. The Exchange Administrator program will automatically connect you to the KMS machine if needed.

2. Open your site's Configuration container and double-click the Encryption object. This object is used to control most KMS settings.

3. Select the Security tab in the Encryption Properties dialog box, as shown in Figure 21.7.

   Note that this dialog also allows the administrator to control which encryption algorithms will be used by default in each site.

FIGURE 21.7.

The Security page of the site Encryption *object's property sheet.*

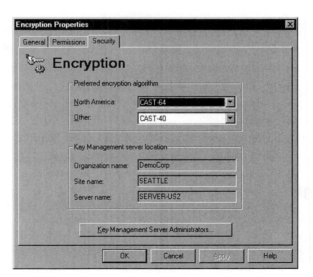

4. At the bottom of the dialog, click the Key Management Server Administrators button. When it prompts you for a password, enter password, which is the initial default password. This dialog also has this option: Remember this password for up to 5 minutes. If you don't check this, you will be prompted for a password for every operation. Although this may be annoying, it is the most secure way to run your Key Management Server—you can walk away from the console at any time, and no one else will be able to walk up and perform KMS admin functions. For security reasons, KMS does not allow you to remember the password for longer than 5 minutes. The password dialog for all KMS administrative functions is illustrated in Figure 21.8.

FIGURE 21.8.

Password dialog for all Key Management Server administrative functions.

5. The Key Management Server Administrators dialog (see Figure 21.9) allows you to add or remove KMS admins and to change the KMS admin password. Initially, there will be one KMS admin account listed: the NT admin account that you used to initially install the KMS. From here, you should add the NT accounts that you want to be able to perform KMS admin functions.

FIGURE 21.9.

Adding or Removing KMS administrators.

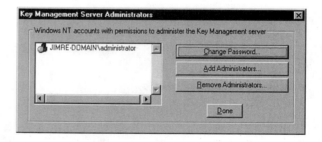

New to
Version 5.0

In Exchange Server 4.0, you can add a maximum of 5 KMS admin accounts. In Exchange Server 5.0, you can add up to 20 KMS admin accounts.

Security-Enabling Your Users

Before your users can begin using digital signatures or message encryption, you must security-enable them. This is the process by which users obtain public and private keys, and the KMS creates *certificates* for them. A KMS administrator can use the Exchange Administrator program to security-enable individual users, or the administrator can use the command-line tool simport.exe to security-enable an entire site of users in bulk.

Only native Exchange mailbox users can be security-enabled. Security keys cannot be issued for custom recipients, distribution lists, or public folders. To security-enable individual users, you can double-click on their mailbox objects to see their properties. Select the Security tab page, and you will see the dialog shown in Figure 21.10.

FIGURE 21.10.

The Security page of an Exchange mailbox.

You will be prompted for the KMS administrator password; you can choose to remember it for up to 5 minutes.

Click the Enable Advanced Security button. The KMS will create a record for the user in the private key archive database, and it will generate a special temporary password, called a *token*. As Figure 21.11 shows, this token is displayed to the administrator. A temporary password is required because the user's e-mail is not yet secure. The user and the KM server will soon be exchanging keys and certificates via e-mail to complete the user's setup. This temporary token will be used to encrypt this initial setup mail until the user has been issued a permanent key. In a sense, the token is a way to bootstrap the user's encryption setup.

FIGURE 21.11.

A user's new temporary token, as displayed in Exchange Administrator.

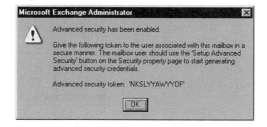

Write this token down or print it (via Print Screen). This token, or temporary password, should be given to the user in some secure method —preferably not via e-mail, because the user's e-mail can't yet be secured with encryption. Some companies might print it on paper and physically deliver it to the user, some might give it to the employee's manager, or some might deliver it via voice mail or phone call. Once the user has this temporary token, he or she will be able to complete the security-enabling process and receive a permanent key.

This dialog also shows the dates for which the user's certificates are valid. The Exchange KMS issues certificates that are valid for 18 months. This time period is hard-coded and cannot be changed in Exchange 4.0 or 5.0.

Completing Security-Enabling—The User's View

Once the user has received a temporary token from the KMS administrator, he or she can complete the security-enabling process. To perform the client-side security setup:

1. The user must log onto his or her Exchange mailbox in *online* mode. Security setup cannot be performed while the user is in offline mode.

2. The user selects the Tools | Options menu and clicks the Security tab page, shown in Figure 21.12.

FIGURE 21.12.

The user's Tools | Options | Security dialog.

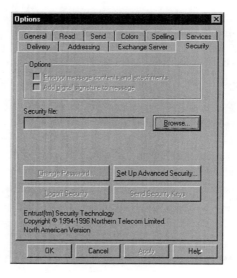

3. From this dialog, the user clicks the Set Up Advanced Security button. This dialog, shown in Figure 21.13, requires several pieces of information from the user, starting with the temporary token he or she was issued.

FIGURE 21.13.
*The Setup Advanced
Security dialog.*

4. Next, the user needs to provide the pathname for a private key file. A default pathname is provided. This private key file (with file extension .EPF) is a local file that the user must carry. It is an encrypted file that will contain the user's private keys for digital signatures and encryption. The user must choose a password that will be used to unlock his or her private key file. This password can be quite long—up to 32 characters. As usual, the longer and more random the password, the harder it will be for an attacker to guess.

5. After choosing and confirming the password, the user clicks OK. The client sends a special encrypted e-mail message (encrypted with the temporary token) to the KMS. The user sees the dialog in Figure 21.14.

FIGURE 21.14.
*The user's security
request has been sent to
the KMS.*

6. The KMS receives the client's e-mail message, decrypts it (because the KMS is the only other party that knows the temporary token), completes the generation of the user's keys and creates X.509 certificates for the user's public signing key and public encryption key. The KMS packages this information into another encrypted e-mail message and sends it back to the client. In a few minutes, the client receives the message from the KMS and is asked for the private key file password, as illustrated in Figure 21.15.

7. The client takes the information from the KMS response (the user's permanent private keys) and stores it securely in the private key file. As part of this last step, the client automatically updates the GAL entry with the new public certificates and some key configuration information, such as whether the client is using 40-bit (exportable) or a 64-bit (North American) client software.

FIGURE 21.15.

The user opens the acknowledgment mail from the KMS.

The user is now security-enabled. Whenever the user performs an operation that requires the private key—such as signing or decrypting a message—the user will be prompted for his or her .EPF file and the password to unlock it.

WHY A PRIVATE KEY FILE?

You may be familiar with network security, where a password is sufficient to allow you to log on. As long as you know the password, you can log on from anywhere. Knowing a single password may be convenient, but it also makes things easier for attackers if they obtain your password. All that's required in that case is "something you know"—your password. So why does Exchange Advanced Security require both a *physical* copy of the private key file and the password to unlock it?

This makes the system more secure. You now need two things to gain access: "something you have" (the .EPF file) and "something you know" (the password). This is very much like your bank ATM card—for someone to be able to withdraw cash from your account they need both the ATM card itself and the PIN (password) that unlocks it. Merely knowing the password doesn't help attackers unless they physically possess the private key file.

Key Recovery

Inevitably, some of your users will lose their private key files, or they will forget the passwords they have chosen. Without their private keys, these users will not be able to read any of their encrypted mail. Similarly, many companies (especially in the U.S.) may require legal access to an employee's encrypted mail files after that employee has left the company. How do users and companies recover encrypted mail data in these cases?

Exchange Key Management Server provides a very powerful solution called *key recovery*. All the permanent private encryption keys issued to users are securely archived in the KMS database. If a user has lost his or her key, a KMS administrator can *recover* that key, and the user will once again be able to read encrypted mail. To recover a user's key, the KMS administrator must go into the user's mailbox properties and, from the Security tab page, click the Recover Security Keys button. This works very much like the initial security setup operation. A new temporary token is displayed to the administrator as Figure 21.16 shows and must be securely given to the user.

FIGURE 21.16.
The temporary token created for key recovery.

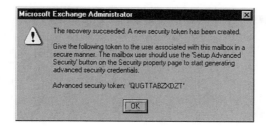

The user goes through the same steps as during initial security setup—selecting the Tool | Options menu, choosing the Security tab page, and clicking the Setup Advanced Security button. The only difference between this and initial security setup is that in the recovery case, the user will receive the entire *history* of private encryption keys in the secure message that comes back from the KMS.

Revoking Advanced Security from a User

If a user leaves the company, or if a security key is stolen or compromised, you will want to ensure that other users no longer trust that user's security keys (certificates). Because the user has physical possession of the private key (in the .EPF file), you can't just disable the ability to use that key. Instead, you can *revoke* the certificate that was issued by the KMS. Revoked certificates are placed on a special *Certificate Revocation List (CRL)* that is updated constantly by the KMS and published in the Exchange Directory Service. All security-enabled clients will check this CRL before using any certificates and will warn the user if he or she attempts to use this certificate.

To revoke a user's security, go into his or her mailbox properties in Exchange Administrator, choose the Security tab page, and click the Revoke Advanced Security button.

Exchange and Outlook clients also cache a local copy of the server's CRL when they log in. This allows the clients to warn about revoked certificates, even when the user is running in *offline* mode. Unfortunately, this local copy can't be updated when running in offline mode. Clients who work offline will see the warning message in Figure 21.17 that reminds them that their local copy of the CRL is not the latest version; additional certificates may have been revoked since they last updated their CRL.

FIGURE 21.17.
Warning showing the user's CRL is not up-to-date.

Renewing User Certificates

With Exchange KMS, the user's certificate has a valid lifetime of 18 months. After that time, it expires and is no longer valid. Before that happens, users must *renew* their security certificates. After about 12 months, the user's Exchange or Outlook client software will automatically begin reminding the user that the certificate is going to expire in the near future. When the user logs onto Advanced Security, the user will see a dialog like the one in Figure 21.18.

FIGURE 21.18.

The user's certificates will expire soon and must be renewed.

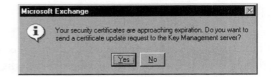

No administrator intervention is required for users to renew their certificates, as long as the users' certificates haven't expired. Users can easily click on the Yes button, and a renewal request will automatically be sent to the KMS. New certificates are created that will be valid for the next 18 months and sent back to the users in secure e-mail messages.

Backup and Restore

Backup of the KMS is done using normal NT file backup software. The primary directory you need to back up is *<path>*\mgrent, where *<path>* is the path where you originally installed KMS (the default is C:\security\mgrent). To ensure that none of the KMS files are in use while you back up, you should stop the KM service while backing up the files and restart it when finished. If you ever need to restore the KMS files, you should restore them to this same directory.

Because the KMS data files are highly sensitive data, you should be careful how you treat the backup tapes. These data files are encrypted so that someone with access to the backup tapes can't directly make use of them. However, remember that backup tapes are *offline* copies of the data. If someone gets an offline copy, he or she can try to break the encryption via brute force (by trying every possible key), and there's little chance that person will be detected, because he or she is offline. So, the person can take all the time needed. For this reason, we recommend that you back up KMS data separately from other data and keep these backup tapes under lock and key.

Planning and Scaling Considerations

Performance

Only a single Key Management Server is used per Exchange organization; large organizations may be concerned with the capacity required to issue and store all the keys for all their users. In actual practice, the amount of data managed by the KMS is relatively small. Here is a quick breakdown of the data that's stored:

Exchange Messaging Security with Key Management Server

CHAPTER 21

525

21

EXCHANGE
MESSAGING
SECURITY

- The KMS private key archive database contains an encrypted text file for each user who has been issued keys. These files are typically 2–4KB in size. For 10,000 users, this would occupy between 20 and 40MB of disk space on the KMS.

- Each security-enabled user's GAL entry contains its public encryption certificate, typically around 700 bytes per user. With 10,000 users, this would increase the DS database size by somewhat over 7MB on each server.

- The Certificate Revocation List (CRL) contains less than 100 bytes of data for each revoked certificate. If your company revokes 10 user certificates per month, the CRL would grow by approximately 12KB per year. The CRL is stored in the directory and downloaded to offline clients.

How All This Works—Cryptography Basics

To make the best use of Exchange Advanced Security and the Key Management Server, it's important to understand some of the basic security technologies behind digital signatures and encryption. The science behind this is called *cryptography*. There are many good textbooks on the subject, and it's taught in many university computer science departments. In this chapter you will explore merely a brief introduction to the concepts of the following: symmetric-key encryption, public-key encryption, hashing, and certificates. You will then learn how these four basic concepts come together to provide digital signatures and encrypted mail.

Symmetric-Key Encryption

Symmetric-key encryption is the most traditional type of encryption technology. Symmetric-key encryption algorithms (sometimes called *secret-key*) use the same key to encrypt and decrypt data. Using such a scheme, if you encrypt e-mail with a particular key, your recipient must have the same key to decrypt it. There are a great number and variety of symmetric key algorithms, most of which can process data at extremely high speeds. This makes symmetric-key algorithms well-suited for encrypted bulk data, such as the contents of e-mail messages. Exchange 5.0 uses two different symmetric-key algorithms: CAST, which uses either 40-bit or 64-bit keys; and DES (Data Encryption Standard), which uses 56-bit keys. Only CAST 40-bit is available in the International version of Exchange, which is sold outside the U.S. and Canada.

Standards

The big drawback to symmetric-key encryption is the need to keep the single key as a secret between sender and recipient. This significantly complicates the distribution of keys. If you want mail to be readable only by you and a given recipient, you need a separate key for every combination of sender and recipient—clearly unworkable. This is where public-key encryption comes to the rescue.

HOW SECURE ARE 40-BIT OR 64-BIT KEYS?

Good symmetric-key encryption algorithms, such as those used in Exchange, don't have any known hidden secrets or back doors. Additionally, the programs that use the algorithms must have good random-number generators; otherwise, someone might be able to guess which keys were chosen to encrypt a given message. If these conditions are met, the only way to crack such algorithms is to try every possible key until you find the correct one. There's no such thing as an uncrackable encryption scheme. Depending on how fast an attacker's computer system can try keys, it's simply a matter of how much time and computing power it takes.

In one widely publicized effort to crack keys in January 1997, a college student with 250 networked RISC workstations at his disposal was able to crack a single 40-bit key in around 3.5 hours. With this computing power, he was able to try over 100 billion keys per hour. A 40-bit key means that there are 2^{40} possible combinations, or slightly over one trillion. In this case, he happened to find the right key less than halfway through; searching all the keys would have taken around 10 hours; the average would be around 5 hours. So what does this mean? It illustrates the relative time and resources (5 hours × 250 RISC workstations) required to crack a single encrypted mail message. Each message is encrypted with a different random key, so, on average, someone equipped with hardware such as this could crack one 40-bit e-mail message every 5 hours.

64-bit keys have 2^{24} times more combinations than 40-bit keys, which means it would take just over *16 million times longer* to crack 64-bit keys than 40-bit keys. With the same hardware as the example above, it would take over 9,000 years to crack a single 64-bit e-mail message. Is 64-bit security good enough? For most cases today, the answer is yes. But keep in mind the following two points: computing power gets faster and cheaper all the time; and some attackers with huge budgets, such as very large companies or governments, might have millions of times more computing power at their disposal than a college computer lab does.

Why use 40-bit keys at all? Why not always use 64-bit keys? The U.S. government currently imposes a 40-bit restriction on hardware and software that can be exported outside the U.S. This means that software built in the U.S., such as Microsoft Exchange, usually comes in 2 flavors: a 40-bit version for export, and a full-strength version for use in the U.S. and Canada.

Public-Key Encryption

Based on some mathematical advances made in the 1970s, *public-key encryption* (sometime called *asymmetric-key*) uses keys that have two parts: a public key and a private key. Together, these are known as a *keypair*. Data encrypted with the public key can be decrypted only by the corresponding private key. Likewise, data encrypted with the private key can be decrypted only by the public key. This provides a neat solution to the key distribution problem. You can publish

Exchange Messaging Security with Key Management Server

CHAPTER 21

527

21

EXCHANGE
MESSAGING
SECURITY

your public key freely to anyone in the world—it's not a secret. You maintain your private key securely and never share it with anyone. Anyone who wants to send you encrypted data can encrypt it with your public key, and only you can read it, because only you have the corresponding private key.

Public-key encryption takes significantly more computation power and is therefore slower than symmetric-key. For this reason, it's generally not used for bulk data encryption, but rather for encrypting small amounts of critical data, such as symmetric keys or message hashes (more on this later). It also generally uses longer key sizes than symmetric-key algorithms. Exchange 4.0 and 5.0 use the RSA public-key algorithm from RSA Data Security, Inc., with 512-bit key pairs.

Hashing

A *hashing* algorithm performs some mathematical operations on data to generate a unique number, similar to a checksum. A good hashing algorithm will always generate a unique hash number based on different data inputs, even if only one bit is different. This property makes hash algorithms well-suited for use in digital signatures to verify the authenticity of some data. If a message is ever tampered with, it will produce a different hash than the original message would. Exchange 4.0 and 5.0 use the MD5 (Message Digest #5) hashing algorithm from RSA Data Security, Inc.

Certificates

As noted previously, public-key encryption allows you to freely publish your public key to anyone so that person can encrypt data for you. Other users must first obtain a copy of your public key before they can do this. Typically, users' public keys are published in a directory service or other type of database. In Exchange Server, for example, they are published in the Global Address Book. How do you know a particular public key really belongs to a particular user? What if someone with access to the directory server switches someone's public key? If you really wanted to be sure, you could physically trade public keys in person with every other user. Obviously, this will work only for a relatively small circle of friends, so any larger organization will need some sort of "trusted authority" to vouch for other users' public keys. This is where certificates some in.

A *certificate* is just someone's public key in a special form that has been *digitally signed* by a **Standards** trusted entity, called a Certificate Authority. A certificate also includes the user's name. In a sense, it's a document from a trusted source that states, "I certify that John Smith's public key is 123456789." Exchange Server follows the CCITT X.509 guidelines for the format of public-key certificates, specifically the X.509 version 1 certificate format. The Exchange Key Management Server acts as the Certificate Authority for your Exchange organization. The public keys for all users are certified by the KMS.

Putting It Together: Digital Signatures in Exchange Clients

Now that you know some of the basic terminology, let's examine how digital signatures actually work. When composing e-mail, Exchange and Outlook client users can easily choose to digitally sign their e-mail message by pressing the Signing button, which is illustrated in Figure 21.19.

FIGURE 21.19.

The Signing button on the Exchange client toolbar.

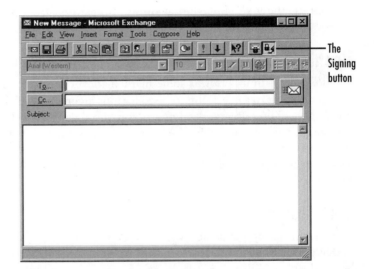

— The Signing button

TIP

By default, the Exchange client ships with the toolbar OFF (just the formatting toolbar is visible). In order to see the Sign/Encrypt toolbar buttons, your users need to choose the View | Toolbar command.

This button is an on/off toggle that indicates that message should be signed when you send it. When you press the Send button, your Exchange client goes through your message's contents—specifically the message body and any attachments—to calculate the *hash value*. This hash is encrypted with the sender's private key and sent along as part of the e-mail message. This means that any recipient with the sender's public key can decrypt the hash. How do recipients get the sender's public signing key? That's easy—it's sent along as part of each signed mail message, in the form of a certificate. At first glance this might not seem secure, because a sender attempting to spoof mail might try to include a fake certificate. Because certificates must be digitally signed by a trusted Certificate Authority, however, the recipient will know immediately whether the certificate in the message is genuine or not.

Exchange or Outlook users can verify a digital signature at any time on mail they have received by clicking the Verify signature button on the message. When they click this button, the client software goes through a series of steps behind the scenes to verify the signature:

1. It extracts the sender's signing certificate from the e-mail message and ensures that it is from a trusted Certificate Authority (the organization's KMS). The recipient will be prompted to enter the password for his or her local keyfile so that the trusted copy of the Certificate Authority's public key can be extracted from the .EPF file. This is used to determine whether the sender's certificate is genuine.

2. Using the public key from the sender's certificate, it decrypts the hash value that was encrypted with the sender's private key.

3. It calculates its own hash value, using the actual message content that it received.

4. It compares the original decrypted hash value with the one it just calculated. If there are any discrepancies, the signature is invalid. In fact, there are four conditions that might cause a signature to be invalid. These will be displayed in the Exchange clients, as shown later. Figure 21.20 illustrates the results if the message has been altered or tampered with since being signed.

FIGURE 21.20.

Indication that signature verification failed, due to message tampering.

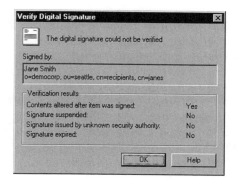

In this example, the message contents were changed because the sender originally signed the message, causing an error to be shown.

Putting It Together: Message Encryption in Exchange Clients

In addition to digital signatures, Exchange and Outlook client users can also choose to encrypt their message contents so that only they and their intended recipients will be able to read them. Encryption can either be used separately from—or simultaneously with—digital signatures. The encryption button on a mail message under composition is also an on/off toggle. In both Exchange and Outlook, the Encryption button is found on the compose note toolbar. Figure

21.21 shows this button in Outlook 97. Selecting it doesn't immediately encrypt the message (because you might not be finished typing yet!), but rather indicates that the message is to be encrypted when it is sent.

FIGURE 21.21.

The Encryption button on the Exchange client toolbar.

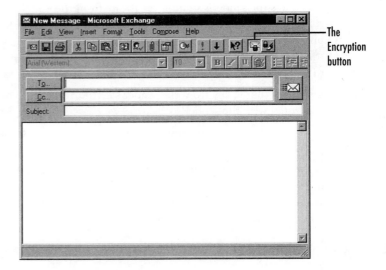

The Encryption button

When you press the Send button, under the covers your client goes through a series of steps to make sure the message contents are encrypted before leaving your machine:

1. The client examines all the recipient addresses and attempts to retrieve public encryption keys (in the form of certificates) from the Global Address List for each recipient. If some of the recipients don't have certificates—either they are "foreign" users or they are not yet security-enabled—the error dialog in Figure 21.22 is displayed, and the user can take corrective action.

FIGURE 21.22.

One or more of the recipients is not security-enabled.

Additionally, the recipients' address book entries are examined to determine whether they are using export-restricted (40-bit) versions of Exchange clients or North American (64-bit) versions. This setting is tracked automatically by the Exchange Directory Server so that users don't have to worry about it. This allows a multinational company to deploy a mixture of 40-bit and 64-bit clients, where appropriate, and have them all interoperate with each other.

> **TIP**
>
> Normally, you obtain other users' certificates from the GAL, but if you are running in offline mode, the Offline Address Book contains all of the other users' certificates. This is only true if you chose to download full details in your Offline Address Book.

2. A random *symmetric encryption key* is chosen for the mail message—either a 40-bit key or a 64-bit key, depending on whether the recipients are using export-restricted clients or the full North American client.

3. The message contents (body and attachments) are encrypted with the random symmetric key, and the encrypted results are stored into a binary "blob" inside the message. The original unencrypted message body and attachments are then deleted. This means that an encrypted message really has *no contents*—it has an empty message body and no attachments. All the encrypted data is carried in the blob property inside the message.

4. Somehow, the random symmetric key that was chosen has to be securely conveyed to the recipients, or they will be unable to decrypt the message. This is where public-key encryption is used. For each recipient, the random symmetric key is encrypted with that user's public key. Microsoft calls the resulting data structure a *lockbox,* because it acts like a secure box that only the recipients can open (only they have the corresponding private key). A lockbox is created for all recipients on the message as well as for the sender so they will be able to go into their Sent Items folders and read this encrypted message.

5. The resulting message is sent. It includes an encrypted blob, instead of actual message contents, and a set of lockboxes.

When the recipient tries to read the encrypted message, he or she just double-clicks to read it as normal. The client software goes through a number of steps to decrypt it:

1. It prompts the user for a local keyfile password, so that the user's private encryption key can be extracted from the .EPF file.

2. It locates the lockbox for the specific recipient, and the user's private encryption key is used to decrypt the lockbox and retrieve the random symmetric key that was used to encrypt the message contents.

3. The symmetric key is used to decrypt the contents of the blob property and display it on the user's screen as the message contents. The on-disk copy of the encrypted message remains encrypted, however; it is decrypted only temporarily while it is displayed on the recipient's screen.

Sending Secure Mail Between Organizations

New to Version 5.0

Exchange 4.0 restricted the use of Advanced Security to users within the same Exchange organization—primarily because you can obtain another user's certificate only through the GAL. With version 5.0, this restriction has been relaxed somewhat. Exchange 5.0 supports a feature called *person-to-person key exchange*, which allows Exchange users in different organizations to send each other digitally signed or encrypted mail over the Internet.

Because users in other Exchange organizations aren't listed in your Global Address List, you need some other mechanism for obtaining their public-key certificates before you can send them encrypted mail. Exchange 5.0 clients include an e-form that allows users to trade certificates with each other and store them in their Personal Address Book for future use. This feature is available on Exchange 5.0 Windows clients only.

To trade certificates with another user:

1. Choose the Tools | Options menu command. Click on the Security tab page. You should see a Send Security Keys button.

> **TIP**
>
> The Send Security Keys button will be disabled if you are running on a Windows 3.x shell—either Windows 3.1, or Windows NT 3.51. If you are running on these platforms, you can launch this e-form manually by choosing the Compose | New Form menu item and selecting Security Key Exchange Form from the Application Forms library (using the drop-down list provided).

2. Click the button. You will see the Security Key Exchange Form, shown in Figure 21.23.

3. Address the form to the Exchange user with whom you are trading keys. Use the user's SMTP (Internet Mail) address. The form includes some personal details about you that will be added to the other person's PAB. Some of the details from your GAL entry are automatically included on the e-form. You can choose to send these or not by using the check boxes for each field. If there are some additional details you want to send that weren't already part of your GAL entry, you can manually fill out those fields.

FIGURE 21.23.

*The Security Key
Exchange e-form used
for Personal Key
Exchange.*

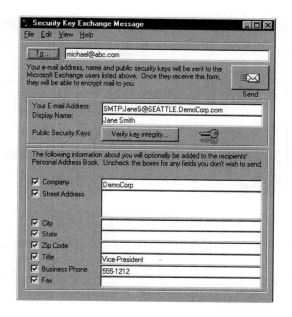

4. Click the Send button.

5. The other person receives the e-form (the user must also have an Exchange 5.0 client) and clicks the Add to Personal Address Book button. This creates an entry for you in the user's PAB, complete with whatever personal details you included on your form and, of course, including your security certificates as well.

6. The other person now performs this same procedure in reverse, using the form to send his or her certificates to you.

   When you are sending these Key Exchange forms over the Internet, your mail is not yet set up to be encrypted. Because you are sending *public* keys and certificates, that's OK. But how can you be sure that the keys weren't intercepted and somehow modified by an attacker when they were flowing over the public Internet? The Security Key Exchange form solves this by providing an *integrity check* feature. You can click this button on the e-form you've received, and you will see a unique message "hash" or "fingerprint," as shown in Figure 21.24. Call the other person on the phone and have that person also click this button on the copy of the e-form sent to you. Read the fingerprint numbers over the phone. If they compare, you know the message wasn't tampered with. In a sense, this is like performing a digital signature verification *manually.*

7. You can now exchange signed or encrypted mail between the two of you, over the Internet.

FIGURE 21.24.

Verifying the integrity of a received Key Exchange e-form.

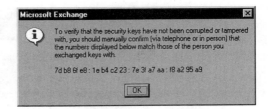

Restrictions on Encryption Software—U.S. Export Regulations

Any encryption software that was created in the United States, including Microsoft Exchange, is currently regulated by U.S. Commerce Department laws, which limit what type of encryption can be exported outside the United States. Under these laws, "strong" encryption software—currently defined by the government to be anything with a key length greater than 40 bits—is considered to be *munitions* or weapons. Export of weapons and munitions is restricted under the U.S. laws known as *ITAR*, or *International Traffic in Arms Regulations*.

Microsoft, therefore, offers two versions of Exchange Server. The North American version is available only inside the U.S. and Canada and contains Exchange clients that can perform 64-bit, 56-bit, or 40-bit encryption. International versions of Exchange Server can be exported to other countries. These contain clients that are capable of only 40-bit encryption. Microsoft makes available the International version only outside the U.S. and Canada.

Note that you cannot purchase the North American version in the United States and then ship it to your overseas offices. In this case, you are now the "exporter" and are subject to the ITAR restrictions. In some cases, it is possible for U.S. companies to obtain their own export licenses that allow them to ship strong encryption software to their overseas offices for internal use. U.S. companies need to contact the U.S. Commerce Department directly to obtain such a license; this is not something Microsoft can provide.

What About Traveling Laptop Users?

A common question is what happens to U.S.-based laptop users who travel outside the U.S. and Canada? If they have the North American Exchange client installed on their machine, potentially they could be breaking the ITAR law every time they travel outside the U.S. Fortunately, the U.S. Government allows an exemption for this case. U.S. citizens who travel overseas are permitted to bring a single copy of North American Exchange client with them for personal use, as long as they agree to bring it back to the U.S. when they return.

This personal exemption law has some minor self-certification record-keeping requirements. The Microsoft BackOffice Resource Kit contains documentation about this law and some sample record-keeping forms you can use.

Defense Messaging System

This chapter has covered the Advanced Security features that are found in the regular **Standards** retail version of Microsoft Exchange Server. There is an additional, specialized version of Microsoft Exchange Server that is custom-tailored to the security needs of the U.S. military. This is called the *Defense Messaging System,* or *DMS* version of Exchange. The Defense Messaging System is a specification created by the U.S. Department of Defense to create a highly secure, standards-based e-mail and messaging system for use by the military and defense community. It is designed to replace the military's current AUTODIN and teletype communications systems. The DMS version of Exchange is certified to comply with these specifications.

The DMS version of Exchange is *not* suitable for any normal commercial company. It uses special message formats that are unique to the U.S. military, and it requires special *hardware-based* encryption-processing cards to be purchased and configured for each user. These hardware-based encryption cards use chips and algorithms based on the U.S. Government's Clipper encryption proposals.

Currently, Lockheed-Martin Federal Systems is the exclusive supplier of DMS-compliant systems to the U.S. Department of Defense, including the Microsoft Exchange Server DMS version. If your organization is in the military or defense area and you are interested in DMS, you can also find further information about the Exchange Server DMS version on Microsoft's Web site at

```
http://www.microsoft.com/exchange/dmsintro.htm
```

Summary

In this chapter, you learned about the advanced security features found in an optional component of Exchange Server, the Exchange Key Management Server (KMS). You also learned about general terminology and concepts that are relevant to the topic of security and how it fits with Exchange. Some of these topics include cryptography basics—symmetric key encryption, 40-bit and 64-bit keys, public key encryption, hashing, and certificates—message encryption, digital signatures, United States export restrictions, and Exchange DMS (Defense Messaging System).

After reading this chapter, you should have a good feel for the breadth of the security features provided by the Exchange Key Management Server, for how to go about implementing KMS, and for the issues that surround advanced security. Exchange 5.0 KMS is very powerful, and if strong end-to-end security is what you need in your Exchange deployment, KMS is the way to get there.

User Management with Exchange

by Greg Todd

IN THIS CHAPTER

CHAPTER 22

One of the many important aspects of using Exchange Server is user management—knowing how to configure and manage the users properly and understanding how it affects the way users interact with the server. Exchange administrators are responsible for a number of things, including the creation and maintenance of user mailboxes and other similar objects, such as distribution lists, custom recipients, public folders, and hidden recipients—objects collectively known as *recipients*.

First, this chapter jumps right in and explores the types of recipients that exist in Exchange Server, but it focuses mainly on the most common one: the mailbox recipient. Also, beginning in this section—and continuing throughout the chapter—you will get a lot of exposure to the Exchange Administrator program. If you are not already familiar with it, you should be by the time you finish.

Then, the chapter reviews some Exchange architectural concepts as they relate to recipient creation, and it addresses management techniques with regard to naming conventions, message size limitations, and storage limitations. These topics will help you plan how to manage your users by giving you a heads-up on relevant Exchange features and functions.

Next, the chapter steps through a range of methods available to create Exchange mailboxes. Microsoft has provided some useful timesaving tools to assist in creating and migrating Exchange users. Examples are included for creating single and multiple mailboxes and for importing users from your NT or NetWare account lists.

Finally, this chapter reviews some of the actual administrative tasks you may undertake for your Exchange organization, such as backing up and restoring mailboxes, updating user information, and moving users within an Exchange site and between two Exchange sites.

Types of Recipients

Exchange identifies a recipient as any object you can send a message to. The following are the five types of recipients:

- Exchange mailboxes
- Distribution lists
- Custom recipients
- Public folders
- Hidden recipients

Figure 22.1 shows examples of the first three types of recipients, which are the most common, in the House Atreides recipients container.

Note that a single public folder called Spice Mining Techniques is also displayed. More on this in a minute.

Hidden recipients are not shown in the listing. To see them, go into Exchange Administrator, select the View menu, and choose Hidden recipients. Note that the mailboxes, distribution lists, and custom recipients will not be shown.

FIGURE 22.1.

There are various types of Exchange recipients in a recipients container.

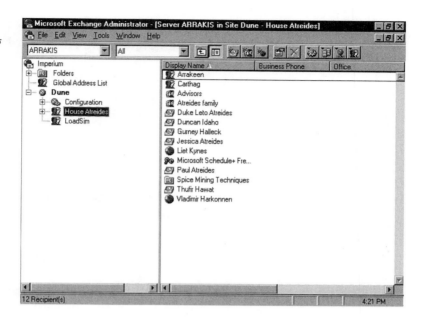

To view all the public folders, open the Public Folders object, as shown in Figure 22.2. You can see that some public folders have a plus sign next to them, such as ArrakisPF1, which indicates the folder has one or more folders within it.

FIGURE 22.2.

Exchange public folders are shown in the Public Folders object.

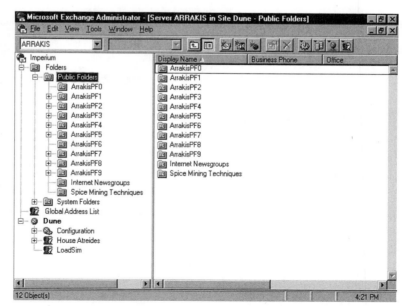

TIP

You can allow public folders to appear in the Global Address List, which will also cause them to appear in a recipients container. From the Administrator, open the properties sheet of the desired public folder by double clicking it (or use Alt+Enter or File | Properties). On the Advanced tab, uncheck the Hide from address book checkbox. The public folder will then appear in the Global Address List in the container shown in the Container name text box. See Figure 22.3.

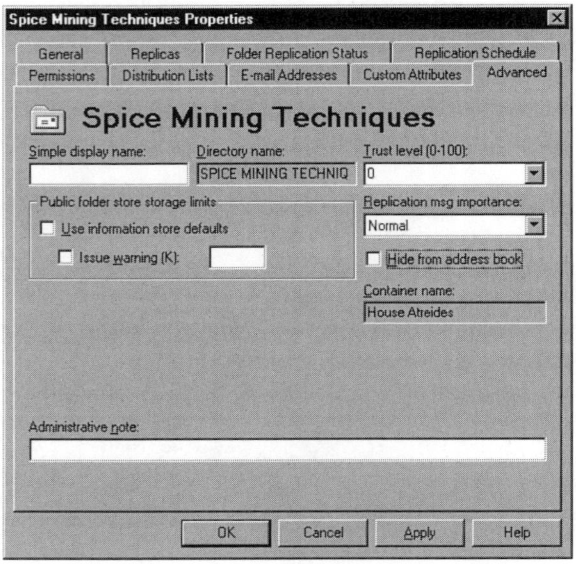

FIGURE 22.3.

You must enable public folders to be displayed in the Global Address List by unchecking Hide from address book.

Recipients Containers

Recipients are stored in recipients containers. They are the objects within the Exchange Directory that hold the various types of recipients. The containers can be named anything you like, and they can be structured to help you keep your Exchange users organized. The organizational structure you use for the containers will be reflected in the Global Address List the clients use when addressing messages.

For example, the server shown in Figure 22.4 has been the subject of an Exchange Load Simulator (LoadSim) run. (For more details on LoadSim, read Chapter 29, "Understanding and Using LoadSim.") Before running LoadSim, you must import the LoadSim "users" into Exchange Directory. When you do that, Exchange creates a recipients container called LoadSim, shown in Figure 22.4. These imported recipients will appear in the LoadSim container in the address book.

FIGURE 22.4.

Here is an example of a dedicated container used for LoadSim recipients.

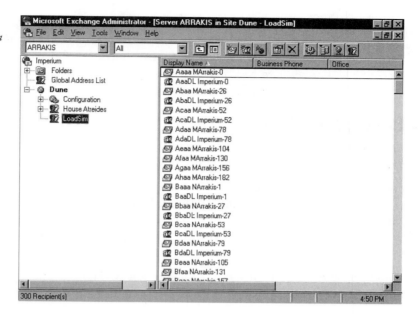

Containers Within Containers

As mentioned previously, if you want to manage your recipients by location within the site, you can structure your site's main recipients container to have multiple recipients containers within it, such as Arrakeen and Carthag, shown in Figure 22.5.

FIGURE 22.5.

For organizational purposes, Exchange recipients containers can be created within other recipients containers.

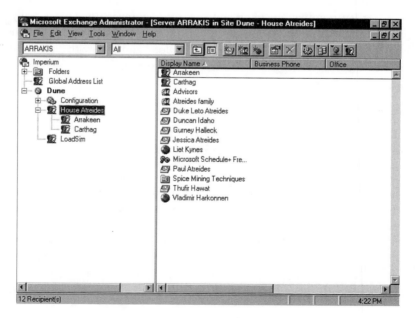

Figure 22.5 depicts the Exchange site called Dune, and it depicts the organizational structure for Dune. The default container called Recipients has been renamed House Atreides. Within the House Atreides container, two additional containers, called Arrakeen and Carthag, have been created. Furthermore, a second recipients container of LoadSim has also been created at the site level. This type of configuration helps structure the users by location and functionality.

Exchange Mailboxes

An Exchange mailbox is the most common type of recipient. Administrators usually create an Exchange mailbox for each user that sends and receives messages on the Exchange server.

For example, if you have 100 users that send and receive mail, you create 100 mailboxes. To create the appropriate mailbox in Exchange Administrator, highlight the desired Site Recipients container and choose File | New Mailbox. This method is best for adding a few users at a time. Fortunately, Exchange also supports creating multiple users at once by importing them into the Exchange Directory.

Both of these methods are discussed in the section "Creating Exchange Recipients," later in this chapter.

Non-User Mailboxes

It is possible to create non-user mailboxes as well as user mailboxes. Although not technically a separate recipient type—they are just mailboxes—non-user mailboxes are merely Exchange mailboxes designated for a particular purpose.

For example, if you have an Employee-of-the-Month program, you can ask your employees to e-mail their nominations to an address called EmployeeOTM. This is really a mailbox with the name EmployeeOTM, and it appears in the Global Address List as such. You can assign someone the access rights to open EmployeeOTM's mailbox and review the nominations. This approach makes it easy to implement solutions of this nature. Of course, you could use public folders to accomplish the same thing.

Security
New to
Version 5.0

Permitted Protocols

One of the new things you can do in Exchange 5.0 is specify which protocols a client is allowed to use when authenticating using HTTP, LDAP, NNTP, and POP3. This can be configured for each individual mailbox and custom recipient on the Protocols tab, as shown in Figure 22.6.

For example, let's say you are an Internet Service Provider (ISP) that uses Exchange Server to provide message, directory, and discussion services. With this new feature, you can specify that some users, who pay $9.95 per month for the "Standard Service," can use POP3 for mail, but they don't get to use NNTP news readers or HTTP Web browsers for access to e-mail and public folders. Meanwhile, other users, who pay $19.95 per month for the "Extended Service," can use any protocol they want. They have full access via mail, news, Web, and POP3 clients.

FIGURE 22.6.

*Exchange 5.0 allows
you to specify which
protocols a client is
allowed to use when
accessing Exchange.*

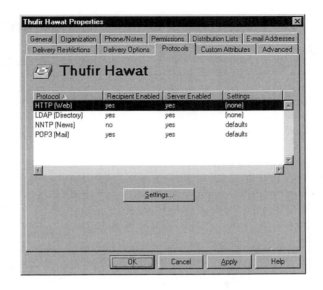

This feature is useful in paid services situations, but it is also useful in performance-related situations. For example, you believe it will help Exchange server performance to limit the number of people who use the Exchange Web Service to read their e-mail from anywhere in the world. You can configure Exchange so that only certain people have that capability. Furthermore, you can customize how all users receive their messages—MIME format or UUENCODEd attachments, plaintext or HTML, and so forth—according to the kind of client software your users use.

All of this can be configured on the Protocols tab, which appears on each mailbox and custom recipient in an Exchange 5.0 site.

Distribution Lists

There are two types of distribution lists (DLs) in Exchange: those that are created by users in their own personal address books (.PAB) and those that are created by administrators for the whole Exchange user community. DLs can have any or all of the five types of recipients as list members. These distribution lists can also be hidden or made visible to the Exchange community in the Global Address List. Figure 22.7 shows the two DLs—Advisors and Atreides family—configured in the House Atreides container. Note that the people in the DL icon are smaller than the people in the recipients icon. There is more information on creating and managing distribution lists in Chapter 23, "The Exchange Directory."

FIGURE 22.7.

Exchange distribution lists are held in a recipients container.

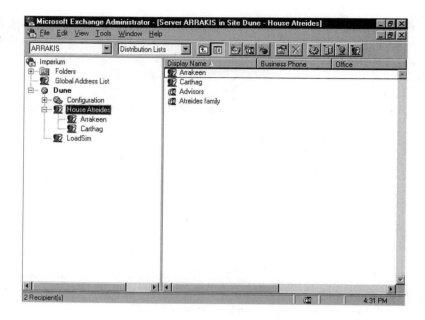

Custom Recipients

You should clearly understand the difference between a mailbox and a custom recipient. A custom recipient is simply a recipient on a foreign system, such as the Internet, X.400, or cc:Mail. Think of a custom recipient as a forwarding address or a pointer, not as an actual Exchange mailbox. Custom recipients do not have an Exchange mailbox account on the Exchange server, in the Exchange site, or in the Exchange organization. Figure 22.8 shows two custom recipients—Liet Kynes and Vladimir Harkonnen—defined in the House Atreides recipients container.

A user can create custom recipients for his or her own use in a Personal Address Book, or the administrator can create custom recipients for all Exchange users in the site to use. Here's how it works:

- *Exchange Client Personal Address Books.* As an Exchange client, you would use the custom recipient addressing method when someone gives you his or her Internet address and you want to send mail to him or her. From the Address Book, select File | New Entry, and select the custom recipient type you want to create. Note that the Exchange client Personal Address Book does not use icons to differentiate between an Exchange mailbox and a custom recipient. Custom recipients are also useful if you have multiple e-mail accounts. For example, you can go on vacation and set up Exchange Client rules to forward your e-mail to a custom recipient that points to your Internet account.

■ *Exchange Administrator.* As an Exchange administrator, you can create custom recipients for your Exchange community to use. There might be times when you will create a few individual custom recipients. However, if you have multiple types of messaging environments in your company, you should create recipients containers for each type of messaging environment or for each location. This is where planning becomes important. Also, the importing facility can help make it less arduous. Simply create the necessary recipients containers and then import your group of custom recipients into it.

FIGURE 22.8.

Exchange custom recipients are held in a recipients container.

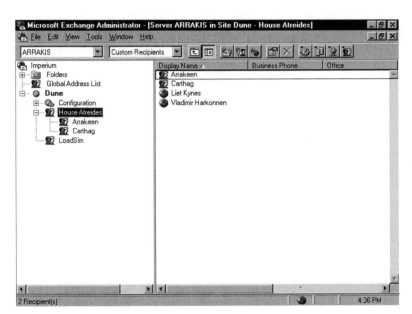

22

USER MANAGE-
MENT WITH
EXCHANGE

CAUTION

If you attempt to create a custom recipient that has the same e-mail address as an existing Exchange user or mailbox, the Exchange Administrator will give you an error.

If you create a custom recipient with an address or name to reside on an Exchange server and the mailbox does not exist, all users that send e-mail to this custom recipient get an undeliverable message from the Exchange System Administrator.

As a new feature in Exchange 5.0, you can now designate a primary Windows NT account for a custom recipient just as you do with a mailbox. You do this on the Advanced tab of the custom recipient properties sheet. This primary account is assigned to be the owner of the custom recipient object and can use it to send and receive messages.

New to
Version 5.0

Another new feature in Exchange 5.0 allows you to specify the message format for individual Internet address (SMTP) custom recipients. When you create the Internet custom recipient, there are now two tabs in the Internet Address properties sheet: one for the actual e-mail address, as usual, and another one for the default message format—MIME or UUENCODE, and plain text or HTML.

Public Folders

The first thing to remember about public folders is that only Exchange clients can create them. Administrators are responsible for managing them and replicating them to other Exchange servers and sites, but they cannot create public folders from the Exchange Administrator program. Administrators must log in with the client software if they want to create public folders. This may seem strange, but it is because public folders are intended to be created and maintained by users. The Administrator just sort of watches over things.

A public folder is a container that can contain messages, postings, and more public folders. Public folders are a central repository of information, not only for the local Exchange environment but also for the Exchange site(s) within the Exchange organization. The integration of Web connectors and browsers makes Exchange folders a powerful tool for your organization's intranet. Public folders can also be members of a distribution list.

For example, you can create a distribution list named Visionary Team that contains all the technical marketing analysts who are responsible for the next generation of computers. If you create a public folder named Visionary Team Topics and include it on the distribution list, every e-mail to the distribution list is copied to the Visionary Team Topics public folder, which in turn can be viewed by those associates with access rights to the folder.

Public folders form a very powerful component of Exchange. Chapter 24, "Public Folders," covers the topic in detail.

Hidden Recipients

Hidden recipients are just that—hidden from the address book. Every object this chapter discusses—mailboxes, distribution lists, custom recipients, and public folders—can be hidden, but only by the Exchange administrator.

To hide an object, highlight it and open its properties page. On the Advanced tab, there is a Hide from address book checkbox. Put a check mark in the box, and the object will be hidden from the address book. A good use for this feature would be to make your CEO's private e-mail address hidden from the Global Address List.

It is also possible to show a distribution list in the address book, but you can then hide (or disable the viewing of) the actual members of the distribution list. If you are using the Exchange Administrator program, you can see the hidden recipients by selecting View | Hidden Recipients from the menu.

Planning for User Management

Now that you understand a bit about recipients, you are just about ready to get into the mechanics of creating mailboxes and managing them. But before you do, let's first explore a few relevant concepts that will make life a bit easier.

Naming Conventions

It is extremely important that you decide on naming conventions when you plan your Exchange topology. Will the users go by first name, then last name; last name, then first name; or something else? Just as there are multiple ways of defining usernames, Exchange Administrator gives you multiple options to customize their format in Exchange Administrator under Tools | Options, as in Figure 22.9.

FIGURE 22.9.

Naming convention customization provides multiple ways to customize the format of names.

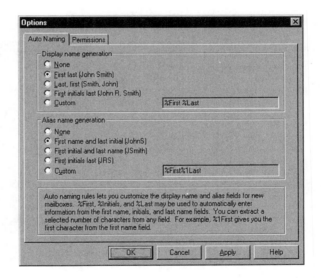

In Alias name generation, the administrator defines how the alias name is generated. As you can see from Figure 22.9, Exchange lets you decide the alias generation format. It can be a combination of initials, names, or characters within the name. The Custom field enables you to create your own specific algorithm if the given options are not appropriate. I recommend keeping alias names eight characters or fewer in length where possible, although Exchange supports up to 64 characters.

Directory Information

You will find that the Exchange Directory is an excellent repository for your organizational data. As you can see in Figures 22.10 through 22.14, the users in your Exchange organization who are running the Exchange client are able to view the property pages for several different things. These figures show the information that can be stored for each entry in the address book, as viewed from the *client*, whether it is in the Exchange Global Address List or in a personal address book. And now that Exchange 5.0 supports LDAP, you can also access the Exchange Directory using an LDAP client.

Information in the Global Address List is modified by the administrator using the Exchange Administrator program. This makes sense, because you wouldn't want people going around willy-nilly, changing the system's public address list. On the other hand, you get to manage personal address books yourself. I find it convenient to store my contact information this way in a personal address book:

- General information (see Figure 22.10)
- Company Organization information (see Figure 22.11)
- Phone/Notes information (see Figure 22.12)
- Distribution list membership (see Figure 22.13)
- E-mail Addresses (see Figure 22.14)

FIGURE 22.10.

General information.

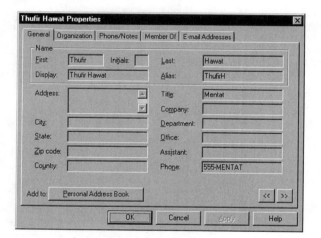

FIGURE 22.11.

Company Organization information.

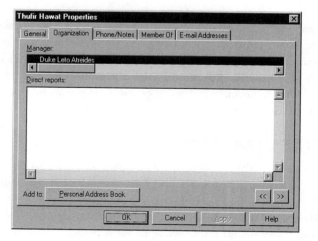

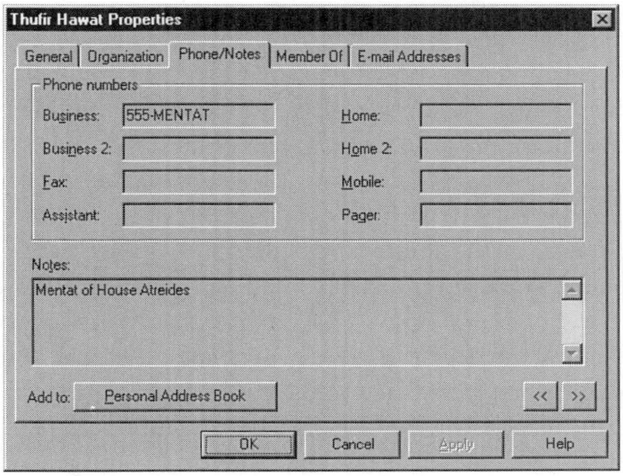

FIGURE 22.12.
*Phone/Notes informa-
tion.*

FIGURE 22.13.
*Distribution list
membership.*

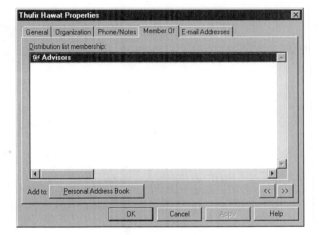

FIGURE 22.14.
E-mail Addresses.

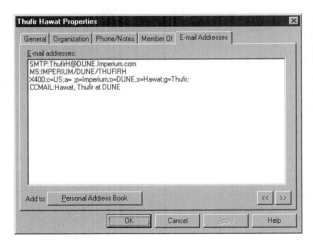

Imposing Mailbox Size Limitations

As Exchange administrator, you are responsible for defining the boundaries of your Exchange system. Boundaries can be placed because of resource limitations as well as organizational philosophy. Administrators can set two types of limitations: message sizes and storage limits.

Message Sizes

Exchange has given the administrator the ability to limit the size of messages going into and leaving the Exchange server. These limitations can be set at the Exchange connector level or at the user level. For example, if you have an Internet Mail Service using a phone line to send and receive mail, you can decide to prevent any messages greater than 1MB from being transmitted into or out of your system. Each connector has a set of property pages that defines limitations. This is normally found on the General tab or the Advanced tab. Figure 22.15 shows an Internet Mail Service (IMS, known as the Internet Mail Connector in Exchange 4.0) that is limiting message sizes to 1MB (1024KB) or less.

FIGURE 22.15.

Message size limits for the IMS are set in the Site Configuration Connections Internet Mail Service object.

You can decide to set limits for each specific user. In this case, you change the mailbox property of the individual user to allow greater sizes of messages outgoing or incoming. This can be done on the Advanced tab of the user's mailbox property pages. Figure 22.16 shows that Paul Atreides is configured for no size limits, which defaults to whatever is set for the information store. However, specific mailbox limits can be designated if necessary.

FIGURE 22.16.

User message size limits for Paul Atreides will default to whatever is set for the information store.

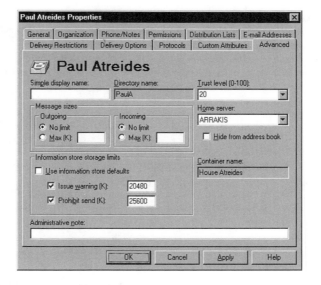

Storage Limits

Each Exchange user has a home server that is the main repository for messages. These messages can be text, bitmaps, video files, sound files, and so on. An Exchange user's individual messages are stored in the Exchange Private Information Store (\exchsrvr\mdbdata\priv.edb). The public messages are stored in the Public Information Store (\exchsrvr\mdbdata\pub.edb). Both are collectively referred to as the *store.* The store is a pair of large databases with transaction logs of all the messaging activity. In versions 4.0 and 5.0, the Private Information Store and Public Information Store cannot grow beyond 16GB of storage each. If your users send large messages or don't delete e-mail, it might be necessary to apply storage limitations.

Storage limitations can be applied at the server level, on the General tab of the Private Information Store properties sheet. Figure 22.17 shows limitations configured on the private store. At 15MB the offending user will be sent a warning message. At 20MB the offending user will be prohibited from sending messages.

Now that limits are set, the users will be sent a warning when they exceed them. There are two types of storage warnings available, in a sort of two-stage warning system:

- *Issue Warning.* This is a warning that Exchange sends to those users who exceed the first set of storage limits. Users are informed by e-mail when they exceed the limits.
- *Prohibit Send.* Users receive another warning that they have exceeded storage limitations. They continue to receive mail but they are prohibited from sending mail until they reduce their storage usage. This usually gets your users to clean out their mailboxes pretty quickly.

FIGURE 22.17.

You can configure default storage limits for the Private Information Store.

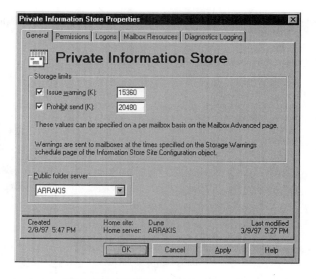

FIGURE 22.17.

You can configure default storage limits for the Private Information Store.

NOTE

Storage limitations for the private store can also be applied at the user level, as you saw in Figure 22.16. In this case, specific mailbox limits are set for Paul Atreides, and the information store's default storage limits are overridden. Note that only an "issue warning" limit can be set for the public store—there is no "prohibit send warning."

Some of you more astute readers might be saying, "Hey, because Exchange implements single-instance storage, and a lot of my users get the same e-mail, what does this storage limit apply to?" In other words, does Exchange ignore single-instance storage when calculating how much storage space a user is consuming? Yes it does. A storage limit applies to each user, regardless of what messages are in the store. So, the logical capacity of the information store can be greater than its physical capacity of 16GB.

Architecture

SINGLE-INSTANCE STORE

When a message comes into Exchange, there is only one copy of the message in the information store. Exchange gives each recipient mailbox a pointer to the message. So, if a 1MB message is sent to 100 users on the same Exchange server, Exchange doesn't store 100 1MB messages, using up 100MB of storage. It stores a single 1MB message with 100 pointers to this message in the database. In this case, Exchange charges 1MB of storage space to each of the 100 users, although the message is actually shared in the database. Thus, the sum of the logical (calculated) storage capacity on the Exchange server can exceed the 16GB physical storage limitations. This is the way Exchange is designed, so it's no problem.

When a user modifies the original message, Exchange creates a modified copy and the user's pointer changes to the newer version.

For example, say there is a server-wide storage limit of 30MB for each user on a server. (See Figure 22.18.) User1 and User2 are in the same group, so they get much of the same e-mail from their team members, about 20MB worth. The single-instance storage proves to be a benefit here. Let's say that in addition to the 20MB of team e-mail, each user has 10MB of other unique e-mail. If User1 and User2 are the only users on their Exchange server, the total size of the private store would be around 40MB rather than 60MB: 20MB of single-instance stored team e-mail, plus 10MB each (20MB total) of e-mail unique to each user. However, both User1 and User2 are charged for the entire 30MB (20MB + 10MB), so they will receive a warning from the system because their limit is 30MB.

FIGURE 22.18.

Here is an example of how the single-instance store works.

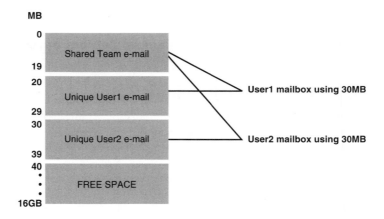

Creating Exchange Recipients

Now that you know more about the implications of user management, you are ready to address the different methods of creating an Exchange mailbox. There are many ways to create Exchange recipients, and each method has its usefulness in the appropriate situation. This section covers methods the Exchange administrator can employ in creating recipients:

- Creating a single mailbox recipient
- Creating multiple mailbox recipients via import
- Extracting accounts from your NT domain account list and then importing them
- Extracting accounts from your Novell account list and then importing them
- Using the command-line interface to create a recipient

This section also covers using the NT User Manager for Domains for creating a single mailbox recipient along with each new NT user account.

It is fairly easy to create an Exchange recipient object. Table 22.1 shows you what you need to do in Exchange Administrator.

Table 22.1. Creating Exchange recipients.

Choose	*To Create*	*Then*
File	New Mailbox	An Exchange Mailbox	Define User/Mailbox attributes
File	New Distribution List	An Exchange Distribution List	Add Members to the new Distribution List
File	New Custom Recipient	A Custom Recipient	Define User attributes
File	New Other	A New Recipient container	Create Recipients within the Container

Again, remember that public folders are created using the Exchange client software, not the Administrator program.

Creating a Single Mailbox Recipient

When you add one or two Exchange mailboxes at a time, you create each user singularly. However, in the long run, you should create one or more mailboxes that will be used as recipient templates to describe generic company users. For example, by creating an engineering template, you can predefine basic information about department name, location, assistants, and so on. That information will be the basis for newly created mailboxes. To create these mailboxes:

1. In Exchange Administrator, choose File | New Mailbox and then complete the Mailbox property pages as generically as possible. Give the new mailbox the display name Engineering Template. Choose Apply and OK to exit this step.

2. Next, in Exchange Administrator, highlight the new mailbox you just created. Choose File | Duplicate. You will see the familiar mailbox property pages with some of the fields already filled in. Pretty handy, huh?

Batch Creating and Importing Recipients

If you want to create multiple mailboxes for your Exchange site and you don't want to enter each individually, it is easy to create a file that Exchange can import. One way to do this is to start with a template and then modify it as you go along.

22

Step 1

The first step is to create a template Import file:

1. To create a template, create at least one mailbox recipient in your Exchange recipients container.

2. In Exchange Administrator, choose Tools | Directory Export. You will see a screen similar to Figure 22.19.

FIGURE 22.19.

The Directory Export dialog box provides a way to export Directory data into an export file.

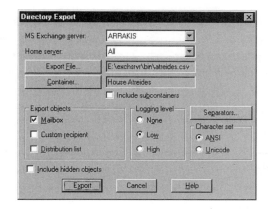

Based on the values you input and select on this form, Exchange Administrator will perform the required tasks you've indicated. The export tool will do the following:

- Export all the selected export objects from the selected container.
- Export the containers themselves (if selected) into the export file you've defined.
- Use the type of separators that you've defined.
- Perform the actual export task.

NOTE

Note that the MS Exchange server entry specifies the server from which the export will be run. The Home server is the server that contains the actual data you want to export. Many times they are the same, but they don't have to be.

Step 2

The second step is to edit your template Import file.

Export produced a CSV (comma-separated variable) file that you can view in Notepad, Edit, or Excel. If you use Notepad or Edit, the fields are separated by commas (or the separator you specified). Excel spreads the data into distinct columns, so you might want to print it out in landscape mode to understand what goes where. I find Excel the most useful when editing mass lines with separators.

The header, or top line of the file, defines the ordering of the user information. Each line after the top header line is specific to each new user. For example, you see something like this:

```
Obj-Class,First Name,Last name,Display Name,Alias Name,Directory Name,
Primary Windows NT Account, Home-Server,E-mail address,E-mail
Addresses,Members,Obj-Container,Hide from AB

Mailbox,Thufir,Hawat,Thufir Hawat,ThufirH,ThufirH,DUNE\ThufirH,ARRAKIS,,
SMTP:ThufirH@DUNE.Imperium.com%MS:IMPERIUM/DUNE/THUFIRH%X400:c=US;a=
;p=Imperium;o=DUNE;s=Hawat;g=Thufir;%"CCMAIL:Hawat,Thufir at DUNE", Recipients/
cn=Advisors,Recipients,
```

However, deciphering this data in columns makes the editing task easier. The following separates this data into fields for easier viewing:

Field	Value
Obj-Class	Mailbox
First Name	Thufir
Last Name	Hawat
Display Name	Thufir Hawat
Alias Name	ThufirH
Directory Name	ThufirH
Primary Windows NT Account	DUNE\ThufirH
Home-Server	ARRAKIS
E-mail Addresses	
SMTP:ThufirH@DUNE.Imperium.com	
MS:IMPERIUM/DUNE/THUFIRH	
X400:c=US;a=;p=Imperium;o=DUNE;s=Hawat;g=Thufir;	
"CCMAIL:Hawat,Thufir at DUNE"	
Obj-Container	Recipients/cn=Advisors
Hide from AB	*blank*

An appendix in the *Microsoft Exchange Administrator's Guide* manual details the significance of each field. Note that because every property page field is not exported, you might need to add additional fields if your organization requires them.

TIP

A trick to figure out what goes in each field is to first run the Exchange Administrator in raw mode. Use the /r parameter:

```
c:\exchsrvr\bin\admin /r
```

After you get into Exchange Administrator, highlight a recipient's mailbox object and choose File | Raw Properties. A Raw Property Page window pops up with object attributes on the left and values in boxes on the right. Not all of these object attributes correlate directly to field names that you can set and consequently import, but you can use this for a quick guide when you can't find the appendix.

Step 3

The third step is to import your new template file that now has an entry for every user. When you are ready to import these users, choose Tools | Directory Import; you see a dialog box, as shown in Figure 22.20.

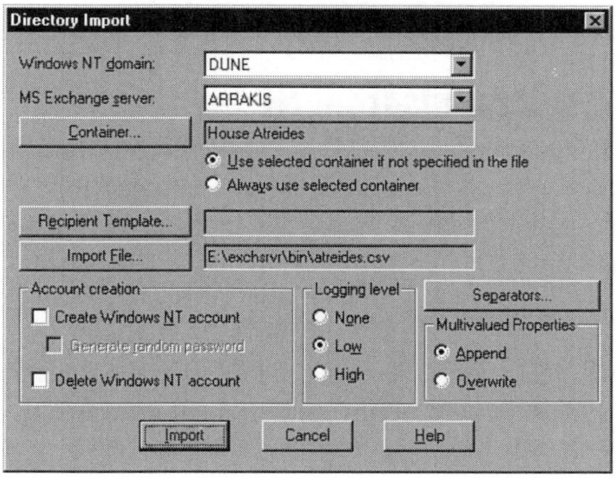

FIGURE 22.20.

The Directory Import dialog box allows you to import recipients into the Exchange Directory.

From this dialog box, you specify several things:

- *NT domain into which you are importing.* (This applies only if you specify that import will also create NT accounts—Exchange relies on the NT security model for user authentication.)
- *Server.* The specific Exchange server where the recipients will be imported.
- *Container.* The container where the recipients will be imported. Note that you can have container names in your .csv file, but you have the option to override these .csv names if needed.

■ *Template.* The recipient template, if you choose to import names and have their mailbox accounts adhere to a predefined template. Here, you might specify the template mailbox we discussed in the previous section.

■ *File.* The location of the import file you just created.

■ *Parameters.* The parameters for creating accounts, including

   Whether you want a corresponding Windows NT account created for each new mailbox.

   Whether you want a random password generated (you are pointed to a password file called BIMPORT.PSW that contains the new passwords). If you don't choose random generation, the passwords are the same as the user's alias name.

■ *Logging level.* Any errors are logged and can be viewed in NT Event Viewer, Application Logs.

■ *Separators.* You have the option to change the separators used in the output file.

■ *Multivalued Properties.* You have the choice of appending imported data to any multivalued property data that exists or overwriting it. Usually you will want to overwrite what is there with new data.

After you import your .csv file, you see all the new mailboxes created in the specified container.

Extracting Accounts from NT

If you implement Exchange into an existing NT environment, it might make sense to create your .csv file by first extracting the NT accounts and then modifying the .csv file with appropriate information. Microsoft has a tool in Exchange Administrator to help you extract these NT user accounts. Here's how to perform the extraction and subsequent import into Exchange.

Step 1

You access the User Extraction utilities from the Tools menu of Administrator. Choose Tools | Extract Windows NT Account List. You should then see a pop-up window similar to the one in Figure 22.21.

FIGURE 22.21.

The Windows NT User Extraction dialog box provides the means to configure NT user account extraction.

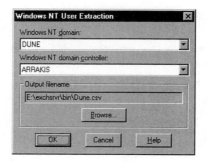

From this window, choose the NT domain from which you want to extract the usernames, the name of the NT domain controller in this NT domain, and finally an output file for the extraction. After you choose and validate these fields, choose OK to run the NT User Extractor tool. You see a resulting pop-up window explaining the number of errors, if any, that occur.

Step 2

Next, you can modify the resulting .csv file, if needed. Your output file might look similar to this:

```
Obj-Class,Common-Name,Display-Name,Home-Server,Comment
Mailbox,Administrator,,~SERVER,Built-in account for administering
➥the computer/domain
Mailbox,dand,Dan Duke,~SERVER,
Mailbox,ExchAdmin,Exchange Administrator,~SERVER,Built-in account for administering
➥the computer/domain
Mailbox,ExchUser,,~SERVER,Built-in account for administering
➥the computer/domain
Mailbox,garyd,Gary Duke,~SERVER,
Mailbox,glend,Glen C. Duke,~SERVER,
Mailbox,Guest,,~SERVER,Built-in account for guest access to the computer/domain
Mailbox,IUSR_ARRAKIS,Internet Guest Account,~SERVER,Internet Server
➥Anonymous Access
Mailbox,katiet,Katie Todd,~SERVER,
Mailbox,mildredd,Mildred Duke,~SERVER,
```

Remove the usernames that are not valid for receiving mail or that already have mailboxes. For example, remove the lines with Administrator, Guest, and IUSR_ARRAKIS.

Next, add fields that your organization requires to the header line, such as Phone or Office, and then add the appropriate information for each user line. If your organization information is the same for each user, it might make sense for you to choose a Recipient Template in the import phase instead. It is up to you to determine the best way for your import.

> **NOTE**
>
> At import time, the value of ~SERVER for Home-Server will simply be replaced with the name of the server from which you are running the import. If you run the import from a different Exchange server computer, and you want the names to be imported to another Exchange server, you must change the ~SERVER value to the name of the destination Home Exchange Server.

Step 3

Next, you must import your modified .csv file. After you have handcrafted your .csv file with the appropriate mailbox accounts and information, choose Tools | Directory Import and follow the steps as discussed in the previous section.

Extracting Accounts from NetWare

If your Exchange implementation is to include Novell NetWare users who already exist, Exchange Administrator provides another extractor tool to handle this. Again, in Exchange Administrator, choose Tools | Extract NetWare Account List, and you see a pop-up window similar to the one in Figure 22.22.

FIGURE 22.22.

The Novell NetWare User Extraction dialog box provides the means to configure NetWare user account extraction.

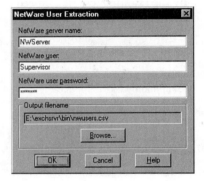

As you can see, it is very similar to the NT User Extraction dialog box. You complete this form with the necessary information:

1. Enter the name of the Novell NetWare server that contains the user account information you want.
2. Enter a NetWare user account that has permission to extract this information, such as Supervisor.
3. Enter the NetWare user's password.
4. Specify an output file for the extraction information.

Follow steps 2 and 3 from the previous section to finish editing and importing the .csv file.

Using the Command-Line Interface

At some point, you may need to do without the Exchange Administrator user interface and do everything from the command prompt. Although not the easiest, most intuitive method to import and export users, it can be done. And sometimes it is necessary.

Appendix B, "Command Reference," covers the command-line parameters for the Administrator program (ADMIN.EXE). Also, if you run the Administrator program with a /? parameter, it opens the online help where all the command-line parameters are described.

Exporting

Assuming you have installed Exchange on drive C:, execute the following command to export information from Exchange Directory. /e means to export, and /d specifies the Exchange server from which you want to export data:

```
c:\exchsrvr\bin\admin /e output.csv /d arrakis
```

The following are other options you can use:

- /n means don't display the progress bar.
- /o means specify export options in an option file.

Importing

To import information into the Exchange Directory, execute the following command. /i means to import, and /d specifies the Exchange server into which you want to import data:

```
c:\exchsrvr\bin\admin /i input.csv /d arrakis
```

As with exporting, you can use these options:

- /n means don't display the progress bar.
- /o means specify import options in an option file.

Using NT User Manager for Domains

One of the great things about Exchange is that Exchange administration is integrated into the NT User Manager for Domains program. There is an Exchange menu added to the menu bar and a property sheet to specify administration options, as shown in Figure 22.23.

FIGURE 22.23.

Exchange mailbox administration is integrated with User Manager for Domains.

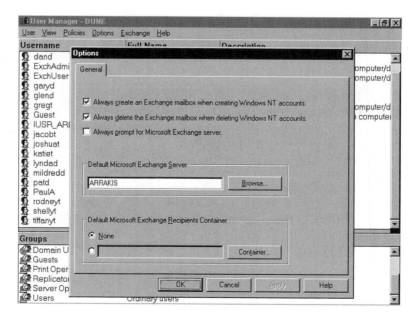

If you add a new user account to the NT domain, you can automatically create an Exchange mailbox for the user at the same time. Likewise, if you delete a user account in the NT domain, you can automatically delete the associated Exchange mailbox.

In NT User Manager for Domains, use the Exchange | Options menu to determine the following:

- Whether User Manager always creates an Exchange mailbox when creating Windows NT accounts
- Whether User Manager always deletes an Exchange mailbox when deleting Windows NT accounts
- Whether User Manager always prompts for the Microsoft Exchange server
- The default Microsoft Exchange server for the new mailbox
- The default recipients container for the new mailbox

You decide upon naming conventions when you plan your Exchange topology. When you use NT User Manager for Domains to create an Exchange mailbox, the username is defined to be the Exchange mailbox name by default. However, you can change the name when you create the mailbox:

1. In User Manager for Domains, choose User | New User (or Copy if you are copying a template user).
2. After you enter the NT information and choose Add, an Exchange mailbox properties sheet appears for the new user. The following fields are normally completed on the new Exchange mailbox:

General tab:	Display Name, Alias Name, Primary Windows NT Account
Advanced tab:	Directory Name, Home Server and Container name (per predefined options)
E-Mail Addresses:	Appropriately generated e-mail addresses

> **NOTE**
>
> You cannot use an Exchange mailbox template when you use NT User Manager to create the Exchange mailboxes. If it is normal in your administration process to use templates, follow these steps:
>
> 1. From the Exchange Options property sheet in User Manager, uncheck Always create an Exchange mailbox when creating Windows NT accounts.
> 2. Use Exchange Administrator to manually create the mailbox for the new NT user.

Mailbox Administration

You may be responsible for adding users, deleting users, monitoring storage limitations, and changing user organization information as the users move around the company. If so, you are also probably responsible for defining a backup and restore policy for the Exchange server and ensuring its implementation. Some of the user management details have already been covered earlier in the chapter. This section focuses on backup and restore policies and on moving users in the organization.

The topic of backups in Exchange is covered in detail in Chapter 25, "Backup and Recovery." Take some time to review this chapter in detail.

Backup and Restore Policies for Users

It is important to set user expectations with regard to restoring deleted mail, because this turns out to be an Exchange administrator's most routine activity. As of the writing of this book, there is not a utility with Exchange Server that can back up or, most importantly, restore a single mailbox. Third-party vendors have products with this capability, but without those products, restorations must be performed at the server level. There are two basic options when determining how to restore a message or a specific mailbox for a user: no restore, or restoring to a test server.

No Restore

Some organizations have a policy of not restoring users' e-mail. Users are on their own. This kind of policy will definitely set users' expectations and make them a bit fearful of their Delete key. Consequently, you will see your Exchange store size grow. However, you will have to restore someone's e-mail one day—possibly yours—so the next section describes a more realistic approach.

Restore to Test Server

Assume that you have a valid backup of your Exchange server. Because you are looking for only one user's mailbox or a specific message, you have to restore the entire Exchange Server database first, find the mailbox, copy the messages to a dummy .pst, and then copy them from the dummy .pst back to the Exchange server. The following section guides you through these steps. You will have to do some work from the administrator menu, as well as some work from the client interface.

You will first log on as an administrator, use the NT Backup and Restore program, and then use Exchange Administrator:

1. Restore the specific backup to a test server that has both NT and Exchange installed. If you restore the backup tape to the original Exchange server, you will overwrite the entire production database, which is not what you have in mind.

2. After you restore the Exchange database to the test server, you create mailboxes to access this data. Exchange has a great tool to resolve such inconsistencies. From Exchange Administrator, highlight the Server name and choose File Properties to view the server's properties. From the Advanced tab, change DS/IS consistency adjustment to All inconsistencies and then choose Adjust. DS/IS consistency adjustment re-creates valid users for the directory service to access the mailboxes in your restored information store.

3. In steps 3 and 4, you will act as an administrator using the Exchange Client interface. Now that you have both valid users and valid data, you must log on to the test Exchange server as a valid Exchange client and access the mailbox and messages. From a system that has Exchange client installed, create an Exchange profile to connect to the desired mailbox on the test Exchange server. Make sure the NT domain name you logged on as has permissions to access this mailbox. Also, create a personal folder information service (.pst) called restore.pst. Name it Restored Folders.

4. Run Exchange client and choose the profile you just created. You see the user's mailbox with all of his or her messages, as well as a Restored Folders container in the Exchange client. Copy the necessary messages from the user's folders into the Restored Folders container. Exit the Exchange client and save a copy of restore.pst to a floppy or to a shared network drive.

5. You can give the restore.pst file to the user so he or she can restore the desired files, or you can do it yourself as Exchange Administrator. Both methods are detailed next.

For the user, at his or her desktop in the production site:

1. Add a personal folder to the user's Exchange profile to enable transfer of restored mail by doing the following:

   From Control Panel, run the Mail and Fax applet and choose the appropriate user profile. Then choose Add and choose Personal Folders from the list. Specify the restore.pst file you created previously and name it Restored Folders.

2. Next, the user must log on using this profile and should now be able to see his or her lost mail in the Restored Folders container. The user should now copy all the desired messages from the Restored Folders container to the Personal Folders container.

3. The user must then remove the restore.pst folder from his or her profile, either through the Mail and Fax applet in Control Panel, or through the Tools | Services menu of the client.

As Exchange administrator, at a desktop in the production site:

1. Ensure that the Exchange Administrator account has permissions on the user's mailbox.

2. From Control Panel, run the Mail and Fax applet and then choose Show Profiles | Add | Manually configure. Create a test user profile name and then Add | Microsoft Exchange Server for the production server with the user's mailbox name.

3. Select Add |Personal Folder to the profile to enable the restored mail to be transferred. To add the folder, choose the restore.pst file from the floppy or shared drive and name the file Restored Folders.

4. Log on as the user and copy all mail in the Restored Folders container to the Personal Folders container.

5. Log off and go to the Mail/Fax icon to remove the restore.pst folder from the profile.

6. E-mail the user that his or her mail has been restored.

Updating User Movement

Moving a user in the organization might be as simple as updating just his or her mailbox information to reflect new phone numbers and office numbers. However, you might also need to change the following:

- Reporting structure
- Distribution lists
- Access to public folders
- Location of his or her public folder home server
- Permission to other users' mailboxes

If a user relocates, you might need to also relocate his or her Exchange mailbox from one Exchange server to another. However, many times users don't move physically from their office but move their communication paths to different organization members. Therefore, users will communicate with a different set of people. In this case, you will want to optimize storage usage and transmissions between Exchange servers. Therefore, it might make sense to move one user's mailbox to an Exchange server that hosts the new user's department members' mailboxes. It will make things more efficient for Exchange to handle the user's e-mail if the user and the majority of recipients are on the same server.

Moving Users Within the Same Site

If your user remains in the same Exchange site, the Exchange Administrator has a tool that moves the user's mailbox from one Exchange server to another. An intrasite move requires the administrator to move the mailbox to the new server, and then the user must change the profile to reflect the new server path. The following steps detail what each person should do:

As an administrator:

1. Make sure the Exchange user is logged off from the Exchange client.

2. In Exchange Administrator, highlight the user's mailbox.

3. Choose Tools | Move Mailbox, and a pop-up window appears with a selection of Exchange servers within your Exchange site.

4. Select the new Exchange Server and click OK.

5. Exchange moves the mailbox.

As the Exchange client/user:

1. After notification from the Exchange Administrator, the user can go into the Exchange profile (using either the Mail/Fax icon or the Tools I Services menu in the Exchange client) and remove the Microsoft Exchange Server information service.

2. Add a Microsoft Exchange Server information service that points to the new Exchange server.

3. The user might need to copy his or her personal address book (.pab) from one system to another, which means the user should modify the personal address book information service path as well.

Moving Users Between Sites

If your users move from one Exchange site to another, moving users between sites requires more effort on both parties. The Move Mailbox tool is only for intrasite movement. As of the writing of this book, there isn't a tool for moving mailboxes from one site to another.

Moving mailboxes from Site A to Site B requires both the user and the administrator to perform tasks in sequence. The tasks are detailed in the following list beginning at Site A and then moving the data to Site B.

At Site A, on the client desktop, the user must add a personal folder to the user's profile to act as a backup copy of all server mail:

1. From Control Panel, run the Mail and Fax applet and choose Add I Personal Folder Service. Create a backup.pst file and name it Backup Folders.

2. The user logs on and then copies all mail from the Mailbox (private folders) on the server to the Backup Folders container.

3. The user logs off.

4. The user must save the backup.pst file to a floppy or shared network drive to use later.

5. The user must save his or her personal address book (mailbox.pab) to a floppy or shared network drive to use later.

At Site B, the administrator needs to create the user's new mailbox.

Then, at Site B the user will create a new user profile to access the new Exchange server and copy his or her backed-up mailbox to the new server-based mailbox. The user should execute the following steps:

1. Make sure backup.pst and mailbox.pab can be accessed from the client desktop.

2. From Control Panel, run the Mail and Fax applet, and then choose Show Profiles I Add I Manually configure. Enter a user profile name and then select Add I Microsoft Exchange Server for the new server with the user's mailbox name. Select Add I Personal Address Book and choose the mailbox.pab file.

3. Add a Personal Folder to the user's profile to enable the transfer of backed-up mail by selecting Add | Personal Folders. Select the backup.pst file and name it Backup Folders.

4. When the user logs on, all mail in the Backup Folders container should be copied to the Mailbox (private folders) container.

5. When the user logs off, he or she can go to the Mail and Fax applet to remove the backup.pst folder from the profile.

At Site A, the administrator can now delete the user's mailbox.

Cleaning Mailboxes

As discussed earlier in this chapter, you will want to monitor your users for storage usage in their mailboxes. One way to perform maintenance on mailboxes is by using the Clean Mailbox tool in the Exchange Administrator. To clean (or reduce the size of) a mailbox, run the Clean Mailbox tool as shown in Figure 22.24.

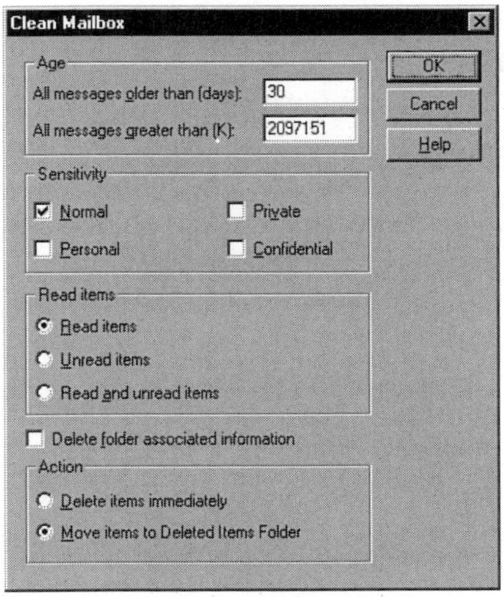

FIGURE 22.24.

The Clean Mailbox utility is useful for uniformly removing messages from mailboxes.

In this example, all read messages of normal sensitivity over 30 days old were moved into the Deleted Items folder. In this example, the maximum value for size is specified because I did not want to remove messages based on their size. Rather, I wanted to remove e-mail based on age.

Summary

This chapter covered the very important topic of user management, a main topic of administration. You learned about the types of recipients that exist in Exchange Server, focusing mainly on the mailbox recipient. The chapter reviewed some Exchange architectural concepts and user management techniques that will help you with planning how to manage your users. I covered a range of methods available to create Exchange mailboxes, including some useful tools from Microsoft. You learned about some of the actual administrative tasks you may perform for your Exchange organization, such as backing up and restoring mailboxes, updating user information, and moving users within an Exchange site and between two Exchange sites. And finally, throughout the chapter you got a lot of valuable exposure to the Exchange Administrator program.

A few final words of advice. It is important to determine the types of Exchange recipients you will have in your Exchange site and to place them in appropriate containers at the beginning of your implementation. Take time to plan for the different messaging subsystems your users will connect to, and then create containers and custom recipients to facilitate it. When you are populating your Exchange server for the first time, use the tools available with Exchange. When your site is up and running, create templates to help you create subsequent mailboxes. You probably already know the requirements for restoring deleted messages, and it will help to have a test server in your lab to be used for emergency restores. Finally, keep informed about new Exchange administration tools that can make your job easier. As time goes on, no doubt Microsoft and third-party ISVs will produce products that make user management for Exchange even easier.

The Exchange Directory

by David Mosier
Revised by Kevin Kaufmann

IN THIS CHAPTER

This chapter provides an overview of directories and covers the administration of the Exchange Directory. It quickly covers the concepts of International Standards Organization (ISO) X.500 Directory Services, the foundation of the Exchange Directory. Next, the chapter explains the major objects in the Exchange Directory and how to administer the security options. It also explains the tools for importing and exporting information with the Exchange Directory. This chapter provides an understanding of what the Exchange Directory is and how to manage it. You should also get an idea of how the Exchange Directory relates to the X.500 directory standard.

Directory Concepts

A directory is a hierarchical database of descriptive information organized for fast and efficient retrieval. Each entry in the directory can have several pieces of information, or attributes, associated with it. One of the best examples of a directory is the residential telephone book. Despite the fact that there can be tens of thousands of entries in a two- or three-inch telephone book, given a person's name, you can generally find their address and telephone number in less than a minute.

A directory is similar to a relational database, but there are some significant differences. Unlike most relational database systems, a directory is read much more often than it is updated. Because the information is more static than a relational database, a directory can use a simple replication process to distribute entries across multiple systems rather than the more complex two- or three-phase commit protocols employed by distributed relational databases. Also, whereas a relational database is organized around tables of interrelated information, a directory is organized around a hierarchy of objects, each with attributes that describe their associated entry.

A computer-based directory service provides a structure for information storage as well as the methods for the secure and reliable entry and retrieval of information. A directory service that is distributed across multiple computers must also provide a method for sharing or replicating the entries in each computer with all the other computers participating in the directory service.

Exchange uses a distributed directory service to store entries about system configuration and about each user. Each entry is referred to as a directory object. Each group of objects—for instance mailboxes, distribution lists, or link monitors—is referred to as an object class. Object classes have specific attributes or properties. Some attributes are required, such as the directory name for a mailbox object, and others, such as middle initial, are optional. The object class is responsible for knowing what attributes it has, which ones are optional, and which ones are required. Object classes allow the Exchange Directory to store virtually any kind of information. Exchange needs to keep track only of the object class of a directory entry; the object class keeps track of the structure of the information in the entry.

X.500 Concepts

The X.500 standard is actually a family of interrelated standards. Each section of the family is a standards document in its own right. In addition, X.500 references other standards for such things as data formatting and remote processing. The following is a list of the standards documents that together make up what is commonly referred to as the X.500 standard:

- X.500, The Directory: Overview of Concepts, Models, and Services
- X.501, The Directory: Models
- X.511, The Directory: Abstract Service Definition
- X.509, The Directory: Authentication Framework
- X.518, The Directory: Procedures for Distributed Operation
- X.519, The Directory: Protocol Specifications
- X.520, The Directory: Selected Attribute Types
- X.521, The Directory: Selected Object Classes
- X.525, The Directory: Replication
- X.581, Directory Access Protocol: Protocol Implementation Conformance
- X.582, Directory System Protocol: Protocol Implementation Conformance
- X.208, Specification of Abstract Syntax Notation (ASN.1)
- X.209, Specification of Basic Encoding rules for Abstract Syntax Notation One (ASN.1)
- X.216, Presentation Service Definition for OSI
- X.217, Association Control Service Definition for OSI
- X.219, Remote Operations: Model, Notation, and Service Definition
- X.227, Connection-oriented protocol specification for the association control service element
- X.229, Remote Operations: Protocol Specification

The X.200 family of standards provides high-level functions for communication, including data format, remote operations, and session setup. These functions provide a basic framework over which the directory services operate.

Recommendation X.500 and X.501 provide the logical structure of the directory and the models for administration and control. Combined with recommendations X.520 and X.521, which define basic object classes and their attribute type, these documents define both the Directory Information Base (DIB) and the Directory Information Tree (DIT). The rest of the X.500 recommendations specify how the various elements of a directory interact with one another.

In the development of the Exchange 5.0 directory, Microsoft closely followed X.500, X.501, X.520, and X.521. The rest of the X.500 family of standards were either not implemented or not fully implemented. Therefore, Exchange 5.0 directory is based on X.500 but is not fully X.500-compliant. Microsoft has committed support for X.518, X.519, and X.525 in the next release of Exchange, allowing for interaction with other X.500 directories.

The X.500 Model

The X.500 model describes a directory service distributed across one or more servers. Each of the servers participating in the directory service is referred to as a directory service agent (DSA). DSAs store the directory information base (DIB) and present it to directory users as the directory information tree (DIT). Directory users, either individuals or programs, access the directory through a directory user agent (DUA). The DUA accesses the DSA through a protocol called directory access protocol (DAP). Communication between the distributed DSA systems is accomplished through the directory system protocol (DSP), the directory operational binding management protocol (DOP), and the directory information shadowing protocol (DISP). DSP allows one DSA to look up an entry in another DSA, usually on behalf of a client DUA. DSA systems use DOP to establish a working relationship and security context. A DSA uses DISP to replicate all or part of its entries to another DSA. Figure 23.1 illustrates the X.500 model and where each protocol is used.

FIGURE 23.1.

The X.500 directory and protocols.

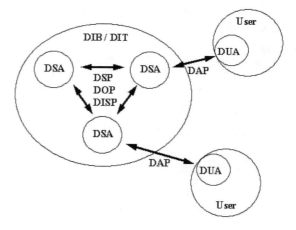

The X.500 standard uses three models or views to outline the directory: the directory user information model, the directory operational and administrative information model, and the directory service agent information model. The directory user information model identifies how entries are named and guarantees each has a unique name. The directory operational and administrative information model identifies how the directory is administered. Administration covers the type of entries that can be stored in a given part of the directory and who can access them. The two previous models look at the directory as a single entity. The directory service agent information model defines how the directory information is distributed and accessed across multiple systems.

The Physical and Logical Directory

The information defined in all three models is referred to collectively as the directory information base (DIB). The DIB is a series of entries where each entry is an object with associated attributes. The entries are related to one another hierarchically. The hierarchy, or logical structure, of the DIB is referred to as the directory information tree (DIT). Thus, the DIB is the raw collection of information, and the DIT is the structured view of the information. For users and administrators alike, it is usually the DIT that is of interest. Figure 23.2 demonstrates the difference between the DIB view of information and the DIT view.

FIGURE 23.2.

Comparison of DIB and DIT.

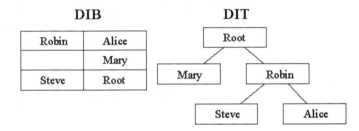

Any significant directory has a schema. A *schema* is the set of rules that ensures order in the directory. It determines what type of objects can be stored in the directory, where they can be stored, what attributes the objects can have, and what values the attributes can hold. The schema is the map that allows users to make sense of the information in the directory.

Every object in the directory must have a name. The X.500 standard refers to two types of names: the distinguished name (DN) and the relative distinguished name (RDN). The RDN identifies an object within a collection of objects with the same parent. Thus, two objects can have the same RDN as long as they do not have the same parent. As an example, you can have two towns named Columbia as long as one is in the state of Maryland and the other is in the state of South Carolina.

The DN is a concatenation of the RDN of each ancestor, starting at the root of the directory and proceeding down through all the parent directories to the RDN of the specific object. The file system is a good example of this. Assume there is a root directory called PlantLife with a subdirectory called Trees, and in the Trees directory is a file named Oak. From within the Trees subdirectory, the file Oak can be referenced simply as Oak. This corresponds to the RDN. However, the full pathname of the file Oak is /PlantLife/Trees/Oak. This corresponds to the DN. Figure 23.3 shows how the RDN relates to the DN and how the DN relates to the DIT.

FIGURE 23.3.

Naming conventions in X.500.

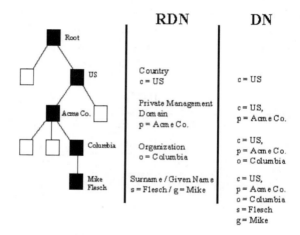

X.500 Security

Security

X.500 security is based on authentication and access control lists. The standard defines two types of authentication: simple authentication and strong authentication.

Simple authentication is essentially the exchange of an ID/password combination. The password may be sent as clear text, encrypted text, or a token derived from the password, which may be sent instead of the actual password. Simple authentication can be quite effective but it can break down in a distributed directory. The primary drawback to simple authentication is the requirement for a secure link outside the directory system for each messaging system or user to establish and update ID/password combinations. As directories and connections grow, administration becomes unwieldy.

Strong authentication involves using public and private keypairs to encrypt messages and to generate digital signatures. Strong authentication has two main advantages over simple authentication. First, it is unaffected if the transmission channel crosses an unsecured link such as the Internet. Secondly, the public keys can be registered with a secure system that is trusted by all participants in the directory or even by other directories. By establishing a secure link to the mutually trusted system and maintaining the list of public keys on that system, secure transmissions can flow between any systems without any previously established relationship.

Exchange and X.500

Standards

The ISO X.500 committee is responsible for the directory services standards. They designed a tree-structured directory capable of holding large amounts of information. The standard allows for distributing the information as well as administration over many computer systems. The entire directory, whether it exists on a single system or is distributed over multiple systems, is referred to as the directory information base (DIB). The logical structure or view of the DIB is referred to as the directory information tree (DIT). The X.500 documents specify in detail the ordering or schema of the DIT, as well as the directory access protocol (DAP) used to access the information. DAP is complex and can be difficult to implement. To address these, LDAP has been developed by the Internet community and documented in 1992 by Internet RFC-1487. LDAP has since been updated by RFC-1777.

> **NOTE**
>
> It should be noted that LDAP is an Internet specification and is not OSI-compliant. As such, it is not formally part of the X.500 standard. However, whether the ISO officially recognizes it or not, the use of LDAP within the Internet, combined with the explosive growth of the Internet itself has made LDAP a part of the X.500 landscape.

The Exchange 5.0 DIB follows the 1988 version of the X.500 directory schema. Therefore, in the definition of object classes and attributes, as well as the syntax of data storage and object names, the Exchange Directory is X.500–1988-compliant. Figure 23.4 shows an example of an X.500-style tree structure used by Exchange.

In addition, Exchange 5.0 at least partially implements the DSP protocol for DSA-to-DSA communication. However, rather than breaking the directory into pieces and distributing it across the various site servers, Exchange 5.0 replicates the entire directory to all servers in the organization. Although replicating the entire directory throughout the organization is not the norm in X.500 environments, it is not a violation of the X.500 standard and has the effect of reducing client response times. The Exchange 5.0 partial implementation of DSP does not allow interaction or replication with other X.500-compliant directories.

The only other significant piece of the X.500 1988 standard that Exchange 5.0 does not at least partially implement is the DAP protocol specified in X.519 protocol specifications.

23

THE EXCHANGE
DIRECTORY

FIGURE 23.4.

*A directory tree
structure.*

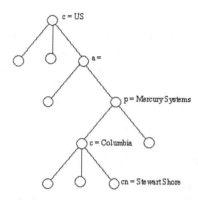

X.500 Name - /c = US /p = Mercury Systems /c = Columbia /cn = Stewart Shore

**Future
Directions**
In 1998, with NT 5.0 Directory Services (also referred to as Active Directory), several pieces of
the NT Registry will move to the directory, including the accounts database and shared resource definition. In addition, this new directory will contain objects unrelated to NT or
Exchange, such as human resource records, enabling the directory to become the corporate
information repository.

Thus, Exchange 5.0 is in a position where the directory itself is X.500-compliant, but no X.500
client applications can access it. In place of DAP, Exchange 5.0 uses an interface called directory application protocol interface (DAPI) to access the directory. It is possible to access the
directory using the mail application protocol interface (MAPI), but the process can involve
more coding and is generally read-only, although it results in faster performance. Additionally,
Exchange 5.0 added read-only support for the de-facto Internet standard LDAP, which is documented in Internet RFC-1777.

The next version of Exchange is expected to implement more of the X.500 directory standard.
In comparison to Figure 23.1, Figure 23.5 illustrates the Exchange Directory and its protocols. Not shown in the figure are the growing numbers of connectors from independent software vendors for connecting to other mail systems, such as IBM PROFS and Lotus Notes.

TIP

If you want to view the actual X.500 directory schema without interpretation, start the
Exchange Administrator in raw mode. Go to a command prompt and type ADMIN /R. You
can then select almost any of the objects in the Administrator interface and press Shift+Enter

to view their attributes. If you want to go all natural, select View and click Raw Directory. A new container called Schema shows up under each site. The Schema container has an alphabetic listing of every object class and attribute in the site.

FIGURE 23.5.

The Exchange Directory and protocols.

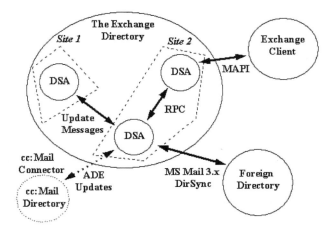

CAUTION

Be extremely careful when you use ADMIN.EXE in raw mode. Do not change anything without direction from support. The destructive force of ADMIN.EXE /R is roughly equivalent to that of REGEDT32.EXE times the number of servers in your Exchange organization.

The Exchange Directory and the NT Registry

Why does Exchange create a complex directory structure to store configuration and user information when NT already has the registry? The Exchange Directory does not replace the NT Registry. It is in addition to the NT Registry and provides Exchange with scalability and adherence to open standards. The NT Registry is intended for use primarily by the local NT system to store its configuration. It does not scale well when storing large amounts of data, and its interface is unique to NT. In fact, the NT Registry's method of storing quickly accessible user information is the primary reason for the limitation of user accounts in a single domain. When NT adopts an X.500 directory for user account information, the number of users permitted in a single domain will no doubt be much higher.

23

THE EXCHANGE
DIRECTORY

Exchange uses both the NT Registry and a directory to store information. Configuration information required by each Exchange server, such as file locations, site name, and protocol parameters, is still stored in that server's NT Registry. But information useful throughout the organization, such as mailboxes, distribution lists, public folder definitions, and link monitors, is stored in the Exchange Directory, where it can be quickly and easily accessed from anywhere in the organization by anyone with the proper authorization. Figure 23.6 illustrates how various information is stored in the NT Registry and the Exchange Directory.

FIGURE 23.6.

Configuration and directory storage in NT and Exchange.

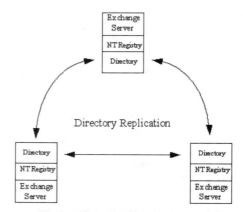

The Exchange Directory Schema

The Exchange DIT represents an organization's users and configuration. Much of the configuration information about Exchange itself is stored in the directory. Also, every detail about every recipient is in the directory. That includes recipients native to the Exchange organization and site as well as remote recipients such as SNADS or foreign X.400 users. This represents hundreds of different object classes and attributes. However, for the purposes of administering the Exchange Directory, the focus is on the following three object classes: mailbox, custom recipient, and distribution list.

Mailbox Object Class

The mailbox object class name is `mailbox`, and it stores attributes for users with accounts in the Exchange organization. These users are sometimes referred to as native Exchange users. Table 23.1 lists all of the attributes associated with the mailbox object class. Only `Object-Class` and `Common Name` are required to create a mailbox object and import information into it. However, to create a functional `mailbox` object, the imported information should include `First Name`,

`Last Name`, `Primary NT Account`, `Home Server`, and `Directory Name`. All other information is derived. Of course, if the defaults do not fulfill your organization's requirements, other attributes can be included.

Table 23.1. The attributes associated with the `mailbox` object class.

Accept Messages from	*Accept Messages from DL*
Address	Admin Note
Admin-Description	Admin-Display-Name
Alias Name	Allow rich text
Alt-Recipient	Alt-Recipient-BL
Alternate Recipient	Ancestor-ID
Assistant	Assistant phone number
Assistant-Name	Assoc-Remote-DXA
Auth-Orig	Auth-Orig-BL
AutoReply	AutoReply-Message
AutoReply-Subject	Business phone number 2
Can-Create-PF-BL	Can-Create-PF-DL-BL
Can-Not-Create-PF-BL	Can-Not-Create-PF-DL-BL
City	Comment
Common-Name	Company
Country	Custom Attribute 1-10
Deliv-Cont-Length	Deliv-EITs
Deliv-Ext-Cont-Types	Deliver to both
Deliver-And-Redirect	Deliverable Information Types
Department	Description
Direct Reports	Directory Name
Display-Name	Display-Name-Printable
DL-Mem-Reject-Perms	DL-Mem-Reject-Perms-BL
DL-Mem-Submit-Perms	DL-Mem-Submit-Perms-BL
DSA Signature	E-mail Addresses
Expiration-Time	Extension Name
Extension-Attribute-1-10	Extension-Data
Extension-Name-Inherited	Fax number

continues

23

THE EXCHANGE DIRECTORY

Table 23.1. continued

Accept Messages from	*Accept Messages from DL*
First Name	Given-Name
Heuristics	Hide-From-AB
Hide-From-Address-Book	Home phone number
Home phone number 2	Home-MDB
Home-MDB-BL	Home-MTA
Imported-From	Incoming message size limit
Initials	Instance-Type
International-ISDN-Number	Is-Deleted
Is-Member-Of-DL	Last name
Locality-Name	Mail-nickname
Maintain-AutoReply-History	Manager
MAPI-Recipient	Master-DSA
Member of	Mobile number
Notes	NT-Security-Descriptor
Obj-Dist-Name	Object-Class
Object-Version	Office
Outgoing message size limit	Owner-BL
Pager number	Period-Rep-Sync-Times
Period-Repl-Stagger	Phone Number
Physical-Delivery-Office-Name	Postal Code
Proxy-Addresses	Public-Delegates
Public-Delegates-BL	Reject messages from
Reject messages from DL	Replication-Sensitivity
Reports	Reps-From
Reps-To	Reps-To-Ext
Secondary-Proxy-Addresses	Security-Protocol
Simple display name	State
State-Or-Province-Name	Sub-Refs
Submission-Cont-Length	Supporting-Stack-BL
Surname	Telephone-Assistant
Telephone-Fax	Telephone-Home
Telephone-Home 2	Telephone-Mobile
Telephone-Number	Telephone-Office1

Accept Messages from	Accept Messages from DL
Telephone-Office2	Telephone-Pager
Teletex-Terminal-Identifier	Telex-Number
Text-Country	Title
Trust level	Unauth-Orig
Unauth-Orig-BL	User-Cert
USN-Changed	USN-Created
USN-DSA-Last-Obj-Removed	USN-Last-Obj-Removed
USN-Source	When-Changed
When-Created	X121-Address
X500-Access -Control-List	Object-Class

There are 140 different attributes that describe a mailbox object. Only 13 of the attributes are exported using the defaults for the Tools | Export Directories menu option in the Exchange Administrator program. To export additional attributes, include their object class names in the header line of the export file. All the directory objects are documented in the Exchange section of the BackOffice SDK 2.0, which is available to MSDN level 3 or Enterprise level subscribers. There is also a utility, HEADERS.EXE, included in the Exchange Server Technical Resource Guide (Microsoft Part No. 098-64705), that can create a header line with any or all of the mailbox object attributes. An explanation of the 13 default attributes exported by the Exchange Administrator program can be found in Table 23.2.

TIP

You can change the automatic name generation for the Display Name and Alias that Admin does for you by selecting Options from the Tools menu in the Exchange Admin program.

Table 23.2. Headers created by the Exchange Administrator program.

Attribute Name	Multivalued?	Purpose
First Name	No	First name of user; used to create default Display Name, Alias, and Directory Name
Last name	No	Last name of user; used to create default Display Name, Alias, and Directory Name

continues

23

THE EXCHANGE DIRECTORY

Table 23.2. continued

Attribute Name	Multivalued?	Purpose
Display Name	No	Name that appears in the address book (for addressing messages, creating distribution lists, and so forth)
Alias Name	No	Mail nickname; a short name that can be used to address messages; also used to generate X.400, SMTP, and MS Mail addresses (that is, alias@site.organization.com)
Directory Name	No	Internal name used by the directory service to reference the user; cannot be changed
Primary Windows NT Account	No	NT domain\account used for security purposes and to authenticate the user
Home-Server	No	The server on which the user's mailbox resides; the server that provides the user with information store and directory store services
E-mail address	No	Not used for mailbox object; used by remote recipient objects (custom recipient) to hold their target-address
E-mail Addresses	Yes	The user's reply-to addresses for any foreign mail systems, such as X.400, SMTP, and MS Mail
Members	Yes	A list of all the distribution lists to which the user belongs
Obj-Container	No	The parent container to which the user belongs; by default, it is Site\Recipients
Hide from AB	No	Indicates whether the user's name should be hidden from the address book

TIP

The Hide from AB attribute can be used during migration to allow users to move from the old mail system to Exchange in manageable groups. Create all the Exchange accounts for a given site or organization, hiding them from the address book. Then, when groups or individuals begin to use their Exchange account, unhide them using the Exchange Administrator program—first click View | Hidden Recipients and then unmark the Hide from Address Book attribute on the Advanced tab of the Site\Recipients\user-name property page.

Custom Recipient Object Class

The custom recipient object class name is `remote`. Remote users in Exchange are really just placeholders. The placeholders permit users on foreign mail systems to appear in the Exchange address book. This allows Exchange users to conveniently address mail to the foreign users, include them in distribution lists, and give the access to Public Folder via NNTP or HTTP. It also allows Exchange administrators to include information about the foreign user, such as telephone number, FAX number, and company, that can make the Exchange Directory more useful for native Exchange users.

The remote object class uses most of the same attributes as the mailbox object class and adds only one additional attribute, `Target-Address`. The target-address attribute holds the address of the recipient in his or her native mail system. For instance, if a FAX gateway is installed in your site, the target-address attribute for a custom recipient available through the FAX gateway may be `FAX:918005551212`.

Distribution List Object Class

The distribution list object class name is `dl`. The dl object class reuses most of the attributes from the mailbox object. However, several additional attributes are required to handle the unique functionality of distribution lists (see Table 23.3).

Table 23.3. Unique distribution list object attributes.

Attribute Name	Multivalued?	Purpose
DL-Member-Rule	Yes	Determines whether distribution lists can be members of this distribution list. This is a hidden attribute. By default, all distribution lists permit distribution lists as members.
Hide-DL-Membership	No	Determines whether the membership of this distribution list is hidden from the address book. The default is false.
Member	Yes	Lists the members of the distribution list.
Member-of	Yes	A backward link to any distribution lists of which this list is a member.

continues

23

The Exchange Directory

Table 23.3. continued

Attribute Name	Multivalued?	Purpose
OOF-Reply-to-Originator	No	Sends mail message back to originator if a member of the distribution list is out of the office.
Owner	No	The full distinguished name (DN) of the owner of the distribution list.
Report-to-Originator	No	Determines whether the message originator receives a report when a message exceeds the size limit for the distribution list.
Report-to-Owner	No	Determines whether the distribution list owner receives a report when a message exceeds the size limit for the distribution list.

CAUTION

If you want to hide the members of the distribution list, you should disable the Report to Originator in addtion to Hide-DL-Membership.

Directory Import

The directory import tool reads information from a text file and updates the Exchange Directory based on the header and contents of the import file. Although the DAPI import function, BImport, is capable of importing any class of object into any part of the Exchange Directory, the tools import function of the Exchange Administrator can import objects only into or below the recipient container. It can import mailbox objects, custom recipient objects, distribution list objects, and container objects. You can run the import utility from within the Exchange Administrator by using menu option Tools | Import, or from the command line.

The import function not only saves hours at installation time, but also it improves accuracy. It can also make directory maintenance significantly easier and faster. With the addition of the Mode field in the import file header, the import function is able to update or delete existing objects. The following example shows an import file that can change the membership of an existing distribution list. A distribution list that has just been created is being populated with three members:

```
Obj-Class, Mode, Directory Name, Members
dl, MODIFY, Managers, Recipients/cn=Kim%Recipients/cn=Megan%Recipients
➥/cn=Morticia
```

When the previous file is imported, Exchange changes the value of the Member attribute for the distribution list object, Managers, and it also changes the Is-member-of-DL attribute for the mailbox objects of Kim, Megan, and Morticia to reflect their membership in the Managers distribution list. As you can see, the import function can be quite powerful. Although this example is trivial, a file with the same basic header can be used with 500 users and 30 different distribution lists.

Exchange Administrator Graphical Import

Figure 23.7 shows the main screen for Tools | Import. The Windows NT domain listbox and MS Exchange server listbox control where the Exchange mailbox is created and where the mailbox gets its security context, respectively. The domain listed in the Windows NT domain listbox is where any NT account is created or deleted. This is especially useful in organizations using the master domain model or the multiple master domain model for their NT domain architecture. The system listed in the MS Exchange server listbox is the home server for any mailboxes or custom recipients created. It is also the only server the import tool looks in for mailboxes to be modified or deleted.

FIGURE 23.7.

Exchange Administrator import utility.

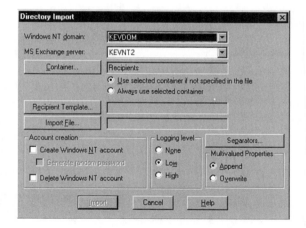

23

THE EXCHANGE
DIRECTORY

TIP

If the Exchange service account for the domain where the import utility is running does not have administrative privileges in the target domain, NT account creation or deletion fails.

Depending on the value of the radio buttons Use selected container if not specified in the file and Always use selected container, the value in container box serves different purposes. If the Use selected container if not specified in the file option is selected, the container is the default for operations where no container is specified. If the Always use selected container option is specified, the container is where all adds, updates, and deletes are performed, no matter what the import file specifies.

> **TIP**
>
> The easiest way to move a large number of users between recipient containers is to export mailboxes from one container, delete them, and then import them into another container. But don't forget these three important steps. Move each user's mailbox messages that are currently stored online to their .pst file. Export all the mailbox attributes, not just defaults for export. See Table 23.1 for the list of possible attributes. Delete the existing profile on the Exchange client and create a new one. The distinguished name (DN) used by the existing profile points to the old container.

The Recipient Template button sets the mailbox object to be used as the source of default information. For instance, you can create templates for different departments that include information such as company name, address, manager, and FAX number. Then you import users grouped by their department, and the template accounts populate the department-specific information.

Account Creation

The account creation options allow the import utility to perform account maintenance on the NT domain specified in the Windows NT domain list box. The settings in this group directly cause accounts to be created or deleted. These settings tell the import utility what to do regarding NT accounts in the event that there are entries in the import file instructing the import utility to either create or delete a mailbox object. When an NT account is created or searched for in the target domain, the default for the NT account name is the value of the common name attribute, unless a value is given for the primary Windows NT account attribute.

> **TIP**
>
> In the Exchange Directory, common name and directory name are two names for the same attribute. They make up the last part of an object's X.500 distinguished name (DN).

If Create Windows NT Account is selected, the option Generate random password becomes undimmed. If this box is selected, a random password is generated that has at least four characters—more if required by the account policies of the target NT domain. If this option is not selected, the password is set to the value of the common name attribute. If the common name attribute is not long enough to fulfill the requirements of the account policies of the target domain, the password is left-justified and the spaces are filled with a lowercase *x*. Whether a random password is generated or not, the password is written to a file with the same name as the import file and the extension of .PSW. If an NT account already exists in the target NT domain, no changes are made to that NT account.

CAUTION

If an NT account is created, a password is always created for the new account. However, the option to require users to change their passwords at the next login is not selected.

Logging Level

The logging level during the import function can be set to three levels. Setting logging level to None allows only two entries into the event log: begin import and end import. No other information is recorded. The Low logging level permits errors to be logged as well as start and finish messages. The High logging level logs the same information as the Low logging level, but it also logs warnings and informational messages. Informational messages are usually letting you know that the error file or export already existed and had to be renamed. Warnings and errors are written to the application log of the NT event log.

The entries that cause an error are written to a file with the extension of .ERR and the same name as the import file. So, an import file named Marketing.CSV that generated an error has an associated error file named Marketing.ERR. This feature makes it fast and easy to determine which entries caused errors, to fix the entry, and to import just the entries that were not previously imported.

Multi-Valued Properties

Care should be taken when setting the value of the Multi-valued properties radio buttons. Multi-valued properties are attributes that can have more than one value. SMTP addresses are an example. One mailbox object can have more than one SMTP address. In some cases, as when you are trying to replace the existing SMTP address, the Multi-valued properties radio button should be set to Overwrite. In other cases, as when you want to add an additional SMTP address to the existing address, the Multi-valued properties radio button should be set to Append. If you don't know which value to use, leave it on Append.

Command-Line Import

So far, this chapter has focused on the graphical interface to the import function. However, the import function can also be called as a command-line utility. By default, the ADMIN.EXE program is in the \exchsrvr\bin directory. The command-line parameters are defined in Table 23.4, and the syntax for the command-line version is as follows:

```
admin /i <import file> /d <directory server name> /n /o <options file>
```

Table 23.4. Command-line parameters for import utility.

Parameters	Description
/i	Tells ADMIN.EXE to run in command-line batch import mode. This parameter is required.
<import file>	The file containing the directory information to be imported. This parameter is required.
/d <directory server>	The name of the server whose directory is to be updated. This is the same as the MS Exchange server listbox.
/n	Prevents the progress bar from displaying during the import process.
/o <options file>	The file containing the options that control the import process. Most of the options are the same as the graphical mode.

Import Options File

The import options file takes the place of the user interface of the Exchange Administrator Tools | Import menu option. Most of the items in the import file have equivalent options in the graphical import utility. DirectoryService is the same as the MS Exchange server list box in the graphical version. OverwriteProperties is the same as Multi-valued properties.

ApplyNTSecurity, RawMode, and CodePage are all unique to the command-line version of the import utility. Applying NT security means matching the mailbox with an existing NT account. CodePage controls the character set used: -1 equals Unicode, 0 equals the active codepage, and any other number refers to other codepages. The InformationLevel option accepts None for no logging, Minimal for logging of errors only, and High for logging of errors and warnings. Table 23.5 describes all the items in the import options file and provides their defaults.

Table 23.5. The Import Options file.

Item	Default	Description
DirectoryService	N/A	The computer name of the directory server into which the utility imports the entries
BasePoint	The local site	The X.500 DN of the target site for the import
Container	Recipients	The RDN or common name of the target for the import
InformationLevel	Minimal	The amount of logging that is performed during the import
RecipientTemplate	None	The X.500 DN of a mailbox object to be used for the defaults for any undefined attributes

Item	Default	Description
NTDomain	Logon domain	The NT domain where accounts are searched for, created, or deleted
OverwriteProperties	No	Determines whether attributes capable of holding multiple values, such as SMTP address, are overwritten or appended
CreateNTAccounts	No	Determines whether NT accounts that do not exist in the domain specified in the NTDomain option are created in UPDATE or CREATE mode, or an error generated
DeleteNTAccounts	No	Determines whether NT accounts that do exist in the domain specified in the NTDomain option are deleted in DELETE mode
ApplyNTSecurity	Yes	Determines whether NT accounts that do exist in the domain specified in the NTDomain option are matched to the target mailbox in UPDATE or CREATE mode
GeneratePassword	No	Determines whether a random password is generated, or if the value of the common name attribute is used for the password of NT accounts that are created
RawMode	No	No attributes are inherited, constructed, or so forth; aliases for attribute and class names are not recognized
CodePage	Current	The codepage that the import file uses

23

THE EXCHANGE DIRECTORY

Most of the alternate values for items in Table 23.5 are obvious. InformationLevel and CodePage are discussed here. InformationLevel also accepts None for no logging and High to log all warnings and errors. CodePage accepts -1 for Unicode, 0 for the current ANSI codepage, or any other codepage number.

CAUTION

RawMode should be used only by individuals with much experience in the Exchange Directory, and even then requires good typing skills. Essentially, raw mode turns off the automatic generation of attribute values, such as Display Name, which by default is First Name Last Name. This allows the import utility to directly enter values for any attribute. However, there is no error checking in raw mode. If the import file instructs the import utility to make modifications that harm the directory, the import utility makes the modifications anyway.

Import File Format

The format of the import file is, for the most part, self-documenting. The first line of the file contains a header that defines the format of the lines that follow. There is no limit imposed by the import utility on the number of entries in the header or the number of data lines following the header. The contents of the header are object class names from the Exchange Directory schema. The import utility reads either ANSI text or Unicode and automatically senses which format is used. Table 23.6 shows the common types of objects that can be imported with the import utility and their required fields. The separators for the import file and the defaults are shown in Table 23.7. The command line import utility does not allow the default separators to be modified. However, the graphical version does allow the defaults to be modified.

Table 23.6. Common importable object classes with the import utility.

Object Class	Description	Required Fields
mailbox	Native Exchange user	Directory Name, Home Server
dl	Distribution list	Directory Name
remote	Custom recipient	Directory Name, Target Address
container	Recipients container	Directory Name

Table 23.7. Separators for import utility.

Character	Separator Type	Default
, (comma)	Field separator	Yes
(tab)	Field separator	No
(space)	Field separator	No
% (percent)	Value separator	Yes
! (exclamation)	Value separator	No
# (pound)	Value separator	No
$ (dollar)	Value separator	No
& (ampersand)	Value separator	No
* (asterisk)	Value separator	No
@ (at symbol)	Value separator	No
^ (control symbol)	Value separator	No
" (double quote)	Encloses text with imbedded spaces	Yes
' (single quote)	Encloses text with imbedded spaces	No

23

THE EXCHANGE
DIRECTORY

NOTE

Although the import utility does not enforce any limits on the size of the header or the number of data lines, the program or utility that you use to manage the import file might. For example, Excel 7.0 can handle spread sheets of 16,384 rows by 256 columns, and an individual column can be 255 characters wide. These numbers are impressive for a spreadsheet, but even a medium-sized distribution list can easily exceed the 255-character limit for column width.

There are two required fields in every import file: Obj-Class and Common Name. Obj-Class must be the first field in the header. It tells the import utility what class of object must be created, deleted, or modified. Given the object class, the import utility knows what attributes are required for the imported entry and what attributes are optional. Common Name identifies which unique object in the Exchange Directory is the target for the import operation. Common Name is actually only a relative distinguished name (RDN), but when combined with the distinguished name (DN) of the object's container, it becomes the DN for the target object. The DN of the parent container is specified in the setup screen for the graphical import utility (MS Exchange Server\Container) and in the options file of the command-line import utility (BasePoint\Container).

The Mode field enables the import utility to be used for more than just initial installation of Exchange and importing new entries from time to time. The Mode field is not a required field. If the Mode field is present, it must be the second field in the header. If it is not present, the import utility assumes the mode is update. The legal values for Mode are create, delete, modify, and update. The create mode tells the import utility to create a new object. If the object already exists, an error is generated. The delete mode tells the import utility to delete an existing object. If the object does not exist, an error is generated. The modify mode tells the import utility to look for an existing object to change. If the object does not exist, an error is generated. The update mode first attempts to locate an existing object, and if one is not found, an object is created.

TIP

If you do not know the object class names to use for the headers of the import file you are creating, use the Export function. Go to the Exchange Administrator menu item Tools | Export Directory. Click on Export File. Type the name of a file that does not exist and click the OK button. When prompted to create the file, answer yes. Now select whichever of the Export objects the selected container has least (to reduce processing time). When you click the Export button, the file is created and populated. Now open the file in Notepad. Delete all the entries after the first line. The first line of the file is the default headers required for an import file.

Listings 23.1 and 23.2 are two examples of the use of the Mode field. The first example import file creates a distribution list and populates it with two members. The second example import file modifies an existing list called Mail Witches by adding MarieD to the list of members.

Listing 23.1. Import file: example one.

```
Obj-Class, Mode, Directory Name, Members
dl, CREATE, "East Coast", Recipients/cn=Marilyn%Recipients/cn=Georgia
```

Listing 23.2. Import file: example two.

```
Obj-Class, Mode, Directory Name, Members, Home-Server, Address
dl, MODIFY, "Mail Witches", Recipients/cn=MarieD,,
mailbox, UPDATE, MarieD,,ARLF2,"1320 Blue House Road"
```

In Listing 23.1, the following must be true, or errors are logged in the event log:

■ The East Coast distribution list must *not* already exist.

■ The recipients Marilyn and Georgia must exist in the recipients container. They may be native Exchange users, custom recipients, or even another distribution list.

In Listing 23.2, the following should be noted:

■ The Mail Witches distribution list must already exist.

■ There must not be a custom recipient with a directory name, display name, or alias equal to MarieD.

■ The native Exchange user MarieD may or may not already exist in the recipients container. If it does not exist, it is created.

The import utility can import entries into the recipients container or any of its subcontainers. It cannot import entries into any other containers. This means that you can import containers, mailboxes, custom recipients, and distribution lists. You cannot import public folder schema or configuration information. The BImport function on which the import utility is based can import into any container. If you require an import utility with more flexibility, you can modify the sample application in the BackOffice SDK. But remember, with the increased flexibility comes increased ability to do harm to the directory.

Directory Export

Directory export is essentially the reverse of the import process, although the export process is by its nature less complicated than the import process. The export process need only dump out data that is already known and previously sorted into meaningful information. The export process has no interaction with NT security and little if any interaction with any other DSA than the one providing the entries being exported.

As Figure 23.8 illustrates, the user interface of the export utility is very similar to the user interface of the import utility. The primary changes to the interface are that the export utility does not affect any NT accounts, and the interface allows you to export all recipient objects or just specific object types. The import file format and the export file format are identical. The header information is exactly the same and in the same order:

```
admin /e <export file> /d <directory server name> /n /o <options file>
```

FIGURE 23.8.
The Exchange Administrator export utility.

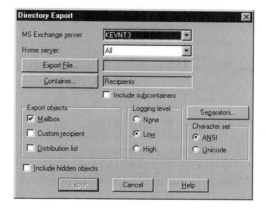

> **TIP**
>
> The Exchange Server Technical Resource CD-ROM includes a utility named HEADERS that creates properly formatted header files for import and export. It has every attribute for most of the object classes.

The command line of the export utility is almost identical to the command line of the import utility. The only difference is that /e is substituted for /i as the first switch.

Export Options File

The format of the export options file is different from the format of the import options file. Table 23.8 describes the items in the file and provides their defaults.

Table 23.8. The export options file.

Item	Default	Description
DirectoryService	N/A	The computer name of the directory server from which the utility exports the entries
HomeServer		The home server of the objects to be exported

continues

Table 23.8. continued

Item	*Default*	*Description*
Basepoint	Local site	The X.500 distinguished name (DN) of the site from which the utility exports the entries
Container	Recipients	The X.500 relative distinguished name (RDN) of the container from which the utility exports the entries
ExportObject	Mailbox	The object class name of the type of object to be exported
InformationLevel	Minimal	The amount of logging that is performed during the export
BasepointOnly	No	Exports only the requested attributes from the BasePoint object specified in the Basepoint option
Hidden	No	Determines whether hidden objects are exported
Subcontainers	No	Determines whether to export all the subcontainers of the container object specified by the container option
CodePage	Current	The codepage that the import file uses

Most of the alternate values for items in Table 23.8 are obvious. ExportObject and InformationLevel are discussed here. ExportObject also accepts the values DL for distribution lists, Remote for custom recipients, and All for all three types of recipient containers. InformationLevel also accepts None for no logging and High to log all warnings and errors.

Directory Security
Security

Security services can be divided into two classes:

- Authentication services
- Access control services

Exchange allows NT to provide authentication services. Before accessing an Exchange mailbox, a user must first logon to an NT domain with a proper user ID and password, thus proving his or her identity. Exchange security is concerned with access control.

Access control is accomplished through the use of rights, roles, and inheritance. In the Exchange Directory, there are five predefined roles:

- Admin
- Permissions admin

- Service account admin
- Send as
- User

The five roles are granted various rights. There are seven basic rights:

- Add child
- Modify user attributes
- Modify admin attributes
- Delete
- Send as
- Mailbox owner
- Modify permissions

Individual NT accounts or NT groups can be granted permissions to access a container object, such as recipients. When they are granted permission to the object, they are assigned a role, and the role determines exactly what rights they have in the container object. Whatever rights users have on a container object, they also have on any objects within the container object. That is referred to as *inheritance*. The child object inherits the permissions—or in X.500 terms, the access control list—from its parent container object. Figure 23.9 shows the permission screen for the recipients container.

FIGURE 23.9.

Permissions on the recipients container.

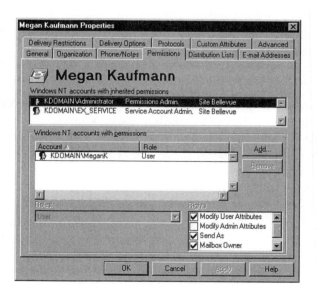

Permissions can also be set on child objects within container objects, such as user Charlie Smith in the recipients container. However, the Exchange Administrator assumes that manually setting permissions on individual child objects is the exception rather than the rule. The default behavior of the Exchange Administrator program is to not show the permission page for non-container, or leaf node objects. To change this, from Tools | Options, select the Permissions page and check the Show Permissions Page for all Objects box. Figure 23.10 shows the Permissions page of Tools | Options.

FIGURE 23.10.

The Permissions page of Tools | Options.

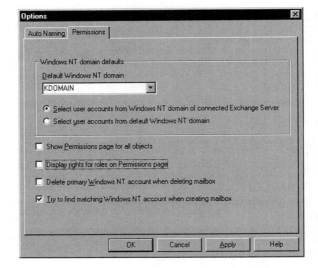

After the Permissions page has been enabled for all objects, there are three ways to have the Exchange Administrator display the Permission page for a specific object. First, to select a recipient, click once on the object in the Exchange Administrator program. Then, either press Alt+Enter, click File | Properties, or double-click the object. Any one of these methods displays the properties page for the object, and the Permissions page will be available.

The Permissions page for an individual object illustrates how the Exchange security model works. Notice in Figure 23.11 that in the box labeled Windows NT accounts with permissions, user CharlieS has been granted user role permissions. Also notice that in the box labeled Windows NT accounts with inherited permissions, CATLAND\mosied has inherited the Admin permission role from the parent container.

FIGURE 23.11.

The Permissions tab for an individual user.

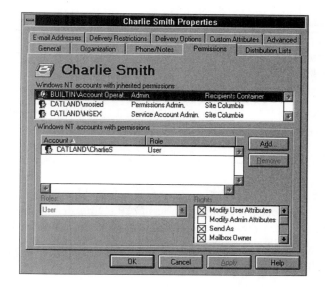

Lightweight Directory Access Protocol (LDAP)

In Exchange 5.0, Microsoft added several new Internet protocols, including LDAPv2, which is documented in Internet RFC-1777. This allows any LDAP client to read and search the directory for particular mailboxes or configuration information. Note, however, that this implementation is read-only; it is anticipated that Microsoft will add write capabilities in the next version of Exchange.

New to Version 5.0

TIP

All RFCs (Request For Comments) and Internet drafts can be accessed from any Web browser from

```
http://www.ietf.org __http://www.ietf.org_.
```

LDAP, like most Internet standards, is implemented only over TCP/IP and uses IP Port 389. Table 23.9 shows all the LDAP calls that are supported by the Exchange Server.

Standards

23

THE EXCHANGE DIRECTORY

Table 23.9. List of supported LDAP calls.

LDAP Call	Description
BindRequest	Client-side request to initiate a new session
BindResponse	Sent by server to accept/reject the BindRequest
UnBindRequest	Client-side request to terminate the session
SearchRequest	Client-side request for seaching the directory
SearchResponse	Server response to SearchRequest

In Exchange, LDAP can be configure for site from LDAP (Directory) Site Defaults object under the \Site\Protocols container or the LDAP (Directory) Settings under the Servers\Protocol container. From these objects, you can disable the protocol, set LDAP security and search options, and time-out options.

Performance   To get the best performance for your LDAP clients, you set the Search option to read any substring searchs and initial substring search (see Figure 23.12). So, when a client submits a SearchRequest for firstname=*bert*, the Exchange server would not find Robert, but would find Bert or Bertha. If you select Allow all substring search, Robert would be found; however, the search time would increase significantly, because the Exchange server would need to perform a nonindexed search through every firstname looking for the string bert.

FIGURE 23.12.
LDAP search options.

As discussed previously in the chapter, the Exchange Directory has a rich security model. Some of this functionality is utilized to determine the set of attributes that is exposed to anonymous and authenticated LDAP clients. From the DS Site Configuration object under the

\Site\Configuration container (shown in Figure 23.13), you can configure the set of attributes that are available to LDAP clients.

FIGURE 23.13.

You can configure the set of attributes that are available to LDAP clients.

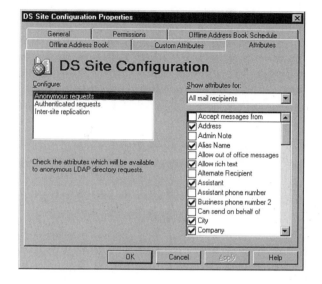

Address Book Views

Address Book Views are a powerful feature added to Exchange 5.0 directory that allow you to organize your mailboxes into a set of logical containers independent of the Exchange Site or Recipient Container in which they are physically located.

New to Version 5.0

> **TIP**
>
> You should always try to use Address Books instead of recipient containers to logically group your recipients. It is not possible to move users between Recipient Containers (you actually have to delete and re-add them), but you can easily move a user to a different Address Book View by changing a single attribute on the mailbox.

Summary

The X.500 family of standards defines the logical format of an X.500-compliant directory and how the various elements of the directory, including the user elements, communicate and interact. Exchange 5.0 adheres to the logical format of X.500; full X.500 compliance is scheduled for late 1996 and 1997.

23

THE EXCHANGE DIRECTORY

The Exchange Directory will not replace the NT Registry, but the directory will take on a larger role within NT. Certain elements of the Registry, such as the accounts database, will move to the directory, and server-specific elements, such as filename and location of the Information Store of a given server, will remain in the server's Registry.

Armed with the knowledge of the attributes for the mailbox, custom recipient, and distribution list object classes, an Exchange administrator can use the directory export and import functions to make many modifications. Changing the display order from `FirstName, LastName` to `LastName, FirstName` can be accomplished quickly and with 100 percent accuracy. Creating a new distribution list and adding hundreds of new members becomes a small task.

Public Folders

by Ken Ewert

IN THIS CHAPTER

## CHAPTER 24

What Is a Public Folder?

As a new user to Exchange, one of the first questions you find yourself asking is, "What are these things called public folders?" Essentially, public folders are the same as your personal mailbox folders, with the difference being that public folder hierarchy is published to the entire Exchange organization, and your personal folder hierarchy is not. Because the folder itself is published and can be made accessible to other users, it is a good place to store data that is to be shared among a group of users.

An instance of a given public folder can reside on any Exchange server in the Exchange organization. This data layer abstraction allows the user to access organizational data without having to worry about where the data is physically located (that is, which specific Exchange server), but only where the data logically is within the public folder hierarchy.

Public folder access is maintained by a set of Access Control Lists (ACLs) that can be set on a per folder basis. Folder access can be granted on a default basis or individually for specific users, or to the entire membership of an Exchange Distribution List (DL). If you assign permissions to a DL, any member of the DL inherits those permissions as well. You are not limited to a single permission ACL on a given folder, because you can grant various access modes to multiple users or multiple DLs. For detailed information regarding how to set access permissions on public folders, see the section "Administration of Public Folders," later in this chapter.

What Do I Put in Public Folders?

A public folder can be a repository of many types of data objects, including mail messages, document files, and electronic forms. Figure 24.1 shows an example of a public folder that contains various data objects.

Mail Messages

Mail messages are the most common object you will find in public folders. Messages can be manually moved or copied into a public folder via the client. Because a public folder is just another type of recipient in Exchange, mail messages also can be addressed to and sent directly to a public folder.

Document Files

You can also store documents in public folders. The document is not an attachment in a mail message; instead, the document file is the object itself. Just as you can save a Word document or Excel spreadsheet into a file system folder on your hard drive, you can put individual files into a public folder. Because public folders are available to multiple users, any permitted user can open, edit, and resave these documents right from the public folder, allowing collaboration of work in a single document.

FIGURE 24.1.

Public folder with various data objects.

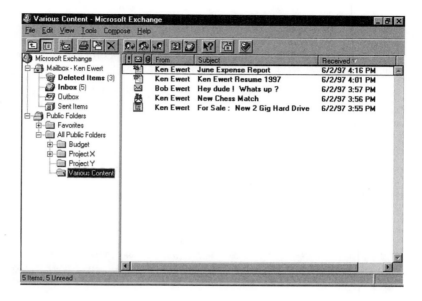

Electronic Forms

Electronic forms provide users the ability to both gather and display information in custom layouts for a specific application or process. For example, you can send a survey to a group of users asking what word processor they are using, or you can ask users to vote for an internal awards program. For a detailed discussion of electronic forms, see Chapter 30, "The Exchange Electronic Forms Designer."

How Do Things Get into Public Folders?

Public folders work similarly to the folders in your private mailbox. Objects can be moved or copied to public folders by a number of familiar methods:

- Users can use a mouse to drag and drop items from one folder to another.
- Users can set up Inbox Assistant rules on their own personal inbox to move or copy specific mail to a public folder.
- Users can post an item to a public folder by using the New Post in This Folder item under the Exchange client's Compose menu item. This method is used to generate a new entry into a public folder without having to create it elsewhere and move or copy it to the public folder. It uses a special form to assist the user in filling out appropriate information for the posting.
- Users can send e-mail messages directly to a public folder. Public folders can appear in the Exchange Address book and therefore can be addressed on a piece of mail, or they can even be a member of a distribution list. For more information on public folders sending and receiving mail, see the next section.

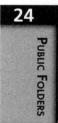

Public Folders as an E-Mail Recipient

Public folders are another kind of Exchange recipient, along with mailboxes, distribution lists, and custom recipients. Essentially, this means that mail can be sent to and from these objects. They all have e-mail addresses associated with them that are obviously valid internally to Exchange, but they are valid to external as well. For instance, someone on the Internet could send mail to a public folder to submit a purchase order for some type of goods. Instead of sending all such purchase orders to a single mailbox, sending it to a public folder makes the data available potentially to a group of order entry clerks, or better yet, to an automated process that will enter the orders into the corporate purchase system.

Because they are addressable, you have the choice of whether to publish them in the Exchange Address Book. By default, public folders are not published in the Address Book, but regardless of whether they are published, public folders can still receive mail sent to them.

TIP

Even if a public folder is not published in the Address book, individual users can still put the public folder's into their Personal Address Books (PABs) and then address it from there. To put a public folder's address in a PAB do the following:

1. From the Exchange client's left pane, select the public folder you want to put in your PAB.
2. Select Properties from the File menu or put the mouse pointer on the folder, right-click, and choose Properties.
3. Go to the Administration tab.
4. Press the Add Folder Address to : Personal Address Book button.

TIP

This allows administrators to maintain a specific policy of which folders get published to the address book, while still providing the individual users the ability to mail to public folders they may require for specific applications.

Another thing you can do with a public folder is make it a member of a distribution list. Being a member of a DL means that any message sent to the DL will wind up in the public folder. A good example of why you might want to do this would be to keep an archive of conversations or decisions made over e-mail so that when a new person joins your group, you can point that person to this archive as a place to start gathering information on what has happened. This will help them come up to speed quicker.

One of the things you might not expect to be able to do with a public folder is send mail FROM or AS public folder. A good example of why you might want to send a message FROM a public folder would be that you are asking a group of people for some type of information and you want to gather that information by having people reply to the message. By having the original message sent from the public folder, all replies will go back to the public folder. As you will read in later sections, public folders have the capability of having rules placed on them similar to those available in the Inbox Assistant for personal mailboxes, which include the capability of forwarding mail as well as replying to the message with a specific reply, depending on the text of the original message.

SUBSCRIBING PUBLIC FOLDERS TO INTERNET LISTSERVERS

A good example use of public folders is to subscribe public folders to Internet listservers. Subscribing a single folder to the listserver can mean a great savings in SMTP traffic through your Internet Mail Service. If individual users are allowed to sign up for listservers on their own, you could potentially have thousands of copies of the same message from the same listserver delivered to your corporate gateway destined for each individual user. By subscribing a public folder to the listserver, only one copy is needed to be sent to your corporate Internet gateway, but you also help to keep the distribution and maintenance issues for that listserver down, which ultimately means as a consumer of this information, it will get to you faster and more reliably.

The usual method to signing up to a listserver is to mail a specific Internet address and request to be subscribed. Newer listservers will accept requests from *any* Internet address by asking the user to include the SMTP address to be used in the subscription. Older and/ or more strict listservers require that the address requesting the subscription (the public folder in this case) be the address that is used to make the subscription request. For those older systems, a user will need to send the request as the public folder. To be able to send as a public folder, do the following:

1. From the Exchange administrators program, go to the Tool | Options | Permissions tab and make sure the Show Permissions page for all objects checkbox is checked. Select OK.

2. Select the public folder from the left pane of the administrator's program and press Alt+Enter to display its property pages. Notice that now there is a new property page called Permissions.

3. Select the Permissions tab.

4. Select the Add button and enter the NT account of the user that needs to be sending as the public folder.

5. From the Roles drop-down list box, select a user role of Send As for that NT account and press OK.

continues

continued

6. From the Exchange client, open a new send note.

7. Select the View menu option and choose the From Box entry. Now, each new message note that you create will have a From box above the To and Cc addressing wells you are used to.

8. When sending the subscribe message to the Internet listserver, place the public folder you are attempting to send as into the FROM well. This assumes that the folder is either published in the Exchange Address book or is an entry in the users PAB.

9. Send the message.

> **NOTE**
>
> For public folders that are subscribed to listservers or other bulletin board, news, or digest type services, please ensure that the Default permissions include the Create items permission. This will allow arbitrary Internet users to submit messages to the public folder. Failure to do so will cause the submission to fail to the public folder, the message to be returned to the listserver administrator, and in all likelihood eventually the address to be removed from the listserver's distribution.

Special Public Folders

There are a number of special public folders in an Exchange Organization. They are not visible to the average user, and most users will most likely use them without even knowing it. The following are the functions these folders serve:

- Free and Busy Scheduling information—1 per Exchange site
- Off-Line Address book—1 per Exchange site
- Electronic Forms registry—1 per supported language in an Exchange Organization

Figure 24.2 shows the Exchange Administrator view of special public folders.

Free and Busy Scheduling Information

For each Exchange user running either Schedule Plus or the Outlook client, certain information about your personal schedule is available for other users to see. This information is the collection of times you are either free (no item on your schedule) or busy (an item on your schedule). This is the information that is then available to other users when looking at the Meeting Planner portion of the Schedule Plus and Outlook clients. Using this free/busy information makes it possible to plan meetings for either a single person or a group of people and to allow the meeting to be scheduled for a time when everybody is available to attend. Note that detailed information about the actual items on your schedule is not available in this folder, but it can be made available to specific users and groups if the owner of the schedule gives appropriate access permissions to his or her personal calendar.

FIGURE 24.2.
Admin view of special public folders.

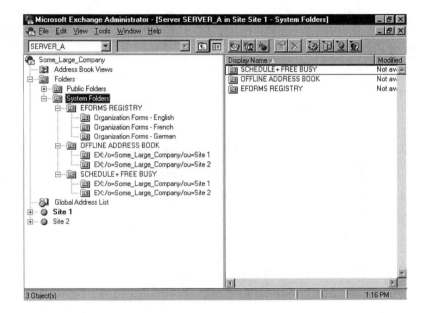

Each site has one of these folders, which is most often located on the first Exchange server installed in the site.

Off-Line Address Book

In each Exchange site, one Exchange server is responsible for calculating the Off-Line Address Book (OAB) that site will use. The OAB is a downloadable copy of the Exchange Address Book that provides Exchange users access to the Exchange Addresses Book while the client is in an offline state. This allows the user to originate and address mail to other users in the online Exchange Address Book while in an offline state without having to make individual entries into a Personal Address Book (PAB) for each of them.

In each site, after configuring which Exchange server will generate this data on a given schedule, the administrator is given a choice of how much data content will be available in the OAB. The choice is for full user detail information (name, location, phone number, and so forth) or just the user's e-mail address. Both will allow mail to be addressed while in an offline state; the difference is in the amount of data the client has to download to the client and the granularity of data available in the offline state.

Electronic Forms Registry

The Electronic Forms Registry is the repository for all organizational electronic forms. Having them in a single repository prevents the need of locally installing all corporate forms on each local user's computer before it can be accessed. The registry works in the following way: A user opens a form object either in a personal or public folder. That form object refers to a specific form. If the form is not installed locally on the user's computer, the organizational registry is checked. If the form is registered, a copy will be made and installed on the local user's computer. If the form is already installed locally on the user's computer, the version installed locally is checked with the version in the registry. If they are the same version, the client will use the local version of the form. If the version of the form in the registry is newer, the local copy of the form is updated.

Because the Exchange server supports multiple language clients, each form can be separately localized and registered for each supported language. When a client of a specific language checks the registry for a form, it will first try to find the form in the language-specific registry of the client, and if it is not there, it will check the default registry (English). This way, French clients will get the French version of the form, and so forth.

To read more on creating and managing the electronic forms registry, see Chapter 28, "Diagnosing the Cause of a Problem."

Public Folder Favorites

Because the public folder hierarchy can grow to multiple thousands of folders, navigating the tree to find specific folders that a user opens often can be a daunting and time-consuming tasks. For this reason, Exchange has come up with the concept of *Folder Favorites*, as shown in Figure 24.3. Essentially, the Favorites feature gives the user the ability to pick a subset of public folders they use often or are interested in and put them in a special section of the lefthand pane in the client. When a public folder is marked as a user's favorite, the user no longer needs to traverse the entire hierarchy to that specific folder, but just open the Favorites section in the lefthand pane, and that folder will be there.

When choosing a specific folder to be a favorite, the user can configure the favorite entry to be

- The single public folder itself
- The public folder and its immediate subfolders
- The public folder and all subfolders below it

Just like users' personal folders in their personal mailboxes, public folders marked as favorites share common features. When opened, the Favorite folders section will provide an indication of the number of unread messages in a given folder. This is displayed in blue parentheses next to the folder name. Favorite folders also are individually available for replication to the local client for use in the offline state. Any changes made while in the offline mode will be propagated back to the server next time the user connects to the server and initiates replication again.

FIGURE 24.3.

Client view of public folder favorites.

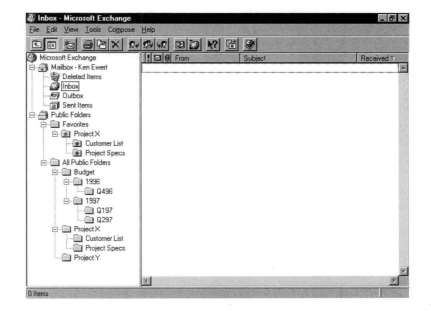

Public Folder Instances/Replicas

As mentioned previously, the user doesn't need to know where the physical location of the folder and its contents are, just where the folder is in the hierarchy. From a user's perspective, that is all that's needed. Administrators, on the other hand, need to know more. Where is this data located? Which Exchange server does this information actually reside on? To answer these questions, administrators need to understand the concept of *instances* of public folders.

By default, a public folder has only a single instance, as well as having what is called a *Home Server*. Initially, both are the same server and the only copy of the folder and its contents. If nothing is done to change this configuration, all users in the Exchange Organization will connect to this specific Exchange server to access the data in that folder. Depending on the required use of this data, the current capacity load on a given Exchange server, or even certain network bandwidth considerations, it may not be desirable to have all users connect to a single Exchange server for access to folder data. In this case, you would want to place multiple instances of the folder on multiple Exchange servers in the organization to better load balance access to the data.

Determining which servers have which instances of which public folders can be approached in two ways. You can configure it from a per folder perspective or from a per server perspective. You can choose a specific public folder from the Exchange Administration tool and configure which specific Exchange servers on which you want to have instances located. You also can choose a specific Exchange server and choose which public folders you would like to have an instance of.

Figure 24.4 shows the Exchange Administrator view of public folder replicas. Figure 24.5 shows a list of public folders with an instance on a server.

FIGURE 24.4.

Admin view of Public Folder Replicas.

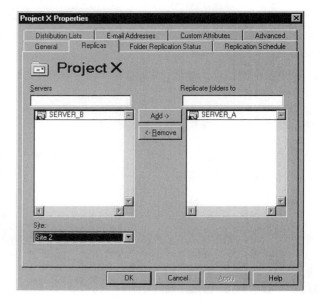

FIGURE 24.5.

List of public folders with an instance/replica on a server.

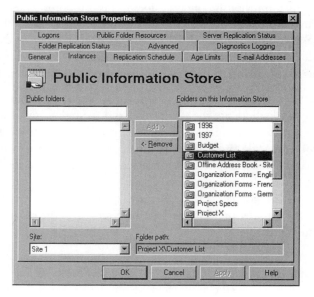

Each instance of the folder is then kept in sync via a replication scheme that updates all instances of the public folder data when objects are added, removed, or modified. Replication is mail-based. This means that each server packages up the changes made to the local copies of the data in its public folders and mails those changes to the other Exchange servers for which there is an instance of that public folder. For more information about configuring public folder replication, see the later section on "Administration of Public Folders."

What happens if two users modify two copies of the same object at the same time? The replication process tries to merge the multiple changes if it is possible. If automatic merging of the data is not possible, the public folder owner and contact is mailed a special form, which is called a *conflict resolution message.* This form notifies the owner of the folder that a merge of two conflicting posts could not take place and allows the owner to do either a manual merge or pick one set of changes to be the new master and resubmit this into the public folder.

Access to Public Folders in Another Exchange Site

In order for users in other Exchange sites to have access to the data in a public folder that is homed in another Exchange site, one of two things needs to happen. One is to have the administrator create a replica of the folder on an Exchange server in the site of the user(s) wanting access to the folder. This would result in two replicas of the data, thereby increasing the overall storage requirements for that selection of data. The better way to access this data is to have the administrator set up what is known as *Public Folder Affinity.* This is set on the Site Information Store Configuration object located in the Configuration container. Adding affinity between sites is as simple as choosing which other Exchange sites you want to give access to your folder replicas and a relative cost or weighting for that access. The cost comes into play in the cases where there is no replica of a folder in your local site but there are replicas in at least two sites for which affinity has been set up. The choice of which site to connect to is then based on the relative cost differences. The order that Exchange attempts to connect to public folders is prioritized from lowest cost to highest cost.

> **NOTE**
>
> In order to use Public Folder Affinity to connect to public folders that are available only in other sites, the user must have network connectivity to the Exchange server in that site, and that connectivity must support RPC connections.

Folder Assistant Rules

Just as a user's personal inbox has the Inbox Assistant, public folders can also have a rules engine called the Folder Assistant that can process mail put in the folder. You have all the same criteria as available with the Inbox Assistant to describe which messages the rule will be triggered on; the only real difference is in the actions available. Actions on the rules are limited to Delete, Reply, and Forward. You can also designate the order in which rules are triggered and can, at any rule, stop the processing of any subsequent rules that may also be triggered by the incoming message.

To configure a rule on a public folder:

1. From the Exchange client's left pane, select the public folder you want to configure.
2. Select Properties from the File menu or put the mouse pointer on the folder and right-click and choose Properties.
3. Select the Administration tab, as shown in Figure 24.6.
4. Select the Folder Assistant button; the list of current rules will show up.
5. At this point, you can choose to either add, edit, or remove a rule by choosing the appropriate button, or you can individually turn existing rules on or off by checking or unchecking the checkbox beside it.

Figure 24.6.

Administration tab for a public folder.

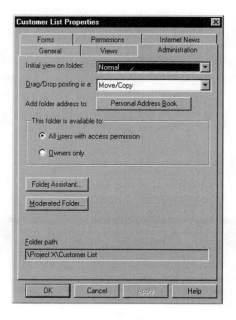

NOTE

Any new rule configured in the Folder Assistant does not act on existing data in a public folder, because it fires only on new data as it enters the public folder.

Moderated Public Folders

New to
Version 5.0

A new feature in Exchange 5.0 is the idea of a *moderated public folder*. The idea of moderating folders is not a new concept; it is widely used in some areas, such as Internet newsgroups. When an Exchange public folder is a moderated folder, it allows you to review contents submitted to the folder before accepting that content into the folder for general access. A good example of its use would be the ability to control the content of a public folder in order to maintain compliance with policies possibly set from your corporate policy maker (that is, Human Resources) or even state or federal law regarding offensive or political content.

Here is how moderated folders work: When a user attempts to submit content to the folder, that content is forwarded to either user, distribution list, or another public folder. Then, any user specifically designated as a moderator for the folder can view the content and either approve or reject the content. If approved, the content will appear in the public folder. If rejected, the content will not appear, and the moderator has the option of sending the content back to the user that originated the content.

If users do not know that a specific folder is moderated, they may not know why their posting is not immediately available in the public folder. To help here, owners of the folder can set up an automatic reply, either with a standard default message stating that the folder is moderated and that there may be a delay in their content being made available, or with a custom message sent to the user with any reply text the moderator wants.

Location

New to
Version 5.0

Another new concept in Exchange 5.0 is the concept of *Location*. The Location concept allows administrators to arrange Exchange servers with public information stores on them into logical groups in order to manage the behavior of public folders within a site more effectively. One of the main reasons for this feature is to help administrators maintain larger Exchange sites and avoid the unnecessary creation of multiple smaller Exchange sites to gain the detailed control of folder access that separate sites allow. Because system administration complexity grows in proportion to the number of sites in an Exchange organization, being able to minimize the number of sites while still maintaining control of access issues is a big win for administrators.

Besides easing administration complexity, Locations can also provide a performance **Performance** and bandwidth increase by allowing slower links that may have previously forced an Exchange site split due to uncontrolled access over them to be used within an Exchange site. These links are usually fast enough so that if they are used occasionally, performance is still acceptable, but allowing preference for the faster links and only using the slower links in fail-over scenarios allows them to be included in the site.

24

PUBLIC FOLDERS

The following are some of the benefits of the Location concept:

- Exchange Servers will first look to other servers in that same Location grouping for folder replication updates before requesting updates from a server outside its Location grouping for updates.
- When there are multiple replicas of a given public folder within the same Exchange site, users will attempt to connect to replicas of folders on Exchange servers within the same Location as their public folder servers before trying to connect to replicas available on other servers in the same Exchange site.

To configure a server's Location value:

1. From the Exchange Administrator's program, select the server you want to configure. This is located in the Servers container located under the Configuration container.
2. Once the server is selected, press Alt+Enter to bring up the server's property pages, as shown in Figure 24.7.
3. On the General property page, enter the value of the Server Location you wish this server to join.

FIGURE 24.7.

General tab on a server object.

Administration of Public Folders

Administration of public folders is done jointly between the Exchange client and the Exchange Administration program. Some functionality, such as setting Client Access Permissions, is available from both programs. Individually, public folders tend not to have a great need for daily administration, but instead require some initial configuration needs to be done, followed by progressive tuning and expansion of its configuration based on system expansion and growth.

Creation and Deletion of Public Folders

Creation and deletion of public folders occurs only from the Exchange client. The Exchange administrative program cannot create or delete public folders.

To create public folders:

1. From the Exchange client, select an existing public folder (or the root of the public folder tree if none exists yet).
2. Select the New Folder item from the client's File menu.
3. Enter the new folder name and press Enter.

Restrictions are placed on exactly who can create folders at the top level of the public folder tree. This allows the administrators to control the overall direction the public folder tree will take. To permit specific users to be able to create top-level folders, do the following:

1. Select the Configuration container for the site where the user you want to give permission to is located.
2. Select the Site Information Store Configuratioin object.
3. Select the Top Level Folder Creation tab.
4. Select the appropriate Modify button for those people you explicitly want to give to or prohibit this permission.

NOTE

You can use an Exchange Distribution List as an object for which you can assign these permissions. All members of that DL then inherit this permission as well.

TIP

If you want to use a distribution list to assign permissions but there is a subset of members on the DL you specifically want to exclude from creating top level folders, put the DL on the ALLOWED side of the dialog and then explicitly state those users you want to exclude on the NOT ALLOWED side. This will prevent you from either having to manually enter all the individuals explicitly on the ALLOWED side or having to create another DL just for this purpose.

You can delete public folders with the following steps:

1. From the Exchange client, select the public folder you wish to delete.
2. Either press the Delete key on the keyboard or use the Remove Folder item from the client's File menu.

> **NOTE**
>
> A user must be an owner of the public folder before he or she can delete it.

Public Folder Properties

To administer a public folder, you configure that folder's property pages. To find a public folder's property pages:

1. Open the Exchange Administration program.
2. In the left pane, expand the public folder hierarchy tree until you find the specific folder.
3. Select the public folder and press Alt+Enter to bring up its Property Pages, as shown in Figure 24.8.

FIGURE 24.8.

General tab on a public folder object.

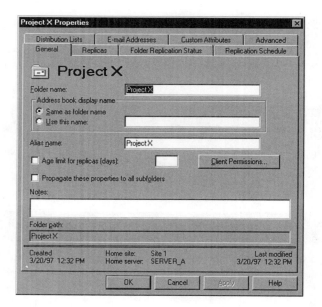

Client Access Permissions

Once the public folder has been created from the Exchange client, the next thing you need to do is set up access privileges to the folder. Access permissions can be administered from the Exchange client as well as from the Exchange Administrators program:

- From the Exchange client, place the mouse pointer on the public folder itself, right-click the mouse, and select the Properties menu item. From this dialog, choose the Permissions tab, as shown in Figure 24.9.

■ From the Exchange Administration program, use the Client Permissions button on the public folder properties General tab.

FIGURE 24.9.

Client access permis-sions for a public folder object.

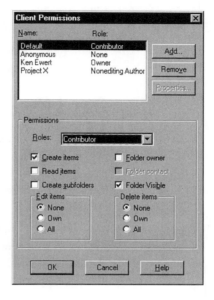

Permission Types

These permissions determine who can access the public folder data and what actions they can do to that data. The access permissions available include predefined roles, as well as the ability to set custom access rights on a per user basis. They are as follows:

Permissions types	
Access	Create Items, Read Items, Create Sub-Folders, Folder Owner, Folder Contact, Folder Visible
Edit Items permissions	None, Own, All
Delete Items permissions	None, Own, All

Predefined roles	
Contributor	Read Items, Edit None, Delete None
Reviewer	Read Items
Non-Editing Author	Create Items, Read Items, Edit None, Delete Own
Author	Create Items, Read Items, Edit Own, Delete Own

continues

24

PUBLIC FOLDERS

Predefined roles

Publishing Author	Create Items, Read Items, Create Sub-Folders, Edit Own, Delete Own
Editor	Create Items, Read Items, Edit All, Delete All
Publishing Editor	Create Items, Read Items, Create Sub-Folders Edit All, Delete All
Owner	Create Items, Read Items, Create Sub-Folders, Folder Owner, Folder Contact, Edit All, Delete All
Custom	Any combination of permission types that are not defined in a predefined role

To set permission access:

1. Choose the New button, and the familiar Address Book dialog box will appear.

2. Select the entry you want to grant the permissions to (mailbox, custom recipient, distribution list, another public folder) and press Enter.

3. Select either a predefined role from the drop-down listbox or configure the desired individual permissions manually. If the individual selections you made wind up being the same as a predefined role, the displayed role will change from Custom to the predefined role to which it equates.

Any object that does not get specifically assigned a set of permissions will use the permissions assigned to the Default permission settings.

The only permission that needs extra explanation, and which is new in Exchange Server 5.0, is the Folder Visible permission. This permission controls whether a user can see a public folder in the public folder tree, based on the user having any permissions on that folder. If the user has None permissions on the folder and the Folder Visible is checked off, that user will not see the public folder in the Public Folder tree. If the user has None permissions but the Folder Visible permission is checked on, the user will see the folder in the Public Folder hierarchy but will not be able to open that folder. The client will be returned with an access denied error. Note that the latter case was the default behavior in Exchange Server 4.0.

> **TIP**
>
> If you give the folder's Default access control object the Create items privilege, anybody can put a data object into the public folder, including both Exchange and external users sending mail directly to the public folder. If you give only specific users Create items, only those users will be able to put or mail data objects into the public folder. If the Create items privilege is restricted to certain users, any other Exchange users or external users will receive a non-delivery report stating a lack of appropriate permissions if they attempt to send mail to the public folder.

Propagation of Public Folder Configuration to Subfolders

New to
Version 5.0

Another new feature in the Exchange 5.0 server is to allow administrators to set specific configurations on an entire tree or subtree of the public folder hierarchy. To do this, the administrator needs to configure all the property pages on the topmost public folder of the tree or subtree he or she wants to bulk-administer. Before pressing the OK button on the General page, select the Propagate These Properties To All Subfolders checkbox. After the folder has been configured, pressing the OK or APPLY button will bring up a dialog allowing the administrator to choose which specific configurations will be bulk-propagated, as shown in Figure 24.10. The choices are the following:

- Client Permissions
- Replication Schedule
- Replicas
- Replication Message Importance
- Age Limit For All Replicas
- Whether To Hide From The Address Book

Choose any combination of properties for bulk propagation by checking the checkbox beside each property. When the OK button is pressed, a progress-type dialog will appear as the propagation process is being carried out.

FIGURE 24.10.

Option values that can
be propagated down a
tree of public folders.

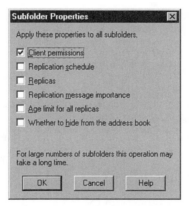

24

PUBLIC FOLDERS

NOTE

Using the permit tree feature on a public folder hierarchy to bulk-set folder permissions will overwrite any existing permissions that existed on any specific folder in that hierarchy, with the permissions being propagated down. The final result of the operation will be that every public folder in the tree or subtree will have identical access permissions.

Expiration of Public Folder Contents

Setting the folder expiration value determines when entries in the public folder automatically get deleted. As with most configurations in Exchange, you can configure default behavior for most things at the server level, as well as at the individual object level. Configuring folder expiration works the same way. Setting the value on this dialog will set up the default expiry schedule for all instances of this public folder.

You can also set a default expiry schedule on a per server basis by going to the Public Information Store object for any given Exchange server. Setting a value on the Age Limits tab will set the default expiry for all public folders on this server. When both defaults have been configured with a value, the effective expiry schedule for a given replica on a given server is the smaller of either the server or folder schedule.

> **NOTE**
>
> By leaving the value on the public folder's General tab blank, no expiry will occur on any replica of the public folder, regardless of any specific server level expiry configuration.

Public Folder Replication

Public folders objects are replicated across the entire Exchange enterprise. Although the entire folder hierarchy is replicated to each Exchange Server running a public information store, individual and specific folder content is not replicated unless specifically configured to do so.

Replicas

Configuring which Exchange servers contain replicas of which public folders can be done in two ways. The first is from the public folder's perspective and defines which servers will have a replica of the folder. The second is from the Exchange server perspective and defines which public folders are replicated to a specific Exchange server.

To configure per folder:

1. Select the Replicas tab from the public folder property pages, as shown in Figure 24.11. The list on the right shows which servers currently have a replica of this public folder.

2. Choose the site of the server you want to replicate the folder to by picking it out of the drop-down listbox at the bottom.

3. From the list of servers that appear in the lefthand list, select the sever(s) you want to put a replica of the folder on and press the Add button. The selected server(s) will move from the list on the left to the list on the right.

4. Repeat for as many replicas as needed in as many sites as needed.

> **NOTE**
>
> You cannot remove the last replica of a public folder from the Exchange administration program. There must always be at least one replica of a public folder. To delete the last replica, you must use the Exchange client to delete the public folder from the public folder hierarchy.

FIGURE 24.11.

The Replicas tab on a public folder object lists all public information stores on which a replica of this public folder exists.

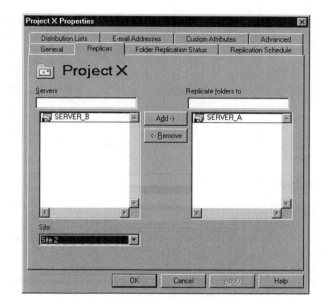

To configure per server:

1. Select the server from Servers container located under the site Configuration container.

2. From the righthand pane, double-click the Public Information Store object.

3. Select the Instances tab, as shown in Figure 24.12. The list on the right shows all public folders that currently have a replica on this server.

4. From the drop-down listbox at the bottom, choose the site where the public folder is homed.

5. From the list of public folders that appear in the lefthand list, select the folders for which you would like a replica to be on this Exchange server and press the Add button. The selected folders will move from the list on the left to the list on the right.

6. Repeat for as many servers as needed.

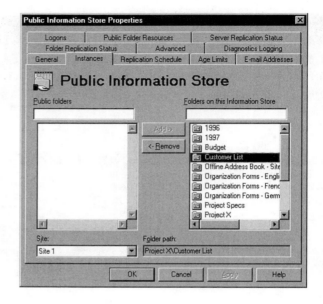

FIGURE 24.12.

*Instances tab on a
Public Information
Store object. Lists all
public folders for which
a replica exists on this
information store
object.*

Replication Schedules

Public folder replication is accomplished via mail messages containing the new or modified folder data being sent to other Exchange servers. To configure how often this public folder will replicate new or changed folder content to other replicas of the folder, you need to define a schedule. Your choices for a schedule are the following:

- Selecting Use Information Store default will use the server's replication schedule as configured on the server's Public Information Store object.
- Selecting Always will cause the folder to replicate by default every 15 minutes. This 15-minute setting is configurable and is located on the Advanced tab of the Public Information Store object, as shown in Figure 24.13.
- Selecting Never will prevent the folder from replicating at any time.
- Selecting Per Schedule allows the administrator to configure a custom schedule for this specific folder by marking explicit times the folder should replicate. The administrator can choose individual times for individual days by selecting individual sections of the schedule grid, or the administrator can select the same schedule each day by choosing top grid point of various time slots causing the entire time slot to be marked for each day.

Replication Status

As it states, this page will give you the status of folder replication for this specific folder. Information such as last time the folder received an update as well as the average time replication transmission time took are displayed to the administrator. Figure 24.14 shows the tab that contains replication status.

FIGURE 24.13.
Replication Schedule tab on a public folder object.

FIGURE 24.14.
Folder Replication Status tab on a public folder object.

Properties of a Public Folder as an E-Mail Recipient

Because a public folder is a special type of recipient in Exchange, it has properties and configurations common to other Exchange recipient types:

■ *E-mail Addresses* lists all the defined e-mail addresses for this public folder. See Figure 24.15.

- *Distribution Lists* lists all the distribution lists of which this public folder is a member. See Figure 24.16.

- *Custom Attributes* uses the custom attributes as defined on the Site Directory Configuration object. These are the same custom attributes available for Mailbox users.

For more information about public folders participating as an Exchange recipient, see the discussion on this topic in the section "Public Folders as an E-Mail Recipient," at the beginning of this chapter.

Advanced Tab

The Advanced tab for a public folder object is shown in Figure 24.17. On this tab, you can configure the following:

- *Set up a simple display name.* This will be used by systems that cannot display the normal display name of the folder

- *Set public folder storage limits.* You can elect Use the default values as set on the server's Public Information Store. Not checking this box means there are no default storage limit quotas on this folder. You also can configure a storage limit threshold; if the folder's storage surpasses this value, the owner(s) of the public folder can be issued a warning stating so.

- *Set the trust level.* The trust level controls whether information about the folder is replicated to a specific recipient. If the trust level set for the folder is larger than the trust level of the recipient, the information is not replicated.

- *Set the importance of the replication message.* Because public folder replication is mail-based, you can determine the importance and priority of the replication mail message being sent to the other servers. In general, messages with higher importance are given priority in their delivery, and therefore you can determine whether replication of this folder should take precedence over regular mail by making the value set to High, or whether the replication of this folder is of less importance and should be prioritized behind regular mail traffic. If so, set the value to Low.

- *Hide from the Address book.* This is checked on by default for all public folders, and only administrators can change this value. If unchecked, the public folder will show up as an entry in the Exchange Address book.

- *Display of the container name.* The name of the container in which this public folder resides.

- *Setting the Administrative Note.* This is an edit box visible only via the Exchange administration program and allows administrators to keep notes on the public folder. A good example is information such as whom to contact before modifying any configuration of the folder.

Figure 24.17.

Advanced tab on a public folder object.

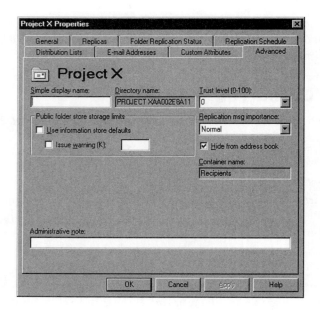

Public Information Store Property Pages

I've referenced this object throughout this chapter on many occasions when the public folder configuration being considered used either a per folder setting on the public folder object or a server-configured default setting. This is the object where those server-specific settings are configured. The tabs on the property pages will seem very familiar to the administrator, because they are essentially the same pages available to public folder objects. In this case, however, the scope of the configuration is at a server level instead of a folder level.

Figure 24.18 depicts the property sheet for the public information store object. Here is a brief summary of the tabs:

- *General.* Default configuration of folder storage limits. Individual public folders can choose to use this setting or one specific to the folder itself.
- *Instances.* Listing of all available public folders in the organization, as well as a list of those folders with a replica on this Exchange server.
- *Replication Schedule.* Default configuration of the Exchange Servers public folder replication schedule. Specific folders can choose to use this schedule or use one specific to the folder itself.

- *Age Limits.* Default configuration for folder content expiry for this Exchange server. Because expiry of content can be different for different replicas stored on different Exchange servers, this page shows the effective expiry per folder on this Exchange server as well as the specific expiry limit set on the public folder itself. Remember, the effective expiry for a folder on this server is the lower of these two limits.

- *E-mail Addresses.* The e-mail address of the public information store. Used in public folder replication.

- *Advanced.* Where the value for the replication setting of Always is configured. Replication message limit size is the maximum size a replication message can be. Multiple updates can be included in a single replication message up to the set limit, and any updates that are larger than this limit are broken up into multiple messages for replication.

The following status information is available both as tabs on the Public Information Store object and virtual objects hanging below the Public Information Store object. The reason they are virtual objects as well is so they can provide the data in the righthand pane column view of the Exchange Administration program, giving the administrator more room to view the data than is available on the property page tab. These columns are all sortable:

- *Folder Replication Status.* The replication status of all folders with replicas on this Exchange server. Information such as last update time, number of replicas a folder has across all Exchange Servers in the Exchange Organization, and whether they are in sync.

- *Logons.* Listing of mailboxes and the NT account that they are currently logged in with, the time the user logged onto the public store, and the time the user last accessed data from the public store.

- *Public Folder Resources.* List of public folders, total number of objects in the folder, the amount of storage the folder is using, the create date of the folder, the date the folder was last accessed, the number of folder owners, and the number of folder contacts. This information allows administrators to manage overactive and inactive folders, as well as any folders that are not explicitly owned by a user.

- *Server Replication Status.* Shows the status of public folder replication between this server and all other servers in the organization with which it replicates public folders. Status includes whether the folder is in sync or has changes yet to be replicated, last time replication updates were received, the time the last replication transmission took, and the average time replication updates take to a given Exchange Server.

24

PUBLIC FOLDERS

FIGURE 24.18.

Public Information Store object.

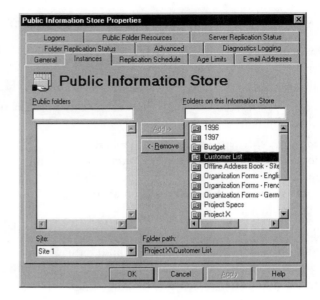

Summary

This chapter is meant as a starting point in your discovery of Exchange public folders. However, the subject is so broad that far more than a single chapter could be written on the topic. After reading this chapter, you should be able to understand some key concepts in public folder usage and administration. These will provide a foundation as you explore and use public folders in your own installation.

In this chapter, you learned what can go in a public folder and how it gets put there. You looked at special public folders and public folder favorites. Finally, you explored the administration and configuration of public folders.

As you can see, Exchange public folders are a simple, yet powerful tool, and they serve as the building blocks for providing data-centric sharing of information across your entire Exchange enterprise.

Backup and Recovery

by Kevin Kaufmann

IN THIS CHAPTER

Silence. That's what I heard from the other end of the telephone when I asked the Exchange administrator when he did his last backup. We had been working on a problem where the Information Store would not start (it turned out they had unknowingly deleted the Information Store database to save disk space). This was a small company with a single Exchange server, and without the backup, all their users had lost several months of saved mail.

The single most important reason to do backup is to recover all your information from some disaster. Disasters can be caused by the following:

- Hardware failure
- A malicious or disgruntled employee
- Administrative error, such as the one mentioned previously, or accidentally deleting a mailbox or public folder
- User error—it's always the CEO who deleted that really important piece of mail that the future of the company depends upon

This chapter provides all the information you will need to ensure that you can recover an Exchange server in the case of a disaster. You will learn how and where data is stored on the Exchange server, including the Jet database, which is used by the Information Store and Directory Service. You will explore how to back up the data and the strategies that will work best for you. Finally, and perhaps most importantly, this chapter will provide detailed information on how to recover from a disaster.

Exchange Data

Before jumping into the different modes of backup and recovery that Exchange provides, it is useful to understand how and where Exchange stores data. Table 25.1 provides a listing of directories that are created under the \EXCHSRVR subdirectory and what information is stored in each directory.

Table 25.1. Data directories.

ccmcdata	cc:Mail temporary data
dsadata	Directory database (DIR.EDB) and log files
dxadata	MS Mail Dir-Sync database and log files
imcdata	Internet Mail Service temporary message queues
insdata	Internet News Service
mdbdata	Information Store database (PRIV.EDB and PUB.EDB) and transaction log files
mtadata	Message Transfer Agent temporary message queues
webdata	Web Service HTML and ASP pages
connect\msmcon	MS Mail Connector Postoffice

Other Directories

Add-ins	Exchange Admin extensions
Bin	Exchange Admin, services and other executables
Res	Event log messages
Tracking.log	Message tracking logs

The most critical data on your Exchange server is kept by the Information Store (database for mailboxes and public folders) and Directory Service (recipient and configuration objects) and is stored in the same underlying database that is known as the Exchange database (AKA Jet). The Exchange database is a rich database engine that provides scalability, full recoverability, and single-instance storage for the Exchange server.

> **NOTE**
>
> The Exchange database is limited to 16GB. It sounds like a lot, but this really limits the number of users that a single Exchange server can hold to 500 if each user is allocated 30MB of disk space. This will be increased to 16TB (terabytes) in the next release.

Future
Directions

The Exchange database uses transaction logs to recover from abnormal shutdowns (for example, power outage) and in case of database corruption. All database transactions are first written to a log file EDB.LOG (which is always created as a 5MB file) before they are committed to the database file. When the file is full of transactions, it is renamed to a filename of the format EDB#####.LOG, where ###### is an incrementing value, and then a new EDB.LOG file is created.

If, for example, the power goes out to an Exchange server, the Exchange database will know the database is in an inconsistent state at startup and automatically enter recovery mode. In recovery mode, any transactions that were not committed to the database will be replayed into the database to bring the database into a consistent state.

It is important to note that, by default, the Exchange server will overwrite old .LOG files (this is known as circular logging) to minimize the amount of disk space the LOG files will use. The disadvantage of doing this is that should the database become corrupt, you can only recover the database to the point in time your last backup was made. If you disable circular logging (that is, keep old .LOG files), you could recover the database with absolutely no loss of information (that is, no mail will be lost). If you decide to disable circular logging (which provides maximum data recoverability), you must back up your database, which will then remove the unneeded log files. The bottom line is that if it is acceptable for you to lose all the data (mail messages) since your last backup and disk space is a concern, you should keep circular logging enabled.

25

BACKUP AND
RECOVERY

Performance

> **TIP**
>
> It is recommended that the transaction logs be stored on a different disk drive than the database files. Not only will this significantly improve overall performance of the system, it will ensure that if only the physical hard drive that contains the database fails, you can still recover all your data.

Backing Up the Exchange Server

One of the initial design goals for Exchange was to provide a system that can truly run 7×24. It was also well understood that organizations required regular backup to their databases. To satisfy both of these requirements, the concept of online backups was derived: provide a tool that can back up a live database with no downtime (see Figure 25.1).

FIGURE 25.1.

The Windows NT Backup utility.

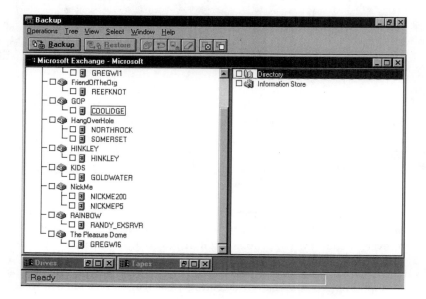

The Windows NT Backup utility was extended, so you can back up the Information Store and/or Directory while users are logged on and sending or receiving mail (see Figure 25.2). There are several modes of online backup, shown in Table 25.2.

Table 25.2. Online backup modes.

Normal (Full)	Backs up the entire Information Store and/or Directory databases (.EDB). All transaction logs are backed up and then deleted.
Copy	Same as the Full backup, except log files are not deleted. You may want to do a Copy before you make a major change to the database. Generally, you will not use this mode on a regular basis.
Incremental	Backs up only the transaction log files (.LOG) and then deletes them. This is normally done on a regular schedule between the Full backups. This is only applicable if circular logging is disabled.
Differential	.LOG files are backed up but they are not deleted from disk. This is only applicable if circular logging is disabled.

FIGURE 25.2.

Online backup of Information Store.

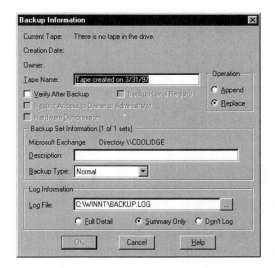

> **TIP**
>
> You should do your online backup during nonpeak hours, because it will significantly impact the performance of the Exchange server. The amount of time to back up the server will depend greatly on the tape drive you are using.

Performance

25

BACKUP AND RECOVERY

Offline is simply a file-based backup. You stop all Microsoft Exchange services and then run the NTBACKUP program to back up all files on the desired drives. See the section "Backup Strategies," later in this chapter, for when and how often you should perform offline backups.

> **NOTE**
>
> In order to perform an online or offline backup, you must have a tape drive installed on the machine you are running the backup from (which is not necessarily the Exchange Server). For best backup performance, you should run the backup directly on the Exchange server. If you decide to back up over the network to centralize your backup servers, you should consider the overall impact it will cause other users of the network.
>
> You can install the Exchange version of NTBACKUP.EXE on a backup server, by installing the Exchange Admin program on the machine.

Backup Command-Line Options

The Exchange version of NTBACKUP provides command-line options, in addition to the standard NTBACKUP options listed in Table 25.3, that can be used to automate the backup process in your company.

Table 25.3. Windows NT backup command-line options.

Parameter	*Purpose*
/a	Causes backup sets to be added or appended after the last backup set on the tape.
/v	Verifies the operation.
/r	Restricts access.
/d "text"	Specifies a description of the backup contents.
/b	Specifies that the local registry be backed up.
/hc:on or off	Specifies that hardware compression is on or off.
/t {option}	Specifies the backup type. *option* can be one of the following: normal, copy, incremental, differential.
/l "filename"	Specifies the filename for the backup log.
/e	Specifies that the backup log includes exceptions only.
/tape:{n}	Specifies the tape drive to which the files should be backed up. *n* is a number from 0 to 9 that corresponds to the number the drive was assigned when the tape drive was installed.

The general format of the new option is the following:

```
NTBACKUP /server \\servername
```

Here is an example:

```
NTBACKUP backup /IS \\EXServer1 /DS \\EXServer1_
```

Backup Strategies

Different companies will have varying configurations and requirements. The following are some common backup strategies for large and small companies:

- *Full Daily Backup.* This works best for an Exchange server that has a relatively small database (that is, 100–200MB). Backups will take longer to perform (because the entire database will be backed up), but restoring the database requires only the single tape. If you use this strategy, you should strongly consider disabling circular logging unless disk space is at a premium; because the log file will be purged every night, the number of transactions associated with a smaller database should not be significant.

- *Full Plus One Incremental.* This method (alternating between Full and Incremental backup each night) requires fewer tapes and less time, because you back up only the changes (that is, transaction logs) every other night. Restoring is slightly more cumbersome, because you need to restore the Full backup and then the Incremental; and the database startup time will be longer because it needs to replay all the log files from the incremental backup. With this strategy, circular logging must be disabled.

- *Full Plus Two Incremental.* This schedule is appropriate for large databases (that is, greater than 3GB). This will minimize even further the amount of data that is physically backed up to tape and thus requires fewer tapes and less backup time. Restore can require up to three different tapes, and the startup time will be longer after a restore. Again, with this strategy, circular logging must be disabled.

Whichever backup strategy you decide on, you should keep a full week (or more) of backups. Additionally, it is absolutely critical for you to verify that the backups are working. When you first set up your backup schedule, you should restore every Exchange server to an alternate server (covered later in this chapter) to verify that the backup is working correctly. Then, you should have an ongoing restoration schedule that rotates through each of your Exchange servers to verify that the backup is working properly.

Offline backup should be done after you install the Exchange server and after any significant changes to the Exchange server configuration (for example, after adding a new site to your organization or configuring the MS Mail Connector). Weekly offline backup provides an extra level of insurance in case of failed online backups.

Recovering from a Disaster

This section discusses the most common situations that require recovering data from your backup tapes (see Figure 25.3):

- Recovering an accidentally deleted mailbox or message from a mailbox
- Recovering an entire Exchange server
- Recovering the Directory

FIGURE 25.3.

Restoring from tape.

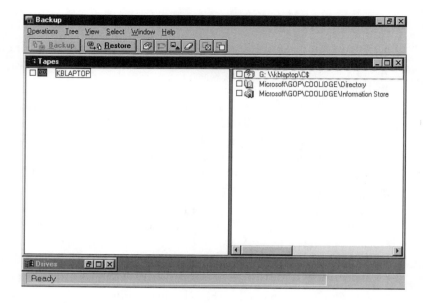

Recovering a Deleted Mailbox or a Deleted Mail Message from a Mailbox

To restore a mailbox that was accidentally deleted, you need to restore the entire private Information Store databases (PRIV.EDB) to an alternate Exchange server (running the same version and service pack as the Exchange server the mailbox resided on). The alternate server must have sufficient disk space for the Exchange server installation and PRIV.EDB file.

First, on the alternate Windows NT server, install the Microsoft Exchange Server and create a new site with the same Organization and Site name that the mailbox resided on.

WARNING

Do not install the server into the existing Exchange site or the procedure will not work. The server you install should be in a stand-alone environment.

Next, use the Windows NT Backup to restore the Information Store from your backup tape (see Figure 25.4). If this is an online backup, specify the name of the alternate Exchange server in the Destination Server field, select the Erase all existing data option, Private and Public options, and Start Service After Restore. If this is an offline backup, restore the PRIV.EDB and PUB.EDB and run `isinteg -patch` and start the Information Store. The `isinteg` utility is covered in Chapter 28, "Diagnosing the Cause of a Problem."

FIGURE 25.4.

Restoring the
Information Store.

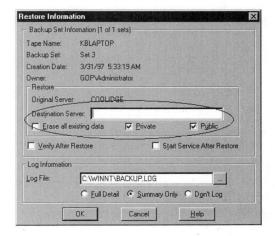

Start the Exchange Administrator program and run the DS/IS Consistency Adjustment from the Advance property page on the Exchange Server object. Now, you should see the mailbox in the Recipients Container. Select the mailbox you want to restore and set the Primary Windows NT account to the account you are logged in as.

Start the Exchange client and, if you are restoring the entire mailbox, copy all the mail messages and folders into a PST. Finally, give the users the PST with all their mail messages.

Recovering an Exchange Server

This section discusses issues with restoring an Exchange server to a different physical machine. In this scenario, the original Exchange server computer was permanently destroyed and a new server will be replacing it. In summary, you need to install Windows NT on the new server with the same Windows NT computer name into the same Windows NT Domain. You then install Exchange Server onto the new server and then restore the Information Store and Directory database.

> **NOTE**
>
> The following assumes that the Exchange server is not the Primary Domain Controller. In general, the Exchange server should run on a member server so it will not be burdened with the task of NT User validations.

First, if the Exchange server is the Primary Domain Controller (PDC) and you have a Backup Domain Controller (BDC) in place, promote a BDC to assume the role of the PDC. With the NT Server Manager tool, delete the old Exchange server from the domain and then re-create it (this will re-create a new SID for the machine account). Next, you install Windows NT and all the appropriate service packs onto the new Exchange server with the same Windows NT computer name as the previous Exchange server.

Next, run Setup /r from the Exchange installation CD to install the Exchange server onto the new machine; you must create a new site (do not join the existing site) with the same Site and Organization names that were set on the original server. When prompted for the service account, select the same service account that was used on the old Exchange server.

Finally, use the NTBACKUP utility to restore the Exchange backup. Select to restore the Directory and Information Store and then the Erase all existing data option and Start Services After Restore. Note that if you are restoring from an offline backup, you also need to run isinteg -patch after you start the Directory service, but before you start the Information Store.

Restoring the Directory Service

If your Directory Service will not start, and you suspect the database (DIR.EDB) is corrupted, you might want to restore the Directory from a backup. As with restoring the Information Store, use the Windows NT Backup to restore the Directory from your backup tape.

Summary

Backups are a critical part of maintaining an Exchange system. In this chapter, you explored the different types of data that are stored by the Exchange server and how the Exchange database provides a scalable, recoverable, and single-instance storage for the Information Store and Directory.

Additionally, you learned how to perform an online and offline backup of the Exchange server. You looked at several backup strategies that can be tailored to the large or small company. Finally, you learned how to recover from various disasters with no loss of information.

V

PART

Maintenance and Troubleshooting

Maintaining Exchange

by Kimmo Bergius
Revised by Greg Todd

IN THIS CHAPTER

After you have your Exchange environment all configured and up and running, it is time to start maintaining the environment. Most of the server maintenance is automatically performed by the Exchange services, with the administrator mostly monitoring the operations. There are, however, some maintenance tasks the administrator should be aware of. Some of them even need to be performed manually.

Maintenance for the Exchange environment can be divided into three categories:

- Maintaining users and public folders
- Maintaining the server and site
- Maintaining connections between servers, sites, and foreign systems

User maintenance mainly consists of defining and modifying mailboxes and other recipients. The administrator also has to monitor storage levels per user and for the whole private information store.

Public folder maintenance mainly consists of checking the storage levels for public folders and also checking that folder replication works properly. Most of the other public folder definitions—for example, public folder creation and configuration—are done at the client level by users.

Administrators do most of their daily work at user and server level, so maintaining the server and site are important. The administrator has to configure and modify the system, monitor server and service operation, free storage space, database files and, most importantly, perform backups for the server.

Connection maintenance consists mostly of monitoring different message queues and checking that messages are delivered from sender to recipient as efficiently and as smoothly as possible.

There are several tools for accomplishing these tasks, some of which are discussed in this chapter and some in the following chapters.

Maintenance Tools

Maintenance tools can be divided into two categories: tools used to maintain the client environment and tools used to maintain the server environment. Some of the maintenance tools are shipped either with the Exchange server or the Exchange client. Other tools used to maintain the Exchange server are part of the Windows NT Server operating system. Still others are provided by third parties. In this chapter, I will focus on tools that come with Exchange Server and NT.

Tools Used to Maintain the Client Environment

There are a few tools that come with Exchange that you can use to maintain the client environment:

- *Setup Editor.* You use this tool to customize the client environment before the client is installed. You can use the Setup Editor to define organization-wide settings, such as the default binding order and other user specific settings. The Setup Editor is covered in detail in Chapter 14, "Installing Microsoft Exchange Clients."

- *Inbox Repair tool.* You use this tool to repair corrupted personal store (.PST) files. A .PST file can become corrupted if the client is terminated abnormally for some reason or another, or if you have stored the .PST file onto a network file server and the network connection is broken. When you start the Exchange client, and you have defined a .PST file in your profile, the client will inform you if the file is corrupted. In such a case, you should run the Inbox Repair tool to fix the .PST file.

- *Exchange Profile Manager.* You use this tool to create and modify Microsoft Exchange client profiles. It can either be accessed by the Mail applet in the Control Panel or by the Tools | Services menu from within the Exchange client. Profiles are covered in detail in Chapter 15, "Configuring Microsoft Exchange Clients."

- *RPCPing.* Use this tool to check the Remote Procedure Call (RPC) connection between two machines. Exchange uses RPCs for communication between a client and a server and between two servers within the same site. You can find the RPCPing tool in the EXCHSRVR\RPCPING directory along with a document detailing its use. RPCPing is covered in detail in Chapter 28, "Diagnosing the Cause of a Problem."

Tools Used to Maintain the Server Environment

The server maintenance tools can be further divided into two categories, tools that are a part of the Exchange Server environment and tools that come with Windows NT Server.

Exchange Server Tools

There are several tools available to you that are specific to the Exchange server itself:

- *Exchange Administrator.* The most important of the Exchange administrator's tools is the Administrator program. Most of the configuration and maintenance of an Exchange server is done with it. The Administrator program is covered in detail in Chapter 5, "Administrative Concepts," and in Chapter 22, "User Management with Exchange."

- *Link and server monitors.* These monitors can be used to monitor a connection between two servers or the health of a single server. These monitors are discussed more in Chapter 27, "Monitoring and Preventing Problems."

- *Exchange Performance Optimizer.* This tool is usually run right after the Exchange server software has been installed. This tool has one main goal: to optimize the Exchange server configuration for best performance on the computer where you installed it. The Exchange configuration is optimized by setting values for parameters stored in the Registry values. Furthermore, Optimizer examines different hard drives and partitions on the system, suggesting the best locations for each of the Exchange components to achieve best performance, and moving the files, if necessary. You should run this tool each time you change the hardware on the system or you change the basic parameters of the Exchange environment. See Chapter 6, "Planning for Optimal Server Performance," for more information on the Optimizer.

- *Exchange utilities.* Even though most of the administration of the Exchange environment is done with the graphical Administrator program, the environment also includes some command-line utilities, such as the EDBUTIL.EXE and ISINTEG.EXE database utilities or the MTACHECK.EXE utility. These utilities are discussed in Chapter 28.

Windows NT Server Tools

The following are the Windows NT Server tools:

- *Control Panel.* You can use the Services applet in the Control Panel to start and stop Exchange services on the local server, and also to change the startup parameters of a service. Additionally, you can use the Network applet to configure the network options on an NT Server that has Exchange installed.

- *Server Manager.* You can use the Server Manager to maintain the services on remote servers. Server Manager is found in the Administrative Tools menu.

- *User Manager for Domains.* NT's User Manager for Domains is used to create and maintain NT domain accounts. When you install the Exchange server (or the Exchange Administrator program) on an NT machine, the installation program will also install an extension to the User Manager. When you use the User Manager to create a new NT user ID, the program will ask you whether you want to create an Exchange account for the user as well (this can be set from the User Manager). Conversely, when you create a new account with Administrator, it can be configured to create a new NT account.

■ *Event Viewer.* When you turn on diagnostics logging for any Exchange server component, the logged events will be stored in NT's event logging system. These logs can be
viewed using the NT Event Viewer, found in the Administrative Tools folder.
Exchange diagnostics log events can be found in any of Event Viewer's logs—Application, System, and Security. The default size of NT's log files is 512KB, so you might
want to change this if you enable logging in Exchange. The default size is changed
from within Event Viewer.

Performance

> **TIP**
>
> You should normally keep all diagnostics logging options in the None or Minimum setting;
> otherwise, the Exchange services will create so many logging events that you will end up
> wasting a lot of disk space. Only when you have detected or suspect an error or malfunc-
> tion in the system should you set the diagnostics logging to Maximum for the specific
> function you are trying to trace, and then follow the events logged in Event Viewer.

■ *Performance Monitor.* When you install Exchange on an NT server, the installation
program will add some Exchange-specific counters to NT's Performance Monitor.
You can use these counters to monitor the health, performance, and usage level of the
Exchange server and services and identify possible bottlenecks or problems in server
performance. The Exchange installation program will also add some predefined
Performance Monitor icons to the Exchange program group. The use of Performance
Monitor to monitor the Exchange environment is discussed in detail in Chapter 27.

> **TIP**
>
> The predefined Performance Monitor icons are the easiest ways for an administrator to
> monitor the daily operation of an Exchange server (for example, the lengths of MTA and
> connector queues). These are automatically installed with Exchange Server, and they are
> discussed in detail in Chapter 12, "Installing Microsoft Exchange Server."

The Exchange Directory Tree

When you install Exchange on a server computer, the installation program will create a directory structure on the disk that you choose. All files and directories related to the Exchange server
are located under a main directory off the root, usually called EXCHSRVR, as in Figure 26.1.

Even though it is not usually necessary to examine or delete these files, an Exchange administrator should be aware of the contents of the subdirectories in the directory structure and of the files that the subdirectories contain.

In a single-drive environment, all files related to Exchange are stored on the same drive. In a multi-drive environment you can, however, choose to store some files on different drives. If this is the case, an EXCHSRVR directory will be created on all selected drives and the appropriate subdirectories created underneath it. If you run the Exchange Optimizer, it will examine the drives on your server system and suggest possible different locations for the directories. The Optimizer will also move the directories and files into their proper positions and change the values in the NT Registry to ensure they are pointing to these files.

FIGURE 26.1.

There are several subdirectories in the Exchange Server directory tree.

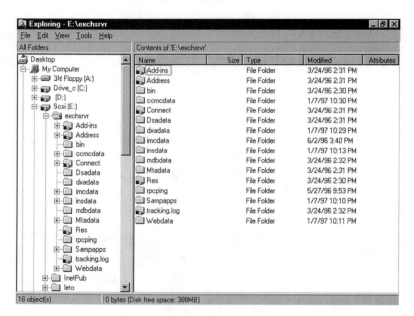

The following list details the subdirectories under the EXCHSRVR directory, what each of the subdirectories contains, and whether they are shared or not.

ADD-INS

The ADD-INS subdirectory contains the administration extensions for the various connectors that will be used in the Administrator program to show the connector's property page. After a full installation, this directory will contain subdirectories and DLLs for the Microsoft Mail Connector, the Microsoft Schedule+ Free/busy Connector, and the

Internet Mail Connector. These DLLs are further divided into subdirectories according to the platform on which they can be run. The installation program automatically shares the ADD-INS subdirectory using the share name ADD-INS.

ADDRESS

The ADDRESS subdirectory contains the address proxy generator DLLs for the three default address types: Microsoft Mail, SMTP, and X.400 addresses. These DLLs are stored in subdirectories according to the address type and platform. The installation program automatically shares the ADDRESS subdirectory using the share name ADDRESS.

BIN

The BIN subdirectory contains the executable files and components of the Exchange server and the Administrator program. This subdirectory also contains many of the Exchange Server diagnostic tools, such as ISINTEG, EDBUTIL, and MDBCHECK.

CCMCDATA

The CCMCDATA subdirectory is used by the cc:Mail Connector to store the temporary data files it needs during message delivery and conversion. There is another set of subdirectories within it that actually contain the data for the messages as they flow in and out of the server.

New to
Version 5.0

CONNECT

The CONNECT subdirectory contains executables and components for the Exchange connectors. After a full installation, there are subdirectories for the Microsoft Mail Connector, the Microsoft Schedule+ Free/busy Connector, and the Internet Mail Connector. In addition, the CONNECT subdirectory contains a subdirectory for various character translation tables. The installation program automatically shares the CONNECT subdirectory using the share name CONNECT.

The subdirectory for the Microsoft Mail Connector, MSMCON, contains two subdirectories: the BIN directory, which contains the executables and components for the Connector itself, and the MAILDATA directory, which contains the Microsoft Mail Connector's shadow post office. The MAILDATA subdirectory contains a directory structure that is almost identical to that of a normal Microsoft Mail post

		office. This directory structure is used to connect the Exchange server to an MS Mail post office. The installation program automatically shares the MAILDATA subdirectory using the share name MAILDAT$ (the share name ends in a dollar sign ($) so that the share will not be visible to normal users when they browse the server's resources).
	DSADATA	The DSADATA subdirectory contains the Exchange Directory database file (DIR.EDB) and its associated transaction logs. These files are discussed in detail in the section "Maintaining the Exchange Databases," later in this chapter.
	DXADATA	The DXADATA subdirectory contains the Directory Synchronization database file (XDIR.EDB) and its associated transaction logs. These files are discussed in detail in the section "Maintaining the Exchange Databases," later in this chapter.
	IMCDATA	The IMCDATA subdirectory is used by the Internet Mail Connector (also called Internet Mail Service or IMS) to store the temporary data files it needs during message delivery and conversion. The IMC also stores some of its logs into these directories. If you turn on SMTP logging in the IMC's Diagnostic Logging database, the log files will be stored in the LOG subdirectory. Also included in the IMC's diagnostics logging is a function called message archival. This function will store a copy of each outgoing or incoming message into the ARCHIVE subdirectories under IN and OUT.
New to Version 5.0	INSDATA	The INSDATA subdirectory contains the files used by the Internet News feeds. It serves a purpose analogous to the MTADATA and IMCDATA directories. If you are not using Internet News, this directory will be empty.
	MDBDATA	The MDBDATA subdirectory contains the database files for the private (PRIV.EDB) and public (PUB.EDB) information stores plus all associated transaction log files. These files are discussed in detail in the section, "Maintaining the Exchange Databases," later in this chapter.
	MTADATA	The MTADATA subdirectory contains various configuration, template, and log files for the Exchange server's Message Transfer Agent (MTA).
New to Version 5.0	RES	The RES subdirectory contains resources for the event logging files. After server installation, this subdirectory is shared using the name RESOURCES.
New to Version 5.0	RPCPING	The RPCPING subdirectory contains the RPC Ping application and documentation. More on RPC Ping in Chapter 28.

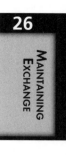

SAMPAPPS | The SAMPAPPS subdirectory contains sample applications and forms written for the Exchange server and client by Microsoft. The installation program automatically shares the CLIENT subdirectory under the SAMPAPPS subdirectory using the share name SAMPLES.

TRACKING.LOG | The TRACKING.LOG subdirectory contains the log files for the Message Tracking function. The installation program automatically shares the TRACKING.LOG subdirectory using the share name TRACKING.LOG.

WEBDATA | The WEBDATA subdirectory contains Active Server Pages and other Web-related files and directories pertaining to the Exchange Web Component.

Exchange Server Registry Entries

Many of the settings for the various Microsoft Exchange server services and features are stored in the NT server Registry in the same way as any NT service or application. You can control and edit most of these settings using the Administrator program, so normally an administrator would not edit them directly in the server's Registry. It might, however, be helpful for the administrator to be aware of the location of the different Registry entries. Furthermore, some entries can be changed only by using the Registry editor.

> **WARNING**
>
> Here's the standard warning about the Registry. If you are not sure how to change the settings in the NT Registry or are unsure about the effects of a particular modification, don't mess with it. An incorrect setting can prevent NT or one of the Exchange services from starting.

All the Registry settings for the Microsoft Exchange server are stored in the HKEY_LOCAL_MACHINE subtree under two hives, SOFTWARE and SYSTEM.

The key name SOFTWARE\Microsoft\Exchange is used to store the settings for the Exchange client, as well as some information on the server. The Setup program uses the subkey SOFTWARE\Microsoft\Exchange\Setup to store information on the Exchange installation. This information is stored when the setup has completed successfully, and it will be used by the setup program to detect whether Exchange has been installed, and if so, where it has been installed.

Performance The values under the subkey SOFTWARE\Microsoft\Exchange\Exchange Provider define which protocols will be used in client-to-server communications (Rpc_Binding_Order) and in server-to-server communications (Rpc_Svr_Binding_Order). The administrator should change these values to include only those protocols that are actually being used. If not, it could cause delays while the client or server waits for unused protocols to time out.

> **NOTE**
>
> The purpose of this section is only to illustrate to the reader the location of the various Exchange Registry entries. Several entries are discussed in detail in various parts of this book, but a detailed discussion of all the entries is beyond the scope of this book.

The settings for the various Exchange services are stored under SYSTEM\CurrentControlSet\Services\<Exchange service>, where <Exchange service> is the name of the service, as detailed in Table 26.1.

Table 26.1. Descriptions for the Exchange Server services used in the Registry.

Exchange Service	*Service Description*
MSExchangeCCMC	Microsoft Exchange Connector for Lotus cc:Mail
MSExchangeDS	Microsoft Exchange Directory
MSExchangeDX	Microsoft Exchange Directory Synchronization
MSExchangeFB	MS Schedule+ Free/Busy Connector
MSExchangeIMC	Microsoft Exchange Internet Mail Connector
MSExchangeIS	Microsoft Exchange Information Store
MSExchangeKMS	Microsoft Exchange Key Manager
MSExchangeMSMI	MS Mail Connector Interchange
MSExchangeMTA	Microsoft Exchange Message Transfer Agent
MSExchangePCMTA	MS Mail Connector (PC) MTA
MSExchangeSA	Microsoft Exchange System Attendant
MSExchangeWEB	Microsoft Exchange Web Component

The Event Log settings for the various Exchange services are stored under SYSTEM\CurrentControlSet\Services\EventLog\Application\<Exchange service>, where <Exchange service> is the name of the service as detailed in Table 26.1. Note that there are some additional names found there, such as NNTP and POP3 interfaces, which are not listed in Table 26.1.

The licensing information for the Exchange server is stored under SYSTEM\CurrentControlSet \Services\LicenseInfo\MSExchangeIS.

You can use the NT License Manager to change the licensing information.

User Maintenance

User maintenance mostly consists of creating and modifying recipients and distribution lists and monitoring the storage space allocated for each user. Recipient and distribution list creation and modification are discussed in Chapter 22 and Chapter 23, "The Exchange Directory," so this chapter concentrates on tasks related to monitoring user storage space.

You can set the maximum amount of disk space allowable for a user by defining the storage limit values on the General property page in the Private Information Store property window. There are two levels of storage limits; users that exceed the first one are given a warning, and when they exceed the second limit, the system will disable them from sending any messages. The default settings defined on the General property page can be bypassed by defining user-specific storage limits on the Advanced property page of the user's mailbox.

NOTE

You can set storage limits on two levels: individual users and the whole Private Information Store. Storage space cannot be limited on the level of user groups or distribution lists.

You can monitor disk space used by each user by opening the Private Information Store property page under the server you want to monitor. The Logons property page lists all the users currently logged onto the system. The Mailbox Resources property page lists all the users defined on the server, the number of messages stored in their mailboxes, and the storage space (in kilobytes) the messages take.

NOTE

The Private Information Store (and the Public IS, for that matter) is based on a single-instance storage principle, which means that each message is stored only once in the private information store database, even though it might appear in several users' mailboxes. The total storage space reported for each user on the Mailbox Resources will, however, include the storage space used by the message separately for each of the users that have that particular message in their mailboxes. The same applies to the user level storage limits. Bottom line: if you add up all the storage space "used" by each user, it will quite likely be larger than the actual size of the store itself. This is proof of the single-instance storage principle at work.

Architecture

Cleaning Mailboxes

The administrator can clean—in other words, delete—selected messages from one or more mailboxes using the Clean Mailbox function. To clean mailboxes, first select the mailboxes you want to clean and then select Tools | Clean Mailbox (see Figure 26.2). The program will display a dialog box that enables you to define the messages you want cleaned from the selected mailboxes.

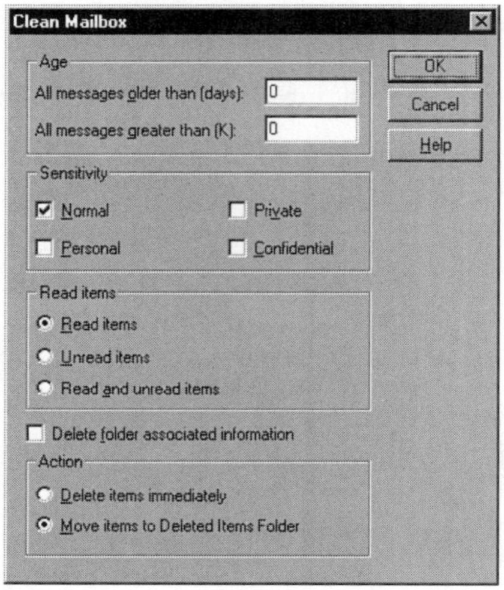

FIGURE 26.2.

The Clean Mailbox dialog box is used to delete mail from mailboxes.

CAUTION

Use the Clean Mailbox function with caution, because it will delete all the specified messages without discrimination. It is generally more advisable to specify a mailbox storage limit and let the users clean their own mailboxes. The maximum storage levels defined to users are very powerful; when users exceed the first limit, they will be notified. But when users exceed the second limit, they will not be able to send any mail until they have cleaned their mailboxes and the storage space used is again under the second limit.

Moving Users

Sometimes, you might have to move a user from one server to another within an Exchange site, or even to another site. Moving a user from server to server within a site is very simple; you just select the mailbox or mailboxes you want to move in the administrator program, select Move Mailbox from the Tools menu, and select the target server from the displayed dialog box. The administrator program will move the user and the user's mailbox to the specified server.

Moving a user to a server in another site is a bit more complicated; you cannot use any single function to do this. You should first copy all the user's folders and messages to a .PST file, delete the user ID from the old server, create the user manually on the new server, and then add a Personal Folders information service to the user's profile and point it to the .PST file created earlier. Then users can copy all their folders and messages to their new mailboxes on the server.

Maintaining Public Folders

Maintaining public folders consists of two tasks: monitoring storage space used by each public folder and all public folders in total, and monitoring the replication of public folders to specified servers.

The default maximum storage space allowed for each public folder is defined on the General property page of the server's property window. You can bypass this setting by specifying a folder specific storage limit on the Advanced property page on the public folder's property window.

Folder replication is monitored from the Replication Status property page of the Public Folder's property window. This page lists all servers to which the folder has been defined to be replicated and the status of the replication to each of the servers.

Moving a Public Folder

You can move a public folder from one server to another server by first replicating the folder to a new server and then deleting the replica from the old server.

> **NOTE**
>
> You cannot delete the last replica of a particular public folder in a site using the Administrator program. To delete the public folder, use the Exchange client.

Maintaining the Exchange Databases

The Exchange Server uses relational fault-tolerant databases to store most of the user and configuration information and user data. This database technology was chosen for Exchange because some of its features—mainly, the relatively compact sizes of the databases and the database engine, and the capability of storing records of varying lengths efficiently—suited the Exchange environment better than some other database solutions, such as the SQL Server engine.

> **NOTE**
>
> The JET database engine used in Exchange Server is not to be confused with the JET database engine used in Microsoft Access. They are completely different, and they are not related at all.

The Exchange database is used to store information for three different services:

- Directory service
- Information Store service
- Directory Synchronization service

The Directory Synchronization database differs from the other two databases, because it is used to store changes in data rather than the actual data. Furthermore, the Directory Synchronization database does not usually need any maintenance. This chapter therefore focuses on maintaining the Directory and Information Store databases. The same methods apply, however, to the Directory Synchronization database as well.

Storing Data

The database files for the different services are stored in the Exchange server's directory structure under the subdirectories for the respective services. The directories contain three different types of files:

- .EDB, the database files
- .LOG, the transaction log files
- .CHK, the checkpoint files

Transaction Logs Explained

When you make a change to the Exchange directory or store an object in your mailbox, the changes are stored into the appropriate database. The database engine does not, however, write the change directly to the database file (.EDB). The change—or transaction—is first written to a transaction log file (.LOG), and the database engine will copy the change to the actual database file (.EDB) at a later time. This method provides some advantages, including the following:

Performance

- *Performance.* The data is written to the transaction log in a sequential manner, always appended to the end of the file. When data is stored into a database file, however, the database engine must access data in a random fashion, because data is rarely stored sequentially in a database. This means that writing the data into a transaction log first is much faster because the data can be written to the actual database at a later time.

■ *Reliability.* After reading about the performance benefits, you're probably concerned about reliability. And rightly so. What happens if the system crashes before the data gets to the database? Simple. The data is still in the logs, so just "replay" all the transactions from the log into the database, beginning at the last checkpoint, and you're back in business. If the database file itself becomes corrupt or is destroyed, you can use the same technique to re-create the actual database file. The catch is that you must maintain the integrity of the log files, so always store them on a fault-tolerant drive system.

Both of these advantages imply that storing the database files and the transaction logs on different drives is more efficient than storing them both on the same drive. If you store the transaction logs on a separate drive, the database engine can store data simultaneously to the transaction logs while the other Exchange services use the other drive(s) for other purposes. Furthermore, if the drive containing the database files fails, you can always re-create the database from the transaction logs. Again, if you split the logs and the database files, always ensure the logs are on a fault-tolerant drive system.

When you install Exchange, you have the option of running the Exchange Optimizer. This program will examine the hard disks attached to the system and suggest the best possible location for each of the components. It will generally suggest locating the database files and transaction logs on different drives. To achieve the best possible performance, you should usually let the Optimizer move the files the way it suggests.

Performance

TIP

One way to improve a server's performance is to locate the transaction logs on a partition formatted with the FAT file system. FAT is a bit faster than the NTFS file system for storing sequential data. All the other server components should be located on an NTFS partition.

Performance

The size of a transaction log is always exactly 5MB (except for the Directory Synchronization database, which uses 1MB transaction log files), or more specifically 5,242,880 bytes. If a log file is a different size, it is most likely corrupt.

Checkpoint Files

Because the changes to any database are written first to the transaction logs and then to the database itself, the most current data will be the database plus the latest transactions in the transaction log. The point in the transaction log where data is guaranteed to have been committed to the database is called a *checkpoint*. Checkpoint information is kept in a checkpoint file called EDB.CHK.

Old Log Files

There are several transaction log files (.LOG) in each of the data directories. The one in use is called EDB.LOG. When this file becomes full, it will be renamed EDB00001.LOG and a new file will be opened and named EDB.LOG. When this file becomes full, it will be renamed EDB00002.LOG and a new EDB.LOG file will be created, and so on, counting in hex. The log files other than the EDB.LOG are called "old log files;" the smaller the number the older the log file is.

The old log files together with a backup of the database file can be used to recover a database in case of a hardware failure or any event that will corrupt the database. You do the recovery by restoring the old transaction files using the backup program and then letting the information store service "replay" the transaction logs into the database.

The database engine will not delete the old log files, and in time they can grow to take all available disk space. The administrator can delete the log files by hand, but this is an extremely unadvisable solution because the administrator cannot know which of the transaction logs have been written into the database file, and therefore might inadvertently delete some data. Also, if the log files are deleted they cannot be used to recover the database in case of a hardware failure. A controlled way to delete the log files is to use backup software that supports Exchange, such as the NT Backup program. After all files, the database file, and the transaction logs have been successfully backed up, the backup program will delete all log files that have been actually committed to the database. The backup and restore processes are discussed in detail in the section "Backing Up and Restoring the Exchange Environment," later in this chapter.

Circular Logging

The administrator can also configure the directory and information store services so that they will reuse log files after the transactions they contain are committed to the database. This function is called *circular logging,* and you set it from the Advanced property page on the server's property window. Circular logging means that the transactions will be written into the transaction log file as usual, but the database engine will overwrite transaction log files after its transactions have been committed into the database file. This means that you will save a lot of disk space because there will be fewer transaction log files to store. On the other hand, you cannot perform the differential and incremental backups, which are faster than full backups.

The Reserved Log Files

In each data directory, there are two log files called RES1.LOG and RES2.LOG. These files are called the *reserved logs.* The purpose of these files is to reserve some room on the log file disk in case the disk fills up. When the EDB.LOG file becomes full, the service stores the file as an old log file and tries to create a new EDB.LOG file. If there is not enough space to create the new file, the database engine will inform the MSExchangeIS service of this and request that the service terminate itself. To ensure that no data is lost, the service will use the reserved logs to store all uncommitted transactions and then terminate itself.

Maintaining Database Files

In time, the data in the database files can become spread out and fragmented, causing decreased server performance. There are two ways to perform maintenance on the database files. Most of the maintenance is automatic and is done while the server is up and running. This maintenance is called *online maintenance,* and is governed by two settings in the administrator's program:

■ Directory database online maintenance. The Garbage Collection Interval value on the General property page in the DS Site Configuration property window defines how often the directory service will perform online maintenance. This value defines how often the directory service will permanently delete all the expired deleted objects (tombstones) from the directory database and defragment the database. The default is set to 12 hours. You shouldn't change this value.

■ Information Store database online maintenance. The schedule defined on the IS Maintenance property page on the server's property window determines when online maintenance will be performed on the private and public store databases. You can set the schedule to Always, or you can define a time in the schedule by using the Selected times option. During online maintenance, the databases will be scanned for deleted objects, the space taken up by the deleted objects will be marked free, and the database will be defragmented. You should try to schedule the IS maintenance during off-peak time so that normal server performance is not decreased by the maintenance function.

NOTE

Online maintenance will defragment the databases, but it will not decrease the size of the databases. Space will only be freed from deleted objects and marked available to other objects. If you wish to decrease the size of the database files and reclaim unused disk space, you have to perform offline maintenance.

As an administrator, you can also perform offline maintenance on the database files, but to do this you first must stop the corresponding service. In other words, offline maintenance cannot be performed while the server is in use. You use the EDBUTIL.EXE database utility to perform offline maintenance.

> **TIP**
>
> You should perform offline maintenance on a new server at least once a month. Monitor closely the performance of the server, particularly the directory and information store databases before and after running the EDBUTIL.EXE utility (for details on monitoring your Exchange server, see Chapter 27). The amount of performance you gain after running EDBUTIL can help you determine how often to perform offline maintenance.

The maintenance utilities, including EDBUTIL and ISINTEG, are covered in more detail in Chapter 28.

Maintaining the Message Transfer Agent (MTA)

The Exchange Message Transfer Agent is one of the core services of an Exchange server—it must be running before the server can be considered usable. The following are some common functions of the MTA:

- The MTA takes care of limited message transfer within the server from one component to another (for example, from MS Mail Connector to Information Store).
- The MTA runs the Site Connector and X.400 Connector. These connectors are really considered to be configurations of the MTA rather than separate components like the Internet Mail Connector or a third-party gateway.
- The MTA is the service that expands distribution lists.
- In message transfer between Exchange servers, one server's MTA talks directly to another server's MTA. This MTA-to-MTA communication occurs whether the servers are in the same site or in different sites.
- When two servers in different sites are replicating Directory Service information, the data is passed from MTA to MTA rather than from DS to DS.

The most important thing about maintaining the MTA, and arguably the entire Exchange server, is to constantly keep an eye on the MTA queues. This is especially true of installations where there are multiple servers exchange messages among themselves.

There are several ways to monitor the MTA queues. You can open the MTA property window in the Administrator program and look at the Queues property page, as shown in Figure 26.3. The Queue name drop-down list contains one line for each of the queues defined on this server. The list will also show the number of items in each of the queues. You can view the details of messages in the queue and delete messages, if necessary.

FIGURE 26.3.
The MTA Queues property page is one way to monitor the MTA queues.

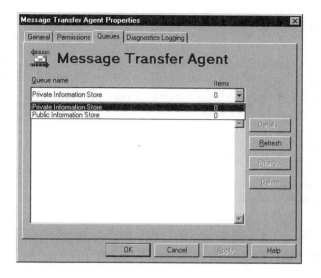

Another way to monitor the MTA queues is to use the counters found in the Performance Monitor MSExchangeMTA object. The are several counters you can monitor that will tell you how the Exchange server's MTA is doing. The Performance Monitor is discussed in detail in Chapter 27.

The MTACHECK Utility

The MTA can become corrupted sometimes, and that will prevent it from starting. In such a case, you should use the MTACHECK utility to fix errors within the MTA environment. This utility examines the MTA database files (.DAT) for damaged objects, which it will then place into files that the administrator can examine. You should be careful when you run the MTACHECK utility, because it can remove data from the database that cannot be restored. When you run the MTACHECK all the damaged objects will be placed into .DAT files in the MTADATA\MTACHECK.OUT directory.

Before you run the MTACHECK utility, you should always empty the MTACHECK.OUT directory of any old .DAT files. Then you can go into the EXCHSRVR\BIN directory and run the MTACHECK.EXE utility. The utility will find the MTA files automatically, and it will report any damaged objects found.

Maintaining the Connectors

In order to ensure smooth operation of the different connectors configured in the system, the administrator should constantly monitor the connector queues. The MTA queues were discussed earlier in this chapter. In addition to the MTA queues, the Internet Mail Connector (now called the Internet Mail Service, or IMS) and the MS Mail Connector have their own queues, which can be seen through each connector's property window:

- *Internet Mail Service.* Select the Queues tab in the connector's property window. The Queues property page shows a list of four queues, two outbound and two inbound. Use this page to view and delete queued messages or manually force the connector to retry sending the message.

- *cc:Mail Connector.* Select the Queues tab in the connector's property window to determine the number of messages in a queue, to view a message in a queue, and to delete a pending message, which will return it to the sender. This property page shows two queues for monitoring outbound and inbound messages: MTS-OUT and MTS-IN, respectively.

- *MS Mail Connector.* This connector maintains MS Mail post office-specific queues. Select the Connections tab in the connector's property window. Then select the post office that you want to monitor and click Queue. The Queue window will show all queued messages, and you can view and delete them if necessary.

As with the MTA queues, all the connector queues can be monitored through the NT Performance Monitor. Various connector queues are typically found in their own PerfMon object, such as in MSExchangeIMC for the Internet Mail Connector and in MSExchangeCCMC for the cc:Mail Connector.

Backing Up and Restoring the Exchange Environment

You need to back up the Exchange system the way you do any important data processing system. You can use several tools to create backups of the Exchange system. The best results can be achieved by using backup software that supports Exchange, such as the NT Backup utility. This section provides an overview of the backup process, but the subject is covered in detail in Chapter 25, "Backup and Recovery."

You have two ways to back up an Exchange system: you can take a backup offline or online.

Offline Backup and Restore

Taking an offline backup means that you stop the Exchange server and take a file-level backup of the whole Exchange directory structure or of selected subdirectories. This method has several disadvantages:

■ You must stop the server in order to make the backup and then restart it when you're finished. This means that users cannot use the server during the backup, and no mail will be delivered during backup.

■ The backup will not delete the old log files, and you as the administrator will have to delete the log files manually or use circular logging.

■ The backup process will copy all the database files onto the tapes, which can take a considerable amount of time compared to an online backup. An online backup can be defined to back up only changed data.

Furthermore, when you restore a file-level backup, some of the global unique identifiers (GUIDs) used in the restored database will probably be in conflict with existing GUIDs. This will result in a failure to start the Information Store service with the error -1011. To correct this, you have to run the ISINTEG.EXE utility with the -patch switch. See Chapter 28.

Troubleshooting

TIP

When you have installed a new server, take a full offline backup of the whole server, including the NT and the Exchange environment. When you take online backups in the future, only the information store and the directory databases will be backed up. If you happen to lose the whole server, it will be easier to restore it from a backup than start installing it from scratch.

You should also have a backup of your NT Server environment that includes the Registry.

Online Backup

Online backup means that you take the backup when the Exchange server is up and running. This is the preferred backup method, because the procedure will also purge the log files. When you do an online backup, it is also possible to use incremental and differential backup methods, which will enable you to take a backup of a large site as well.

NOTE

Making an online backup will create a backup of only the information store and directory databases. If you want to back up the other Exchange components, you must use the offline backup method. It is recommended that you take a full offline file backup of the Exchange server files right after the server has been installed, and keep updating the backup every now and then.

Compatibility When you install the Exchange server or administrator program on an NT server, the installation program will also install a new copy of the Windows NT Backup utility. The new version includes some new functionality that enables you to make online backups from an Exchange server.

> **TIP**
>
> If you do not want to install a complete copy of the administrator program on the NT machine from which you want to take the backups, you can also copy the new version of NT Backup from the Exchange server CD. The file is called NTBACKUP.EXE and can be found in the platform-specific directory under SETUP.

The new backup utility has a new function in the Operations menu called Microsoft Exchange. When you select this function, the backup utility will display a window asking for the name of an Exchange server to which to connect, as shown in Figure 26.4. You can also start the Exchange Directory and Information Store services if necessary. The server does not have to be the one you want to back up—any one in the desired organization will do. Regardless, I usually select the one I plan to back up.

FIGURE 26.4.

Select an Exchange Server in the Organization before beginning the backup process.

After you select the server, the backup program will establish a connection to the selected server and get some information about the server's organization. The backup program will then show a list of all the sites and servers within the organization, as shown in Figure 26.5. You can back up any server in the organization to which you have an RPC-capable connection. In this window, you can also select to back up only the Information Store or the Directory database, or both, on selected servers.

FIGURE 26.5.

*NTBackup allows you
to select the databases in
the Exchange
organization to be
backed up.*

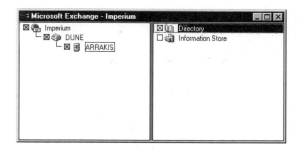

After you select the servers and databases to be backed up, click the Backup button. The program will display the Backup Information dialog box, in which you can define the settings for the backup process, as shown in Figure 26.6:

- *Tape name.* Specify a name that will uniquely identify the backup tape and will tell the administrator what the tape contains.

- *Operation.* Specify whether to append the backed-up data to the data already on the tape or to replace any data the tape contains.

- *Verify After Backup.* Specify whether to have NTBackup compare what it just put on tape to what is on the disk. I recommend this option for offline file backups to ensure you have a reliable backup.

- *Restrict Access to Owner or Administrator.* This setting is necessary only if you want to be the only one with access to the backup.

- *Backup Set Information.* This is description for the backup and the backup method. The different backup methods are discussed in detail later in this chapter.

- *Log Information.* Specify log filename and logging type.

FIGURE 26.6.

*The Backup Informa-
tion dialog box allows
you to set backup
options.*

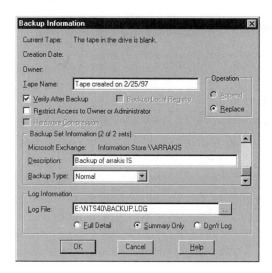

When you have selected the appropriate options, click OK. The program will display the Backup Status dialog box, which shows the status of the backup process, as in Figure 26.7. Note that there are no physical files being backed up, but rather the Exchange component itself.

FIGURE 26.7.

The Backup Status dialog box shows the progress of the currently running backup.

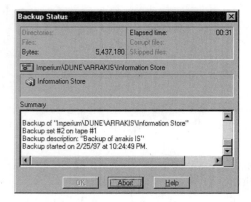

How Does the Online Backup Work?

When you connect to an Exchange server using the NTBACKUP program to perform a full backup, the server will first store the current checkpoint from the EDB.CHK file. This checkpoint points to the record in the transaction log files that has been last committed to the database. The next step is to back up the database files (.EDB). In the beginning of the database backup, the server will create a patch file (.PAT) that will be used to store all changes to the transaction logs written during the backup process.

After the databases have been backed up, all transaction logs created during the backup process will be backed up. After this, the process will write any patch files onto the backup tape. Finally the process will delete all transaction log files created before the current checkpoint stored in the beginning of the process.

The process is a bit different if you are using the differential or incremental backup method, because these methods take only a backup of the transaction logs.

Backup Methods

There are four different backup methods you can use when making an online backup:

- *Normal (Full).* This backup method will take a full backup of the selected databases—that is, back up all the files for the selected databases, whether or not they have changed since the last backup. The backup will also purge the transaction logs—that is, delete the log files that have been committed to the actual database. This will mark the files for a differential or incremental backup.

The advantage of this backup method is that you will need only one tape for a restore operation, because all the data will be backed up at once. The disadvantage is that the backup will take a fairly long time, because all the data will be written to the tape.

■ *Copy.* This method is similar to the normal method, except that the log files are not purged or the files marked for differential or incremental backups.

■ *Incremental.* This method will take a backup of only the data that has changed since the last normal or incremental backup (whichever was last). During the backup, only the changed transaction log files are written to the backup tape. After the backup has been completed, the process will delete the backed-up transaction log files.

The advantage of this backup method is that it is the quickest; only information that has changed since the last backup will be backed up. The disadvantage is that in the case of a database failure you will need the last full backup and all the incremental backups made after the full backup.

■ *Differential.* This method will take a backup of all the data that has changed since the last full backup. The differential backup does not purge the transaction logs, which means that they will be purged during the next full backup.

The advantage of this backup method is that you will never need more than two backup tapes to restore the system: the last full backup and the last differential backup. The disadvantage of this method is the time it takes to complete. The backup time will vary from day to day; it will always be longer than an incremental backup but shorter than a full backup.

Combining Backup Methods

The best possible backup solution is to take a full backup every night of all Exchange databases. When your site grows in size, this can become impossible, because you will not be able to take a full backup during one night. In such a case, you can either upgrade your backup hardware, use more than one device to take the backup, or combine full backup with either the incremental backup or differential backup.

NOTE

Never combine the incremental and differential backup methods together. Both methods take backups only of data that has changed since the last backup, but if you're not careful, you could inadvertently exclude data that needs to be backed up.

If you want to combine two backup methods, you should select the time to take the full backup so that it will not matter whether the backup process is not finished during one night. Usually, selecting Friday for the full backup is the best option. Then, on Monday evening take the first incremental or differential backup, on Tuesday the second, and so on. The selection of the second backup method is based on the amount of data to be backed up. If you use incremental backup, only the changes made since the last backup (full or incremental) will need to be backed up, thus minimizing the time to take the backups during the week. If you use differential backup, the backup process will take a backup of all changes made since the last full backup on a Friday, thus increasing the backup time toward the end of the week.

Another thing to consider is the time you need for a full restore in case of a system failure. If you use full/incremental backup, you need the full backup tape plus all the incremental backups to do a full restore. If you use the full/differential backup method, you will need only the full backup plus the last differential backup to do a full restore.

Restoring Data from a Backup

Unlike the backup process, you must run the restore process offline. To perform an offline restore, any Exchange services have to be stopped.

> **TIP**
>
> As mentioned earlier, you should take a full offline (file level) backup of the Exchange server every now and then, so that in case of a total system failure you can restore the entire Exchange environment without having to reinstall Exchange. When you restore a file-level backup, some of the Globally Unique IDentifiers (GUIDs) used in the restored database may be in conflict with existing GUIDs. This will result in a failure to start the Information Store service with the error -1011. To correct this you have to run the ISINTEG utility with the `-patch` switch.

The first thing you do for a restore is establish a connection to an Exchange server in the organization. After that you can select the server(s) and database(s) that you want to restore, as shown in Figure 26.8.

When you click on the Restore button, the program will display the Restore Information dialog box, where you can select the following options for the restore process, as shown in Figure 26.9:

■ *Erase all existing data.* NTBackup will erase the data in the destination before beginning the restore. You might choose this option if you are restoring IS data to a different server than the one from which the data was originally backed up.

■ *Destination Server.* This option is available only if you are restoring the Information Store. You can specify the original server or a different server to receive the restored IS data. However, a destination server must be specified. If you are restoring the Directory, this option does not apply because the Directory must be restored to the server from which it was backed up.

■ *Private* and *Public.* These options are available only if you are restoring the IS—you specify whether to restore the public or the private IS databases, or both.

■ *Start Service After Restore.* Use this option to automatically restart the IS or Directory service after the restore process completes.

FIGURE 26.8.

NTBackup allows you to select the databases in the backup set to be restored.

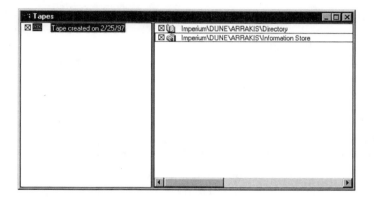

FIGURE 26.9.

The Restore Information dialog box allows you to set restore options.

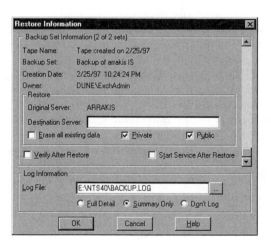

When you have selected the appropriate options, click OK. The program will display the Restore Status dialog box showing the status of the restore process, as in Figure 26.10.

FIGURE 26.10.

The Restore Status dialog box shows the progress of the currently running restore.

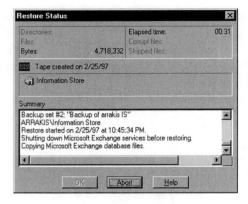

Performance After the restore process is finished, the restored service may take a while longer than usual to start. That is normal, because Exchange is running internal consistency checks on the database. The length of time it takes depends on the size of the database and the speed of your computer. If you're really concerned, you should run the IS/DS Consistency Check to check the consistency in the Information Store and the Directory databases.

Backup and Restore Considerations

After you have installed your Exchange server, you should plan a suitable backup method and also go through the steps needed to perform a restore of your backup. In any large site, you should always have an ample supply of backup hardware available. In some sites it might even be justifiable to keep a backup server available, ready with NT installed on it. In case of a system failure, the only thing you need to do is rename the server appropriately and restore your backups on the server—and you're up and running again.

All the administration access rights information on the Exchange server is stored in the Directory database. The administration rights are always defined to a certain NT user security identifier (SID). Because the SIDs are unique and will never be reused after they are deleted, you should always have a backup of the NT operating system files, as well as Exchange files. If for some reason you have to restore a whole directory database, you will not be able to start any services if you do not have access to the same domain database that the original server was using—that is, if you cannot use the same user account (the same SID) to start and administer the service. Therefore, it is highly risky to install the Exchange server onto a Primary Domain Controller in a domain with no Backup Domain Controllers; if you happen to lose the machine, you will lose the domain database, and you will not be able to restore your directory database and use it.

If you do not want to use the NT Backup program to take backups of the Exchange environment, many independent software vendors are including Exchange support in their backup products. Some are mentioned in Appendix A, "Third-Party Add-On Products." You can also check out Microsoft's Web site. Search for the word Backup to obtain a list of vendors producing backup software for Exchange.

Summary

In this chapter, you got a broad overview of things involved in maintaining Exchange. User and private store maintenance, public folder maintenance, server maintenance, and connection maintenance—all constitute a large part of the administrator's responsibilities.

These various maintenance tasks consist of defining and modifying mailboxes and recipients, monitoring storage levels, verifying public folder replication, configuring and modifying the server, monitoring server and service operation, monitoring available storage, monitoring messages queues, and performing regular backups.

User maintenance mainly consists of defining and modifying mailboxes and other recipients. The administrator also has to monitor storage levels per user and for the whole private information store.

There are several tools available for accomplishing these tasks, some of which are discussed in this chapter and some in the following chapters. Understanding these tools is important to properly administering an Exchange server. You don't have to know everything about everything, but it is important to have a working knowledge of the type of things involved in administering a server.

Monitoring and Preventing Problems

by Greg Todd

IN THIS CHAPTER

CHAPTER 27

Troubleshooting One key aspect of effectively managing an Exchange server is keeping a watchful eye on the server's behavior. This behavior will manifest itself in at least three ways: availability, performance, and functionality. In other words: Is my server up? How fast is my server responding? Am I able to send and receive e-mail from the Internet? This chapter provides some suggestions on how to monitor Exchange Server so that you can prevent server problems by catching them before they happen.

The idea is simple: If you can keep the server healthy, you can keep your users up and running. That makes everyone happy.

The focus of this chapter is to introduce you to useful tools for preventive maintenance. The following are the main tools that help you with this task:

- Windows NT Performance Monitor
- Auto-installed Performance Monitor workspaces
- Exchange-specific Performance Monitor counters
- Windows NT Performance Monitor counters
- Microsoft Exchange Server Monitors
- Information Store maintenance

First, you examine one of the most useful tools available to anyone monitoring an Exchange Server: Windows NT Performance Monitor (PerfMon). This tool is quite powerful, and used in the correct way, it can provide a wealth of information about the health of the server.

After you look at Performance Monitor, checking out the auto-installed PerfMon workspaces included with Exchange makes sense. These "canned" views of data are great for monitoring an Exchange server.

Then you examine some useful counters that will help you monitor the most critical aspects of an Exchange server. I include both Exchange-specific counters and generic Windows NT counters.

Next, you wrap up the chapter by looking at a few areas of monitoring and maintenance provided by the Exchange Administrator program: Server Monitor, Link Monitor, and automatic IS maintenance. They provide additional capability for ensuring that connections and services are up and running, for keeping system clocks among Exchange servers in sync, and for keeping the IS databases clean and defragmented.

Furthermore, if you're interested in monitoring the following items in the Exchange Server system, this chapter is for you:

- Exceeded thresholds
- Services that have stopped running
- Connections that have failed
- Server clocks that are out of sync

So get comfortable—and get ready to jump into the stimulating world of the finer points of monitoring an Exchange Server.

27

MONITORING AND
PREVENTING
PROBLEMS

Windows NT Performance Monitor

Performance

First, I want to spend some time going over the Windows NT Performance Monitor (PerfMon) application because it is an extremely valuable tool. This is a fairly comprehensive look at PerfMon, because I want you to get a sense for how to use PerfMon and what you can do with it.

For example, PerfMon gives you the ability to monitor how many messages your Exchange server is handling at any given time. You can also see how many users are logged on to the Exchange Information Store. Or what the database buffer cache hit rate is. Or how much paging activity is occurring. Or what the CPU utilization is. All these, and more, are important data points to know when managing an Exchange Server computer.

Think of PerfMon as a wide-angle lens looking at a very large picture, the very large picture being all the performance data available in Windows NT. You can bring many things into focus with the lens, and you can look at a large number of things. Some things you can even get a fairly close look at. If, however, you really need to zoom in on one specific detail, you probably need to switch to a macro zoom lens. In that case, PerfMon might not be the right tool to use.

So, although PerfMon isn't everything to everyone, chances are it will be enough to at least point you in the right direction for what to do next. And for many monitoring tasks, it will be all you need. I know it works that way for me.

Objects and Counters

The first thing to understand about PerfMon is that it relays data to you in an orderly fashion. Because you can monitor so much information in a Windows NT system, it must have some structure; otherwise, you could never get through it all.

The highest-level item on which Windows NT reports performance is called an *object*, and objects are organized into *counters*. The counters actually convey the performance data related to a particular object.

In fact, in its architecture, Windows NT is composed of many objects that represent system resources, such as processes, physical devices, and memory. So, when you use PerfMon monitor performance in a Windows NT system, you are monitoring the behavior of its objects. Figure 27.1 shows a PerfMon screen with a counter of an object's Processor, System, Process, and Memory displayed.

FIGURE 27.1.

Monitoring multiple counters and multiple objects is simple using PerfMon.

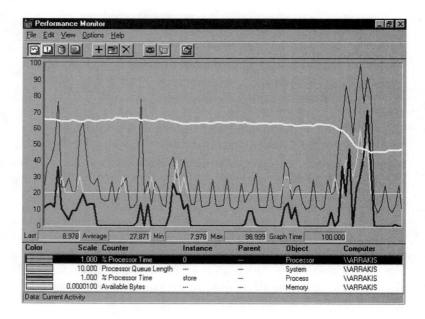

Table 27.1 shows some of the objects you find in Windows NT.

Table 27.1. Some PerfMon objects found in Windows NT.

Object	Contains Counters For
Browser	NT network browser information
Cache	NT system cache information
Logical Disk	All logical disks in the system
Memory	System memory information
Objects	The quantity of high-level system objects, such as processes, threads, semaphores, and so on
Paging File	NT page file(s)
Physical Disk	All physical disks in the system

Object	Contains Counters For
Process	Active processes in the system; similar to Thread object
Processor	System processor(s)
Server	Miscellaneous server-related information about the system
System	Miscellaneous system-wide counters
Thread	All active threads in the system; similar to Process object

Your system probably has the objects listed in Table 27.1, plus some others, depending on what software components have been installed. If you install TCP/IP, for example, TCP, IP, and UDP objects are available to monitor.

When Exchange Server is installed, additional Exchange-specific objects are available as well. You learn more details about these objects and their counters in the section "Exchange-Specific Performance Monitor Counters," later in this chapter.

Ways to View Data

You might think that the features I've already covered are enough for anyone to wield for monitoring an Exchange server. Well, maybe so, but there's more to PerfMon. In addition to being able to view the data graphically in real time with the Chart view, as in Figure 27.1, you can employ the three other views to help you sort out your data: Alert view, Log view, and Report view.

The following sections will discuss these four views and show examples of each.

Chart View

The Chart view, shown in Figure 27.2, is the view on which I have focused the majority of discussion so far. It is also probably the one you will spend the most time using when you are monitoring a server. Also, it's the one I tend to associate most often with PerfMon because of the graphical screen it provides.

Chart view gives you a graphical real-time look at various performance counters in the system. Or you can use it for a graphical look at logged data saved previously. In Figure 27.2 you can easily see paging activity on the server \\arrakis.

TIP

If you press the Backspace key—or Ctrl+H—the line on the graph associated with the highlighted chart line changes from colored to bold white so you can see it better. This capability is especially useful when you're working with crowded Chart views while scrolling through counters on the chart line.

Figure 27.2.

In the Chart view, Performance Monitor graphically conveys performance counter data.

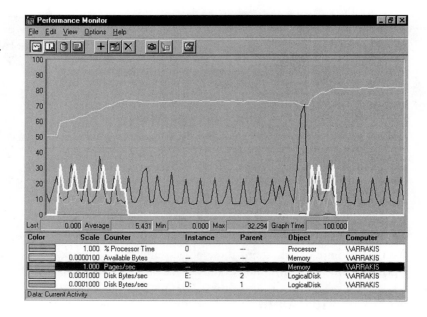

You set the options, such as periodic update, grid lines, legend, and so on with the Chart Options dialog box. From the PerfMon menu, choose Options | Chart—or Ctrl+O—to open this dialog box. Most of the options are self-explanatory.

You add counters to the view by clicking the + (plus) button on the toolbar or by choosing Edit | Add to Chart. The Add to Chart dialog box then appears, as shown in Figure 27.3. The Tab button also does the same thing, and I usually use it because it's faster.

Figure 27.3.

Any available objects and counters for the server \\ARRAKIS are selected in the Add to Chart dialog box.

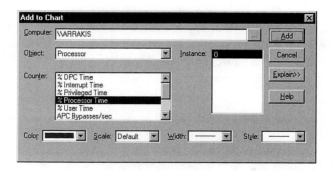

In the Counter list box, you can see all the available counters of the Processor object. By clicking the Object drop-down list box, you can see all the available objects in the system.

> **TIP**
>
> If you don't know what a counter represents, you can click the Explain button, which is a handy aid in the Add to Chart dialog box. At the bottom of the dialog box you will see a brief description of the counter you've highlighted. Using this feature can be helpful on some of the more obscure counters. You might not be exactly sure, for example, what the `Cache:Async MDL Reads/sec` counter is. The Explain button might cast some light on the subject.

The Legend

After you add a counter in the Add to Chart dialog box and click Done (the Cancel button changes to Done after you add a counter), the counter appears in the *legend* at the bottom of the Chart view in what is called a *chart line*. The chart line gives a summary of the system resource being monitored.

As you might have noticed in Figure 27.2, several columns of characteristics about each chart line are displayed in the legend. The columns displayed are specific to the Chart view. Let's take a closer look at them:

- *Color* specifies the color of the line that appears on the display, presuming you have a color monitor. If you don't have a color monitor, the screen becomes difficult to read very quickly as you add more counters, but you can modify the line style to be dashed, dotted, and so on.

   You can change the graph color of the highlighted counter. Just double-click the line (or highlight a line and choose Edit | Edit Chart Line), and a dialog box appears enabling you to change, among other things, the color of the line as it appears in the graph. You also can alter Scale, Width, and Style.

- *Scale* describes the multiplier applied to the data value for display on the PerfMon screen. If you're looking at a counter, for example, and all its values are below 10, you might want to select a multiplier of 10 so that its values show better on the graph, which ranges from 0 to 100. Changing the scale does not alter the actual data value in any way. As with Color, you can set the scale in the Edit Chart Line dialog box.

- *Counter* indicates the actual PerfMon counter being monitored. The general form of reference to a counter is `object:counter`; shown here is the `counter` portion of that. The amount of memory available in the system, for example, is written as `Memory:Available Bytes`. In this way, you know to go to the `Memory` object and select the `Available Bytes` counter.

- *Instance* shows which one of multiple instances of an object you are monitoring. This applies only if that object can have more than one instance. For some objects, such as `Memory`, instance is not applicable, so dashes appear in the column. Other objects, such as `Processor` or `Logical Disk`, can have multiple instances of their counters.

If you have two processors in a system, for example, you have two instances of the Processor object, 0 and 1. You can monitor all the counters in the Processor object for each instance of 0 and 1. Doing so gives you a separate set of counters for each object instance, or for each processor in this case.

Here is another example: if the system has three disks called C:, D:, and E:, it has three instances of the Logical Disk object: 0 ==> C:, 1 ==> D:, and 2 ==> E:. You can monitor a full set of Logical Disk counters, such as Disk Reads/sec, Disk Write Bytes/sec, Free Megabytes, and so on for any drive in the system.

As you might imagine, these two objects, Processor and Logical Disk, are key when monitoring performance of a system. Others are important as well, but these are two of the most common and useful. I recommend you become familiar with these two objects and their associated counters.

■ *Parent* indicates the parent of the object, if applicable. For most objects, this characteristic does not apply, so dashes appear in the column. But if you choose to monitor a counter in the Thread object, you see many instances of threads. They all have parents, and they show in the column.

In Figure 27.2, the parent of the Logical Disk:Disk Bytes/sec counter is really an instance of the Physical Disk object. In other words, drive D:'s parent is instance 1 of the Physical Disk object (the second physical disk in the system). Drive E:'s parent is instance 2 of the Physical Disk object (the third physical disk in the system). If physical disk 1 had multiple logical disk partitions on it, the parent for each would be 1.

So, for example, if you want to monitor % Processor Time of the first thread of the Exchange Information Store process (it has many threads), in the Add to Chart dialog box, you would add the Thread:% Processor Time counter. Then, under Instance, select store ==> 0. After you click Done, on the chart line you would see a 0 in the Instance column, store in the Parent column, and Thread in the Object column. If you had selected the second thread (thread 1), everything would be the same except for a 1 in the Instance column.

■ *Object* tells you which object is being monitored. I'm not sure why it is not situated beside Counter; I would have liked it to the left of the Counter column. But, hey, I didn't write the software. Regardless of its place on the chart line, this is a very important column. Coupled with Counter, you can tell exactly which resource in the system you are monitoring.

To reiterate, an object is the highest level in the hierarchy of the performance items in the system, and objects represent various Windows NT resources such as processor, memory, logical disk, and so on. Fortunately, with objects, unlike some of the counters, you can usually know you're monitoring simply by the name of the object. Some of the counter names are less intuitive.

■ *Computer* is simply the computer name that is being monitored. Some of you really astute readers might be scratching your head, thinking "Hey, does that mean we can monitor the counters on other computers?" If you were thinking that, you are exactly right! PerfMon enables you to monitor other computers on the network. This feature of the software is both powerful and useful, and it is covered in the section "Monitoring Data on Other Computers" later in the chapter.

You remove counters from the view by clicking the X button on the toolbar, or by choosing Edit | Del from Chart. I usually just highlight the chart line to be deleted and press the Delete key, which is much faster.

The Value Bar

Just above the chart line in the Chart view is the *value bar*. The value bar contains the relevant values for the highlighted chart line. It shows fields for the Last, Average, Min, Max, and Graph Time values of the highlighted chart line. If you don't see the value bar, make sure that the Legend and Value Bar check boxes are checked in the Chart Options dialog box. The numbers shown in these fields are the precise values for the counters selected.

> **TIP**
>
> Sometimes, reading counter data from the value bar is easier than reading it from the graph itself. The graph is great for spotting trends. The counter is best for seeing instantaneous values.

The Status Bar

At the bottom of the screen is the *status bar*. Like most status bars, this one tells what is going on in the program. In Figure 27.2, the caption in the status bar indicates that data is being graphed from the current activity in the system; that is, the data is real time. If you were viewing captured data, for example, the status bar would show the log file being used as the source (you learn more about capturing data later in this chapter in the "Logging Data" section). If the status bar is not present, you can toggle it on by choosing Options | Status Bar or pressing Ctrl+S.

Alert View

Figure 27.4 shows an example of an Alert view screen. Note that it looks generally different from the Chart view, but a few things are similar. The toolbar and the status bar are the same. Alert view, however, displays data in a very different way.

The Alert Legend contains the same columns as the Chart View Legend, except that Scale is replaced by Value and the color is represented as a dot rather than a line. Value shows the threshold of the counter being monitored. Any data that violates the threshold value will trigger an alert.

FIGURE 27.4.

In the Alert view, Performance Monitor monitors thresholds of various counters.

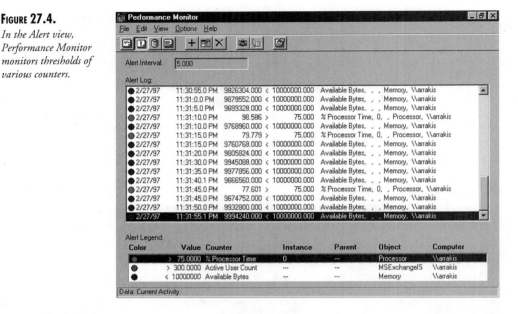

The Alert view is useful if you want to know whether a counter exceeds or falls below a certain threshold value. This way, you don't see all the individual data points, but you are notified if a counter gets out of line.

In Figure 27.4, for example, three alerts are configured. The first of the configured alerts will occur if the Processor:% Processor Time counter exceeds 75 percent. You can see that PerfMon has posted several alerts; the date, time, counter value, threshold, and counter information are all displayed on one line for each alert.

The second of the configured alerts will occur if the MSExchangeIS:Active User Count exceeds 300. This has not happened, but one like it is good to have around so you can see when Exchange Server is getting loaded down with users.

The third of the configured alerts will occur if the Memory:Available Bytes falls below 10 million (~10MB). Several of these alerts have occurred. Because you know that if the system runs short on memory, performance will degrade, this is an example of a valuable use for Alert view.

You configure these thresholds in the Add to Alert dialog box. As in the Chart view, you can choose Edit | Add to Alert, press Tab, or click the + (plus) button in the toolbar to display it, as shown in Figure 27.5.

This dialog box looks similar to the Add to Chart dialog box explained previously, except at the bottom of the dialog box, you can set the threshold type—Over or Under—and you can enter a program to run when an alert occurs. When you are finished, press Esc or click the Done button (the Cancel button changes to Done after a counter is added).

FIGURE 27.5.

Using the Add to Alert dialog box, you can add alerts with thresholds to monitor for each counter.

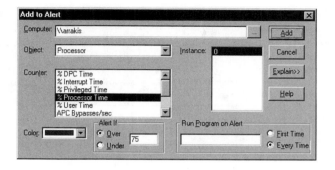

One other noteworthy item is the Alert Interval just below the toolbar in the Alert view. The Alert Interval is how often PerfMon samples the counters to see whether there is a threshold violation occurring at that moment. It defaults to once every 5 seconds, but you can set it to other values. You can also configure other alert options in the Alert Options dialog box, as shown in Figure 27.6. To get there, choose Options | Alert from the PerfMon menu or just press Ctrl+O.

FIGURE 27.6.

You configure Alert View options in the Alert Options dialog box.

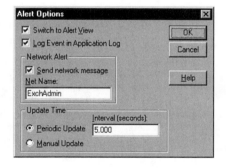

As I mentioned before, the Alert view is useful if you want to have PerfMon notify you when a threshold violation occurs. If you enable the Network Alert section in the Alert Options dialog box, PerfMon sends a network message when a threshold is violated. You can also have PerfMon switch to the Alert view or log an event in the NT Event Log when a threshold violation occurs.

Log View

You use the Log view strictly for logging data to a disk file, not for displaying data in any way. It is quite different compared to the other views—the only similarity is the menus, the toolbar, and the status bar. Figure 27.7 illustrates an example of the Log view. (You learn more details relevant to capturing data later in this chapter in the section "Logging Data.")

FIGURE 27.7.

In the Log view, Performance Monitor logs data to disk that records the activity of system objects and their counters.

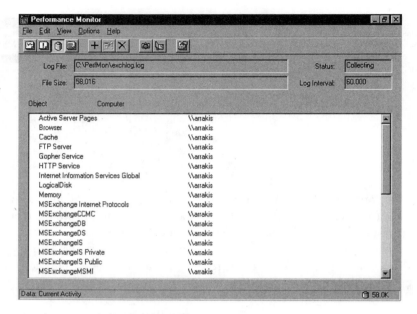

This view is pretty unexciting to look at, but in Figure 27.7 data is being collected once every 60 seconds for each of the objects that belong to the computer \\arrakis.

NOTE

Note that *all* counters for these objects are logged; you do not select specific counters to be logged, only objects. At first, this all-or-nothing logging might seem to be overkill, but it actually proves quite handy. This way, you don't have to worry about not having data for that one counter you didn't log.

You add objects to the list using the Tab or + (plus) button, as in the other views. After you add them, however, the only thing that shows is the object name and the computer that owns the object. If you're wondering whether you can log data from multiple computers here in one centralized place, you can indeed.

The Log File text box at the top of the Log view shows which file is holding the logged data. You cannot modify it directly. Instead, you must use the Log Options dialog box. Access it by choosing Options | Log, or Ctrl+O. Here, you see a common dialog box for choosing your destination log file, along with a way to specify the update interval in seconds. After you select a log file, the Start Log button becomes available. Click it, and PerfMon starts logging data. In Figure 27.7, I am logging to EXCHLOG.LOG. Notice the size of the log file is also displayed in the File Size text box.

The Status text box shows Collecting, which means data is being collected into the log file. If you look at the status bar at the bottom, you also see a little cylinder at the right and a number next to it. This serves as a visual cue—which shows in the status bar of all views—indicating that PerfMon is actively logging data and the current size of the log file.

If you stop data collection (go back into the Log Options dialog box and click Stop Log), the Status text box changes to Closed, and the cylinder disappears from the status bar.

The Log Interval text box reflects the data collection time interval, in seconds, that you set in the Log Options dialog box.

Any time you need to log data on a server, you can visit this view. It is great for logging a typical day in the life of an Exchange server. After the data is captured, you can easily view and analyze it to see whether any server problems are lurking. You should play around with the Log view—learning how to log data and manipulate logged data will make PerfMon much more valuable. Also read the section later in this chapter, "Logging Data."

Report View

You use the Report view, which is complementary to the Chart view, to view tabular data in real time. You can use it if you want a quick summary of counter values in tabular text format. You can view data as it is happening in real time, or you can use logged data.

When you first open a Report view, you see only a blank screen—no dialog boxes, no legend, nothing. Only the menu, the toolbar, and the status bar are the same as the other views. As you add counters, they appear on the screen. Figure 27.8 shows an example.

FIGURE 27.8.

In the Report view, Performance Monitor conveys a tabular summary of performance counter data.

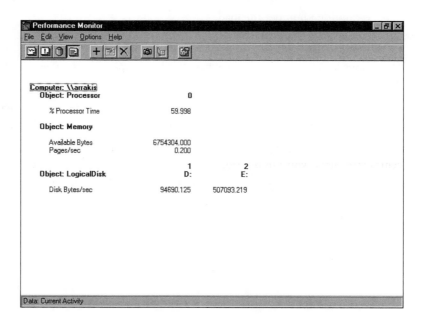

The counters shown in Figure 27.8 are the same ones shown in the Chart view in Figure 27.2 (although the data is different). These figures should give you a feel for the difference in the way the data is presented. Basically, the numbers here correspond to the numbers in the Last field of the Chart view's value bar.

Sometimes having a quick look at some data is nice, especially if a spreadsheet is not handy. Report view serves that purpose. Usually, for more formal data analysis, I instead use PerfMon's export feature to export my logged data to a spreadsheet so I can get more detailed results and analysis.

Logging Data

Fortunately, as mentioned previously, PerfMon can save performance data to a disk file as it is reading it. This feature is incredibly useful, and it is quite valuable for analyzing the health of an Exchange server.

To capture data, you go to the Log view and add objects to the list for which you want to gather performance data. Then you open the Log Options dialog box and tell PerfMon which file to log the data in and what collection interval to use. Click Start Log, and you're off to the races. The process is that simple. As I mentioned before, all counters for the selected object(s) are captured.

You can start capturing data on an Exchange server during a typical day, walk away, and come back the next day. The data is captured for you, and you can export it into a CSV (comma-separated variable) or a TSV (tab-separated variable) file for easy importing into your favorite spreadsheet program. From there, you can analyze the data at your convenience to see how the server is holding up under the load.

Viewing Logged Data

You've logged some data. So now what? Well, a couple things come to mind.

Suppose you want to view a graph of the paging activity during the day when users are on the server. Presuming that you have logged the Memory object, viewing this activity will be easy. Yes, I did say the Memory object; the paging counters are not contained in the Paging File object.

First, switch PerfMon from showing current real-time data to showing logged data. To do so, choose Options | Data From to get the Data From dialog box. Click the Log File radio button, and either type in the log filename or click the ... (ellipses) button to find it.

After you select the log file, the path and filename appear in the status bar at the bottom of the screen. Make sure that you are in Chart view; then add the Memory:Pages/sec counter to the view.

> **TIP**
>
> At this point, all views are now using this same log file. In other words, none of your views are showing you real-time data anymore. The fact that all views are tied to the same log file is a little nonintuitive at first, but after you use PerfMon awhile, it makes sense.

A couple of things are different now. First, if you capture data only for the Memory object, Memory will be the only object available in the Add to Chart dialog box. From there, you can add any counter from the Memory object to the display, and it will appear like it does when you're viewing real-time data.

Second, the graph might look funny—maybe compressed if you captured a lot of data. The default for a screen full of data in the Chart view is 100 samples. Therefore, if you sample your data at one time per second, you can get 100 seconds worth on the graph. But if your test is more than 100 seconds, you will still see all the data; it will just be crammed onto the screen in the graph.

Of course, you can get around viewing this compressed data. Just specify the time interval you want to view. Choose Edit | Time Window, and the Input Log File Timeframe dialog box appears. In this dialog box, you can zoom in to specific regions of the data.

Exporting Logged Data

You now need to export this data so that you can import it into your spreadsheet program and get some real work done. Choose File | Export Chart, and in the File Name box type the name of a file to export into. The format can be either CSV or TSV—you choose.

After you click OK, you have a file ready for importing into your spreadsheet program, complete with headings and everything. Any counter you have on your Chart view screen is exported into the file. So if you have only the Memory:Pages/sec counter in the view, that's all you get in the export file. This feature is one of the keys to using PerfMon.

You also can export data from the other views. When you export data from the Alert view, you get the alert data shown on the screen. When you export data from the Log view, you get a summary of the objects being logged. When you export data from the Report view, you get a file containing the summary data shown in the view.

Monitoring Data on Other Computers

Up to this point, I have assumed that PerfMon is capturing data on the same computer where it's running. This doesn't have to be the case. In fact, not running PerfMon on the same computer where you are capturing data is usually better for two reasons. One, you don't want to skew the data you are capturing with PerfMon overhead. Two, you don't want to place more stress on the system being measured, especially if it is your Exchange server.

Sometimes you might want to view or capture data from one or more Exchange servers on the network. Perhaps you are running a server that supports many users, and you don't want to incur the overhead of running PerfMon on that machine. Or perhaps you are monitoring a machine that is not nearby. Or maybe you just want to see how busy your neighbors' machines are because you think they're goofing off again. Accomplishing any of these tasks is easy with the remote monitoring feature of Performance Monitor.

To use the remote feature, there is (fortunately) no change to the user interface at all. Neither do you have to install or use another piece of software. Simply select the computer name when you are adding counters to be monitored or collected.

Say, for example, you're running PerfMon on your desktop computer, and you want to use the Chart view to monitor objects on an Exchange server. In the Add to Chart dialog box (refer to Figure 27.3 to refresh your memory), you can either type the name directly in the Computer text box, or you can click the ... (ellipsis) button at the end of the text box. A list of the computers available on the network appears. After you select the desired computer name, the available counters for that computer are available for you to choose from.

Figure 27.9 shows a Chart view of data being collected from two different computers, \\arrakis and \\fremen.

FIGURE 27.9.

Viewing counters on multiple computers at once in real time is simple with Performance Monitor.

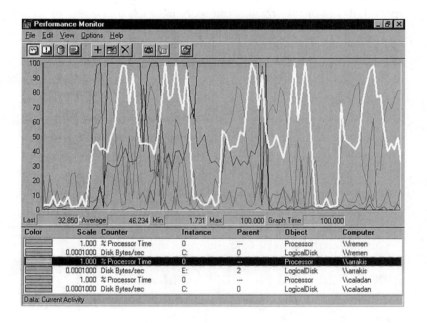

The interface is quite seamless. It looks exactly the same as monitoring information on a local computer. As expected, the computer name appears in the Computer column, and the other information appears in the other columns.

In a stroke of good luck—or more likely, good design—the same principle applies to the remaining three views as well. In the Alert view, you can view alerts from other computers. In the Log view, you can log data from other computers. And in the Report view, you can get tabular summary reports on data from other computers.

> **TIP**
>
> You can save the current view, as you will learn in the next section, so you can use it later. As an improvement to PerfMon in NT 4.0, you can open the view on a different computer running PerfMon, and you will still be monitoring the same computer(s) you were on the original machine. With PerfMon in NT 3.51, that was not the case; the PerfMon views generally were not transportable.

Saving Your Work

One other important feature of PerfMon is the capability of saving your Performance Monitor views.

Suppose you've been working on getting that perfect Chart view configured so that you can monitor performance on your Exchange servers. You probably don't want to reconfigure the view each time you start PerfMon, right? Right. You can save your Chart view settings into a .PMC file for later use. Choose File | Save Chart Settings, and type a name in the File Name box.

You can choose from five different file formats, one for each of the four view types, and one for the global PerfMon workspace, which contains all four views.

Chart view	.PMC
Alert view	.PMA
Log view	.PML
Report view	.PMR
Workspace (all views)	.PMW

I use .PMC the most, but of course the others are handy as well. I recommend creating a few different .PMC files that contain related information so that you can have them at your disposal.

You might, for example, create one called CPU.PMC, which contains some processor-related counters. Or you might create EXCHSRVR.PMC, which contains processor, disk, and network counters specifically selected for monitoring your Exchange server. Then you could simply load this .PMC file on any computer running PerfMon, and you would instantly be looking at the performance of your Exchange server.

Why would you use a .PMW file? Simple. A PerfMon workspace contains all the four views stored in a single file. So, you could configure any combination of views and save them in a workspace file. In fact, some .PMW files get installed when you complete the setup of Exchange Server; they appear in your Microsoft Exchange folder automatically. You learn more about these individual workspaces later in the chapter, in the section "Auto-Installed Performance Monitor Workspaces."

Last Words About Performance Monitor

Whew! You've learned a lot about PerfMon, but there's plenty more where that came from. I encourage you to play around with it on your own—that's the best way to learn it. Before we wrap up, I'd like to leave you two final bits of information. They are important to note, and I saved them until the end of this topic because I didn't want them to get lost in the shuffle.

Performance Monitor Has Overhead

Performance Monitor has overhead. Yes, that's right, all this great performance information isn't exactly free. Fortunately, the overhead is relatively low for such a powerful tool, but the idea is to disturb the server being monitored as little as possible. Here are a few points to think about when monitoring an Exchange server with PerfMon. Keep in mind that all these points have trade-offs, but I hope they will get you started.

■ Use PerfMon remotely, and capture data over the network from another machine.

Doing so offloads the overhead of running PerfMon from the Exchange server being monitored, because it would not have to sustain PerfMon in addition to its normal activities. And assuming the collection interval is fairly long, say 10 seconds or more, the slight I/O overhead will be unnoticed. Using PerfMon remotely is an excellent option if you don't plan to measure LAN traffic—this method does introduce additional traffic at each collection time.

■ If your network is heavily utilized, but you still need to capture data remotely, install a second network card in your server.

With a second network card in your server, you can set up a small two-node network consisting only of the Exchange server to be monitored and your PerfMon machine. Using this approach, a small, isolated "dead network" is dedicated to gathering the performance data, and it won't disturb the main network or your main network card. The Exchange server would, however, incur incremental overhead to handle the second network card, so keep that in mind. If your collection interval is far enough apart—say one minute or greater—you probably don't need to use this approach. Just use the regular network.

■ Consider increasing the time interval for collecting data. In other words, collect data less frequently.

You can set the collection interval to be as small as one second, but if you are collecting a lot of counters, this method can generate pretty heavy activity. You might get away with capturing data every two or three seconds if you need very high granularity. That would cut the total overhead to one-half and one-third, respectively, when compared to one second. For long periods of data capture, like several hours or more, use a 30–60 second interval, or longer. Watch the size of your log file—it can get pretty large, depending upon how many objects are being logged.

■ Consider gathering data for fewer PerfMon objects.

Instead of just automatically gathering data on every object in the server, systematically reduce the ones being captured to the ones you really care about. This way, you can keep the log file sizes from getting unnecessarily bloated. And it will reduce the data collection overhead caused by PerfMon. The Thread and Process objects are usually the most expensive ones, so you can start there.

You Must Activate Disk Counters

Most counters in the system begin working automatically from the time they are installed. The one major exception is any disk-related object—namely, Logical Disk and Physical Disk. These counters all show zeros unless you activate disk performance measurement. You do so by entering the following line at an NT command prompt:

```
diskperf -y
```

This command activates the disk counters on the local NT computer. You can also activate disk counters from a remote computer by entering the following:

```
diskperf -y \\anycomputer
```

This command activates the disk counters on the computer named anycomputer, provided it can be reached on the network. Full syntax of the command is available if you enter the following:

```
diskperf -?
```

Some overhead—albeit pretty minimal—is associated with these counters. Regardless, I suggest turning them off after you finish gathering performance data on your server to restore peak disk performance. You deactivate them by entering the following line at an NT command prompt:

```
diskperf -n
```

This overhead is especially apparent in less powerful systems, such as 80486-based models with slower disk subsystems. With most newer, more powerful machines, however, the overhead has very little discernible effect. Of course, now that you're a whiz at this stuff, you could always use PerfMon to measure the effect for yourself.

> **NOTE**
>
> You must reboot the computer for any changes made with the `diskperf` command to take effect.

Auto-Installed Performance Monitor Workspaces

Following your enlightening run through PerfMon, here's an opportunity to put your newfound knowledge to work.

After you install Microsoft Exchange Server, you should be able to find a folder under Programs in the Start menu named Microsoft Exchange. This folder contains several icons, as shown in Figure 27.10. You first learned about these icons in Chapter 12, "Installing Microsoft Exchange Server," but I want to revisit them in more detail.

FIGURE 27.10.

Microsoft Exchange Server Setup automatically installs several Performance Manager icons in a common Program Manager group.

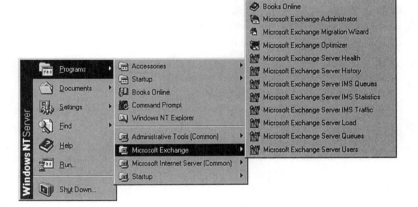

In Figure 27.10, you can see the five icons that represent PerfMon workspaces.

- Microsoft Exchange Server Health
- Microsoft Exchange Server History
- Microsoft Exchange Server Load
- Microsoft Exchange Server Queues
- Microsoft Exchange Server Users

Remember earlier in the chapter in the "Saving Your Work" section, you learned about the five different types of PerfMon files. Now you will see one of them at work already—the Workspace, or .PMW file. The thoughtful engineers at Microsoft decided to provide something to help you start monitoring an Exchange server. (I'm glad they did, because it opens up a whole realm of ideas about how to monitor your server.)

The workspaces are ready-made views of various Exchange Server performance counters to help you start monitoring performance of the server. The .PMW files are located in the `BIN` subdirectory in which you installed Exchange Server—for example, `C:\EXCHSRVR\BIN`.

> **NOTE**
>
> These workspaces are not designed to work remotely; that is, they must be run using PerfMon on the same machine as your Exchange server. You might not want to do this based on what you learned previously in this chapter in the section "Performance Monitor Has Overhead." If you want to monitor the counters remotely, you have to create your own workspaces with the counters you want pointing to the Exchange server you want.

Microsoft Exchange Server Health

The Health chart, shown in Figure 27.11, represents a summary of your Exchange Server's state of being. It is mainly a CPU utilization chart that shows counters for overall system CPU utilization and for how the main processes within Exchange Server are using the CPU. Overall system Paging is also included.

FIGURE 27.11.

The Microsoft Exchange Server Health chart monitors various CPU utilization counters.

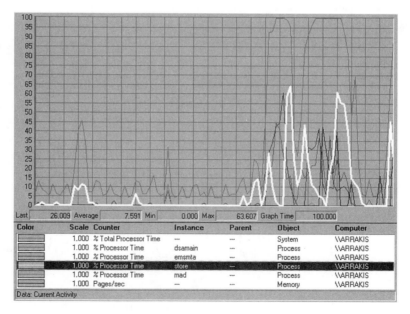

The refresh time is one second, so you use this chart to get a detailed look at your server's status. It would be a great workspace to add other relevant counters to, such as `Memory:Available Bytes` or `System:Processor Queue Length`.

TIP

If you use the `Processor Queue Length` counter in the `System` object, don't forget that you also have to monitor a counter in the `Thread` object to activate it. Any thread counter will do—just pick one.

The following is a summary of the counters:

- `System:% Total Processor Time`

  This counter is a current indication of the server's entire processor subsystem utilization, regardless of the number of CPUs present in the system.

- `Process:% Processor Time <dsamain>`

  The Exchange Directory Service runs as the process dsamain.exe. This counter shows how much CPU that process is using.

- `Process:% Processor Time <emsmta>`

  The Exchange MTA Service runs as the process emsmta.exe. This counter shows how much CPU that process is using.

- `Process:% Processor Time <store>`

  The Exchange Information Service runs as the process store.exe. This counter shows how much CPU that process is using.

- `Process:% Processor Time <mad>`

  The Exchange System Attendant service runs as the process mad.exe. This counter shows how much CPU that process is using.

- `Memory:Pages/sec`

  This counter shows the frequency of overall system paging. It increases as the system runs short on memory.

Microsoft Exchange Server History

The History chart, shown in Figure 27.12, is designed to give you a high-level look at what your server has been doing over the past 100 minutes. This chart mainly shows message activity in the public and private stores, along with user count, MTA work queue, and amount of paging.

This graph is a good one to bring up and let sit so that you can glance at it periodically. Watching the Work Queue Length of the MTA is very useful if you have multiple Exchange servers sending mail to each other. Also, the counters are excellent ones to monitor on a more frequent basis if you need finer granularity than 60-second intervals. I regularly watch `User Count`, `MTA Work Queue Length`, and `Pages/sec`.

FIGURE 27.12.

The Microsoft Exchange Server History chart monitors traffic on your server.

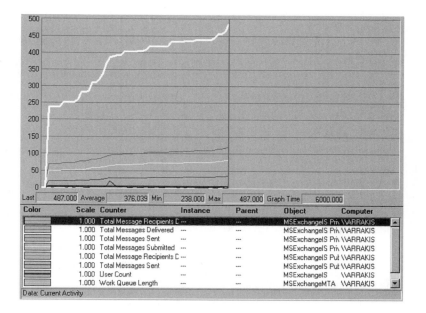

Note that I changed the scale on the first six counters from their default of 0.001 to 1.0 so we could see the trends better. Depending on the values, over time you will probably need to adjust the scale for the same reason. The scale does not affect the actual data, however.

> **NOTE**
>
> All the PerfMon workspaces loaded with Exchange Server use the Chart view.

The following is a summary of the counters:

- `MSExchangeIS Private:Total Message Recipients Delivered`

  This counter shows a running count—since the server was started—of the total number of recipients in the private store that have received messages.

- `MSExchangeIS Private:Total Messages Delivered`

  This counter shows a running count—since the server was started—of the total number of messages delivered to all recipients in the private store. Assuming all private store messages are making it to their destinations, this count will be at least equal to MSExchangeIS Private:Total Messages Submitted. It will be higher as there are messages submitted to distribution lists.

- **MSExchangeIS Private:Total Messages Sent**

  This counter shows a running count—since the server was started—of the total number of private store messages that were sent through the MTA to other systems. In addition to other MTA activity, messages sent to distribution lists will show up here.

- **MSExchangeIS Private:Total Messages Submitted**

  This counter shows a running count—since the server was started—of the total number of messages submitted to the server's private store by clients.

- **MSExchangeIS Public:Total Message Recipients Delivered**

  This counter shows a running count—since the server was started—of the total number of recipients in the public store that have received messages.

- **MSExchangeIS Public:Total Messages Sent**

  This counter shows a running count—since the server was started—of the total number of public store messages that were sent through the MTA to other systems.

- **MSExchangeIS:User Count**

  This counter shows the number of client computers connected to the Information Store, plus one. One user is always connected to the IS after Exchange Server starts.

- **MSExchangeMTA:Work Queue Length**

  This counter shows the number of messages that have yet to be processed by the MTA. This counter is roughly analogous to the MSExchangeIS Private:Send Queue Size and MSExchangeIS Public:Send Queue Size counters.

- **Memory:Pages/sec** (not shown in figure)

  This counter shows the frequency of overall system paging. This number increases as the system runs short on memory.

Microsoft Exchange Server Load

The Load chart, shown in Figure 27.13, is slightly different from Health. Although the load on your server ultimately can affect its health, this workspace gives insight into how much traffic your server is managing.

Note that I changed the scale on two counters from their default of 1.0 to 10.0 so you could see the trends better. Depending on the values, over time you will probably need to adjust the scale for the same reason. The scale does not affect the actual data, however.

This chart only scratches the surface of showing how much load is on your server; you can also look at many more counters, such as Logical Disk, CPU, Network Interface, and so on, to get a picture of overall server load. You can use this chart as a quick view into generic server load. The update interval is a bit longer—10 seconds—so you get a bigger picture of how the server's load is going over the last 16 to 17 minutes.

FIGURE 27.13.

The Microsoft Exchange Server Load chart monitors traffic loads on your server.

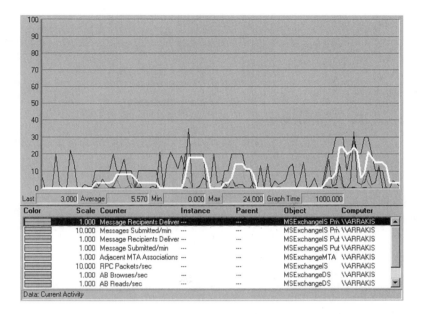

TIP

When you open these Performance Monitor workspaces, they have no menu bar. Double-click in the graph area (or just press Enter) to make it appear. You can still resize the window or check chart options to see what's being depicted on the chart.

The following is a summary of the counters:

■ `MSExchangeIS Private:Message Recipients Delivered/min`

This counter shows the rate that Exchange recipients are receiving messages in the private store.

■ `MSExchangeIS Public:Message Recipients Delivered/min`

This counter shows the rate that Exchange recipients are receiving messages in the public store.

■ `MSExchangeIS Private:Messages Submitted/min`

This counter shows the rate the messages are submitted by clients to the private store.

■ `MSExchangeIS Public:Messages Submitted/min`

This counter shows the rate the messages are submitted by clients to the public store.

■ `MSExchangeMTA:Adjacent MTA Associations`

This counter shows the number of open associations this server's MTA has to other servers' MTAs. It shows values only if multiple Exchange servers are available.

■ `MSExchangeIS:RPC Packets/sec`

This counter shows the rate the server is processing Remote Procedure Call packets.

■ `MSExchangeDS:AB Browses/sec`

This counter shows the rate the Directory Service is processing Address Book browses by clients accessing the server.

■ `MSExchangeDS:AB Reads/sec`

This counter shows the rate the Directory Service is processing Address Book reads by clients accessing the server.

■ `MSExchangeDS:ExDS Reads/sec` (not shown in figure)

This counter shows the rate the Directory Service is processing reads by Extended Directory Service clients, such as other Exchange services and the Exchange Administrator program.

■ `MSExchangeDS:Replication Updates/sec` (not shown in figure)

This counter shows the rate the Directory Service is applying replication updates. It is an indication of how much Directory replication load is on the server.

Microsoft Exchange Server Queues

The Queues chart, shown in Figure 27.14, shows five major queues in Microsoft Exchange Server, updated every 10 seconds.

FIGURE 27.14.

The Microsoft Exchange Server Queues chart monitors the critical work queues on your server.

These counters are critical to system performance, and if any of them starts to become backlogged, you will notice a delay in delivery of messages, accompanied by a drop in user response time. The slowdown also probably indicates a bottleneck somewhere in the system.

NOTE

The Users and Queues charts have the *Histogram* option of the Chart view enabled rather than the *Graph* option, so the data displays as bars rather than as graph lines. You set this option in the Chart Options dialog box.

This graph is a good one to open periodically to get a quick check on the status of the system queues. The window doesn't show what queue each bar represents, but if you enlarge the window, you can see the legend at the bottom. If any of these queues starts growing steadily, or stays above the 10–50 range without coming back down, you should start investigating why.

The following is a summary of the counters, corresponding to the bars from left to right:

- MSExchangeMTA:Work Queue Length

    This counter shows the number of messages not processed by the MTA. This counter is roughly analogous to the MSExchangeIS Private:Send Queue Size and MSExchangeIS Public:Send Queue Size counters.

- MSExchangeIS Private:Send Queue Size

    This counter shows the number of messages waiting to be sent by the private store.

- MSExchangeIS Public:Send Queue Size

    This counter shows the number of messages waiting to be sent by the public store.

- MSExchangeIS Private:Receive Queue Size

    This counter shows the number of messages waiting to be delivered to private store recipients.

- MSExchangeIS Public:Receive Queue Size

    This counter shows the number of messages waiting to be delivered to public store recipients.

In this figure, the MSExchangeMTA:Work Queue Length and the MSExchangeIS Private:Receive Queue Size each have a value of 1.

Microsoft Exchange Server Users

The Users chart, shown in Figure 27.15, is a simple PerfMon chart that shows only the number of client machines connected to Exchange Server, updated every 10 seconds.

Having this graph open in the corner of the screen is useful for giving you a quick visual indicator of how many users are on the server at any given time.

The only counter in this chart is MSExchangeIS:User Count, which was explained in the earlier section, "Microsoft Exchange Server History."

In the figure, there are 50 client machines connected to the Exchange Server Information Store.

27

MONITORING AND
PREVENTING
PROBLEMS

FIGURE 27.15.
The Microsoft Exchange Server Users chart monitors the number of users on your server.

Other Charts

Three other PerfMon workspace files are located in the \EXCHSRVR\BIN directory in case you are using the Internet Mail Service (IMS), called the Internet Mail Connector (IMC) in Exchange 4.0. The names can be used interchangeably.

Although installed by Setup, the following three IMS-related workspaces will not show any data if the Internet Mail Service has not been installed. These workspaces get their data from the counters in the MSExchangeIMC PerfMon object, which is only installed along with the IMS. These three charts basically show the flow of messages through the IMS and associated counters.

■ *Microsoft Exchange Server IMS Queues* is a bar chart which shows the status of four main Internet Mail Service queues. These queues are important to exchanging messages with the Internet or other SMTP mail services.

This chart is updated every second to give you a very current look at each queue. For example, if messages are not making it out of Exchange onto the Internet, or from the Internet into Exchange mailboxes, these queues might provide a clue as to why.

■ *Microsoft Exchange Server IMS Statistics* is a simple graph that shows the total number of inbound and outbound messages that have been passed by the Internet Mail Service during the past 50 minutes.

If you are interested in monitoring how many messages the server's Internet Mail Service has handled over time, this is a good graph to monitor. The counters are cumulative over time.

■ *Microsoft Exchange Server IMS Traffic* is a graph that depicts traffic through the Internet Mail Service and the number of inbound and outbound connections.

This graph is updated every second to provide a real-time view of the traffic being handled by the MSExchangeIMC. This is a good one to fire up if you are concerned that the traffic on your server may be getting too heavy, or if the data from another chart suggests there may be a problem in the IMS.

Again, if you have not installed the Exchange Internet Mail Service, the MSExchangeIMC PerfMon object is not installed; therefore, these counters will not function.

Exchange-Specific Performance Monitor Counters

Performance

Some applications have their own performance objects. They can make your life much easier when you're tracking performance or system behavior. Table 27.2 lists the Exchange-specific objects that are automatically installed in Performance Monitor during setup. These are all useful in one way or another, and they provide a wealth of information on the behavior of your Exchange Server computer. I encourage you to explore them on your own and get familiar with them.

Note that the following PerfMon objects are new to Exchange 5.0: MSExchangeCCMC, MSExchangeMSMI, and MSExchangeWEB.

New to Version 5.0

27

MONITORING AND PREVENTING PROBLEMS

Table 27.2. Exchange objects installed in Performance Monitor.

Object Name	Description
MSExchangeCCMC	Contains counters pertaining to the cc:Mail Connector (CCMC). *Counters available only if the cc:Mail Connector is installed.*
MSExchangeDB	Contains counters pertaining to the Exchange Server database engine (DB).
MSExchangeDS	Contains counters pertaining to the Exchange Directory Service (DS).
MSExchangeDX	Contains counters pertaining to the MS Mail Directory Synchronization (DX). *Counters available only if MS Mail DirSync is installed.*
MSExchangeIMC	Contains counters pertaining to the Internet Mail Connector (IMC). *Counters available only if the Internet Mail Service is installed.*
MSExchangeIS	Contains general counters for the Exchange Server Information Store (IS).
MSExchangeISPrivate	Contains counters pertaining to the Exchange Private Information Store.

continues

Table 27.2. continued

Object Name	Description
MSExchangeISPublic	Contains counters pertaining to the Exchange Public Information Store.
MSExchangeMSMI	Contains counters pertaining to the MS Mail Connector Interchange (MSMI). *Counters available only if the MS Mail Connector is installed.*
MSExchangeMTA	Contains counters pertaining to the Exchange Mail Transfer Agent (MTA).
MSExchangeMTA Connections	Contains counters pertaining to connections to the MTA.
MSExchangePCMTA	Contains counters pertaining to the MS Mail Connector MTA for PCs (PCMTA). *Counters available only if the MS Mail Connector is installed.*
MSExchangeWEB	Contains counters pertaining to the Exchange Web Service. *Counters available only if the Web Connector is installed.*

Dozens of Exchange Server counters are included in these objects. Table 27.3 contains some general Exchange counters to get you going.

Table 27.3. Useful Exchange counters.

Object Name	Counter	Description
MSExchangeDB	% Buffer Available	(Instance=Information Store) The percentage of the database buffer cache that is available for use. This counter and the following one help monitor how effective your database buffer cache is.
MSExchangeDB	% Buffer Cache Hit	(Instance=Information Store) The percentage of requests for store data that were satisfied from the database buffer cache.
MSExchangeIS	User Count	The number of client machines connected to the IS.
MSExchangeISPrivate	Messages Submitted/min	The rate messages are being submitted by clients. If the rate is consistently higher than Messages Delivered/min, the server might not be able to keep up with the delivery load.

Object Name	Counter	Description
MSExchangeISPrivate	Messages Delivered/min	The rate messages are delivered to all recipients. If the rate is consistently lower than Messages Submitted/min, the server might not be able to keep up with delivery load.
MSExchangeISPrivate	Send Queue Size	Number of messages in the message send queue for the private IS. It is another counter that can indicate when the server is overloaded.
MSExchangeISPublic		(Same counters as MSExchangeISPrivate)

Windows NT Performance Monitor Counters

This section presents some generic PerfMon objects and counters that are installed as a part of Windows NT. Table 27.4 contains a list of some of these generic objects that I have found useful for monitoring an Exchange Server.

Table 27.4. Windows NT objects installed in Performance Monitor.

Object Name	Description
Cache	Contains counters pertaining to the NT System Cache.
Logical Disk	Contains counters pertaining to the logical disk drives in the system. *You must enable these counters with diskperf -y and reboot.*
Memory	Contains counters pertaining to memory usage in the operating system.
Paging File	Contains counters pertaining to the status of the NT page file.
Process	Contains counters pertaining to every process running under NT.
Processor	Contains counters pertaining to the system processor(s).
Server	Contains general counters pertaining to the server service of the system.
System	Contains general counters pertaining to the operating system itself.

Again, there are dozens of counters included in these objects. Table 27.5 contains some useful counters to get you going.

27

MONITORING AND
PREVENTING
PROBLEMS

Table 27.5. Useful generic counters.

Object Name	Counter	Description
Cache	Data Map Hits %	The percentage of successful references to the in-memory system data cache.
Logical Disk	% Disk Time	The percentage of time the disk is busy servicing I/O requests.
Logical Disk	Avg. Disk sec/ Transfer	The average amount of seconds it takes the disk to satisfy a disk transfer (read or write).
Logical Disk	Disk Bytes/sec	The rate at which data is transferred to or from the disk during I/O operations.
Memory	Available Bytes	The amount of virtual memory in the system available for use.
Memory	Cache Bytes	Size of the NT System Cache. Note that the system cache is for both disk and LAN.
Memory	Pages/sec	Indicates overall paging activity—the rate at which memory pages are written to or read from the disk.
Paging File	% Usage	Shows what percentage of the page file is in use. Could indicate whether you need to increase your page file size.
Processor	% Processor Time	Amount of time the processor is busy doing work. This is User and Privileged time combined.
Process	Working Set	Shows the number of bytes in the working set of the selected process (Instance). A working set of memory is memory that was recently used by threads in the process, that is, the set of memory with which the process is currently working.
Process	Page Faults/sec	Shows the rate of page faults by all threads executing in the selected process. Can indicate there is memory pressure in the system. If Memory:Pages/sec is also getting activity, there could be a memory shortage in the server.
Server	Bytes Total/sec	The rate at which the server is sending data to and receiving data from the network.
System	Processor Queue Length	The number of threads waiting in the processor queue. Values consistently above 2 can indicate processor congestion. (You must also monitor at least one thread from the Thread object for this counter to be nonzero.)

> **CAUTION**
>
> Be careful how you interpret the `Logical Disk:% Disk Time` counter, especially when using hardware RAID sets. Because an array can handle multiple I/Os simultaneously, having some I/Os queued and waiting for the array is not bad. This counter shows 100 percent busy in that scenario, however, when, in fact, the disk subsystem might not be 100 percent busy. More reliable indicators are `Disk Reads/sec` and `Disk Writes/sec`. You should be able to calculate how many reads and writes per second your array is capable of and compare that number with what PerfMon reports.

27

MONITORING AND
PREVENTING
PROBLEMS

Microsoft Exchange Server Monitors

Now you're ready to move on from the PerfMon tool. Although the Performance Monitor is quite powerful, other resources available in Exchange can also help you monitor how the server is doing.

Because the Exchange Server documentation covers this subject nicely in the *Administrator's Guide*, Chapter 16, "Monitoring Your Organization," I'm going to keep this discussion brief. I do, however, want you to know what monitors are so that you can dig into them further.

You can use the two basic types of monitors:

- ■ Server monitor
- ■ Link monitor

You can find monitors in the Exchange Administrator, under the `organization\site\Configuration\Monitors` object.

You can use monitors to configure notifications, synchronize clocks among Exchange servers, monitor NT services, and so on.

> **NOTE**
>
> After you configure a monitor, it does not automatically start working; you must activate it. You do so by highlighting the monitor and then choosing Tools | Start Monitor from the Exchange Administrator. A child window within the Administrator then appears, showing the status of the monitor you just activated. Monitors can also be started automatically if you place the Administrator program in the NT Startup group and use the /m parameter with ADMIN.EXE. Refer to Appendix B, "Command Reference" for details on using parameters with ADMIN.EXE.

Server Monitor

You can use a Server monitor to do the following:

- Verify Windows NT services are running on the Exchange server being monitored
- Synchronize the clocks among multiple Exchange server computers
- Restart computers or services on computers

To create a new Server monitor, highlight the Monitors object, and choose File | New Other | Server Monitor from the Exchange Administrator. A properties sheet similar to the one shown in Figure 27.16 then appears.

FIGURE 27.16.

The Server Monitor is configured with both a directory name and a display name.

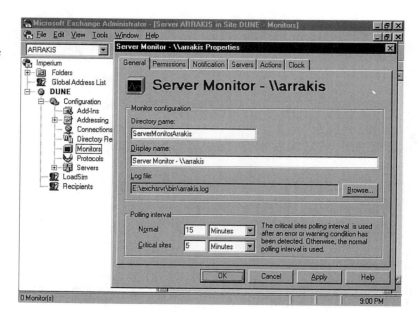

From here, configuring what you want the monitor to do is easy. On the General tab, you specify the monitor's name, log file, and polling intervals.

On the Permissions tab you set Windows NT accounts that have permissions for the server monitor.

TIP

To cause the Permissions tab to appear on all property pages you use in the Exchange Administrator, enable the Show Permissions page for all objects checkbox on the Options property page in the Tools | Options menu of the Administrator. You should also enable the Display rights for roles on Permissions page checkbox.

On the Notification tab, you specify the type of notification to occur when a server goes into a warning or alert state. Click the New button if you don't have any notifications configured. The following are the three types of notification:

- *Launch a process* causes the computer running Exchange Administrator, not the monitored server, to launch the specified process. The process can be any program you want.
- *Mail message* causes an Exchange e-mail to be sent to the specified recipient.
- *Windows NT alert* causes a network message to be sent to the specified computer on the network. This notification is similar to the Send network message feature in the Alert Options of the PerfMon Alert view.

On the Servers tab, you specify which Exchange Servers to monitor. It can be any server in any Site you have access to.

On the Actions tab, you specify actions to take when a service is stopped on a monitored server. You can have the monitor do one of three things:

- Take no action
- Restart the service
- Restart the computer

Finally, on the Clock tab, you specify the tolerances for the monitored clock. This setting determines how far out of sync the monitored computer's system clock can be compared to the monitor. You can also optionally have the monitored server's clock forced into sync with the monitor.

If you have several Exchange server computers, it is useful to keep the clocks synchronized. One reason is that if something happens anywhere on your Exchange network, you can easily track down the sequence of events knowing the clocks are all in sync among the various servers. Another reason is that if you have time-sensitive tasks to be executed on the servers—such as backup or other types of maintenance—you can be sure all the servers have the correct time on them.

Link Monitor

You can use a Link monitor to ensure that the message transport mechanism between two servers is working properly. It does so by sending a message via the MTA to the other server. Then it checks to see whether the message made the trip successfully.

A Link monitor can monitor round-trip time for a ping message sent from one Exchange server to another, or from an Exchange server to a foreign messaging system. More often, it is for the latter case.

If the ping message takes longer than expected to make the round trip—called the *bounce duration*—a notification occurs. The type of notification depends on how you configure notifications. Basically, they're just like Server monitor notifications.

To create a new Link monitor, highlight the Monitors object and then choose File | New Other | Link Monitor from the Exchange Administrator. A properties sheet similar to the one in Figure 27.17 then appears.

FIGURE 27.17.

The Link Monitor is configured with both a directory name and a display name.

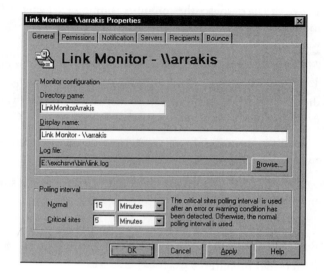

As with the Server monitor, configuring what you want the monitor to do is easy:

- The General, Permissions, Notification, and Servers tabs are identical in function to those in the Server monitor.
- On the Recipients tab, you specify the recipients who will receive the test message (also called a *ping*).
- On the Bounce tab, you specify the *bounce duration*, or the maximum amount of time it is acceptable for a test message to make a round trip from the Link monitor to the destination and back.

Information Store Maintenance

Wouldn't it be handy if the IS could automatically perform its own database maintenance and defragmentation on the fly? Turns out you're in luck this time—it can be done. Any Exchange server can be configured to perform online maintenance at specified intervals. You can schedule the maintenance to occur at whatever time of day or night you prefer.

This capability is useful because as the IS gets pounded, over time it might start to exhibit diminished response time. Running daily automatic maintenance on the IS helps prevent this situation from happening because the database is kept fresh and defragmented.

You access this feature via the Exchange Administrator program. The configuration is located on the IS Maintenance tab of the properties page for `\organization\site\Configuration\ Servers\servername`. Just highlight the server and press Alt+Enter, or select File | Properties from the Administrator menu. Figure 27.18 shows the IS Maintenance tab.

FIGURE 27.18.

The IS Maintenance server feature is useful for automatically keeping the database store in good shape.

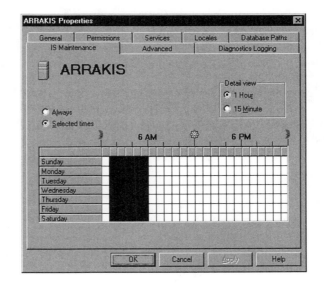

In Figure 27.18, the maintenance is scheduled to start sometime between 1:00 a.m. and 6:00 a.m. every day of the week. Using this schedule is a good idea for two reasons. First, the maintenance is scheduled for a (likely) slow time of the day. Second, the maintenance is done once daily, which is about how often you should perform this maintenance anyway.

Unlike EDBUTIL's defragmenter, with IS Maintenance the entire store (public and private databases) is defragmented while still online; that is, the MSExchangeIS service runs the entire time. The following are two caveats:

- The size of the database is not reduced after this utility runs. Instead, unused space is marked as available for use by anything that needs it. So, although the database doesn't actually shrink, it back-fills the empty space before growing the database size.

- User response time degrades while the online maintenance is occurring. This problem is temporary, and better response will resume after the maintenance finishes.

Summary

In this chapter, you learned about major tools and system resources to assist in monitoring Exchange Server computers, such as Windows NT Performance Monitor, auto-installed Exchange PerfMon workspaces, Exchange-specific PerfMon counters, Windows NT PerfMon counters, Microsoft Exchange Server Monitors, and Exchange Server Information Store maintenance.

These items help you monitor servers that have exceeded thresholds, that have services that have stopped running, that have failed connections, that have server clocks that are out of sync, and much more.

The topic of monitoring an Exchange server is broad, as you can see, but you have covered a significant chunk of it here. This information is enough to give you some useful ideas about how to proceed with monitoring your own servers.

Armed with this information as your foundation, you are better prepared to move into Chapter 28, "Diagnosing the Cause of a Problem." There, I extend some of the ideas presented in this chapter to assist you in figuring out what has happened when something goes wrong with an Exchange server system.

CHAPTER 28

Diagnosing the Cause of a Problem

by Greg Todd

IN THIS CHAPTER

Troubleshooting

So how do you diagnose a problem with Microsoft Exchange Server? There are so many variables in a complex system such as Exchange Server, it causes the scope of troubleshooting to be huge. That's the bad news. The good news is that there are several tools and techniques available to help with the task.

There's an old proverb that goes something like this: I can give you food and you will be hungry again, or I can teach you to fish and you will never be hungry. To do well at diagnosing Exchange problems, you'll have to learn to fish.

Basically, troubleshooting is a process of elimination. But if you have several tools in your repertoire, you can apply them to see what light they shed on the problem. Usually, at least one tool points you to the cause of the problem. Often, more than one tool points to the same thing or illuminates different aspects of a more complex problem.

Most often, diagnosing the cause of a problem is a matter of using several tools together. For example, if a user experiences poor response time, you can check Windows NT Performance Monitor (discussed in Chapter 27, "Monitoring and Preventing Problems") to see if the server is heavily loaded. If the server looks okay, you can try RPC Ping to see whether the connectivity is working properly between the client and the server. You can also check the NT Event Log for any strange-looking entries.

The *Microsoft Exchange Server Administrator Guide* spends about 100 pages dedicated to troubleshooting—specifically, Chapter 17, "Troubleshooting Tools and Resources," and Chapter 18, "Troubleshooting Your System." I encourage you to read these chapters for additional insight.

The Microsoft Exchange Resource Kit is also available. If you have used a Microsoft resource kit before, you know they can be quite helpful. The Exchange Resource Kit is no exception. It contains valuable tools and helpful information.

So, rather than rewrite the Microsoft documentation or detail all the specific problems, this chapter highlights some of the more valuable tools and describes why you want to use them. You will find these tools help track down the cause of a problem. Look at this chapter as a complement to the product documentation and to the tools introduced in Chapter 27.

The following are the main diagnostic tools that Exchange and Windows NT provide:

- General diagnostic utilities
- Message tracking
- Windows NT administrative tools

First, this chapter discusses diagnostic tools included with Microsoft Exchange Server, including RPC Ping, ISINTEG, EDBUTIL, MTACHECK, and others.

Next, the chapter looks at the message tracking center, which is the message tracking utility included in the Exchange Administrator. This utility provides the capability to track the path of a message through the system.

Then, the chapter covers a few Windows NT Server administrative tools that prove helpful in troubleshooting such as Server Manager, User Manager for Domains, and Windows NT Event Viewer.

The scope of problems referred to in this chapter is limited to those problems that occur on an Exchange server. Examples are messages that don't make it to their destination, Exchange servers that don't talk to each other, a server that cannot be reached by the client, and errors that Exchange itself encounters.

This chapter does not attempt to address other issues that might still impact the server, such as network problems, hardware problems, improper Windows NT configuration, and poor performance.

General Diagnostic Utilities

There are several diagnostic utilities and tools included with Microsoft Exchange Server and Windows NT. For the administrator who is trying to troubleshoot problems in the Exchange Server environment, they prove invaluable:

- RPC Ping
- ISINTEG
- EDBUTIL
- MTACHECK
- Exchange optimizer
- Inbox repair tool

With the exception of the Inbox repair tool, these utilities are run on the server. RPC Ping can use both the client and the server.

RPC Ping

If you are familiar with TCP/IP, you probably know about ping. RPC Ping serves a similar purpose to ping, but instead it uses RPCs (remote procedure calls) to ensure connectivity with the destination. RPC Ping is a handy utility to have around.

RPC Ping is located on the Microsoft Exchange Server directory, in the \EXCHSRVR \RPCPING directory. There is a small documentation file included there as well, which you might find useful.

There are two components to RPC Ping that make it work:

- *RPC Ping Server*, which runs on the Exchange Server computer you are trying to ping.
- *RPC Ping Client*, which runs on the Exchange Client computer you are trying to ping from.

RPC Ping Server

The RPC Ping Server is available for three NT platforms:

- RPINGS.EXE—Intel
- RPINGS_A.EXE—Alpha
- RPINGS_M.EXE—MIPS

If you want to use the Ping Only mode or the Rping endpoint, you must have the RPC Ping Server process running.

When the server process starts, it activates all possible protocols it can find on the server, by default, as shown in Figure 28.1.

FIGURE 28.1.

The RPC Ping Server program has started with several protocols loaded and is ready for pinging.

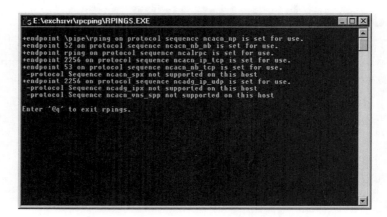

Optionally, you can configure the server process to start a single protocol. This is useful if you only want to test one protocol at a time. The syntax is as follows:

```
RPINGS [-p protocol]
```

where *protocol* can be any one of the following:

- namedpipes for Named Pipes
- tcpip for TCP/IP
- ipx/spx for IPX/SPX
- netbios for NetBIOS over NetBEUI
- vines for VINES IP

RPC Ping Client

The RPC Ping client comes in five versions:

- RPINGC32.EXE—32-bit version for Intel-based Windows NT and Windows 95
- RPINGC16.EXE—16-bit version for Windows 3.*x*
- RPINGDOS.EXE—DOS version for use on MS-DOS
- RPINGC_A.EXE—version for Alpha-based Windows NT
- RPINGC_M.EXE—version for MIPS-based Windows NT

In Figure 28.2, a ping has been sent to the Exchange Server called arrakis by way of TCP/IP to the store endpoint. arrakis responds with the appropriate responses, indicating that it is available to talk with clients. This section goes more into detail about using RPC Ping. By the end, you should understand exactly what the screen in Figure 28.2 is telling you.

FIGURE 28.2.

The RPC Ping utility is useful for checking connectivity from a client to an Exchange server.

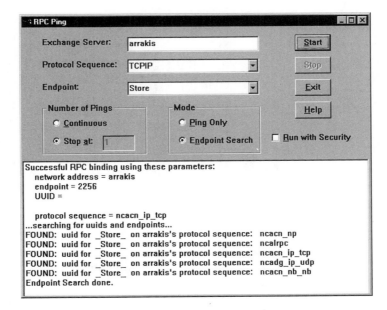

There are multiple RPC methods the Exchange client uses to establish a connection with the Exchange server. RPC Ping supports all of these, so you can test them as needed.

After ensuring the RPINGS.EXE process is running on your Exchange Server computer, you must specify three parameters in the client program before you initiate a ping:

- Exchange Server
- Protocol Sequence
- Endpoint

First, the Exchange Server field specifies the name of the server to ping. You can also specify an IP address here if you're using TCP/IP.

Second, the Protocol Sequence field specifies the configuration of the RPC mechanism that is used for the NCA connection between the client and server. In order for RPC Ping to work, the client and server must both be using the same protocol sequence.

Table 28.1 shows a listing of the protocols that RPC Ping supports.

Table 28.1. Supported protocols in RPC Ping.

Protocol Sequence	Transport Mechanism
ncacn_np	Named Pipes
ncacn_nb_nb	NetBIOS over NetBEUI
ncacn_nb_tcp	NetBIOS over TCP/IP
ncacn_ip_tcp	TCP/IP
ncacn_spx	SPX
ncacn_vns_spp	Banyan VINES
ncadg_ip_udp	UDP datagram TCP/IP
ncadg_ipx	IPX datagram IPX
ncalrpc	Local procedure call (LPC)

Third, the Endpoint field specifies the protocol-specific port with which the RPC Ping client communicates on the other computers. The RPC Ping clients can communicate in one of three ways, as selected in the Endpoint field:

- Rping

  This option attempts communication with RPC Ping Server. If RPC Ping Server is not up and running, the ping will not be successful regardless of which mode is selected in the Mode box.

- Store

  This option attempts communication with the Exchange Server Information Store. Assuming Endpoint Search is set in the Mode box, RPC Ping Server does not have to be up and running. This method is useful for a simple test if you cannot run RPC Ping Server on your Exchange Server computer, but you want to check connectivity between client and server. If Ping Only is set in the Mode box, RPC Ping Server must be up and running.

■ Admin

This option attempts communication with the Exchange Server Admin. Assuming `Endpoint Search` is set in the `Mode` box, RPC Ping Server does not have to be up and running. This method is also useful for a simple test if you cannot run RPC Ping Server on your Exchange Server computer, but you want to check connectivity between client and server. If `Ping Only` is set in the `Mode` box, RPC Ping Server must be up and running.

Optionally, you can select the mode for RPC Ping operation. The selections in the `Mode` box determine how the RPC ping is carried out:

■ Ping Only

This mode causes RPC Ping Server to echo the ping character sent to it. This is the simplest connectivity test because it does not require Exchange Server to be up and running. However, you must have RPC Ping Server up and running on the destination computer.

■ Endpoint Search

This mode simply searches for the endpoint selected in the `Endpoint` field, and it lists all the different protocol sequences running on the server computer. If `Rping` is the selected endpoint, RPC Ping Server must be up on the Exchange Server computer; if `Store` or `Admin` is the selected endpoint, Exchange Server must be up on the server computer. `Endpoint Search` is useful for seeing which protocols are being used between the client and the server computers. It is also a simple connectivity test between client and server.

Finally, the `Number of Pings` box is self-explanatory—it specifies the number of times the ping operation will be carried out when the `Mode` is set to `Ping Only`.

ISINTEG

ISINTEG is the Microsoft Exchange information store integrity checker. The executable, ISINTEG.EXE, is automatically installed in the \EXCHSRVR\BIN directory on the Exchange Server during setup.

You must run ISINTEG on the Exchange Server machine, and you must stop the `MSExchangeIS` service before using ISINTEG.

TIP

You don't have to stop all the Exchange Services when you run ISINTEG, only `MSExchangeIS`. In fact, if you do not leave the `MSExchangeDS` and `MSExchangeSA` services running, you will get a `DS_E_COMMUNICATIONS_PROBLEM` error when ISINTEG attempts to update the store. However, if you just stop `MSExchangeIS`, the other required services are left running. Then, when ISINTEG is finished, you can restart the `MSExchangeIS` service.

See Appendix B, "Command Reference," for the syntax of ISINTEG. If you prefer to see the syntax on the screen, you can run ISINTEG with no parameters from a Windows NT command prompt.

ISINTEG serves three main purposes:

- To patch the IS after an offline restore
- To test and optionally fix the IS
- To provide a dump of the IS

So why would you want to do these things?

Patch

In Exchange terminology, an *offline* backup of the Information Store is a file-level backup of the IS that does not occur when Exchange Server is not up and running. Remember, the IS is composed of two main files, PRIV.EDB and PUB.EDB, which are open while Exchange Server is running. Therefore, performing an offline backup of the IS is fundamentally a matter of shutting down Exchange Server and backing up these two files.

An *offline* restore of the Information Store is a file-level restore that does not support restoring the IS while Exchange Server is up and running. An offline restore of the IS is typically performed using an offline backup set or some other method that replaces PRIV.EDB and PUB.EDB.

The -PATCH option comes into play after the restore. After you perform an offline restore of the IS, you must use ISINTEG to patch the database before you can use it. Among other things, Patch replaces GUIDs (Globally Unique IDs) in the database so all entries in the database will be handled properly by Exchange.

For example, suppose you bring down the Exchange Server and save a copy of the IS—both public and private stores—somewhere, be it on tape or disk. Sometime later you restore those IS files, replacing the existing IS. When you try to start the MSExchangeIS service, you get an error and the service doesn't start. You must run ISINTEG using the following syntax to patch the IS and prepare it for use:

```
ISINTEG -PATCH
```

ISINTEG patches both the public and private stores automatically—there is currently no way to patch one or the other. It doesn't take that long—usually under a minute, depending on the size of your IS and the speed of your computer.

> **TIP**
>
> I find using ISINTEG useful when I am doing performance tests with Exchange Server. I want to always start with the IS in the same state before each test run, so I stop MSExchangeIS, restore the master IS from the backup, and use ISINTEG to patch it. After rebooting the server (not necessary, but I always do), I'm ready for the next run.

Test and Fix

If your private or public store seems to be acting funny, run ISINTEG and see what it finds. When ISINTEG executes, it runs a suite of 22 tests on your IS—either private store, public store, or both.

An example of using ISINTEG to test the public store would look like this:

```
ISINTEG -PUB
```

Using ISINTEG to test and fix the public store would look like this:

```
ISINTEG -PUB -FIX
```

For convenience, test and fix have a verbose mode. Also, you can instruct ISINTEG to log the output to a file for later reference.

ISINTEG can take a while to run, depending on the size of your database and the speed of the computer. A 100MB database check can take up to 10 minutes to run all the tests.

For example, a common usage of ISINTEG is for checking the private store with verbose output and logging the results in the default ASCII text file called ISINTEG.PRI (the default output file is ISINTEG.PUB if the test is run on the public store). No fixes will be performed. The command looks like this:

```
ISINTEG -PRI -VERBOSE -L
```

If ISINTEG finds a problem and you want to fix it, add the -FIX parameter to the end of the parameter list and run ISINTEG again.

For example, say the power goes out while Exchange is running. When you restart the server, you find that the MSExchangeIS service logs an error on initialization and it doesn't start. The first step is to run ISINTEG and EDBUTIL (covered in the next section) to see what's going on.

Technically, in this scenario there should not be a problem. When you start Exchange Server, the database automatically rolls back to the last checkpoint, and the logs are applied to the database to restore it to the point of failure. But if something goes wrong there, ISINTEG can come in handy to help set things straight.

Dump

Like -FIX and -PATCH, -DUMP is another parameter of ISINTEG. However, most users don't have a need for Dump, because it is mainly for diagnostic purposes used by people who know what the dump contents mean. But if you are the curious type (like me) and want to see what a dump of the IS looks like, you can run one—it won't hurt anything.

EDBUTIL

EDBUTIL is another useful tool for analyzing the state of the Exchange databases. It is a companion to ISINTEG. But whereas ISINTEG looks at only the public and private stores, EDBUTIL additionally looks at the Directory Service database (DS). The executable, EDBUTIL.EXE, is automatically installed in the \EXCHSRVR\BIN directory on the Exchange server during setup.

You must run EDBUTIL on the Exchange Server machine, and you must stop the MSExchangeIS service before you use any EDBUTIL utility.

See Appendix B to see the complete syntax. Also, you can run EDBUTIL with no parameters from a Windows NT command prompt to list the syntax on the screen.

EDBUTIL is really a suite of database utilities, and you invoke a particular utility in the suite by running EDBUTIL with the appropriate parameter. The EDBUTIL utilities do the following for you:

- Perform database defragmentation
- Perform a database recovery
- Verify database consistency
- Perform a database upgrade to the current version
- Perform a dump of a database header or checkpoint file

Let's look at why you use these utilities.

Defragmentation

In the case of Exchange databases, defragmenting the database is synonymous with compacting the database. You can run defragmentation on the information store and the directory.

Everyone knows about the benefits of defragmentation for a hard drive. It organizes the data to be stored in a more efficient manner by making the data on the drive contiguous. In the case of a hard drive, it doesn't necessarily save space, but it puts all the data together rather than spreading it out over the drive.

With Exchange databases, defragmentation can save disk space.

An Exchange database takes up space on the hard disk. In a fragmented database, there is active data mixed in with unused or deleted data. This deleted data doesn't always get cleaned up as the database grows, so the database gets larger as time goes on. Eventually, for example, you may have a 1GB database, but only 75 percent of that is active data. The other 25 percent is trash. After a defragmentation, all the active data is collected and put together contiguously so as to require only 75 percent of its former bulk to store it. The other 25 percent is then released. In this case, defragmentation just bought back 250MB of disk space.

The command to compact the private store looks like the following:

```
EDBUTIL /D /ISPRIV
```

Using the /ISPRIV, /ISPUB, and /DS switches, the utility automatically finds the databases based on their locations recorded in the Windows NT Registry.

There are several handy options in the deframentation utility, so check the syntax closely for more details.

The amount of time it takes to run EDBUTIL depends on the database size and the speed of the computer. A 100MB database should defragment in less than 10 minutes.

> **CAUTION**
>
> You must have enough free disk space to run defragment. The maximum amount of free disk space required is equal to the size of the database that is being defragmented. This is because EDBUTIL makes its compacted copy of the database as it works. For example, if you have a 2GB database to defragment, a maximum of 2GB free space will be enough for EDBUTIL to perform the defragmentation. Because it is writing the defragmented copy as it works, EDBUTIL might not actually use up all 2GB.

28

DIAGNOSING THE CAUSE OF A PROBLEM

Recovery

Recovery performs the task of committing all the transaction logs to a database. This utility "plays back" the transactions that are logged and commits them into the database.

Run Recovery *only* if you have a good reason to run it. Why? Because the IS normally manages its logs just fine on its own. And if you happen to damage the database logs, you can really mess up your IS databases.

Usually you run this utility because someone at Microsoft technical support told you to. I do not advise running it just to see what happens.

Consistency

Consistency is a read-only utility used for scanning the database to find any unreadable records. It is similar to ISINTEG in that it seeks out problems in the target database. But unlike ISINTEG, it doesn't try to fix them.

It's mainly just another way to check out an Exchange database to see if there are any problems with it. The length of time to complete depends on the database size and the speed of your server. You can check a 100MB private store in less than 10 minutes.

Upgrade

Upgrade upgrades an existing database to a new version of Microsoft Exchange Server.

For example, suppose you have been running on Exchange 4.0 for a while. Now Exchange Server 5.0 is out and you want to upgrade to it and retain all your database information. However, the database architecture has had some improvements in 5.0, so a 4.0 database doesn't work with the 5.0 executables. You can use the upgrade feature of EDBUTIL to upgrade your database to the new revision.

You probably won't have to worry about using this feature. The upgrade process will handle this for you. See Chapter 8, "Exchange Server 4.0 to 5.0: Migration and Coexistence," for more details.

File Dump

As with ISINTEG, the dump utility is mainly for diagnostic purposes. Go ahead and run it to see what it looks like. It's harmless.

MTACHECK

MTACHECK is a straightforward utility. Basically, you can run it with no parameters for it to do its job.

MTACHECK is to the Exchange Server MTA what ISINTEG and EDBUTIL are to the Exchange Server IS. Neither ISINTEG nor EDBUTIL do anything with the MTA—that's where MTACHECK comes into the picture.

The executable, MTACHECK.EXE, is automatically installed in the \EXCHSRVR\BIN directory on the Exchange Server during setup.

MTACHECK cleans up the MTA. This means it looks for and removes old objects lying around in the MTA queue that are causing problems. For example, if the MTA doesn't seem to be routing messages, if it's routing very slowly, or if the MSExchangeMTA service doesn't start at all, there might be something in the queue causing the problem. MTACHECK removes anything that shouldn't be there, and it rebuilds the queue so the MSExchangeMTA service starts again.

Its syntax is simple:

```
MTACHECK /V
```

You can run MTACHECK with a /? to produce the syntax. The options are very limited, however. Basically you can specify a verbose mode with /V, and you can specify an output file with /F, and that's about it.

You must stop the MSExchangeMTA service before running MTACHECK. Also, the directory called MTACHECK.OUT must be empty—that is where MTACHECK puts its trash.

Exchange Optimizer

Microsoft Exchange Optimizer is another useful tool that helps you troubleshoot an Exchange system. It sets the Exchange system parameters to the proper values.

If Exchange system parameters are set improperly—maybe someone messed around with them, or maybe they weren't set after installation—the Exchange server doesn't run well. So if your Exchange server seems to be performing worse than you think it should, run Exchange Optimizer and let it make some suggestions about how to set your Exchange system parameters.

The Exchange Optimizer is covered in detail in Chapter 6, "Planning for Optimal Server Performance."

Inbox Repair Tool

You use the Inbox Repair tool to repair defective personal store (PST) files; you use it if something is wrong with your PST file.

The executable, SCANPST.EXE, is actually installed with the client, not the server, and it is represented by one of the icons in the Exchange group. It is similar in function to the check MMF feature found in MS Mail.

Inbox Repair performs several checks on the selected PST file. Its basic goal is to validate, to scavenge, and to rebuild the structure of the personal store in order to get it back in operating condition again. After you initiate it, Inbox Repair functions without user intervention unless it finds a problem. Although rare, if it does discover something wrong with your PST file, and it needs to inform you of something or needs your input, the Inbox Repair tool will prompt you.

Message Tracking

You use the Message Tracking facility in the Exchange Administrator to track the path of messages through entry and exit points in the Exchange server.

Messages are tracked in two main places:

- In the Information Store (IS)
- In the Message Transfer Agent (MTA)

These two Exchange Server entities handle all the messages on a particular server, so if you track messages that pass through them, you track all the messages on the server.

Optionally, you can track messages in the Internet Mail Service (IMS) and the Microsoft Mail Connector if you have them installed.

Enabling Message Tracking

Enable message tracking in the IS to handle those messages that do not leave the local server. For example, if Shelly sends Katie an e-mail and they both have their mailboxes on the same Exchange server, the message never has to go to the MTA. It is handled solely by the IS.

Enable message tracking in the MTA to handle those messages that go outside the local Exchange server. For example, if Shelly sends Tiffany an e-mail, and they have their mailboxes on separate Exchange servers, although both servers reside on the same network, the message must be handled by the MTA. Additionally, enabling message tracking provides tracking of messages sent to distribution lists because the MTA is responsible for expanding distribution lists.

However, be advised that message tracking does not follow a message onto the Internet or an X.400 public carrier. There is no way to track e-mail during the time it is outside the Exchange network.

For example, Shelly and Lynda both work for the same company, but Shelly is based in Texas and Lynda is based in Florida. When Shelly sends e-mail to Lynda via the Internet, the e-mail proceeds from Shelly's Exchange server to Lynda's Exchange server via the Internet, using the MTA and the IMS on each server. The administrator can track messages up to the point where they are handed off from the MTA of Shelly's Exchange server to go out to the Internet, and then again at the time they are picked up by the MTA of Lynda's Exchange server after coming in from the Internet. But the e-mail cannot be tracked in transit from Texas to Florida because it is not being handled by an Exchange server.

> **NOTE**
>
> When message tracking is enabled, it applies to all Exchange servers in the Exchange site, not just to a single server.

Message tracking is not automatically enabled; it is enabled by way of the Exchange Administrator program. For the IS and MTA you can find the message tracking feature in the Information Store Site Configuration and the MTA Site Configuration objects, respectively. These are located in the Exchange Administrator under organization\site\Configuration as shown in Figure 28.3.

For each object, open the properties page, look in the General tab, and check the Enable message tracking checkbox.

As soon as message tracking is enabled, all messages that pass through that object—either the IS or the MTA—are tracked in an ASCII log file kept in the \EXCHSRVR\TRACKING.LOG directory. A new file is created each day, based on Greenwich mean time, and it is named using a format of yyyymmdd.log. For example, if you enable tracking on June 5, 1997, the filename is 19970605.LOG.

FIGURE 28.3.

Message tracking is enabled in two places in the Exchange Administrator.

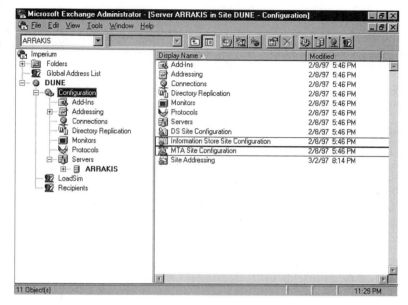

Disabling Message Tracking

Enabling message tracking enables it for all Exchange servers in the site. But what if you don't want that? What if you want to disable tracking on a server?

You disable message tracking on a particular Exchange server with the Windows NT Registry on that computer. After you disable the computer, it is excluded from the message tracking activities.

You disable the IS and the MTA separately as you do when you enable message tracking. If you have the IMC and MS Mail connector installed, you must separately disable it for those as well.

> **NOTE**
>
> You must enable message tracking on all Exchange servers for a message to be fully tracked up to the point of delivery. If one server in the path has message tracking disabled, the message is tracked until it reaches the server that doesn't have message tracking enabled.

IS

To disable message tracking for the IS of a particular Exchange Server computer, look in the Registry under HKEY_LOCAL_MACHINE and find and highlight the key \SYSTEM\

CurrentControlSet\Services\MSExchangeIS\ParamtersPrivate. Under this key, there is a value called X.400 Service Event Log. If it is there, set it to 0 (zero). If it is not there, create it by selecting Edit | Add Value. Type X.400 Service Event Log in the Value Name box, and set its data type to REG_DWORD. Then click OK and set the value in the Data box to 0.

To re-enable IS tracking for this computer, set the value to 1 or remove X.400 Service Event Log.

MTA

To disable message tracking for the MTA of a particular Exchange Server computer, look in the Registry under HKEY_LOCAL_MACHINE and find the key \SYSTEM\ CurrentControlSet\Services\MSExchangeMTA. Under this key there is a value called X.400 Service Event Log. If it is there, set it to 0 (zero). If it is not there, create it by selecting Edit | Add Value. Type X.400 Service Event Log in the Value Name box, and set its data type to REG_DWORD. Then click OK and set the value in the Data box to 0.

To re-enable MTA tracking for this computer, set the value to 1 or remove X.400 Service Event Log.

Using Message Tracking

After you enable message tracking, you must restart the Exchange services to activate the message tracking facility.

To actually use the facility, from the Exchange Administrator select Tools | Track Message. It asks you which server you want to connect to and then brings up the message tracking center. You are immediately prompted to enter parameters to select a message to track as shown in Figure 28.4.

The details of operating the message tracking center are covered in the *Microsoft Exchange Server Administrator's Guide* in Chapter 17.

CAUTION

Tracking can cause server performance degradation. For example, if you enable tracking on everything in all servers in the site, expect to see some performance degradation. The degree of degradation is impossible to say. It depends on how much tracking is going on, how powerful the servers are, how much message activity there is, and other factors.

FIGURE 28.4.

The message tracking center is activated from within the Exchange Administrator.

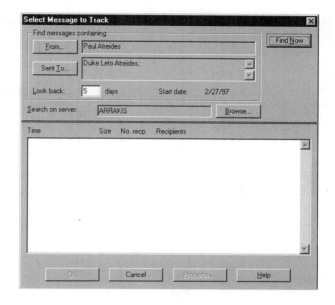

Windows NT Administrative Tools

Microsoft Exchange Server includes some useful tools to help you troubleshoot a server. However, it doesn't stop there. Windows NT Server itself has some tools that are also helpful in diagnosing problems with an Exchange Server:

- Event Viewer
- Server Manager
- User Manager for Domains

Each of these three tools is found in the Administrative Tools folder that is installed with Windows NT Server.

Event Viewer

Probably the most useful of these three tools is Event Viewer. In fact, Event Viewer is usually the first place you should look if something goes wrong with anything in Windows NT.

An *event* is simply anything noteworthy that happens in Windows NT that gets logged in the event log. So, any entry listed in the event log is referred to as an event.

Figure 28.5 shows a typical event log screen. This one just happens to be a view of the system log events.

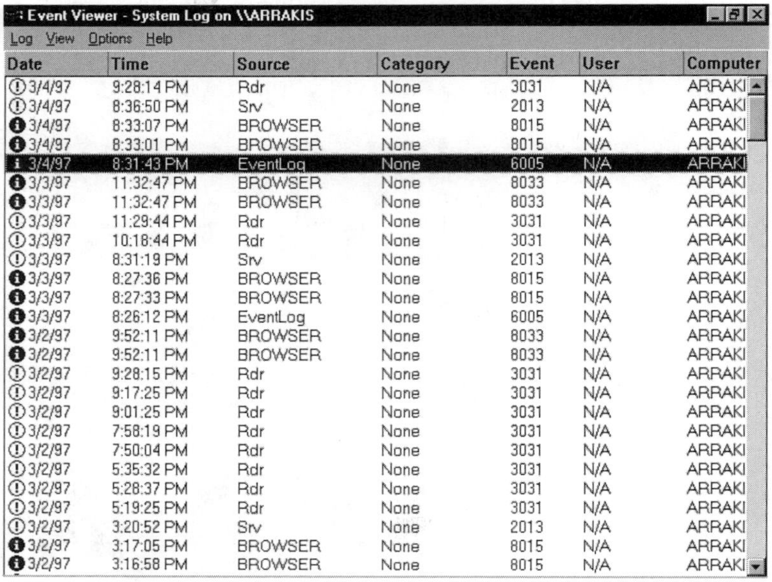

FIGURE 28.5.

The Windows NT Event Viewer contains entries for each event that happens in Windows NT.

The event log is continuous; that is, it does not distinguish between days or weeks or months. It logs each event as it happens with a date and time stamp. It's easy to see where the log starts. There is always an event with a source of EventLog in the system log that marks where the event log starts. The one highlighted in Figure 28.5 illustrates this.

There are three types of events that are logged: system, security, and application. Of those three, system and application usually get the most activity under normal circumstances:

■ *System* events pertain to operating system–level components, such as the server, the redirector, the browser, system devices, and the event log itself.

■ *Security* events pertain to Windows NT security. The types of events logged here include log on and log off, file access, security policy changes, and system restarts. Most of the events in this log are controlled by the Audit Policy settings configured in the User Manager for Domains application.

■ *Application* events are those that pertain to applications running under Windows NT, such as Exchange Server.

TIP

Many times when there is an event in one log, there is a corresponding event in one (or both) of the other two logs that provides additional detail. Always check all three logs for related event entries so you can get as much information as possible about the event. The Time field will help you determine which events occurred simultaneously.

When something goes wrong with Exchange Server, the event log is a good place to start looking for the problem. Exchange is very good about logging what happens to it, and many times it points you directly to the problem.

Using Event Viewer

For example, if an Exchange server service does not start, an event is logged in either the system log or the application log, or both. There is usually a description of the problem along with relevant error codes and information.

Figure 28.6 shows a sample Application Log with some Exchange events in it.

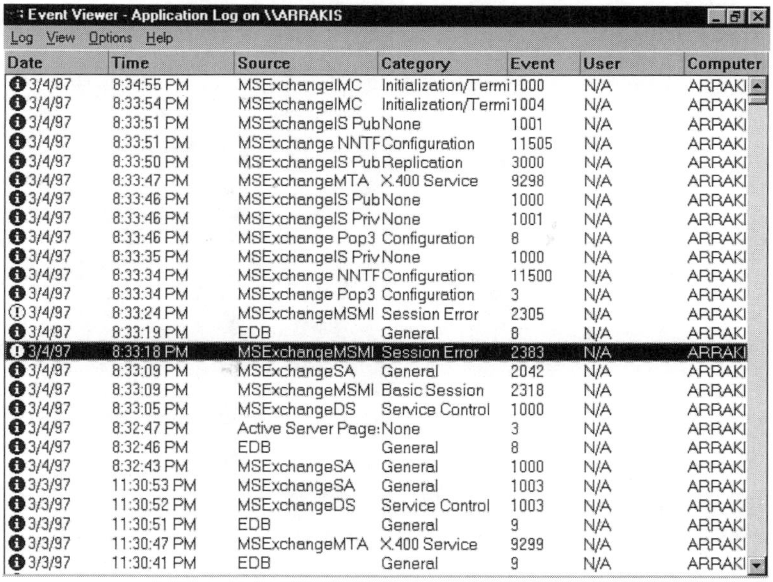

Event Viewer - Application Log on \\ARRAKIS

Log View Options Help

Date	Time	Source	Category	Event	User	Computer
3/4/97	8:34:55 PM	MSExchangeIMC	Initialization/Termi	1000	N/A	ARRAKI
3/4/97	8:33:54 PM	MSExchangeIMC	Initialization/Termi	1004	N/A	ARRAKI
3/4/97	8:33:51 PM	MSExchangeIS Pub	None	1001	N/A	ARRAKI
3/4/97	8:33:51 PM	MSExchange NNTF	Configuration	11505	N/A	ARRAKI
3/4/97	8:33:50 PM	MSExchangeIS Pub	Replication	3000	N/A	ARRAKI
3/4/97	8:33:47 PM	MSExchangeMTA	X.400 Service	9298	N/A	ARRAKI
3/4/97	8:33:46 PM	MSExchangeIS Pub	None	1000	N/A	ARRAKI
3/4/97	8:33:46 PM	MSExchangeIS Priv	None	1001	N/A	ARRAKI
3/4/97	8:33:46 PM	MSExchange Pop3	Configuration	8	N/A	ARRAKI
3/4/97	8:33:35 PM	MSExchangeIS Priv	None	1000	N/A	ARRAKI
3/4/97	8:33:34 PM	MSExchange NNTF	Configuration	11500	N/A	ARRAKI
3/4/97	8:33:34 PM	MSExchange Pop3	Configuration	3	N/A	ARRAKI
3/4/97	8:33:24 PM	MSExchangeMSMI	Session Error	2305	N/A	ARRAKI
3/4/97	8:33:19 PM	EDB	General	8	N/A	ARRAKI
3/4/97	8:33:18 PM	MSExchangeMSMI	Session Error	2383	N/A	ARRAKI
3/4/97	8:33:09 PM	MSExchangeSA	General	2042	N/A	ARRAKI
3/4/97	8:33:09 PM	MSExchangeMSMI	Basic Session	2318	N/A	ARRAKI
3/4/97	8:33:05 PM	MSExchangeDS	Service Control	1000	N/A	ARRAKI
3/4/97	8:32:47 PM	Active Server Page:	None	3	N/A	ARRAKI
3/4/97	8:32:46 PM	EDB	General	8	N/A	ARRAKI
3/4/97	8:32:43 PM	MSExchangeSA	General	1000	N/A	ARRAKI
3/3/97	11:30:53 PM	MSExchangeSA	General	1003	N/A	ARRAKI
3/3/97	11:30:52 PM	MSExchangeDS	Service Control	1003	N/A	ARRAKI
3/3/97	11:30:51 PM	EDB	General	9	N/A	ARRAKI
3/3/97	11:30:47 PM	MSExchangeMTA	X.400 Service	9299	N/A	ARRAKI
3/3/97	11:30:41 PM	EDB	General	9	N/A	ARRAKI

FIGURE 28.6.
The Exchange-specific events are logged in the Application Log.

As you can see, there are several application events. Although some of the letters in the Source column are cut off (unfortunately, the column cannot be widened), among the events are Exchange-specific events:

- `MSExchangeIMC`—Internet Mail connector
- `MSExchangeIS Pub`, `MSExchangeIS Priv`—Information Store
- `MSExchangeNNTP`—Exchange Network News interface
- `MSExchangeMTA`—Message Transfer Agent
- `MSExchangePop3`—Exchange POP3 interface
- `MSExchangeMSMI`—MS Mail Connector Interchange
- `Active Server Pages`—Exchange Active Server Page facility

■ EDB—Exchange database engine

■ MSExchangeSA—System Attendant

■ MSExchangeDS—Directory Service

This is a busy server.

Figure 28.7 gives you a feeling for how helpful the events can be. In this figure, the event highlighted in Figure 28.6 is opened to show the event detail.

FIGURE 28.7.

The event log can be quite helpful in assisting with diagnosing the cause of problems with Exchange services.

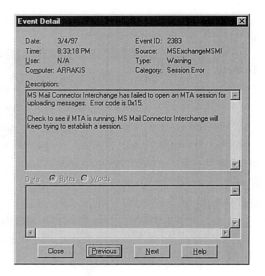

In this case, there is a warning because the MS Mail Connector Interchange (MSMI) can't get a session with the MTA. The MSMI tried twice before being successful. A pretty simple thing, but without this log entry it is one of those subtle problems that can go on unnoticed for awhile.

Unfortunately, not everything is always this perfect. The level of detail in the log depends upon the type of error. Sometimes it is cut and dry as in the example. But sometimes it isn't quite so specific. That's where the other tools discussed come in handy.

However, most of the time, the event log doesn't let you down. It at least points in the right direction and gets you on the road to correcting the problem.

TIP

I recommend you check the event logs each day. Sometimes things can be going on in the system that aren't obvious. If you check the logs regularly, it helps ensure there isn't anything going on you don't know about. You may even want to clear the events in the log each day if you don't need them.

Viewing Logs on Other Servers

Another convenient feature of Event Viewer is that it provides a way to view event logs on other computers on the network. This can be handy, especially if you are trying to diagnose a problem just by looking from your desktop.

Select Log | Select Computer, and choose the domain and computer whose logs you want to examine. Assuming you have the necessary permissions, the destination machine's event logs will appear. It's that simple.

Server Manager

You use the Windows NT Server Manager for several different tasks in the context of Windows NT networking. However, in the context of Microsoft Exchange Server, it is the most useful for enabling you to examine the services on a Windows NT Server on the network that is running Exchange Server.

From the main screen of Server Manager, highlight the computer name whose services you want to check, and select Computer | Services. You then get a list of the services—and their status—on that computer.

Suppose you discover that an Exchange server has suddenly stopped responding to users. Every time a user attempts to connect, he or she cannot open the information store.

The first thing to do is check to ensure all the Exchange Server services are running on the server, especially the MSExchangeIS service. By opening the Server Manager and checking the services, it is simple to check and see if the proper services are actually up and running on the server.

Of course, there are the other standard Windows NT security items you can check with Server Manager. For example, you can make sure the Exchange Server computer name is listed in the NT domain. If it isn't, the computer won't be able to function in the domain. Maybe there are problems with shares; those can be checked too. Also, you can check what user sessions are active on a server to see if anything looks funny that way.

28

DIAGNOSING
THE CAUSE OF
A PROBLEM

EXCHANGE SERVER AND SYSTEMS MANAGEMENT

Some readers may be interested in taking this idea of managing a server to the next level of sophistication. Fortunately, the idea of viewing logs or being alerted when a service is down or when a counter exceeds a threshold is not a new one. There is an entire segment of the software market dedicated to *systems management* that addresses these very issues. Software companies in this market—such as BMC Software and Computer Associates, for example—provide software solutions specifically for managing systems and applications.

continues

continued

For example, you could configure BMC's PATROL Application Management product to monitor your server to ensure that it doesn't post a critical event in the Event Log. If that happens, you would be notified immediately. That may seem a bit redundant, but consider what you could do if you wanted to monitor a few dozen servers at once. Or maybe a hundred—all from a single console. Perhaps you want to know when an NT service has stopped running or would prefer to be paged or sent e-mail rather than having to rely on checking the Event Viewer or Server Manager applications. Or maybe you also need to manage non–NT-based servers with your NT-based servers. These requirements are clearly outside the reach of the tools discussed here. For these advanced needs, you require software specifically designed to provide these features.

As computer systems grow in complexity, it becomes more important to be able to manage the systems rather than just deploy them and hope they stay up and running. Systems-management software is designed to provide you with the powerful features required to help you stay on top of things. Take a look at some of the systems-management vendors' product offerings. You could find just what you need.

User Manager for Domains

User Manager for Domains is another troubleshooting tool. Like Server Manager, you use this program to administer NT security for the domain. The subject of NT security is one thing to always keep in mind when you are troubleshooting an Exchange server. Many problems can occur simply because someone doesn't have the proper user rights.

Aside from all the usual security issues, there is one special thing about User Manager for Domains. When Exchange Server is installed, the menu User Manager for Domains is enhanced with an Exchange menu extension as shown in Figure 28.8.

This feature enables you to set an option to create and delete Exchange mailboxes when you create and delete NT user accounts. It also enables you to view Exchange property pages for the selected NT user account.

Although this particular tool might not help much with tracking down why your server crashed, it certainly helps when you are trying to sift through lists of users to see if the proper permissions exist on different mailboxes.

FIGURE 28.8.

The Exchange Setup program automatically installs an extension to User Manager for Domains.

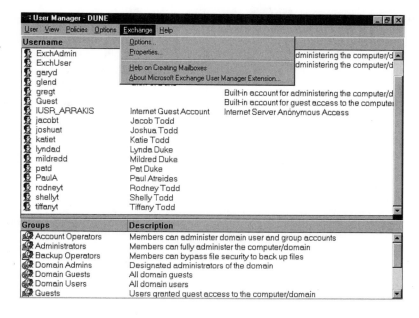

Summary

This chapter covers several tools available to assist in diagnosing the cause of a problem with an Exchange Server computer:

- General diagnostic utilities
- Message tracking
- Windows NT administrative tools

First, it discusses the diagnostic tools included with Microsoft Exchange Server: RPC Ping, ISINTEG, EDBUTIL, MTACHECK, and some others.

Next, it looks at the message tracking center, which is the message tracking utility included in the Exchange Administrator. This utility provides the capability to track the path of a message through the system.

The chapter finishes by covering a few Windows NT Server administrative tools that prove helpful in troubleshooting: Server Manager, User Manager for Domains, and Windows NT Event Viewer.

Let's hope you won't have to use the tools covered in this chapter very often for diagnostic purposes. It would be great if your Exchange installation has no problems, wouldn't it? Unfortunately, it's not a matter of *if* problems occur, but *when*.

With that in mind, the main point to remember about troubleshooting is that there are no hard and fast rules about how to diagnose the cause of a problem. It's really a matter of using the tools you have, knowing what the tools are telling you, and learning how to fish.

VI

PART

IN THIS PART

More Than Just E-Mail

Understanding and Using LoadSim

by Greg Todd

IN THIS CHAPTER

Performance

This chapter is intended to help you understand the Microsoft Exchange Server Load Simulator program, commonly referred to as LoadSim. If you expect ever to use LoadSim, you should definitely read this chapter. If you don't expect to use LoadSim, you could still skim this chapter to get some insights about Exchange. Might as well get your money's worth, right?

LoadSim is quite a powerful tool, and along with that power comes a degree of complexity. To help you get going, this chapter explains the major aspects of the program so you can start using it quickly.

First, the chapter introduces the LoadSim program and explains some key concepts about it, such as user profiles and suggested number of users you can simulate with it. The idea is to give you some explanation of the when, where, and why to use the program.

Next, you walk through a sample LoadSim scenario and look at an example of how to install, configure, and run LoadSim. The sample gives you a good idea of how to actually use the program, and from there you can adapt it to your own needs.

Finally, you learn the data collection aspect. LoadSim wouldn't be useful without a way to collect data about the effects it has on Microsoft Exchange Server, so I will cover proven techniques for gathering accurate data.

When you finish reading this chapter, you should be able to set up LoadSim yourself on your own machines and start simulating.

Here is some common terminology referred to throughout the chapter:

- *LoadSim* refers to the Exchange Load Simulator software.

- A LoadSim *client* refers to the machine that runs the LoadSim software. This client machine must have the Microsoft Exchange Client software installed on it.

- A LoadSim *user* refers to a single, synthetic Exchange user that LoadSim creates and simulates. You normally run multiple LoadSim users on a LoadSim client.

- A LoadSim user *profile* (or user *type)* refers to the type of Exchange user, whether it is a heavy hitter or one that hardly uses the system at all. There are three predefined profiles in LoadSim: Light, Medium, and Heavy. These are defined later in the chapter. I will often use the terms *profile* and *type* interchangeably.

- An Exchange Server *user load* refers to the amount of stress placed on an Exchange Server computer by one or more LoadSim clients simulating multiple LoadSim users based on a particular user profile.

Finally, you should be aware that LoadSim is not officially supported software. Although it was designed and written by Microsoft, it is made available as a tool that is used "as is."

> **NOTE**
>
> If you've been looking for LoadSim on the Exchange CDs, don't bother looking any further. Unlike the LoadSim that shipped with Exchange Server 4.0, the Exchange 5.0 version of LoadSim is not included anywhere on the Exchange Server CDs.
>
> Microsoft does make LoadSim available, but you have to ask for it. Simply contact Microsoft directly and request LoadSim. Unless you ask for additional protocols, what you will get is the LoadSim program along with MAPI protocol support—basically what you got with LoadSim 4.0. If you would like the additional protocol support, you must request that as well.

What's New in LoadSim 5.0?

New to Version 5.0

There are several enhancements in LoadSim for Exchange Server 5.0. You can still use LoadSim 4.0 against Exchange 5.0 servers—no problem. However, you might want to use the latest version for the added feature set, new capabilities, and increased load accuracy. Plus, if you're like me, you always like to be using the latest version of software. Call it a character flaw.

One of the most obvious enhancements is the user interface. Microsoft has done a lot of work in this area. If you are familiar with LoadSim 4.0, you'll find the menus, dialog boxes, and property sheets are rearranged a lot. It should not be a problem to find things, though, because most of the features from LoadSim 4.0 are still in place. Overall, things are better organized and more efficient.

LoadSim 5.0 now provides the capability of running tests against Exchange Server using multiple protocols—namely LDAP, NNTP, and POP3—in addition to MAPI. There will be more protocol support as Microsoft develops it. The multiple protocol support for LoadSim mirrors that which you get with Exchange Server.

Microsoft has made some refinements with regard to load accuracy. LoadSim 4.0 did not have any really major problems along these lines. In the process of redesigning LoadSim to support multiple protocols, however, the engineers were able to do some tweaking to the LoadSim engine to make its loads more accurate. If the loads are more accurate, the results are more repeatable, and that makes for more reliable data so you can make better decisions.

Unlike with LoadSim 4.0, with LoadSim 5.0, you no longer have to specify both senders and recipients. Now the LoadSim users specified in the test are both the senders *and* the recipients. It's less confusing this way. You'll see more about this later in the section, "How to Use LoadSim."

29

UNDERSTANDING AND USING LOADSIM

Microsoft worked on increasing the number of users you can simulate with a single LoadSim client. To accomplish this, LoadSim 5.0 now has a thread pooling feature. It is mostly useful for protocols, such as POP3 and NNTP, where the clients are idle most of the time. Unfortunately, the number of simultaneous MAPI users you can simulate on one LoadSim client has not been increased over LoadSim 4.0.

Finally, one other feature has changed that is worth mentioning. Although this feature is somewhat esoteric, if you used LoadSim 4.0 a lot you will miss it. LoadSim 4.0 had the capability to simultaneously support multiple LoadSim clients using a single LoadSim test setup (.SIM file). Just specify the LoadSim clients in the test, and go. With LoadSim 5.0 you must configure a separate .SIM file for each LoadSim client. It's a bit less convenient this way, but the data produced is no different. Microsoft may put this feature back into a future revision of LoadSim, but for now you should know it's not there.

Introduction to LoadSim

Architecture

LoadSim has a single purpose in life: to provide a way to simulate a user load on a Microsoft Exchange Server computer. That's it. Everything about LoadSim is focused on the purpose of simulating a specific number of users on an Exchange server. If you want to do performance testing on Microsoft Exchange Server, your main goal is to disturb the system under test as little as possible. LoadSim makes this possible.

Suppose you want to simulate a hundred simultaneous users on a server. To do it without LoadSim, you have to have 100 identically configured Exchange client machines, each running some kind of script that regulates the activity. Then you must have a way to measure all the response times and keep track of the activities of each user. A real pain, believe me.

Using LoadSim, you can accomplish this 100-user simulation with a single powerful machine. A Pentium/100 with 48MB RAM, a fast hard drive, and a good network card will do perfectly. This requirement hasn't changed much since LoadSim was first introduced. Fortunately, hardware prices have—for the better—making good simulations that much more attainable.

NOTE

LoadSim should not run on the Microsoft Exchange Server machine itself, although you technically could do so if you also install the Exchange Client on the server.

Instead, LoadSim should run on a separate machine. You don't want to run it on your server machine, because running LoadSim puts extra stress on the server that isn't there normally. This disturbs the server being tested and skews the results. Again, you want to keep from disturbing the system under test as much as possible.

As clear and simple as this purpose sounds, there is much to the notion of simulating a user load in this way.

Issues of Simulating a User Load

For starters, there are several issues about simulating a user load. You may have even thought of some of these yourself:

- How can you actually create an accurate load that represents many users by using one LoadSim client, without causing a bottleneck on the LoadSim machine?

- If the LoadSim client is simulating multiple users on a single machine, how can you be assured that each simulated user is delivering the same load as all the others?

- How many users can you realistically simulate on a single machine?

- How will the test be structured so it has some bearing on the real world? For that matter, is it important to make the test relate to the real world? Why not simply create a benchmark that produces a number for comparing one Exchange Server machine to another?

- Is it possible to configure the program to simulate a specific customized user profile?

- How do you track the LoadSim user response time?

- How do you collect data and make the administration of the tests manageable?

- Under what circumstances do you use a program such as LoadSim?

These are just some of the questions that might come to mind when you are considering a program such as LoadSim. Rest assured the engineers at Microsoft, and those of us who beta-tested LoadSim during its development, have invested much time and effort into making LoadSim address all these issues—and more.

The next few sections cover topics that answer these questions either directly or indirectly and will give you some insight into how LoadSim works.

LoadSim Theory

LoadSim takes full advantage of Windows NT's capabilities to be able to reliably simulate multiple users. It is a multi-threaded, multi-process program that enables a single machine running Windows NT to simulate one user or many users. Each LoadSim process has one or more threads in it, with each thread performing the task of a single LoadSim user. Because LoadSim relies on the inner workings of Windows NT to handle running each thread, you can be assured each thread, or user, gets equal attention from NT. That means each simulated user produces the same load on the targeted Exchange server.

LoadSim requires Windows NT Workstation (or Server) 3.51 or higher. It uses the Microsoft Exchange Client software for Windows NT to talk to Exchange server, just like a real Exchange user does. So, you must install the Microsoft Exchange client for Windows NT on the LoadSim client before you get underway.

> **NOTE**
>
> The same version of LoadSim also runs under Microsoft Windows 95. However, due to the way processes are implemented in Windows 95, LoadSim supports simulating only a single user. If you want to simulate multiple users with a single machine, run LoadSim under Windows NT Workstation or Windows NT Server. You can run only one instance of LoadSim for each LoadSim client machine.

By design, LoadSim does not disturb the Microsoft Exchange Server being tested. That way, Exchange Server thinks it is seeing a real user load, and you can measure how it performs. Because the LoadSim client is a separate machine from the Exchange Server computer, and because LoadSim uses the Exchange Client software to talk to Exchange Server, the LoadSim users are treated like real users by Exchange Server.

There are other features incorporated into LoadSim that make it act like real users. The idea is to minimize the number of performance artifacts caused by LoadSim itself. You want the load imposed to be as natural as possible.

For example, there are realistic "think times" built into the LoadSim users. These delays simulate the time users spend typing, reading, or whatever, before they actually perform a task, such as sending mail or opening a folder.

The artificial user names produced by LoadSim are not in any particular pattern. This ensures that there are no unfair efficiencies gained by Exchange Server processing names that are similar or follow a pattern.

Finally, there is also a random element in the LoadSim users, making the load they generate less regular so LoadSim doesn't cause predictable patterns of performance—but not so much that LoadSim won't generate reproducible results.

These are just a few features LoadSim has, but they illustrate the fine line to walk in designing such a program.

OK, enough LoadSim theory. Let's move on to some of the more practical aspects of the program.

LoadSim User Profiles

In LoadSim, there is the concept of a user profile. The profile of a user determines how much load that simulated user places on Microsoft Exchange Server. There are three user profiles—Light, Medium, and Heavy—that represent three classes of users that come "stock" in LoadSim. They are listed in Table 29.1.

Table 29.1. Default LoadSim user profiles.

LoadSim User Attribute	Light	Medium	Heavy
LENGTH OF A DAY (hours)	8	8	8
READING MAIL			
New mail (times/day)	12	12	12
Existing mail (times/day)	5	15	20
AFTER READING MAIL			
Reply to it	5%	7%	15%
Reply All to it	3%	5%	7%
Forward it	5%	7%	7%
Move it	20%	20%	20%
Copy it	0%	0%	0%
Delete it	40%	40%	40%
Do nothing to it	27%	21%	11%
RUN/LOAD MAIL ATTACHMENT (if one exists)	25%	25%	25%
SENDING MAIL			
New mail (times/day)	2	4	6
Save a copy in Sent Mail Folder?	YES	YES	YES
Number of random recipients	3	3	3
How often to add a Distribution List	30%	30%	30%
Message Priority	Normal	Normal	Normal
Delivery Receipt?	No	No	No
Read Receipt?	No	No	No
NEW MAIL MESSAGE CONTENT			
Text-only, no attachment			
1KB body (ups1K.msg)	90%	64%	50%
2KB body (ups2K.msg)	0%	17%	10%
4KB body (ups4K.msg)	0%	4%	5%
1KB mail body, with attachment			
10KB attachment (ups10Kat.msg)	10%	5%	10%
Embedded bitmap object (upsBMobj.msg)	0%	2%	5%
Word attachment (upsWDatt.msg)	0%	2%	5%
Excel attachment (upsXLatt.msg)	0%	4%	5%
Embedded Excel object (upsXLobj.msg)	0%	2%	10%

continues

Table 29.1. continued

LoadSim User Attribute	Light	Medium	Heavy
SCHEDULE+ CHANGES			
Changes per day	1	5	
Update Free/Busy information	No	No	No
Schedule File Size (Avg)	22KB	22KB	22KB
PUBLIC FOLDER ACTIVITY	None	None	None
APPROXIMATE MESSAGE TRAFFIC (per user, per day)			
Total mail received	22.94	66.30	118.89
Total mail sent	4.70	14.18	30.67
Mail sent as New mail	2.00	4.00	6.00
Mail sent as a Reply	1.05	3.76	13.03
Mail sent as a Reply to All	0.60	2.67	5.82
Mail sent as a Forward	1.05	3.76	5.82
Average # recipients for each mail	4.88	4.68	3.88

Don't be confused by all the attributes and their associated values. If you don't know what an entry means, don't worry—it should become evident by the end of the chapter. Each of the attributes is needed in order to properly simulate an Exchange user.

These three user profiles give you an idea of the different loads you can place on Exchange Server with LoadSim. More importantly, you can now analyze these user loads and determine which one fits best into your organization.

NOTE

The calculated daily user load figures are based on the values in the table. For example, if you increase the amount of new mail sent per day, the calculated numbers go up accordingly.

The Heavy profile is most useful as a stress test rather than as an actual user test. It does not represent a realistic user profile, because its load is so intense. However, if you need to pound on your server to test its limits or to see if something in software breaks, the Heavy profile is a good way to do it.

The Medium profile most closely reflects users in "e-mail–intensive" environments who rely on their e-mail systems. A good example of this profile is a Fortune 500 corporate e-mail user who depends upon e-mail as a regular, integral part of corporate communications. This also makes it a good practical upper limit, or worst-case scenario, for estimating the number of users LoadSim can support. In other words, if the Exchange Server can support 300 Medium users with acceptable client response time and server performance, you can plan to support 300 real users on the server in real life.

The Light profile most closely reflects those users who employ e-mail sometimes or irregularly. A good example is a user at a smaller company or at a company that has just started using e-mail. The users do not rely heavily on it yet, so their usage pattern is light. The converse of Medium users, Light represents a good practical best-case scenario for many circumstances.

> **TIP**
>
> Of course, you aren't stuck with only three canned profiles in LoadSim. They're mainly there to get you started and to provide a common frame of reference for comparing LoadSim data to other LoadSim data. Arguably, the most powerful feature of LoadSim is that user profiles can be configured to mirror your particular users. In this sense, LoadSim is infinitely configurable. Well okay, maybe not infinitely. But there are many combinations.

For example, suppose your users receive about 30 e-mails per day and they sent around seven. Most of the messages are short, but once in awhile, there is an attachment. Looking at the LoadSim users, you find your users are close to the Light LoadSim profile. In fact, after a few tweaks of parameters, you can simulate your users very closely. All you have to do is configure LoadSim to reflect those exact characteristics, and you can generate a realistic picture of your user load. This helps you to predict server performance and assists you in selecting proper server hardware.

How Many Users Can I Simulate?

So your next question might be, "How many users can I simulate?" A good question. There are two answers.

First, the limit to the *total* number of users you can simulate is dictated only by the number of LoadSim clients you have and by the number of actual users supported by Microsoft Exchange Server. It is possible, for example, to simulate 20,000 users—if you have enough LoadSim machines and a powerful enough Exchange Server.

Second, the actual number of users a *single* LoadSim client can simulate depends upon the class of hardware it's running on. As I said before, you have to be running Windows NT, so factor that in. Table 29.2 shows some typical hardware recommendations for a LoadSim client.

29

UNDERSTANDING AND USING LOADSIM

Table 29.2. Hardware recommendations for a LoadSim client running MAPI.

User Type	Quantity per Client	Minimum Recommended Hardware
Light	Up to 50	Pentium/66, 32MB RAM, 1 disk
Light	Up to 100	Pentium/66, 48MB RAM, 1 disk
Light	Up to 200	Pentium/90, 64MB RAM, 1 fast disk
Medium	Up to 50	Pentium/100, 32MB RAM, 1 disk
Medium	Up to 100	Pentium/100, 48MB RAM, 1 fast disk
Medium	Up to 200	Pentium/133, 64MB RAM, 1 fast disk
Heavy	Up to 50	Pentium/100, 32MB RAM, 1 fast disk
Heavy	Up to 100	Pentium/133, 64MB RAM, 1 fast disk

CAUTION

These estimates are conservative, but I don't recommend exceeding these numbers of simulated users per LoadSim client if you want a valid user load to be produced on the Exchange Server computer.

Furthermore, if you plan to rely on the score produced by a particular LoadSim client, do not simulate more than 100 users of any profile on that client. If you attempt more users, your score will likely be skewed higher than it should be. The higher score will make Exchange Server appear as though it is performing worse than it really is. However, if you stay within the guidelines listed in Table 29.2, the user load placed on the server will still be accurate. The result? Although the score on the LoadSim client is inaccurate, the Exchange Server performance data remains valid. In fact, this is a way to squeeze more simulated users out of fewer machines. See the sections "Configuration Example 1" and "Configuration Example 2," later in this chapter, for more on this idea.

Finally, you should realize that when you simulate a significantly higher number of LoadSim users on a single client—for example, 300 or more—the LoadSim client itself will eventually bottleneck, especially running the MAPI protocol. If this happens, Loadsim will not produce the intended load on the Exchange Server computer. The result is that both the LoadSim score and the Exchange Server performance data will be completely unusable.

You may be able to get away with more users per LoadSim client with the other protocols, such as NNTP, LDAP, or POP3. This chapter covers the MAPI (Exchange) protocol.

Suppose you want to simulate 500 Light users on your Microsoft Exchange Server. There are a couple of ways to go about properly configuring your LoadSim clients and gathering data. These techniques are discussed further in the section "Techniques for Gathering Useful Data," later in the chapter.

Configuration Example 1

If you want to rely on the score produced by each LoadSim client in the test, you should not exceed 100 LoadSim users per client. Therefore, according to Table 29.2 you would need five LoadSim clients, each configured with at least a Pentium/66, 48MB RAM, and a hard drive. This is an optimal configuration for testing 500 Light users, although it might not be optimal for your budget. However, with this configuration you would be able to use the score from all five LoadSim clients, so the score would be more reliable statistically. See "Use Scores from Multiple Clients," later in the chapter, for more about this approach.

Configuration Example 2

Alternatively, you could get by with using only three LoadSim clients for this test. Using the preceding guidelines from Table 29.2, to simulate 500 Light users you need at least three LoadSim client machines: two to support 200 users each with a Pentium/90, 64MB RAM, 1 fast hard disk; and one to support 100 users with a Pentium/66, 48MB RAM, 1 hard disk. All three LoadSim clients would place the proper load on the server, but you would use only the score from the LoadSim client running 100 users. The score produced by the other two LoadSim clients will be higher, so disregard them. See "Use a Dedicated Monitor Client," later in the chapter, for more about this approach.

Bear in mind these are not hard and fast rules, but guidelines based on experience. You can always monitor your LoadSim client with PerfMon to see whether it is getting overloaded. The two most crucial areas to watch on the LoadSim client are network utilization and CPU utilization, in that order. Because LoadSim is simulating usage for many Exchange users, these system resources are usually the first ones to get used up on the LoadSim client. When they do, LoadSim no longer generates the load you think it is. As a result, your performance result is skewed.

What Should I Look at in a LoadSim Run?

There are basically two items to glean from a LoadSim run against Microsoft Exchange Server:

- The load placed on Exchange Server
- The response time (score) of the LoadSim client

Observing the load placed on Exchange Server is the more complex of the two. Windows NT Performance Monitor is the best overall tool to accomplish this. There are PerfMon objects and counters that are generic to Windows NT and those that are specific to Microsoft Exchange Server. These tell a large part of the story about how your server is faring under the load.

Of course, you don't have to run LoadSim to monitor these counters. They are also useful for observing a server under a real user load. There are some preconfigured PerfMon workspaces that are installed with Microsoft Exchange Server. These are covered in more detail in Chapter 27, "Monitoring and Preventing Problems." If you need to keep an eye on things, become familiar with them.

The second task to do is analyze the *score* on the LoadSim client. This represents LoadSim's main performance metric. The score is simply an indication of the average LoadSim client response time, in milliseconds. This is covered later in the section called "Analyzing the LoadSim Score."

The LoadSim Screen

Figure 29.1 depicts a LoadSim 5.0 screen during execution. If you used LoadSim 4.0 you'll notice some changes, but for the most part you should recognize it. I will spend some time in this chapter going over how things work in this version.

FIGURE 29.1.

A typical LoadSim screen during a run contains much useful information.

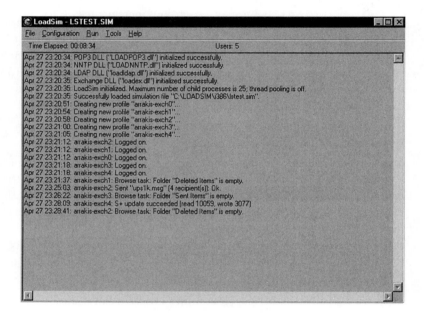

As you can see, there is a lot of information presented to you. At the top of the screen, there are two fields: Time Elapsed and Users. Time Elapsed is simply how long the test has been running. Users shows how many LoadSim users are logged on from this LoadSim client.

If you look in the body of the screen, there is some useful information there, too.

The first four lines represent something new for LoadSim 5.0: multiple protocols. In this screen, POP3, NNTP, LDAP, and Exchange—or MAPI—protocols are loaded. As I mentioned at the onset of this chapter, you will have to get the non-MAPI protocol support directly from Microsoft. But I wanted to show it here so you'd know what it looks like.

The next two lines represent some initialization information. LoadSim is configured to run with a maximum of 25 processes. That means that no matter how many LoadSim users you simulate with this client, only 25 processes will be spawned. Although I don't recommend changing it, this is configurable. I cover it later in the section called, "Setting LoadSim Options." On the next line, the SIM file LSTEST.SIM is loaded, which contains all the simulation settings for this test.

For simplicity, the run shown in the figure simulates only five LoadSim users. In the next five lines, you see LoadSim creating messaging profiles for those five users because they weren't already in the Registry. The next time LoadSim is run, this won't be necessary.

The next five lines show the five LoadSim users successfully logging on to the Exchange server. This shows up in every run, so you can see the users are logged on. As they log on, the number beside the Users field at the top of the screen is incremented.

In the final five lines you see some actual LoadSim user activity.

Each line shows the activity detail for each LoadSim user. For example, in the last entry you see the date and time (hh:mm:ss) of the activity, followed by the LoadSim user name, followed by the activity detail. In this entry, at 23:28:41, the user called `arrakis-exch2` performed a task where it browsed its Deleted Items folder for existing messages, and found there were no messages there. Guess I need to run Initialize Database, covered later in the section, "Initializing the Exchange Database." If the database is initialized properly, LoadSim won't find empty folders like that.

> **NOTE**
>
> During a LoadSim run, the default is to write all this data to log files LOADSIM.SUM, LOADSIM.OUT, and LOADSIM.LOG. There is a utility that comes with LoadSim called LSLOG that enables you to analyze the scores from a LoadSim log. There is more on this later in the section called "Analyzing the LoadSim Score."

29

UNDERSTANDING AND USING LOADSIM

How to Use LoadSim

So far, this chapter has covered basic LoadSim topics in order to give you a foundation for the rest of the chapter. Because the best way to learn something is usually to jump in and try it, I have set up an example scenario in the next section. Here, you look at the details of how to install, configure, and run LoadSim.

Sample LoadSim Scenario

In the example, Microsoft Exchange Server is up and running. But before you deploy it and put real users on it, including your boss, you might think it's a good idea to see how it holds up against the required user load. I tend to agree.

There are two main requirements for your test scenario:

1. The first requirement is to ensure that a single server sufficiently handles 300 users that closely match LoadSim's Medium user profile. Performance is not an exact science, so close is good enough. You just want to make sure the server doesn't fall over and die when you turn users loose on it, right?

2. The second requirement is to have response times of one second or less. This is a standard value, and users generally don't get impatient if response time stays in this range.

This example looks at the simplest case, where there is only one server in the Exchange organization. There are parameters in LoadSim that enable you to do multiple server tests, but I focus on the single server scenario because that covers the majority of the parameters. If you understand those, it is an incremental step to configuring LoadSim to do a multiple server test.

Collecting the User Profile Parameters

To collect the user profile parameters, let's review the ones introduced earlier in Table 29.1. Table 29.3 shows the required parameters for a Medium user, which is the target. The table goes through the areas in LoadSim where all these parameters are set, so if you want to change some of them for your specific requirements you'll know where to do it.

> **TIP**
>
> It's a good idea to create a blank form with each of these parameters on it. Then you can fill in the blanks with the proper parameters for your user requirements. That makes it easier to configure LoadSim for your specific user profile.

Table 29.3. User profile for a Medium user.

LoadSim User Attribute	Medium
LENGTH OF A DAY (hours)	8
READING MAIL	
New mail (times/day)	12
Existing mail (times/day)	15
AFTER READING MAIL	
Reply to it	7%
Reply All to it	5%
Forward it	7%
Move it	20%
Copy it	0%
Delete it	40%

LoadSim User Attribute	Medium
Do nothing to it	21%
RUN/LOAD MAIL ATTACHMENT (if one exists)	25%
SENDING MAIL	
New mail (times/day)	4
Save a copy in Sent Mail Folder?	YES
Number of random recipients	3
How often to add a Distribution List	30%
Message Priority	Normal
Delivery Receipt?	No
Read Receipt?	No
NEW MAIL MESSAGE CONTENT	
Text-only, no attachment	
1KB body (ups1K.msg)	64%
2KB body (ups2K.msg)	17%
4KB body (ups4K.msg)	4%
1KB mail body, with attachment	
10KB attachment (ups10Kat.msg)	5%
Embedded bitmap object (upsBMobj.msg)	2%
Word attachment (upsWDatt.msg)	2%
Excel attachment (upsXLatt.msg)	4%
Embedded Excel object (upsXLobj.msg)	2%
SCHEDULE+ CHANGES	
Changes per day	5
Update Free/Busy information	No
Schedule File Size (Avg)	22KB
PUBLIC FOLDER ACTIVITY	None
APPROXIMATE MESSAGE TRAFFIC (per user, per day)	
Total mail received	66.30
Total mail sent	14.18
Mail sent as New mail	4.00
Mail sent as a Reply	3.76
Mail sent as a Reply to All	2.67
Mail sent as a Forward	3.76
Average # recipients for each mail	4.68

29

UNDERSTANDING
AND USING
LOADSIM

Now that you've collected the required data for your test user profile, you are ready to configure LoadSim.

> **NOTE**
>
> LoadSim provides the capability of simulating public folder tasks. The focus in this example is configuring for e-mail tasks, but configuring for public folders is very similar and uses similar principles. Along the way, where appropriate, I mention specific public folder options so they aren't totally unfamiliar when you're finished.

Installing LoadSim

Installing LoadSim on a machine is easy. There are two parts:

1. First, you must install the Microsoft Exchange Client software for Windows NT, which is covered in Chapter 14, "Installing Microsoft Exchange Clients." This is crucial, because LoadSim cannot talk to Microsoft Exchange Server on its own—it must have the client software.

2. Next, you install the LoadSim software. There is no setup program; it's a simple matter of copying the files to a directory on the LoadSim client's hard drive.

As I mentioned at the beginning of the chapter, LoadSim is not included on the Exchange Server 5.0 CDs. You can request a version with full MAPI support directly from Microsoft. In essence, it is equivalent to that shipped with Exchange Server 4.0.

Copy these files to a directory on your LoadSim client's hard drive, for example, \LOADSIM. For convenience, you can make a shortcut for LoadSim in a location of your choice in Windows NT. I usually put it in the same group as the other Microsoft Exchange client stuff.

Configuring and Running LoadSim

There are several main steps in configuring LoadSim. This section goes through them one by one to get LoadSim up and running:

1. Configure the LoadSim Test Topology properties.
2. Configure distribution lists.
3. Configure the LoadSim Test Properties.
4. Create the LoadSim Test Topology, import users into Exchange.
5. Set LoadSim options.
6. Save your work and LoadSim settings.
7. Initialize the Exchange database.
8. Run the test.

When you bring up LoadSim for the first time after installing it, you see a screen like Figure 29.2.

FIGURE 29.2.

The initial LoadSim opening screen looks like this.

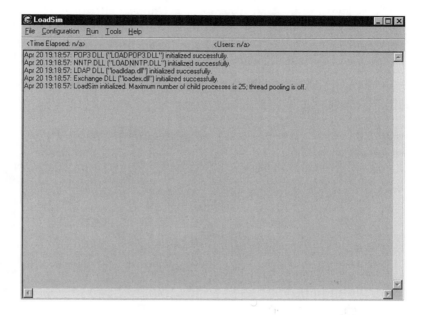

Fortunately, the way LoadSim is structured, you go through the Configuration, Run, and Tools menus pretty much in order to get up and running. So although there's a lot of information in some of the menus, bear that order in mind and you won't go wrong.

At this point you have a blank slate with LoadSim. From here, it's a matter of filling in the menus and saving your work.

TIP

LoadSim 4.0 had the capability of configuring a single LoadSim test (.SIM file) to simultaneously support multiple LoadSim clients. As it pertains to this example, you could specify the test to contain three LoadSim clients and to simulate 300 users. When you ran the test, LoadSim would automatically know to divide the clients evenly between the three machines. The result is that each of the three LoadSim clients would simulate 100 LoadSim users.

This capability has been removed from LoadSim 5.0, but the feature should be included in a future revision. For now, you must manually configure each LoadSim client individually, with its own .SIM file and its own set of LoadSim users to simulate.

29

UNDERSTANDING
AND USING
LOADSIM

Configuring LoadSim Topology Properties

The *topology properties* are the first thing to configure in LoadSim. Don't let the name bother you. Topology is just a fancy name for specifying the infrastructure of your test, such as the name of the server(s) under test, public folder configuration, quantity of clients and client protocols, and distribution lists. The topology properties are very important, however, because they are the basis for the remainder of the test configuration.

From the Configuration menu, select Topology Properties. Figure 29.3 shows the resulting properties sheet.

FIGURE 29.3.

The topology properties are ready to be configured.

Right now there's nothing there, so you're going to add the relevant information about the server to be tested. Select the Add button, and the Server Properties sheet appears, displaying the Type tab. After you fill in the blanks, it looks like Figure 29.4.

FIGURE 29.4.

The Server Properties Type tab provides a place to enter information about the server to be tested.

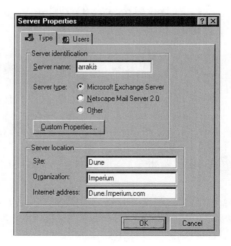

There are two parts to complete in the server properties, the Type tab and the Users tab. You must enter the information about the Exchange Server to be tested in the Type tab before you can continue to the Users tab. The organization, site, and server text boxes must be entered exactly as you configured Microsoft Exchange Server.

CUSTOM PROPERTIES FOR PUBLIC FOLDERS

If you are setting up for public folder tasks, you need to put some information in the dialog box accessed by the Custom Properties button. Configuration is pretty simple. Basically, you just tell LoadSim how many root folders and non-root folders you want, how deep you want the folder tree to be, and how many messages you want in each folder. This information will be used by LoadSim when you run Public Folder Initialization.

After you complete the Type tab, you can open the Users tab, which provides a place to configure the number of LoadSim users in the topology. The completed Users tab is shown in Figure 29.5.

FIGURE 29.5.

The Server Properties Users tab provides a place to enter how many users you want to configure.

29

UNDERSTANDING
AND USING
LOADSIM

NOTE

Note that the number of users specified here is not *necessarily* the number of users this particular machine will simulate. Bear in mind that in this property sheet you are configuring the properties of the *topology* for the entire test, not just for this machine. You'll get to configuring the number of users for this particular machine shortly.

If you have LoadSim configured to support client protocols in addition to MAPI—such as LDAP, NNTP, and POP3—you can specify the mixture of users the topology will have for each protocol type. This test uses 300 clients with the Exchange (MAPI) protocol only, so don't worry about the other protocols in this example.

After you click OK, you return to the Test Topology dialog box. The entry you just made is listed as shown in Figure 29.6.

FIGURE 29.6.

The Exchange Server to be tested is now listed in the topology properties.

Notice it shows the name of the server along with the site, organization, and number of users. This becomes important later, because the number of users entered here dictates the number of users available when you are configuring the test. You see that later in this section.

Click OK to close the dialog box, and you are ready for the next step.

LOGON SECURITY

In this version of LoadSim, Microsoft added the ability to configure which NT user account the LoadSim user would use when it logs in. The default is to use a separate account for each user, because that's the way it would work in the real world—each user would have his or her own NT user account. However, sometimes it's convenient to be able to use one NT account for all LoadSim users. I recommend using the default.

Configuring Distribution Lists

Using distribution lists (DLs) is an optional part of any LoadSim test. But because the example user profile says the user adds a DL to the address list 30 percent of the time, you need to ensure that use of DLs is enabled. You don't configure the 30 percent usage here—this is where you turn DLs on and configure their content.

Open the Configuration menu, and select Distribution Lists. Figure 29.7 shows the dialog box.

You see that the default is for DLs to be enabled, so leave the Use distribution lists box checked. Also, you find some customization parameters for DLs here:

- The DLs per site entry configures how many distribution lists you can have in the site. Here, the default is 30. Keep in mind that a given recipient might be in one or more DL.

- The last three entries configure how many users are on each of the DLs. You can specify whatever you want, as long as it doesn't exceed the total number of users you have. Here, the average number of recipients on the DL is the default, 10. Changing this number affects the calculated number of e-mails sent and received in a day.

Click OK and move to the next step.

Configuring LoadSim Test Properties

Configuring test properties is the central part of LoadSim. So pay attention to this part.

From the Configuration menu on the main LoadSim screen, select Test Properties. You are presented with the Test Properties dialog box, as shown in Figure 29.8.

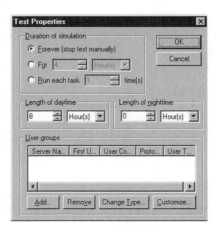

- Settings in the Duration of simulation section determine how long the test runs. The default is to run Forever, which means until you manually stop it.

- Setting the test to run for a certain number of hours is useful for unattended tests, because LoadSim stops the test automatically.

- Running each task a specified number of times is used mainly for stress testing, because LoadSim executes the tasks as quickly as possible the number of times you specify. I rarely use this setting.

- Length of daytime specifies how long LoadSim's artificial "day" will be. In other words, this is the span of time in which LoadSim user tasks will be performed. The Length of nighttime is how long each LoadSim user will "rest" before restarting another day's work. In this case, the LoadSim users will work for eight real hours, take no rest, and start again the next day. Just the kind of users bosses love.

> **CAUTION**
>
> Be careful messing around with Length of daytime. Although it's not obvious here, understand that for Light, Medium, and Heavy users, a LoadSim day is based on 8 hours. That means they are supposed to complete their assigned tasks over a span of 8 hours. Why is that important? For example, if you were to specify 4 hours for Length of daytime, LoadSim would cram an 8-hour workload into 4 hours, effectively doubling the stress your LoadSim users impose on the server. If you want to run the test over only one LoadSim day, configure the Duration of simulation to be 8 hours, and LoadSim will stop the tests automatically after one full day. Or, you could configure the Duration of simulation to be Forever, and you would have to stop the tests manually. In both cases, however, the load imposed by LoadSim would be correct according to the user load specifications.

If you are familiar with LoadSim 4.0, you will notice that there are no tabs for configuring the many test parameters. With this version, you access them through the Customize button at the bottom. I'll get to that in a minute, but for now notice that there is nothing in the list in the User groups section. You need to add something there before you do anything else.

Click the Add button to add a user group to the list. This will be where you specify the main parameters about the test. Figure 29.9 shows what the resulting dialog box looks like:

- Server specifies the name of the Exchange server that the test will run against. Our server is called arrakis.

- Protocol specifies which protocol this Exchange client will use. In this case, Exchange (MAPI) is the selected protocol. Only protocols for which you configured users in the Topology Properties are available here.

- User type specifies the LoadSim user profile to use. Our test calls for the Medium profile.

- First user specifies which one of the 300 users this client will start simulating. Here, it will start with the first user, user 0.

- Number of users specifies how many users this LoadSim client will simulate. As our test calls for, this client will simulate 100 users.

- Users covered is automatically calculated based on First User and Number of Users. This LoadSim client is simulating users 0–99.

FIGURE 29.9.

Edit User Group is the dialog where the main test parameters are specified.

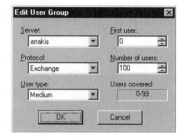

This dialog box is one of the most important as to how the test runs. Its contents determine how many actual LoadSim users are simulated on this particular LoadSim client, regardless of the total number of LoadSim clients. It also controls which users *send* e-mail and which users *receive* e-mail.

Let me repeat that, because this is new in version 5.0. The contents of this tab determine how many actual LoadSim users are simulated on this LoadSim client, regardless of whether you have one LoadSim client or twenty. The selected users send e-mail only to themselves.

New to
Version 5.0

29
UNDERSTANDING
AND USING
LOADSIM

TIP

In LoadSim 4.0, you could specify both senders *and* recipients. In LoadSim 5.0, the users you choose to be in a User Group send e-mail only to themselves. For example, suppose you have 500 total LoadSim users in the Exchange Directory, and you configure a single User Group that contains the first 100 users (0-99). If you run the test using this one User Group, only users 0-99 will send and receive e-mail; users 100-499 will neither send *nor* receive e-mail. The one caveat is that Distribution Lists can contain any of the 500 users, so e-mail sent to a DL could end up going to users 100-499.

TIP

Here's something that may not be very obvious to the casual observer. You might have been expecting a simple parameter somewhere that says, "Number of users to simulate." There's not one—the Edit User Group dialog is where you specify it. More people get confused about this than anything else.

Click OK to return to the Test Properties dialog. Now you will see your entry in the list. Some of the headings are cut off due to size limitations of the dialog box, but you can see a summary of the selections you just made for the user group. Figure 29.10 shows the result.

FIGURE 29.10.

The Test Properties lists the User groups that have been configured.

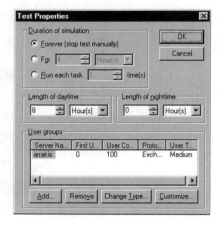

Customizing LoadSim Test Properties

At this point, you're actually ready to run the test. In fact, since your scenario calls for the Medium profile, you can really skip this section because there are no parameter changes needed. You specified a Medium User Type in the prior section, so you don't want to mess things up. However, you may want to customize the parameters sometime in the future, and it's good to know where various parameters and settings are specified. So let's take a couple minutes while we're at this point and look at customizing.

Again, if you're not interested in customizing, you can just skip to the section, "Creating the LoadSim Test Topology."

As you might have guessed, the Customize button on the Test Properties dialog is how you access the custom properties. There are several property sheets in there, and probably the best way to understand them is to go through and discuss each one.

Click the Customize button, and the Customize Test property sheet appears, as shown in Figure 29.11.

There are three tabs on this property sheet:

- The Tasks tab provides a way to customize all the parameters for the various user tasks. This chapter focuses most of your attention on this part of customization.

■ The Test/Logon tab provides a way to configure how the LoadSim user handles logging on and off during the test.

■ The Initialization tab provides a way to configure how the Exchange database will be set up during the Initialize Test process. See the section in this chapter, "Initializing the Exchange Database," for more information.

FIGURE 29.11.

The Customize Test property sheet is the way to customize an individual test.

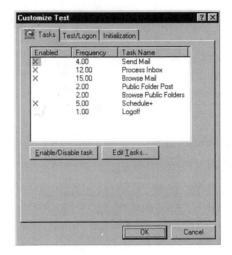

Customizing Tasks

The most important tab, and the one that you will be most concerned with when customizing, is the Tasks tab. In Figure 29.11, you can see seven tasks listed. Each of these tasks represents some activity the LoadSim user can perform on the Exchange server.

You can enable or disable any of these tasks by highlighting the line with the desired task and clicking the Enable/Disable button. This way, you can set up any task mix you want. In Figure 29.11, there are four tasks enabled: Send Mail, Process Inbox, Browse Mail, and Schedule+. Indeed, these four are the most common tasks a LoadSim user will perform. They are likely the most common tasks your real-world users will perform, too.

Finally, you see a number in the Frequency column, which represents the number of times each day the particular task will be executed. For example, this LoadSim user will send mail 4 times a day, process the Inbox 12 times a day, browse mail 15 times a day, and perform a Schedule+ action 5 times a day.

All this stuff is configurable, so let's take a look at how to do it. Click on the Edit Tasks button. You will see the Task Properties sheet, as shown in Figure 29.12.

29

UNDERSTANDING
AND USING
LOADSIM

FIGURE 29.12.

*The Task Properties
sheet is where all the
LoadSim tasks are
customized.*

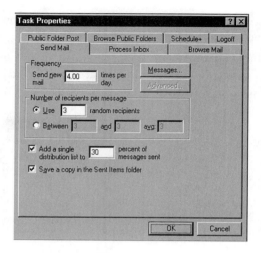

There are seven tabs on this property sheet, which correspond to the seven tasks shown in Figure 29.11. You will normally leave the parameters in the tabs as default because they need to be changed only when you want to customize something. Some of the tabs pertain to public folders, which you aren't concerned with in this test.

The first tab you see, shown above in Figure 29.12, is the Send Mail tab. This is a key tab in configuring the user load as it pertains to sending e-mail. The values in these boxes directly correspond to the values in the user profile. They also change as you select the Light, Medium, and Heavy User Type from the Edit User Group dialog:

- The profile calls for sending new mail four times a day, reflected in the Frequency entry at the top. The messages LoadSim uses to send are configured in the Messages button. See the "Configuring Messages" sidebar for an explanation of how messages are configured in LoadSim.

- Number of recipients per message defaults to Use 3 random recipients. That means there are always precisely three recipients of an e-mail, but they are selected randomly. The Between option is probably more like the real world, because you don't always send e-mail to the same number of users; there is usually a range.

- Thirty percent of the time, a distribution list is added to the address list. Note that this is *in addition to* the addressees in the above section, not in place of.

- A copy of the sent e-mail is saved in the Sent Items folder, as specified in the original user profile.

CONFIGURING MESSAGES

What content does LoadSim use when it is sending e-mail? There are a set of default files that comprise the content of messages, and you can even customize LoadSim with your own if you like. The explanation here pertains both to e-mail and to public folder file activity.

Figure 29.13 shows the Send Message Options dialog that appears when you click the Messages button in the Send Mail tab.

When a user composes an e-mail or sends an attachment, these are the source files that are used. Basically LoadSim pulls them into the mail message when it needs them.

How does LoadSim know when it needs a file? If you notice, each file is assigned a weighting. As you highlight the number in the Weight column, you can modify it if you like. This weight determines how often the file is used in e-mail.

Each file was originally created using the Microsoft Exchange Client and it is saved in *message format*. This format is specific to Microsoft Exchange and it contains everything in the mail message including text, formatting, attachments, embedded objects, and so on. With this in mind, you don't have to explicitly specify to LoadSim how many messages have attachments, embedded objects, rich text, and so on. Because all these attributes are included in the .MSG file, specifying a weighting for the file implicitly handles this all in one location.

If you add the weightings for all the .MSG files, they should equal 100. They don't have to, but that makes it easy to figure the percentage of how often each file is used by LoadSim. This percentage maps directly to the original user profile parameters in Table 29.3.

(If you look closely in this case, the default Medium weightings actually add up to 95, but assume they add up to 100 for simplicity's sake.)

Here is an explanation of each file in the list, and what it contains. They are each located in your LoadSim program directory:

- UPS1K.MSG, weighting = 60. This message contains 1KB of rich text and no attachment. It is sent 60% of the time.
- UPS2K.MSG, weighting = 16. This message contains 2KB of rich text and no attachment. It is sent 16% of the time.
- UPS4K.MSG, weighting = 4. This message contains 4KB of rich text and no attachment. It is sent 4% of the time.
- UPS10KATT.MSG, weighting = 5. This message contains some rich text and a 10KB attachment. The amount of text isn't as important as the fact that it has an attachment. In this test profile, it is sent 5% of the time.

continues

continued

- UPSXLATT.MSG, weighting = 4. This message contains some rich text and a Microsoft Excel attachment. It is sent 4% of the time.
- UPSWDATT.MSG, weighting = 2. This message contains some rich text and a Microsoft Word attachment. It is sent 2% of the time.
- UPSBMOBJ.MSG, weighting = 2. This message contains some rich text and an embedded bitmap object. It is sent 2% of the time.
- UPSXLOBJ.MSG, weighting = 2. This message contains some rich text and an embedded Microsoft Excel object. It is sent 2% of the time.

You can use your own files if you want. Simply create them with the Microsoft Exchange Client and save each file in message format (.MSG). Then add them into this list with the Add Files button and assign them a weighting. Likewise, you can remove files if you don't want to use them anymore.

Finally, Set priority and Request receipts sections control what percentage of messages have priorities and receipts configured. These options apply only to the mail that is sent each day.

FIGURE 29.13.

The Send Message Options dialog is where you customize how files are used in LoadSim.

Customize Inbox tab is a key section that controls the part of the user load pertaining to reading new e-mail. The numbers in these boxes directly correspond to the values in the Medium user profile in Table 29.3. They also change as you select the Light, Medium, and Heavy usage profiles. Figure 29.14 shows the Process Inbox tab.

FIGURE 29.14.

You configure the number of times a day new messages are read with the Process Inbox tab.

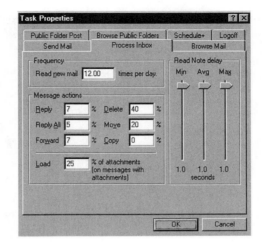

The following provides a description of the Process Inbox tab:

- The Frequency section controls how many times the user reads new mail during a day. Remember, a day is defined in the Test Properties sheet. Keep in mind that each user is constantly getting sent mail from other users, and if you run Initialize Test, there is existing mail for the user to read. So in this case, no matter how many new e-mails the user gets in a day, only twelve are read.

- The Message actions section is one of the key parts of this tab. Again, the numbers in the user profile map exactly to these entries. The Load entry refers to how often an attachment is actually opened and loaded. This might simulate a user opening an Excel spreadsheet, for example, which is attached to the mail message.

- The Read note delay section is generally left at 1 second. This represents how long the user pauses to read the mail message before closing it.

The Browse Mail tab is a counterpart to the Process Inbox tab. Whereas Process Inbox has to do with new messages, Browse Mail has to do with existing read messages. It's configuration is simple, as shown in Figure 29.15.

The Frequency of 15 times a day reflects the value specified in the Medium user profile.

The next two tabs—the Public Folder Post and the Browse Public Folders tabs—pertain to LoadSim user activity with public folders. They work just like their private store counterparts, so configuring them is easy.

29

UNDERSTANDING AND USING LOADSIM

Figure 29.15.

The Browse Mail tab is where you configure the number of times at day existing messages are read.

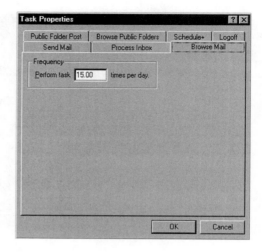

The Public Folder Post tab is configured much like the Messages button in the Send Mail tab. And the Browse Public Folders tab is configured much like a combination of the Process Inbox tab and Browse Mail tabs.

Next is the Public Folders tab. The settings in this tab are disregarded in the test because you didn't check the Public Folders Task Option in the General tab.

Figures 29.16 and 29.17 show the Public Folder Post and Browse Public Folders tabs.

Figure 29.16.

The Public Folder Post tab of Task Properties.

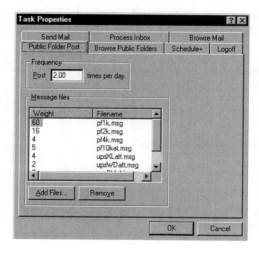

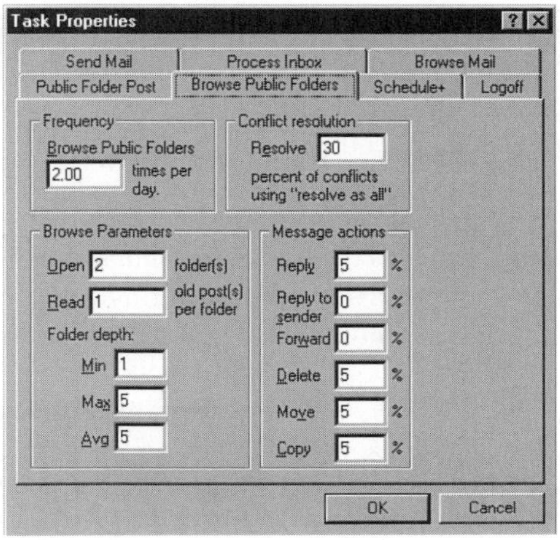

FIGURE 29.17.

The Browse Public Folders tab of Task Properties.

Most of the parameters function similarly to sending mail. For example, there is the number of times each day to post into public folders—sort of like how many times to send new mail—along with a frequency for browsing and message actions for after reading.

> **NOTE**
>
> If you disable the corresponding public folder activities on the Tasks tab of Customize Test, these settings are disregarded by LoadSim.

Next is the Schedule+ tab. This tab is very simple and it doesn't require much attention. It is self-explanatory, especially if you are familiar with Microsoft Schedule+. Figure 29.18 shows the Schedule+ tab.

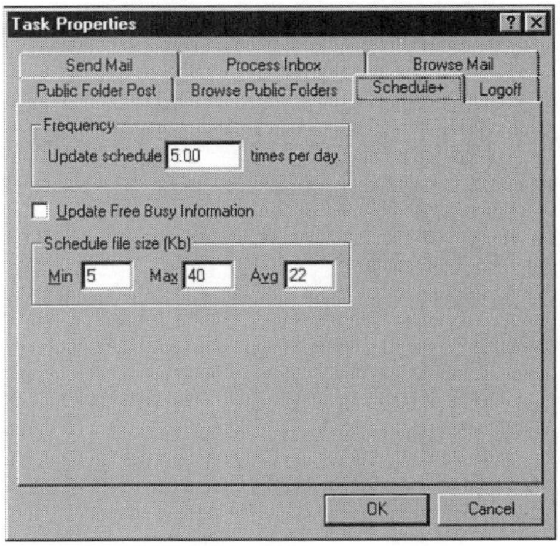

FIGURE 29.18.

The Schedule+ tab is where Schedule+ actions are configured.

> **NOTE**
>
> If you disable the Schedule+ Actions Task Option in the Tasks tab of the Customize Test property sheet, these settings are disregarded.

Next is the Logoff tab. This tab is also very simple and it doesn't require much attention. Basically, it is how you specify the number of times the LoadSim users are to log off from Exchange Server during the course of a day. Figure 29.19 shows the Logoff tab.

FIGURE 29.19.

The Logoff tab, where the clients are configured to log off each day.

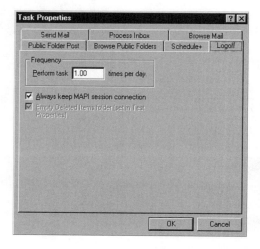

> **NOTE**
>
> If you disable the Logoff task in the Tasks tab of the Customize Test property sheet, these settings are disregarded.

Unless you want to simulate users completely logging off the system, you will want to keep the MAPI session alive while the LoadSim users log off from Exchange. There is extra overhead associated with having to reestablish the MAPI session each time.

Customizing Test/Logon

Back to the Customize Test property sheet—you have two more tabs left. They won't be as involved as the Tasks tab, I promise.

There are two main sections to this tab: the Logon/off properties section and the Test report section, as shown in Figure 29.20.

FIGURE 29.20.

The Test/Logon tab, where you specify overall logon and logoff settings.

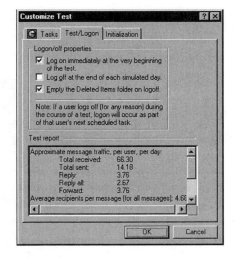

The Logon/off properties section covers overall user configuration regarding logging on and off:

- Log on immediately at the very beginning of the test is always left checked. That way, as soon as you start LoadSim, the users immediately start logging on.

- Log off at the end of each day is optional, but if you run only a single day's worth or less, it doesn't matter. It only lets you control how the users behave with regard to logging off and on. This actually works in addition to the number of times you specify for the users to log off each day.

- Empty the Deleted Items folder on logoff is usually left checked, but you should set it to the way you prefer the users to perform the test.

The Test report section gives an overview of how much work the LoadSim user will be producing. Its purpose is purely informational. These numbers are calculated based upon the various parameter settings, and they should correspond precisely with the Medium user setting in Table 29.3 for this example.

For example, if you select the Light user profile, these numbers change to reflect that selection. If you change the average number of recipients in the Distribution lists dialog box, the numbers change. There are several parameters in LoadSim that affect the calculations on this page.

Customizing Initialization

Before running any tests against Exchange Server, you need to initialize the database with some information. In effect, you're seeding the Exchange database store. This is covered in the section "Initializing the Exchange Database." Somewhere you have to set the properties for

29

UNDERSTANDING
AND USING
LOADSIM

Initialize Test—this is the place. When you run Initialize Test, the LoadSim client will begin methodically stuffing mailboxes on the server with messages according to the parameters specified for Initialization in the Test Properties, as shown in Figure 29.21.

FIGURE 29.21.
*The Initialization
property tab is where
the Initialize Test
parameters are set.*

All the parameters for Initialize Test were automatically set when you added a User Group with a specific User type to the Test Properties. The numbers shown in the figure directly relate to whether you selected a Light, Medium, or Heavy User type. Bottom line: you don't have to worry about it, but I wanted you to know where the Initialization properties are coming from.

Creating the LoadSim Test Topology

All right, you're ready to leave the Configuration menu and move to the Run menu. Previously, you configured the topology. The next thing to do is create the topology.

This step creates a list of users and DLs and attempts to import them into the Exchange Directory. LoadSim does not use any users or mailboxes you might have created in your Exchange Server. Instead, it creates its own user names and mailboxes (and distribution lists, assuming you enabled the use of DLs). After everything is imported into the Exchange Directory, the recipients are placed in their own recipient container in the Exchange Directory called LoadSim. That keeps things nice and tidy so as not to interfere with any existing Directory entries.

Open the Run menu and select Create Topology. There is no further configuration to do; the file containing the user list is generated and the Directory import is attempted automatically.

TIP

When you create the topology, LoadSim automatically *attempts* to perform a Directory import of the LoadSim users it just generated. Figure 29.22 shows a sample output screen, beginning with Begin Topology Creation and ending with End Topology Creation.

The automatic import usually works fine, but in some cases, as depicted in the figure, you will get an error message during the import. The most common cause is that your LoadSim client does not have administrative privileges on the Exchange server where the import is being attempted. If you look in the Application Event Log, you will see the reason for the failure.

Don't worry. If this happens, the user information has been created in a .CSV file, but you will need to perform a manual import (as it suggests on the next to last line on the screen) to get the information into the Exchange Directory. This process is explained next.

FIGURE 29.22.

The directory import file is created by LoadSim.

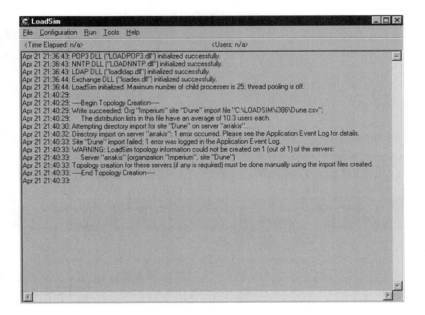

The topology creation should happen almost instantaneously in this case, because you are creating only 300 users. Even if you are creating more users, the process is still very fast because LoadSim is just creating an ASCII file. The directory import takes a bit longer.

During the topology creation, a file is created and its name is listed on the screen. This file is a .CSV (comma-separated variable) ASCII text file, and it is the appropriate format for importing into the Microsoft Exchange Server Directory. The file, DUNE.CSV in this case, is located in the directory where you installed LoadSim. It is named using the convention *site.csv*. It contains the 300 user names and the 30 distribution lists specified earlier. This is the file you will import into the Directory.

Now you are ready to import the files. My preferred method is to copy DUNE.CSV to the \EXCHSRVR\BIN directory on the Exchange Server machine itself or share the file over the network. Then perform a directory import from the Tools menu of the Microsoft Exchange administrator, as shown in Figure 29.23.

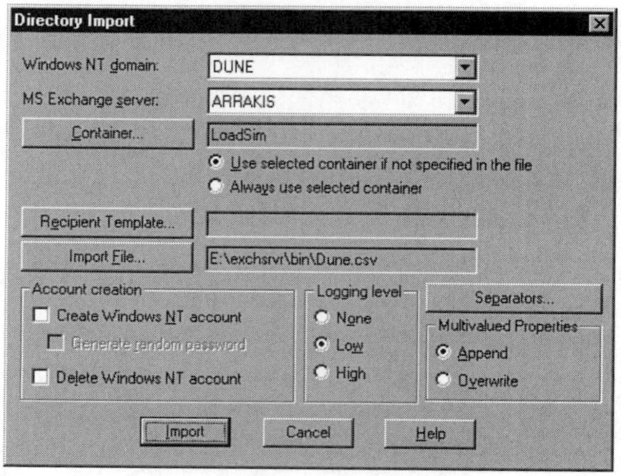

FIGURE 29.23.

The Directory import can be performed from the Exchange Administrator program.

If you use this method, it is not necessary to create NT accounts for each imported LoadSim user. With this method, you also don't have to worry about setting site permissions for the LoadSim client to allow the import.

TIP

Providing you don't change the test configuration, each time you run Create Topology, LoadSim creates an identical output file. For example, if you run it for 300 users, then again for 400 users, the first 300 entries for both sets of files are identical. This is because LoadSim uses a consistent algorithm to generate user names. If you examine the .CSV file, you see user names derived from the Exchange Server name. It's usually best to generate the maximum number of users you plan to use, import them all, then run your tests. That way you won't have to mess with it later when you're trying to get some testing done.

Setting LoadSim Options

You're almost finished configuring the test, but take a minute and review the LoadSim program options. You might find some of these useful.

When you select Tools | Options from the LoadSim menu, there are two tabs that appear on the Options property sheet. These enable you to configure various global LoadSim parameters. These values are stored in LOADSIM.INI, which is kept in the %SystemRoot% directory.

The first tab is Logging, as shown in Figure 29.24.

FIGURE 29.24.

Set general LoadSim logging options using the Logging tab.

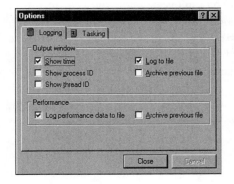

Here, you can specify general operating parameters for LoadSim:

■ The Output window section contains checkboxes that determine what appears on the LoadSim screen during a run. The default selections are shown here, and I usually leave them. Show time is important because you want time stamps on all the activities. Showing process and thread ID information is optional, and they should be selected only when you are trying to debug a problem or something. Log to file is a good idea if you want a log of exactly what is printed on the LoadSim screen during the run. The default filename is LOADSIM.OUT. If you don't want to overwrite previous LOADSIM.OUT files, check the Archive previous file checkbox.

■ Log performance data to file is an important entry. You must enable this if you want to generate logs that can be parsed with LSLOG to produce scores. Typically, you want to overwrite old logs so you don't end up accidentally mixing them between separate runs. The default is LOADSIM.LOG. If you don't want to overwrite previous LOADSIM.LOG files, check the Archive previous file checkbox.

The second tab is Tasking, as shown in Figure 29.25:

■ Maximum number of LoadSim processes tells LoadSim how many instances of LoadSim processes to crank up. LoadSim can be a very resource-intensive program, so this should be left at a low number, such as 25. If you increase it too much, NT will create too many processes to be managed effectively, and that will impact the accuracy of LoadSim.

29

UNDERSTANDING
AND USING
LOADSIM

■ The Threads section is probably something you won't need to alter very often. Threads are managed by LoadSim itself, allocating a thread for each LoadSim user, so you usually will leave the Allow thread pooling checkbox unchecked. But there are times when you might want to use a pool of threads for all the users rather than one thread per user. LoadSim will calculate the optimum number of threads to use for you, but you can override it if you need to with the checkbox. The good news is that thread pooling allows LoadSim to scale better so it can simulate many more users on a single LoadSim client. The bad news is that it should be used only for clients that are mostly idle, such as POP3 and maybe NNTP. If you start messing around with this setting, you can adversely affect LoadSim's accuracy and spoil your test results.

FIGURE 29.25.

Set LoadSim tasking options using the Tasking tab.

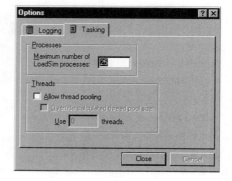

CAUTION

You should *not* enable thread pooling for Exchange (MAPI) clients. LoadSim users running the MAPI protocol need to have one thread dedicated to each of them. Thread pooling mostly applies to simulating users with Internet protocols, NNTP, POP3, LDAP, and so forth. Bottom line: don't change the thread pooling configuration unless you know what you're changing.

Saving Your Work and LoadSim Settings

Now you are completely finished configuring LoadSim, so don't forget to save your work. From the File menu, select Save, and you are presented with the familiar common dialog box. Give the file a name. For this example, name it LSTEST.SIM. Now your .SIM file is saved in your LoadSim directory for later use. Here's an overview of where LoadSim keeps different files:

■ A .SIM file contains the specific test information, such as the number of LoadSim clients, names of tests, test parameters, and so forth. Its format resembles that of an .INI file. You probably want to name the file something relevant to the type of test it represents, such as MED100.SIM if your configuration is for simulating 100 Medium users. LoadSim defaults to saving this file in the LoadSim home directory, but you can save it anywhere.

- ■ .SUM, .LOG, and .OUT files contain the information described earlier. They are usually stored in the same directory as the LoadSim program files.

- ■ LOADSIM.INI contains overall program settings set in the Options property sheets, such as maximum LoadSim processes, recently opened files, and so on. Note this file is not stored in the LoadSim directory; it is stored in %SystemRoot%.

Initializing the Exchange Database

Now that you have fully configured LoadSim and there are names in the Exchange Server Directory, you need to initialize the Exchange database for the test. Currently, there is nothing in the mailboxes of the users who were imported, so Run | Initialize Test is a way to populate the e-mail database—called the private store or PRIV.EDB—with some data. This simulates having some mail in each mailbox in the database as though the LoadSim users had been using it all along.

If you recall our Medium profile, the LoadSim users read existing mail 15 times a day. The Initialize Test process is where that existing mail comes from. Also, having some data in the database doesn't give the Exchange store an unfair performance advantage of dealing with an empty database.

NOTE

Running Initialize Test adds data to PRIV.EDB. If you plan to run LoadSim against a live database, be aware that this adds data to your live database in the LoadSim container. You can always delete the data, but just be aware of it.

Basically, when you run Initialize Test, the LoadSim client begins methodically stuffing mailboxes on the server with messages according to the parameters specified for Initialization in the Test Properties, as shown previously in Figure 29.21.

You can initialize the public store—PUB.EDB—with messages, just as you can the private store. When you run Initialize Test, it will ask you whether you want to initialize public folders too. Click Yes if that's what you want to do. This worked differently in LoadSim 4.0, where there was an explicit Public Folder Initialization process. With LoadSim 5.0, it's a part of Initialize Test.

New to Version 5.0

It's time to actually run Initialize Test. Open the Run menu and click Initialize Test. LoadSim starts initializing the database. You can run this on a single LoadSim client, walk away, and come back when it's finished. Then you'll be ready to run the real tests and start gathering some data.

29

UNDERSTANDING AND USING LOADSIM

At the Medium Usage setting, Initialize Test increases the PRIV.EDB database by about 2MB for each user. So for 300 users, expect to end up with about a 600MB database. The Light Usage setting is about 500KB for each user.

Running the Test

Finally, you're ready to run the test. Assuming your Exchange Server is up and running, and you've prepared properly, things should go OK.

Open the Run menu and select Run Simulation. LoadSim starts churning away, and you see processes start up and LoadSim users start to log on. This activity shows as increasing numbers at the top of the screen beside Users. There isn't any other activity on the screen at first unless LoadSim needs to create Exchange profiles for its users. When all the users are logged in, profiles are created, and LoadSim has started its work, you might see something like Figure 29.26.

FIGURE 29.26.

All five LoadSim users are logged in and have started their tasks.

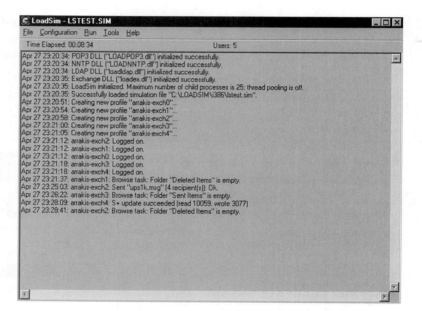

Depending on what you want to accomplish, you let the test run for a fixed amount of time. If you want reliable scores, let LoadSim run for at least five hours. Then you can use the LSLOG utility to parse the LoadSim logs. The next section goes into this in more detail.

Analyzing the LoadSim Score

By now, at least five hours have passed and your LoadSim run is over. Now it's time to analyze the data LoadSim has gathered so you can see how the Exchange Server performed.

LSLOG is the utility to parse the LoadSim logs and give you the score information for the run. It is included with LoadSim as one of the program executables. See Appendix B, "Command Reference," for the full command syntax of LSLOG.

By default, when you run LSLOG against a LoadSim log, it shows you the 95th percentile score. So, if you are simulating 100 users and the score shown by LSLOG is 1100, that means 95 of the simulated users are experiencing an average response time of 1.1 seconds or better. You must use LSLOG to derive the score that you will use for any data analysis.

Obtaining a set of scores becomes useful if you want to see how fast Exchange Server is servicing client requests. Furthermore, if you impose performance goals of subsecond client response time, you expect the score to show around 1000 or less during a LoadSim run.

Figure 29.27 shows a typical output of LSLOG.

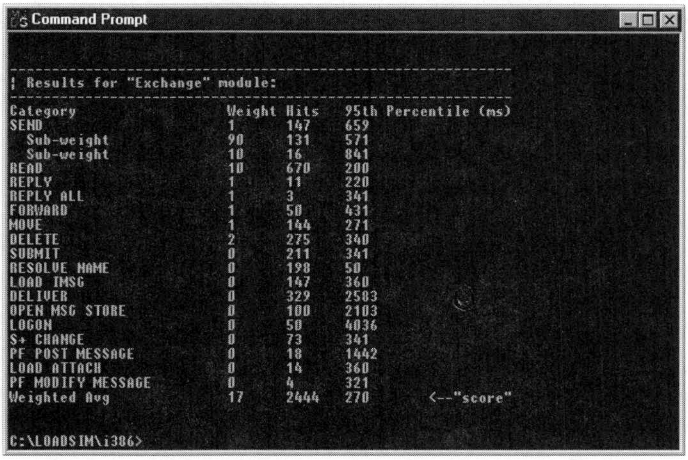

FIGURE 29.27.
LSLOG provides a summary of the LoadSim score for a run.

How did we do on our example run? Assuming Figure 29.27 represents the output for our example test, you can see from the Weighted Avg line at the bottom, indicated by "score," that the 95th percentile score is 270. That is to say that 95 percent of the users can expect to experience a response time of .27 seconds or less. Realistically, this means that most users will experience half-second response time, or better, for most operations. Not bad.

This result is well below the subsecond requirement imposed in the example criteria, so the conclusion from the run is that the Exchange Server is providing adequate response time for the users. Assuming there is nothing weird in the NT Performance Monitor data on the Exchange Server computer, you are ready to deploy 300 users on the server—with confidence.

NOTE

There are other scores listed here. They are broken out for each activity type in LoadSim. You can see the weighting each task is given and the number of times the task occurred (hits), as well as the respective 95th percentile score. The final average is most definitely a weighted average.

Also note that the data is from the Exchange module. That is, the LSLOG summary is derived from the performance of MAPI clients. If you were running other protocols in LoadSim, you would see a similar summary for each protocol.

ABOUT LOADSIM DATA

Due to both the ways LoadSim operates and the fact it is simulating many clients, allow LoadSim to run for more than an hour—preferably five hours—before using the score as a meaningful number. LoadSim takes about an hour to reach steady state, so if you throw away the first hour—referred to as "hour 0"—and use the second through fourth hours (hours 1–3), the scores are the most usable. LSLOG makes this process easy. See Appendix B for the syntax.

Even so, there is still some margin of error in the score. Typically, the longer you let LoadSim run—up to a point— the more accurate the score is. Identical runs don't produce identical scores, but they are within a hundred milliseconds. Often, they are within 50 or less. The theoretical minimum score (depending on the Exchange Server hardware) is in the 100–200 range.

As LoadSim runs, conditions may tend to degrade over long periods of time. For example, if you allow a test to run for days on end, you will likely see fluctuations in the response-time trends. So longer is not necessarily better when it comes to LoadSim runs. The idea in taking the first five hours of data is to get a good sampling of how the system is expected to run with no degraded conditions.

COMPARING RESULTS FROM LOADSIM 4.0 AND LOADSIM 5.0

Compatibility

It is not recommended that you compare the results obtained from LoadSim 4.0 and LoadSim 5.0. They will likely not be exactly the same. In other words, if you perform identical runs on identical LoadSim clients on identical Exchange servers, the scores produced by LoadSim 4.0 and 5.0 will probably be different, the LoadSim 5.0 scores usually being a lower number.

This difference in score is not the result of something wrong with one or the other versions of LoadSim. And it does not invalidate any of your prior tests with LoadSim 4.0. Rather, there were changes in the LoadSim 5.0 engine to make it more efficient and more accurate in the load it imparts on Exchange. I recommend you use LoadSim 5.0 because it's more accurate, if for no other reason.

Techniques for Gathering Useful Data

There are different ways to use LoadSim to gather data that are useful to you. Three are summarized in this section, but as you work with LoadSim—or even as you read this—you might think of other methods. Try them out and see what works for you.

Use Scores from Multiple Clients

One technique for gathering accurate scores is to run multiple, identically configured LoadSim clients. The idea is to ensure that each LoadSim client is producing accurate scores, then average them for more accuracy.

Using the example of testing 300 users, and based on the recommendations in Table 29.2, you need three LoadSim clients. Each machine is a Pentium/100 with at least 48MB RAM and a fast disk. Each LoadSim client can easily handle 100 Medium users, and the score reflected is reliable because the LoadSim client is not bottlenecked.

Run LSLOG as explained, and take the average score produced by each LoadSim client to produce the final score for the run. If things are running correctly, each score should be within 50 points, plus or minus, of the average.

This technique is probably the best, but it requires a lot of hardware resources, especially if you intend to simulate many clients. It is also more trouble to keep track of all the .LOG files as the number of LoadSim clients increases. However, the scores produced using this technique are probably as accurate as they can be.

Use a Dedicated Monitor Client

Another technique for gathering accurate LoadSim scores is to dedicate a LoadSim client as a score machine. The trick here is to ensure that the dedicated LoadSim client is not overloaded. In fact, it should be under-loaded. This machine is always assured of having a fair score regardless of whether the other LoadSim clients are overloaded.

This technique is based on the idea that although a heavily loaded LoadSim client might not produce an accurate score, it still produces an accurate *load*. Up to a point, this is true. That is, you probably can't accurately simulate 500 Medium users on a single LoadSim client, but you can squeeze more users out of a LoadSim client if you don't care about the score the client produces.

For example, run a test with multiple LoadSim clients, each one simulating a number of users greater than Table 29.2 recommends—but still a reasonable amount. In the example scenario with 300 Medium users, simulate 250 of the 300 users with two slightly lesser machines—for example, at least Pentium/66 machines with at least 32MB RAM and a fast disk. They don't even have to be configured the same. That's 125 users for each LoadSim client rather than 100. Then, with a separate LoadSim client—for example, a Pentium/100 with 64MB RAM and a fast disk—simulate the remaining 50 users. This is the dedicated monitor client. Only use the score from this monitor client and disregard the scores from the other two.

This technique is useful if you don't have quite enough hardware to configure multiple identical high performance LoadSim clients. Because the LoadSim clients that produce the bulk of the load don't have to be identical, and because you only need to have one high performance machine from which to get the score, this is a good option. However, you don't get the benefit of averaging scores. Still, scores compared from identical runs should be within 100 points or so.

Plot a Users-Per-Server Graph

Of course, the most useful piece of information that can be gleaned from this entire exercise is the number of users a server supports. That's the question everyone wants to answer anyway. So use the techniques outlined above and plot your own graph.

Taking the sample scenario one step further, say you want to see how much "headroom" the server has. You already know the example Exchange Server yields a score of 270 for 300 Medium users. But how does it do all the way up to 800 Medium users? Simple. Reconfigure the test for 100 users, repeat the process to get another data point. Then repeat for 200, 400, and so on, until you test through 800 users. Skip 300, of course, because you already have it. Then plot the data points. The resulting graph might look like Figure 29.28.

FIGURE 29.28.

A typical Users per Server graph might look like this.

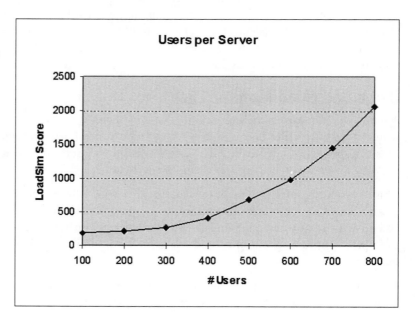

You can get useful information from a Users per Server graph at a glance. It's clear to see that the current hardware on the Exchange server easily takes you to 600 users before it starts encroaching on the subsecond response time requirement.

Correlate Scores with PerfMon Data

The data points for a Users per Server graph take time to generate, but the resulting graph is an excellent picture of how the server performs. To augment this picture, I recommend gathering PerfMon data during each LoadSim run, too. I find it very interesting and insightful.

Observe the PerfMon data from the LoadSim run to see what's going on in your server. A graph of the data can easily be viewed using PerfMon itself, or you can export the data into Excel for detailed analysis. You can correlate the scores LoadSim produces with the Exchange server's PerfMon data from each run, and soon you will begin to spot trends for which subsystems in the server are beginning to get used up. At that point, you have excellent insight into what's going on with Exchange. Then you're well on your way to mastering the performance of your server.

Stay Consistent

One final word about conducting your performance tests: stay consistent. If you select a method of gathering data, producing scores, or running tests, stay with it. Consistency is the single most important aspect of getting meaningful performance data. Any variables introduced into the system can cause havoc and produce results that have you scratching your head. Remember, performance is not an exact science; there's some subjectivity to it as well. If something does not make sense, it's probably because something is wrong somewhere. Run the test again just to be sure. The time invested to be sure of yourself is always much better than proceeding on a false premise. And if the results look good, and they're repeatable, you are probably on the right track. Good luck!

Summary

This chapter covers a lot of ground. You learned what's new with LoadSim 5.0. The user interface has changed a lot, along with several other notable things in the program. You also learned about the philosophy behind LoadSim, how to actually use LoadSim, and how to collect and analyze data in a useful fashion. Finally, you got some tips and advice from me about how to proceed with your own performance testing.

After reading this chapter, it should be apparent that LoadSim is quite a powerful tool, but along with that power comes a degree of complexity. However, it is clear that if you are willing to invest the time and effort, the results can be quite useful. You also see that LoadSim is not really as complex as it appears at first glance. After examining the program, each item is there for a reason and it makes sense.

Now you are ready to set up LoadSim on your own machines and start running simulations. And because of the information provided in this chapter, you should have minimal problems. As an additional resource, you could refer to a helpful Microsoft white paper that covers LoadSim and the concept of users per server. The paper is entitled, "MS Exchange Performance: Concurrent Users per Server," and it was available beginning with the May 1996 edition of Microsoft TechNet. You can also refer to the Microsoft Knowledge Base article Q155417, revised April 29, 1997.

CHAPTER 30

The Exchange Electronic Forms Designer

By Diane Andrews and Rick Andrews

IN THIS CHAPTER

Most organizations (if not all) use custom forms in some way to communicate, move, tabulate, survey, and record information in the workplace, whether the workplace is an in-home small business or a worldwide enterprise. Often, you or another individual within the company is responsible for creating some of these forms because your company has specific needs that require customized forms (that is, forms that are not readily available from a supplier). Creating these forms the old-fashioned way meant simply drawing boxes on a piece of paper (with text identifying each box's purpose) in an organized collection, printing multiple copies of these forms, and making them available to others in your workplace.

Microsoft Exchange Forms Designer (EFD), a new application that comes with Microsoft Exchange, provides a way to create electronic forms (forms that are sent electronically across the computer network) to replace the old-fashioned forms to which you are accustomed. The Forms Designer does the same things for electronic forms that your pencil, typewriter, and printer do for paper forms. In this chapter, you use EFD to create an Expense Report form that you can use in your company. The techniques demonstrated in this chapter are applicable to any type of EFD you will want to design.

What Is EFD?

The Exchange Forms Designer (EFD) is a tool that enables you to easily create custom e-mail forms for your organization without writing a single line of code; you don't have to be a programmer to design Exchange forms! EFD provides a simple, easy-to-use, drag-and-drop interface that enables you to visually create your forms. A simple wizard gets you started, and EFD then makes it easy for you to design the form and install it in Exchange, making it available to everyone in your organization.

If you want to add functionality to your Exchange form that is beyond what is provided in EFD, EFD creates forms that are *extensible*. This means that after you create a fully working Exchange form application with EFD, you can go further and make custom modifications to it using the Microsoft Visual Basic programming language. After you design your form with EFD, EFD produces the Visual Basic source code that builds the form. You can ignore this source code and let EFD do everything for you automatically. However, if you are a programmer, or someone interested in programming, you can view the source code to study the internals of e-mail messaging in Microsoft Windows, modify the source code, and rebuild and install the form with added functionality or special customization. Note that the subject of extending your Exchange forms with Visual Basic is covered lightly at the end of this chapter in the section, "Extending the Expense Report Form with Visual Basic," but is not considered within the scope of the topic discussed here. This chapter primarily focuses on developing forms without programming. For more information on extending forms, read the *Application Designer's Guide* that came with your Microsoft Exchange Forms Designer.

What Are Exchange Forms?

To many, it is not obvious what exactly an Exchange form is. Assuming that you are familiar with what a standard e-mail message is (see Figure 30.1), start by recognizing your standard e-mail message as nothing more than a simple form that contains only envelope fields (the place where you enter To:, Cc:, Subject:, and so on) and a single message body field (the place where you type or read your actual message).

Forms can be made up of several windows, and forms you design with EFD will generally have more than one. For example, a standard e-mail message you could create in EFD might have a Compose window, a Read window, a Forward window, and a Reply window. Each window represents a different view of the form for each context in which the form will be used (for example, a Reply window appears when you want to reply to an e-mail message; that is, you use this window to type in your reply). Together, the windows define the form.

FIGURE 30.1.

A standard e-mail form.

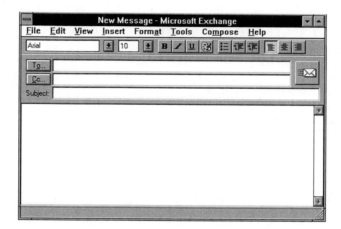

All you are doing with EFD is creating more functional forms that, besides the basic envelope and message body fields, might have list boxes from which users make selections, multiple text fields into which they enter data, or even picture boxes so you can decorate your form with pictures.

Exchange Forms in the Workplace

How do forms fit into the workplace? As the Exchange administrator, it is probably be your responsibility to address this problem in your organization. Generally, whenever you need to obtain information in an organized fashion, you should use forms. Several very useful forms ship with the sample applications that come with EFD. You'll also find several forms from independent Exchange form developers; some of these might be perfect for your organization. Because designing forms is so easy with EFD, you'll probably find that several people in your own organization will design them when the need arises (or even just for fun). But often, it will be up to you to determine what forms are needed and then to design them.

You can design a form for practically every type of activity in your organization—a form that enables employees to check out books from the company library; perform a company-wide inventory of computer equipment at everyone's workstation; conduct surveys, employment reviews, or job interviews; or disperse reports to all the employees. And you aren't limited to just your local workplace. If your business has people at remote locations, they can access the forms created by EFD, too. All they need is the Exchange Client running on their computer and a way to connect to the Exchange server (by WAN, modem, or ISDN).

After you've created a form, EFD makes it easy for you to install the form into the Exchange server so that all the Exchange users in your organization can send and receive the forms.

Administrator's Roles

As the Exchange administrator, you have certain roles to perform to incorporate EFD into your company. This section summarizes what these roles are. For more information, refer to your Exchange Server documentation.

Installing EFD

You need to install the EFD software before you can begin to design Exchange forms. You can find the installation files for EFD on the same distribution CD and subdirectory as the Exchange client software, under EFDSETUP. Note that EFD setup cannot be completed unless you already have an Exchange client installed.

From the \EFDSETUP subdirectory of the Exchange Client CD, run setup.exe. Choose the Typical setup option to install all of EFD's available features. This will include the installation of some of the sample applications that come with Exchange. These sample application files will be installed under \EFDFORMS\SAMPLES.

> **TIP**
>
> Opening these sample application files in EFD and examining them is an excellent way to familiarize yourself with how EFD can be used.

Other people in your organization who will be designing forms will also need to have EFD installed. We suggest you create a share point (a shared directory) on your Exchange server from which others can install EFD. To do so, simply copy the entire EFDSETUP directory from your CD to this share point.

Setting Up the Organization Forms Library

In order to make forms available for Exchange users, you must place the forms into a forms library that is available to your Exchange users. The Organization Forms library is such a library. Examples of other forms libraries are Personal Forms Library, Public Folder Library, and Personal Folder Library, but these are not necessarily available to all users. For example, forms installed into your Personal Forms Library are accessible only to you.

> **NOTE**
>
> A library is located in Exchange where you put your forms so users can access them. You can choose to have one library where all your company's forms are located, or you can make separate libraries to organize your forms according to topic, security access, departments, and so on.

Establishing an Organization Forms Library

You use the Microsoft Exchange Administrator to establish an organization forms library (see Chapter 12, "Installing Microsoft Exchange Server," for an overview of the Administrator program). (We assume use of the default name of "Organization Forms," but you can modify this name as you wish when you create the library.)

To create an Organization Forms Library, follow these steps:

1. Start the Exchange Administrator program.
2. Select Forms Administrator from the Tools menu. The Organization Forms Library Administrator dialog box will appear.
3. Click New. The Create New Forms Library dialog box will appear.
4. Select the appropriate language from the Language list.
5. Click OK.

The Organization Forms library you just established is now visible in the Organization Forms Library Administrator dialog box. Leave this dialog box open; next, you'll need to set permissions to use the Organization Forms library.

Setting Permissions to Install Forms in the Organization Forms Library

The permission level for the Organization Forms library is set to Reviewer by default. A user with Reviewer permission can read only existing items—similar to having read-only access to a file on your hard drive or on a network share.

As the administrator, you need to give yourself Owner permissions to the Organization Forms library so that you can fully administer your company's forms.

To do so, follow these steps:

1. Open the Organization Forms Library dialog box (see previous section) if it is not already open.
2. Select Organization Forms.
3. Click Permissions. The Forms Library Permissions dialog box will appear.
4. Click Add. The Add Users dialog box will appear.
5. Locate your Exchange Client user name in the list on the left.
6. Add your user name to the list on the right.
7. Click OK. You'll return to the Forms Library Permissions dialog box.
8. Select your name.
9. Set the Roles (under Permissions) to Owner.
10. Click OK.

You will now be able to perform every available administration task on the Organization Forms library, including the installation of forms.

Creating and Providing Exchange Forms

As the Exchange administrator, you might be responsible for providing forms to your Exchange users that they can use in their daily work to improve communication and efficiency in the workplace. Your first thought might be to create these forms yourself. However, you should be aware that there are other resources available from which you can obtain forms that can do the job you need. Besides creating the forms yourself, you might want to consider looking for other solutions, such as the Exchange Application Farm (see the section "Other Sources of Information" at the end of this chapter) page on the Web. The Exchange Application Farm is a place where you can find and contribute application forms for others to share. Other sites where you can locate consultants who develop Exchange form applications should be available.

Creating Folders

As the administrator, you will probably want to create public folders for some of your forms. Forms in public folders can provide information updates to the entire organization quickly and in one central location. You can build custom views for the public folders in the Exchange Viewer and enable users to see important information at a glance. When users post forms to a specially designed public folder, they can use the Exchange Viewer to quickly view the information from the forms.

Basic Design Process

The following is a quick overview of the entire design process involved in building a custom form with EFD. Later, in the section "A Sample Expense Report," you build a sample expense report Exchange application that takes you through this design process in more detail.

Planning a Form

As with any design process, the first thing you need to do is plan. Make sure you know what you want before you get started. What does the form need to do? What problem is it trying to solve? Where is this form supposed to go—to other users or a public folder? Do you want the recipient(s) to see the information in the form differently than the way the sender sees it? You should answer questions like these before you begin creating the form.

Using the Wizard to Create a Skeleton Form

Without EFD, creating forms can be extremely complicated if you are not a skilled developer familiar with Exchange messaging concepts. For this reason, EFD begins with a Wizard to help you establish the basics of your form. The Wizard asks you a series of questions about the type of form application you want to create and then it creates a skeleton "working" form ready for you to customize. It does the hard part and leaves the easy, fun part for you.

Adding Fields to the Form

The next step is an easy drag-and-drop operation. You choose fields, such as Entry fields, ListBox fields, and OptionButton fields, from the ToolBox window of EFD, add them to the window of your form, and position them as you want. Fields are the main elements that make up a form. They are used to display information and get input.

Setting Properties for Fields, Windows, and Forms

Just about everything in EFD has properties (for example, Font size, Background color, and Window name) to set. There are properties specific to the form, properties specific for each window, and properties specific for each field. In most cases, you should be able to use most of the default property settings that were initialized when you first created the object (form, window, or field). But you need to change some properties to fit the requirements of your individual form. You use the Property Inspector and the Field Appearance Palette to change most of the properties that need changing. The Property Inspector and Field Appearance Palette are discussed later in the sections "The Property Inspector" and "The Field Appearance Palette."

Finishing Up

After you have designed your form, you'll want to install it into the Exchange Server so your organization can use it. You do this by selecting Install from the File menu or by clicking the

Install toolbar button. Either action launches a four-step process that results in the final form. (By the way, unless you are a programmer who wants to extend the form with custom programming, you probably won't care much about these steps; the important thing to know is that when these steps are completed, your form will be installed and ready to use.) Here are the four steps:

1. Save Form to .EFP file.

   The file type used by EFD is called EFP. Your Exchange Forms Project (EFP) file is a database containing all the information needed to define the form's structure and functionality. Perform this step only if you have not manually saved your project by using the Save command in the File menu or clicking the Save toolbar button.

2. Generate VB Source Code.

   EFD next uses the information in the EFP file to generate Microsoft Visual Basic (VB) source code that implements the runtime version of your form. Until now, you've been dealing with the design-time version of the form. The *design-time* version of the form is what you use in EFD when you are designing the form. The *runtime* version is what your users will actually send, receive, post, and reply to on the Exchange network. The EFP file contains the information for both the design-time and runtime versions of the form.

3. *Compile VB Source Code.* Next, EFD compiles the VB source code into an EXE file that can be executed by Exchange. Note that you will not be able to easily run this EXE as a stand-alone application because it expects to receive commands (events) from Exchange that tell it what to do. Without these messages, no window will ever appear.

4. *Install Form.* Finally, the form is installed into the Exchange server and is available for use. Don't forget to test it thoroughly before everyone on Exchange starts using it.

That's the whole process from beginning to end. To summarize, you start by planning the form you want to design. You then use the EFD Forms Wizard to create a basic form to get you started. Next, you add fields and then set properties to customize the form to fit your design needs. Finally, you instruct EFD to generate and install your form.

You are now going to take a close look at EFD and look at the tools and methods it provides to make designing forms easier.

A Quick Tour of EFD

This section takes you through a quick tour of the features and tools in EFD that you'll use to design forms.

The Basic Windows of EFD

There are several important windows in EFD that you will use while you design your form. This section lightly touches on each one to give you a feel for the overall structure of EFD.

The Layout Window

The layout window is where you actually place the fields you want on your form. It represents a window of the final form itself, but at this point it has no functionality other than enabling you to place and position fields. Figure 30.2 shows the layout window with some fields already on it.

FIGURE 30.2.

The EFD layout window.

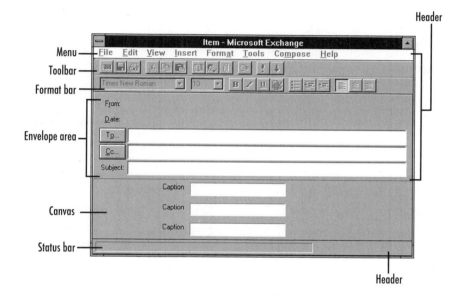

Note that there are several parts to the layout window. The *canvas* is where most of the design activity will take place. The canvas represents the body of your form. You choose fields from the toolbox and place them on the canvas. The *envelope* area is where your envelope fields go. Envelope fields are the From, Date, To, Cc, Bcc, and Subject fields that appear in an e-mail message so the user can enter and/or read header information regarding the message and its recipient(s). The *menu, toolbar,* and *status bar* on the canvas are nonfunctional, except that you can change the menu captions. These pieces are here mainly for cosmetic reasons to give you a feel for the final look of your form. Collectively, the envelope area, menu, toolbar, and status bar are referred to as the *header*, distinguished from the canvas. As you'll see later, you can hide the header to give you more room for working on the canvas.

The Menu Bar

The menu bar, not to be confused with the nonfunctional menu on the layout window, includes a toolbar and is where you can process commands that affect the layout window and other windows. (See Figure 30.3.)

FIGURE 30.3.

The menu bar.

The Toolbox

The toolbox is where you select fields to place on the canvas. It has two parts. The top part contains buttons from which you choose envelope fields, and the bottom part is where you choose body fields to place on the canvas. (See Figure 30.4.)

FIGURE 30.4.

The toolbox.

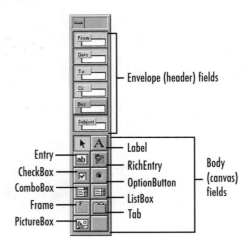

The Envelope Fields

You place envelope fields on the canvas by clicking the button of the envelope field you want. Clicking it again removes the envelope field. You cannot position these fields; they can only be turned on and off. Envelope fields are often referred to as *header* fields.

Body Fields

You add the body fields to the canvas by clicking the desired field in the toolbox and then clicking on the canvas. A field with default size is placed where you click the canvas. The individual fields are discussed shortly in the section "The Body Fields of EFD." Body fields are often referred to as *canvas* fields.

TIP

If you hold down the Ctrl key when you click the body field on the toolbox, that field becomes "sticky" and you can place several copies of this field on the canvas by repeatedly clicking on the canvas. Clicking anywhere outside the canvas or back on the toolbox causes this sticky mode to end and return to normal.

The Property Inspector

Each field you place on the layout window has several properties that you can customize. For example, you can change the caption, back color, size, and location of most fields. You also can set properties for each window that makes up your form and for the form itself. You set and view these properties using the property inspector (PI); it can be displayed from the View menu. There are three types of property inspectors: one for form properties (the Form PI), one for window properties (the Window PI), and one for field properties (the Field PI). Only one can be shown at a time.

All three PIs are made up of tabbed dialog boxes and are described in the following sections.

The Form PI

You set and view properties for your overall form in the Form PI.

On the General tab of the Form PI, you can change properties such as the name of your form and the icons associated with it.

On the Events tab, you can specify or view the action that will take place or the window to show when the user performs certain events (for example, clicking the Reply or Print button). These settings are called the form's Events Properties.

> **NOTE**
>
> *Events Properties* refers to a collection of properties that define how the form will react when certain events occur. For example, when Exchange tells you that a Print event occurred (for example, the user clicked the Print button on the toolbar), you will probably want to set the Print event's properties to print the active window. Figure 30.5 shows the General tab of the Form PI.

The Window PI

You set properties specific to each window in your form in the Window PI. You'll probably want to provide different windows that the users see when they are, for example, composing a new form to send as opposed to reading a form they just received. EFD enables you to create several windows for various purposes, and each has its own individual properties. Examples of window properties are the window caption, background color, and menu captions. Figure 30.6 shows the Menus tab of the Window PI.

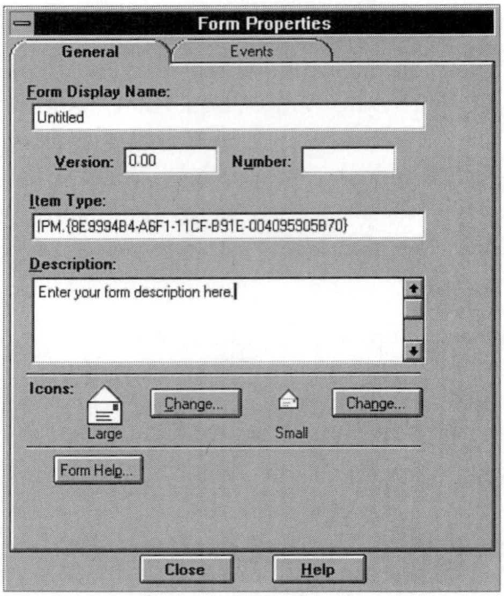

FIGURE 30.5.

*The Form PI showing
the General tab.*

FIGURE 30.6.

*The Window PI
showing the Menus tab.*

The Field PI

Each field you place on the canvas has its own properties to set or view. If you click on different fields of the canvas while the Field PI is displayed, the Field PI changes to reflect the properties of the selected field. As you change field types, the settings available also change to those appropriate for the selected field's type. For example, a CheckBox field will have a property setting for declaring whether the check box should be initially checked or unchecked; such a property wouldn't make sense for an Entry field that shows only text. The CheckBox and Entry fields are described later in the sections "The CheckBox Field" and "The Entry Field," respectively. Figure 30.7 shows the Format tab of the Field PI.

FIGURE 30.7.

The Field PI showing the Format tab.

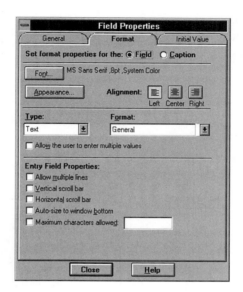

The Field Appearance Palette

Not all field properties can be set by the PI (for example, 3D and border properties can't be set using the PI). The Field Appearance Palette enables you to set the background and foreground colors of each field and modify its 3D or flat appearance. For example, you can show an entry field that has a very wide border with a raised 3D look to give it special emphasis. Giving it red text on a green background might be just what you want for the company's Christmas forms. Figure 30.8 shows the Field Appearance Palette. Note that the two rows of small boxes labeled Fore Color and Back Color each display a set of colors you can change for these properties.

FIGURE 30.8.

The Field Appearance Palette.

The Body Fields of EFD

There are ten field types, plus variations of some of the types, which you can place on the canvas (body) part of the form. Figure 30.4, earlier in this chapter, shows which toolbox button creates each of these fields. Figure 30.9 shows an example of each field, including some variations, after the field has been placed on the canvas. They will look different in the final runtime form (for example, the list box will probably be populated with items you specified in its properties), but their sizes and positions will remain the same in most cases. Note that some fields, such as the ComboBox field, can take on different appearances depending on their properties. Also, some fields (the Frame, PictureBox, and Tab fields) are known as *container* fields. A container field is a special type of field that can contain other fields. This is described in more detail in the section "The Frame Field."

FIGURE 30.9.
EFD field types.

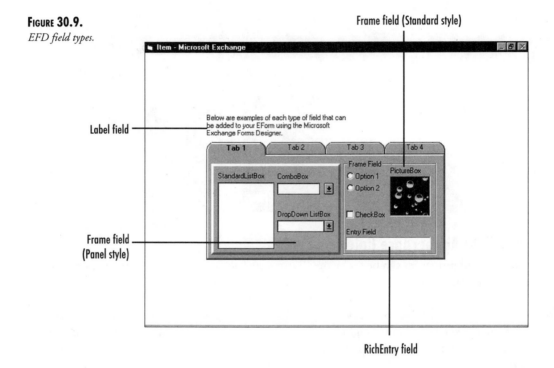

The Label Field

The Label field is a simple field for displaying read-only text on the canvas. The text will word-wrap if there is more text than will fit within the width of the field.

The Entry Field

The Entry field is a field in which the user can enter text. You will often use the Entry field when you want to require the user to enter formatted data, such as dates, currency, or numbers. You can also use it for entering plain text, but the RichEntry field (described next) is better suited for this purpose.

The RichEntry Field

You also use the RichEntry field to enter text, but unlike the Entry field, the user can change the font, color, size, and so on of individual characters within the field at runtime; text that can be changed like this is commonly referred to as *rich text*. You can also embed OLE objects, such as Excel spreadsheets, within the body of the RichEntry field at runtime. Note that at design time, the Entry field and RichEntry field appear identical. For this reason, only one is shown in Figure 30.9.

The CheckBox Field

The CheckBox field enables you to prompt the reader for simple yes/no type of input. It's a great field to use for surveys.

The OptionButton Field

The OptionButton field is also commonly used in surveys. Option buttons, unlike check boxes, operate together in groups. When you place an option button on the canvas, it is automatically contained within a Frame field (see "The Frame Field," later in this chapter). The OptionButton field cannot exist outside a Frame field. If you try to move it out of the Frame field and place it directly on the canvas, another Frame field will automatically be created to contain it. You can place multiple OptionButton fields within the same Frame field, and that is exactly what you want to do. When you have multiple option buttons within the same Frame field, only one can be selected at a time. Whenever you select another option button, the one currently selected becomes unselected.

TIP

If you want to make the option buttons appear as if they are not within a frame, you can set the properties of the containing frame to have no border or caption and a background color that matches the background color of the canvas (or the frame's container). This gives the appearance that the frame is invisible. The option buttons are still in a frame, but the frame appears invisible. To do this, follow these steps:

1. Place your option button on the canvas.
2. Display the Field Appearance Palette (Ctrl+A).
3. Select the first option button labeled None to make the option button non-3D.
4. Select the Frame field that contains the new OptionButton field.
5. Change the Frame Style to Panel in the Field PI's Format tab.
6. Display the Field Appearance Palette while the Frame field is still selected.
7. Click the blank button on the far right in the row of buttons labeled Width. (Refer to Figure 30.8.)

continues

continued

Your Frame field's background color will change to match the background color of the canvas (or container). If you later change the background color of the canvas (or container), the background color of the frame will also change to match, thus keeping it virtually invisible. It will not appear invisible, though, if you put a picture behind it.

The ComboBox Field

The ComboBox field gives you a field that can contain a list of items from which the user can select and/or enter his or her own new item. Note that when the user enters a new item, it is not added to the list, but it does remain in the entry part of the ComboBox. Whatever item the user selects or adds is displayed as the active item to the recipient of the form.

When first dropped on the canvas, the ComboBox has the Dropdown ComboBox style. You can change it, though, to a Standard List or Dropdown List field by changing its style property in the Field PI. The list box and drop-down list box styles enable you to add items to their respective lists at design time, but at runtime the users cannot type in their own choices as they can with the ComboBox style. Again, the selected item in the list remains the selected item when the recipient receives the form. Each style of the ComboBox field can be seen in Figure 30.9.

The ListBox Field

The ListBox field is exactly the same as the ComboBox field except that when it is dropped on the canvas it is initialized with the ListBox style instead of the ComboBox style. See "The ComboBox Field" earlier for more information.

The Frame Field

The Frame field is the first of the container fields. *Container fields* are fields in which you can place other fields. For example, Figure 30.9 shows a frame field containing two OptionButton fields, a CheckBox field, an Entry field, and a PictureBox field (described later in the section "The PictureBox Field"). These fields aren't merely positioned in front of the Frame field, they are actually contained by it. If you reposition the Frame field, all its contained fields will move along with it.

The Frame field can take on one of two styles, Standard or Panel, when you set its Frame Style property in the Field PI. In Figure 30.9, the frame on the right is the Standard style. To the left of the Standard style Frame field is a Panel style Frame field containing the three styles of the ComboBox (or ListBox) field. You can change the look of the Panel style to be either raised or inset 3D, or you can make it appear invisible by giving it no border at all using the Field Appearance Palette. When you remove the border from the Panel style, it takes on a new feature; its background color will now always match the background color of either its container or the canvas if it's not in another container.

Note that container fields can be contained within other container fields. This is called *nesting*.

> **NOTE**
>
> *Nesting* means that you place a field within another field. It is said that one field is nested within the other. Only container fields can nest other fields. Sometimes, the container field is referred to as the *parent* and the nested field is referred to as the *child*.

The Tab Field

When there is not enough room on the canvas to hold all the fields you need for your form, or you want to organize the fields on your form into logical groupings, the Tab field comes to the rescue. Like the Frame field, the Tab field is a container field, but with multiple containers. Only one container can be seen at a time, but you can easily switch from one to the other by clicking the tabs at the top of the field. By setting properties in the PI, you can change the number of tabs in your Tab field. You can change the captions of the individual tabs by clicking the selected tab's caption and typing in a new one.

> **NOTE**
>
> You can have only one Tab field per window of your form.

The PictureBox Field

The PictureBox field enables you to display a bitmap, icon, or metafile on your form. By setting properties in the Field PI, you can configure the PictureBox field to automatically size itself to the size of the picture or to stretch the picture to fit the size of the control. Like the Frame and Tab fields, the PictureBox field is also a container field in which you can nest other fields.

The Form Template Wizard

The Form Template Wizard is similar to other wizards you might have used with other software applications. By answering the Wizard's questions, you can create a template in which the number of windows, default envelope fields, form types, and form event properties are already defined. You then add fields and customize the properties for your fields, windows, and the form.

Form Types Created By the Wizard

There are two basic form types created by EFD's Wizard: forms to send information and forms to post information. As the names imply, a Send form is used to send information from point A to point B, and a Post form is used to post information in a specific location (most commonly in a public folder). See Figure 30.10 for an example of the Form Template Wizard.

FIGURE 30.10.

The Where will your information go? screen of the Wizard.

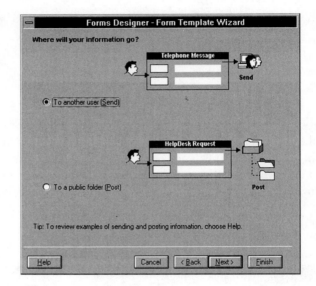

These two basic form types each fall into two categories: a Send category and a Reply category. Send and Post forms used for sending information are very straightforward to design and use. Send and Post Reply forms, though, are a bit more complicated, because to use them you must integrate them with another form—that is, the form to which you are replying. You must modify the other form's event properties to make this connection. The primary difference between the Send and Reply forms is the types and handling of envelope fields. A Reply form will automatically initialize some of its envelope fields. For example, it will automatically address the reply to the sender of the original message. A Send form's envelope fields will automatically be blank. (Note that you can change any of the settings using the Field and Form Property Inspectors—the settings discussed here refer to Wizard default settings.) Figure 30.11 shows the Wizard screen where you tell EFD whether your form will be used to send a new message or send a response.

After you become familiar with using EFD and setting form properties, Reply forms will not seem as complex. For more information on using Reply forms, refer to the *Application Designer's Guide* or EFD's online help.

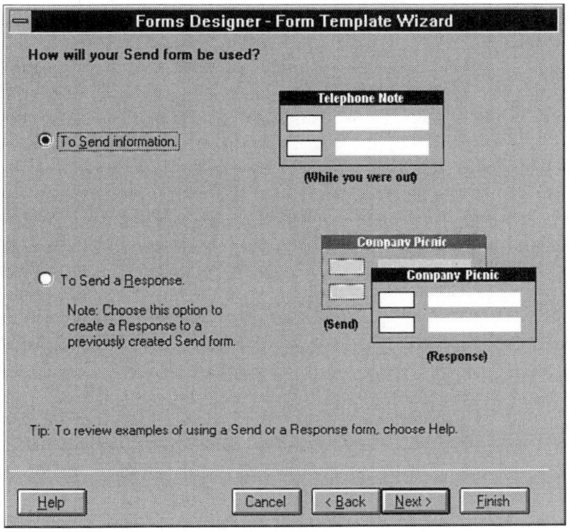

FIGURE 30.11.

*The How will your
Send form be used?
screen of the Wizard.*

Window Types Created By the Wizard

The Form Template Wizard can create a one-window form or a two-window form for both
the Send and Post forms. With a one-window form, you get a single window that is used for
both composing and reading a note. With a two-window form, you get separate windows for
composing and reading. You use the Compose window to compose the information to be sent
or posted. You use the Read window to view the information after it has been sent or posted.
The Read window also has additional fields (such as From) that are initialized with information from the Compose window. Figure 30.12 shows the Wizard screen in which you specify
whether you want a one-window or a two-window form.

If you ask the Wizard for a form with two windows, the Wizard will create windows named
Compose and Read, respectively.

If you ask for a one-window form, it will be named simply Window1. Again, the same window
is used for both composing and reading.

There are several occasions on which a two-window form is advantageous, if not necessary. For
example, the Expense Report form (which you will design later in this chapter) has a specific
need for two windows. You need to allow the employee to enter expense items in the form, but
you must not allow the employee's manager to alter it. To meet this need, use two windows; in
the Compose window, all fields on the form can be written to, but in the Read window, the
window read by the manager, the expense item fields have been "locked" from use (made read-
only). This easily shows the same information to both users without allowing the manager to
modify the pertinent data.

FIGURE 30.12.

The Wizard screen that asks, "Do you want one window or two windows in your form?"

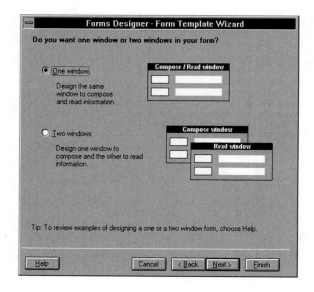

Another occasion on which a two-window form would be appropriate is for an information-gathering form used over and over by a specific department. For example, perhaps your Human Resources department sends out a form to every new employee requesting routine data such as his or her name, address, phone number, and so on. The Compose window might need only the To: and Subject: envelope fields. The Read window, though, would look like a standard data entry form, with field names and places for the employee to type in the required data. Rather than show all the empty data fields to Human Resources repeatedly, you can simply show them a small form with To: and Subject: fields.

Any time your form's composer and your form's reader don't need to see the same information, a two-window form might be in order.

Summary of Form Types Created By the Wizard

To summarize, depending on your answers to the Wizard's questions, the Wizard will produce one of the following eight types of forms:

- *A one-window Send note.* A form for sending and receiving messages between users using the same window. The sender sees the same window the recipient sees.

- *A two-window Send note.* Same as the one-window Send note except that the sender composes the note in a different window from the one in which the reader will read it.

- *A one-window Post note.* Same as the one-window Send note except that the destination of the form is a public folder. Users reading the note in the public folder see the same window in which the sender composed the note.

- *A two-window Post note.* Same as the one-window Post note except that the sender composes the note in a different window from the one in which the reader will read it (in the public folder).

■ *A one-window send-response note.* A form for replying (responding) to a Send note a user received. The person replying and the reply's recipient see the same window.

■ *A two-window send-response note.* Same as the one-window Send-response note except that the person replying composes the reply in a different window from the one in which the recipient of the reply reads it.

■ *A one-window post-response note.* A form for replying (responding) to a Post note a user read in a public folder. The reply becomes another post in the public folder. The form with which the person replying creates his or her reply is the same as the one someone else will use to read the reply in the public folder.

■ *A two-window post-response note.* Same as the one-window post-response note except that the person replying composes the reply in a different window from the one in which the recipient of the reply reads it (in the public folder).

General Usage

As the last part of the quick tour of EFD, make a simple form and install it. You'll make a simple Send note, similar to the standard message window in which you currently compose mail with Exchange. This will simply be a form with the standard envelope fields and a RichEntry field. The following are the steps you should take:

1. Start EFD.

2. Use the Wizard to make a simple one-window Send note. Simply clicking Next and then Finish will do this for you. Because you used the Wizard, the envelope fields are already added to your form.

3. Add a RichEntry field to the canvas of the form. Just click the RichEntry button on EFD's toolbox and then click on the canvas. A RichEntry field with default size and properties will appear on the canvas. Figure 30.13 shows the canvas after the RichEntry field is added.

4. Position the main part of the RichEntry field in the upper-left corner of the canvas. To do so, simply click the main part of the field (most field types in EFD have two parts: the main part and the caption) and drag it to the upper-left corner while you hold the mouse button down. Let the caption move off the screen to the left; it isn't important for this form. (Alternatively, you could set the Left and Top properties of the field in the Field PI to get more precise placement; close is good enough for now.)

   Notice that the field has stretch handles (boxes in the corners of the field—see Figure 30.13) that you can use to size it. Because you are making a Message Body field, you will later set properties so it will size itself at runtime to fill the window, so don't worry about sizing it now. If you want, you can try out the sizing handles to get a feel for how they work. The large box in the upper-left corner does not size the field; instead, it gives you a way to move the main part of the field independent of its caption. Figure 30.14 shows the RichEntry field after you've moved it to the upper-left corner of the canvas.

FIGURE 30.13.

Placing the RichEntry field onto the canvas.

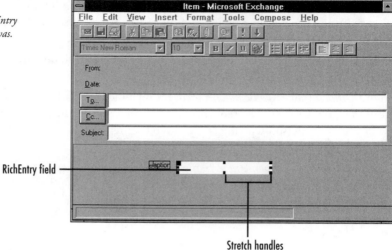

RichEntry field ——

Stretch handles

FIGURE 30.14.

The RichEntry field moved to the upper-left corner of the canvas.

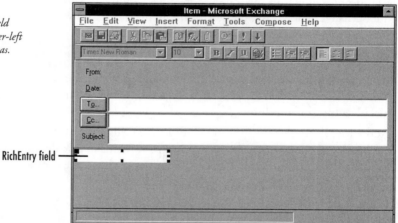

RichEntry field ——

5. Press F4 to display the Field PI. Make sure the RichEntry field is still selected.

6. Select the Format tab.

7. Check the "Vertical scroll bar" and "Auto-size to window bottom" checkboxes. The "Vertical scroll bar" check box will cause a vertical scrollbar to appear in the runtime form whenever more lines of text are entered into the window than will fit. "Auto-size to window bottom" will cause the RichEntry field to grow (to the right and down) when the window is resized so it always uses as much space as is available. Note that only one RichEntry field on any one window can have the auto-size property set. You'll get an error if you try to set it on a second one.

8. Select Form Properties from the View menu to display the Form PI. Make sure it is on the General tab.

9. Enter `My First Form` in the Form Display Name field. When you want to open the runtime form later, this is the name that will appear in the list of available forms.

10. Enter `One-Window Send Note` in the Description field. When you want to open the runtime form later, this is the description that will appear when you select this form from the list of available forms.

11. Click Save from the File menu and save your form as myform.efp.

12. Click Install from the File menu to install the form into Exchange.

    In a few moments, the Set Library To dialog box will appear (see Figure 30.15). This is where you specify where you want your form installed. For this exercise, just install it to your Personal Forms Library. This makes the form available only to you, which is great for testing your form. If you have set up other libraries on Exchange (see the section "Setting Up the Organization Forms Library," earlier in this chapter), you could select those instead. For now, though, stick with the Personal Forms Library.

FIGURE 30.15.

The Set Library To dialog box.

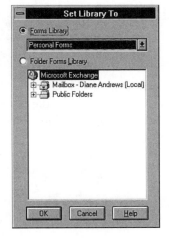

13. Click OK in the Set Library To dialog box after verifying that the Forms Library option button is selected and that Personal Forms is selected in the drop-down list box.

14. Click OK when the Form Properties dialog box appears. You already set the important properties shown here in step 9 and 10. The form will finish installing and focus will return to EFD when it's complete.

    You are now ready to test the runtime form.

15. Start up the Microsoft Exchange client.

16. Select New Form from the Compose menu in Exchange.

17. Select Personal Forms from the list box at the top of the New Form dialog box. You should see your form My First Form in the list of available forms that appears. (See Figure 30.16.)

FIGURE 30.16.

The New Form dialog box.

18. Select My First Form from the list and click OK.

In a moment, your runtime form should appear. Notice that the RichEntry field (the Body field) you added to the form now fills up the entire canvas. This is the result of checking the Auto-size to window bottom property. Notice how much Figure 30.17 looks like the standard e-mail note shown in Figure 30.1.

FIGURE 30.17.

The runtime form showing the RichEntry field filling the canvas.

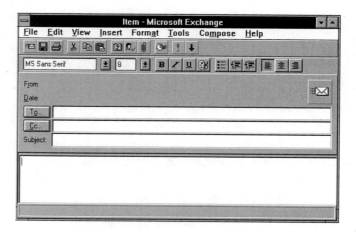

Enter some text in the body field (because it's a RichText field, try using various font styles, sizes, colors, and so on) and send the form to yourself. Open it up when it appears in your inbox.

That completes the quick tour of EFD. Without going into great detail, you have seen all the elements for designing forms with the Microsoft Exchange Forms Designer. You are now ready to jump in and build a more complex form, the Expense Report form, which should be useful within your organization.

> **TIP**
>
> The form you just created does not enable you to insert files into the body of the message. You can add this capability easily in EFD by going to the Field PI's General tab (when the RichEntry field is selected on the canvas) and selecting MAPI_Body_Custom from the Reference Name drop-down list box. That's all you need to do. When you reinstall the form (see the following tip), it will now enable you to insert files into the body field.

A Sample Expense Report

In this section, you will design, install, and integrate three forms that will work together as an expense report Exchange application. Your objective is to create a method for employees to create expense reports electronically and submit them to their managers for approval. The managers need the capability of either approving the expense reports for payment and forwarding them to another department for processing or of declining approval and returning the expense report to the employee with comments explaining why the report was declined. To implement this, you will design and build the following three forms:

- *Expense Report Form.* This will be a two-window Send note. The employee will use the Compose window (see Figure 30.18) to enter expenses, and the manager will use the Read window (see Figure 30.19) to review the expenses. All the expense fields will be locked (read-only) in the Read window but not in the Compose window; therefore, a two-window Send note is required.

- *Approve Form.* This will be a one-window response note. Assuming the manager approves the expense report, this form will appear pre-addressed to the Accounting department marked as approved. The Accounting department will read the same form that the manager sends. See Figure 30.20 for an example of the Approve form's window.

FIGURE 30.18.

The Compose window of the Expense Report form.

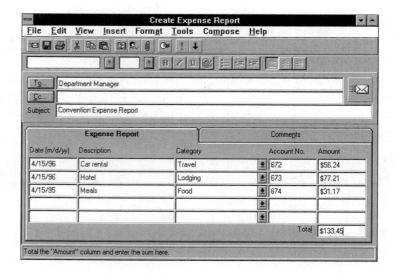

FIGURE 30.19.

The Read window of the Expense Report form.

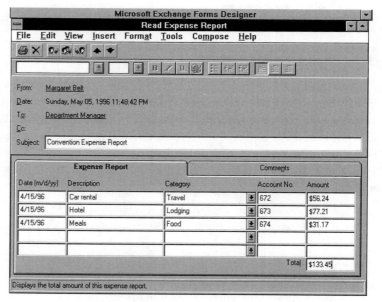

■ *Decline Form.* This will be a two-window response note. If there is a problem with the expense report submitted by the employee, the manager will decline it. When doing so, this form's Compose window will appear (see Figure 30.21), and the manager will enter comments explaining the reason for the decline. The manager will send it back to the employee, who will read the comments in the Read window (see Figure 30.22). The difference in the two windows, and thus the reason for a two-window form, will be the menu choices available in each case.

FIGURE 30.20.

The Approve form's window.

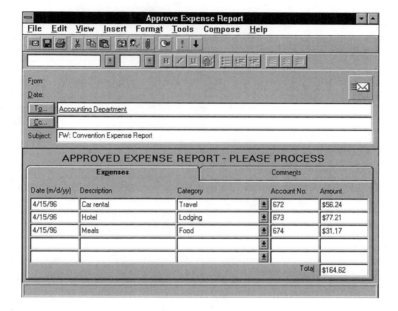

FIGURE 30.21.

The Compose window for the Decline form.

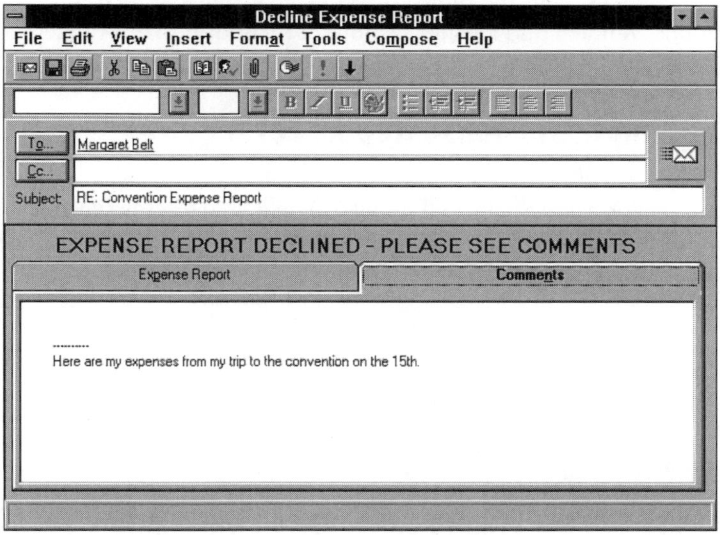

FIGURE 30.22.

The Read window for the Decline form showing the Comments tab with comments thread.

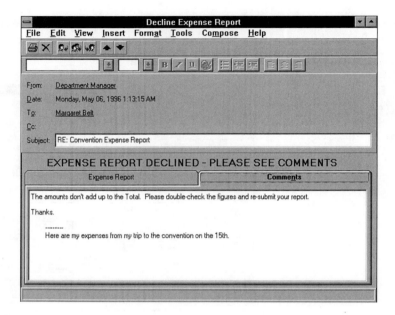

You design these three forms entirely within the EFD environment—there will be no programming required. Later, you'll add a custom feature to the form to learn how to make programming changes to the form if you want.

First, you will build the three forms one at a time and then integrate them. In the following sections, you will find a major section for each form that is broken down into steps for you to follow.

Building the Expense Report Form

The Expense Report form is the form in which the employee will enter expenses. First you'll build the form and then you'll install it. You'll then test the runtime form to verify that it works properly on its own before you proceed with building the other two forms.

As you learned earlier, when you build a form with EFD, you will do the following:

1. Use the Wizard to create a two-window send form.
2. Design the Compose window.
3. Design the Read window.
4. Set Form properties.

Step 1: Use the Wizard to Create a Two-Window Send Form

Start EFD. In the opening window, select Form Template Wizard and then click Next. Continue through the Wizard and answer its questions according to Table 30.1.

Table 30.1. Creating a two-window Send form.

When Asked This:	Choose This and Then Click Next:
Where will your information go?	To another user (Send)
How will your Send form be used?	To Send information
Do you want one window or two windows in your form?	Two windows

The Wizard will now prompt you for a form name and description. Enter `Expense Report` as the form name. Enter `Expense Report Form` as the form description.

> **NOTE**
>
> The Form Display Name represents how your form will be identified to the users of Exchange. After your form is installed in the Organization Forms Library, the form name will be visible in the New Form dialog box whenever a user selects New Form from the Exchange Viewer's Compose menu.
>
> The Description tells the users about your form. It is also visible in the New Form dialog box and other places in Exchange. It is good practice to include a short but clear description of your form's purpose in its Description field so that users can easily tell from the New Form dialog box what your form can do for them.

Click Next and then click Finish. The Wizard will now create and display the form you requested.

Before proceeding, save your work. From EFD's File menu, select Save. In the Save As dialog box, enter `EXPENSE.EFP` as the filename. Click OK. Your form is now saved as ...\EFDFORMS\ EXPENSE.EFP.

Step 2: Design the Compose Window

To design the Compose window, you will go through the steps described in the following sections:

1. Add Tab and Expense Report fields.
2. Set field properties of the Tab and Expense Report fields.
3. Add a Comments field to the Tab field.
4. Set field properties of the Comments field.
5. Set properties for the window.

30

THE EXCHANGE ELECTRONIC FORMS DESIGNER

Adding Tab and Expense Report Fields

Using the method discussed earlier in the "General Usage" section, add the fields shown in Table 30.2 to the canvas in the following order: start with the Tab field and place the remaining fields inside of Tab 1 of the Tab field (make sure that Tab 1 is the current tab page). After all the fields have been added to the canvas, put them in the proper position by setting their properties in the Field PI.

Table 30.2. Adding fields to the expense report Compose window.

Field Name	Number of Fields
Tab field	1
Label field	5
Entry field	21
ComboBox field	5

Setting Field Properties of Tab and Expense Report Fields

The next step is to set the field's properties. To set a field's properties, you must first select the field. Because there are a large number of fields in this window of the form, it will be difficult to select a field by clicking on it as you did before. Instead, select the field in the Fields drop-down list box (located at the far right side of EFD's menu window). After the field is selected, the Field PI will show its properties so you can change them.

The following list shows the fields whose properties need setting and the order in which we will proceed:

- Tab field
- Label fields for the column headings
- Entry fields for the date column
- Entry fields for the Description column
- ComboBox fields for the Category column
- Entry fields for the Account No. column
- Entry fields for the Amount column
- Total field

First, select the Tab field and then press F4 to load the Field PI (or select Field Properties from the View menu). By default, the General properties tab of the Field PI is loaded. Set the General properties shown in Table 30.3 for the Tab field. If Table 30.3 does not specify a property setting, leave the default setting alone.

Table 30.3. Setting the General properties for the Tab field.

General Property	Value
Left	75
Top	90
Width	8670
Height	2820

NOTE

Instead of setting the Left, Top, Width, and Height properties in the PI, you could drag the field to its location with your mouse. Entering the property values in the PI, though, allows better precision, so use this method to build the expense report.

Click the Format tab on the Field PI. The Expense Report form uses only two tabs, so you need to remove Tab 3 and Tab 4 from the Tab field. Locate the Pages list (in the middle of the Format tab of the Field PI). Select Tab 3 and click the Remove button. Repeat the process for Tab 4. This should leave only Tab 1 and Tab 2.

Set the Format properties shown in Table 30.4 for the Tab field. If Table 30.4 does not specify a property setting, leave the default setting alone.

Table 30.4. Setting Format properties for the Tab field.

Format Property	Value
Tabs per row	2
Tab 1 caption	Ex&penses
Tab 2 caption	Comme&nts

TIP

For detailed information on any of the available field properties, select the property and press F1 to display EFD's online help, or refer to the *Application Designer's Guide*.

To change the tab captions, double-click the tab name in the Pages field of the Format tab. A dialog box in which you can change the caption will appear. Alternatively, you can edit the

30

THE EXCHANGE
ELECTRONIC
FORMS DESIGNER

caption directly in-place on the tab itself by moving the mouse cursor over the tab and clicking it when the mouse cursor changes to an I-beam.

> **TIP**
>
> Notice that the ampersand (&) character becomes an underline of the following character when you accept your entry. The underlined character is now a hot key, which enables the user to reach either tab page simply by pressing Alt+P (to reach the Expenses tab page) or Alt+N (to reach the Comments tab page).

Now you set the properties for the Label fields. You will use the Label fields for the column headings in the expense report. Start by selecting Label1; this will be the heading for the column in which the employee enters the date of the expense. Note that when you select Label1, the Field PI automatically updates to display its properties. Click the General tab of the Field PI. Set the General properties for Label1 as shown in Table 30.5.

Table 30.5. Setting General properties for Label1.

Property	Value
Reference Name	`LabelDate`
Left	`60`
Top	`35`
Width	`1200`
Height	`300`

> **NOTE**
>
> The reference name is just a name you give to the field that identifies it to you later. You could leave it with its default name, but it will make your design easier if you give it a meaningful name. Later, you will be copying information from fields in one form to fields in another form; you will use the reference name to identify the fields you are copying from and to.

Click the Initial Value tab of the Field PI and enter the following in the Initial Text field:

`Date (m/d/yy)`

This will be the text of the heading for the date column.

Set field properties for Label2 through Label5. Go back to the General tab of the Field PI, and for each field use the same values as those used for Label1, substituting the Reference Name and Left values as shown in Table 30.6. (Remember, to select a field, choose it from the drop-down list box on the right side of EFD's menu bar.)

Table 30.6. Setting General properties for Label2 through Label5.

Label Number	Property/Value
Label2	Reference Name = `LabelDescription`
	Left = `1290`
Label3	Reference Name = `LabelCategory`
	Left = `3720`
Label4	Reference Name = `LabelAccountNo`
	Left = `6045`
Label5	Reference Name = `LabelAmount`
	Left = `7275`

Click the Initial Value tab of the Field PI. Enter `Initial Text` for Label2 through Label5 as shown in Table 30.7. Recall that these will be the column headings for the expense report.

Table 30.7. Setting initial values for Label2 through Label5.

Label Reference Name	Initial Text
LabelDescription	`Description`
LabelCategory	`Category`
LabelAccountNo	`Account No.`
LabelAmount	`Amount`

Next, you set the properties for the Entry fields for the date column. Users will enter the date of the expense in the date column—for example, `1/1/96`.

Locate Entry1 in the Fields drop-down list box on EFD's menu bar. Set General properties for Entry1 as shown in Table 30.8.

30

THE EXCHANGE ELECTRONIC FORMS DESIGNER

Table 30.8. Setting field General properties for the Entry1 field.

General Tab Property	Value
Reference Name	Date1
Left	60
Top	335
Width	1200
Height	300

You also need to set properties for Field Help. Click the Field Help button on the General tab of the Field PI to display the Field Help for Users dialog box. In the Status Bar field, enter the following:

```
Enter the expense date in the following format: m/d/yy.
```

> **NOTE**
>
> Field Help is displayed when the user of the runtime form presses F1 from within a field. Instructions on what type of information goes in a field and how to enter it can be put into Field Help. When you enter status bar text for your fields, the text is visible on the runtime form's status bar whenever the field has focus.

Set field Format properties for Entry1 as shown in Table 30.9.

Table 30.9. Setting field Format properties for the Entry1 field.

Format Tab Property	Value
Type	Date
Format	System Default (Short)

> **NOTE**
>
> The Type and Format properties are available for the Entry and Label fields. These properties control what kind of data can be used by the field. There are six different types: Text, Integer, Date, Time, Currency, and Floating Point. For each type except Text, there are several predefined formats from which you can select. The Text field type enables you to enter any kind of data. The Date field, like that used here, enables the

user to enter only dates. If the field contains data that does not correspond with its Type/Format properties, Exchange will not enable the message to be sent until the data is corrected.

NOTE

Some Format properties are available only for the field itself and not for the field's caption. You control which properties are visible by selecting Field or Caption at the top of the Format tab.

Set field properties for Entry2 through Entry5. For each field, use the same values as those used for Entry1, substituting the Reference Name and Top values as shown in Table 30.10.

Table 30.10. Setting the field properties for Entry2 through Entry5.

Field Number	Property/Value
Entry2	Reference Name = Date2
	Top = 665
Entry3	Reference Name = Date3
	Top = 995
Entry4	Reference Name = Date4
	Top = 1325
Entry5	Reference Name = Date5
	Top = 1655

Next, you set the properties for the Entry fields for the Description column. In the Description column, the user will be able to enter a brief description of the expense—for example, Lunch meeting with Sam to discuss budget issues.

Set the properties for Entry6 as shown in Table 30.11.

Table 30.11. Setting properties for Entry6.

General Property	Value
Reference Name	Description1
Left	1290

continues

30

THE EXCHANGE
ELECTRONIC
FORMS DESIGNER

Table 30.11. continued

General Property	Value
Top	335
Width	2400
Height	300
Status Bar	Enter a brief description of the expense item.
Field Help—QuickHelp caption	Description
Field Help—QuickHelp body text	Enter a brief description of the expense item. Example: Lunch meeting with Sam to discuss budget issues.

Remember, to set Field Help properties, you must first click the Field Help button on the General tab of the Field PI.

Set field properties for Entry7 through Entry10. For each field, use the same values as those used for Entry6, substituting the Reference Name and Top values as shown in Table 30.12.

Table 30.12. Setting properties for Entry7 through Entry10.

Field Number	Property/Value
Entry7	Reference Name = Description2
	Top = 665
Entry8	Reference Name = Description3
	Top = 995
Entry9	Reference Name = Description4
	Top = 1325
Entry10	Reference Name = Description5
	Top = 1655

Now you set the properties for the ComboBox fields for the Category column. Expenses generally fall into categories such as Meals and Lodging. The Category column is where the user will select under which category each expense belongs. At times, an expense will not fit into one of the predefined categories and the user will need to enter a new category. The ComboBox field is perfect for this type of situation, so for this exercise use ComboBox fields for the Category column.

Set properties for ComboBox1 as shown in Table 30.13.

Table 30.13. Setting properties for ComboBox1.

General Property	Value
Reference Name	Category1
Left	3720
Top	335
Width	2295
Field Help—Status Bar	Select an expense category from the list.
Field Help—QuickHelp caption	Category
Field Help—QuickHelp body text	Select an expense category from the list. To see the list of available choices, click on the arrow located at the right-hand side of the Category field.

Note that you did not set the Height property for ComboBox1. This is because ComboBox fields have a fixed size.

Set field Initial Value properties for ComboBox1 as shown in Table 30.14.

Table 30.14. Setting field Initial Value properties for the ComboBox1 field.

Initial Value Tab Property	Value
List values	Entertainment
	Food
	Lodging
	Office Supplies
	Other
	Telephone
	Training
	Travel

NOTE

Initial Value properties set and display the initial entry contained in the field when the form is first displayed at runtime. In the case of the Category combo box, you are setting the initial value to the different available expense categories. Other fields also have initial value properties. For example, you use the Initial Value tab to give an entry field an initial value that users can type over if they choose to.

30
THE EXCHANGE
ELECTRONIC
FORMS DESIGNER

Set field properties for ComboBox2 through ComboBox5. For each field, use the same values as those used for ComboBox1, including the Initial Value properties, substituting the Reference Name and Top values as shown in Table 30.15.

Table 30.15. Setting properties for Category2 through Category5.

Field Number	Property/Value
ComboBox2	Reference Name = Category2
	Top = 665
ComboBox3	Reference Name = Category3
	Top = 995
ComboBox4	Reference Name = Category4
	Top = 1325
ComboBox5	Reference Name = Category5
	Top = 1655

Next, you set the properties for the Entry fields for the Account No. column. You might want to have an account number for the employee's use in entering their expense item—for example, 001 could be food, 002 could be supplies, and so on.

Set properties for the Entry11 field as shown in Table 30.16.

Table 30.16. Setting properties for Entry11.

General Property	Value
Reference Name	AccountNo1
Left	6045
Top	335
Width	1200
Height	300
Field Help—Status Bar	Enter the expense account number.
Field Help—No Help	Selected
Format Tab Property	Value
Type	Integer
Format	0

Set field properties for Entry12 through Entry15. For each field, use the same values as those used for Entry11, substituting the Reference Name and Top values as shown in Table 30.17.

Table 30.17. Setting properties for Entry12 through Entry15.

Field Number	Property/Value
Entry12	Reference Name = AccountNo2
	Top = 665
Entry13	Reference Name = AccountNo3
	Top = 995
Entry14	Reference Name = AccountNo4
	Top = 1325
Entry15	Reference Name = AccountNo5
	Top = 1655

Now you set the properties for the Entry fields for the Amount column. Employees will need to enter the amount of each expense item in the amount column.

Set properties for Entry16 as shown in Table 30.18.

Table 30.18. Setting properties for Entry16.

General Property	Value
Reference Name	Amount1
Left	7275
Top	335
Width	1200
Height	300
Field Help—Status Bar	Enter the expense amount in dollars and cents (for example, 10.95).
Field Help—No Help	Selected
Format Tab Property	Value
Type	Currency
Format	General

Set field properties for Entry17 through Entry20. For each field, use the same values as those used for Entry16, substituting the Reference Name and Top values as shown in Table 30.19.

Table 30.19. Setting properties for Entry17 through Entry20.

Field Number	*Property/Value*
Entry17	Reference Name = `Amount2`
	Top = `665`
Entry18	Reference Name = `Amount3`
	Top = `995`
Entry19	Reference Name = `Amount4`
	Top = `1325`
Entry20	Reference Name = `Amount25`
	Top = `1655`

Next, you set the properties for the Total field. The employee enters in the Total field the total of all amounts in the Amount column.

Set properties for Entry21 as shown in Table 30.20.

Table 30.20. Setting properties for Entry21.

General Property	*Value*
Reference Name	`Total`
Left	`7275`
Top	`1985`
Width	`1200`
Height	`300`
Required	`Checked`
Field Caption	`Tota&l`
Field Help—Status Bar	`Total the "Amount" column and enter the sum here.`
Field Help—No Help	`Selected`
Format Tab Property	`Value`
Type	`Currency`
Format	`General`

NOTE

"Required" is a property that specifies that the user must enter something. He or she won't be able to send the form without doing so. In this case, you are specifying that the user must total his or her expense report before sending it. How many times have you turned in an Expense Report without a total and had the form sent back to you without payment because of the missing total?

The Expense Report tab page is now complete.

Adding Comments Field to Tab Field

Click on the Comments tab page and then use the toolbar to add a RichEntry field to the Comments tab. This field will give the form's users a place in which to enter their comments.

Setting Field Properties of Comments Field

Set field properties for the RichEntry field as shown in Table 30.21.

Table 30.21. Setting field properties for the RichEntry field.

General Property	Value
Reference Name	`MAPI_Body_Custom` (set this by selecting it in the Reference Name list box by clicking on the arrow at the right side of the field)
Left	`45`
Top	`30`
Width	`8475`
Height	`2310`
Field Caption—Position	None
Field Help—Status Bar	`Use this field to add your comments.`
Field Help—No Help	`Selected`
Format Tab Property	`Value`
Vertical Scroll Bar	`Checked`

> **NOTE**
>
> Recall that MAPI_Body_Custom is a special reference name available only for the RichEntry field that, when set, enables the user to attach files to the field in the runtime form. To learn more about the MAPI_Body_Custom field, put the focus in the Reference Name field of the Field PI and press F1.

You are now finished setting field properties for the Compose window. From EFD's File menu, select Save to save your changes before proceeding.

> **TIP**
>
> After you become more familiar with using EFD, you might find it easier to use the Clipboard to copy and paste similar fields when you are adding several fields of the same type. For example, you could have copied the first row of entry fields (Date1 through Amount1) to the Clipboard and then pasted four copies onto the Expense Report tab to make the other four rows. Most of the properties will be copied with the fields, but you will still have to reposition the fields and enter a new Reference Name for each one.

Setting Window Properties

To set window properties, display the Window PI by pressing Ctrl+W (or select Window Properties from the View menu). By default, the General properties tab of the Window PI is loaded. Set the Compose window's General properties as shown in Table 30.22. If Table 30.22 does not specify a property setting, leave the default setting alone.

Table 30.22. Setting General properties for the Compose window.

Property	Value
Window Name	Compose
Window Caption	Create Expense Report
Field Tab Order	(see text following this table)
Window Help—caption	Expense Report
Window Help—body field	Use this form to prepare an expense report for manager's review.

First, you set the properties for the Field Tab Order on the General tab. The Field Tab Order section of the Window PI enables you to add your fields to the form's tab order (the order in which the cursor moves through fields each time you press the Tab key). By default, EFD always includes the envelope fields (that is, the To and Subject fields) first in the form's tab order. Generally, the envelope fields should always remain at the top of the window's tab order. To add a field from the Available Fields list to the Fields in Tab Order list, first click the field you want to add in the left column and then click the (>>) button to move the field to the right column (it will be placed after the field currently selected in the right column). Finally, use the Up and Down arrows to position the field in the proper order, the top field being number one in the tab order.

Add the Compose window's fields to the form's Tab Order in the following order:

1. Click Date1 in the left column and then click MAPI_Subject in the right column (note that MAPI_Subject is the default reference name for the envelope subject field).

2. Click the >> button.

3. Add Description1 from the left column to the right column (to follow Date1). Then add Category1, AccountNo1, and Amount1.

4. Repeat this process for Date2 through Amount2. Continue adding the next three rows of fields from the Compose window, finishing with the Total field as the last field in the tab order.

To set properties on the Format tab, click the Format tab of the Window PI. Set Format properties for the Compose window as shown in Table 30.23.

Table 30.23. Setting Format properties for the Compose window.

Property	Value
Maximize Button	Checked
Minimize Button	Checked
Toolbar	Checked
Status Bar	Checked
Formatting Toolbar	Checked
Window Icon	C:\EXCHANGE\EFDFORMS\ICONS\NOTE2L.ICO
Window Sizing Options	Fixed Size

NOTE

The minimize and maximize properties control whether your runtime form can be minimized or maximized. Note that maximizing a runtime form does not have any effect on the size or location of the form's fields—keep this in mind when you are deciding whether to include a maximize button on your form. If the form is minimized, the Window icon will be the visible representation of your form on the user's desktop.

The toolbar properties control whether your runtime form will display the specified toolbars. Typically, forms should always have a toolbar. You use the Formatting toolbar to format the contents of the RichEntry field. The status bar displays status-bar text for fields and menu command items.

EFD uses the Window icon to represent the minimized window on the user's desktop (note that the path specified in Table 30.23 assumes you installed EFD in the default location; if you installed it elsewhere, you need to modify this property setting accordingly).

You use the Background property to control the background color of the window.

The Window Sizing Options control whether your window can be sized with the mouse (by using the mouse to drag the window borders to a desired size). This property is separate from the Maximize and Minimize properties (that is, a Fixed Size window can still be maximized or minimized if these properties are checked in the Format page of the Window PI).

Congratulations! You've just finished the toughest part of the Expense Report Exchange Application. From EFD's File menu, select Save to save your changes before proceeding.

Step 3: Design the Read Window

You are now ready to design the Read window. From EFD's Window menu, select Read. EFD will load the Expense Report form's Read window. The Read window will be seen by recipients of the expense report (when an employee sends an expense report to his or her manager for approval, the manager will see the form's Read window when he or she opens the item in his or her Exchange inbox).

Inserting the Tab Field from the Compose Window

The Read window is going to look just like the Compose window, except that most of the fields will be locked (read-only). Because the Read and Compose windows are so similar, make things easy by copying the fields from the Compose window using EFD's Insert Fields feature:

1. Select Field from EFD's Insert menu. The Fields from Expense Report dialog box will be displayed.
2. Select Tab and then click the Insert button. EFD will place a copy of the Tab field and its contained fields in the center of the Read window (you might need to resize the Read window so that the entire tab is visible).
3. Click the Close button.

Modifying Field Properties

Because you used the Insert Fields feature, most of the field properties are already set appropriately for the Read window. However, you need to do the following:

1. Reposition the Tab field.
2. Set the Locked property on all the Entry fields and ComboBox fields on the Expense Report tab.
3. Modify the Field Help to make it relevant.

Click on the Tab field and press F4 to load the Field PI. In the General tab of the Field PI, set the tab's Left property to 75 and the Top property to 90.

After the employee completes and sends his or her expense report, you (the form designer) need to make the form do the right thing with the employee's information. In this case, you need to make sure that the expense report items cannot be modified after the employee has sent the form. You can do this by setting a single property for every Entry field and ComboBox field on the Read window (Date1 through Date5, Description1 through Description5, Category1 through Category5, AccountNo1 through AccountNo5, Amount1 through Amount5, and Total). Each of these fields on the Read window must be set to Locked (read-only). This will ensure that the employee's expense items cannot be modified after the employee sends the form. Go ahead now and set the Locked property for these fields. You'll find it on the General tab of the Field PI.

Now that the Entry and ComboBox fields are locked, you need to modify the help text. Because viewers of the Read window cannot make entries to these fields, change their help text to describe what the field contains (for example, change Enter the date of the expense item to something like Displays the date of the expense item). Go ahead now and modify the help text for each of the fields on the Expense Report tab page. Recall that you set the Field Help properties by clicking the Field Help button on the Field PI's General tab.

The Comments tab and its contained field (the MAPI_Body_Custom RichEntry field) require no changes. The manager will be allowed to enter comments into this field, just as the employee can.

Setting Window Properties

You should set the Read window's window properties identical to those for the Compose window, with two exceptions: the window Name should be Read and the window Caption should be changed to Read Expense Report. Refer to Tables 30.22 and 30.23 to set the Read window's remaining properties. Go ahead and set these properties now.

You are finished setting the Read window's properties. From EFD's File menu, select Save to save your changes before proceeding.

Step 4: Set Form Properties

The last thing you need to do before this form is finished is set the Form properties themselves. There are two types of properties you will be setting:

- General properties
- Events properties

Setting the Form's General Properties

To set the form's General properties, display the Form PI by pressing Ctrl+F (or select Form Properties from the View menu). By default, the General properties tab of the Form PI is loaded. Notice that the form name and description you entered when you first started with the Wizard are displayed in the Form PI.

Enter values for the rest of the form's General properties as specified in Table 30.24.

Table 30.24. Setting the Expense Report form's General properties.

Property	Value
Version	1.00
Item Type	IPM.Send.ExpenseReport
Large Icon	C:\EXCHANGE\EFDFORMS\ICONS\NOTE2L.ICO
Small Icon	C:\EXCHANGE\EFDFORMS\ICONS\NOTE2S.ICO
Form Help—Caption	Expense Report
Form Help—body text	Use this form to send an Expense Report to your manager for approval.

NOTE

Use the Version property to track changes to your .EFP file. When you add new features or revise existing ones, update your Version property accordingly. (Usually, if you make minor modifications to an existing form design, the Version number will become 1.1. If you make major modifications, or if you redesign the form, the Version number will become 2.0.)

Exchange uses the form's Item Type to locate the form in the Forms Library. For example, when you ask Exchange to load the Expense Report form later in this chapter in the section "Testing the Form," Exchange will search through the Forms Library for a form with the item type `IPM.Send.ExpenseReport` (the Expense Report form's item type) It is very important that this item type be unique to all other forms that might be used in your system. You don't need to enter a value here if you prefer not to. EFD automatically generates one for you that is guaranteed to be unique. The advantage to creating your own is you can give it a name that is meaningful and easier to refer to. Later, when you integrate the three forms, you will use the item type to identify each one.

The form's large and small icons are visible to the user in different Exchange locations. The large icon is displayed in various Exchange dialog boxes, such as the New Form dialog box and the Forms Manager dialog box. The small icon is visible in the Item Type column in the Exchange Viewer. Several pairs of matched large and small icons are shipped with EFD, and they reside in the `C:\EXCHANGE\EFDFORMS\ICONS` directory, but you can use any icons you want to with your forms. Note that the small icon consists of approximately the upper-left 16×16 pixels of a regular icon. Anything beyond this area in the small icon property will not be visible in the Viewer.

Use Form Help to tell the user about your form. Forms can also work with external help files. For specific instructions on implementing Form Help, refer to the *Application Designer's Guide* or EFD's online help.

Setting the Form's Events Properties

You will use the Expense Report form's Events properties to integrate the form with the Approve and Decline forms, which you will design later in this chapter in the sections "The Approve Form" and "The Decline Form." Wait until then to set these properties.

NOTE

All the functions that users can perform with a form are *events*. Examples are Printing, Saving, Replying, and Forwarding. Notice that these are some of the same items that appear in the form's Compose menu and File menu. You use the Compose menu to create new messages and to respond to messages you receive. The Events properties

continues

continued

are probably the most complex properties of forms and will typically be modified only by advanced users of EFD. Note that the Wizard automatically sets the Events properties of each form it creates. When you design the Decline Form later in this chapter, you will be shown exactly how to set the form's Events properties so that Exchange will know when to display each of the form's windows to the user.

For more detailed information on setting form Events properties, click the Help button on the Form Properties dialog box, or refer to the *Application Designer's Guide*.

Installing the Form into Your Personal Forms Library

Before you can use the form in Exchange, you need to create a runtime version of the form. You do this by "installing" the form into Exchange.

Select Install from EFD's File menu. EFD will now generate VB source code, create an executable file (.EXE) for your form, and install the .EXE into Exchange. At the end of this process, you will be prompted to select the Forms library into which you want to install the form. For now, select Personal Forms and click OK. (Later, after the application is complete and tested, you'll move it into the Organization Forms Library.)

TIP

After you install your form into a Forms library, you should test it to verify that it behaves as you intended before making it available to Exchange users. A good practice to follow is to install your form into your Personal Forms library and test the form's behavior locally (send the form to yourself and use it as you expect users to). After you have verified that it is ready for general use, copy the form to the Organization Forms library.

The Form Properties dialog box will appear next; enter yourself as the contact name (the name of the person who should be contacted with questions about the form). Note that all the other properties were set during the design process. Click OK to complete the installation of the Expense Report form into your Personal Forms library.

Testing the Form

Your first form is complete. Test it now and verify that it works as expected.

From the Exchange Compose menu, select New Form. In the New Form dialog box, locate Expense Report in your Personal Forms library. Select the form and click OK. When the form is loaded, try using the form as you would expect users to and verify that all the fields function as intended. Verify the status bar text for the different fields by putting focus on the field and observing the status bar of the form. Try sending the form without totaling the items. The form should not enable you to send without completing the Total field. Verify that you can enter data in all the fields of the Compose window. Send the form to yourself and verify that you can see all the information in the Read window. Verify that you cannot modify the Expense Report items in the Read window. Verify that you can enter comments in both the Compose window and the Read window.

If you find errors, go back to EFD and make the necessary corrections. Then choose Install from EFD's File menu and repeat the code generation and form installation process. Re-test to verify that any problems were corrected.

The Approve Form

When a manager receives an expense report, he or she will either approve it for payment and forward the report for processing or decline approval and return the report to the employee for correction. In order to preserve the employee's original information and transfer it from the Expense Report form to the Approve form, use the fields you've already created in the Expense Report form to build the Approve form.

An important difference between the Approve form and the Expense Report form is that the Approve form will have only one window. It has only one window because after the expense report is approved, nothing changes from what the manager sees and what the Accounting department sees. Recall that you use two windows if the form's sender and the form's recipient need to see different information (for example, in the case of the Expense Report form, the expense item fields are locked in the Read window, but not in the Compose window); in this case they are seeing the same information (the fields are locked for both the sender and the recipient), therefore you need only one window.

Building the Approve Form

To build the form, you will do the following:

1. Use the Wizard to create a one-window send form.
2. Design the window.
3. Set Form properties.

Step 1: Use the Wizard to Create a One-Window Send Form

Use the Wizard and answer its questions according to Table 30.25.

Table 30.25. Creating a one-window Send form.

When Asked This:	*Choose This and Then Click Next:*
Where will your information go?	To another user (Send)
How will your Send form be used?	To Send information
Do you want one window or two windows in your form?	One window

Enter Approve Expense Report as the form name and enter Form for approving Expense Report as the form description. Click Next and then click Finish. The Wizard will now create and display the form.

Now save your form as APPROVE.EFP.

Step 2: Design the Window

To design the window, you will do the following:

1. Insert the Tab field from the Expense Report form's Read window.
2. Modify the Tab field properties.
3. Add the Label field.
4. Set Label field properties.
5. Set the window properties.

To insert the Tab field from the Expense Report form's Read window, you will again (as you did for the Expense Report form's Read window) copy the fields you have already created using the Insert Field feature. You are inserting the fields from the Read window because these fields have already been set to locked, which is what you want for the Approve form.

Follow these instructions to insert the fields:

1. Select Field from EFD's Insert menu. The Fields from... dialog box is displayed.
2. In the Fields from... dialog box, click the Browse button. The Select Project dialog box is displayed.
3. In the Select Project dialog box, locate your EXPENSE.EFP file. Select it and click OK.
4. In the Window list, choose Read. In the Fields list, scroll down to locate Tab, select it, click the Insert button, and then click Close. EFD will insert a copy of the Tab field onto the Approve form's canvas. You are now ready to modify the fields to suit the purpose of the Approve form.

To modify the Tab field properties, position the Tab field by setting its Left property to 75 and its Top property to 420.

Next, add a Label field directly to the canvas (not to the Tab field, as you did for the Expense Report form).

Set field properties for the Label field according to Table 30.26, Table 30.27, and Table 30.28.

Table 30.26. Setting field general properties for new Label field.

General Property	*Value*
Reference Name	LabelApprove
Left	75
Top	90
Width	8370
Height	300

Table 30.27. Setting field format properties for new Label field.

Format Property	*Value*
Font	12 pt, Bold
Alignment	Center

> **NOTE**
>
> Clicking the Font button on the Format tab displays the Font dialog box, which is used to set font attributes for the entire Label field (you can't mix fonts or font attributes in the same Label field).
>
> The alignment buttons enable you to left-, center-, or right-justify the field's text.

Table 30.28. Setting field initial value properties for new Label field.

Initial Value Property	*Value*
Initial Text	APPROVED EXPENSE REPORT - PLEASE PROCESS

You are now finished modifying the field properties. Save your changes before proceeding.

To set the window properties, select Window Properties from the View menu. Set the window's General properties as shown in Table 30.29. If Table 30.29 does not specify a property setting, leave the default setting alone.

Table 30.29. Setting the window's General properties.

Property	Value
Window Caption	Approve Expense Report
Field Tab Order	(see the section "Setting Window Properties," earlier in this chapter)
Window Help—caption	Approve Expense Report
Window Help—body field	This Expense Report has been approved for payment by the employee's manager.

Set the window's Format properties as shown in Table 30.30.

Table 30.30. Setting the window's Format properties.

Property	Value
Window Icon	C:\EXCHANGE\EFDFORMS\ICONS\PENL.ICO
Window Sizing Options	Fixed Size

For descriptions of the different window properties, refer to the subsection "Setting Window Properties" in the section "A Sample Expense Report," earlier in this chapter.

Save your changes before proceeding.

Step 3: Set Form Properties

The last thing you need to do before this form is finished is set the Form properties themselves. There are two types of properties you will be setting:

- General properties
- Events properties

To set the form's General properties, select Form Properties from the View menu. Enter values for the form's General properties as described in Table 30.31.

Table 30.31. Setting the Approve form's General properties.

Property	Value
Version	1.00
Item Type	IPM.Approve.ExpenseReport
Large Icon	C:\EXCHANGE\EFDFORMS\ICONS\PENL.ICO

Property	Value
Small Icon	C:\EXCHANGE\EFDFORMS\ICONS\PENS.ICO
Form Help—caption	Approve Expense Report
Form Help—body text	This form is used for approving payment of expense reports.

You are now ready to set the form's Events properties. Save your changes before proceeding.

There is only one Events property that needs to be modified for the Approve form. Because this form is used only to forward an approved Expense Report form for processing, this form will never be opened as an original form; therefore, the user does not need to see it in the Forms Library. Set the form's Viewer Menu Command property to Hidden. This will prevent it from showing in the New Forms dialog box.

To set the Hidden property, follow these steps:

1. Go to the Events tab in the Form PI.
2. Select Hidden from the Viewer Menu Command drop-down list.

Save your changes before proceeding.

Installing the Approve Form into Your Personal Forms Library

As you did with the Expense Report form earlier in this chapter, you need to install the Approve form into Exchange before you can use the runtime form. Do this by selecting Install from EFD's File menu. For more information about the Install process, refer to the earlier section for the Expense Report form, "Installing the Form into Your Personal Forms Library."

Because this form was designed specifically to work with the Expense Report form, there is no way to properly test it until you integrate the forms. Therefore, don't test this form now. Later in this section, after you install the Decline form into your Personal Forms library, you will test all three forms together to verify that they behave as expected.

The Decline Form

If a manager chooses to decline approval of an Expense Report form for any reason, he or she will use the Decline form to return the expense report to the employee who submitted it. Use the fields you've already created in the Approve form to build the Decline form. This will enable you to continue transferring the employee's original information as you send the expense report and its related forms through Exchange.

Now that you've created two forms, you've gained a lot of expertise in using EFD. To give you more exposure to working with EFD, for the Decline form you will rely less on the Wizard and, instead, set more of the event-handling properties yourself.

Building the Decline Form

To build the form, you will do the following:

1. Use the Wizard to create a simple blank form.
2. Design the Compose window.
3. Create the Read window.
4. Set Form properties.

Step 1: Use the Wizard to Create a Simple Blank Form

This time, start EFD, click Next, and then click Finish. This will create a blank form.

Save your form as DECLINE.EFP.

Step 2: Design the Compose Window

To design the window, you will do the following:

1. Insert the Tab field from the Expense Report form's Read window.
2. Modify the Tab and Label field properties.
3. Set the window properties.

Inserting the Tab Field from the Expense Report Form's Read Window

From EFD's Insert menu, select Field. In the Fields from... dialog box, click the Browse button. In the Select Project dialog box, locate your EXPENSE.EFP file. Select it and click OK. Select Read from the Window drop-down list. In the Fields list, scroll down to locate Tab, select it, and click the Insert button. EFD will insert a copy of the Tab field onto the Decline form's canvas. Click Close. You are now ready to modify the fields of the Decline form.

Modifying the Tab and Label Field Properties

In the Field list box on EFD's main window, locate LabelApprove. Select it in the list box and press F4 to display the Field PI (or select Field Properties from EFD's View menu). Modify field properties according to Table 30.32 and Table 30.33.

Table 30.32. Modifying field general properties for the Label field.

General Property	Value
Reference Name	LabelDecline
Left	75
Top	90

Table 30.33. Modifying field initial value properties for the Label field.

Initial Value Property	*Value*
Initial Text	EXPENSE REPORT DECLINED - PLEASE SEE COMMENTS

Reposition the Tab field by setting its Left property to 75 and its Top property to 420.

You are now finished modifying the field properties. Save your changes before proceeding.

Setting the Window Properties

To set the window properties, select Window Properties from the View menu. Set the window's General properties as shown in Table 30.34. If Table 30.34 does not specify a property setting, leave the default setting alone.

Table 30.34. Setting the window's General properties.

Property	*Value*
Window Name	Compose
Window Caption	Decline Expense Report
Field Tab Order	(see the section "Setting Window Properties," earlier in this chapter)
Window Help—caption	Decline Expense Report
Window Help—body field	Use this form to return an Expense Report to the originating employee for corrections. Explain your reason for not approving this report in the Comments tab.

Set the window's Format properties as shown in Table 30.35.

Table 30.35. Setting the window's Format properties.

Property	*Value*
Window Icon	C:\EXCHANGE\EFDFORMS\ICONS\NOTE1L.ICO
Window Sizing Options	Fixed Size

For descriptions of the different window properties, refer to the subsection "Setting Window Properties" in the section "A Sample Expense Report," earlier in this chapter.

You are now ready to create the Decline form's Read window. Save your changes before proceeding.

Step 3: Create the Read Window

Earlier, when you created the Expense Report form, you used the Wizard to create a two-window Send form. When the Wizard created the form for you, it automatically set all the necessary Events properties so that Exchange would know which of your form's windows to display for specific events. This time, you will create the second window for your Decline form by copying it from the existing Compose window and then manually set all of the form's Events properties to control which window Exchange displays for the different form events.

To create the Read window, you will do the following:

1. Copy the Compose window.
2. Modify the window properties.

Copying the Compose Window

To copy the Compose window to create a new window, following these steps:

1. Select New Window from EFD's Edit menu. The Create New Window dialog box will appear.
2. Change the Window Name to Read.
3. Select Copy of: to make a copy of the Compose window.
4. Click OK.

EFD will create the new window, and the window will automatically have the same fields and window properties as those in the Compose window, except for the window name, which you set to Read.

There is no need to modify field properties—the properties copied from the Compose window meet the needs of the Read window as is.

Modifying the Window Properties

To modify the window properties, select Window Properties from the View menu. Modify the window's General properties as shown in Table 30.36.

Table 30.36. Modifying the Read window's General properties.

Property	Value
Window Help—body field	This Expense Report has been returned to you by your manager. Please refer to the Comments section of the form for details.

Copying the Compose window to create the Read window preserved all of the window properties that you already set, including the Field Tab Order. As you can see, using the New Window dialog box with the "Copy of" feature selected can save a great deal of design time in this type of form (a form that uses the same fields, layout, names, and so on, in more than one window).

Save your changes before proceeding.

Step 4: Set Form Properties

The last thing you need to do before this form is finished is set the form properties themselves. There are two types of properties you will be setting:

■ General properties
■ Events properties

Setting the Form's General Properties

To set the form's General properties, select Form Properties from the View menu. Enter values for the form's General properties as described in Table 30.37.

Table 30.37. Setting form properties for the Decline form.

General Property	Value
Form Display Name	Decline Expense Report
Version	1.00
Item Type	IPM.Decline.ExpenseReport
Description	Used to decline approval of a submitted Expense Report form.
Large Icon	C:\EXCHANGE\EFDFORMS\ICONS\NOTE1L.ICO
Small Icon	C:\EXCHANGE\EFDFORMS\ICONS\NOTE1S.ICO
Form Help—caption	Decline Expense Report
Form Help—body text	Use this form to return an Expense Report to the originating employee for corrections or changes.

Save your changes before proceeding.

Setting the Form's Events Properties

You need to manually set the form's Events properties so that Exchange will display the appropriate window for each of the form's events. You also set the Hidden property for the form like you did with the Approve form.

When the Wizard creates a form, it automatically sets the form's Events properties appropriately. For example, all events that involve an *unsubmitted* item are set to the Compose window, and all events that involve a *submitted* item are set to the Read window.

> **NOTE**
>
> *Submitted* and *unsubmitted* might be new terms to you. Until a Send form has been sent, or until a Post form has been posted, the item is considered unsubmitted, meaning that it has not been given to Exchange for processing and delivery. After a form has been sent or posted, it becomes a submitted item—an item that has gone through Exchange and been processed and delivered. The events for a single-window form will be set either to Window1 or to Unsupported (meaning that the event is not available to the user).

Select Form Properties from EFD's View menu. Enter values for the form's Events properties as described in Table 30.38. To set Events properties on the Events tab of the Form PI, do the following:

1. Select the event shown in the left column of Table 30.38 from the For This Event: drop-down list.
2. Select the Pass To Window: option.
3. Choose the property in the right column of Table 30.38 from the drop-down list associated with the Pass To Window: option.

Table 30.38. Setting the Decline form's Events properties.

Event	Pass to Window Property/Value
Create new item	Compose
Open unsubmitted item	Compose
Open submitted item	Read
Print unsubmitted item	Compose
Print submitted item	Read
Save unsubmitted item as text	Compose
Save submitted item as text	Read

Select the Create new item event again and set the Viewer Menu Command property to Hidden.

Save your changes before proceeding.

Installing the Decline Form into Your Personal Forms Library

As you did with the Expense Report and Approve forms earlier in this chapter, you need to install the Decline form into Exchange before you can use the runtime form. Do this by selecting Install from EFD's File menu. For more information about the Install process, refer to the earlier section for the Expense Report form, "Installing the Form into Your Personal Forms Library."

Because the Decline form (like the Approve form) was designed specifically to work with the Expense Report form, there is no way to properly test it until you integrate the forms, which you will do next. Then you will test all three forms together to verify that they behave as expected.

Integrating the Expense Report, Approve, and Decline Forms

To make the three forms you have created work together in Exchange, you need to customize some of the properties for the forms' Events properties. The changes you are about to make will tell Exchange what forms to display for which events. This is how you will give the manager Approve and Decline options for the employee's expense report. You will also provide an option for the employee to make corrections to a declined expense report and resubmit it for approval.

To modify the Expense Report and Decline forms, you first open each form separately in EFD and then make the necessary modifications.

The Approve form requires no further modifications to work with the Expense Report form, because after the manager sends it to the Accounting department, its task is finished.

Customizing the Expense Report Form

You now customize the Expense Report form to include Approve Expense Report and Decline Expense Report menu items on the Exchange Client Viewer's Compose menu and on the Read window's Compose menu. To do this, you set properties for Custom Response events for the Expense Report form.

Custom Response events are special events that you can define in addition to the standard, default events. You usually use Custom Response events to enable the user to open other custom forms (EFD forms) from your current form's menu, as you will do here.

The Custom Response properties are set in two places:

- The Form PI's Events tab is where you set menu items that are shown on the Exchange Viewer's Compose menu.
- The Window PI's Menus tab is where you set menu items that are shown on the form window's Compose menu.

This can be a little confusing. It is important to understand that each Custom Response menu item (as well as each default Response menu item) is displayed in two places:

- On the Exchange Viewer menu
- On the form window's menu

You need to change each of these places separately (changing one does not change the other). To begin customizing the Expense Report form, select Open from EFD's File menu. Use the Open dialog box to locate and open your EXPENSE.EFP file.

To add the Approve Expense Report menu item to the Exchange Viewer's Compose menu and prepare it for integration, do the following:

1. Select Form Properties from EFD's View menu and go to the Events page of the Form PI.
2. Select Custom Response 1 in the For This Event: list.
3. Change the Viewer Menu Command: to Approve &Expense Report. (Note that the Viewer Menu Command refers to the Exchange Client Viewer.)
4. Select the Create Response option.
5. Set Response Form's Item Type: to IPM.Approve.ExpenseReport (IPM.Reply.Approve is the Approve form's item type; this is how you tie the two forms together). You can do this either by typing the item type directly into the field or clicking the Browse button and then using the Select Form's Item Type dialog box to locate and select the DECLINE.EFP file.
6. Set Response Style: to Forward.
7. Check Initialize new items when created.
8. Click the Options button. The Response Form Initial Values dialog box will appear.
9. In the Response Form Initial Values dialog box, add all the fields in the Field: list to the Fields copied: list. (See the following note.)
10. Check both the Add response item to conversation thread and Initialize To, CC, and Subject values in response item check boxes. The first check box will cause new comments to be added to the previous comments on the Comments tab. The second check box will make sure the envelope fields are initialized when a person is approving or declining the form.
11. Click OK.

> **NOTE**
>
> Adding the fields to the Fields copied: list in step 9 is how your field values get copied from one form to the next. That is, this is how the expense items the employee entered in the original expense report show up in the same places in the Approve and Decline

forms; otherwise, the fields would all be blank. This works because the Field Reference Names are identical in both forms.

To add the Decline Expense Report menu item to the Exchange Viewer's Compose menu and prepare it for integration, do the following:

1. Select Form Properties from EFD's View menu and go to the Events page of the Form PI.
2. Select Custom Response 2 in the For This Event: list.
3. Change the Viewer Menu Command: to &Decline Expense Report.
4. Select the Create Response option.
5. Set Response Form's Item Type: to IPM.Decline.ExpenseReport (the Decline form's item type).
6. Set Response Style: to Reply.
7. Check Initialize new items when created.
8. Click the Options button. The Response Form Initial Values dialog box will appear.
9. In the Response Form Initial Values dialog box, add all of the fields in the Field: list to the Fields copied: list.
10. Check both the Add response item to conversation thread and Initialize To, CC, and Subject values in response item check boxes.
11. Click OK.

To add the Approve Expense Report and Decline Expense Report menu items to the Read window's Compose menu, do the following:

1. Select Read from EFD's Window menu. The Read window will be displayed.
2. Press Ctrl+W to display the Read window's Window PI and go to the Menus tab.
3. Select Compose in the Menu list.
4. Select Custom Response 1 in the Commands list.
5. Change the Command Caption for Custom Response 1 to Approve &Expense Report.
6. Select Custom Response 2 in the Commands list.
7. Change the Command Caption for Custom Response 2 to &Decline Expense Report.
8. Close the Window PI.

NOTE

The Menus tab of the Window PI is where you set properties for all the window's menu items (that is, you can change the command name of a menu item or add status bar text). Note that these properties are preset by default, and you will usually not make changes to the settings. In the case of your Expense Report Exchange Application, though, you need to make some minor modifications, as shown in the preceding steps.

The Menu list contains all the menu items that make up a window's menu bar. The Menu Caption property applies to the menu bar item currently selected in the Menu list.

The Commands list contains all the individual menu options for the currently selected Menu list item. The Command Caption property applies to the individual menu option currently selected in the Commands list. Note that on a Windows menu, the items typically on the menu bar (File, Edit, View, and so on) are the menu items, and the items that appear in the submenu when you click one of these menu items are the menu commands.

For more information on window menu properties, refer to the *Application Designer's Guide*, or EFD's online help.

In order to incorporate the preceding changes into the runtime form, you need to reinstall the form into your Personal Forms library. Select Install from EFD's File menu to reinstall the form.

The Expense Report form is now integrated with the Approve and Decline forms.

Customizing the Decline Form

Now you add a Correct Expense Report option to the Decline form, which will enable employees to make corrections to their expense reports. This option simply opens a new Expense Report form and copies the field values from the Decline form to the new Expense Report form. This effectively gives the employees their original expense items, which can now be modified as necessary.

As you did for the Expense Report form, set the necessary properties for the Decline form to add this new option to the Exchange Client Viewer's Compose menu and to the Read window's Compose menu.

To begin customizing the Decline form, select Open from EFD's File menu. Use the Open dialog box to locate and open your DECLINE.EFP file.

To add the Correct Expense Report menu item to the Exchange Viewer's Compose menu and prepare it for integration, do the following:

1. Select Form Properties from EFD's View menu and go to the Events page of the Form PI.
2. Select Custom Response 1 in the For This Event: list.

3. Change the Viewer Menu Command: to &Correct Expense Report.

4. Select the Create Response option.

5. Set Response Form's Item Type: to IPM.Send.ExpenseReport
   (IPM.Send.ExpenseReport is the Expense Report form's item type; this is how you tie
   the two forms together).

6. Set Response Style: to None.

7. Check Initialize new items when created.

8. Click the Options button. The Response Form Initial Values dialog box will appear.

9. In the Response Form Initial Values dialog box, add all of the fields in the Field: list
   to the Fields copied: list.

10. Check the Add response item to conversation thread check box.

11. Click OK.

To add the Correct Expense Report menu item to the Read window's Compose menu, do the
following:

1. Select Read from EFD's Window menu. The Read window will be displayed.

2. Press Ctrl+W to display the Read window's Window PI and go to the Menus page.

3. Select Compose in the Menu list.

4. Select Custom Response 1 in the Commands list.

5. Change the Command Caption for Custom Response 1 to &Correct Expense Report.

6. Close the Window PI.

Again, as with the Expense Report, in order to incorporate these changes into the runtime form,
you need to reinstall the form into your Personal Forms Library. Select Install from EFD's File
menu to reinstall the form.

Testing the Integration of the Forms

Now open the runtime Expense Report form and use it as you would expect users to. This is
how you test the runtime form to verify that it behaves as you intended.

To open the runtime Expense Report form, follow these steps:

1. Start your Exchange Client.

2. Select New Form from the Compose menu. The New Form dialog box will appear.

3. Select Personal Forms from the drop-down list at the very top of the New Form
   dialog box.

4. Select Expense Report and click OK.

When the Create Expense Report window is displayed, complete at least the first row of expense items, enter the total of the amount column, enter comments on the Comments tab, and send it to yourself.

When the Expense Report form arrives in your inbox, open it as you would any other mail message. From the Read Expense Report window's Compose menu, select Decline Expense Report. When the Decline Expense Report window is displayed, verify that the To: field already contains your address and that the Subject: field reads RE: followed by the subject you entered for the Expense Report. Verify that the expense items and total that you entered in the Expense Report are visible in the Decline Expense Report window. Verify that your comments are contained in the Comments field. Enter new comments into the Comments field and then send the form.

Open the Decline form in your inbox. Verify that the expense report items are still intact and that the original comments, along with the additions you made, are still intact. From the form's Compose menu, select Correct Expense Report. Verify that the expense items and comments are intact. Make modifications to the Expense Report, including adding more comments, and send the form to yourself.

When the corrected Expense Report arrives in your inbox, open it and verify that your changes are visible. From the form's Compose menu, select Approve Expense Report. When the Approve form is displayed, again verify that all information has been preserved as expected. The Approve form's To: field should be empty, and the Subject: field should read FW: followed by the subject from your corrected Expense Report. Address the form to yourself, send it, and then open the item when it arrives in your inbox and verify that all information is intact and that you cannot modify any of the fields on the Expense Report tab.

If you find any problems, go back to EFD to make the necessary corrections and then reinstall the forms and repeat the testing process.

After the forms pass the testing process, you are ready to make them available to the users of Exchange.

Placing the Forms in the Organization Forms Library

To make the forms automatically available to all the Exchange users, you need to place them in the Organization Forms library. Because the forms currently reside in your Personal Forms library, you can simply copy them to the Organization Forms library.

From the Exchange Tools menu, select Options. From the Options dialog box, select the Exchange Server tab. Under Exchange Server, click Manage Forms. In the Forms Manager dialog box, you should see a list of organization forms on the left and a list of personal forms on the right. Under Personal Forms, select the three forms (Approve Expense Report, Decline Expense Report, and Expense Report) and then click Copy. The Forms Manager will copy the three forms to the Organization Forms library.

The forms are now installed in the Organization Forms library, and the Expense Report form will be visible to Exchange users and available for their use. Because the Approve and Decline forms are hidden, they will not be visible to Exchange users, but Exchange will display them whenever the appropriate menu items are selected from the Expense Report form's Compose menu.

You're finished! Your Expense Report Exchange Application can now be used by everyone in your organization.

Advanced Topics

This section looks at what else you can do with your forms beyond what is provided by EFD. Three topics are covered here:

- Making the Expense Report a public folder application
- Creating an Expense Report view in Microsoft Exchange
- Extending the Expense Report form with Visual Basic

Making the Expense Report a Public Folder Application

The Approve form you made as part of the Expense Report Exchange Application will lend itself nicely to a public folder application, because by putting the approved expense reports into a public folder, the Accounting department, the manager, and the employee can easily review them. Furthermore, after they are in a public folder, you can create a custom view for that folder so all the expense reports will be listed with the fields of interest shown as columns in the viewer.

In this section, you create a public folder called Expense Reports, add the folder to your personal address book, and then set the initial value of the Approve form's To: envelope field to the folder's address. You also create a custom view in the public folder for viewing the Approve form items.

Note that this topic will require that you have public folders set up on your Exchange Server and that you have a personal address book (PAB) on your client.

Preparing the Folder in Microsoft Exchange

You must first create a public folder. In the left column of your Exchange client, locate Public Folders. Open the public folders and select All Public Folders. From the File menu, select New Folder. In the New Folder dialog box, enter Expense Reports and click OK.

> **TIP**
>
> To keep other users from accessing this folder until you are finished setting it up and testing the forms, set the Default Permission Role to None. To do so, display the Properties dialog box for the folder by selecting the folder and clicking the right mouse button. In the Permissions tab, change the Default Role to None by selecting Default in the list box and then selecting None in the drop-down list labeled Roles.

Modifying the Form In EFD

To modify the form in EFD, you must first set the Initial Value property of the Approve form's To: field. To complete this step, you need to add the Expense Reports public folder (which you just created) to your personal address book (PAB). This ensures that the folder's address is available to you from the Approve form's Form PI.

To add the Expense Reports folder to your PAB, first click the Expense Reports folder with the right mouse button and select Properties. Click the Administration tab in the Properties dialog box and click on the Personal Address Book button to add the folder address to your PAB. Click OK to close the Properties dialog box.

Start EFD and open APPROVE.EFP. Select the To: field in the Approve form's window and press F4 to display the Field PI. Go to the Initial Value tab and click the To button. In the Address Book dialog box that appears, select Personal Address Book in the Show Names from the: list. Select the Expense Reports folder on the left and click the To...-> button to add the folder to the Message Recipients list on the right. Click OK.

Click the Subject field on the Approve form. Set the Subject field's initial value to Approved Expense Report.

Setting these initial values automatically addresses your Approve form to the Expense Reports public folder and enters the subject text Approved Expense Report whenever a user selects Approve Expense Report from the Expense Report form's Read window.

Save your changes before proceeding.

You next must install the form into a public folder. As part of converting the Expense Report and its related forms to a Public Folder application, you should first remove the forms from the Organization Forms library. This ensures that Exchange users are not creating their expense reports with the wrong forms and using an outdated process. You use the Exchange Client's Forms Manager dialog box to copy the forms to the Public Folder library and then delete the forms from the Organization Forms library.

To do this, select Options from the Exchange Tools menu. In the Options dialog box, go to the Exchange Server tab and click Manage Forms. In the Forms Manager dialog box, set one side (either side is OK) of the dialog box to Organization Forms Library and the other side to the Expense Reports Public Folder. Select the Expense Report and Decline forms in the Organization Forms list and click Copy. Exchange will copy the forms to the Expense Reports folder. (You don't copy the Approve form because you have to install the revised form into the public folder.) Now select the Expense Report, Approve, and Decline forms again in the Organization Forms library and click Delete. The forms will be deleted from the Organization Forms library. Close the Forms Manager dialog box and then close the Options dialog box.

Now install the revised Approve form into the Expense Reports public folder. From EFD's File menu select Install. When prompted to Set Forms Library, set it to the Expense Reports public folder.

The Expense Report forms, including your newly modified Approve form, are now installed in the Expense Reports public folder. Whenever an Expense Report is approved, the Approved form will automatically be sent to the Expense Reports public folder.

Creating an Expense Report View in Microsoft Exchange

You will now create a custom view for the Expense Reports folder. By creating custom views, you can control and arrange the information displayed in the Viewer so that Exchange users immediately see the relevant data whenever they open the Expense Reports folder. Creating custom views is an excellent way to make it easy for users to get the information they need from public folders. This can greatly increase the usability of your folders and encourage user participation.

Preparing the Form in EFD

To prepare a form to be used in a custom view, set the Microsoft Exchange Column Name property in EFD's Field PI for each field of your form that you want shown as a column name in the view. When you designed the Expense Report forms, you already prepared the forms for public folder views when you set the field captions (changing the field caption automatically changes the Microsoft Exchange column name to match, unless you manually change the Microsoft Exchange Column Name property).

Defining the View in the Public Folder

Follow these steps to define the view in the public folder:

1. From your Exchange Client, right-click the Expense Reports public folder.
2. Select Properties from the menu list.
3. In the Properties dialog box, go to the Views tab. Select Folder views and click New.
4. Enter `By Expense Report` as the View name. Click the Columns button.
5. Remove the following fields from the "Show the following" list (on the right) by selecting the item and clicking the Remove button: Importance, Attachment, Subject, and Size.
6. In the Available columns list, locate Total and add it to the "Show the following" list.

7. Click OK to accept your changes.

8. Click OK to close the New View dialog box, and again to close the Expense Report Properties dialog box.

You now see the column names you just set in the right side of the Viewer. When new Approved Expense Report messages are sent to the folder, they will automatically be displayed by the columns you just set in your By Expense Report view.

Testing the Folder Application

To test the Folder application, select the Expense Reports folder and click the Compose menu. At the bottom of the Compose menu, you see New Expense Report. When forms are installed into public folders, they are automatically added to the folder's Compose menu (and their name is automatically preceded by New). Select New Expense Report to open a new form. Complete the form and send it to yourself. Open the item in your inbox and select Approve Expense Report from its Compose menu. When the Approve form is displayed, verify that it is already addressed to the Expense Reports public folder and that the subject line reads Approved Expense Report. Send the form. When it arrives in the Expense Reports public folder, verify that it is displayed correctly in the Viewer.

After you are satisfied that the Expense Report public folder application is working properly, you need to change the default permission role so that Exchange users can access the folder and use its forms. From your Exchange client, select the Expense Reports folder and click the right mouse button. Select Properties from the menu list. In the Properties dialog box, go to the Permissions tab. Change the Default Role to Author.

The Expense Reports public folder is now ready for use.

Extending the Expense Report Form with Visual Basic

After you've designed and installed your form using EFD, you can use Visual Basic for Microsoft Exchange Server to customize your form even further. To do this step, you must be familiar with programming in the Visual Basic programming language. Depending on what you want to customize, you might also need to be familiar with the Microsoft Message API (MAPI) to extend your form. Both of these subjects are beyond the scope of this book, but you can learn more about Visual Basic and MAPI by referring to the *Application Designer's Guide* and the Visual Basic documentation.

The following is just a brief example of how to extend your form with Visual Basic. In this example, you will add a CommandButton control to the sample Expense Report form you made earlier in this chapter. When you click this button it will add up the expenses in the last column and insert the total in the bottom right cell of the expense report.

> **CAUTION**
>
> If you modify the form's code using Visual Basic, you will not be able to load the form back into EFD to make modifications without losing the changes you made by hand. We suggest you make a copy of your hand code before making additional changes to your form in EFD. This will make it easy to insert your code afterward.

Loading Source Code into Visual Basic

When you installed EFD onto your system, you also installed a special version of Visual Basic for EFD called "Visual Basic for Microsoft Exchange Server." It should have been installed into the Exchange\EFDFORMS\VB directory. Start up this version of VB.

The first thing you want to do is load the VB project that EFD automatically generated when you clicked File | Install on EFD's menu bar. EFD created a subdirectory below the directory in which your EFP file was saved. This directory, Expense.vb, contains the VB source code that EFD generated. In this directory, you'll find the Expense Report form's project file, Expense.vbp. Load that file into VB as you would load any other Visual Basic project file.

Replacing the Total Label with the Total Command Button

Display the Compose window's VB form, which is named COMPOSE.FRM. This form should look a lot like the form you created in EFD except that things have been moved around a bit. First, temporarily reposition the canvas a bit to make your work easier.

Select the control named Canvas_Ctrl in the VB properties window. Canvas_Ctrl is the control that EFD generated for your canvas. Notice that it is a standard VB picture box control.

Note that the Top property of Canvas_Ctrl is currently set to -30. Change that to -1000 to move the interesting part of the canvas up into better view. Remember the original setting of -30, because you'll want to move it back later.

Step 1: Add the Total Command Button to the Form

Select a command button control from VB's toolbox and place it in the same location as the Label control whose caption is Total. For simplicity here, place the command button on top of the label to hide it. You could choose to remove the Label control altogether, but then you'd have to also remove any code that references it. Position the command button as shown in Figure 30.23. Name the command button control cmdTotal. Give it the caption Tota&l.

FIGURE 30.23.

Adding the Total button to the runtime form in Visual Basic.

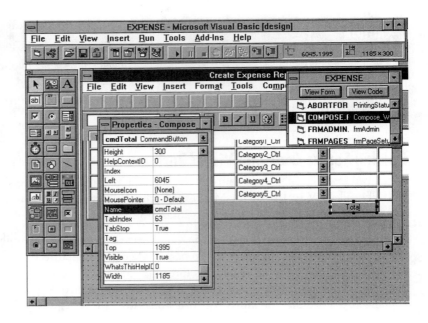

Set the Top property of Canvas_Ctrl back to -30.

Step 2: Write Code for the Total Command Button

Add the following code to the `cmdTotal_Click` event in COMPOSE.FRM. This is the only code you need to add to allow your expense form to total the expenses:

```
Private Sub cmdTotal_Click()
Dim curTotal As Currency

    curTotal = _
    CCur(IIf(Amount1_Ctrl.Text = vbNullString, 0, Amount1_Ctrl.Text)) + _
    CCur(IIf(Amount2_Ctrl.Text = vbNullString, 0, Amount2_Ctrl.Text)) + _
    CCur(IIf(Amount3_Ctrl.Text = vbNullString, 0, Amount3_Ctrl.Text)) + _
    CCur(IIf(Amount4_Ctrl.Text = vbNullString, 0, Amount4_Ctrl.Text)) + _
    CCur(IIf(Amount5_Ctrl.Text = vbNullString, 0, Amount5_Ctrl.Text))

    Total_Ctrl.Text = Format(curTotal, "Currency")
End Sub
```

> **TIP**
>
> If you are making a lot of hand-coded changes to your EFD-generated code, we suggest you add separate forms, classes, and/or modules, as appropriate, to the EFD-generated project instead of adding your code to the existing forms, classes, and/or modules. By doing this you can separate your hand code from the generated code. This will make maintenance

of your code more manageable, plus it will make it easier for you to regenerate your code with EFD without losing your hand-coded changes.

Building the New Compose Form EXE

Now build a new EXE to replace the one generated by EFD; choose Make EXE File from VB's File menu. Do not change the name of the EXE from the one that appears. The name was randomly generated by EFD, and changing it will cause problems when you install the form.

Now exit VB. You are finished with the hand coding. Don't forget to save your changes if you want to keep them.

> **NOTE**
>
> If you made a mistake when you enter the code or something goes wrong at this stage and your form doesn't work when you install it, you can simply start over by regenerating the code again from EFD. Of course, you will have to enter your hand-coded changes again from scratch.

Installing the Form into the Expense Report Public Folder

For the purposes of this example, assume that the Expense Report form is currently installed into the Expense Report public folder. If it is in the Organization Forms library, you need to make the appropriate changes when you are following the instructions:

1. From the Exchange Client's Tools menu, select Options.

2. In the Options dialog box, click the Exchange Server tab.

3. On the Exchange Server tab, click Manage Forms.

4. In the Forms Manager dialog box, set the right-hand forms list to the Expense Report public folder (click the Set button; then in the Set Library To dialog box, choose the Expense Report public folder under Forms Library).

5. On the Forms Manager dialog box, click the Install button.

6. In the Open dialog box's Directories list, locate and select the Expense.vb directory. A file named Expense.cfg will appear in the File Name list.

7. Select the Expense.cfg file and click OK.

8. Make any desired modifications in the Form Properties dialog box (for example, enter your name as Contact Name) and then click OK.

The Forms Manager will install the form into the Expense Report public folder.

> **NOTE**
>
> If you want to add a new control when you are customizing code and you want the contents of that control to show in the Viewer, you need to make appropriate changes to the .CFG file. The .CFG file is a text file that you can edit using any text editor. For information on making changes to the .CFG file, see the *Application Designer's Guide*.

Testing the Form

When you test the form, select New Expense Report from the Expense Report public folder's Compose menu. Complete two or more lines of expense items and then click the Total button. Verify that the Total field receives a value and that the value is the sum of all amounts in the Amount column. Send the form to yourself. Open the Expense Report in your inbox and verify that the Total value is intact.

Related Topics

This section looks at additional resources that may be helpful to you for using EFD and designing custom forms. Two topics are covered here:

- Microsoft Exchange sample applications
- Other sources of information

Microsoft Exchange Sample Applications

The Exchange product comes with a collection of sample applications. These samples demonstrate how to use EFD to provide real-world solutions.

You find the sample applications on the Exchange server (in the same location as the Exchange clients), under the SAMPAPPS subdirectory. Within the SAMPAPPS directory, you will find several subdirectories, a readme.wri file, and a sampapps.pst file. The readme.wri file contains detailed instructions for setting up the sample applications in Exchange Server's public folders. The sampapps.pst file is a preconstructed folder that contains all of the installed sample application folders, forms, and sample items that demonstrate how to use the individual forms and folder applications. The sample application folders come with predefined custom views (when applicable).

Within each of the subdirectories under \SAMPAPPS, you will find .EFP files, readme.wri files, and any Visual Basic hand code (if applicable) for that particular sample application. The readme.wri files contain detailed information about the samples, including how to use the forms and how to set up the folders.

You can open the .EFP files in EFD, where you can examine the properties to see how the forms are designed. You can also modify the forms to customize them for use within your organization. For additional information about any given form's design, consult the form's

Designer Notes from within EFD (open the .EFP file in EFD and then press Ctrl+F1 to display Designer Notes, or select Designer Notes from EFD's Help menu).

Other Sources of Information

There are several other locations where you might want to look for additional information on designing forms with Microsoft Exchange Forms Designer. Some are listed in the following sections.

Online Help

EFD comes with extensive context-sensitive online help. Most of your questions should be easily answered by simply pressing the F1 key.

Application Designer's Guide

The *Application Designer's Guide* is the printed documentation that comes with EFD. It goes into much more detail than this chapter can, particularly with respect to extending forms and working with MAPI.

MAPI Documentation

If you really want to get down to the level of basic Messaging API coding, you'll want to study MAPI. You can get more information on MAPI from Microsoft and you can find it on the Microsoft Developer's Network (MSDN). To find out how to subscribe to MSDN, check the Web at

```
http://www.microsoft.com/msdn
```

Microsoft Web Site

Microsoft maintains a Web site specifically devoted to Microsoft Exchange. You should check this site frequently for additional information and new developments regarding Microsoft Exchange and EFD. As additional software and tools become available, you will probably find information about them here. You can find the Web site at the following:

```
http://www.microsoft.com/exchange
```

Microsoft Application Farm

The Application Farm is another Web page maintained by Microsoft. It is a place to look for a variety of sample applications for Microsoft Exchange. You can find the Web site at the following:

```
http://www.microsoft.com/technet/boes/bo/mailexch/exch/tools/appfarm/appfarm1.htm
```

Exchange Newsgroups

Microsoft maintains a peer-to-peer newsgroup on the Internet specifically designed for discussing

Exchange. It's called `microsoft.public.exchange.applications` and can be accessed on the `msnews.microsoft.com` server. Here, you can ask questions and discuss topics related to EFD with other EFD users. Check

`http://www.microsoft.com/exchange`

for information on how to get to this newsgroup.

Summary

In this chapter, you learned how to create Microsoft Exchange forms using the Microsoft Exchange Forms Designer. This chapter covered how to use the EFD Wizard to start your form, how to customize the form by adding windows and fields and setting their properties, how to join forms together into an Exchange application, how to install your completed form into the Exchange Server, and finally, advanced topics on extending the capabilities of EFD.

Workflow with Exchange: Keyfile's Keyflow

by Greg Todd

So what is workflow anyway? You probably have heard it used pretty often in the press, especially as a great product feature. But what does it really do for you? How does it work, and how does Exchange fit into the picture?

In this chapter, I'm going to take a bit of a departure from the other chapters in this book, and introduce you to a product from Keyfile Corporation called Keyflow. During the course of the chapter, I plan to answer those questions and, in the process, showcase an aspect of Exchange that takes it beyond messaging.

There is a lot of great third-party software available for Exchange. So why did I choose Keyflow? Aside from the fact that it happens to be one product I am familiar with, I believe Keyflow is important to examine for a couple reasons.

First, Keyflow is a great example of the extensibility of Exchange Server. Exchange was built from the beginning to be open, with the capability to extend the product programmatically to do what you need it to do. With this kind of open architecture, Exchange can really go beyond just e-mail. Keyflow exploits this aspect of Exchange's openness.

Second, Keyflow provides a solution for a valid business need. All businesses have processes that are executed every day. No matter whether you are requesting office supplies or making strategic decisions, there are certain processes in place that allow the event to happen. Keyflow helps to automate and track these business processes.

Basically, if you already have Exchange deployed in your organization, you can easily deploy a product such as Keyflow right on top of it. And if you don't have Exchange already, the functionality a product like Keyflow provides can definitely help justify the purchase of Exchange.

In this chapter, I will cover several aspects of workflow with Exchange. First, I will introduce workflow along with some key business drivers for the technology and relevant terms and concepts. This will help you understand what Keyfile is trying to accomplish with Keyflow.

Next, I will discuss how Keyflow is integrated with Exchange Server. One of Keyflow's strengths is that it sits right on top of Exchange, leveraging the underlying architecture of the system.

Following the integration topic, I will discuss the architecture of Keyflow itself. You will see figures that depict the structure of Keyflow "under the covers." Then I will step through a sample installation and a sample application so you can see how Keyflow works.

Finally, I will include a section with some sample code that shows how to start a flow using VBA (Visual Basic for Applications) from within Word 97.

One more thing. As with all the other chapters in this book, I don't want to attempt to rewrite the manuals in this chapter. Although there will perhaps be some overlap, I expect to add value to the product documentation by covering some of the things I encountered while using the product. In addition, I want to provide some information that may not be readily apparent in the documentation.

If you have not yet purchased Keyflow, this chapter should help you in your assessment of the product to see whether it meets your needs and how it fits into your Exchange environment.

Introduction to Workflow

One of the first things you might wonder about a workflow product is why you would use it. Sure, the technology is great. But what will it do for you, and why do you need it?

Next, before moving into a deeper discussion of Keyflow itself, you need to understand some foundational workflow terminology.

This section discusses these two basic ideas surrounding the topic of workflow. Then you can move into more of the actual details of Keyflow.

Key Business Drivers

There are several principal business drivers forcing companies worldwide to use technology such as Keyflow to address mission-critical business problems. These are pretty universal, so you will probably be able to relate to at least one of them in your own business:

- Re-engineering business processes
- Competing more effectively
- Responding to external pressures
- Doing more with fewer resources
- Contributing to the bottom line

Many companies have adopted the need to re-engineer business processes, work more efficiently, streamline processes, and empower workers to find ever more rapid ways of getting the job done and keeping the customer happy.

Competitors who use technology in innovative ways are better able to attack new markets more cost-effectively than those who do not. If your company wants to stay on the edge, it needs to employ technology to stay competitive.

External pressures, such as competitive threats, government regulations, and the need to improve customer service quality, are forcing businesses to take action. Standing still is not an option.

Companies cannot afford to simply add more people and spend more money and time to do more work. They quickly reach the point of diminishing returns.

Whatever you do must contribute to bottom-line profitability—and quickly. Million-dollar technology systems that require several years to realize a return on investment are difficult to justify.

Workflow software is commonly accepted worldwide as the principal method for streamlining and automating business processes.

Case Management

By way of example, one of the primary areas within companies that dramatically affects the cost of doing business is case management. These activities often—if not always—involve responding to external events: a customer call, a competitive threat, a problem with a strategic account, a defective part, or a new business relationship that needs to be documented and contracted.

These external events are essential to, and an integral part of, our business activities. They require us to bring together all kinds of paper and electronic information—assembling and organizing the information in whatever manner the particular transaction requires—and follow a flexible, disciplined process as the decisions are made.

The decisions need to be tracked, reported, and audited so they can be used to speed customer responsiveness and thereby increase customer satisfaction. In fact, any area that has contact with customers probably involves case management activities today. Keyflow provides a way to accomplish the task, simplifying it and making it more efficient at the same time.

User Requirements

In any product that is as complex as Keyflow, there are requirements the user places on the product. They are probably items you would want in such a product, too:

- Ease of use
- Ease of development
- Ease of administration
- Integration with mail and database platforms
- Support for de facto standards
- Good price/performance ratio
- Reusability of custom tasks
- Ability to modify flows "on the fly"

Keyflow provides these features, and the benefits are easy to see. Those who need the information have it when and where it's needed. End users can control their own destiny, rather than being forced to the end of the IS department's backlog for applications development. Only those with authorization are able to create and edit workflow processes. Finally, flows can be reused and modified simply and easily.

Having said all that, it's time now to move into a discussion of the main terminology pertaining to workflow and Keyflow in particular.

Workflow with Exchange: Keyfile's Keyflow

CHAPTER 31

859

31

WORKFLOW WITH
EXCHANGE:
KEYFILE'S KEYFLOW

Workflow Terminology

When discussing workflow, there are some important terms that should be defined from the start. Read over this section carefully, as I will be using these terms throughout the rest of the chapter.

As I mentioned before, all businesses have processes occurring throughout the day that define the work done by the business. Your process could be simple—distributing information to a few recipients— or more complex—routing approval forms to multiple managers for a major purchase.

This flow of work can be described within Keyflow as a *workflow*, an electronic version of your paper-based business process. A workflow is based on a *flow template* that helps you visualize the process and follow it through every step. Flow templates are physically stored in the Exchange database store, usually in the public folder area. By using a flow template, a workflow can be used over and over again by everyone.

Workflows are made up of *steps* in a business process. A step can be simply delivering a message, having someone approve and forward a message, or requiring someone to reply with their opinion.

You combine steps to circulate information, distribute attachments, gather responses, and assign specific tasks. When you put the steps together, they can be made to graphically represent the individual tasks that complete each part of the process.

Keyflow provides a way to graphically construct the workflow on the computer and define exactly how the workflow will be executed. You use your Exchange mailbox combined with the Keyflow client software to participate in workflows. You may receive messages, tasks, or requests that require your response.

Of course, the really cool thing about electronic workflows is that there are no boundaries. You can have participants from various departments, or from all over the world. Literally. It doesn't matter.

Keyflow uses *step icons* to graphically represent each step in a process, as shown in Figure 31.1.

Connectors—lines between step icons—indicate the flow of steps. Some steps, such as the step labeled Response, require a response from a user; others do not. You can configure steps to react differently, depending on the status of a user's response to a previous step. In other words, Keyflow won't perform a step unless the *prerequisite* is met. Words next to a connector represent the step's prerequisite. In the example, the Response step won't execute unless the Start step is done. The steps FYI1 and FYI2 won't execute unless a VoteCount prerequisite is met. Finally, the Done step won't execute unless both the FYI steps have been executed.

FIGURE 31.1.

Keyflow uses step icons to graphically represent each step in a process.

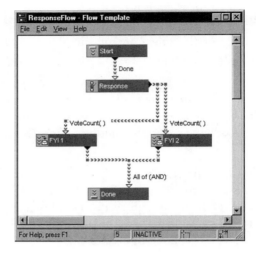

Integration with Exchange and Windows NT

Keyflow is exclusively integrated with Exchange and NT, both on the server side and on the client side. Keyflow takes advantage of the messaging, addressing, public folder, and replication features of Exchange.

For Keyflow server support, you will install a Keyflow Server on one or more Microsoft Exchange servers, depending on the load distribution you require.

For Keyflow client support, you install the client software on top of the existing Exchange client. This is done for each user who will be creating and editing flow templates, starting flows, and receiving task messages. Keyflow leverages the existing Exchange client interface and extends it with features unique to Keyflow.

Server Integration

On the server side, the Keyflow Server runs as a Windows NT service—called, appropriately enough, Keyflow Server—that works in conjunction with the Exchange server. The operation of the Keyflow Server is completely transparent to the user; its purpose in life is to process the workflows that the clients initiate.

The Keyflow Server must have a mailbox—the Keyflow Server Account—on the Exchange server where you've installed Keyflow. When you start Keyflow, it needs to log on to MAPI so it can process messages; that is why it needs a mailbox. However, a MAPI profile is not necessary because you specify the required information when you configure the service after installation. You'll learn more about this in the later section "Installing and Configuring the Keyflow Server."

> **NOTE**
>
> If you are using the Demo Keyflow Server, you need to establish an MAPI profile that points to the Keyflow Server Account mailbox. You select the profile when you start the demo server, and it will use the profile when it logs on to MAPI.

The Keyflow Server has an interface to the Windows NT Service Control Manager. It uses the NT Event Log for logging events, and there are specific NT Performance Monitor (PerfMon) counters installed under the Keyflow Server PerfMon object. I will cover the PerfMon counters in the later section "New Performance Monitor Counters."

Client Integration

The client side is where the integration is the most visible to the user. Figure 31.2 shows a typical Exchange 5.0 client with Keyflow installed.

FIGURE 31.2.

The Keyflow software is tightly integrated with the Exchange client software.

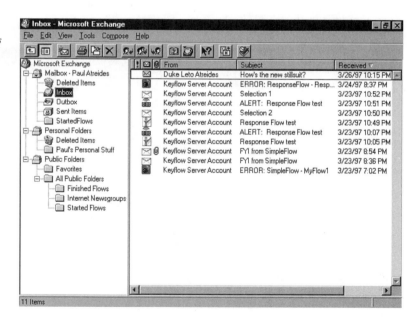

From the figure, you can see there are Keyflow messages in the regular Inbox, mixed with an e-mail message. This is a significant point, because it is proof that Exchange is delivering on the original promise of serving as a universal Inbox. Exchange really is a messaging system that embraces various types of information.

NOTE

The Keyflow client software requires the Exchange 4.0 (or higher) client software for either Windows 95 or Windows NT. The Windows Messaging client that comes with NT 4.0 and the Exchange client that comes with Windows 95 will not work.

OLE Objects as Attachments

As a convenient feature, you can include attachments in your flow template. You can use one or more files, links to files, or embedded OLE objects as attachments to a flow template. When a user open an FYI or Response task message, your originators and recipients can use these attachments while processing the flow.

You use the Attachments page on the Flow Template designer to include attachments with a flow, as shown in Figure 31.3.

FIGURE 31.3.

Attachments can be included in the flow template.

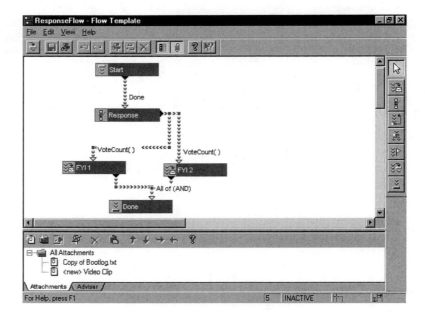

Workflow with Exchange: Keyfile's Keyflow
CHAPTER 31

863

31

WORKFLOW WITH
EXCHANGE:
KEYFILE'S KEYFLOW

NOTE

Keyfile Corporation's flagship document management product is called Keyfile. If your Keyflow recipients also use Keyfile, which is a separate network-based product, you can add Keyfile object references as attachments in the flow. Recipients can access these types of attachments if they are Keyfile users on the same Keyfile Document Server on the same network as the author. All they have to do is establish a connection to the Keyfile server, whether it is over a LAN, WAN, or whatever.

Graphically Map Business Processes

Your business processes are probably not drawn out anywhere. Instead, they are probably just in people's heads, or at best, written down.

A better way to manage a process is to have a picture of it—a picture is worth a thousand words, you know. The flow template designer provides a way to depict your business process graphically. In fact, drawing a picture of the process is precisely the way you design new workflows using the Keyflow client.

Integrated with BackOffice

Keyflow meets the requirements for BackOffice compliance, and the product carries the BackOffice Software logo. That by itself is a significant point of credibility.

Right now, the BackOffice requirements include the following for the server portion Keyflow:

- Runs as a Windows NT Server service
- Network independence—that is, it supports both IPX/SPX and TCP/IP using RPC, OLE, Named Pipes, or WinSock
- Supports the Windows NT unified logon
- Installable using Microsoft Systems Management Server

For the client portion of Keyflow, these are the BackOffice requirements:

- Uses MAPI for send and post, or uses OLE/Messaging and/or OLE/Scheduling
- Installable using Microsoft Systems Management Server
- Has a 32-bit Windows-based client
- Uses the MAPI APIs to talk to Exchange Server

Integrated with Exchange Security

Keyflow uses Microsoft Exchange's security to control user access to flow templates. Because flow templates are usually kept in Exchange public folders, the security inherent in Exchange is in place for Keyflow.

Furthermore, because Exchange's security is integrated with Windows NT's security, there is an added measure of protection. In other words, if you can log in to NT, and you can log in to Exchange, and you have the appropriate permissions registered with both NT and Exchange, then you can access your flows.

This is a crucial point because it means the developers at Keyfile didn't have to construct their own security system. As a result, the robustness of the NT and Exchange security model is completely leveraged for Keyflow.

Architecture

At this point in the discussion, it might be helpful to take a peek at the Keyflow Server architecture. Figure 31.4 shows a diagram that depicts the structure and general flow of operation through the various components. Take a minute to look over this figure.

FIGURE 31.4.

The Keyflow Server architecture.

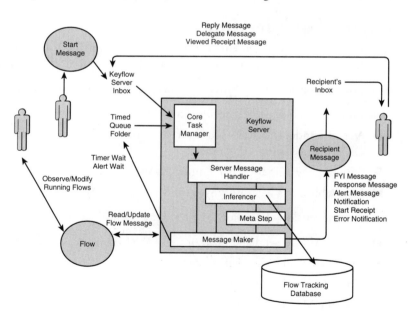

Beginning with the Start Message circle, you can see how the process flows through the components of the Keyflow Server. The flow moves to the Server Inbox and then into the Keyflow Server itself. From there, a few things happen to it.

First, the flow tracking database is updated so you can see where the flow is in the process. Also, if you actually choose to observe or modify a running flow, the Server handles that request. The flow might enter a timed wait queue—in which case, it will wait the allotted time and loop back into the server.

Finally, the flow will be routed to a recipient's Inbox for the recipient to read or respond to. If there are alerts, errors, or notifications, they are also forwarded to the recipient.

New Performance Monitor Counters

Performance

When you install the Keyflow Server, a PerfMon object called Keyflow Server is also installed so you can monitor performance counters related to Keyflow. Within this object are 42 counters, described in Table 31.1.

> **NOTE**
>
> These counters are available only if you are running Keyflow Server as a Windows NT service.

Table 31.1. Keyflow Server counters installed in Performance Monitor.

Counter Name	Description
Failed Flows	The total failed flows seen and referenced from incoming request messages since Keyflow Server service started.
Failed Request Messages	The total failed incoming Keyflow Server request messages since this service started.
Failed Sent Messages	The total number of outbound messages that either received errors immediately upon attempts to send or later resulted in receipt of a non-delivery report since this service started.
Flows Completed	The total number of flows that completed all their relevant steps, causing them to transition to an inactive state.

continues

Table 31.1. continued

Counter Name	Description
Flows Completed/sec	The number of flows completed per second, averaged over the specified display update interval.
Flows Started	The total number of flows started since the Keyflow Server service was started.
Flows Started/sec	The number of flows started per second, averaged over the specified display update interval.
Messages in Inbox	The number of Keyflow Server request messages in this server's private store Inbox.
Messages in Keyflow Deleted Items	The number of messages in this Keyflow Server's Deleted Items folder.
Messages in Timer Queue	The number of messages in this Keyflow Server's Timer Queue folder.
Received Activate New Messages	The number of Activate-New messages received since the Keyflow Server service was started.
Received Activate This Step Messages	The number of Activate-This-Step messages received since the Keyflow Server service was started.
Received Alert Wait Messages	The number of Alert-Wait messages received since the Keyflow Server service was started.
Received Bytes	The total number of bytes in all messages received (both Timer and Inbox requests) since this Keyflow Server service was started.
Received Bytes/hour	The number of message bytes (both Timer and Inbox requests) received per hour, as a rolling average with a half life of about 10 minutes.
Received Bytes/sec	The number of message bytes (both Timer and Inbox requests) received per second, averaged over the specified display update interval.
Received Delegate Messages	The number of Delegate messages received since the Keyflow Server service was started.
Received Messages	The total number of all messages received (both Timer and Inbox requests) since this Keyflow Server service was started.

Counter Name	Description
Received Messages/hour	The number of messages (both Timer and Inbox requests) received per hour, as a rolling average with a half life of about 10 minutes.
Received Messages/sec	The number of messages (both Timer and Inbox requests) received per second, averaged over the specified display update interval.
Received Non-Delivery Reports	The number of non-delivery report messages received since the Keyflow Server service was started.
Received Reply Messages	The number of Reply messages received since the Keyflow Server service was started.
Received Resolve Conflict Messages	The number of Resolve Conflict messages that were sent (outbound from service private store) since the Keyflow Server service was started.
Received Start Messages	The number of Start messages received since the Keyflow Server service was started.
Received Step Status Messages	The number of Step-Status messages received since the Keyflow Server service was started.
Received Timer Alert Messages	The number of Timer or Alert messages received since the Keyflow Server service was started.
Sent Alert Messages	The number of Alert messages that were sent (outbound from service private store) since the Keyflow Server service was started.
Sent Bytes	The total number of bytes in all message mailed out from this Keyflow Server since this service started.
Sent Bytes/hour	The total number of bytes sent (outbound from the service private store) per hour, as a rolling average with a half life of about 10 minutes.
Sent Bytes/sec	The total number of bytes sent (outbound from the service private store) per second, averaged over the specified display update interval.
Sent Delegate Messages	The number of Delegate messages that were sent (outbound from service private store) since the Keyflow Server service was started.

continues

Table 31.1. continued

Counter Name	Description
Sent Error Messages	The number of Error messages that were sent (outbound from service private store) since the Keyflow Server service was started.
Sent FYI Messages	The number of FYI messages that were sent (outbound from service private store) since the Keyflow Server service was started.
Sent Messages	The total number of all messages mailed out from this Keyflow Server since this service started.
Sent Messages/hour	The total number of messages sent (outbound from the service private store) per hour, as a rolling average with a half life of about 10 minutes.
Sent Messages/sec	The total number of messages sent (outbound from the service private store) per second, averaged over the specified display update interval.
Sent Notification Messages	The number of Notification messages that were sent (outbound from service private store) since the Keyflow Server service was started.
Sent Response Messages	The number of Response messages that were sent (outbound from service private store) since the Keyflow Server service was started.
Sent Start Receipt Messages	The number of Start-Receipt messages that were sent (outbound from service private store) since the Keyflow Server service was started.
Server Running Hours	Hours elapsed since Keyflow Server service started.
Steps Executed	The total number of flow steps executed since the Keyflow Server service was started.
Steps Executed/sec	The number of flow steps executed per second, averaged over the specified display update interval.

As you can see, there is a very rich set of counters available to the Keyflow Server administrator. Fortunately, most of the counters and their uses are self-explanatory. What are the most important counters? It really depends upon what you are trying to monitor within Keyflow.

Workflow with Exchange: Keyfile's Keyflow

CHAPTER 31

869

31

WORKFLOW WITH
EXCHANGE:
KEYFILE'S KEYFLOW

For example, if you are concerned that your Keyflow Server may be getting overloaded, you might want to watch at the /sec counters along with the Messages in Inbox counter. If the latter counter starts to increase steadily, especially if the /sec counters are high, you may be experiencing a server backlog.

Maybe you are most interested in seeing when errors occur in flows—then you want to watch Failed Flows along with the Error and Alert Message counters.

Perhaps you just want to know general statistics, such as how many messages and flows are being processed (or not processed), and how long Keyflow has been up. Counters such as Received Non-Delivery Reports, Flows Completed, Sent Messages, and Server Running Hours will provide the information you want.

Installing and Configuring the Keyflow Server

Installing Keyflow is a simple task. The most important thing is understanding beforehand what is expected so you will be prepared for what's coming during install. If you're new to Keyflow, there are a couple things that might be slightly non-intuitive about getting things up and running. But once you get the hang of it, things work just fine, and it all makes sense. Aren't you glad you bought this book?

TIP

The Keyflow Server can be installed and run as a stand-alone program rather than as an NT service, but I don't recommend it for production purposes. You don't get the Keyflow-specific PerfMon counters, and you won't get the benefits that come with having the server exist as a service. The option is there mainly for demo purposes or for other temporary uses. The remainder of the chapter will presume you are installing Keyflow Server as an NT service.

NOTE

This chapter is based on the demo version of the Keyflow product, just like the one included on the CD that accompanies this book. The demo is functionally identical to the retail product, except that it expires after a predefined period of time. Version 1.1, which fully supports Exchange 5.0, was just released as of this writing, and it should be in full production swing by the time you read this. The version on the CD that accompanies this book is v1.01, but you can get a v1.1 demo directly from Keyfile at www.keyfile.com.

Getting Started

The Keyflow documentation goes into detail about specifying what kind of machine is required to install the software. Suffice it to say, if you have Exchange Server running on it, you can most likely install Keyflow.

After you find and run the Keyflow setup program, it will check the configuration of your system. After a couple of screens with copyrights and general information, you will see a screen that presents you with three installation options:

- *Typical* provides an easy way to install all the components of the software, including help files and examples. However, you don't get to specify what directory the software is installed—the default is *SystemDrive*\Program Files\Keyfile Corp.

- *Compact* provides a way to install only the core software. No help files or examples are installed.

- *Custom* provides a way to manually select which components of the software you want to install. You also get to select in which directory the software will be installed.

If you choose the Custom installation option, you can install the Keyflow Server as an NT service, as shown in Figure 31.5.

FIGURE 31.5.

You should choose the Custom option if you want to configure the Keyflow Server to run as a Windows NT service.

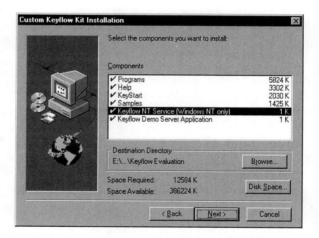

After you click the Next button, you get one more screen to review your options before proceeding with the actual install. Following the install, there is a new folder created for the Keyflow program icons, as shown in Figure 31.6.

Now that the basic installation is completed, it's time to configure the Keyflow Server service. This is a crucial task to getting Keyflow to work properly, so stay with me.

FIGURE 31.6.

Setup creates a new folder for the Keyflow program icons.

Configuring the Keyflow Server Service

You probably noticed the Configure Keyflow Server icon in Figure 31.6. This is the program we will focus on. The others are not needed to configure the service.

> **NOTE**
>
> The entry called Demo Keyflow Server is the program you run when you don't want to run Keyflow as a service. This is strictly for demo purposes. As mentioned before, you must have the proper MAPI profile configured prior to execution.

There are a few things you need to prepare for before configuring the Keyflow Server service:

1. You need to create or designate an NT account that will serve as the Keyflow Server Account. You must grant this account the "logon as a service" advanced user right. This right is granted in the User Manager for Domains program, under the Policies | User Rights menu. This account must also be a member of the Domain Administrator group.

2. You need to create or designate an Exchange mailbox to be the Keyflow Server mailbox. This mailbox is sometimes referred to by the Keyflow client as the "Keyflow Server," although technically it is merely the mailbox the Keyflow Server uses.

3. The NT account that is the Keyflow Server Account must be designated as the primary account on the Keyflow Server Account's Exchange mailbox. This is shown in Figure 31.7.

4. Finally, the Keyflow Server Account must also be the mailbox owner of the Exchange mailbox, as shown in Figure 31.8.

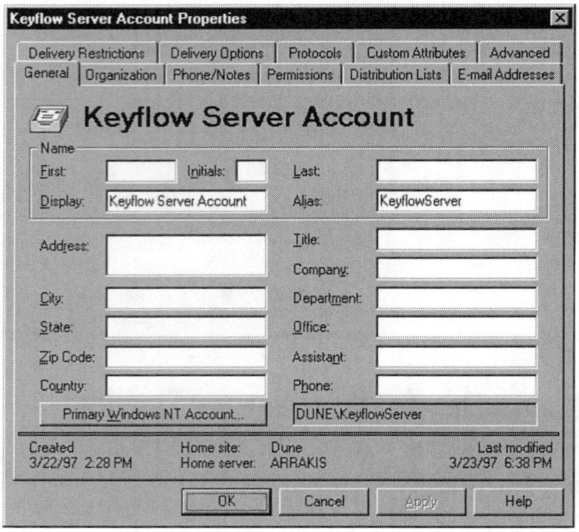

FIGURE 31.7.

The NT account called
KeyflowServer *must be*
designated as the
primary account on the
Keyflow Server Account
mailbox.

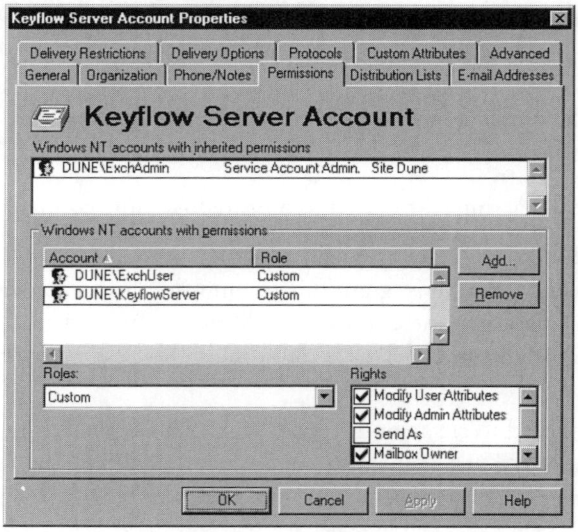

FIGURE 31.8.

Ensure the Keyflow
Server Account has
Mailbox Owner *and*
Modify User
Attributes *rights on*
the Exchange mailbox.

After you have made the preparations, run the Configure Keyflow Server program. A large dialog box appears, as shown in Figure 31.9. It is here that you will configure the Keyflow Server service.

FIGURE 31.9.

The Keyflow Server is up and running as a Windows NT service.

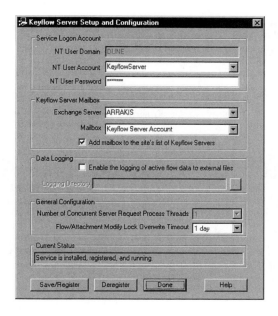

In the preceding figure, the Keyflow Server is installed, registered with the NT service control manager, and running. While all this is covered in the documentation, you can get through this in four easy steps. If you completed the previous preparations, completing this dialog box correctly will be a snap—you'll be up and running in no time:

1. Ensure that the name in the NT User Account box is the one from step 1 in the previous steps. Enter the appropriate password in the box below it.

2. Ensure that the name in the Exchange Server box is correct. It should be the one on which you just installed Keyflow.

3. Ensure that the name in the Mailbox box is the name of the Exchange mailbox from step 2 in the previous steps.

4. Place a check in the Add mailbox to the site's list of Keyflow Servers checkbox.

After you've complete these steps, simply click the Save/Register button. That initiates a few tasks, including saving your settings, registering the Keyflow Server service with the NT service control manager, installing PerfMon counters, and starting the Keyflow Server service.

You're finished! Now you're ready to get clients up and running so you can start sending workflows around the network. The next section summarizes how to install and use the Keyflow client.

Installing the Keyflow Client

Installing the Keyflow client software is done using the same setup routine as the Keyflow Server, so don't let that confuse things. Essentially, both client and server software are installed each time you run setup.

The main requirement is that you must have the Exchange client already installed before installing the Keyflow client.

NOTE

The Keyflow client software requires the Exchange 4.0 (or higher) client software for either Windows 95 or Windows NT. The Windows Messaging client that comes with NT 4.0 and the Exchange client that comes with Windows 95 will not work.

Version 1.01 of Keyflow will work with Exchange 5.0, but version 1.1 provides official support for Exchange 5.0.

Figure 31.10 shows the setup program with the appropriate selections for the client installation. After it is installed, the Keyflow client will be integrated with the Exchange client.

FIGURE 31.10.

The client setup is much the same as the server setup.

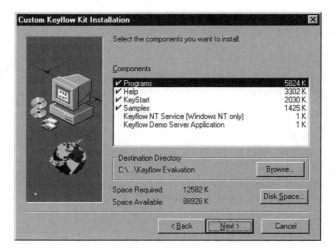

Using the Keyflow Client

Once you get the Keyflow client software installed, it's time to create some workflows and really get things going.

In this section, I would like to walk you through a typical use of Keyflow with a straightforward example of a workflow that we all have to deal with—purchase orders. It is the classic

Workflow with Exchange: Keyfile's Keyflow

CHAPTER 31

875

31

WORKFLOW WITH
EXCHANGE:
KEYFILE'S KEYFLOW

example of routing a form to various people in the purchase approval chain so what you want to buy will be bought. Although the example is rudimentary, it is actually something you could use as a starting point in your own business setting.

First, you might want to draw an actual diagram (yes, on paper) of the workflow you'd like to model. Draw lines between each step in the process that you want included. Continue drawing steps and connector lines, and setting properties until each step in your business process is represented. Or you may simply want to draw the flow in the flow designer while you're creating the flow template. What a great idea! Either way is fine, but the end result is a completed flow template—a reusable version of the actual workflow. Flow templates are the basis of all workflows in Keyflow.

After you create the flow template, you will start the flow. Keyflow creates an instance of the flow template and uses that during the actual execution of the flow. If you need to, you can check the status of the flow while it's in progress. When the flow completes, you will have done your first workflow. You will be well on your way to understanding better how workflows actually function and how you can use them.

Creating a Flow Template

Creating workflow applications requires the use of graphical workflow design tools, such as Keyflow's design window. You know best how to design your own workflow, and Keyflow's graphical authoring software makes it simple.

Because your workflow is dynamic and highly individualized, Keyflow gives you the ability to choose the various *steps* in your workflow. The resulting workflow is called a flow template, which is a reusable electronic representation of your workflow.

To create a flow template representing your own business process, simply select Compose | New Form from the Exchange client menu. You will see a new application form called Keyflow Flow Template, as shown in Figure 31.11.

FIGURE 31.11.

You use the Keyflow Flow Template form to create a new flow template.

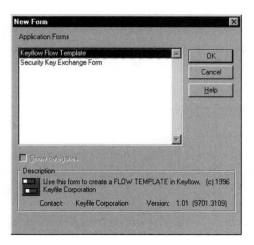

Template Properties

As soon as you open the Keyflow Flow Template form, the Keyflow client opens and you are presented with a dialog box similar to Figure 31.12.

FIGURE 31.12.

*Each flow template has
its own set of default
properties.*

Each workflow template has its own set of default properties, which you assign before designing the flow.

You need to fill in the Title box with the name to use for the template. This can be anything descriptive of what the flow will be, such as a Purchase Order.

In the box labeled Start flows using this server, you must put in the Keyflow Server Account that you established earlier. Note that you do *not* specify the name of the Keyflow Server itself. This is a bit confusing at first, so take note of it. You can change these properties when you run the flow if desired.

Finally, in the box labeled Place started flows in this folder, you must enter the fully distinguished name of the folder where you want running flows to exist. A default name is already shown but you should specify the one you want. In Figure 31.12, I have specified a public folder.

When flows are completed, you can opt to leave them in the same folder where they were running, or you can specify to move the completed flow into a different folder. In the figure, I chose to place completed flows in a public folder called Finished Flows. Again note that the folder name must be fully distinguished. I generally choose to move the completed flows to a different folder so I can tell which flows have been completed. You may encounter a need to leave finished flows in the same folder where they were running, so the option is there for you.

Workflow with Exchange: Keyfile's Keyflow

CHAPTER 31

877

31

WORKFLOW WITH
EXCHANGE:
KEYFILE'S KEYFLOW

NOTE

The original flow template always stays in the folder where you created it and are storing it. It is actually an instance of the flow that is moved around to the folders you specify in this dialog box.

Flow Steps

After completing the Flow Template Properties dialog, you will find yourself in the flow designer, as shown in Figure 31.13. At this point, you have started the actual design of the flow.

FIGURE 31.13.

The first step of every flow is always the Start *step.*

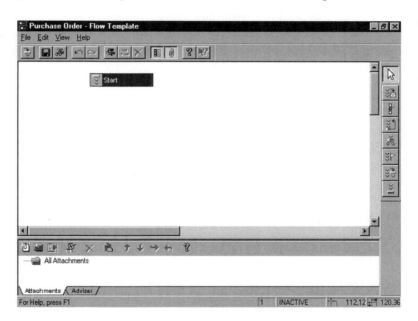

Note the Start step at the top of the screen in Figure 31.13. Every flow begins with one. There are actually eight different *steps* that you will use as building blocks to create your flow—Start is just one of them:

- *Start.* There is one Start step for each flow. When the flow starts, the start step will prompt you for role notation recipients. The Design Window adds this step to each new flow template automatically.

- *FYI.* The FYI step distributes a task to the specified recipients. Use this step when you don't want or need a response. This step is complete when it is distributed to all recipients.

- ■ *Response.* The Response step distributes a task that requires a response—which you define—before the step is considered complete.

- ■ *Loop.* The Loop step repeats a previous step, creating a loop in your flow. This step is complete when the next step becomes active.

- ■ *Milestone.* The Milestone step sets a "marker" in the flow that, when reached, alerts the flow author that the milestone has been reached.

- ■ *Split Path.* The Split Path step creates parallel steps that all have the same prerequisites and all become active at the same time. This step is considered complete when the next step begins.

- ■ *Launch.* The Launch step initiates the start of another flow template. It is used to spawn another flow from within a flow. Similar to the Start step, but it is used within a flow.

- ■ *Done.* The Done step ends the flow after the step is complete. It does not send a message to anyone signaling the end.

Except for the Start step, the steps are kept in the Step Palette at the right of the screen in Figure 31.13.

Each step type has its own set of configuration properties—similar to those shown previously in Figure 31.12—such as recipients, prompts, messages, prerequisites, due dates, conditions, and many more. I'll leave it to the Keyflow documentation to explain all these in detail; let's keep stepping through the example so you'll get a general feel for how they work together.

Creating Flow Steps

Now that you have your starting point, you're halfway there. The first thing you want to do in your purchase order flow is to send the request to your manager for approval, which serves to initiate the process. Click on the Response icon from the step palette and click in the open space below the Start step. A step named Response1 appears. Draw a line between the Start step and the Response step by clicking at the bottom of the Start step until the pointer changes to a pencil, then drag a line down to the Response step and release. The result is shown in Figure 31.14.

TIP

If you have ever programmed in Visual Basic, the process is similar. You create instances of objects from a palette and then modify the properties of the objects. There is no programming here, but the idea is similar.

Workflow with Exchange: Keyfile's Keyflow
CHAPTER 31

879

31

WORKFLOW WITH
EXCHANGE:
KEYFILE'S KEYFLOW

FIGURE 31.14.

The first step after starting the flow is a Response *step.*

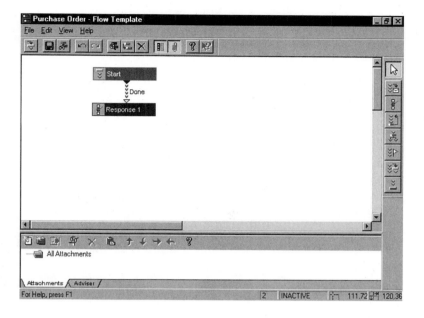

Let's configure the Response to ask your manager for approval. Double-click the leftmost part of the step to bring up the Response1 properties sheet, as shown in Figure 31.15. There is nothing in this sheet for the moment, but you will fill it out next.

FIGURE 31.15.

The Response *step properties sheet lets you specify how the step will function.*

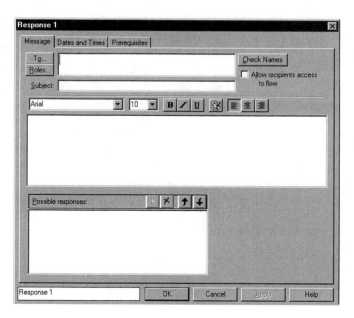

The Response step is a way to send a message to someone and require a response before the flow will continue. As you might imagine, this step is very commonly used, so take a couple minutes and look it over.

Basically, you need to define to whom the response message will go. That person is your manager—let's call him MyManager—and his name will go in the To box. Then you put something descriptive in the Subject field and the message body. Because you don't want to give your boss too many options, you create two possible responses in the Possible Responses box: Approved and Denied. Finally, you update the name in the lower-left box to reflect what the step actually does—that is, Manager Approval. Things should look something like Figure 31.16.

FIGURE 31.16.

The Response *step properties sheet is configured to ask* MyManager *for a purchase decision.*

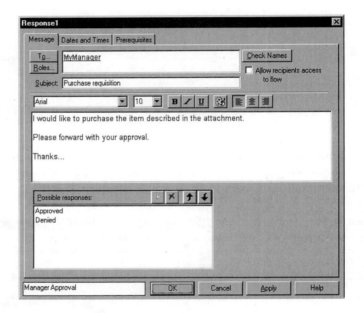

If MyManager approves the requisition, it will go to your director, MyDirector. If the requisition is approved at that level, the requisition will land in the Inbox of your administrative person—you guessed it—MyAdmin, to be purchased. Then you will receive a notification message in your Inbox that the purchase was approved. If either MyManager or MyDirector decides you don't need what you're trying to purchase, you will receive a message about that as well.

When it's all designed, the completed flow template should look something like Figure 31.17.

To save the flow template, choose File | Close, and the template will be saved into the folder you had open when you initiated the process with Compose | New Form.

FIGURE 31.17.

The Purchase Order flow template is complete.

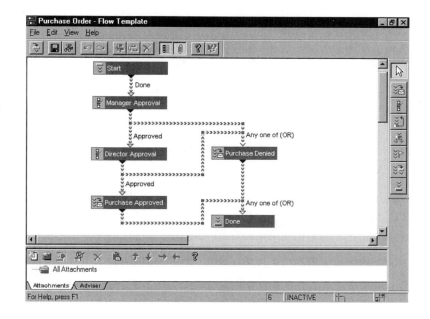

The flow template is usually stored in an Exchange public folder, which can include replicated public folders. For that matter, it can be stored in any folder, but public folders are the most convenient for everyone to access. You may copy, move, and use these flow templates as an object. Figure 31.18 shows the Purchase Order flow template we just created stored in the public folder called Workflows.

FIGURE 31.18.

The Purchase Order flow template is stored in a public folder called Workflows.

Starting and Running a Flow

Now you're ready to run the workflow. It's simple; just highlight the flow template and choose Compose | Start Flow from the menu in the Exchange client.

You will provide a name for the instance of the flow. Then you decide which attachment documents or OLE objects to send along with the flow. You can include an existing file or object by simply entering its path, or you can create a new file or object by pushing the Create New button.

After that, you send it on its way. At this point, the instance of the flow template is running, and it is officially called a *flow*.

When the flow is completed, it will land in the Finished Flows folder.

Checking Workflow Status

You can quickly check the status of a running flow by looking at the graphical representation of the workflow. Just open the appropriate flow folder.

Recall that, when designing the flow template, one of the first steps is to specify the folder where the started flows would reside. It was configured in the example to be a folder called Started Flows. By opening that folder, you can display the current status of the workflow and its progress is shown, as in Figure 31.19.

The flow is waiting for Manager approval. From the bottom of the screen, it shows that the request has not been opened yet. Time to go knock on someone's door.

FIGURE 31.19.

The Purchase Order flow is waiting for Manager approval.

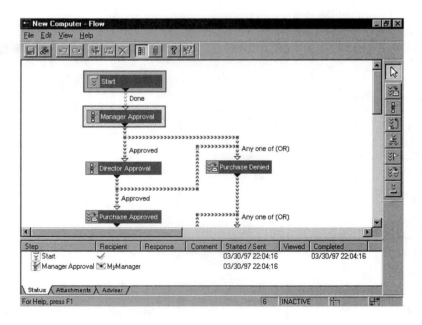

Sample Flow Templates

In every industry, there are examples of processes that are a normal part of the everyday business activity. Included with the Keyflow are several sample flow templates to help get you going. I highly recommend looking these over for ideas and techniques from the people who designed Keyflow.

If you elected to install the sample flow templates during the setup phase, the flows are stored in the SAMPLES directory in a personal folder called SAMPLES.PST. Just add this folder to your Exchange profile, and you will have complete access to all the flow templates. There are flow templates in there for a wide range of tasks, from credit approval to customer service and sales.

Starting a Flow from a Word 97 Macro

Microsoft Word 97 (or Version 8.0) contains a Visual Basic Script Editor that is very similar to the Visual Basic programming environment. There may be cases where you would want to start a flow from within MS Word. This example starts a flow from a Word Macro using VBA. To extend the Word user interface, you can use the Visual Basic Script Editor to write a macro and then associate it with a Word menu item, toolbar button, or custom form.

The following procedure shows you how to create a start flow macro, add a new menu and a menu item to Word, and associate that menu item with the start flow macro.

Compatibility

For this example, you can start only flow templates that do not contain prompted roles. The code assumes that there is a flow named "Approve Purchase Order" in the user's Inbox. The macro prompts the user to save any changes to the document if it has been modified, adds the active document as an attachment to the flow, and starts the flow.

Follow these steps:

1. From Word, select Macro from the Tools menu.
2. Select the Visual Basic Editor submenu item.
   The Visual Basic Editor window opens.
3. Select Macro from the Tools menu.
   The Macros dialog box opens.
4. Type the name of the macro, such as StartFlow, and press Create.
   This creates an empty macro in the Visual Basic Editor window.

5. Add the following code:

```
Sub StartFlow()
    DIM sTemplateName

    ' ==== Keyflow template name ====
    '
    sTemplateName="Approve Purchase Order"

    ' Set an error handler
    On Error GoTo StartFlowError


    ' ==== Word Document Check ====
    '
    ' Make sure at least one document is opened
    If Documents.Count >= 1 Then
        ' Prompt user to save changes if active document has been modified
        If ActiveDocument.Saved = False Then
            Dim Response As Integer
            Dim strChanges As String
            strChanges = "Do you want to save changes to " &
ActiveDocument.Name & "?"
            Response = MsgBox(strChanges, vbYesNo, "Start Flow")
            If Response = vbYes Then
                ' Save the active document
                ActiveDocument.Save
            End If
        End If
    Else
        MsgBox "No documents are open"
        Exit Sub
    End If


    ' ==== MAPI setup ====

    ' Session object
    Dim objSession As Object

    ' Start a MAPI session
    Set objSession = CreateObject("MAPI.Session")

    ' Logon to Exchange only if not already logged on
    objSession.Logon newSession:=False


    ' ==== Keyflow Automation setup ====

    ' Keyflow StartFlow automation object
    Dim objStartFlow As Object

    ' Create a start flow object
    Set objStartFlow = CreateObject("StartFlow.Document")

    ' Set the session in the Keyflow automation server
    objStartFlow.Session = objSession.MAPIOBJECT
```

```
' ==== Find the Keyflow template in the Inbox ====

Dim objInboxFolder As Object
Dim objInMessages As Object
Dim objMsg As Object

' Search Inbox
Set objInboxFolder = objSession.Inbox
Set objInMessages = objInboxFolder.Messages

' Provide filter for getting template message only (quicker)
Set objMsg = objInMessages.GetFirst("IPM.Keyflow.Flow.Template")

' Look for template that has a subject of 'sTemplateName'
Do While Not objMsg Is Nothing
    If objMsg.Subject = sTemplateName Then
        Exit Do
    Else
        Set objMsg = objInMessages.GetNext
    End If
Loop

' Notify user if flow template not found
If objMsg Is Nothing Then
    MsgBox sTemplateName & " template not found"
    Exit Sub
End if


' ==== Load the Keyflow StartFlow Message ====

' Set flow template message in Keyflow automation server
objStartFlow.FlowTemplateMessage = objMsg.MAPIOBJECT

' Create StartFlow message object
Dim objStartMessage As Object

' Create a message in outbox that will be used as a StartFlow message
Set objStartMessage = objSession.Outbox.Messages.Add

' Set new StartFlow message in Keyflow automation server
objStartFlow.StartFlowMessage = objStartMessage.MAPIOBJECT

' Construct the StartFlow message from the template message
objStartFlow.construct


' ==== Attach this Word Document to the Workflow ====

' Create an attachment object
Dim objAttachment As Object
Set objAttachment = objStartFlow.Folder.AddAttachment

' Make attachment a copy not a link
objAttachment.Type = 0
' Add the active document as an attachment to the flow
objAttachment.FileName = ActiveDocument.FullName
```

```
        ' Set the name of the attachment
        objAttachment.Name = ActiveDocument.Name


        ' ==== Save and Send the StartFlow message ====

        ' Save the StartFlow message
        objStartFlow.Update

        ' Send the StartFlow message, to start the flow on the Keyflow Server
        objStartFlow.Send


        ' ==== Finished with MAPI ====

        ' Logoff from MAPI
        objSession.Logoff

        MsgBox sTemplateName & " started", vbYes, "Start Flow"
        Exit Sub


    ' ==== Error handling ====

    StartFlowError:
        ' Show Error Message unless the user pressed Cancel
        If Err <> &H80040113 Then   (MAPI_E_USER_CANCEL)
            MsgBox Err.Description
        End If
        Exit Sub

    End Sub
```

I don't know what will happen if you attempt to run it in other contexts, although it should work fine if you remove the MS Word–specific stuff.

Aside from being intended for MS Word, this example has two aspects that are not generic:

- It attaches the *current document* in Word as an attachment to the flow.
- It looks for the template (called sTemplateName in the code) in the user's Inbox. The template might actually be in a different folder, but you can change it to whatever you want.

This code should be enough to get you started using VBA and Keyflow. The code is in a Word template file (.DOT) stored on the Sams Publishing Code Center, a Web page dedicated to software included with Sams books at www.mcp.com/sams/codecenter.html.

Summary

In this chapter, you explored workflow, along with some key business drivers for the technology and relevant terms and concepts. This helped you understand what Keyfile is trying to accomplish with the Keyflow product. Next, you learned how Keyflow is integrated with Exchange Server, leveraging the underlying architecture of the system. Following the integration topic, you examined the architecture of Keyflow itself. You stepped through a sample installation of Keyflow and a sample application, and finally you saw some sample VBA code used for starting a flow from within MS Word 97.

It's easy to see that collaboration and messaging products, such as Exchange, and workflow products, such as Keyflow, are integrating tightly to provide real benefits to end users. This kind integration allows for easy creation of coordinated and structured workflow processes. This chapter gave you a glimpse of how the integration of Exchange Server and Keyflow provides a great example of these benefits.

You can access Keyfile's Web site at `www.keyfile.com`.

Exchange Server as Part of the Active Server Platform

by Paul Garner

IN THIS CHAPTER

CHAPTER 32

A significant portion of the total effort being put into application development at the moment is being put into development for the Web. Starting with HTML and with the addition of scripting, ActiveX components, and Java, the Web browser is rapidly becoming the main client application runtime environment, and the Web server the major server application runtime environment.

Exchange Server, in addition to being a great e-mail and collaboration system used through its own clients, also provides applications with a number of services. Applications written to take advantage of it can use it for messaging and to host discussions, and can use the flexible distributed object storage and directory components to their advantage.

This chapter introduces the notion of combining Exchange Server with Microsoft's Internet Information Server (IIS) to become part of what is being called the Active Server Platform. You learn how that integration works, explore the object models that make it possible, and go over some example code to see the essentials of building applications for the Web with this technology.

There are a few assumptions I'm going to make in this chapter in order to keep it to a manageable length. I am going to assume that

- You have at least some understanding of the technologies and protocols on which the World Wide Web is based.
- You understand basic HTML or can get a reference to help you—I'm not going to explain the HTML tags that I use in the examples.
- You can read Visual Basic script and make sense of it. Again, there is plenty of reference material to help you with this.

What's So Cool About Exchange Applications on the Web?

Until now, most people have thought of Exchange applications as, well, just that, Exchange applications—in a kind of class on their own. The concepts you thought in terms of were folders, forms, and items, and you could easily do some powerful things, such as thread items and filter views. But the UI that was available to interact with those applications wasn't very flexible or customizable. It always had a set of folders on the left and a view of items in a folder on the right; when you clicked on an item, up came a plain gray form. On the Web, most applications were standard, static HTML documents that, while rich, rarely changed. Although Web applications are becoming more and more dynamic by using database technology, it still requires a lot of effort to build them. So, combining the collaboration semantics provided by Exchange with the user interface richness of the Web provides some very compelling applications.

Bringing Collaboration Functionality to the Web

First, it is very easy to incorporate discussions into a Web site so that, rather than go to a separate newsgroup, people coming into the site can use the discussions there and then (see Figure 32.1). On the Internet, it makes the Web sites more dynamic and interesting, and internally it enables other information to be combined in the UI with the discussion application. For instance, I can put today's company news headlines on one side of the pane and a news discussion on the other.

FIGURE 32.1.

The Exchange Community Web site uses Exchange to deliver the news.

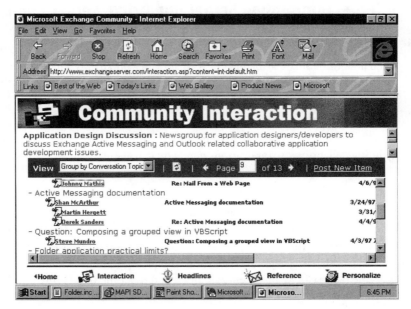

The discussion functionality in particular is especially powerful because of Exchange's support for the NNTP protocols and its own native clients. The interaction with NNTP newsreaders and Exchange and Outlook users enables everyone to participate in the same discussion, reading the same newsgroup from a variety of different clients.

Using the storage features in Exchange makes it easier to build some applications than it would if you were using a database such as SQL Server or Oracle. The main reason for this is the dynamic schema that Exchange provides. If you want a new field in a table, you just start adding it to new items; as you add them, the storage just takes care of it.

The Basics—Understanding IIS, Active Server Pages, and Exchange

Before going into any detail about the things you need to consider when writing such an application for your Web site or your intranet, I want to talk about the basic components so that you can see how it works.

Internet Information Server and Active Server Pages

The first thing to understand is how IIS and Active Server Pages (ASP) work. You can then look at how they integrate with Exchange using the Active Messaging library to enable data in Exchange to be made available on Web sites. If you already know about Active Server Pages and understand how they work, you can probably skip to the next section without missing anything. Otherwise, read on.

IIS provides a Web server that interacts with Web browsers using the HTTP protocol. It runs on a Windows NT server and on Windows 95, although because we are talking primarily about building collaboration applications here, you can assume that we're talking about running IIS on an Windows NT Server.

One of the main features of IIS is that it can build dynamic Web pages using a combination of HTML and a scripting language (usually VBScript). This feature is called Active Server Pages. The Web pages, which are in ASP files, contain both script and HTML. The scripts get run on the server before the Web page is sent to the client, so instead of sending a static HTML page or using a separate program to generate the page content—which is what other Web servers do—the pages can be both self-contained and dynamic (see Figure 32.2).

Here's how it works:

1. An HTTP request comes into the server from a browser, referencing an ASP page.
2. The server loads in the page and evaluates any script it contains.
3. The resulting HTML is placed in the response to the browser.

FIGURE 32.2.

ASP scripts create dynamic Web pages.

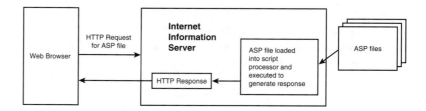

> **NOTE**
>
> VBScript is documented in the Active Server Pages help files, and there are sample applications to that ship with IIS that demonstrate the concepts behind using script to generate dynamic HTML pages and the use of the Active Server Pages objects.

Security Options with IIS and Active Server Pages

IIS provides three security mechanisms for interaction with browsers. One is used for **Security** any user who accesses the server from the Internet, and two can be used when the browser user has an identity on the Windows NT network. The user in these cases has an account in the NT domain that the server is running in or in one that has an NT trust relationship with it.

It is important to understand these different mechanisms when using Exchange and IIS together in the same application.

Anonymous access provides a generic Windows NT account that users who do not have an account on the system, and therefore no authenticated identity, use. When their browsers request a page from the NT server, any process that the server runs to generate that page—a script, for instance—is run in the context of the anonymous account. If the server is set up to allow anonymous access, this is what happens by default, regardless of whether the users have an NT account in the system. It's cheaper to do this, and for many Web applications where the content isn't restricted, it is all that is needed.

The other two access options allow users driving the Web browser to authenticate themselves with their identity in the system. The processes and/or scripts that IIS runs to generate the response to the browser are then run in the users' security identities. This is especially important for Web applications that access databases to update or retrieve information when access to the information is restricted to particular users. An Exchange mailbox, for example, should be accessed only by the person—or people—who have privileges to access it. It clearly wouldn't be good if the mailbox and its contents were accessible by the Web server so that anyone with a browser could get to it. It is therefore important that the script that is run by the Web server to access the mailbox is using the security identity of the user to which it is sending the Web page it builds.

The two security options that IIS supports that enable this are Basic Authentication and NT Authentication.

NT Authentication can be used with browsers that support it, such as Internet Explorer. If the server requires authentication before responding to a request from the browser, the browser can obtain a security token for the currently logged-in user from the operating system and send it to the Web server. The Web server then uses that token to impersonate the user that the request came from while it is processed.

Basic Authentication requires users to enter a username and password to authenticate themselves with an identity at the server. These credentials are then sent to the Web server by the browser, and the Web server uses them to log on to the NT system in order to then process the HTTP request using the correct security identity. It is mainly used when a user is accessing the Web site from outside the NT domain in which his or her identity exists—in which case, the workstation that is running the browser can't be logged in—or when his or her browser doesn't support NT Authentication.

If NT Authentication is enabled on the server, and the browser supports it and can get the security token associated with the logged-on user, this is what will be used first. In this way, users don't get prompted for a userid and password when they have already logged into their NT domains from their workstations.

I/O with Active Server Pages

Scripts that generate the HTML output from active server pages can manipulate the input and output, or request and response data streams. Normally, when an HTML file is the target of an HTTP request, the Web server just reads the file out into the HTTP response and sends it back to the browser. When an ASP file is targeted by a request, the HTML in the file is also put into the response stream and sent to the browser, but it is modified by the script mixed with it inside the ASP file. The Active Server reads the ASP file and runs the script it contains. Whenever the process comes to any HTML text in the file, it copies it to the response stream. For example, by putting some HTML inside a script loop, the piece of HTML is repeated each time the loop is iterated (in the code snippets I'm using here, the <% and %> delimiters bind the VBScript inside an ASP file and separate it from the HTML):

```
<%
For i = 1 to 10
%>
<FONT FACE=ARIAL SIZE=4>
Repeat after me 10 times....
</FONT> <BR>
<%
Next
%>
```

The script can also directly modify the response stream by using the `Response` object provided by the server. For example, a script can call the `Response.Write` method to send some text to the browser.

```
<%
For i = 1 to 10
    Response.Write("Repeat after me 10 times ....")
Next
%>
```

The script can also get information about the HTTP request that invoked it using the server's request object. About the most common use of this is to get content from the query string in the URL that caused this page to be invoked. (The query string is the portion of the URL after a question mark (?).) Using name value pairs in the query string allows the request object to return a named section of the query string to the script:

```
<%
bstrFolderID = Request.QueryString("FolderID")
%>
```

This mechanism is particularly important for Exchange scripts that rely on getting the id of the message or folder that they should retrieve from Exchange to display to the user in the HTML page in the response.

Session and State Management in Active Server Pages

HTTP, as you probably know, is essentially a connectionless protocol. No connection or session is maintained by the protocol from one request-response between browser and server and another. This becomes a problem when you are using script or code on the server to interact with the user on the other end of the browser, because the state has to be maintained from one request to the next. In the case of an Exchange application, this issue is particularly apparent because the Active Server Pages Web server logs on to an Exchange account and stores the objects necessary to access the information in the Exchange system. When a user clicks on the page in his or her browser to get the next page of information from Exchange, a new HTTP request is generated, and when it arrives at the Web server, the script it invokes needs to be able to go to the Exchange server and get the data for the next page.

The session and application objects in Active Server Pages provide the capability for an application to manage its state across many requests from a client and keep that state separate from a session being maintained in the same application for a different user.

The server tracks sessions with cookies for you. It sends a cookie to the browser in response to the initial request and uses that cookie in every subsequent request to map to the session information it is maintaining for that browser. Two intrinsic objects provided by Active Server Pages provide the storage for state information between requests: the application object and the session object. You can save objects and variables into the ASP session object while processing a request, and thanks to the cookie mechanism, when your script is called again to process the next request from the browser, the state information you saved in the session object can be retrieved and used.

The application object behaves in much the same way, except that its state storage lasts for the duration of the whole application and is accessible from different sessions.

Active Server Pages supports four events for which you can write procedures in a file called global.asa in the root of the application. You can use these to initialize and clean up your application and carry out any initialization and clean-up procedures for each session:

On_Application_Start() is called when the first HTTP request for the application comes in from any browser.

On_Session_Start() is called when the first HTTP request for the application comes in from each browser.

On_Session_End() is called after a configurable timeout after the last request from a particular browser.

On_Application_End() is called when the server is shut down or the Web server virtual root containing the application is disabled.

Here's a quick summary of the behavior of the Active Server Pages Session and Application objects:

- *Session objects* are maintained across HTTP requests from a single browser. They can be set up and initialized in the On_Session_Start() procedure and are cleaned up after a timeout after the last request from a browser and the On_Session_End() event procedure have been run.

- *Application objects* are maintained across the life of an application, from the time of the first HTTP request for the application to when the server is shut down. The On_Application_Start() event procedure is often used to initialize its content, and the On_Application_End() event procedure is often used to clean up its content.

The Internet Information Server (3.0 or later) comes with comprehensive online documentation that describes the Active Server Pages objects and the event procedures—how they work and what you can do with them. Take a look at that documentation for more in depth information.

Interaction with Exchange

So far you've learned that

- An Active Server Pages server can execute script to dynamically build an HTML data stream to send to a browser in response to an HTTP request.

- The server supports a security mechanism that allows the scripts to be run in the security context of the user driving the browser when necessary.

- The server uses cookies and a combination of session and application objects to maintain a session for the browser.

All this functionality is important in order to build Web applications using Exchange. The Active Server Pages Web server maintains a "session" for a browser using the application where it stores the objects that manage the interaction with Exchange. The script can run in a security context specific to the user of the browser, so Exchange can manage access to the information in the system in much the same way as with any other client application.

A convenient way to think about it is that the Web server maintains a proxy Exchange client application within itself to service each of the browsers that are connected to it. The scripts in the Web server are responsible for taking the data from Exchange, presenting it as an HTML stream to the browser, and allowing the user to navigate through the data.

The objects that the Web server uses to interact with Exchange are called the Active Messaging Objects. I'll describe in a lot more detail how they work in a later section, but for now let's just walk through a quick scenario and see what happens.

For the purposes of this scenario, imagine that the Web server and the Exchange server are on different machines sitting next to each other. (They needn't be on different machines or sitting next to each other, but it helps with the visualization if you think of them like that.) The Web server is IIS 3.0 or later with Active Server Pages and the Exchange Active Server components installed on it, and both servers are configured in the same NT domain.

The Web server contains a virtual root containing the Web site that constitutes the Exchange application. (A *virtual root* is the subdivision of a Web server where an application lives. With IIS, the virtual root maps to a specific directory tree in the file system containing the files, the HTML files, the script files, and so forth, that make up the application.)

Here's what happens:

1. When the user points his Web browser to the application's virtual root on the Web server, the application initializes a session for the browser and presents a logon page that enables the user to specify a mailbox on Exchange to which to log on. At this point, the scripts on the server are running in the anonymous account's security context.

2. When a user enters a mailbox name, the application attempts to get the server to authenticate the browser. Usually, this means that a dialog box will appear on the browser requiring the user to enter his or her NT credentials as Basic Authentication.

3. If a user is authenticated, the application creates a session between the Web server and the mailbox on the Exchange server using the user's identity.

4. The set of objects that are required to render the content of the Exchange mailbox is instantiated on the Web server, and the scripts then use it to render the content of the mailbox as HTML and send it to the browser.

5. The objects on the Web server that are used to manage the connection with the Exchange server on behalf of the browser user are stored in the Active server's session object and can be retrieved to process the next request from that browser session.

6. The user, having been presented with an HTML view of his or her inbox clicks on a link to a message in the inbox. The HTTP request is sent to the Web server containing the URL of the script file that reads the message from the Exchange store and renders its content into HTML.

There are differences to this procedure when the data is being accessed by an anonymous user, but you learn about that later in the section "Logging On to Exchange."

NOTE

When you install Exchange, you have the option in Setup of installing the Active Server Components. These are the Active Messaging object libraries and the set of scripts that the Web server runs to provide Web access to the system (see Figure 32.3).

FIGURE 32.3.

Active Server Pages interacting with Exchange using Active Messaging Objects.

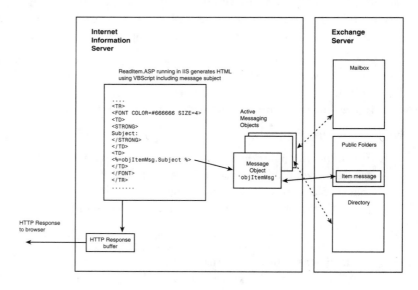

You learned about the security options that IIS provides in the previous section. If the browser is using anonymous access to the Web site, it means that the user's identity isn't known to the system, and the scripts on the Web server are running in the special Anonymous security context on the server. The mechanism is essentially the same as the one described previously except that no authentication takes place, and the scripts can only access resources and data in the Exchange system on which they have been given explicit permissions.

Only folders in the Exchange public folder store and the address book can be made available to applications using the anonymous account. The administrator or the folder owners have to give specific permissions to them in the folder's permissions property sheet or use the Exchange Administrator program.

NOTE

An application that requires authentication to interact with Exchange will likely be limited to Basic Authentication. The reason is that the Web server, whether it is located on the same physical server as the Exchange server it is connected to or not, will likely need to access another server to get public folder data or a mailbox located on a different server. NT doesn't yet provide the ability to chain security tokens from one server to another after they have been obtained from the client, so the second server can't impersonate the client in order to check for access to resources. However, in the case of Basic Authentication, the server itself logs in to the NT domain, using the credentials that the user supplies on the browser. The Web server is then effectively a client to the remote Exchange Server, which in turn can impersonate that client security context.

URLs and Exchange Objects

When you use the Exchange Web client, you may see the URLs that Exchange uses to link to the objects that it displays. (A *URL* or *Uniform Resource Locator* is the address you typically use at the top of your Web browser—many of them start with http://www.....) The URL for a Web page that displays the content of a folder, for instance, will likely contain the MAPI entry identifier for the folder. The entry identifier is a string containing a hex number that uniquely identifies the folder to Exchange. This identifier is held in the query string portion of the URL, which is passed to the ASP file that displays the object.

Each message can also be referenced by its entry identifier. When a Web page displaying a list of items in a folder is generated by an ASP file on the server, it contains links to each item in the folder with the item's entry identifier in the query string. So, when you click on one of those links, the ASP file that is pointed to by the URL in the link is invoked and the message is passed to it.

Active Messaging

Now that you have a picture of how IIS and the Active Server Pages server works and how it can interact with Exchange through this thing called Active Messaging, let's delve into Active Messaging a little. You will need to have an understanding of it in order to write even simple scripts.

Active Messaging Architecture

Architecture

Active Messaging consists of two parts. The first is the core library, which provides a high-level programming interface on MAPI which is the low-level messaging API provided by Microsoft, and reflects the MAPI object model to a large degree (see Figure 32.4). The second is the Active Messaging rendering objects, which help with creating HTML representations of the data in Exchange.

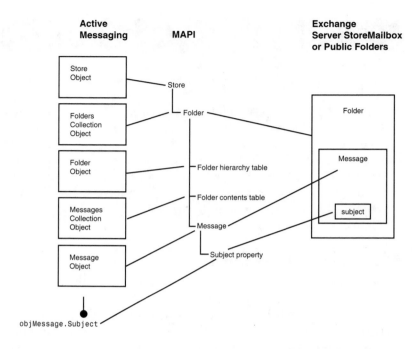

FIGURE 32.4.

Active Messaging and MAPI.

I'm not going to go into great detail about Active Messaging, what each object does, and how you call each function, or even give you a complete picture of the object model, because you can get that information from the documentation provided with Exchange. I do want to outline the major concepts, so that later you can understand how the Exchange Web client uses the libraries and how, in general, you can use them to create Exchange applications on the Web.

A Quick Overview of the Active Messaging Objects

Active Messaging objects are arranged in a hierarchy, and the hierarchy is used to access them. The hierarchy starts at the top with the Session object, which you use to log on to Exchange. Once you have logged on, you can access the child objects in the hierarchy to get at information stores, folders, messages, address books, and so forth. Once you have a folder object, for instance, you can access the set of message objects that represent the contents of the folder.

Sessions

The session is the root object of the Active Messaging object model. You instantiate a session object first and derive all other objects from that. Before you can use a session object or any of the other objects, though, you need to connect it to Exchange using the object's logon method.

Don't mix up the Active Messaging session to the Exchange Server with the session provided by Active Server Pages to enable you to manage your interaction with the Web browser across multiple HTTP requests. Looking at script code, it is very easy to confuse the two. A reference to "Session" in the script will be an active server page's session object. The Active Messaging session object should be named something different in the script.

Stores

Once an Active Messaging session is configured and bound to a mailbox on the Exchange server, you can obtain the list of stores that are accessible through the session. A session with an Exchange server will, in most cases, have two stores associated with it: a mailbox store and a public store. These appear in much the same way as you will see when logged on with an Exchange or Outlook client. When you've programmatically selected and opened a store, you can access any of the folders or messages inside it using the message and folder objects.

Folders

The folder objects allow you to programmatically access folders inside the Exchange store. There is an object that you can use to manipulate a single folder, and there is the Folders collection object, which allows you to get at the list of subfolders in a folder. Using the functions on these objects, you can programmatically navigate around the folder hierarchy in a store, manipulate the view of the contents of a folder that you can see, and get the list of items in the folder. A second way of binding a folder object to a particular folder is to identify it uniquely, using its entry identifier, and retrieve it using the getfolder method on the Session object.

TIP

Be careful with entry identifiers for folders. There are two kinds, and in some circumstances you can pick up the wrong kind without knowing it. One kind is the short-term entryid, and the other is known as the long-term entryid. Within the same session, you can use either without any issues. But if you are storing the identifier—in a link in a Web page, for instance—so that it can be sued in subsequent sessions, a short-term entryid will not enable you to open the folder in another session. You always need to use the long-term entryid in this case. The problem is that, because of the way it works internally, Active Messaging can return either kind depending on what it has cached. The easy way to check what you get when you ask for an entryid from Active Messaging is to look at the length of the entryid. A long-term id—the one you want—will be longer—48 bytes. A short-term id will be significantly less than that. If you get a short-term id, you can go back and ask for a long-term id explicitly using code like the following:

```
Folder.Fields.Item('&H66700102')
```

You should try using the Folder.ID property first, though, because this method will work only if you were first returned the short-term id. If you are getting unexpected folder-not-found errors when you've written your code, this could be the reason.

Messages

Message objects allow you to access items in folders—any item, that is, not just messages. You also use message objects to create new items, either to save into folders or address as a message and send through the mail system.

So what about the content of the items? You can get at the core data within the item with the standard properties on the message object:

- `Message.Subject` is the subject line.
- `Message.Text` is the body of the message.

If you want to use other properties on the message, properties you are defining yourself or that others have defined, you should use the field objects.

In order to read through the list of items in a folder you can use the "messages collection" object derived from the folder object. This will enumerate the messages in the folder for you and can be sorted and filtered as you want. You can then navigate down the list, retrieving and processing each item in turn, using the `getnext` and `getprevious` methods on the messages collection object, which return to you the individual message objects for the items that make up the list.

Fields

An individual item in a folder—or a folder itself, for that matter—can have properties that are outside the normal range of predefined properties—predefined by MAPI, that is. You can create or access these properties using the fields collection object and field object.

Profiles

Unfortunately, it is necessary to understand, at least in outline, the use of MAPI profiles in order to use Active Messaging. This is the case even though the version that works with Active Server Pages has automated the process of creating a profile for Exchange.

Profiles give MAPI its flexibility for use as an interface for multiple messaging services of different kinds. There is normally at least one client profile per client application containing the configuration information the client needs to connect to the service transparently.

In the Exchange case, it points to a server and a mailbox to connect to so that the client application knows where to go to log on to an Exchange Server. Normally, from a client application you would configure the profile before you can log on to Exchange, but because the Web server has to create profiles "on the fly" for anyone that connects to it, the Active Messaging system provides the ability to specify an Exchange server and mailbox programmatically, which it then uses to create a profile and log on to the Exchange mailbox. You simply create a string containing the server name and a mailbox name and pass it to the logon function instead of a profile name:

```
bstrProfileInfo = bstrServerName + chr(10) + bstrMailboxName
AMSession.logon(,,,,,,,bstrProfileInfo)
```

Performance

The Active Messaging Rendering Library

The rendering objects are used to provide high-performance rendering of the data in Exchange into HTML to be sent by the Web server to a client browser. You can achieve the same content rendering by using the core Active Messaging objects and iterating through them in the script. But for repetitive operations, such as reading the rows from a view table on an Exchange folder and displaying them in an HTML view, it is much more efficient to use these high-performance libraries.

Using the rendering libraries is simple once they've been configured to generate the HTML you want. You set up an HTML frame for them to work in, point them at the folder or address book container that you want displayed, and then simply add a line that does the rendering.

So, there are two reasons to use the rendering objects: performance and ease-of-use for repetitive operations.

The biggest challenge for using them is configuring them. The library provides objects to allow you to specify "formats" and "patterns" for the HTML you want emitted to the browser for each property that gets rendered. By setting the HTML prefixing and suffixing the data, you can control the way it looks in the Web browser. Once you have set up a pattern for a particular messaging object or field type in a table, it will use that format whenever that field is included in a view, unless you later override it.

The following sections give you a quick overview of the key objects in the Active Messaging Rendering library. To get more detailed information on each of these objects and how to use them, take a look at the Active Messaging documentation that comes online with Exchange Server.

RenderingApplication

`RenderingApplication` is the top-level object from which the other objects in the library can be derived. It is normally the first one you instantiate and provides a global configuration context that is inherited by the derived rendering objects. If you set a format for a particular property on the `RenderingApplication` object, it will be inherited by the renderers created from it.

The `RenderingApplication` object also has functions that get global configuration information from the server registry and from the Exchange directory.

There are two classes of rendering object you can create with the rendering application object: a container renderer and an object renderer.

ContainerRenderer

The `ContainerRenderer` object takes a folder or an address book object and produces an HTML table displaying the content of the folder or address book in a format specified by an associated `TableView` object. This is the rendering object you are likely to use most in an application, because it makes the formating of tables relatively easy.

ObjectRenderer

The `ObjectRenderer` is used to produce HTML representations of the properties on an `ActiveMessaging` object. If you want a small set of the properties from the objects you are interested in, and you don't want them presented in a tabular form, use this rendering object rather than the `ContainerRenderer`. The following objects all control the output generated by the rendering objects. You can set them up and they will then control the formatting of the output of the `ContainerRenderer` objects to which they are applied.

Views

The Views collection provides storage for the selection of views that can be used for rendering a container object. Each renderer may have several views associated with it, which may be defined on the folder by an Exchange client application or created programmatically and added to the collection by your application for its own use. A view specifies the columns that are visible and how they will be formatted, the way the view is sorted, and the grouping of messages in the view.

Column

The column object enables you to specify the format for one property in a table view. On each view there is a columns collection that defines the set of columns and their formatting for that view. You use them most often to define which columns appear in the rendering and how each of them is to be displayed. This code example shows the setting of the format for the message size column to make it appear in kilobytes with a `K` following it.

```
<%
For iCol= 1 to objView.Columns.Count
If objView.Columns.Item( iCol).Property= ActMsgPR_MESSAGE_SIZE Then
        objView.Columns.Item( iCol).RenderUsing= "%kvalue%K"
End If
Next
%>
```

Using the Rendering Library

Here is what you have to do to set up a renderer to display a view on a folder:

1. Instantiate the renderering application object and configure it by calling its `LoadConfiguration` method.

2. Create a `ContainerRenderer` and point it at a messages collection from a folder by setting the `DataSource` property and a view using the `CurrentView` property.

3. For each different column that you want to specifically format in the table, set up a column object in the format of the object specifying the way that you want a specific type of object rendered. You can control the HTML that is sent before and after the data, so you can change the font style and color or even substitute an image in a GIF file for a particular value. If you don't want to change the default format, you can just leave out a format for the row.

4. Specify any special HTML you want emitted at the head of the table or in the heading portion of any column.

5. Tell it to render the table using the render method.

Now that you have the rendering object set up, what does it do? When you call the render method, the rendering object uses low-level MAPI calls to navigate through a table on a folder, an address book container, or a particular object; merges the data in each row with the HTML specified in the column, format, and pattern configuration objects; and injects it straight into the HTTP response stream to the browser (see Figure 32.5).

FIGURE 32.5.

Using a rendering object.

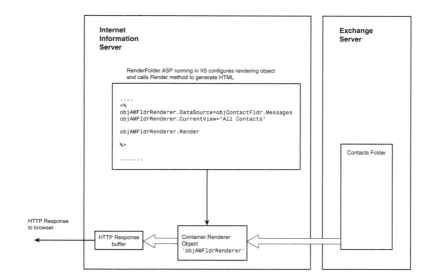

The Active Messaging rendering library is incredibly flexible, and this chapter can't give it full treatment, but you've learned about the most frequent use of it, and this should have given you a feel for what you can do. Using the documentation that comes with Exchange, you can modify the output formatting to serve the needs of most applications using information in Exchange server.

Designing an Application

Before you build your application, during the design phase, there are a number of things you should consider. Understanding these issues up front and making decisions before you build and deploy an application, will save a considerable amount of time. The following are the key things to think about:

- The security model you want to use
- The permissions users need to access the information in Exchange
- Whether to use the rendering library

Let's go through each of them in turn.

Security Options

I've already outlined the various security options that Internet Information Server provides: anonymous access and two kinds of authenticated access (see Figure 32.6). It is important to decide which of these you'll use for your application, because it affects what you will implement, how you write your scripts, and how you deploy the application. Which of them you'll want to use depends on the application and who the users of the application are.

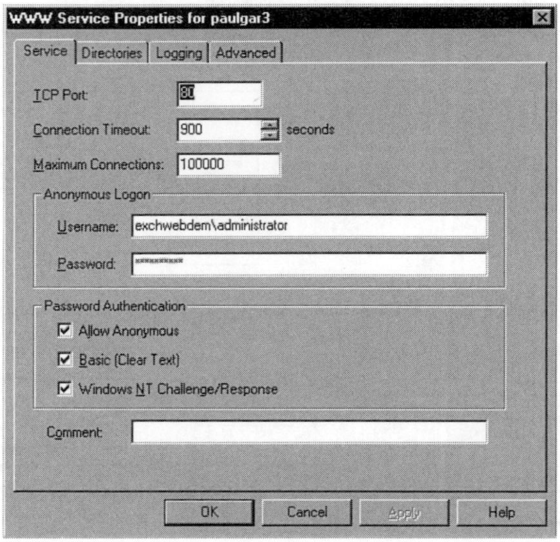

FIGURE 32.6.

The Internet Information Server Manager program allows you to configure security options for the Web site.

Use anonymous access when

- You are building a public Web site and providing freely available information stored in Exchange public folders.
- You don't know the identities of all the people who will be visiting the site to get information.

Use Basic Authentication when

- You are building a corporate or intercorporate application.
- You want to restrict access to particular people.
- Those people have accounts on your network.
- Those people are using non-NT networking security-compatible machines— non–Windows NT or Windows 95 or browser software that doesn't support NT authentication.

Use NT Authentication when

- You are building a corporate or intercorporate application.
- You want to restrict access to particular people.
- Those people have accounts on your network.
- They are connecting from workstations on the network that support the Windows NT domain and security model and are running browser software compatible with NT authentication. This usually occurs only in an intranet configuration.

An advantage that comes with using anonymous access is that the Active Server Pages   **Performance**
Web server has to maintain only a single MAPI session to handle all incoming browser
requests, rather than an individual session and associated objects for each connected user. This
reduces memory overhead on the server and has a better performance for a given number of
users, allowing more connected users than would be possible in the other cases on the same
hardware.

Permissions on Folders

The folders you are using for your application have to be set up with the correct permissions to
enable your Web application to be able to get at the data on behalf of a user. If you require
authenticated access to your application, the scripts that make up the application will be running in the security context of the user who logged in, and they will have to have permissions
on the data in Exchange in order for your scripts to access it. You can either set the default
permissions for anyone to access the folder, or you can specify the users who will be using the
application individually or as a group using the folder properties Permissions tab in the
Exchange client program. (See Figure 32.7.)

FIGURE 32.7.

The folder
Permissions tab.

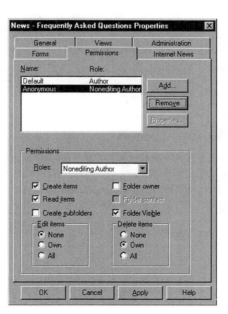

32
THE ACTIVE
SERVER PLATFORM

If you are setting up your application to be accessed by anonymous users, the anonymous account has to be given the appropriate permissions on the folder. The default anonymous permission on most folders in the public folder store is None, so you normally would have to change the permission.

The permissions that are granted on the folder can govern what different people can do in your application. For instance, you could grant the group of people organizing a conference create and edit permissions on a folder containing the conference agenda, and grant anonymous users read permissions. If, on the conference Web site, there is the application you have written to interrogate that folder and display the up-to-date conference agenda, users coming into the site anonymously from the Internet would be able to read the information, and the organizers would be able to update the agenda.

> **NOTE**
>
> The Exchange administrator program allows you to set the top-level folders that an anonymous user will see in his or her Web client view of Exchange. If you are using anonymous access to specific folders, you don't need to configure the folders you are going to use in the administrator program as you do if you are using the Exchange Web client. The administrator user interface is shown in Figure 32.8. In the case of the Exchange Web client, when you open the public store with an anonymous account, the script can't access the root folder and get the list of top-level folders in the store. The list that the administrator provides in the admin program provides a set of root folders in the public store for the Web client to display to anonymous users as top-level folders to give them a point from which to navigate. If you are using a folder with a link that is hard-coded into your site, you don't need to use the list in admin; you can reference the folder entryids directly from an HTML page.
>
> If, on the other hand, you want to use the admin program to select arbitrary folders to use with your Web site for anonymous access, you can use this facility to store the links you want to use at the top level. If you are going to do this, you need to use the rendering object that displays the folder hierarchy.

Using Rendering Objects

Performance

The use of rendering objects in your application can provide an essential performance benefit if the application at any time has to display a long list of the items in a folder, the folder hierarchy, or the contents of the Exchange Address Book. They can, however, make the code you need to write significantly more complicated to achieve a simple task if the length of the list is going to remain small, so making the right choice over the use of the rendering objects is important. Use them if

- You need a table displayed with the items rendered in well-defined formats.
- You want to use views defined in the Exchange client or in Outlook.
- The list of items in the table is large or will grow. When I say large, I mean anything over 20 or 30 items.

FIGURE 32.8.

The Exchange Admin anonymous folder list for anonymous users.

Building an Application

You've explored the various components that go together to make this Web application environment and how they interact, and you've learned the key things to consider up front when designing an application. Now it's time to put it all together and actually build something that works. In this section, I'll take you through the main steps of getting a Web server application up and running and talking to your Exchange server. I'm going to focus on the script code you need rather than the niceties of the HTML content or formatting.

There are many more resources you can use to help you here. First, is the sample code that is on the CD accompanying this book. Then, there is the sample code provided on the Microsoft.com Web site:

http://Microsoft.com/Exchange

Last, but not least, there is the Web client that Microsoft ships with Exchange, which you can use for reference. Although it is a bit on the large size and unwieldy for use as sample code, it does provide some useful insight into how some things work. You can find it on a disk on which you have done an Exchange Server install in the Exchsrvr\webdata directory.

TIP

By the time this book is in print, it is very likely that there will be tools available to automate much of the process of putting Exchange functionality into Web sites. Those tools will make most of this process much easier.

Setting Up the Environment

If you are using anonymous access to Exchange, you can set up the Active Messaging session with Exchange when the application first starts up and store it away in the application object, thereby making it available to all subsequent sessions between the server and Web browsers. Then you can derive child objects as necessary in order to service requests from that browser or any other browser.

If you are using authenticated access, most of the Active Messaging session setup will be after each session with the browser starts and the user of the browser has been authenticated.

When the application starts—that is, in the Application_OnStart() event procedure in the global.asa file if you are using the rendering library to display the content of Exchange folders or address books—you should create the RenderingApplication object, the root object of the renderer object hierarchy, and configure it.

From Global.asa, use this:

```
Sub Application_OnStart
    On Error Resume Next
    Set objRenderApp = Server.CreateObject("AMHTML.Application")
    If Err = 0 Then
        Set Application("RenderApplication") = objRenderApp
        Set Application("AMAnonSession") = Nothing
    Else
        Application("startupFatal") = Err.Number
        Application("startupFatalDescription") = "Failed to create application
        ➡object<br>" & Err.Description
        End If
    Application("hImp") = Empty

    Err.Clear

End Sub
```

> **TIP**
>
> Use the MAPI property definitions provided by Microsoft. In order to access MAPI object properties for which there is no explicit Active Messaging property (such as `Message.Subject`) defined, you need to know the property tag—a seven-digit hexadecimal number that identifies the property to MAPI. For example, to access the MAPI property `ActMsgPR_BUSINESS_TELEPHONE_NUMBER`, which has a property tag of &H3A08001F, you use something like the following line:
>
> ```
> Folder.Fields.Item("&H3A08001F")
> ```
>
> This isn't very readable, and it's difficult to remember the tags for the properties you use. The Exchange Web connector code and many of the sample applications from Microsoft include a file that declares constants for each of the MAPI property tags so you can use the property name as a literal. The file is called AMPROPS.INC. You can find it on the Sams Publishing Code Center, a Web page dedicated to software included with Sams books:
>
> ```
> http://www.mcp.com/sams/codecenter.html.
> ```
>
> The previous line would become this:
>
> ```
> Folder.Fields.Item(ActMsgPR_BUSINESS_TELEPHONE_NUMBER)
> ```
>
> which is a good deal more readable if a little more long-winded.

Logging On to Exchange

One of the first things you will want to do from your application is log on to your Exchange server so that you can retrieve information from it. Again, how you do this will depend on the type of access, authenticated or anonymous, you are using. If you need to use both in your application in order to allow authenticated users to do more, you can. Have one script process a request for anonymous access and another for authenticated access.

Using Anonymous Access

Do the following in your script:

1. Include the file anlogon.inc, which contains some functions that will set up the anonymous session for you. This is from the sample code that Microsoft provides for the purpose.

2. Call the `CheckAMAnonSession` function as follows:

```
If CheckAMAnonSession Then
    Set objAMAnonSession= Application( "AMAnonSession")
Else
    Response.Write("Cannot logon to Exchange Server")
    Response.End
End If
```

If you do this at the top of each script that can be invoked directly on your site, you will be sure that you always have an Active Messaging session object logged on for anonymous access stored in the application object. Of course you may want to do something more sophisticated if an error occurs logging onto Exchange.

Remember, in order for this code to work, you need to have enabled anonymous HTTP access on the Exchange server from the Exchange administrator program.

> **TIP**
>
> To help with debugging scripts, use `Response.write`. The Active Server Pages environment in version 3.0 has one serious drawback for coding: its support for debugging, or rather the lack of it. The most effective way of getting a picture of what is happening to a code path or a variable is to use `Response.write()` statements in the script. These send output straight to the browser. Once you've debugged your code, you can comment out the `Response.write`:
>
> ```
> Response.Write("Debug: Folder ID =" & Folder.ID)
> ```

Using an Authenticated Session

Logging on to Exchange with an authenticated session is very similar, in terms of what you have to include. The main difference is that the function that creates the session and does the logon for you also checks that the session between the Web server and the browser is authenticated. If it isn't, it sends an HTTP response to the browser requesting that it authenticate, before attempting to log on to Exchange.

The functions that do this for you are supplied in sample code by Microsoft in the file logon.inc, which you should #include at the top of any script that uses the functions:

```
<!--#include file="logon.inc"-->
```

Calling the `CheckAMSession` function supplied in this file will make sure that you have an authenticated Active Messaging session open and ready to use. Your script should look something like this:

```
set objAMSession= Session( "AMSession")
    if objAMSession Is Nothing Then
        ' CheckAMSession was unable to retrieve or create a session
        Response.Write( "GetAMSession returned nothing!<br>")
    End If
```

If an authenticated session with the Exchange server mailbox doesn't already exist, the `CheckAMSession` function will attempt to create one and log on. In order to be able to do the logon, however, the user must have been authenticated so that the script is running in the right security context when it attempts to log on to the user's mailbox. Another function,

BAuthenticateUser is called from within the `CheckAMSession` function to request the authentication. The following code shows how this function builds the response to send to the browser to get it authenticated:

```
Public Function BAuthenticateUser
    On Error Resume Next
    BAuthenticateUser = False
    bstrAT = Request.ServerVariables("AUTH_TYPE")
    If InStr(1, "_BasicNTLM", bstrAT, vbTextCompare) < 2 Then
        Response.Buffer = TRUE
        Response.Status = ("401 Unauthorized")
        Response.AddHeader "WWW.Authenticate", "Basic"
        Response.End
    Else
        BAuthenticateUser = True
    End If
```

Opening a Folder

Once you've logged on to Exchange, you'll likely want to either get some information out of an Exchange folder or post information into an Exchange folder. Either way, the chances are you are going to want to open up a folder. The first job is to decide whether it is a fixed folder you are going to open, one that can be hard-coded to your Web site in some way, or whether you need to present the user with a dynamic set of folders that they can access. The normal approach, and one that is used throughout the sample code that Microsoft provides, is to use one script to access the folders and put the entryid of the folder to open in the URL to that script in the link from a parent Web page. The URL is typically something like the following:

```
http://mysite.com/discussions/
folder.asp?FolderID=000002A238F750E2370A430B30C02FF340023
```

`folder.asp` is the script that displays the folders, and the string after the question mark is the entryid of a particular folder.

You can make the parent Web page static and just embed a fixed set of links to folder entryids, or you can make the page dynamic and retrieve the set of ids from the folders and place them in the links "on the fly" using script; just run down the list of subfolders in a folder and present the user with a link for each one on the resulting Web page. If you are going to use this mechanism in an application accessible by anonymous users, the top-level folder that is accessible in the application has to be either hard-coded into the script or Web page, or retrieved from the server's list of top-level folders created by the Exchange admin.

Whatever you choose here, the basic mechanism to open a folder is roughly the same: You get the entryid of the folder, which is the identifier that uniquely identifies the folder to Exchange, and then use the `getfolder` method on the Active Messaging session object.

Here's the code from inside folder.asp that gets the id from the string in the URL and opens the folder:

```
bstrFolderID= Request.QueryString( "FolderID")
Set objFolder= objAMAnonSession.GetFolder( bstrFolderID, NULL)
         If err.Number <> 0 Then
             Response.Write( bstrFolderID & "<br>")
             Response.Write( err.number & ": " & err.description & "<br>")
             ReportError1 "Cannot open requested folder"
         End If
```

The first line gets the "FolderID" from the HTTP request query string (the string after the ? in the previous URL), and then that entryid is passed to the Active Messaging session object's GetFolder method. If the GetFolder method succeeds, you have an Active Messaging folder object pointing to the folder you want. If it fails, it is usually because the entryid isn't right or because the account you are using doesn't have the necessary permissions on the folder.

> **CAUTION**
>
> The Active Messaging Library that ships with Exchange 5.0 doesn't support access to the favorites folder, so don't expect to be able to add a folder to your favorites and then be able to access it with a Web application.

Displaying the Contents of a Folder

Now you have the folder you want, and an Active Messaging folder object pointing to it called, appropriately enough, objFolder. In many cases, you'll want to display the content of the folder in tabular form in a frame on your Web page so you get a similar effect to the right pane in the Exchange or Outlook clients. This is basically very easy to achieve, but if you want to do something sophisticated, it can get quite tricky. As mentioned previously, there are two ways of doing this. First, you can write script that walks down the list of items in a folder and generates the HTML you want to send to the browser. The main issue with this is that it can be slow and hurt the performance of your Web server if there are a lot of items in the folder that you need to display. It also doesn't let you take advantage of the views on the data that are already configured in Exchange. The second option is to use the rendering objects that the Exchange Web client uses. Doing this has the following advantages:

- It improves performance.
- It formats the HTML output with the same columns as in the Exchange views configured on the folder.
- It automatically divides the view into pages.

On the downside, it can be difficult to reconfigure the rendering object to format the output the way you want it.

Iterating Through the Folder

First, get a messages collection object on the folder. Then you can iterate through that and build up the HTML you want to send. In the next code snippet, you run down the items in the folder, pulling out the subject line displaying it in the Web page. You also get the message id and make the subject line a hot link to the message by putting in a URL to a script read.asp that renders the message. The parameter that is passed to the read script is the id of the message whose subject line you are displaying on this line. The result is a list down the page of all the subject lines in the folder. If you click on any of them, the message containing that subject line will be opened:

```
<%
  Set objMessages = objFolder.messages
  Set objMessage = objMessages.GetFirst
  szTopic = ""
  On Error Resume Next
  Do While Not objMessage is Nothing
bstrURL = "/read.asp?obj=" & objMessage.ID
        %>
        <TR bgcolor=#E7E7D6>
        <STRONG>
        <TD  ALIGN=LEFT>
        <A HREF="<%=bstrURL%>">
        <STRONG>
        <FONT SIZE=3 COLOR="#600000"><%=objMessage.Subject%></FONT>
</A>
</TD>
        </STRONG>
        </TR>
        <%
        Set objMessage = objMessages.GetNext
  Loop
%>
```

Rendering a View

The script code in the ASP file that does the same as the previous code example, but uses a rendering object to build the table, is a lot simpler:

```
<% objFRenderer.Render 1, iPage, 0, Response %>
```

where `iPage` has previously been set to the page number to display, and `Response` is the Active Server Pages response object that contains the stream to send back to the browser.

However, quite a bit of work has to be done up front to set up the formatting of the output of the renderer object to get the right results. The following script code is from the `GetMessagesRenderer` function that is included in the script the previous line was taken from and called to configure the rendering object:

```
'from
Set objFormat = objRenderer.Formats.Add(ActMsgPR_SENT_REPRESENTING_NAME, Null)
objFormat.Patterns.Add "*", "<FONT SIZE=2 " + bstrFace + ">%value%</FONT>"
```

32

THE ACTIVE SERVER PLATFORM

```
'subject
Set objFormat = objRenderer.Formats.Add(ActMsgPR_SUBJECT, Null)
objFormat.Patterns.Add "*", "<FONT SIZE=2 " + bstrFace + ">%value%</FONT>"
```

These lines are just part of the process to set up the rendering object. They specify the HTML that formats the From field and the Subject field when any content of those properties is output into the HTTP response stream by the rendering object.

So you can see that although the rendering objects can take quite a lot of setting up, once there, the scripts that call them are very easy to write.

Using Your Web Application

There are a few other things to discuss that are relevant to the deployment of your applications and that you should consider early in the process of planning your applications:

- How many Web servers do you need?
- Do the Web servers have sufficient access to Exchange?
- What needs to be installed on the Web server?

Number of Web Servers

You can connect multiple Active Server Pages Web servers to a single Exchange server, because it is the Web servers that have to do the most work when interacting with users. You can think of the Web servers as multiuser Exchange clients. Think about how many people will be using your application. If it is an application that is going to be used on a departmental level, you'll likely need only one Web server, and it could easily reside on the same physical machine as the Exchange Server. If, on the other hand, you are building a high-traffic Internet site or a corporatewide application and you expect several hundred or thousand concurrent users, you'll likely want to use more than one Web server.

As is always the case, this is a little like asking how long that proverbial piece of string is. It does depend to a certain extent on whether the users will be anonymous or authenticated users. There is less memory overhead to support anonymous users, because they share the same Active Messaging session, and, of course, it will vary with the type of hardware you are using. A useful rule of thumb: a single processor pentium pro server with something of the order of 128MB of RAM running IIS 3.0 and Exchange 5.0 Active Server Components will probably support up to 100 concurrent authenticated users, or a few more anonymous users. This number is likely to go up with subsequent releases of the products as they become more optimized.

Access to Exchange Server

Clearly, if a Web server is to act as a proxy for a user on the Internet, it needs to be able to log on to Exchange. It is therefore important that the Web server and the Exchange server are in the same NT domain, or in domains that trust each other.

What Needs to Be Installed on the Web Server?

You can get most of this information from the various pieces of documentation, but I thought that I'd consolidate it here. With the current (at the time of writing) release of Exchange, which is release 5.0, you need

- Windows NT 4.0 SP2 on the Web server
- Internet Information Server 3.0 and Active Server Pages
- Exchange Active Server Components

You should confirm compatible versions with later releases of the product when they are available.

Summary

This chapter introduced the concept of using Exchange server as a back-end for Web applications and showed how Exchange integrates with Internet Information Server, using Active Messaging to create a flexible application environment. Combining Exchange with traditional Web sites enables you to add discussion groups—one of Exchange's main strengths—and easily build other kinds of collaborative applications.

You learned how these components fit together using the scripting capability in Active Server Pages to call the Active Messaging objects and the Active Messaging rendering library, and then you walked through some of the techniques you can use to put these applications together.

Finally, I recommend that you do the following:

- Take a look at the sample applications that are being made available on the Internet. The Microsoft Web site at www.Microsoft.com/Exchange is a good source.
- Consider how the capabilities of Exchange, especially the public folders, can help you build compelling Web applications, either for use internally or out on the Internet.
- Look out for tools coming from Microsoft and third parties that make this kind of application easier to build. Given the right tools, it will be possible to do this with little or no coding—although even when using high-level tools, it is still useful to understand the concepts behind the code that they generate.

VII
PART

IN THIS PART

Appendixes

Third-Party Add-On Products

by Greg Todd

Microsoft Exchange is a powerful product by itself. However, its real power comes from its extensibility, that is, its capability of interacting or interfacing with add-on products. Exchange 5.0 is, in large part, a demonstration of that. Furthermore, because of Exchange's architecture, Independent Software Vendors (ISVs) can create software that works with Exchange and extends its features and usability. You've seen an example of that in Chapter 31, "Workflow: Keyfile Corporation's Keyflow."

This appendix lists several ISVs that are either currently shipping products for Exchange or are developing new products for Exchange.

This appendix's purpose is twofold. First, I want to provide you with contact information for some of the players in the Exchange industry. Second, and perhaps more important, I want to give you some idea of what is possible with Microsoft Exchange. That should get the creative juices flowing so you can go forth and solve all your problems. Well, OK, maybe just most of them.

NOTE

Here is my standard disclaimer about information such as this. I have tried to ensure that all the contact information, addresses, phone numbers, product names, and so on are accurate. But you and I both know this is a fast-paced and dynamic industry, so this information might have changed by the time this book makes it to print.

The *Windows NT Magazine's Microsoft Exchange Server Sampler CD* that accompanies this book also contains a lot of valuable Exchange ISV information, such as product names, descriptions, and contact data. There are even full working demo versions of some very neat products for Exchange. Look for the notation **<CD-ROM>** next to the product names for software that can be found on the CD-ROM bundled with this book. If your computer supports the AutoPlay feature, a cool demo will start when you load the CD. You can also access the CD directly using Windows Explorer or a Web browser.

Action Technologies, Inc.

1301 Marina Village Parkway, Suite 100
Alameda, CA 94501

510-521-6190

800-967-5356

Fax: 510-769-0596

www.actiontech.com

Action Workflow System

The Action workflow server is a powerful workflow server that integrates with Microsoft Exchange Server via the MAPI workflow framework. This enables customers to use the Microsoft Exchange client to track the status of workflow objects.

Active Voice Corporation

2901 3rd Ave, Suite 500

Seattle, WA 98121

206-441-4700

Fax: 206-441-4254

ActivExchange

2046 Westlake Avenue North, Suite 203

Seattle, WA 98109

206-378-1140

Fax: 206-378-1142

Import Wizard <CD-ROM>

Import Wizard is a wonderful collaborative tool from ActivExchange. This product utilizes the Public Folders feature within Exchange by enabling you to copy information from your own database.

Alcom Corporation

1616 N. Shoreline

Mountain View, CA 94043 USA

800-801-8000

415-694-7000

www.alcom.com

Alcom LanFax NT <CD-ROM>

LanFax for the Windows NT environment enables you to send faxes from various applications, including Exchange.

TeLANphony

TeLANphony for Microsoft Exchange fully integrates Active Voice's voice and fax messaging systems with the Microsoft Exchange client. All messages—e-mail, voice, and fax—are available in a single inbox and can be accessed by phone as well.

ARDIS

300 Knightsbridge Pkwy
Lincolnshire, IL 6006

708-913-1215
800-992-7347
Fax: 708-913-1453

www.ardis.com

ARDIS Mobile Office for Microsoft Exchange Server

ARDIS Mobile Office for Microsoft Exchange Server is an end-to-end solution consisting of a matched set of client and server MAPI agents that optimize the MAPI message for wireless. It enables the user to maintain a single inbox on Exchange Server for the routing of information and communications while in the office or on the road. Additional product components include a MAPI Transport Service Provider, which provides reliable delivery across the ARDIS network, and ARDIS communication drivers supporting the variety of PCMCIA wireless modems available for the ARDIS Network. Physical connectivity options between Exchange Server and the ARDIS Network include X.25 for an enterprise-level solution and a wireless interface for the smaller, departmental solution.

AT&T Wireless Systems Inc., Wireless Data Division

10230 N.E. Points Drive
Kirkland, WA 98033

206-803-4000 (Ask for Microsoft Back Office Programs)

www.attws.com/nohost/data/da.html

Circuit Data Service Packet Data Service

AT&T Wireless Services enables users to remotely access Microsoft Exchange virtually anywhere or any time, using either Circuit Data Service or Packet Data Service.

AT&T's Circuit Data Service and Packet Data Service are complementary offerings. Both can be used to remotely access Microsoft Exchange without modification to the Microsoft Exchange Server or Client software. This can be achieved with Packet Data Service, because it is based on Internet Protocol (IP) and will support standard TCP/IP communications. Circuit Data Service, on the other hand, appears to the application as a standard dial-up asynchronous connection and can therefore be utilized in the client and server with little change.

Attachmate Corporation

> 3617 131st Ave. SE
> Bellevue, WA 98006 USA
>
> 206-644-4010
> 800-426-6283
> Fax: 206-747-9924
>
> www.attachmate.com

EXTRA! Client Connection for PROFS/OV

EXTRA! Client Connection for PROFS/OV supports the user-friendly interface of Microsoft Exchange as a mail client while using IBM PROFS and OfficeVision/VM as the mail server platform. It integrates messaging into the Microsoft Windows desktop environment.

EXTRA! Connector for SNADS

EXTRA! Connector for SNADS is a Windows NT Server-based connector that facilitates enterprisewide messaging by enabling Microsoft Exchange users to share information with users on IBM MVS-based and AS/400-based office systems, including OfficeVision/MVS, OfficeVision/400, IBM Mail Exchange, and Verimation Memo.

EXTRA! Connector for PROFS

Attachmate's Connector for PROFS is a BackOffice solution that allows integrated connectivity between Microsoft Exchange and IBM's PROFS/OV. The Connector for PROFS runs as a Windows NT service and is tightly integrated into SNA Server and Microsoft Exchange Server BackOffice components. Primary features include seamless bidirectional messaging and scheduling between Microsoft Exchange and Schedule+ Windows clients and IBM's PROFS/OV VM/CMS users.

BMC Software

2101 CityWest Blvd.
Houston, TX 77042

713-918-8800 (Corporate)
800-841-2031 (Sales)
800-537-1813 (Technical Support)

www.bmc.com/patrol

PATROL Knowledge Module for Microsoft Exchange Server

Employee productivity can be dramatically affected when access to key systems, such as e-mail, is unavailable. To ensure high availability of systems and applications across the enterprise, the PATROL Management Suite provides automated, continuous monitoring and management for industry-leading applications, databases, messaging and middleware systems, Internet servers, and underlying resources. The PATROL Knowledge Module (KM) for Microsoft Exchange Server provides administrators with management tools and monitoring information necessary to ensure ongoing availability of the server, track current usage, and plan for future capacity needs.

Caere Corporation

100 Cooper Ct.
Los Gatos, CA 95030

800-535-7226(SCAN)
800-654-1187 (Corporate customer service)
Fax: 408-395-7130

OmniForm 2.0

OmniForm 2.0, a Windows 95 native forms conversion software, takes advantage of Microsoft Exchange for easy e-mailing and faxing of forms and also enables routing slips to be added to an electronic form. OmniForm 2.0 shipped in December, 1995.

Cheyenne Software

A Division of Computer Associates
3 Expressway Plaza
Roslyn Heights, NY 11577 USA

516-465-5000
Fax: 516-484-2489 or 516-484-7105

Protection Suite for Microsoft Exchange Server

The Protection Suite for Microsoft Exchange Server provides complete protection for messaging systems in the Windows NT environment and includes the following:

- ARCserve for Windows NT Enterprise Edition
- InocuLAN for Windows NT Single Server Edition
- Backup Agent for Microsoft Exchange Server
- AntiVirus Agent for Microsoft Exchange Server
- Cheyenne AntiVirus Client, Single User

ARCserve for Windows NT <CD-ROM>

Cheyenne's ARCserve product is a very useful restore-and-backup tool for Exchange.

InocuLAN for Windows NT <CD-ROM>

This highly regarded antivirus program from Cheyenne is a very powerful administrative tool in the fight to maintain clean systems.

Seagate Software

1095 West Pender Street, 4th Floor

Vancouver, BC V6E 2M6

800-663-1244

800-877-2340

www.seagatesoftware.com

Crystal Reports v5.0

Crystal Reports for Microsoft Exchange enables you to create, view, and distribute presentation-quality reports containing Microsoft Exchange specific data. This includes information from the Exchange message tracking log, Microsoft Exchange address books, and Microsoft Exchange folder contents.

Desktop Data, Inc.

80 Blanchard Road

Burlington, MA 01803

617-229-3000

800-255-3343

Fax: 617-229-3030

www.desktopdata.com

NewsEDGE for Microsoft Exchange

NewsEDGE for Microsoft Exchange delivers and integrates live news and information from thousands of leading global information sources directly into the Microsoft Exchange environment. Exchange users can easily create personalized profiles and folders and search a 6+ month database of information on a real-time basis. News EDGE provides unlimited access all at a 100-percent fixed cost.

EDISYS Ltd.

Friars Court, Friairage Passage

Aylesbury, BUCKS, HP20 2SJ

United Kingdom

44 1296 330011

Fax: 44 1296 330012

www.premenos.com/resources/organization/edisys.html

Vedi/X

Vedi/X is a Microsoft Exchange Server-based EDI (Electronic Data Interchange) translator running as an Exchange Server Mailbox Agent. EDI is a strategic business solution that facilitates the transfer of business data (purchase orders, invoices, manifests, and so on) in a computer-processable form from the computer-supported business applications in one company to those in another. EDI provides many benefits; the elimination of data rekeying is important when you are confronted with the fact that 70 percent of data keyed into a computer is taken from a computer-produced document. Besides the reduction of clerical errors and improved data accuracy, EDI also provides improved customer service, reduced costs and delivery times, faster trading cycle, lower administration costs, and improved cash flow.

Eicon Technologies

14755 Preston Road

Suite 620

Dallas, TX 75240

214-239-3270

800-803-4266 (US and Canada)

Fax: 214-239-3304

www.eicon.com

WAN Services for Windows NT

Eicon Technology's WAN Services for Windows NT is the first in the industry to extend the IP stack included in Microsoft Windows NT Workstation and Windows NT Server over X.25, Frame Relay, PPP, and ISDN. Using this IP routing functionality, WAN Services for Windows NT provides Internet access for both corporate and mobile users. In addition, it provides WAN communication services complementary to those of Microsoft BackOffice using robust, high-capacity implementations of X.3 PAD for Remote Access Service, SNADIS driver support for SNA Server, and X.25 support for Exchange Server/Mail Server and Systems Management Server.

Ericsson, Inc.

(World Headquarters)

Telefonaktiebolaget LM Ericsson

Telefonplan

S-126 25 Stockholm, Sweden

Tel. +46 8 719 00 00

(United States)

Ericsson Wireless Data and Paging Systems

45C Commerce Way

Totowa, NJ 07512

201-890-3600

Fax: 201-256-8768

www.ericsson.com/us/evo

Virtual Office <CD-ROM>

Ericsson Virtual Office is a client-and-server middleware platform that makes it possible for users to gain access to group, corporate, and public information services across wireless networks and traditional wireline dial-up and TCP/IP LAN/WAN connections. Virtual Office wirelessly enables all MAPI- and ODBC-based applications, including Microsoft Access, Microsoft Excel, Mail, and Microsoft Exchange.

Fenestrae

Fenestrae BV

Loire 128-130

PO Box 77

NL-2260 AB Leidschendam

Netherlands

+31-70-3015100

Fax: +31-70-3015151

Fenestrae Inc.

6455 East Johns Crossing, Suite 175

Johns Creek Technology Park

Duluth, GA 30097 USA

770-622-5445

Fax: 770-622-5465

www.fenestrae.com

Faxination for Microsoft Exchange <CD-ROM>

Faxination for Windows NT is Fenestrae's scaleable Windows NT Fax Server that offers native integration with Microsoft Exchange Server and Microsoft Mail.

By integrating Fax with the environment the user is already familiar with (Microsoft Exchange), the customer can save significantly on fax-related labor cost without adding the overhead of a dedicated LAN fax-only solution.

FileNet Corporation

3565 Harbor Boulevard

Costa Mesa, CA 92626-1420 USA

800-345-3638

FileNet Ensemble <CD-ROM>

The importance of workflow management has become even more vital in the world of e-mail, intranets, and the Internet. FileNet has created a very useful workflow product that will help you sort through your company's productivity plan and maximize efficiency.

Fulcrum Technologies, Inc.

785 Carling Avenue

Ottawa, Canada K1S 5H4

800-FULCRUM

Fax: 613-238-7695

www.fulcrum.com

Fulcrum FIND!

Quick and easy retrieval is vital to an organization's capability to take advantage of the information stored within a Microsoft Exchange Server infrastructure. Fulcrum FIND is a graphical, Windows-based client-server add-on product that provides powerful indexing and content-based searching for information stored in Microsoft Exchange Server public folders.

Fulcrum FIND can help you quickly find all kinds of information, wherever it is stored in public folders. The information can be in the form of messages, message attachments, or form data located in public folders on any Microsoft Exchange Server, remote or local. You can also search by common Microsoft Exchange Server properties or attributes.

Fulcrum FIND includes a client and a server component. Both are seamlessly integrated with the Microsoft Exchange Client and Server, respectively. This means that both have the look and feel you would expect from Microsoft Exchange, no matter what version you are using.

Fulcrum Knowledge Network <CD-ROM>

Knowledge Network from Fulcrum is a powerful way to merge all your various sources of information into one easily accessible source. You can use this software to compile information from the Web, your databases, groupware, and more.

Icom Solution, Ltd.

PO Box 1240 ,Witton,

Birmingham

U.K. B6 7UH

Phone: +44 (0) 121 356 8383

Fax: +44 (0) 121 356 0463

Microsoft Exchange Server Host Migration Tools

SNADS gateway for Microsoft Exchange enables users to exchange mail between Microsoft Exchange and SNADS.

A

THIRD-PARTY
ADD-ON
PRODUCTS

Individual, Inc.

8 New England Executive Park West

Burlington, MA 01803

617-273-6000

Fax: 617-273-6060

www.individual.com

First! for Exchange

First! for Exchange is a customized news service delivered every business day via e-mail to an Exchange-capable workgroup or enterprise. Every day, Individual filters news from over 600 sources worldwide based on a subscriber's profile. This information is then packaged in MAPI format and delivered once each business day to customers running Microsoft Exchange Server. Designed to take full advantage of the native Microsoft Exchange environment, First! for Exchange is a "best of breed" product surpassing any other groupware or e-mail service available from Individual or competitors.

Inmarsat

99 City Road

London EC1Y 1AX

England

+44 (0)171 728 1000

Fax: +44 (0)171 728 1044

www.inmarsat.org/inmarsat

Inmarsat Wireless Messaging Technology

Inmarsat Wireless Messaging Technology (IWMT) is a universal platform for linking mobile communicators with e-mail and other similar applications. IWMT is embedded in Precis Link, Paragon Software's product for wireless messaging with Microsoft Exchange.

Inso Corporation

330 N. Wabash 15th Floor

Chicago, IL 60611 USA

312-329-0700

Fax: 312-670-0820

Quick View Plus <CD-ROM>

Have you ever been sent an e-mail with a file attachment that you can't open? This handy utility enables you to work with hundreds of file formats so that you can view, print, or save that attachment.

Integra Technology International, Inc.

411 108th Avenue NE

Suite 1600

Bellevue, WA 98004

206-637-5600

800-842-8395

Fax: 206-636-5607

www.integra.net

Integra Wireless Messaging Server for Microsoft Exchange

With the Integra Wireless Messaging Server for Microsoft Exchange, you can send wireless messages and pages from your Microsoft Exchange inbox to any digital or alphanumeric pager and also to laptops with onboard paging cards and PDAs.

JetForm Corporation

560 Rochester Street

Ottawa, Ontario K1S 5K2 Canada

800-JetForm (538-3676)

Fax: 613-751-4852

www.jetform.com

JetForm Design

With JetForm Design, customers can enable form fields for use with Microsoft Exchange. Using the JetForm Forms Installer for Microsoft Exchange, customers can install JetForm forms into a Microsoft Exchange public folder.

JetForm Workflow <CD-ROM>

This server version of the JetForm software helps companies convert to electronic processes and documents to help increase productivity and cut down on hard copy or paper documents. The JetForm Filler can be used on the client side to utilize these tools.

JetForm Filler Pro <CD-ROM>

Customers can use JetForm Filler Pro to fill forms and save them into Microsoft Exchange folders. Data that is entered into nominated form fields can be used to group, sort, and filter forms using the Microsoft Exchange viewer.

Keyfile Corporation

22 Cotton Road
Nashua, New Hampshire 03063

603-883-3800
1-800-4-KEYFILE
Fax: 603-889-9259

www.keyfile.com

Keyflow for Microsoft Exchange Server <CD-ROM>

Business processes continually change. We regularly find better ways of getting the job done. The challenge is putting ideas into practice. By combining the comprehensive enterprise information management and communications infrastructure of Microsoft Exchange Server with dynamic workflow software, Keyflow facilitates automating business processes.

Keyflow integrated with Microsoft Exchange Server provides the three most important elements that any workflow solution can offer: the ability for any user to graphically map out and easily create a workflow process; the ability of users in authority to dynamically change the process of a "live" workflow; and the ability, through close integration with Microsoft Exchange Server, to provide interconnected departmental processes throughout the enterprise.

Creating a workflow can be as simple as routing a document to several people for their information. Or it can be as complex as routing documents and decision processes to specific recipients, requesting information based on document contents, and automatically routing the work based on those replies to other individuals—anywhere in the company.

Legato Systems

3210 Porter Drive
Palo Alto, CA 94304 USA

415-812-6000

NetWorker BusinessSuite <CD-ROM>

Legato has put together a very robust administrative tool to help back up and restore your network transaction logs, directory, and more.

The MESA Group, Inc.

29 Crafts Street

Newton, MA 02160

617-964-7400

Fax: 617-964-4240

www.mesa.com

MESA Connection Agent

MESA Connection Agent provides a coexistence and interoperability solution for existing and emerging groupware platforms and information sources, including the Internet, Lotus Notes, MESA Conference, and Microsoft Exchange.

MESA JumpStart

JumpStart is a conversion utility and a subset of the MESA Connection Agent, which provides full coexistence. It converts information from Lotus Notes databases into Microsoft Exchange folders.

Mitel Corporation

350 Legget Drive

P.O. Box 13089

Kanata, Ontario K2K 1X3

Telephone: 613-592-2122

Fax: 613-592-4784

www.mitel.com

Mitel MediaPath

Digital Equipment Corporation (www.digital.com) and Mitel's Client Server Telecom Division are jointly developing a computing and telecommunications-integrated (CTI) solution. The solution combines Digital's MS-Windows NT-based AlphaServer platform, Mitel's MediaPath, and Microsoft Exchange. This open CTI solution will enable voice mail, electronic mail, fax, and other messaging media to converge in a single server platform. A single access point for the user is enabled through Microsoft Exchange's e-mail inbox and browser facility. MediaPath is fully integrated with Windows NT Server and Microsoft Exchange.

Octel Communications Corporation

1001 Murphy Ranch Road

Milipitas, CA 95035

408-321-2000

www.octel.com

Octel's Unified Messaging Strategy

Octel Unified Messaging integrates with Microsoft Exchange's database, directory, and administration. Communications are simplified by merging voice and fax messages into a single Microsoft Exchange Server mailbox and by providing access to all messages from a telephone or PC.

OMTOOL, Ltd.

8 Industrial Way

Salem, NH 03079

800-886-7845

www.omtool.com

Fax Sr. <CD-ROM>

Omtool's Fax Sr. provides full send-and-receive integration with Microsoft Exchange Server, including least-cost routing across the WAN and systemwide management.

Optus Software, Inc.

100 Davidson Ave.

Somerset, NJ 08873

908-271-9568

Fax: 908-271-1044

FACSys server: 908-271-9572

www.facsys.com

FACSys Fax Messaging Gateway <CD-ROM>

FACSys is a completely native 32-bit fax connector for Microsoft Exchange Server. It delivers the power to meet your needs today and the scaleability to grow with your business.

PC DOCS, Inc.

25 Burlington Mall Road

Burlington, MA 01803

617-273-3800

Fax: 617-272-3693

DOCS Interchange for Microsoft Exchange

DOCS Interchange for Microsoft Exchange provides a set of tools for publishing documents and accessing information through Microsoft Exchange. Documents created within DOCS Open can be published into Microsoft Exchange folders for dissemination and discussion.

Pivotal Software, Inc.

310 260 West Esplanade

North Vancouver, B.C.

Canada V7M 3G7

604-988-9982 (then press 2)

Fax: 604-988-0035

`www.pivotal.com`

Pivotal Relationship <CD-ROM>

Pivotal Relationship is an enterprise-wide customer interaction software that increases sales and profitability by giving you the competitive advantage of superior technology to find, win, understand, and keep customers, and it is fully integrated with Microsoft Exchange.

Reach Software Corporation

872 Hermosa Drive

Sunnyvale, CA 94086 USA

800-624-5356

WorkMAN Route&Track <CD-ROM>

This graphical workflow tool from WorkMAN enables you to take advantage of Exchanges features to help you be productive with your postings, documents, and more.

Sax Software

950 Patterson Street

Eugene, OR 97401 USA

800-645-3729

Sax mPower <CD-ROM>

Would you like to create your own little utilities or tools to help you manage Exchange or Outlook better? mPower can be a great augmentation to Visual Basic so that you can create Exchange e-form applications.

Seagate Software, Network & Storage Management Group

37 Skyline Drive

Lake Mary, FL 32746

407-333-7500

Fax: 407-333-7720

www.smg.seagate.com

Microsoft Exchange Server Agent Windows NT

Seagate Software is shipping Microsoft Exchange Agents for its Backup Director and Storage Manager products that automate Microsoft Exchange backup by integrating it into existing network data protection. Features include online support, bricked or monolithic backup, and selective restores.

Backup Exec for Windows NT Exchange Server Module

Seagate Software is shipping a Microsoft Exchange Server Module for its Backup Exec software that provides the integration of unattended Microsoft Exchange backup into existing network backup routines. Features include online support, autoloader support, and software data compression.

SpectraFAX Corporation

3050 N. Horseshoe Drive Suite 100

Naples, FL 34104-7908 USA

800-325-7732

Fax Liaison <CD-ROM>

SpectraFAX's powerful fax utility for the Windows NT environment enables you to manage your fax needs via the network, broadcast, or various other avenues.

Symantec Corporation, The Delrina Group

10201 Torre Ave

Cupertino, CA 95014-2132

408-253-9600 (Corporate)

800-228-1848 (Sales)

800-441-7234 (Customer Service / Technical Support)

Fax: 408-366-5987

www.delrina.com

FormFlow 2.0

FormFlow 2.0 electronic forms software enables organizations to leverage existing technology to automate business processes. New capabilities include graphical forms routing/workflow, enhanced application development and security, and full integration with Microsoft Exchange.

FormFlow 2.0 forms can be registered to private, public, or global folders in Microsoft Exchange, providing access to those forms from the Microsoft Exchange client and taking full advantage of Microsoft Exchange Server's distribution and replication of folders. This ensures that the correct version of the form is available to all users, who can access them either through the FormFlow Form Library or through the Microsoft Exchange Compose menu, where a list of all forms registered in that folder appears.

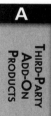

A

THIRD-PARTY
ADD-ON
PRODUCTS

Telesis North Inc.

90 Sheppard Avenue East

North York, Ontario M2N 3A1 Canada

416-229-9666

OnAir Mobile <CD-ROM>

These wireless communication protocols maximize Microsoft Exchange capabilities and administration, especially for remote mail.

Trax Software, Inc.

5840 Uplander Way

Culver City, CA 90230-6620

310-649-5800

800-FOR-TRAX (367-8729)

Fax: 310-649-6200

www.traxsoft.com

Team Talk 2.0 for Microsoft Exchange

TeamTalk is a powerful, yet easy-to-use, group discussion application that makes it easy for groups to make the transition to team-based, collaboration software.

TeamTalk is the easiest way to tap into the powerful features of Microsoft Exchange. Adding a Group Discussion application to Microsoft Exchange can help ensure that Microsoft Exchange becomes an instant success in any organization by making it easier to use, more fun, and a more productive activity right from the start.

TeamTalk provides a transcript view of the contents of a folder, membership, and notification, as well as the capability of viewing the contents while adding a new comment. One-button access to newly added comments and TeamTalk's trademark Stickers (emotional icons) round out the Microsoft Exchange enhancing features. These features combine with the many features of Microsoft Exchange so you can use Microsoft Exchange as your group discussion platform.

Trend Micro, Inc.

20245 Stevens Creek Blvd

Cupertino, CA 95014 USA

800-228 5651

ScanMail <CD-ROM>

Just as the name of this product indicates, ScanMail will check all your Exchange mail for any virus that may be lurking and remove any potential problems before they hit your system through shared files or attachments.

Verity, Inc.

1550 Plymouth St.
Mountain View, CA 94043

415-960-7600
Fax: 415-960-7698

www.verity.com

topicSEARCH for Microsoft Exchange

topicSEARCH for Microsoft Exchange complements the groupware aspects of Microsoft Exchange with the power of the Verity search engine, enabling users to intelligently find relevant information in the Microsoft Exchange environment and beyond.

Web Directory for Microsoft Exchange

topicWEB Organizer is a Microsoft groupware application that provides a single, organized environment for administrators to track and manage Web pages. This enables users to easily find and access information published on the corporate intranet and on the broader Internet.

Team Conference for Microsoft Exchange

topicTEAM is a Microsoft Exchange groupware application that enables distributed workgroups to track and share information—no matter where they are located or when they participate. A team moderator defines the group's goals and objectives and creates the environment for the electronic conference. Team members can quickly and easily view and contribute to the discussion, promoting strong interaction and involvement from the entire working group.

Search'97 Personal <CD-ROM>

This Verity search tool is geared for the individual's Exchange mail and helps you locate any incoming and outgoing messages more efficiently.

Wang Software

600 Technology Park Dr.
Billerica, MA 01821-4130 USA

800-229-2973

THIRD-PARTY ADD-ON PRODUCTS

OPEN/workflow <CD-ROM>

Wang's workflow program takes work management to the next level. OPEN/workflow can be launched on client-server or enterprise platforms to enable companies to be creative yet efficient with critical applications.

Worldtalk Corporation

5155 Old Ironsides Dr.
Santa Clara, CA 95054 USA

408-567-1500

NetTalk <CD-ROM>

NetTalk is a powerful intranet e-mail and directory-solutions link from Worldtalk that smoothly manages to integrate LAN-based e-mail, such as cc:Mail, to groupware mail, such as Exchange. Starting with POP3 and MTA, NetTalk includes connectors to Notes, Exchange, and others.

Secure Messenger <CD-ROM>

This desktop or client communications tool uses the S/MIME (Secure MIME) protocol to interact between remote sites, LAN-based e-mail systems, Exchange, and more.

Summary

This appendix is more for reference than anything else. Although this list is not exhaustive, by the time this goes to print there will likely be even more products available for Exchange Server.

For more Exchange ISV information, you can check the *Windows NT Magazine's Exchange Server Sampler CD* that accompanies this book. You can also use the following Microsoft Web site to check for additional updated information on Exchange Server, Exchange ISVs, and associated products:

```
www.winntmag.com
```

This appendix will prompt you to think about the possibilities Exchange Server holds. There is much you can do with Exchange, as evidenced by all the third-party add-on products available. And if something introduced in this appendix helps you solve a single problem, then my purpose will have been served by including it.

<div class="appendix-tab">APPENDIX **B**</div>

Command Reference

by Greg Todd

IN THIS APPENDIX

The majority of your time will be spent using the Exchange client, Exchange Administrator, or LoadSim—all graphical user interface programs. So you will interact with these products mostly by way of menus and the mouse. However, there are some command-line options and utility programs you should be familiar with. This appendix covers the more common ones, beginning by pointing out some utilities new to Exchange 5.0. Then, others that were there in Exchange 4.0 are listed. The general format of each section is to list the name of the program, a brief description of its purpose, what type of program it is, and its command-line options.

> **CAUTION**
>
> This appendix is for reference only, and it assumes you know how to apply the utilities covered. Some utilities and parameters for programs listed herein can cause real problems with your Exchange Server if improperly used. Be sure you know what you're doing.

New Utilities in Exchange 5.0

Among all the new features in Exchange 5.0 are some new utilities that you might find useful. These are available to help make life easier, and they certainly help do the job.

You can find these utilities on the Exchange Server CD-ROM in the \support\utils directory. They are described in detail in a file called README.DOC in that directory.

All utilities are available for both Intel and Alpha platforms (except REPLVER). Because these utilites are well-documented, I won't describe them here, but I do want to bring their existence to your attention.

Utility	Title
AUTHREST	Authoritative Restore
ERROR	Error Converter
FILEVER	File Version Utility
IMCDUMP	IMC Queue Dump
IMCCOPY	IMC Configuration Restorer
IMCSAVE	IMC Configuration Extractor
IMSTIMES	Internet Newsfeed Times
MDBVU32	Information Store Viewer (propvu32.dll, statvu32.dll, tblvu32.dll, xvport.dll)

Utility	Title
REPLVER	Public Folder Replication Verification Tool (available only for Intel platforms)
RESTEST	IMC DNS Resolver Test

ADMIN

The Exchange Administrator program is the main interface for managing an Exchange server. It is optionally installed during the server Setup process. You can install Administrator on any machine, not just the Exchange server itself.

ADMIN.EXE is a program that exists in the \EXCHSRVR\BIN directory. If you execute it, the Exchange Administrator program will start. The following sections summarize the command-line switches available for the Administrator program.

/r

The /r parameter starts the Administrator program in raw mode. Raw mode provides access to all directory attributes contained in the schema.

CAUTION

Because the directory is exposed, you should be careful with modifications when using this option. You can really mess up your Exchange server if you don't know what you are doing.

The *schema* defines the structure for information in the directory. The schema defines the rules for structuring information such as which attributes are associated with which objects, and which types of values can be associated with which attributes. The schema also defines the relationship between objects. The directory enforces these rules.

You can also run the Administrator program in raw mode by creating a RawMode entry in the Windows NT Registry. Creating the Registry entry makes the Administrator program run in raw mode at all times. To create the Registry entry, run the Registry Editor and find the following key:

HKEY_CURRENT_USER\Software\Microsoft\Exchange\MSExchangeAdmin\Desktop

Under this key, add a new value as follows:

Value Name: RawMode

Data Type: REG_DWORD

Data:	0 (don't run in raw mode unless forced by /r command-line switch)
	1 (always run in raw mode)
Radix:	Hex

/h or /?

The /h or /? parameter starts the Administrator program and displays the Microsoft Exchange Administrator help.

/s <ServerName>

The /s <ServerName> option starts the Administrator program and connects to the server you specify for *ServerName*.

/m [Site\]MonitorName¦Server

The /m [Site\]MonitorName¦Server option starts the Administrator program and starts the monitor you specify for *MonitorName*. The server *Site* is optional. *MonitorName* is the directory name of the monitor within the site, and *Server* is the server to which the monitor should connect.

/t

The /t option temporarily suspends monitoring on a server that you are taking down for maintenance or backup. This option is used in conjunction with various monitor suspension options, which are explained in the following:

- ▪ /t r: Suspends repairs during the maintenance mode, but sends a notification if a problem is found
- ▪ /t n: Suspends notification during the maintenance mode but initiates any repairs specified by the monitor
- ▪ /t nr: Suspends both notification and repairs during the maintenance mode
- ▪ /t: Resets the monitor to normal mode

NOTE

When you are performing maintenance on a server, you must set the admin /t command to start before the server goes offline. Consider the polling intervals of the monitors and be certain that each monitor receives a maintenance mode notification before the server goes down.

/i <import file> /d <directory server name> /n /o <options file>

This option runs the command-line directory import utility. The /i switch is required, and all other switches are optional.

<import file> is the name of the file that contains the directory information to be imported.

<directory server name> is the name of the server whose directory is to be updated.

/n sets the "no progress" switch. This indicates that you do not want to see the progress bar that is displayed by default during directory import.

<options file> is the name of a file containing options that control how directory information is imported.

/e <export file> /d <directory server name> /n /o <options file>

This option runs the command-line directory export utility. The /e switch is required, and all other switches are optional.

<export file> is the name of the file where you want exported directory information to be written.

<directory server name> is the name of the server from which the directory will be exported.

/n sets the "no progress" switch. This indicates you do not want to see the progress bar that is displayed by default during directory export.

<options file> is the name of a file containing options that control how directory information is imported.

EDBUTIL

EDBUTIL is one of the Exchange Server database utilities. Run it with no command-line options to list a description of the options on the screen.

EDBUTIL.EXE is in the \EXCHSRVR\BIN directory. It can perform five housekeeping functions on a server's databases. Each housekeeping function is described in the following sections (you can also read more about EDBUTIL in Chapter 28, "Diagnosing the Cause of a Problem"):

- Defragmentation: EDBUTIL /d <database name> [options]
- Recovery: EDBUTIL /r [options]
- Backup: EDBUTIL /b <backup path> [options]
- Upgrade: EDBUTIL /u <database name> /d<previous .DLL> [options]
- File Dump: EDBUTIL /m[mode-modifier] <filename>

Defragmentation/Compaction

The defragmentation/compaction function performs offline compaction of a database.

The following is the syntax for defragmentation:

```
EDBUTIL /d <database name> [options]
```

■ `<database name>`: Either the filename of the database to be compacted, or `/ispriv`, `/ispub`, or `/ds`. The switches `/ispriv`, `/ispub`, and `/ds` use the Registry to automatically set the database name, log file path, and system file path for the appropriate Exchange store.

The *options* are zero or more of the following switches, separated by a space:

■ `/l<path>`: The location of the log files. The default is the current directory.
■ `/s<path>`: The location of the system files (for example, the checkpoint file). The default is the current directory.
■ `/r`: Repair the database while defragmenting.
■ `/b<db>`: Make a backup copy under the specified name.
■ `/t<db>`: Set the temporary database name (the default is TEMPDFRG.EDB).
■ `/p`: Preserve the temporary database. (That is, disable instating. When instating is disabled with `/p`, the original database is preserved uncompacted, and the temporary database contains the defragmented version of the database.)
■ `/n`: Dump defragmentation information to DFRGINFO.TXT.
■ `/o`: Suppress the text header identifying the utility, version, and copyright information.

> **NOTE**
>
> Note that before defragmentation begins, soft recovery is always performed automatically to ensure that the database is in a consistent state.

Recovery

The recovery function performs an Information Store recovery, bringing all databases to a consistent state.

The following is the syntax for the recovery function:

```
EDBUTIL /r [options]
```

The *options* are zero or more of the following switches, separated by a space:

- ■ /is or /ds: The special switches /is and /ds use the Registry to automatically set the log file path and system file path for recovery of the appropriate Exchange store(s).
- ■ /l<*path*>: The location of the log files. The default is the current directory.
- ■ /s<*path*>: The location of system files (for example, the checkpoint file). The default is the current directory.
- ■ /o: Suppress the text header identifying the utility, version, and copyright information.

Consistency

The consistency function verifies the consistency of an Exchange database.

The following is the syntax:

```
EDBUTIL /c <database name> [options]
```

The parameters are either <*database name*> (the filename of the database to verify) or /ispriv, /ispub, or /ds. The special switches /ispriv, /ispub, and /ds use the Registry to automatically set the database name for the appropriate Exchange store.

The *options* are zero or more of the following switches, separated by a space:

- ■ /a: Check all nodes, including deleted ones.
- ■ /k: Generate the key usage statistics.
- ■ /p: Generate the page usage information.
- ■ /t<*name*>: Perform a check on the specified table <*name*> only. The default checks all tables in the database.
- ■ /o: Suppress the text header identifying the utility, version, and copyright information.

NOTE

The consistency checker performs no recovery and always assumes that the database is in a consistent state. It returns an error if this is not the case.

Upgrade

The upgrade function upgrades a database (created using a previous release of Microsoft Exchange Server) to the current version.

The following is the syntax:

```
EDBUTIL /u <database name> /d<previous .DLL> [options]
```

The following are the parameters:

- *<database name>*: The filename of the database to upgrade.
- */d<previous .DLL>*: The pathed filename of the .DLL that came with the release of Microsoft Exchange Server from which you're upgrading.

The *options* are zero or more of the following switches, separated by a space:

- */b<db>*: Make backup copy under the specified name.
- */t<db>*: Set temporary database name. The default is TEMPUPGD.EDB.
- */p*: Preserve the temporary database. (That is, disable instating. When instating is disabled with /p, the original database is preserved, and the temporary database contains the upgraded version of the database.)
- */n*: Dump the upgrade information to UPGDINFO.TXT.
- */o*: Suppress the text header identifying the utility, version, and copyright information.

NOTE

First, you should use this utility only to upgrade a database after an internal database format change has taken place. If necessary, this will usually coincide only with the release of a major, new revision of Microsoft Exchange Server.

Second, before you upgrade, the database should be in a consistent state. An error will be returned if otherwise.

File Dump

The File Dump function generates formatted output of various database file types.

The following is the syntax:

```
EDBUTIL /m[mode-modifier] <filename>
```

The following are the parameters:

- *[mode-modifier]*: An optional letter designating the type of file dump to perform. Valid values are h (dump the database header—the default) and k (dump the checkpoint file).
- *<filename>*: The name of the file to dump. The type of the specified file should match the dump type being requested (for example, if you are using /mh, *<filename>* must be the name of a database).

ISINTEG

ISINTEG is one of the Exchange Server database utilities. Run it with no command-line options to list a description of the options on the screen.

ISINTEG.EXE is in the \EXCHSRVR\BIN directory.

There are three main ISINTEG functions: fix, patch/repair, and dump. Each is described in the following sections. For more information on ISINTEG, see Chapter 28.

Fix

The fix function provides a way to check, and optionally fix, the Exchange Information Store. The command syntax is as follows:

```
isinteg -pri¦-pub [-fix] [-verbose] [-l logfilename] [-test testname,...]
```

The following summarizes the parameters for the fix function:

- `-pri`: Run against the private store
- `-pub`: Run against the public store
- `-fix`: Check *and* correct (default is check only)
- `-verbose`: Report verbosely
- `-l logfilename`: (default is isinteg.pri or isinteg.pub in current directory)
- `-test testname`: (default is all tests, listed next)

  Main tests: `folder, message, aclitem, mailbox, delfld, acllist, rcvfld, timedev, rowcounts, attach, morefld, oofhist, peruser, global, searchq, dlvrto, namedprop`

  Ref count tests: `msgref, attachref, acllistref, aclitemref, fldrcv, fldsub`

  Special tests: `deleteextracolumns` (not included in all)

Patch/Repair

The Patch/Repair function will repair the Exchange Information Store after an offline restore.

If you have restored a database—either PRIV.EDB or PUB.EDB—from a backup, you must run the patch/repair utility before the MSExchangeIS service will start.

> **NOTE**
>
> To run this utility, the MSExchangeDS and MSExchangeSA services must be running and the MSExchangeIS service must be stopped.

Following is the typical syntax for patch/repair:

```
isinteg -patch
```

Dump

The dump function generates a verbose dump of the Exchange Information Store data. Following is the command syntax:

```
isinteg -pri¦-pub -dump [-l logfilename]
```

The following summarizes the parameters for the dump function:

- -pri: Run against the private store
- -pub: Run against the public store
- -dump: Dump the specified database
- -l logfilename: Dump the data into the file logfilename

LoadSim

LoadSim is the Microsoft Exchange Client load simulation tool provided with Exchange Server. See Chapter 29, "Understanding and Using LoadSim," for more details on using LoadSim.

For convenience, LoadSim has some optional command-line options that can help automate running LoadSim scripts.

The following is the syntax, and each part is described in the following sections:

```
LOADSIM [simfile[test]] [-q]
```

- simfile: The simfile parameter specifies the .SIM file to open when LoadSim is started. You must use a fully qualified filename if the .SIM file does not exist in the current directory. I always use a fully qualified filename.

- test: The test parameter specifies the name of the test in the .SIM file to run. Upon successfully opening the .SIM file, LoadSim automatically starts the test specified by this parameter.

  It is not valid to specify test without a simfile.

- -q: This parameter sets the Auto-Quit feature. This will cause LoadSim to automatically quit after the currently running test—either specified by the test parameter or manually invoked—completes.

LSLOG

LSLOG is a utility included with LoadSim that is used for parsing and reporting on the LoadSim log files. This utility is quite useful for generating statistics and data based on the performance of the LoadSim client.

The following is the syntax:

```
LSLOG <op> <args>
```

The parameters *<op>* and *<args>* are the operation to perform and its arguments, respectively:

- *<op>*: The LSLOG operation to perform. All operations write to stdout. You can abbreviate the values for *<op>*, as shown in the following examples.
- *<args>*: The arguments of the *<op>*.

Valid operations for *<op>* are as follows. Each operation is explained in a subsequent section:

- truncate
- merge
- answer
- times

truncate

The truncate parameter removes times before the begin time and after the end time. It also truncates the file at end-of-year boundaries.

The following is the syntax for truncate:

```
LSLOG truncate logfile [begin end]
```

- *logfile* is the name of the Loadsim perf log file to truncate.
- *begin* and *end* are the times in hours, and are optional. The default values are 1 and 4, respectively. The hours are zero-based. Hour 0 covers the first 60 minutes; hour 1 covers the second 60 minutes; and so on.

merge

The merge parameter merges two or more log files so that the resulting single log file's events are still in sequential order.

The following is the syntax:

```
LSLOG merge [/r] logfile logfile [logfile ...]
```

If the /r (rebase) flag is specified, all files begin at Jan 01 00:00:00, and are merged accordingly.

merge supports wildcard file specifications.

answer

The answer parameter computes and outputs the Nth percentile single and weighted average response times for the given LoadSim *logfile*. If not specified, the default *pctile* is 95, or the 95th percentile.

B

COMMAND
REFERENCE

The following is the syntax:

```
LSLOG answer [/i] logfile [pctile] [flags...]
```

If the /i (ignore) flag is specified, weight values for specific actions of a given type are ignored; all actions of the same type are weighted equally.

The -w flag can be specified at the end of the command. It means to override the default weight for a given action. The syntax looks like this:

```
-wACTION:N
```

where *ACTION* is the name of the action—for example, READ—and *N* is the new weight. Action names are matched case-insensitive, without spaces, and only up to the number of characters you specify; for example, replya matches REPLY ALL.

You can specify as many flags as you want. For example, you can override the weight values of several different actions (see the example in the "Examples" section).

times

The times parameter outputs the first and last times the given log file was logged into.

The following is the syntax:

```
LSLOG times logfile
```

The times parameter supports wildcard file specifications. The *logfile* is the LoadSim log file to read.

Examples

Following are some examples of LSLOG usage:

```
LSLOG truncate loadsim.log > loadsim.1t4

LSLOG trunc loadsim.log 4 8 > loadsim.4t8

LSLOG merge /r client?.log > mclients.log

LSLOG answer loadsim.log

LSLOG answer -i loadsim.log

LSLOG answer loadsim.log -wread:5 -wsend:5 -wreplya:0

LSLOG times *.log
```

MTACHECK

MTACHECK is one of the Exchange Server database utilities. The MTA database integrity checker performs checks on the MTA objects and does a general cleanup by collecting orphaned objects and discarding them. For more on MTACHECK, see Chapter 28.

MTACHECK.EXE is located in the \EXCHSRVR\BIN directory. Run MTACHECK with no command-line options to execute the MTA check. Run it with the /? parameter to list options on screen.

The following is the syntax:

```
MTACHECK [/V] [/F <filename>]
```

NOTE

To run this utility, the MSExchangeMTA service must be stopped.

/V

The /V option provides verbose output during the execution of the MTA Checker.

/F <filename>

The /F option redirects the output of MTACHECK into the file specified by *filename*.

NEWPROF

The Exchange clients include a utility called NEWPROF.EXE that can be used to automatically generate profiles. This utility generates a profile from the DEFAULT.PRF file.

An administrator can create a customized DEFAULT.PRF using the Setup Editor that contains the home server for the users as well as any other desired configuration information. After users install the client, they can use NEWPROF.EXE with the installed DEFAULT.PRF, as customized by the administrator, to generate their profile. This should be easier for the user, because the user doesn't have to answer any questions when the client first starts.

When the client is installed, both NEWPROFS.EXE and DEFAULT.PRF are installed in the directory in which the client is installed—for example, \EXCHANGE.

NEWPROF.EXE must be started from a command prompt and uses the following syntax:

```
NEWPROF -s <path\><filename>.PRF
```

Client Command-Line Switches

There are several command-line switches available for both the Windows-based and MS-DOS Exchange clients. These optional parameters can make using the client more convenient.

The Windows-based Exchange clients support the following switches:

B

COMMAND
REFERENCE

Switch	Purpose
`<filename>`	Creates a new note, attaching the specified file
`/n`	Creates a new note
`/f<filename>`	Opens the message in the specified `.MSG` file
`/s`	Opens a new find dialog box
`/a`	Opens the address book
`/i`	Opens the Inbox
`/e`	Embeds an OLE command line

The MS-DOS Exchange client supports the following command-line switches:

Switch	Purpose
`-p[profile]`	Used to specify the user profile to open on startup
`-s`	Displays the profile settings
`-m`	Starts in monitor mode
`-[25¦43¦50]`	Sets the display mode for the number of times to display in the client

NET Commands

There are several NET commands that can be entered from the NT command prompt to start and stop Exchange Server services. The next four sections highlight the NET command for the four core services of Exchange Server. If your server has more services, you can start and stop them also with a console NET command.

MSExchangeIS

MSExchangeIS is the Windows NT service name for the Microsoft Exchange Information Store (IS):

■ NET STOP MSEXCHANGEIS stops the service.

■ NET START MSEXCHANGEIS starts the service. It also starts the MSExchangeDS and MSExchangeSA services if they are not started.

MSExchangeMTA

MSExchangeMTA is the Windows NT service name for the Microsoft Exchange Message Transfer Agent (MTA):

■ NET STOP MSEXCHANGEMTA stops the service.

■ NET START MSEXCHANGMTA starts the service. It also starts the MSExchangeDS and MSExchangeSA services if they are not started.

MSExchangeDS

MSExchangeDS is the Windows NT service name for the Microsoft Exchange Directory Service (DS):

- ■ NET STOP MSEXCHANGEDS stops the service. It also stops the MSExchangeIS and MSExchangeMTA services if they are running.
- ■ NET START MSEXCHANGEDS starts the service. It also starts the MSExchangeSA service.

MSExchangeSA

MSExchangeSA is the Windows NT service name for the Microsoft Exchange System Attendant (SA):

- ■ NET STOP MSEXCHANGESA stops the service. It also stops the MSExchangeDS, MSExchangeIS, and MSExchangeMTA services if they are running.
- ■ NET START MSEXCHANGESA starts the service.

Summary

This appendix was intended to give you a quick and handy command reference for some of the more common utilities used with Exchange Server. It is by no means exhaustive, but it should help provide clarification to help you survive out there using Exchange Server.

Glossary

by Greg Todd

Address Book   A collection of one or more lists of recipients. An address book organizes the recipient data into containers (lists of recipients). *See also Global Address List, Personal Address Book.*

Address Book Provider   A MAPI address book provider provides access to any existing central database that holds information on all users and recipients in a messaging system. The Exchange directory service is an example of an address book provider.

Address List   A collection of recipients in the address book, organized by their recipients container. *See also Global Address List, Personal Address Book.*

Address Space   A set of address information associated with a connector or gateway that identifies a certain type or group of recipients and the route messages to those recipients should take. The address space exists so the Exchange MTA can determine how to get a message to its final destinations. *See also Connector.*

Administrator Program   A graphical user interface that administrators use to manage and configure Microsoft Exchange Server objects, such as organizations, sites, and servers.

Advanced Security   Provides administrators and users with the ability to protect and verify messages.

Alias   Typically, a shortened version of the mailbox owner's name, used to address messages. This item is specified in the Recipient properties page.

Authentication   Validation of a user's Windows NT Server login information. *See also Trust Relationships.*

Backbone   A network connection—usually high-speed to handle heavy traffic—between local area network (LAN) segments. A backbone connects two or more LANs.

Bridgehead Server   A Microsoft Exchange Server computer that acts as an endpoint of a connection between two Exchange sites. It is responsible for routing messages through the site connection.

Certificate   An authentication method used in security that contains information that actually authenticates a signed or sealed message. A certificate is only available to security-enabled users. It primarily houses a user's public key and is transported through the Exchange network via the Directory service. A certificate is analogous to a notary public's seal on a document, verifying its authenticity. *See also Certification Authority, Key.*

Certification Authority (CA)   In Exchange advanced security, the central process that generates the public and private keypairs. The CA is responsible for creating and maintaining security keypairs and special certificates. *See also Certificate.*

Client Installation Point   A shared directory on a file server to which users can connect in order to install the Microsoft Exchange Client. *See also Network Share.*

Client-Server Architecture   In a client-server system, the client sends requests to a server, the server carries out the instructions, and the results are sent back to the client. Client-server is the underlying architecture of Microsoft Exchange Server. *See also Shared File Architecture.*

Common Message Calls (CMC)   A set of 10 high-level functions for quick and easy implementation of simple messaging.

Connector   A component of Exchange that routes messages between Microsoft Exchange Server sites and other messaging systems. For example, the Internet Mail connector enables Microsoft Exchange users to send and receive messages with other users on the Internet. *See also Address Space.*

Container   In the Administrator program, an object that contains other objects. For example, the recipients container is composed of recipient objects.

Custom Recipient   A recipient in a foreign system whose address is specified in the address book. For example, if your Microsoft Exchange system is connected to a different e-mail system by way of the Internet Mail connector, the recipients in that e-mail system have custom recipient address entries in the address book.

Delegate   In Exchange, a person with permission to manage and/or send e-mail for another user.

Delivery Receipt (DR)   A notice confirming that a message has been delivered to its intended recipient. *See also Read-Receipt (RR).*

Digital Signature   An advanced security feature of Exchange that enables users to verify the source of messages and to verify that the contents of the message have not been modified during transit. *See also Encryption, Key, Signing.*

Directory   The Exchange directory stores all the information about an organization's resources and users such as sites, recipients, and servers. Other Exchange components use the directory to address and route messages. On an Exchange server, the directory, also called Directory Service (DS), is a Windows NT service—MSExchangeDS. It is one of the four core Microsoft Exchange Server services. *See also Information Store, Message Transfer Agent, System Attendant.*

Directory Object   A record in the directory, such as a server, a mailbox, or a distribution list. Every object has properties that can be defined.

Directory Replication   The process of updating the directories of all Exchange servers within and between Exchange sites.

Directory Replication Bridgehead Server   A specialized bridgehead server—an Exchange server that acts as the endpoint of a directory replication connection between its site and a remote site. This server requests directory updates from the remote Exchange site.

Directory Synchronization   The process of synchronizing an Exchange server directory with the directories from MS Mail systems, either PC or AppleTalk. On an Exchange server this is managed by a Windows NT service, the Directory Synchronization Agent, MSExchangeDXA.

Distribution List (DL)   A collection of recipients commonly addressed together as a single recipient. A DL makes it easier and more convenient to manage and address multiple recipients. Administrators can create DLs that are available in the address book. Users can create DLs and add them to their personal address book.

Domain   A Windows NT domain is a group of computers running Windows NT Server, minimally composed of a Windows NT primary domain controller. A domain can also include other types of servers and clients. Usually a Windows NT domain directly corresponds to a Microsoft Exchange site.

Domain Controller   A Windows NT domain controller is the Windows NT server computer that maintains the security database for a domain and authenticates domain logons. Windows NT domains can have one primary domain controller (PDC) and one or more backup domain controllers (BDC).

Dynamic RAS Connector   A Microsoft Exchange Server messaging connector that routes messages between Exchange sites using Windows NT Remote Access Services (RAS). *See also Messaging Connector.*

E-Mail Addresses   A general term that refers to the address or name by which recipients are known to Exchange and to foreign systems.

Encryption   An advanced security feature of Exchange that provides confidentiality by allowing users to scramble data using complex algorithms. The data can only be decrypted by someone with a key. Encrypting a message is also known as "sealing" a message. Data is encrypted as it resides on disk and as it travels over a network. Exchange uses CAST-40 and CAST-64 encryption. *See also Digital Signature, Key, Sealing, Signing.*

Fault Tolerance   A general term that refers to the capability of a system—hardware or software—of responding to an event, such as a power failure or a component failure, so that information is not lost and so that operations continue without interruption.

Foreign System   A messaging system other than Microsoft Exchange Server.

Form   A structure for posting and viewing information. An example is a send form, such as a purchase requisition.

Forms Designer   The Microsoft Exchange Client component that enables you to create custom forms and applications for use with Exchange.

Gateway   Delivers messages from Microsoft Exchange Server to foreign systems. For example, the Internet Mail connector is a type of gateway.

Global Address List   A list containing the names of all mailboxes, custom recipients, distribution lists, and public folders in an organization. *See also Address Book.*

Home Server   From an Exchange user perspective, the specific Microsoft Exchange server that contains a user's mailbox.

HTTP (HyperText Transport Protocol)   One of the newly supported Internet protocols in Exchange 5.0.

Information Service   A "bolt-on" intermediary between MAPI and whatever messaging system is being accessed by way of the Exchange client. It provides a way for the client to access data from an outside information source such as Exchange Server. There are four main information services available to the Exchange client: Microsoft Exchange Server, Microsoft Mail, Personal Address Book, and Personal Folders. There are more available through Microsoft and third parties, such as Internet-related, CompuServe, and other e-mail systems.

Information Store (IS)   The Exchange information store contains the public and private information stores. On an Exchange server, the IS is a Windows NT service—MSExchangeIS. It is one of the four core Microsoft Exchange Server services. *See also Directory, Message Transfer Agent, Private Information Store, Public Information Store, System Attendant.*

Internet Mail Service (IMS)   An Exchange Server messaging connector that enables users to exchange messages with SMTP users. For example, it provides a way to send and receive messages from the Internet, or it can be used to connect Exchange sites over any SMTP backbone. The IMS is, in effect, an SMTP gateway. The IMS is functionally the same as the IMC. Called the Internet Mail Connector (IMC) in Exchange 4.0. *See also Gateway, Messaging Connector, SMTP.*

Key   Used in Exchange for advanced security features. There are four types of keys: two public keys and two private keys. Without a key, no security measures, such as signing and sealing, can be used. *See also Certificate, Digital Signature, Encryption, Key Management Server, Private Key, Public Key, Sealing, Signing.*

Key Management Server (KM Server)   A specific Exchange Server computer that has been installed with the advanced security features of Exchange. On an Exchange Server, these features are managed by a Windows NT service, the Key Management Service. *See also Key.*

LDAP (Lightweight Directory Access Protocol)   One of the newly supported Internet protocols in Exchange 5.0.

LoadSim   Microsoft Exchange Server Load Simulator program. A utility included with Microsoft Exchange Server for placing a reliable, predictable, reproducible load on the server. It provides the capability for a single Windows NT machine (called the LoadSim client) to simulate multiple Exchange users.

LoadSim Client   Any computer running Windows NT Workstation or Windows NT Server and the LoadSim program. A LoadSim client's purpose is to simulate multiple synthetic users to place a load on an Exchange server.

Local Delivery Message   A message sent between recipients that share the same home server. This type of message has the fastest delivery time. The MTA does not participate in delivering local messages unless a distribution list is involved.

C

Mailbox   The fundamental delivery location for a recipient's incoming mail messages.

MAPI (Messaging Application Program Interface)   A standard interface that Exchange Server and Client use to communicate with each other. There are two types of MAPI: *Simple MAPI* and *Extended MAPI*. Simple MAPI contains 12 high-level messaging functions for implementation of simple messaging. Extended MAPI is designed for applications that depend heavily upon messaging. It provides handling complex messages, large numbers of messages, message storage, and complex addressing information. Exchange uses Extended MAPI.

Message Spooler   Contained in the MAPI message transport provider, the spooler works in conjunction with other MAPI processes to call upon information services to access store, transport, and addressing services.

Message Store Provider   A MAPI message store provider serves as the central repository for messages and folders in a messaging system. The main Exchange databases, PRIV.EDB and PUB.EDB, are two examples of a message store provider.

Message Transfer Agent (MTA)   Responsible for routing messages to other Exchange Server MTAs, information stores, connectors, and third-party gateways. It is also responsible for breaking down distribution lists into their individual recipients. On an Exchange server, the MTA is a Windows NT service—MSExchangeMTA. It is one of the four core Microsoft Exchange Server services. *See also Directory, Information Store, System Attendant.*

Message Transport Provider   Provides message transportation services from the local MAPI message system to the message transport medium. This transport medium is usually the network software. It also incorporates a spooler. *See also Message Spooler.*

Messaging Connector   An Exchange Server component that is used to connect two Exchange sites so messages can be transported between the sites. There are four main messaging connectors with Exchange Server: Site Connector, X.400 Connector, Dynamic RAS Connector, and Internet Mail Service (formerly the Internet Mail Connector). Connectors are also used to connect an Exchange server with a foreign messaging system. Examples of such connectors are the cc:Mail Connector, the Internet Mail Service, and the MS Mail Connector.

Messaging Profile   *See Profile.*

Messaging System   A generic term that refers to any messaging system, such as Microsoft Exchange Server, CompuServe, MS Mail 3.*x*, and so forth. Also known as *Messaging Service*.

Microsoft Mail Connector   An Exchange Server component that works with the Exchange MTA to provide connectivity to MS Mail systems (both PC and AppleTalk) and to MS Mail (PC) gateways. On an Exchange server, this is implemented as a Windows NT service, the Mail Connector (PC) MTA. It provides the same functionality as an MS Mail 3.*x* MTA or MMTA.

Microsoft Schedule+ Free/Busy Connector   An Exchange Server component designed to work in conjunction with the Microsoft Mail 3.*x* executables SCHDIST.EXE and ADMINSCH.EXE to exchange free and busy appointment information between an Exchange server and a MS Mail post office. This is managed by a Windows NT service.

Network Share   A shared directory on a Microsoft Windows Network that users can connect to in order to access files over the network. The client installation point is a network share. *See also Client Installation Point.*

NNTP (Network News Transport Protocol)   One of the newly supported Internet protocols in Exchange 5.0.

Non-Delivery Report (NDR)   A notice received by an Exchange client indicating that a message was not delivered to the recipient.

Non-Read Notification (NRN)   A notice received by an Exchange client indicating that a message was deleted before it was read.

Object   In an Exchange system, a general term that refers to a record—such as a site, server, connector, mailbox, or distribution list— in the Exchange Server directory.

Offline Folders   Specific mailbox folders and favorite public folders that are configured to be used both when connected and when not connected to the user's Exchange server.

Organization   A collection of Microsoft Exchange server sites. An organization is the highest level of grouping in the Exchange hierarchy. *See also Server, Site.*

PerfMon   Microsoft Windows NT Performance Monitor. A tool included with Windows NT that provides a way to monitor performance counters in the system.

PerfWiz   Microsoft Exchange Server Performance Optimizer. A utility included with Microsoft Exchange Server that examines the system resources and sets configuration parameters for optimal Exchange Server performance. It is usually run after Microsoft Exchange Server is initially installed. It should also be run any time system resources are altered.

Permission   Authorization to access an object or to perform an action.

Personal Address Book (PAB)   A user-created version of the address book stored locally on the client in a .PAB file. *See also Address Book.*

Personal Folder   A client-based folder that contains any kind of information the user wants to store off the server. You must create your own personal folders after installing the Personal Folders information service. Personal folders are usually stored on the user's local hard drive in a .PST file, and they are displayed under the Personal Folders object in the client.

POP3 (Post Office Protocol 3)   One of the newly supported Internet protocols in Exchange 5.0.

Private Folder   A server-based folder that is part of a user's mailbox. Inbox and Outbox are examples of private folders. Private folders are stored in the private information store on an Exchange Server, and they are displayed under the Mailbox object in the client. *See also Private Information Store.*

Private Information Store   The database on an Exchange Server that contains all the individual users' mail folders. The filename is PRIV.EDB, and it can be found in the \EXCHSRVR\MDBDATA directory. On an Exchange server, the private information store is a part of the Microsoft Exchange information store. *See also Information Store.*

Private Key   A type of key that is only known by a specific user. It is a fixed-length security string that is stored in a local encrypted security file on each user's computer and used to unseal and sign messages. Exchange actually uses two private keys: one for unsealing messages and one for signing messages. *See also Sealing, Signing.*

Profile   An optional service of MAPI that is employed to help users manage the Information services configured on an Exchange client.

Provider   *See Information Service.*

Public Folder   A server-based folder that is available to all users of Exchange, much like a bulletin board. It can contain various types of information, including e-mail, spreadsheets, graphics, and voice mail. Public folders are stored in the public information store on an Exchange server, and they are displayed under the `Public Folders` object in the client. *See also Public Information Store.*

Public Folder Affinity   Enables users in one Exchange site to open public folders on Exchange servers in other sites.

Public Folder Replication   The process of updating the changes to identical copies of a public folder on multiple Exchange Server computers. *See also Public Folder.*

Public Information Store   The database on an Exchange server that contains all the public folders. The filename is PUB.EDB, and it can be found in the \EXCHSRVR\MDBDATA directory. On an Exchange server, the public information store is a part of the Microsoft Exchange information store. *See also Information Store.*

Public Key   A type of key that is available to any user of the Exchange system. It is a fixed-length security string that is stored in publicly available certificates and is used to seal and verify secure messages. Exchange actually uses two public keys: one for sealing messages and one for verifying messages.

Read-Receipt (RR)   A notice received by an Exchange client indicating that a message was read by its intended recipient.

Recipient   A general term that refers to directory entities such as users, mailboxes, distribution lists, public folders, automatic processing agents, and so forth. These entities can receive messages and information.

Remote Procedure Call (RPC)   A standard protocol for client-server communication.

Replication   A general term referring to updating the changes between two copies of the same information. *See also Directory Replication, Public Folder Replication.*

Revocation   A warning users receive when they get a signed message from an originator whose advanced security has been revoked.

Role   A group of permissions.

Routing   The process of transferring and delivering messages.

Routing Table   A special data structure that contains information that the MTA needs to route information.

Roving User   A user who logs on to the Exchange Client from various different computers in an organization.

Schedule File   An .SCD file that stores scheduling information for MS Schedule+ users.

Sealing   A process allowing a sender to encrypt the body part and any attachments of an originating message using a public key. It provides confidentiality of a message as it moves through a Microsoft Exchange system. *See also Encryption, Private Key, Public Key, Unsealing.*

Security Context   A security aspect of Windows NT Server that controls the kind of access a user, a process, or a service has to Windows NT operating system services.

Security File   A CAST-encrypted file stored on the user's local machine as an .EPF file. It contains the user's private signing key, the certification authority's certificate, and the signing and sealing certificates. *See also Certification Authority, Private Key.*

Security Token   A random 8-character string given to users during setup of Advanced Security. This token is used for enabling a number of security features. Some are to create the public and private signing key pair, to send the public signing key to the KM server, to retrieve the sealing key pair stored in the KM database, and to identify the user-defined access password that is used to encrypt a security file. *See also KM Server.*

Server   In an Exchange system, a computer configured with Windows NT Server and the Microsoft Exchange Server software. The Exchange server contains many services the Exchange client accesses. A server is the lowest level of grouping in the Exchange hierarchy. *See also Organization, Site.*

Service Account   A Windows NT user account that is specifically enabled to provide the security context required to run the Microsoft Exchange Server services. All Exchange servers in a site should use the same service account. *See also Security Context.*

Service Provider   *See Information Service.*

Shared File Architecture   In a shared file system, the client is required to process all the user requests. The server in the system is just a network-based repository for information that the client uses. Much less efficient than client-server. MS Mail 3.*x* is a shared file architecture e-mail system. *See also Client-Server Architecture.*

C

GLOSSARY

Signing   When a sender signs a message, it causes the Exchange client to "stamp" a digital signature into the originating message, using one of the user's two private keys. Then, by verifying the message, a recipient can be sure of the identity of the sender and that the content has not been modified during transit. For example, this feature can prevent someone from originating a message under the guise of another identity. *See also Private Key, Public Key, Verifying.*

Site   An Exchange site is one or more Exchange servers that share the same directory information. Usually, servers in a site are connected by LAN or other high-speed connection (greater than 64 Kbits/sec). Servers in a site communicate by way of Remote Procedure Call.

Site Connector   An Exchange Server messaging connector that connects two Exchange sites. This enables users in different Exchange sites residing on the same LAN to send and receive messages. *See also Messaging Connector.*

SMTP (Simple Mail Transfer Protocol)   In an Exchange system, a protocol used by the Internet mail connector to transfer messages between an Exchange site and another SMTP messaging system such as the Internet.

System Attendant (SA)   The Exchange SA is responsible for various server housekeeping tasks. It also interacts with the Advanced Security features of Exchange. On an Exchange server, the SA is a Windows NT service—MSExchangeSA. It is one of the four core Microsoft Exchange Server services. *See also Directory, Information Store, Message Transfer Agent.*

Target Server   An Exchange Server computer that acts as the endpoint of a connection between two Exchange sites.

Token   *See Security Token.*

Transaction Log   A crucial set of files used to provide fault tolerance in the event that the IS or directory databases need to be rolled back so data can be restored. There are separate sets of log files for the IS and the directory databases. Every transaction to these databases is logged in the log files for fault tolerance. The IS logs are stored in \EXCHSRVR\MDBDATA. The directory logs are stored in \EXCHSRVR\DSADATA. All transaction logs should always be stored on a fault-tolerant disk volume.

Trust Relationship   A Windows NT security concept that makes it possible for a user in one Windows NT domain to access a network resource—including an Exchange Server—that resides in another Windows NT domain.

Unsealing   The process of decrypting a received message that was sent encrypted. When a recipient receives a sealed (encrypted) message, the message is unsealed (decrypted) with one of the user's two private keys. *See also Public Key, Private Key, Sealing.*

User Account   A Windows NT entity that contains information such as the username, password, group membership, and permissions. User account information is used directly by the Exchange Client and Server to determine access permissions.

User Profile   *See Profile.*

Verifying   The process of checking the digital signature in a signed message to ensure that the message has not been altered and the originator is not an impostor. When a recipient receives a signed message, the message is verified with a public key. *See also Private Key, Public Key, Signing.*

X.400   Developed by the CCITT and published every four years since 1984, X.400 is a recommendation for computer-based handling of electronic messages. The goal is to enable e-mail users to exchange messages no matter what messaging system they use. X.400 is designed to be hardware/software-independent. Microsoft Exchange is compliant with the 1984 and 1988 X.400 recommendations.

X.400 Connector   An Exchange Server messaging connector that can be configured either to connect two Exchange sites or to route messages to foreign X.400 systems. *See also Messaging Connector.*

I
INDEX

MACMILLAN COMPUTER PUBLISHING USA
A VIACOM COMPANY

Technical ---- Support:

If you need assistance with the information in this book or with a CD/Disk
accompanying the book, please access the Knowledge Base on our Web
site at **http://www.superlibrary.com/general/support**. Our most
Frequently Asked Questions are answered there. If you do not find the
answer to your questions on our Web site, you may contact Macmillan
Technical Support **(317) 581-3833** or e-mail us at **support@mcp.com**.

Windows NT 4 Server Unleashed, Professional Reference Edition

Jason Garms et al.

The Windows NT server has been gaining tremendous market share over Novell, and the new upgrade—which includes a Windows 95 interface—is sure to add momentum to its market drive. *Windows NT 4 Server Unleashed, Professional Reference Edition* is written to meet that growing market. It provides information on disk and file management, integrated networking, BackOffice integration, and TCP/IP protocols. The CD-ROM includes source code from the book and valuable utilities.

$69.99 USA/$98.95 CAN
ISBN: 0-672-31002-3

User level: Accomplished–Expert
1,776 pp.

TCP/IP Unleashed

Timothy Parker, Ph.D.

This book starts with the installation of the most popular TCP/IP products on each platform, then proceeds through configuration and troubleshooting each product. Subsequent chapters increase the reader's understanding of the theory and practice of TCP/IP, from both an administrative and a user point of view. The book also includes configuration and troubleshooting information. The CD-ROM includes source code from the book.

$55.00 USA/$74.95 CAN
ISBN: 0-672-30603-4

User level: New–Casual
880 pp.

Teach Yourself Microsoft Outlook 97 in 24 Hours

Brian Proffitt & Kim Spilker

Microsoft Office is the leading application productivity suite available, and in its next version, it will have Outlook as a personal information manager. Using step-by-step instructions and real-world examples, readers will explore the new features of Outlook and learn how to successfully integrate Outlook with other Office 97 applications—painlessly! Each day focuses on working with Outlook as a single user as well as in a group setting.

$19.99 USA/$28.95 CAN
ISBN: 0-672-31044-9

User level: New–Casual
400 pp.

Microsoft Internet Information Server 3.0 Unleashed, Second Edition

Arthur Knowles

Following in the tradition of the best-selling *Unleashed* series, this all-in-one guide to Microsoft Internet Information Server covers everything users need to know—from installing and configuring the server and working with other BackOffice products to administration and security issues. This book has been updated to cover Microsoft Index Information Server 1.1, Active Server Pages, Netshow Server, and FrontPage 97 IIS extensions. It also covers content development for Web sites, including Visual Basic Scripting and CGI programming, and shows how to use Internet Information Server to work with SQL Server databases. The CD-ROM is loaded with all the source code from the book, as well as examples and third-party software.

$49.99 USA/$70.95 CAN
ISBN: 1-57521-271-4

User level: Accomplished–Expert
1,000 pp.

Add to Your Sams Library Today with the Best Books for Programming, Operating Systems, and New Technologies

The easiest way to order is to pick up the phone and call
1-800-428-5331
between 9:00 a.m. and 5:00 p.m. EST.
For faster service, please have your credit card available.

ISBN	Quantity	Description of Item	Unit Cost	Total Cost
0-672-31002-3		Windows NT 4 Server Unleashed, Professional Reference Edition	$69.99	
0-672-30603-4		TCP/IP Unleashed	$55.00	
0-672-31044-9		Teach Yourself Microsoft Outlook 97 in 24 Hours	$19.99	
1-57521-271-4		Microsoft Internet Information Server 3.0 Unleashed, Second Edition	$49.99	
❏ 3 ½" Disk		Shipping and Handling: See information below.		
❏ 5 ¼" Disk		TOTAL		

Shipping and Handling: $4.00 for the first book and $1.75 for each additional book. Floppy disk: add $1.75 for shipping and handling. If you need to have it NOW, we can ship product to you in 24 hours for an additional charge of approximately $18.00, and you will receive your item overnight or in two days. Overseas shipping and handling add $2.00 per book and $8.00 for up to three disks. Prices subject to change. Call for availability and pricing information on latest editions.

201 W. 103rd Street, Indianapolis, Indiana 46290

1-800-428-5331 — Orders   1-800-835-3202 — FAX   1-800-858-7674 — Customer Service

Book ISBN 0-672-31034-1

What's on the Disc

SAMS Publishing is happy to present the *Windows NT Magazine Microsoft Exchange Server Sampler CD* bundled with this book. This companion CD-ROM contains a wide variety of third-party tools, utilities, and product demos for Microsoft Exchange. Within this multimedia product, you can view information concerning products and companies, and install programs with just a few clicks of the mouse.

Some of the companies and products featured on this CD include:

Alcom LanFax NT by Alcom Corporation

Cheyenne's ARCserve® for Windows NT® and InocuLAN® for Windows NT

Ericsson Inc's EVO

Optus Software, Inc. FACSys Fax Messaging Gate

SpectraFAX® Corp.'s Fax Liaison™ software

Omtool's Fax Sr.package

Faxination by Fenestrae®, Inc.

FileNet® Corporation's FileNet Ensemble™

Fulcrum® Technologies Inc.'s Fulcrum Knowledge Network™

Import Wizard from ActivExchange

JetForm Workflow and Filler Pro from JetForm Corporation

ProKeyfile Corporation's Keyflow

Worldtalk Corporation's NetTalk

NetWorker BusinesSuite by Legato Systems

Telesis North Inc.'s OnAir® Messaging

Wang Software's OPEN/workflow

Pivotal Software Inc's Pivotal Relationship™

Inso® Corporation's Quick View Plus™

Sax Software Corp's Sax mPower™

ScanMail™ for Microsoft® Exchange™ by Trend Micro, Inc.

SEARCH'97™ Personal from Verity™, Inc.

Worldtalk® Corporation's Secure Messenger

WorkMAN Route &Track by Reach Software Corporation

System Requirements

The following configuration is recommended in order to use and install the CD-ROM:

Minimum operating system: Windows NT 3.51 or Windows 95 or later

Recommended operating system: Windows NT 4.0 or later

Memory: 16M RAM minimum for NT; 8M RAM minimum for 95

Display: 256-color display at 640×480 resolution minimum

Peripheral: 2X CD-ROM drive minimum

Options: SoundBlaster-compatible sound card recommended

> **NOTE**
>
> For best results, set your monitor to display between 256 and 64,000 colors. A screen resolution of 800×600 pixels is recommended. If necessary, adjust your monitor settings before using the CD-ROM.

To get started with this CD-ROM, follow these steps:

Windows NT or Windows 95 Installation Instructions

1. Insert the CD-ROM disc into your CD-ROM drive.
2. With Windows NT/95 installed on your computer and the AutoPlay feature enabled, this CD-ROM will automatically start. Follow the directions provided in the installation program.

   If Autoplay is not enabled, using Windows Explorer, choose Start.exe from the root level of the CD-ROM.

Technical Support

If you need assistance with the information in this book or with the CD-ROM accompanying this book, please access the Knowledge Base on our Web site at

http://www.superlibrary.com/general/support

Our most Frequently Asked Questions are answered there. If you do not find the answer to your questions on our Web site, you may contact Macmillan Technical Support at (317) 581-3833 or e-mail us at support@mcp.com.

You may also send inquiries to cd@winntmag.com.